Strategic SPORT Marketing

SPORT MANAGEMENT SERIES
Series editor: Professor David Shilbury

Strategic SPORT Marketing

4TH EDITION

David Shilbury, Hans Westerbeek, Shayne Quick, Daniel Funk and Adam Karg

ALLEN&UNWIN
SYDNEY • MELBOURNE • AUCKLAND • LONDON

This edition published in 2014

First published in 1998

Allen & Unwin
83 Alexander Street
Crows Nest NSW 2065
Australia
Phone: (61 2) 8425 0100
Fax: (61 2) 9906 2218
Email: info@allenandunwin.com
Web: www.allenandunwin.com

Cataloguing-in-Publication details are available
from the National Library of Australia
www.trove.nla.gov.au

ISBN: 978 1 74331 477 7

Index by Puddingburn Publishing Services

Set in 10.5/12 pt Minion Pro by Bookhouse, Sydney
Printed and bound in Australia by Griffin Press

10 9 8 7 6 5 4 3 2

MIX
Paper from responsible sources
FSC® C009448

The paper in this book is FSC certified. FSC promotes environmentally responsible, socially beneficial and economically viable management of the world's forests.

Contents

	Preface	x
	About the authors	xiii
PART I	**INTRODUCTION**	1
1	An overview of sport marketing	3
	Headline story	4
	Marketing defined	6
	Defining the sport marketing mix	7
	Unique characteristics of sport and sport marketing	8
	Importance of marketing in sport management	12
	Sport marketing defined	16
	Overview of this book	17
PART II	**IDENTIFICATION OF MARKETING OPPORTUNITIES**	19
2	The strategic sport-marketing planning process	21
	Headline story	22
	The strategic sport-marketing planning process	25
	Step 1: Understanding the environment in which the sport competes	26
	Step 2: Understanding the internal capabilities of the organisation	30
	Step 3: Examining market research and utilising information systems	33
	Step 4: Determining the marketing mission and objectives	35
	Summary	40
3	Understanding the sport consumer	44
	Headline story	45
	Sport consumer behaviour	46
	The sport consumption decision-making process	47
	Involvement and decision-making	51
	A model of sport consumer behaviour	51
	Involvement in the decision-making process	64
	Summary	66

4 Market research: Segmentation, target markets and positioning 68
Headline story 69
Market research and strategy 70
Developing marketing information systems 70
Data sources for a marketing information system 72
Marketing research in sporting organisations 75
The marketing mission 76
The market research process 77
Segmenting the sport market 80
Target market selection 85
Positioning 86
Summary 87

PART III STRATEGY DETERMINATION 91

5 The sport product 93
Headline story 94
The sport product 94
Sport as a service 97
Service and technology 101
Service quality 101
Positioning the sport product 103
Product development 105
Sport and television 109
Summary 110

6 Pricing strategies 117
Headline story 118
The strategic pricing process in sport 119
Summary 134

7 The place of the sport facility 137
Headline story 138
Facility planning 140
Physical evidence 143
Process 145
People 146
Blueprinting the sport service delivery system 147
Marketing channels for sporting goods and services 148
Summary 150

8 Customer satisfaction and service quality 154
Headline story 155
Defining sport services 156
A relational approach to customers (and the role of satisfaction) 157
Defining and differentiating service quality and customer satisfaction 158

Service quality 160
Satisfaction 164
Role of expectations and 'disconfirmation' in satisfaction 165
Measuring satisfaction in sport services 165
Managing and measuring service quality and satisfaction in organisations 166
Summary 170

9 The sport promotion mix 175
Headline story 176
Defining promotions 177
Communications model 178
Towards a strategic, integrated promotional mix 180
Tools for promotion 182
The promotions process 190
Considerations for the IMC/promotions mix 193
Summary 193

10 Advertising 197
Headline story 198
The advertising management process 200
Advertising strategy 201
Advertising objectives 202
Advertising budget 202
Message strategy 203
Creative strategy 204
Media alternatives 206
Timing and cost 209
Media selection 209
Measuring advertising effectiveness 210
Ambush marketing through advertising 211
Summary 212

11 Sport and television 216
Headline story 217
Television and sport marketing 218
Sport programming 219
Measuring the television audience 222
Advertising during sport programming 227
Advertising effectiveness 230
Television sponsorship 232
The price of this national sponsorship is: 232
Spot packages 232
Pay television 233
Digital television 234
Summary 237

12 Sport and new media 242
Headline story 243
Impact of technology 245
Defining digital 245
Dimensions and characteristics of new media 246
New media and sport marketing 249
Social media and networking 250
Broadcasting and content extensions 252
Second-screen and content marketing 253
Fantasy sport 254
Online communities and fan forums 256
E-commerce, online advertising and interactive web elements 257
Implications for organisations 259
Summary 260

13 How to attract and implement sponsorship 262
Headline story 263
What is sponsorship? 263
The market for sponsors 264
Sponsorship goals: The right to associate . . . 266
Advantages and disadvantages of sport sponsorship 267
Creating win–win situations 268
Sponsoring individual athletes and celebrity marketing 271
The integrated marketing approach 275
Current research trends in sport sponsorship 278
Summary 280

14 Measuring the effectiveness of sponsorship 285
Headline story 286
Measuring sponsorship effectiveness 287
The sponsorship properties: Events and athletes 290
The SPONSEFFECT model 292
Ambush marketing 294
Location dependency of sponsorship 298
Summary 299

15 Public relations 301
Headline story 302
Defining public relations 303
Evaluating public attitudes 304
Linking policies and procedures to the public interest 308
Planning and executing a program of action 311
Reputation management 314
Advantages and disadvantages of public relations 315
Summary 317

16 Promotional licensing 319
Headline story 320
Trademark licensing 321
Building the sporting organisation's licensing program 328
Branding 333
Summary 338

PART IV STRATEGY IMPLEMENTATION, EVALUATION AND ADJUSTMENT 343

17 Coordinating and controlling marketing strategy 345
Headline story 346
Controlling the sport marketing function 346
Measures of success 348
Coordinating and implementing marketing strategy 352
Careers in sport marketing 353
Sport-marketing planning revisited 354

Bibliography 357
Index 376

Preface

The face of sport has changed radically over the last 40 years. What was once just a local Saturday afternoon activity for both participants and spectators now takes place on any night of the week and can be intrastate or interstate, with the fan experience live or mediated. In growing numbers, supporters are demonstrating their allegiance to sport via the merchandise they buy, the literature they read, the television they watch and increasingly the use of social media. Sport in the 2000s is a multi-faceted, multimedia industry, with growing appeal to an ever-increasing number of stakeholders and supporters. What was once a clearly defined, stable activity is now a complex technologically oriented and constantly changing industry. This is the environment in which the current generation of sport marketing practitioners must operate.

The sport experience can present a host of problematic consumer preferences for the sport marketer to target—compounded by the fact that sport no longer faces competition merely from within its own ranks. With decreasing amounts of leisure time and discretionary income judiciously being allocated, sport now has to compete for the consumer dollar with a vast array of both sport and non-sport activities. The various branches of the arts, the increasing proclivity toward short-term tourist activities and the growth of passive recreation all provide viable alternatives to the sport experience for the modern consumer. Sport is now just one component—albeit a very important one—of the entertainment milieu.

Given this cluttered environment, sport attracts consumers not through serendipity, but rather through carefully structured planning, creativity and perseverance. Successful sport marketing is the implementation of clearly defined strategies that are rooted in both perspiration and inspiration. The notion 'if we build it, they will come' is no longer appropriate. Planning processes are now required that view sport not merely as an athletic endeavour, but as an activity in which multiple individuals and groups can engage.

There is little doubt that sport is changing, both on and off the field. While athletes have become fitter, stronger and faster to cope with the demands of the modern game, the management of sport has, at the same time, become a highly professional endeavour. To facilitate this process, and enhance the expertise of those charged with its effective management, education and training are vital components of the sport environment. Increasingly, both the sport industry and educational institutions have realised that sport can no longer be managed by individuals or groups who do not come equipped with certain skills.

It is important to recognise the range of skills required to manage the modern sporting organisation when preparing the educational framework for future sport managers. The growth in sport marketing teaching and practice is accompanied by a growth in sport management education generally. Sport marketing remains a popular area of study, viewed as exciting and attractive to the next generation of sport managers. The challenge of preparing graduates and practitioners for the rigours of sport management lies in balancing the emotion and tribal character of sport with the need for an objective application of business principles. Modern management of sport is more than just a response to traditional actions or present realities. It encompasses a vision for the future, together with the strategies and implementations required for bringing about that vision. This vision is based on a well-rounded curriculum, cognisant of the need to integrate sport industry knowledge with the fundamentals of management, marketing, accounting and finance, and other business studies. Texts such as this one play an important part in this process. They are constructed by groups and individuals who understand the sport experience and what it means to play, watch and officiate, and who also understand the meaning of management. In many instances, they have moved beyond sport and have appropriated from other fields of endeavour those theories and strategies that, when used appropriately, result in a successful sport experience for all concerned.

The ability to translate theory into effective strategic practice is the result of management education programs that utilise business practice to comprehend contemporary sport while simultaneously remaining cognisant of what sport means to the end consumer or fan. The modern consumer is discerning, and needs to be treated as such. Through the provision of theory and examples, this text will result in future generations of sport marketers having the skills critical to the successful promotion of their sport.

Strategic Sport Marketing is unique from two perspectives. It is the first sport marketing text to truly integrate international examples. Case studies, sportviews and examples from myriad national and international sports and events have been used to reinforce theoretical positions and key points. From Australian Rules (AFL) football to European soccer, from the Sydney Kings to the NBA, a concerted effort has been made to include as many popular sports and events as possible.

While this is important, more significant is the fact that there has been a conscious decision to place the text within a framework of strategic decision-making. The three major components of the text underscore this commitment. Part II of *Strategic Sport Marketing* concentrates on identifying market opportunities, focusing on the consumer and the ways in which information can be gathered, collated and utilised in order to establish an effective marketing management process. In this edition, Part III delves into determining the best strategies to use when dealing with a particular component of the sport experience. Included in this section is the recognition that sporting organisations provide a service with an emphasis on service provision, service quality and customer satisfaction. A revised Chapter 8 focuses on customer satisfaction and service quality, and this is followed by a rewritten and reconceptualised Chapter 9 on the sport promotion mix. Technology and its implications on the selection of marketing mix variables are also considered in a rewritten Chapter 12, on 'Sport and New Media', which explores the role of online and new technologies in marketing and their impact on strategic marketing decisions.

A focus on sponsorship and its importance in the promotions mix has been retained in two chapters: Chapter 13, concentrating on how to attract sponsorship, and Chapter 14, on measuring sponsorship effectiveness. Thus Part III develops in some detail the theoretical and practical significance of marketing the sport service. Finally, Part IV establishes mechanisms for the ongoing evaluation, adjustment and maintenance of the strategic marketing process. Collectively, the three sections provide a seamless comprehension of the integration of consumer, activity and process. In addition, this fourth edition of *Strategic Sport Marketing* gathers together a new set of sportviews, case studies and examples to illustrate sport marketing in action.

Strategic Sport Marketing is aimed at senior undergraduates and entry-level graduate sport marketing students. It is also a useful resource for the practitioner engaged in sport marketing. While the case studies provide obvious examples of how the text can be used, we hope this text will be used by sport marketing teachers and practitioners not only to stimulate the thought processes, but to engage with and improve the sport experience for the benefit of all concerned. Finally, it is hoped that the utility of this text will continue to stimulate literary contributions to the field of sport management.

David Shilbury
Hans Westerbeek
Shayne Quick
Daniel Funk
Adam Karg

About the authors

David Shilbury PhD is the Foundation Professor of Sport Management and a former Head of the School of Management and Marketing at Deakin University. In 1990 he was responsible for the implementation of the first business-based programs in sport management in Australia, establishing the Bachelor of Business (Sport Management) and the Master of Business (Sport Management). Prior to commencing at Deakin University, David worked for the Australian Cricket Board in Perth, the City of Stirling and the Western Australian Golf Association. He was a member of the Victorian Sports Council in 1995 and of the AFL Tribunal from 1992 to 2003. In 2011, David won the prestigious North American Society for Sport Management Dr Earle F. Zeigler award for his contributions to sport management scholarship and the field generally. Significantly, he was the first non-North American scholar to be honoured with the Zeigler award. In 2009, he was the inaugural winner of the Sport Management Association of Australian and New Zealand Distinguished Service Award, and in 1999/2000, David won the Eunice Gill Award for Sport Management presented by the Victorian Sports Federation. He was also the Foundation President of the Sport Management Association of Australia and New Zealand between 1995 and 2001.

David is the Senior Associate Editor of the *Journal of Sport Management* and a former editor of *Sport Management Review*, and remains a member of the editorial board of *Sport Management Review*. His most recent textbook, *Sport Management in Australia* (2011), serves as the introductory text to many sport management courses in Australia. David has been published widely in various journals, and has presented papers at conferences in Australia, New Zealand, North America, Europe, South Korea and India. He received a Diploma of Teaching and a BAppSc (Recreation) from Edith Cowan University in 1976 and 1984 respectively, an MSc (Sport Management) from the University of Massachusetts/Amherst in 1989, and a PhD from Monash University in 1995. His principal research interests lie in the areas of sport governance, strategy, sport development and marketing.

Hans Westerbeek PhD is Dean of the College of Sport and Exercise Science at Victoria University, a former Head of the School of Sport, Tourism and Hospitality Management at La Trobe University in Melbourne, Australia and has worked as an academic and consultant in the fields of international marketing and sport business. In addition to a range of 'blue chip' clients, Hans has consulted to a range of professional sport organisations, (inter)national and state sport associations, and local and state governments in multiple countries, such as FIFA, IMG, the Giro d'Italia, Sport Business Group, the government of the United Arab Emirates, PGA Australia, Tennis Australia, the Australian Football League (AFL) and Cricket Australia. Hans is also an experienced corporate facilitator, and has conducted a range of residential professional development programs for organisations such as Coles Myer, Australia Post, the ANZ Bank and the Australian Football League Level I (elite) coaching program, as well as contributing cross-cultural management and leadership, and sport marketing components to the MBA programs of the University of Groningen (Netherlands), the Free University of Brussels (Belgium) and Sport Knowledge Australia. He is the (co)author of more than ten books in the field of sport business, including *Sport Business in the Global Marketplace*, *The Sport Business Future* and (also published by Allen & Unwin) *Managing Sport Facilities and Major Events*.

Prior to moving to Australia, Hans was a marketing manager with Freia Science Services BV in the Netherlands and a member of the Sport Management Committee of the European Union's European network of sport science institutes. He was a founding board member of the Dutch Society for Managers in Sport (NVMS), the European Association for Sport Management (EASM) and the Sport Management Association of Australia and New Zealand (SMAANZ). He is also a Past President of the SMAANZ and the Past President of the Netherlands Chamber of Commerce in Australia (NCCA). He is a member of the Editorial Board of Arko Sports Media (the Netherlands), sits on the Academic Advisory Council of Sport Knowledge Australia and is a member of the editorial board of *Sport in Society*.

He has received numerous academic and industry awards, including outstanding service awards from the Netherlands Chamber of Commerce in Australia and the Sport Management Association of Australia and New Zealand, outstanding achievement awards from Deakin University and, most recently, the Henry Fong Award for Contributions to Global Citizenship by the International Network of Universities. Hans holds a Bachelor's degree in Physical Education, Masters degrees in Human Movement Sciences (MSc) and Business Administration (MBA) and a PhD in International Marketing from Deakin University.

Shayne Quick PhD has taught undergraduate and postgraduate subjects in sport management and sport marketing at universities in both Australia and North America, and is an Adjunct Professor at the Democritus University of Thrace in Greece. He is a former President of the Sport Management Association of Australia and New Zealand. Shayne obtained a BAppSci (PE) from Victoria University of Technology, a BEd from Monash University, an MA from the University of Western Ontario, Canada and a PhD from Ohio State University in the United States. He has been a consultant to the Houston Rockets, the Sydney Kings, the Australian Motorcycle Grand Prix, the New South Wales Waratahs and the Australian Rugby Union, and has been involved with the Sydney 2000, Athens 2004 and Beijing 2008 Olympic Games. Shayne's research has focused on the management of professional sporting organisations in Australia, sport and consumer behaviour and international sport management education. He has published and presented widely on these topics, and is the co-editor of the *International Journal of Sport Management, Recreation and Tourism*.

Daniel C Funk, PhD is Professor and Washburn Senior Research Fellow in the School of Tourism and Hospitality Management at Temple University, USA. Professor Funk also holds an adjunct appointment as Professor of Sport Marketing with the Griffith Business School, Australia. Dr Funk has established an international reputation in the area of sport marketing with an emphasis on sport consumer behaviour. His research evaluates psychological, personal and environmental determinants that shape sport consumer involvement. The application of this research provides marketing and management solutions to organisations dedicated to the delivery of sport, tourism and recreation services and products. Professor Funk has published over 80 refereed articles in scientific journals, authored the book *Consumer Behaviour for Sport & Events: Marketing Action*, currently serves as Editor for *Sport Marketing Quarterly* and is a distinguished fellow in the North American Society for Sport Management and the Sport Marketing Association. Professor Funk continues to work on various international projects examining marketing practices for professional and collegiate sport teams and participation at sporting events. He has given invited presentations at international conferences and seminars in Australia, Canada, Germany, Greece, Japan, New Zealand, Scotland, South Korea and the United States.

Adam Karg PhD is a Lecturer in Sport Management at Deakin University in Melbourne, Australia. His PhD thesis investigated the structural design of sport organisations in Australia. He holds a Bachelor of Commerce, majoring in Sport Management and Sport Economics, with first-class Honours in sport marketing. Adam is Course Director of the Undergraduate program at Deakin and has received teaching and learning awards, having taught undergraduate and postgraduate courses in sport marketing, promotions and public relations, broadcasting and organisation.

He has been engaged in a range of consulting and research projects, and advisory roles, with national and state sporting organisations and governing bodies, charities, sport technology start-ups and more than 25 professional sport clubs in Australia and overseas, including AFL, Big Bash League, A-League, NRL and Super Rugby teams. He has developed a reputation as one of Australia's leading researchers of fan development and season ticket-holder and membership services related to satisfaction, fan engagement and loyalty. He continues to undertake research in consumer behaviour, sponsorship, online engagement, branding, media consumption and fantasy sport.

Adam has presented at leading sport management conferences in Australia, New Zealand, North America and Europe, as well as national and international marketing conferences, and has had articles published in leading international sport management and marketing peer-reviewed journals. He also sits on the board of the Sport Management Association of Australia and New Zealand (SMAANZ). Prior to joining Deakin, Adam developed a background in sport through positions with sport marketing and media companies and worked in equity research within investment banking.

Part I

Introduction

1

An overview of sport marketing

CHAPTER OBJECTIVES

After studying this chapter, you should be able to:

- discuss the role of marketing in organisations
- identify the marketing mix
- describe the importance of marketing in sport organisations
- describe the unique product features of sport and their impact on sport marketing
- define sport marketing.

HEADLINE STORY

Crowded out: The crowds for 50-over internationals are diminishing

Bums on seats have always been a vital indicator of the public's appetite for One-Day International (ODI) cricket. They still are—it's just that instead of those seats being at the ground, increasingly they are in people's homes instead. During the week, the Sydney Cricket Ground (SCG) in Sydney and the Gabba in Brisbane announced they were down to their last few thousand available tickets for their looming ODIs. A decade ago, whenever the Australian team was in town, a near-capacity turn-out was likely for everywhere except Melbourne. Now that situation has become the exception. When New Zealand and South Africa toured in 2001–02, the average ODI tri-series crowd for matches involving Australia was a touch under 40 000 people. In the decade since, it has never been as high—even when bigger drawcards such as England and India have been involved. The plateau of ODI attendances since 2001–02 has transformed to a decline since 2006–07 for two key reasons: allowing unhindered live television coverage in Melbourne and Sydney (and Brisbane three years later), and Twenty20 Internationals gaining a foothold. Since Cricket Australia (CA) decided to schedule more than a single Twenty20 international per summer, from 2007–08, the average crowd for those matches has hovered about 20 000 above the corresponding number for that summer's ODI matches involving Australia. CA's decision to schedule this summer's two Twenty20 internationals at the nation's biggest stadiums—the Melbourne Cricket Ground (MCG) in Melbourne and ANZ Stadium in Sydney—will make that gap between the two limited-overs formats a chasm this season—an average of 60 967 from two Twenty20 internationals compared with 22 034 across Australia's four ODIs so far. Just under 30 000 people attended the series-opening match at the MCG between Australia and India—a hefty proportion of the crowd was supporting the visitors—while the average crowd at the SCG has been below 30 000 in three of the past four seasons. If CA was relying on ticket sales to make ends meet, the issue of ODI crowds would be plunging towards crisis stage. The reason why it is not is simple: television.

To blame all weakened ODI crowds on live TV coverage would be wrong, especially based on the most recent matches in blackout zones Perth and Adelaide. The 13 085 people who attended last Friday's match at Perth's WACA Ground between Australia and Sri Lanka was below that for all five of the Perth Scorchers' home matches in the Big Bash League. Similarly, the 22 728 who last Sunday watched Australia and India at the Adelaide Oval—a venue where ODI crowds have held up well in recent years—was only just above the 21 964 average home crowd for the Adelaide Strikers, one of the laggards of the BBL. One reason why ODI attendances cannot totally be ignored is that in just under three years Australia will, with New Zealand, host the 2015 World Cup. Even more than the yearly international matches in Australia, that event will be geared towards television ratings. But the World Cup is one event where money is not everything. Prestige is crucial too, both in terms of scheduling matches involving Australia and the finals. (Hogan, 2012)

In the technological world of 2014 and beyond, many sports have emerged via the media to challenge for the position of global dominance. Soccer has long remained unchallenged as the world's most globalised sport, a competitive advantage based on high levels of participation and interest in so many countries throughout the world, resulting in soccer being a highly sought-after broadcast commodity. Cricket, which is a popular but not global sport, has sought consistently to expand its market by working to develop new markets and by varying its product to better suit the needs of television. The introduction of the 50-over-per-team ODI format was predicated on the need to expand the market by providing a shortened version of the sport. Twenty20 cricket presents similar dilemmas to those confronted when ODIs were first mooted as a serious component of international cricket fixtures. The compressed format of the sport often leads to more exciting and intense style of cricket and, more importantly, a quick result.

Strategically, cricket has been struggling to find the right fit for its newest product offering. Significantly, its expanding product portfolio has created tensions between the various forms of the game and, in relation to television, live attendances as it tries to balance the needs of its broadcast partners against income derived from attendances. The role of Twenty20 cricket in the product portfolio is clearly growing, but is it a legitimate form of the game that warrants a World Cup format? Indeed, the most recent Twenty20 world championship was played in Sri Lanka in September and October 2012. Alternatively, is the prime role of Twenty20 cricket to entertain and promote the wider features of the sport of cricket?

This is a classic strategic and competitive positioning question confronted by many sport marketers in many different sports. Obviously, the three-hour, 20-over-per-team format is more attractive to television than the two other longer forms of the sport. Moreover, it is also more appealing to cricket fans, but it may simply be redistributing fans among the various forms of the game. In three hours, television executives can expect rapid-fire big hitting, lots of wickets, thrilling catches and run-out opportunities, as well as constant scampering between the wickets by the batsmen. All this action, plus a result without having to hold the viewers' attention for a whole day or more, is very appealing.

Major changes have occurred to the competitive positions of a variety of sports as a consequence of the media's ability to show sporting competitions played in all parts of the world. Domestic competitions also have increased in familiarity through the media. For example, the former Victorian Football League (VFL) has expanded from a twelve-team, state-based competition to become an eighteen-team national competition played in five states. Basketball, too, has capitalised on its increased exposure, creating the National Basketball League (NBL). Television and new media generally have contributed to the emergence of new and restructured competitions. Changing competitive conditions have forced sport managers to develop more complex and subtle marketing strategies for their sports, based on increasingly sophisticated means of sourcing data through a variety of business analytic tools.

The purpose of this book is to examine the role of marketing within the sport context. More specifically, it will consider the role of marketing from a strategic perspective, highlighting the ways in which marketing contributes to the growth and development of various sports. Marketing assumes greater significance than other management functions in sporting organisations, as it remains the principal means by which sports compete off the field. For instance, large firms such as BHP Billiton, PepsiCo and Pacific Dunlop have the option to pursue acquisition-type strategies to build market share, or to engage in product development or diversification. These strategies generally are not available to sporting organisations, the principal responsibility of which is as national governing bodies, such as the Football Federation of Australia, Bowls Australia or Swimming Australia. In the broader context of the sport industry, major manufacturing firms such as Nike, Adidas, Puma and Spalding are large firms that do have the capacity to pursue acquisition-based strategies. In sport, each governing body is responsible for a specific code, and its charter is to develop and enhance that particular sport. Product diversification may occur, but sport-governing bodies rarely use strategies based on acquisition. This is particularly evident for club-based sport systems.

Cricket Australia's consideration of the strategic role of Twenty20 cricket is a classic case of product diversification. The possibility of a Twenty20 league involving domestic teams from Australia, England, South African and India has strategic merit. The creation of this league would diversify cricket's television product offering, with obvious financial benefits from rights revenues. Importantly, it would also provide an additional competitive outlet and financial reward for second-tier cricketers worldwide. It also has the benefit of exposing the next generation of cricketers to future forms of international cricket. Indirectly, television is driving this strategy—largely in response to the competitive forces emerging out of India in relation to the creation of the Indian Premier League (IPL). The main product of this new league is Twenty20 cricket. As always, strategic decisions warrant careful consideration of their impact. Saltau (2007: 17) notes, for example, that: 'In developing the new league, Cricket Australia will be anxious not to cannibalise the traditional forms, which also are lucrative, and to ensure profits are ploughed back into the game.' The importance of marketing strategy in sport management is illustrated by cricket, and is discussed further later in this chapter.

Marketing defined

Marketing, as defined by Kotler et al. (2006: 7), is 'a social and managerial process by which individuals and groups obtain what they need and want through creating and exchanging products and value with others'. The identification of consumer needs and wants is a critical aspect of the marketer's role. Marketing strategies must be based on known consumer needs.

In sport, it has been assumed that the original form of the game is naturally attractive, and therefore satisfies consumer needs. An analysis of sporting organisations in Australia shows this to be an outdated view, however. Many sports have modified rules to make their games more attractive and, in the case of cricket, one-day and Twenty20 matches have become an important part of the range of product offerings. One-Day International matches played throughout an Australian summer have more readily satisfied consumer need for compressed entertainment and a quick result—so much so that Twenty20 is now considered more entertaining and likely to attract new consumers to the sport of cricket. At junior levels, many sports have been modified significantly to satisfy the desire of many more young people to participate in the game. Inherent in this change has been the recognition that juniors wish to develop game skills through actual participation, to have fun, and in general to be with their friends through the sport setting.

The sport marketer must identify what needs and wants are being satisfied through the exchange process. Kotler et al. (2006: 10) identify the process of exchange 'as the act of obtaining a desired object from someone by offering something in return'. What is offered in return for the sport consumer's membership fees or entry fee may include social interaction, physical activity and an avenue for competition, health and fitness, as well as entertainment. Identifying the needs of various segments of the population is the challenge inherent in the early phase of the marketing process. Obtaining this information will allow the sport product's benefits to be communicated in such a way as to define the sport's positioning. For example, the product attributes of one-day cricket matches and five-day Test match cricket are different, and are likely to attract different segments of the market.

Having established the range of product attributes in relation to needs and wants, the sport marketer embarks on the challenge of effecting the exchange. Sporting organisations must develop a mix of marketing strategies to influence consumers to buy their products, via either attendance or participation. Combined, the four variables of product, price, promotion and place are known as the traditional four Ps of marketing.

Defining the sport marketing mix

Figure 1.1 depicts the seven component strategies of the marketing mix, composed of the traditional 4Ps of marketing plus the 3Ps of service—process, people and physical evidence. These 7Ps form the nucleus of this book, and each will be described in more detail in later chapters. A brief description of the 7Ps is as follows:

- *Product*—ensures that product characteristics provide benefits to the consumer (includes identifying the actual product).
- *Price*—ensures that the product is priced at a level that reflects consumer value.
- *Place*—distributes the product to the right place at the right time to allow ease of purchase.
- *Physical evidence*—is the visual and/or tangible clues of the service product, such as the design and construction of the facility, and in general the aesthetic appeal.
- *Process*—represents the convergence of the marketing and operations functions and therefore affects real-time service delivery and quality.
- *People*—are responsible for delivering the event and are a major distinguishing quality factor in the consumption process.
- *Promotion*—communicates the product's ability to satisfy the customer through advertising, personal selling, sales promotions, sponsorship, public relations and promotional licensing.

In sport, the combination and implementation of these marketing mix variables change due to the unique characteristics of the sport product. The most notable change from the traditional 4Ps of marketing is not only in its expansion to 7Ps, but in the order

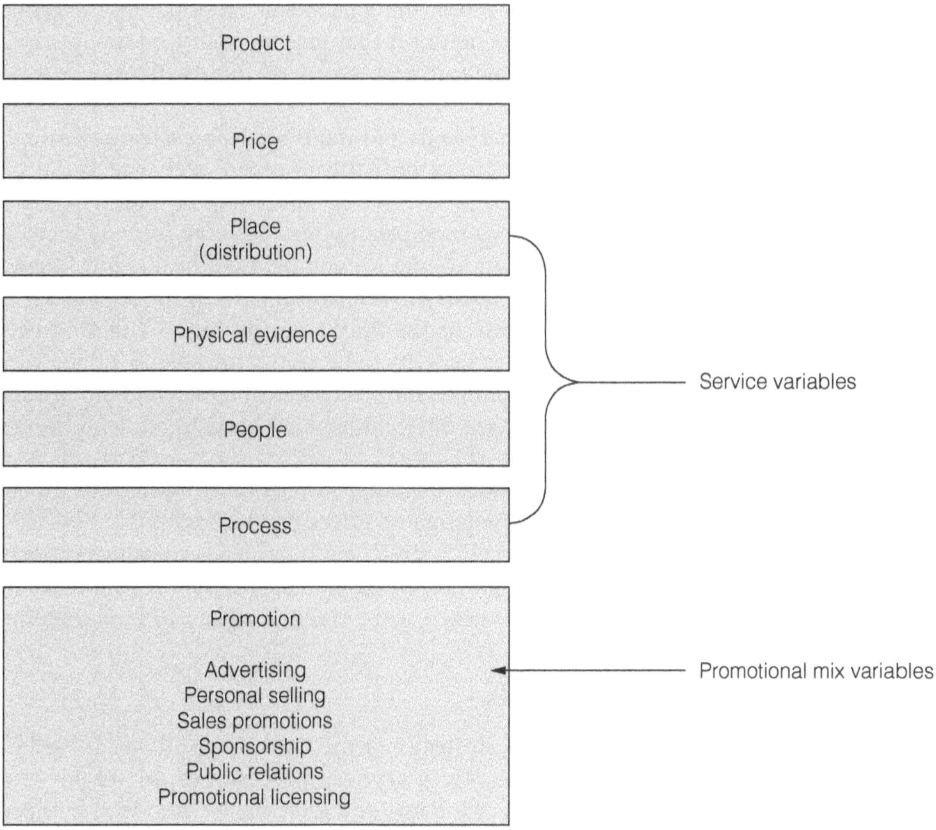

FIGURE 1.1 The marketing mix: The 7Ps

we recommend in determining marketing strategies for sporting organisations—particularly those reliant on facilities to host the sporting contest. This expansion and reordering also take account of the special features of sport, and are described in the next section.

Unique characteristics of sport and sport marketing

In 1980, Mullin identified, for the first time, a series of characteristics of the sport product that affect the marketing process. Mullin argued that sport had progressed from a form of institution that was simply 'administered' to a form of organisation that required 'managing'. In making this distinction, he noted that sport had reached a phase in its development where it was incumbent on the sport manager to be actively seeking ways to expand the revenue base of the organisation. Typically, the administrator is responsible for maintaining the status quo within the sporting organisation. The manager, on the other hand, is responsible for assessing and evaluating environmental trends likely to affect the organisation's survival and, ultimately, its success. The modern sport marketer is charged with one simple responsibility: to increase the sources of revenue for the sport. The tools to achieve this will be discussed in later chapters.

Mullin identified five special characteristics of sport marketing. In examining these characteristics, he notes (1985a: 106):

> Almost every element of marketing requires significantly different approaches when the product being marketed is sport. Predictably, the critical differences lie in the unique aspects of the sport product, and the unusual market conditions facing sport marketers.

The five characteristics noted by Mullin are summarised in Table 1.1. Interestingly, some of these characteristics reflect attributes associated with marketing services. It is uncertain whether this was intentional; clearly, sport is a service product. Service-marketing implications for sport marketing will be developed and integrated further throughout this text.

TABLE 1.1 Unique characteristics of sport marketing

Market for sport products and services

- Sport organisations simultaneously compete and cooperate.
- Partly due to the unpredictability of sport, and partly due to strong personal identification, sport consumers often consider themselves 'experts'.

Sport product

- Sport is invariably intangible and subjective.
- Sport is inconsistent and unpredictable.
- Marketing emphasis must be placed on product extensions rather than the core product.
- Sport is generally publicly consumed, and consumer satisfaction is invariably affected by social facilitation.
- Sport is both a consumer and an industrial product.
- Sport evokes powerful personal identification and emotional attachment.
- Sport has almost universal appeal and pervades all elements of life—that is, geographically, demographically and socioculturally.

Price of sport

- The price of sport paid by the consumer is invariably quite small in comparison with the total cost.
- Indirect revenues (e.g. from television) are often greater than direct operating revenues (e.g. gate receipts).
- Sport programs have rarely been required to operate on a for-profit basis.
- Pricing is often decided by what the consumer will bear rather than by full cost recovery.

Promotion of sport

- Widespread exposure afforded to sport by the media has resulted in a low emphasis on sport marketing and, often, complacency.
- Due to the high visibility of sport, many businesses wish to associate with sport.

Sport distribution system

- Sports generally do not physically distribute their product. Most sport products are produced, delivered and consumed simultaneously at the one location. The exceptions are sporting goods and retail and broadcast sport.

Source: Adjusted from Mullin (1985a).

Consumer involvement

Perhaps the most readily identifiable characteristic is the 'expertise' demonstrated by the sport consumer. On the one hand, this is a disadvantage, as every move made by the sport manager and coaching staff is critically examined and dissected. The 'armchair selector' syndrome is an issue within sport. It is, however, one reason why sport is so popular. The pervasiveness and universal nature of sport, and the ease with which the consumer identifies with the sport product, compensate for the intensity with which the consumer follows sport. Very few businesses in the world are viewed with such simplicity and such personal identification by the consumer.

Unpredictability

As with most service products, the consumer's interpretation and enjoyment of the sport product are open to considerable subjectivity. Participation in and attendance at sporting contests allow the consumer to gain varying forms of gratification. For example, some spectators may enjoy the closeness of the game, others the entertainment surrounding the game and yet others the inherent strategies of the contest. This makes it difficult for the sport marketer to ensure a high probability of satisfaction, and hence repeat attendance. The intangibility and subjective nature of sport spectating and sport attending clearly align sport with the service industry. No tangible product is taken from the sporting contest—as opposed, for example, to the purchase of a washing machine or similar goods. These characteristics of the service experience are examined and extended further in Chapters 5, 7 and 8, which cover service quality, facility management in the context of service delivery and customer satisfaction in sport.

Equally unpredictable is the actual sporting contest, which varies from week to week. This heterogeneity is a feature of sport. It is the unpredictability of the result and the quality of the contest that consumers find attractive. For the sport marketer, this is problematic, as the quality of the contest cannot be guaranteed, no promises can be made in relation to the result and no assurances can be given in respect of the performance of star players. Unlike consumer products, sport cannot and does not display consistency as a key feature of marketing strategies. The sport marketer therefore must avoid marketing strategies based solely on winning, and must instead focus on developing product extensions rather than on the core product (that is, the game itself). Product extensions include the facility, parking, merchandise, souvenirs, food and beverages—in general, anything that affects spectators' enjoyment of the event. In Chapters 5, 7 and 8, we discuss the methods by which sport marketers can develop and improve the quality of product extensions.

Competition and cooperation

Another feature of the sportscape is the peculiar economy that dictates—in professional leagues at least—that clubs must both engage in fierce competition and at the same time cooperate. This is necessary to ensure that each club's contribution to the league enhances the strength of the league. An unusual blend of politics and competition emerges in sports leagues, often amplifying the importance of the public relations function, to be explored further in Chapter 15.

Sponsorship

Sponsorship of sport is also a unique feature of the sport economy. While not necessarily specific to sport, sponsorship has provided—and continues to provide—an opportunity for commercial advertising by corporations and businesses. Sponsorship represents the 'industrial' component of the sport product, and is manifested through commercial advertising of its industrial aspect.

Publicity

Complacency in developing adequate marketing strategies has resulted from an almost unlimited amount of media exposure for sporting clubs, leagues and associations. Sport traditionally has been able to rely on publicity as its principal form of marketing and promotion. The disadvantage of relying on publicity is the amount of negative press that occurs during a season or major event. More recently, major leagues, clubs and associations have become cognisant of the need to develop an effective public relations strategy to counter the issues that typically occur during a season or event. Unfortunately, sporting clubs and athletes must contend with serious issues relating to drug use, gambling and alcohol, and various other misdemeanours that attract the public's attention. This book views the public relations function as a very important aspect of the promotional mix.

Distribution

The final characteristic relates to the distribution system used by sport. As with most service providers, sports participation and spectating revolve around specific facilities for specific sports. To attend a sporting contest, spectators must travel to the venue—usually a major facility within a city. The actual facility becomes an integrated component of the marketing function, as the sport product is produced, consumed and delivered at the same time at the same venue. Many facilities, such as Melbourne's MCG, Medinah Golf Club in Chicago, Eden Park in Auckland, the Wanderers and Ellis Park Stadium in Johannesburg and Wembley Stadium in London, have developed an aura and mystique as a result of heroic performances on the ground over the years.

As a consequence of developments in technology, the distribution system for sport has undergone radical change during the past decade. It is now possible to distribute a game to all parts of the country and the world via television networks, the internet and other technologies such as mobile 4G networks. The introduction of pay television in Australia has further enhanced the distribution network for sport, as well as increasing the number and levels of different sport competitions shown. In general, however, the televised sport product is different from the live event. The mix of benefits is slightly different in each mode of consumption.

Due to the relatively stable nature of distribution (i.e. one major stadium per sport per city), it is vitally important to locate teams and facilities so that they are able to compete effectively in the market. In Australia, product distribution has been the focus of intense debate over the past 25 years. This is particularly evident in the expansion of the former Victorian Football League (VFL) to become the Australian Football League (AFL). In the early 1980s, the VFL was a twelve-team, state-based competition primarily located in Melbourne. By 1991 the league had changed its name to the AFL, as it had relocated the South Melbourne Football Club to Sydney and admitted the Brisbane Football Club and West Coast Football Club in 1987, followed by the Adelaide Crows in 1991. By 1995, a second team from Western Australia (Fremantle) had joined the competition, and a second team from South Australia (Port Adelaide) entered in 1997. In 2011, the Gold Coast Suns were admitted to the competition followed in 2012 by Greater Western Sydney, which served to increase local competition from a marketing perspective in Southeast Queensland and the city of Sydney. However, nine teams remain in Melbourne, a city of approximately 4.1 million people. While this is an example of a league reconfiguring its distribution, once established it should remain relatively stable despite obvious over-capacity in Melbourne.

A comparison between the United States and Australia illustrates just how important location of the product is in terms of developing appropriate marketing strategies, particularly in view of the substantial population differences between the two countries. The United States has a population in excess of 300 million, compared with Australia's 22.6 million. The US national competitions of basketball (National Basketball Association, NBA), football (National Football League, NFL), baseball (Major League Baseball, MLB) and ice hockey (National Hockey League, NHL) have evolved past the point of over-capacity in any one city. Significantly, the three major markets of Greater New York, Los Angeles and Chicago (each with a population of 10–18 million) all host professional franchises. However, not one of these markets hosts more than two teams of any one code. The importance of marketing as a revenue-generating activity for the clubs is important in this issue of location. Over-capacity intensifies competition and reduces the available income for each of the teams located in any one common market. This issue will be acutely on display in Sydney with the arrival of the second AFL team, Greater Western Sydney, in a market that traditionally has not been a stronghold for the AFL. Marketing strategy will play just as important a role as on-field performances in the early years, as the club strives to establish its presence in Sydney, attract spectators and build loyalty leading to club membership sales.

Importance of marketing in sport management

As indicated earlier in this chapter, marketing plays a key role in the sporting organisation's overall planning efforts. This has not always been the case. The professionalisation of sport during the past 30 years has raised the level of importance of the marketing function.

For much of sport history, volunteers have administered organisations in the true spirit of amateur participation. As sport systems founded on club-based models evolved from amateur to professional clubs, leagues and associations, there was a lengthy transition period between what is described as 'kitchen table' administration and professional management. In Australia, this was the period pre-1970. As Figure 1.2(a) illustrates, during this period of voluntary administration, the marketing function was non-existent. The predominant tasks were to ensure the ongoing operation of the club, league or association. Administrators adopted a very narrow view of their organisation, preferring to concentrate on internal operations. Typically, administrators dealt with only half of the accounting and budgetary process: the allocation and control of

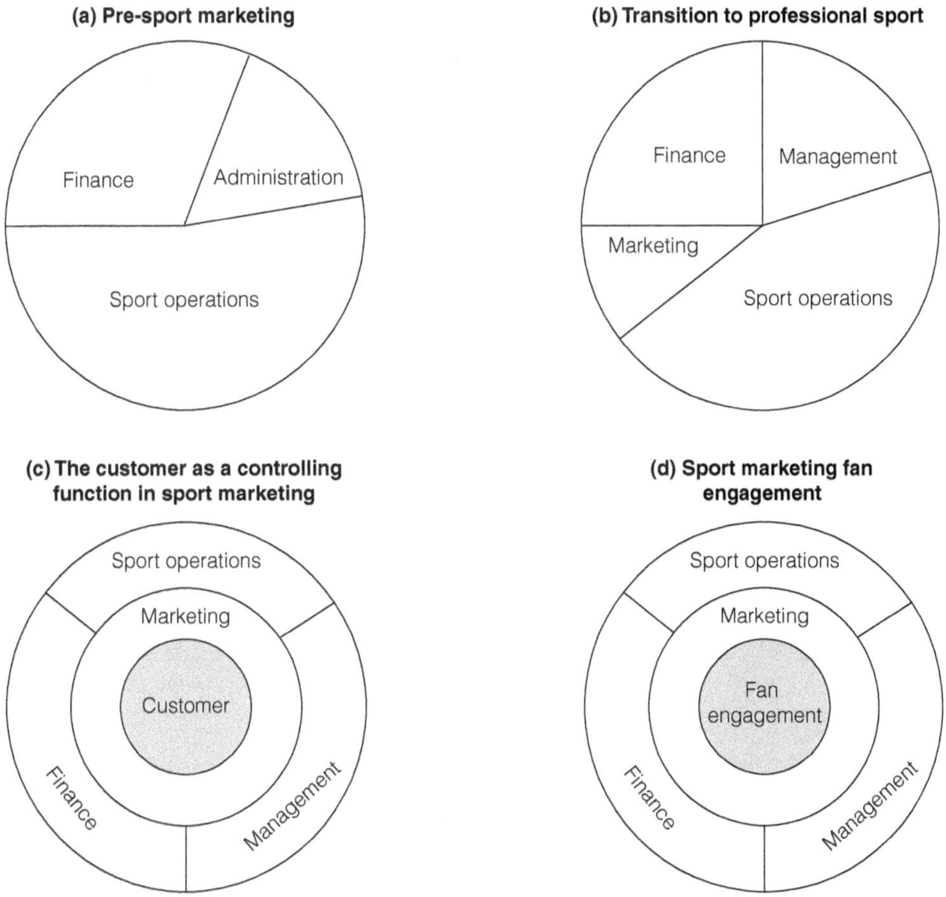

FIGURE 1.2 The importance of sport marketing

expenditures. Even as sporting organisations began to professionalise, the administrator 'culture' lingered for some years.

Figure 1.2(b) displays the progressive movement away from administration to management of organisations. One of the manager's main tasks is to monitor environmental trends and plan for the organisation's ongoing growth. Sport was very reluctant to embrace proactive growth. The Australian Cricket Board's (ACB—now Cricket Australia) dispute with Kerry Packer over television rights, and the players' push for improved remuneration and playing conditions in 1977, are examples of a major sport adopting narrow internal perspectives. The introduction of colour television was an example of a technological change ignored by the ACB. World Series Cricket (WSC) subsequently proved to be the catalyst that forced sporting organisations in Australia to embrace a greater range of business functions. This view is supported by Halbish (1995: 3), who notes that 'looking back traditional cricket had grown out of touch with the fast emerging professionalism of sport in Australia'. By 1980, WSC and the ACB had reconciled their differences;

however, from that point marketing was to become an important element of business activity in sport. Interestingly, during 2007 the Board of Control for Cricket in India (BCCI) was fighting a similar battle to that fought by the ACB 30 years earlier. In 2007, a privately financed Indian Cricket League (ICL) was being formed, with its first tournament held in October 2007 using the lively Twenty20 format, following the officially sanctioned ICC Twenty20 World Cup in South Africa. The ICL had also signalled its intentions to organise traditional 50-over one-day matches in the future; however, the ICL folded in 2009 as the BCCI-controlled IPL gained ascendancy and domination of the Indian Twenty20 cricketing landscape. Nevertheless, once again, a rival competition from outside traditional structures caused a wave of change in the sport.

Myriad issues arise here, not the least being who players are contracted to, and who controls cricket, in India. As was the case in Australia many years earlier, the plight of the players was central to these issues, with full-time professional athletes requiring financial security. More importantly, the increasing importance of the media, and revenues from new and old technologies, drove the ICL and the need to fill airtime and boost subscriptions. India is a developing country, with an under-developed sporting infrastructure. These issues and others are certain to surface during these times of transition to professional sport.

Initially, marketing activities in Australia were outsourced by a number of sports. The ACB, for example, granted marketing rights to a company known as PBL Marketing. Taylor (1984: 13), the managing director of PBL at the time, made the following observations about the status of marketing and sponsorship in sport following the reconciliation:

> Five years ago the Australian Cricket Board did not have a published program . . . Last year more than 300 000 copies of the ACB program were sold and this year almost 20 publications will be on sale. Work has also been put into merchandising . . . it has taken five years to develop 29 licensees, but this season we expect cricket merchandise to top $5 million in retail turn-over and to start producing a satisfactory level of return.

Figure 1.2(c) demonstrates the importance that marketing has taken on, despite a long period of resisting the need to promote and nurture new and fertile markets. For the first time, the identification and nurturing of new markets brought recognition that the customer is central to ongoing organisational survival. Sports had to find ways of generating revenue to sustain the growing costs of professional competitions. One-day cricket is an example of modifying the product to increase market share for the sport, as is the recently introduced Twenty20 cricket and its attractiveness as a televised product as exemplified through the ICL BCCI dispute in India. Focusing on consumer needs and wants via increasingly sophisticated marketing research, sport organisations have continued to develop strategies based on consumer information. Many of these developments focus on product extensions, although changes to game formats and rules are also common.

The centrality of the consumer has been even more important due to the evolving spectrum of social media. Focusing on consumer needs has evolved further to customer or fan engagement. Figure 1.2(d) shows customer/fan engagement to be a pivotal feature of contemporary sport marketing communication strategies—largely the result of evolving social media outlets. Kaplan and Haenlein (2010) created a classification scheme of the different types of social media, which illustrates why sport organisations have now moved to capitalise on the opportunity to develop a closer sense of involvement with fans. The six categories include: collaborative projects (Wikipedia, Dropbox); blogs and microblogs (Twitter); content communities (YouTube); social networking sites (Facebook); virtual game worlds (Fantasy sports); and virtual social worlds (*Second Life*). Of these social media outlets, the creation of fantasy sports has become very popular with sports fans, as they seek to simulate the real-life experiences of team management. Fantasy sports and the other forms of social media will all be developed further in later chapters, and it is in this area that the most significant changes to marketing strategies used by sport organisations can be observed.

Together with sport operations (that is, all that surrounds the management of fielding a team), marketing is a sporting organisation's principal ground for identifying and creating a competitive advantage. Normal acquisition-type strategies associated with for-profit firms are not so readily applicable to sport. Internal growth strategies tend to be the major ground on which sport competes. These strategies are developed further in Chapter 2.

Ethical behaviour

Increasingly, commercial pressures create tension for the sport marketer. That is, sport-marketing executives often find themselves caught between an opportunity to generate revenue for their sport and the consequences of changes that might accompany these revenues. Consider, for example, the staging of an Olympic marathon during the middle and hottest part of the day because a television network asks for it to be staged at that time to maximise ratings. What do you do? Clearly, scheduling the marathon at this time will not be in the best interests of the athletes. Alternatively, what do you do if you work with the NRL and the strategic goal is to reduce the number of clubs in the competition? This was a real-life dilemma, as the South Sydney Rugby League club was removed from the competition as part of a rationalisation strategy. The club subsequently won the right, through a protracted legal battle, for readmission to the NRL competition from 2002. As a sport-marketing manager, with the goal of maximising revenues for the competition, how do you balance commercial interests against the social and community interests in the South Sydney club? These two examples illustrate ethical dilemmas, which are practical problems requiring solutions—often involving equally compelling reasons to act one way or the other. In essence, the sport manager must determine the right thing to do without a definitive 'rule book' available to guide decision-making.

Although space precludes a detailed analysis of ethics and corporate social responsibility here, sport managers must consider their actions within a broader societal framework. DeSensi and Rosenberg (2010: 135) note that

> recognition of ethics and social responsibility has increased in recent years . . . as a sport manager, learning to adopt a social consciousness leading to a commitment to being socially responsible is paramount . . . Questions regarding the nature of the complex relationship between society, sport and the formal organisations of sport are raised within social responsibility.

Given the significant standing of sport in Australian culture, and as a social institution, community expectations in relation to the behaviour of sport managers are often high. There are many examples of sport-marketing decisions that create ethical tensions for individuals, and collectively for organisations, wishing to be good corporate citizens. Some of these are explored in this book—in particular in the chapters on sponsorship, where ambush marketing is a source of considerable ethical frustration for managers.

Sport marketing defined

The term 'sport marketing' was first used in the United States by the *Advertising Age* in 1978. Since then, it has been used to describe a variety of activities associated with sport promotion. Two distinct streams exist within the broad concept of sport marketing: marketing 'of' sport, and marketing 'through' sport.

Marketing 'of' sport

This refers to the use of marketing mix variables to communicate the benefits of sport participation and spectatorship to potential consumers. Ultimately, the goal is to ensure the ongoing survival of the sport in rapidly changing environmental circumstances. This aspect of marketing has only recently developed in sporting organisations. Survival depends largely on the principal purpose of the sporting organisation. National sporting organisations predominantly associated with elite-level professional sporting competitions will be striving to develop their marketing mix to ensure that the sport product is attractive as a form of live entertainment and live broadcast via television, the internet and other mobile outlets. Sports-governing bodies will also be responsible for ensuring that participation in their sport remains healthy. Participants are the lifeblood of sport, as they become the next generation of champions and spectators.

We do not make any notable distinctions in this book between marketing strategies specifically pursued for either spectator or participant sport. The theories posited are equally applicable, regardless of the principal objective of the marketing strategy. As with all marketing strategies, when the objectives change, the actions or strategies used to achieve the objectives also change. The application of the marketing mix does not, although various components of the mix may assume more importance in the two different scenarios. For example, the outlets used to advertise a junior sporting competition would be different from those used to advertise a major sporting event. Students of sport marketing should adapt the concepts of sport marketing to either situation, because each is vital to the ongoing survival and financial well-being of individual sporting organisations.

Marketing 'through' sport

Sponsorship of sport by firms is an example of marketing 'through' sport. Large corporations use sport as a vehicle to promote and advertise their products, usually to specifically identifiable demographic markets known to follow a particular sport. Sports with significant television time are very attractive to firms seeking to promote their products through an association with sport. Developing licensing programs is another example of marketing through sport. Typically, major companies such as Tip Top (bread) or Coca-Cola pay for the right to use a sport logo to place on their products to stimulate sales.

Although the main emphasis of this book is on marketing 'of' sport, the role of corporate sponsorship and licensing in sport marketing is also examined.

Definition

Given these perspectives, and information pertaining to marketing in general, the following definition of sport marketing is offered:

> Sport marketing is a social and managerial process by which the sport manager seeks to obtain what sporting organisations need and want through creating and exchanging products and value with others.

The exchange of value with others recognises the importance of the sport consumer. The many different types of sport consumer are discussed in more detail in Part II of this book.

Overview of this book

The ability to recognise the needs and wants of consumers does not necessarily imply action. It is the action associated with the marketing process in sport that is the focus of this text. This is known as the marketing management process, which is described by Kotler et al. (2006: 13) as 'the analysis, planning, implementing and control of programs designed to create, build and maintain beneficial exchanges with target buyers for the purpose of achieving organisational objectives'.

This chapter has defined marketing and sport marketing, as well as introducing the unique characteristics of sport and how they impinge on the marketing process. The remainder of this book is divided into three parts:

- Part II examines how the sport marketer identifies marketing opportunities. Chapter 2 examines the place of marketing in the planning process and specifically reviews the strategic sport-marketing planning process; Chapter 3 concentrates on understanding the sport consumer; and Chapter 4 focuses on the market research and information systems, and the implications this information has for segmenting the sport marketplace.
- Part III covers the strategy determination stage. It examines the sport marketing mix and the way in which the organisation is positioned in relation to target markets. Selection of the core marketing strategy is significant in this stage, and the contribution of the 7Ps—product, price, place, physical evidence, process, people and promotion—to strategy determination is examined. The issues specific to sport marketing contained in these chapters include the place of the facility in service provision, service quality, customer satisfaction and engagement, sponsorship, public relations, television and its impact on sport marketing, and promotional licensing.
- Finally, Part IV returns to the important marketing management process of implementation and evaluation. This part consists of just one chapter, which examines how the sport marketer evaluates the success of marketing strategies and the coordinating function between the sport marketer and the rest of the organisation. Of particular interest to students will be a section on careers related to sport marketing.

Part II

Identification of marketing opportunities

2

The strategic sport-marketing planning process

Stage 1—Identification of marketing opportunities

Step 1—Analyse external environment (forces, competition, publics)

Step 2—Analyse organisation (mission, objectives, SWOT)

Step 3—Examine market research and marketing information systems

Step 4—Determine marketing mission and objectives

▼

Stage 2—Strategy determination

▼

Stage 3—Strategy implemention, evaluation and adjustment

CHAPTER OBJECTIVES

Chapter 2 identifies three stages that make up the strategic sport-marketing planning process. Within these stages, eight steps are isolated as constituting the marketing planning sequence for sporting organisations. Steps 1–4 are reviewed in this chapter, with the remaining steps covered in Parts III and IV. In sporting organisations, the strategic sport-marketing planning process (SSMPP) assumes great significance because these organisations are often one-product entities, and therefore organisation-wide planning and marketing planning become the same process.

After studying this chapter, you should be able to:

- understand the strategic sport-marketing planning process
- recognise the role of strategic sport-marketing planning in sport
- analyse the forces driving industry competition
- conduct a SWOT analysis
- recognise the principal strategies available in sport marketing.

HEADLINE STORY

Rugby World Cup 2011 boost for all areas of the game

The success of Rugby World Cup 2011 looks set to deliver a significant boost to the ongoing development of Rugby worldwide, after tournament owners Rugby World Cup Limited today announced strong initial financial results for the showcase event. With New Zealand 2011 hailed as an exceptional event, the tournament is on track to achieve a net surplus of more than £90 million [A$143.4 million], making RWC 2011 the second-highest revenue earning event in the history of the tournament. Gross commercial revenues achieved for Rugby World Cup 2011 of £142 million [A$226.3 million] were within 3 per cent of the total achieved for the record-breaking France 2007, reaffirming the tournament as one of the world's premier sporting events.

Previous forecasts indicated the tournament, the seventh Rugby World Cup, would achieve a surplus of £80 million [A$127.5 million], but the strength of the Rugby World Cup brand in the commercial marketplace and increased broadcast exposure, particularly in new markets, contributed to results that will ensure that the game's governing body, the IRB Council, is able to continue to invest significantly in the development of the game at all levels worldwide over the next four-year cycle.

The announcement is another boost for a tournament that exceeded all revenue, ticketing and visitor forecasts for the host nation and tournament organisers, Rugby New Zealand (RNZ) 2011 Limited. This was the largest event ever hosted in the country. More than 1.35 million fans took their seats at 48 matches, with revenue from ticket sales surpassing the NZ$268.5 million [A$223 million] target set by RNZ in 2011. This equated to more than ten times the gross revenue generated by the next biggest sporting event hosted by New Zealand, the 2005 British and Irish Lions tour. In addition, more than 133 000 fans travelled to New Zealand from overseas—nearly double original forecasts. The tournament is estimated to have boosted economic activity in New Zealand by more than NZ$500 million [A$416 million], delivering a significant return for the host nation.

"The financial results also reflect the significant commitment and support of the tournament by our Unions and are a strong endorsement of our long-term hosting strategy. The awarding of Rugby World Cup 2015 to England and Rugby World Cup 2019 to Japan at the same time has provided certainty for our commercial partners and broadcasters and has ultimately enabled the IRB to take a ten-year strategic view to global investment to ensure that our Tier 1 base is strong while maintaining our investment in Tier 2 and 3 and developing Rugby markets." Rugby World Cup is the financial driver of the Global Game, and over the 2009–12 period the IRB is investing £150 million [A$239 million] across all 117 Member Unions at all levels of the game. RWC 2011 will provide the platform for unprecedented investment in Union Grants, tournaments, strategic investments, research and development and player welfare programmes during the next four-year Rugby World Cup cycle. (International Rugby Board, 2012)

According to *The Economist* (2011), New Zealand lived up to its claim to be a stadium of four million during the World Cup. Rugby Union is New Zealand's most significant sport, and arguably the All Blacks are its highest profile brand! After winning the 2011 World Cup, no one in New Zealand would likely argue with this claim. New Zealanders were desperate to host a Rugby World Cup, and even more desperate for the All Blacks to win! The cost of staging the event therefore was almost irrelevant. Such is the passion for the country's foremost sport. As *The Economist* notes, this event cost New Zealand in the region of NZ$300 million (A$249.7 million]. Based on the International Rugby Board (IRB) figures quoted above, the event ran at a surplus, but what is not clear from the figures reported by the IRB and New Zealand Rugby Union (NZRU) is whether this result captures the entire spending on infrastructure to support the World Cup as well as the actual operational costs of staging the event. It is likely that the New Zealand government spent millions more to upgrade facilities, and to improve roads and other infrastructure required to ensure the cities hosting major matches could cope with the influx of spectators.

Regardless of the actual outcomes, it is clear the Rugby World Cup has grown into a major event of economic importance to Rugby. The IRB (2009), in a summary of the finances of the World Cup, noted that the surplus generated from this event has grown from £17.6 million (A$28 million) in 1995, when the first event was hosted in South Africa, to £122.4 million (A$195 million) in 2007. Broadcast revenues have increased from £18.8 million (A$30 million) in 1995 to £82 million (A$130.7 million) in 2007. The £80 million surplus project from 2011 does not reach the heights of 2007, but it is clear that profits from the World Cup provide the security to develop a ten-year strategic view to invest in the game at all levels. This was obvious when both the NZRU and Australian Rugby Union (ARU) complained about lost revenues in the lead-up to the 2011 World Cup because their traditional Tri-Test series and Bledisloe Cup matches had to be scaled back due to the World Cup. Moreover, New Zealand threatened to boycott the 2015 World Cup in England if the financial model was not altered to compensate leading nations for lost revenue as a consequence of a reduced playing schedule. NZRU's Steven Tew, for example, observed that 'the tier one unions collectively lose £48 million [A$76.5 million] of revenue in this World Cup due to the impact on the international match schedule' (Growden, 2011: 17). Imagine a World Cup without the all-conquering and pervasive All Blacks! What would be the marketing and financial consequences for the World Cup? Would this positively or negatively influence the Tri-Nations series and Bledisloe Cup, the traditional profile and revenue generators for Australia and New Zealand Rugby Union? Ultimately, this issue was resolved in 2012 with the IRB agreeing to set aside £10 million to offset the impact of the World Cup on four nations: Australia, New Zealand, Argentina and South Africa.

The profits garnered from the World Cup raise some important strategic questions. Clearly, the sport has been very successful in its transition from an amateur code, but as the forces of commercialisation are realised, it is apparent that tensions are now evident when trying to find the right balance between the IRB securing its financial position and the needs of the major Rugby-playing countries. The most obvious question of strategic importance concerns how the sport will construct its major events schedule in order to maximise revenues for the major Rugby-playing countries. The answers are most likely to be found in the marketing strategies that Rugby formulates to develop its range of products (major events) and how it manages its event schedule and distributes its earnings.

Given the growing profile of Rugby Union, the ARU's desire to become Australia's main winter sport is ambitious, but it is also an example of how sporting organisations need to map out their strategies and adopt a systematic approach in order to achieve their stated goals. Consider the competitive marketplace for the football codes, which include the AFL, NRL and the A-League (soccer), which is played in spring and summer to avoid the competition provided by the AFL, NRL and Super 15s. It is apparent that the ARU will have to know its market. It is clear, however, that Rugby's dream run has commenced. As already indicated, Rugby has made considerable progress in Australia. With competition intensifying due to the move by both the NRL and AFL to national competitions during the 1990s, Rugby's response has been to capitalise on its international prominence through the Tri-Nations Series and Bledisloe Cup matches against New Zealand. Test matches, with the advent of Stadium Australia and its 80 000-plus capacity, boosted Rugby's ability to stage mega-events. In addition, the Super 15s has been the key strategy that has lifted the profile and image of Rugby in Australia. The Super 15s competition is an alliance between Australia, South Africa and New Zealand that has seen club Rugby played internationally. Moreover, it has meant that there exists a constant product for the respective Rugby-governing bodies to market, which provides more games to boost attendances, sponsorship revenues and, significantly, revenue from broadcast rights.

The strategies used to move the code from an amateur to a professional structure have been crafted carefully in a way cognisant of the importance of marketing strategy. The ARU's dream run continued with the sole staging of the World Cup in 2003, after New Zealand was not able to fulfil International Rugby Union conditions in relation to the provision of clean stadiums (stadiums free of existing advertising). This hallmark event was an important opportunity to market the game throughout Australia and beyond. Equally, the World Cup held in France during 2007 and New Zealand in 2011 provided the ARU and Rugby worldwide with further opportunities to expose the code and, significantly, a healthy surplus to continue growing the sport. Given that marketing is primarily concerned with consumer needs, it is the responsibility of the company to satisfy these needs. The ARU, for example, must satisfy multiple demands from:

- the *players*, who need matches and tournaments with attractive financial rewards
- the *sponsors*, who require star players and close, quality contests to ensure that their financial investment in Rugby attracts maximum exposure via the media, and
- the *paying public*, who want to see Rugby played at the optimum level.

Recognising and satisfying consumer needs ensures maximum market share, market development opportunities and growth. The ARU's challenge has been to develop its product by identifying opportunities for growth. To some extent, there existed latent demand for Rugby Union, as its former amateur structure did not aim to harness the potential of the sport by maximising playing opportunities. Spectators and players now have ample opportunity to watch or play at the elite level.

In this book, the strategic marketing planning process is specific in its reference to sport, and is labelled the strategic sport-marketing planning process (SSMPP). Figure 2.1 illustrates the SSMPP, which includes the eight steps listed opposite.

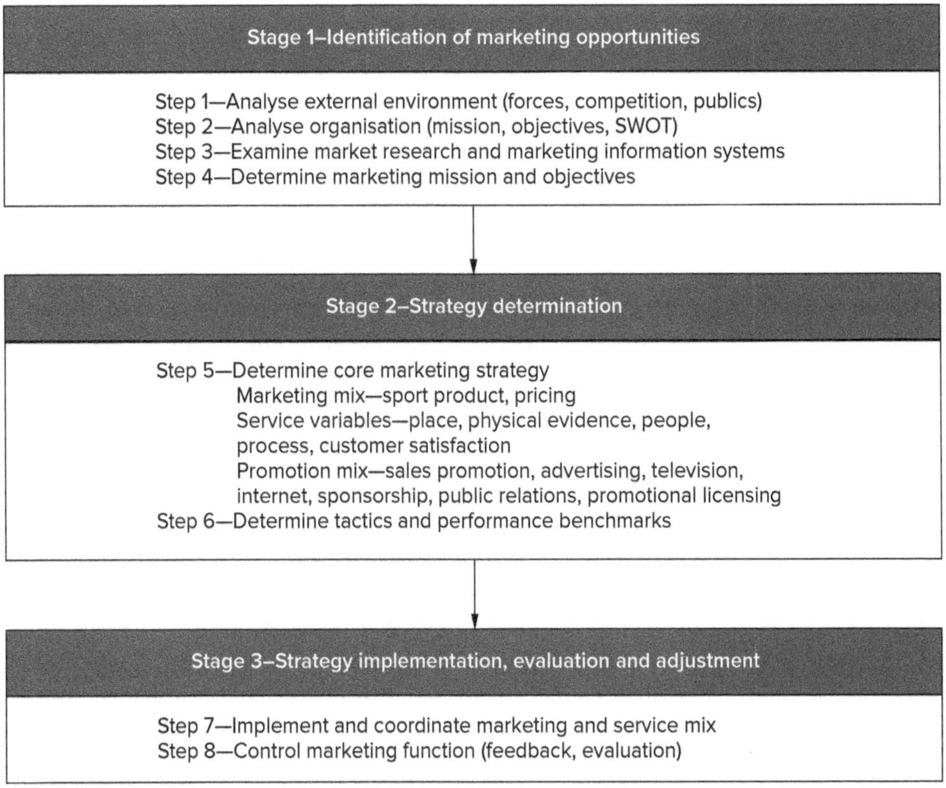

FIGURE 2.1 The strategic sport-marketing planning process

The strategic sport-marketing planning process

1 Analyse the external environment, the forces driving industry competition and the publics to be served.
2 Analyse the sporting organisation internally, to determine mission, goals and objectives, and to assess strengths, weaknesses, opportunities and threats (SWOT).
3 Examine market intelligence data in relation to the existing product range.
4 Determine the specific marketing mission and objectives for the prescribed period of the plan.
5 Determine the core marketing strategy using marketing mix variables, identifying and selecting the desired competitive position in relation to an identified sustainable competitive advantage.
6 Establish tactics to achieve objectives, and formulate benchmarks to measure progress.
7 Implement and operationalise the planned strategies.
8 Measure the success of core strategies, and adjust strategies where necessary.

This chapter examines Steps 1–4 of the SSMPP. Later chapters deal with individual aspects of the marketing and service mix variables, detailing the factors to consider in selecting a core marketing strategy, and Steps 7 and 8 are encapsulated in the final chapter. First, we examine both the external and internal environments and the forces driving competition.

Step 1: Understanding the environment in which the sport competes

A marketing program is not delivered in isolation of the organisation-wide planning process. In normal circumstances, the marketing planning process must reflect the overall plans for the organisation. In sport, as indicated by the Rugby Union example above, there is often little difference between organisation-wide planning and the marketing planning process. The ARU's overall direction and success are based solely on its major product offerings: Test matches and Super 15 Rugby. Determining the difference between organisation-wide planning and marketing planning requires careful attention by sport marketers.

The first step of the SSMPP is equivalent to conducting an inventory. The data collected form the basis of decisions made later in the process.

External forces

Figure 2.2 shows the environmental factors requiring consideration, which are the forces that affect an organisation indirectly. They include government legislation, economic climate, technology, political forces, and demographic and social trends. It is important for sporting organisations to monitor changes in each of these forces. Government legislation, for example, can alter the economic infrastructure of an industry through legislative changes. For instance, when pay TV was introduced to Australia in the 1990s, government legislation dictated that pay TV operators would not be able to sell advertising time for the first five years. This was designed to protect the free-to-air networks; and, given the importance of sports programming to television revenues, this policy reduced pay TV's capacity to generate revenue and, in turn, its capacity to pay for rights to broadcast sport. Technology can also change the ways in which businesses operate. The internet, via Twitter, smartphones, tablets and apps, has altered the means through which organisations can communicate with members, players, coaches and officials. It is also an important source of information for fans. The role of the new media in the marketing mix, and specifically the promotions mix, is considered in detail in Chapter 12.

At a macro level, political forces might involve government policy directly affecting an industry. In Australian sport, the Australian Sports Commission is the agency responsible for implementing government policy. Similar entities exist in other countries, including the Singapore Sports Council, the UK Sports Council and Sport New Zealand. A change of government often leads to new policies. The most obvious and important policy for many sports relates to funding support. Most national and state sport organisations are non-profit, with limited sources of revenue. Government funding is critical for ongoing development. One simple example of government policy is the focus of funding and programs on the elite or on mass-participatory programs. Demographic and social trends refer to the changing population makeup of Australia. For example, the increasingly multicultural composition of Australian communities will affect when, why and how sport marketers communicate with the community. It cannot be assumed that all sport consumers in a diversified society will respond in the same way to all

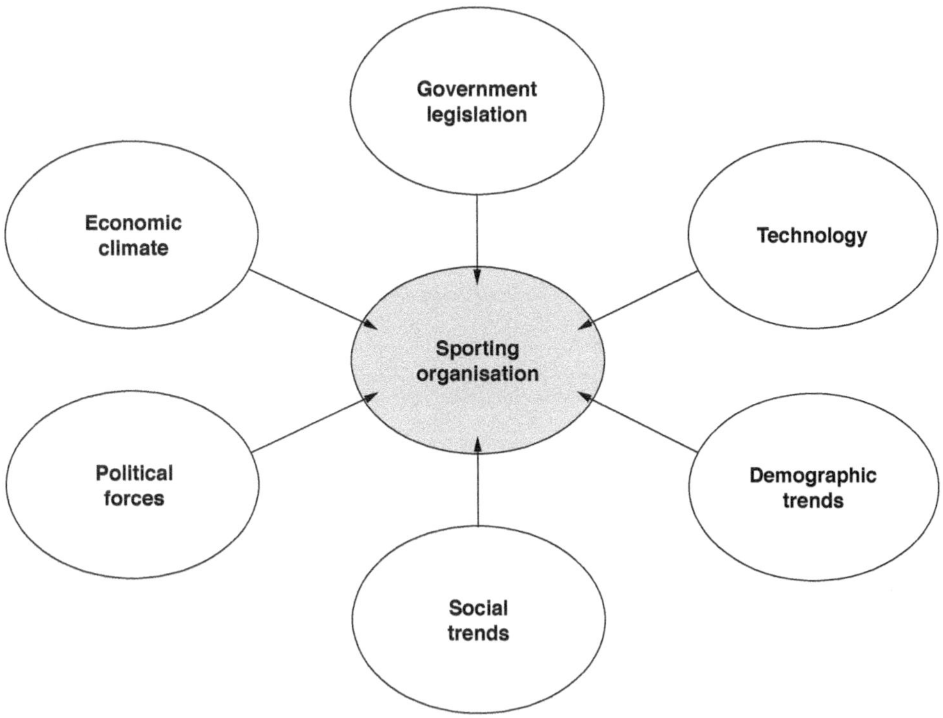

FIGURE 2.2 External environmental forces

marketing strategies, or that everyone will respond to the same sports. For many years, sport organisations neglected to examine these forces and the impact that a changing environment might have on their sport. The example of the Australian Cricket Board cited in Chapter 1 indicates this past neglect.

Industry competition

On a more direct level, sporting organisations need to monitor the industry in which they compete. Figure 2.3 incorporates an adapted version of Porter's (1980) competitive forces model. Porter described five forces that managers should review when examining competition and the attractiveness of an industry:

1 the intensity of competition between existing firms within an industry
2 the bargaining power of buyers
3 the threat of substitute products
4 the bargaining power of suppliers, and
5 the threat of new entrants.

The attractiveness of an industry typically is measured by profitability, which is not always the main goal of non-profit and sporting organisations. Viability and winning games are important outcomes, and become the primary measure of attractiveness for sporting organisations. In professional sports leagues, for example, the number and

FIGURE 2.3
Forces driving industry competition

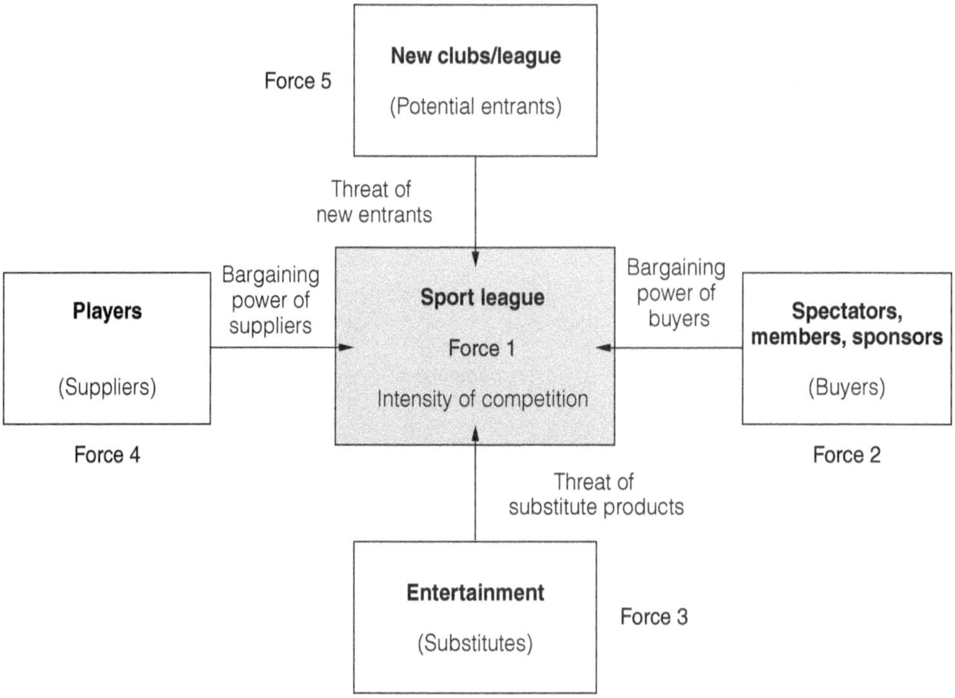

Source: Adjusted from Porter (1985).

location of teams in respective markets require the league to assess the attractiveness of a market in terms of viability. Other questions indicative of industry attractiveness may include: Is the economic base of a city or region large enough to sustain just one or more than one team? How many other professional sports already exist in this market? What other recreation and leisure pursuits are potentially competing for disposable income? A brief review of Porter's five forces follows.

Professional leagues for football will be used to illustrate the applicability of Porter's model. The model in this instance assumes that a professional sport league can be considered an industry, although this industry is subject to the broader market and competitive pressures of the entertainment and leisure sectors. The turnover of the Australian Football League (AFL) and its member clubs, for example, is closing in on A$1 billion, making the AFL a large and significant economic entity.

Force 1: Intensity of competition

The first force is the intensity of competition within the industry. In the case of a sporting league, the number of teams and their location are the first indicators of the intensity of competition. Obviously, nine AFL clubs based in Melbourne and nine professional Rugby League clubs based in Sydney intensify competition in these markets. This competition is further heightened by the presence of other sporting codes seeking sponsor dollars, spectators and members. In both codes, despite the large number of teams in each market, exit barriers have remained very high. This highlights the peculiar economics associated with leagues. Tradition, emotion and club loyalties often override the economic deficiencies experienced by some clubs, explaining why it has not been so easy to achieve a better geographical balance of teams competing in these national leagues.

Force 2: Bargaining power of buyers

The second force—the buyers or consumers of sport—is finite in relation to the number of teams located in one market, hence the intensity of competition by clubs to attract spectators, members and sponsors. Attendance, membership and sponsorship revenues are the main sources of income generated by sporting clubs. Typically, customers can force prices down, demand higher quality and play competitors off against each other. Too many teams located in one market can exacerbate the leverage of consumers, although sports consumers in some sport leagues have less leverage in this regard, as club membership tends to be price-standardised throughout a league and the cost of attendance common to all games—although there is evidence of change in relation to members and spectators now being able to purchase premium seating at many stadia. Most bargaining power lies with sponsors seeking to choose the best range of benefits from clubs. Sponsor bargaining power strengthens as the number of clubs based in a market increases.

Force 3: Threat of substitute products

Another major force comes from the substitutability of products—that is, other recreation and leisure activities offering similar benefits to those provided by participation in sport. It is this force that provides the greatest range of competitive forces for a sport league. Under the broad heading of 'entertainment', a variety of products have the potential to attract the consumer's money normally available for leisure pursuits. These may include other sports, the movies, videos and the theatre. A major determinant of the strength of these potential substitutes is the switching cost associated with each product. Switching cost refers to the cost of changing brands or products. If the cost is low, both financially and psychologically, then consumers are more likely to switch, and a product becomes susceptible to substitution. This, of course, has the potential to erode profits. A major advantage possessed by various sports is that brand loyalty (to the sport or club) is very high. Psychological association with a sport or club is often far more important than economic considerations. In part, this explains the fanatical support for some sports and clubs, such as for soccer clubs worldwide and for AFL clubs in Australia.

Force 4: Bargaining power of suppliers

Suppliers can exert bargaining power on participants in an industry by raising or reducing the quality of purchased goods and services. In a sport league, the major supply required to operate successfully is the players. No one source has exclusive control over player supply and, with the exception of some sports like soccer, it no longer costs clubs to buy players. This is also the area that the sport marketer has least control over in terms of product quality. The bargaining power of the players has the potential to erode industry profits via their salary demands, rather than through what it costs to procure players from specific suppliers. In their quest for the ultimate prize—a premiership or championship—clubs often accede to the demands of high-priced athletes, explaining why the sport economy is often regulated by the use of salary caps.

Force 5: Threat of new entrants

New clubs or a new rival league can reduce industry profits and specific market share for the existing clubs and/or league. The commencement in 1997 (for just one year) of the Superleague competition in Rugby League is an example of a rival league's entry. Superleague, owned by News Ltd, was established to form a breakaway league, enticing existing clubs and players in the Australian Rugby League's (ARL) New South Wales competition to defect to Superleague. In the process, contractual obligations of both players and clubs were displaced, ultimately creating serious divisions within the league. In attempting to overcome the barriers to entry, the structure and product offerings of the ARL competition were seriously threatened. The gravity of this threat largely depended on the barriers to entry. The major barrier in this case was provided by the established and recognised keeper of the code—the ARL—through the New South Wales Rugby League competition. A similar scenario was also obvious during 2007, with plans by the International Cricket League to form a new league in India. Access to a supply of talented players is usually a major barrier to entry.

Publics

Examination of the external environment can be concluded by identifying the publics to which the sport is responsible. To an extent, some of these will have been identified from the competitive analysis conducted using the Porter (1980) framework. Kotler and Andreasen (2003: 74) define a public as 'a distinct group of people, organisations, or both whose actual or potential needs must in some sense be served'. The competitive forces model has already shown that diverse publics exist for a club competing in a professional league. Figure 2.4 illustrates the publics that may exist for a professional sport club.

Another group of publics exists within the organisation. This leads us to consider Step 2 in the SSMPP.

Step 2: Understanding the internal capabilities of the organisation

Sport managers gauge the significance of a sport's internal competencies on the basis of the opportunities and threats present in the sport's competitive environment. For example, the arrival of colour television in Australia in 1974 represented an opportunity for sport, as have the internet and smartphone technologies more recently. The ACB, as previously discussed, did not possess the internal capabilities at the time to capitalise on this development; however, given this experience, and the professionalisation of sport, it was much better placed to cope with the new media in the 1990s and 2000s. Similarly, the globalisation of sporting competitions via the media has opened a window of opportunity for the professionalisation of Rugby Union.

SWOT analysis

An important foundation for understanding the internal capabilities of a sport is the ability of the sport manager or marketer to match strengths and weaknesses with industry opportunities and threats. The international Rugby Union community clearly identified the threat of being overrun by the larger and more powerful professional football codes.

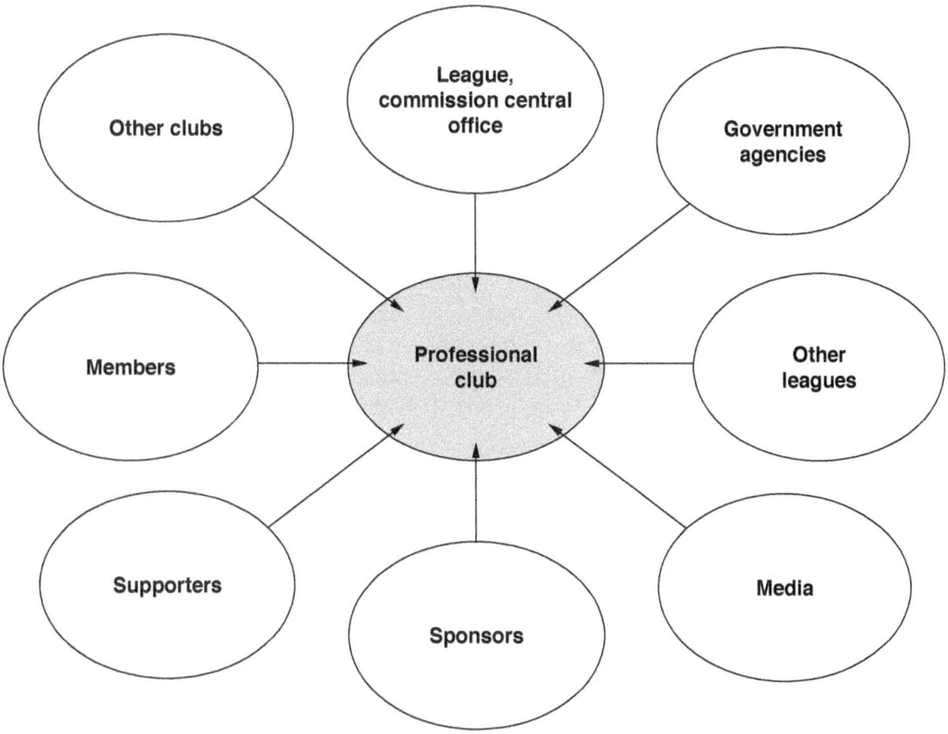

FIGURE 2.4 Publics impacting on a professional club

The choice of the ARU to engage in an alliance with New Zealand and South Africa is evidence of a sport recognising an opportunity to share the production and professionalisation of Rugby Union, rather than be forced to expand the code in limited markets in each country. The strengths, weaknesses, opportunities and threats (SWOT) analysis is a commonly accepted tool used by managers to assess the current capabilities of their organisations. In essence, it provides a structure for their analysis:

- Strengths are resources, skills or other advantages relative to competitors.
- Weaknesses are limitations or deficiencies in resources, skills and capabilities that inhibit a sport's effectiveness in relation to competitors.
- Opportunities are major favourable situations in a sport's environment.
- Threats are major unfavourable situations in a sport's environment.

Mission, objectives and goals

Having established the internal capabilities, it is necessary to ascertain the mission of the organisation, followed by a review of the organisation's principal goals and objectives. The mission statement provides direction for the sport, defining and clarifying its meaning and reason for existence. To be unambiguous, a mission statement should clearly answer 'What is our business?' For example, the Australian Sports Commission's mission statement is deceptively simple: 'To enrich the lives of all Australians through sport.'

In 2012, following the creation of an independent commission to govern the NRL, a new strategic plan was formulated for the period 2013–17. The mission stated in that plan is interesting, and is similar to that of the Australian Sports Commission: 'To bring people together and enrich their lives' (National Rugby League, 2012). The key to defining a mission for a sport organisation is to ensure that the mission statement is not so narrow that it limits its scope of operations or is simply a list of services provided. In this case, the mission of the NRL captures all the 'touch points' for the sport—or, in other words, all the means through which people can connect through playing, attending games or watching via various broadcast media. In all instances, the implicit message is that Rugby League brings people together for a common interest, and in so doing creates mini-communities. The NRL vision is also interesting, in that it is clearly aspirational: 'Rugby League—The Greatest Game of All. The most entertaining, most engaging and most respected sport' (National Rugby League, 2012). Both the NRL vision and mission serve to provide direction for the strategic sport marketing planning process. Whether Rugby League can become the greatest game of all will surely stimulate robust debate among sport fans.

In the context of sport, another factor impinges on formulating mission statements. Most sports are non-profit entities, and as such exist to achieve a common group of objectives by a relatively homogeneous group of people. Non-profits by definition exist to fight a cause. This cause becomes the operating charter, which is generally less flexible than the mission statement of a for-profit firm. If the cause ceases to exist, so too will the organisation. If profits cease to exist, the for-profit firm has the choice of redefining the business in which it wishes to be, and hence its range of product offerings. If, for instance, the ARU's alliance with other countries is not successful, professional Rugby Union could disappear—and with it the Super 15s. Defining the mission implicitly defines the broad goals to be pursued by an organisation.

Organisational goals refer to the broad aims that organisations strive to achieve. In sport, these may include ensuring financial viability, increasing participation, raising the number of members and stimulating public interest in the sport. Each of these goals contributes to the key targets a sport organisation seeks to achieve. The NRL has established eight targets against which to measure progress by 2017. These targets are also aligned with key aspects of the vision. For example, a target of 400 000 club members has been set to achieve the 'most entertaining' goal, and 700 000 players as the measure of the 'most engaging'. Other measures include 5.8 million people in social media reach, 1.65 million Rugby League experiences and 1.8 million people engaged in community programs. These three measures in particular highlight the importance of social and new media as avenues through which to engage and reach fans. An interesting inclusion is the 'most respected' measure, in which the NRL strives to achieve 84 per cent of players in education or training; this target has understandably been driven by the off-field player behaviour issues that have beset the sport in recent years. Finally, money talks! Buoyed by the new five-year broadcast deal of nearly $1 billion signed in 2012, the NRL has the resources to tackle its aspirational vision and associated targets. The goal of the NRL is to further build financial strength to over $300 million in central revenue and to over $200 million in growth fund investments (National Rugby League, 2012).

Examples of key initiatives, or actions, are shown in Table 2.1, using the NRL strategic plan 2013–17. Broad goals become the focus for devising more specific initiatives, which are shown also for each key result area. At least three of the key result areas are marketing related: achieve deeper engagement; generate positive presence, profile and brand; and grow our fan base. Of these three areas, achieving deeper engagement reflects the greatest change to sport marketing strategy in the last five years. Developing a digital strategy to build deeper fan engagement has become paramount and, given the NRL's increasing resource base, the league is in a position to capitalise on these initiatives. This approach also has the benefit of delivering to the sport marketer rich and varied data pertaining to consumer behaviour. How to use social media and develop a digital strategy will be developed further in Chapter 12. It is also worthwhile noting the importance of improving the game-day experience in the key result area 'grow our fan base'. In strategic terms, this action fits within the range of service variables outlined as part of the 7Ps contained in the marketing mix. The importance of these service variables when formulating and implementing sport marketing strategy will also be considered in later chapters. When formulating these strategic initiatives, it is important to consider the necessary detail to achieve key result areas and seek to establish SMART objectives. SMART objectives are:

S—Specific
M—Measurable
A—Achievable
R—Realistic
T—Timebound.

Step 3: Examining market research and utilising information systems

Step 3 recognises that the important phase of marketing research is undertaken to ensure that decisions made in relation to marketing missions and objectives are based on a sound understanding of the marketplace. Basically, market research in sporting organisations seeks to answer six questions about consumers in relation to their consumption of the product. Initially, sporting organisations need to know WHO their consumers are, but this is only the tip of the iceberg. WHY they choose the particular sport product, and WHEN and WHERE that consumption takes place, are equally important. WHAT that consumption entails in terms of pre- and post-event activities, and HOW the product is used, also are critical in terms of establishing a complete consumer profile.

To make informed decisions, organisations need information—and lots of it. Yet the collection of this material is only a starting point for the construction of a management information system (MIS). Once compiled, this information must be integrated, analysed and used to guide the direction of the organisation. Stanton et al. (1995: 48) believe that an MIS is an 'ongoing, organised set of procedures and methods designed to generate, analyse, disseminate, store and later retrieve information for use in decision making'. Nevertheless, they also acknowledge that, for the MIS to be successful, the data should not only be of high quality but must also be used in a realistic manner and adopted as a source of decision-making by the organisation. Information collated through market research and organised into meaningful data sets provides the foundation for sport

TABLE 2.1 NRL key initiatives 2013–17

Provide elite clubs with the fundamental for growth	Create a performance-based club funding model that: • attracts and rewards the best athletes • drives high standards of operation across all clubs • provides funding for strategic initiatives that drive club growth • delivers a Club Services Unit to work with clubs to maximise growth opportunities.
Create and refine pathways	Refine 'whole-of-game' structure and pathways that: • support players through a lifelong association with the game and offer targeted growth opportunities at each stage of their development • establish the highest standards in refereeing, coaching and support staff • develop skills, values and opportunities that extend beyond Rugby League.
Achieve deeper engagement	Engage more deeply with the Rugby League Family using digital and social media through: • innovative data acquisition, database management and digital marketing initiatives • investment in the quality and growth of our digital and social media presence • building a detailed knowledge of every fan's interaction with the game • the establishment of a Rugby League media unit that generates new content, products and technologies, and that enhances the game's digital brand.
Generate positive presence, profile and brand	Grow profile and positive presence through: • heartland strategies that strengthen support for the game in traditional areas • integrated strategies for marketing, communications, corporate partnerships and government relations • increasing the profile of elite players in non-sporting media, events and activities • expanding Rugby League's presence through strategic placement and national exposure of matches and events • conducting a formal review after the 2014 season to consider the merits of expansion.
Grow participation at all levels	Create a comprehensive program for grassroots growth through: • a single, integrated national development model • providing tools to enable grassroots clubs to grow, including investments in research, co-investment in local facilities and a volunteer assistance strategy • a world-class first-contact program for players in both metropolitan and regional locations • partnerships with recreational forms of the game.
Grow our fan base	Consolidate the current fan base and generate new fans by: • improving the game-day experience • directly engaging with members and fans • targeting specific marketing initiatives at potential fans • delivering a five-year membership plan • pursuing a stadium strategy that places matches in optimal locations.
Deliver community outcomes	Create, deliver and promote programs that provide positive community outcomes through: • a national framework and delivery model that aligns and empowers the game's stakeholders • the use of current and former players who inspire others through their involvement • the creation of specific social inclusion programs • a focus on building positive legacies in our communities.
Increasing financial resources	Consolidate the game's financial base by: • doubling non-broadcast revenues and maintaining a focus on efficiency • ensuring all funding is aligned to the strategic plan and is performance based • building strategies to optimise the next broadcast deal.

Sources: National Rugby League (2012); <www.nrl.com/portals/nrl/RadEditor/Documents/The_Game_Plan.pdf>, viewed 20 April 2013.

marketers to determine marketing strategies. In other words, this information helps sport marketers to refine and develop their sports, to know where and when to offer them, and to what age groups and at what times. These are just a few examples of how this information underpins marketing strategy decisions.

Step 4: Determining the marketing mission and objectives

Marketing must devise its own specific plans, complementary to the organisation's overall mission, goals and objectives. The purpose of the planning process is to establish a competitive advantage over rival firms. The mission of marketing is to develop a range of product offerings that reflects a firm's organisation-wide mission statement. These products may be in the form of goods or services or both, depending on the nature of the business. In sport, the product offerings tend to be limited, although they are clearly in the service domain. Inherent in the challenge confronting the sport marketer is designing this portfolio of product offerings to achieve a competitive advantage.

Competitive advantage

Porter (1985: 26) describes competitive advantage as 'the way a firm can choose and implement a generic strategy to achieve and sustain a competitive advantage'. This definition is specific to three generic strategies that he describes, which will be discussed later in this chapter. The concept of competitive advantage, however, is broader than Porter's direct application to his theories. Implicit in this concept is the notion of sustainability. Without sustainability, a competitive advantage becomes elusive. Coyne (1986: 55) posits three conditions that must be met for a firm to have achieved a sustainable competitive advantage:

- Customers perceive a consistent difference in important attributes between the producer's products or services and those of competitors.
- That difference is the direct consequence of a capability gap between the producer and competitors.
- Both the difference in important attributes and the capability gap can be expected to endure over time.

The key to sustainability is differentiation among competitor products. Coyne (1986: 55) further notes that:

> for a producer to enjoy a competitive advantage in a product/market segment, the difference or differences between him [sic] and his competitors must be felt in the marketplace: that is, they must be reflected in some product/delivery attribute that is the key buying criterion for the market.

Each individual sport has its own unique set of product attributes, due to its particular nature. In this regard, some sports are inherently more appealing to some segments of the population. For many years, sports believed that these unique features of their game would remain popular forever. In Australian sport, however, this was proved not to be the case. The traditional sports of cricket, Australian Rules football, netball and softball suddenly found that their competitive advantage was being eroded by changing attitudes towards leisure options. Increasing diversity of recreational and sporting opportunities saw these sports struggling in the late 1970s and early 1980s, and as a consequence they had to re-examine their key buying criteria and look to reposition themselves. One technique that these sports could have used to examine their range of product offerings is covered in the next section.

Product market expansion

Ansoff (1957) devised the product/market expansion grid, shown in Figure 2.5, to help managers to balance their product offerings.

FIGURE 2.5 Product/market expansion grid

	Existing products	New products
Existing markets	1 Marketing penetration	3 Product development
New markets	2 Market development	4 Diversification

Source: Adjusted from Ansoff (1957).

Market penetration

Market penetration (or concentration) refers to making more sales to existing customers without changing the product. Typically, this involves intensifying the advertising and promotions campaign to attract consumer attention. Often this strategy also involves a price reduction aimed at moving consumers away from competitors' products. The former New South Wales Rugby League (NSWRL) advertising and promotional campaign 'Simply the best', featuring Tina Turner, is an example of a market-penetration strategy in sport. Although there were some minor adjustments to the game in terms of a crackdown on excessive on-field violence during the 1980s, the game itself remained unchanged. The NSWRL was successful in stimulating interest in the game, which translated into flourishing attendances and television viewership. The 'Simply the best' advertising campaign is considered to be one of the most sophisticated, inspiring, modern promotional campaigns seen in Australian sport, and can be accessed on YouTube at <www.youtube.com/watch?v=Z-P0085ii4Q>.

Market development

A market development strategy is a relatively inexpensive way of creating new markets for existing products. It typically involves few risks, and requires only minor modification to the product. It depends on sound research indicating that new segments of the population are willing to buy the product.

Sportview 2.1 describes how the Football Federation of Australia (FFA) responded to market feedback and a deteriorating A-league competition in terms of key measures and perceptions about the future of the competition. A series of initiatives were put in place, most of them falling within the range of marketing mix variables, including the decision to delay the start of the season to avoid being swamped by end-of-season grand finals in both the AFL and NRL. Once again, the use of a digital media strategy to engage 14–24-year-olds was part of the mix of strategies used to enhance the profile and awareness of the competition.

SPORTVIEW 2.1

Clever strategies help turn the A-League around

This time last year, the mood around the A-League was at best muted. At worst, it was morbid. Talk that the competition itself was at risk had plenty of traction. Something had to change, and it did. Football Federation Australia (FFA) gets its fair share of criticism, but now it deserves some credit. It's one quarter of the way into the new season, and by every significant measure the A-League is booming. Again.

What a difference a year makes. 'A year ago, a lot of people were saying the A-League had hit a wall, and there was some truth in that,' A-League boss Lyall Gorman says. 'But I'd like to think we've gone a long way towards changing that perception. The talk around the game—good or bad—has never been stronger. But the largest percentage of that talk is positive, and the perception continues to change. It's been a tremendously encouraging start, but of course we can't take our foot off the pedal.' Let's talk facts. Television ratings—up 80 per cent. Crowds—up 49 per cent. Membership—up 17 per cent. Website traffic—up 30 per cent. Early days, perhaps, but they're still good numbers. It's great timing, given negotiations for the next TV deal are due to start early next year. 'Our partners have never been more satisfied with the work we're doing to bring the TV deal to life,' Gorman says.

Credit where it's due, and the FFA has made the right call on a number of key strategies:

- a later kick-off (first week of October), to avoid being swamped by the business end of the AFL and NRL seasons
- careful fixturing, after listening to the special needs of each club
- a rivalry round to build tradition
- a reduction in midweek fixtures
- a campaign to engage the 14–24 years demographic through social and digital media
- accommodating changes to the Fox Sports coverage
- opening the dressing room door—in some cases, literally—to the media to generate more and better stories
- a community round, which kicks off next weekend (December 4) in Morwell, and will engage regional cities such as Launceston, Dunedin and Bathurst.

Even something as seemingly innocuous as allowing the clubs to contract their own apparel suppliers has created a lot of positive feedback about the playing strips, and that's been reflected in merchandise sales, which are up 10 per cent.

The A-League looks better, and is better. All good then? Not completely. Gorman isn't paid to relax. He's paid to worry. That means keeping an eye on potential obstacles. He sees a few. Player payments, for one. The current deal with the players' union expires in mid-2013. 'We must maintain a close eye on salaries, and the salary cap,' he says. 'We work with the clubs every day to make sure they live within their means, and that includes their discretionary spend.' Gorman knows the sporting environment is super-competitive, and perhaps the biggest challenge for the A-League, he says, is 'to capture our fair share, and by that I mean a share which reflects the fact we have the largest participation rate of any sport in the country'.

Source: Extract from Cockerill (2011).

Product development

A product development strategy involves offering a modified or new product to current markets. Australian cricket's introduction of one-day cricket is an example of a sport exhibiting aspects of both market development and product development. One-day cricket can be considered to be the same product as four- and five-day cricket. Notably, the condensed version of the game has attracted a large following among women, which Test match cricket did not. On the other hand, one-day cricket can be considered to be a modified form of the game, and may thus better be described as a product development strategy by Cricket Australia. The weakness in this view is that one-day cricket has obviously had the capacity to expand the market interest in cricket. The traditional form of the game was not creating this expansion, although in recent times an exciting brand of cricket has been a feature of Test matches. This has largely been the result of rule changes that allow for extended hours to make up for time lost due to rain, and the need to bowl a minimum number of overs in a day's play. Combined with an aggressive and relentless approach by the Australian cricket team during the Waugh, Ponting, Warne, Hayden, Gilchrist, McGrath era, Test match cricket experienced a resurgence in interest. It also illustrates the impact sport managers can have on the product through rule changes, such as those shown in cricket.

Regardless of the final distinction and product form responsible for growing cricket, it raises an interesting dilemma in sport marketing: namely, the point at which the game has been modified to such an extent that it is in effect a new product offering. In one-day cricket, for example, the basic elements of the game are still apparent: batting, bowling and fielding. The condensed version of the game forces more action, but whether this constitutes a new or different product is debatable, and illustrates the conflict that can exist between the 'purists' and those who prefer non-stop excitement in sport. With the introduction of Twenty20 cricket, the same questions can be posed. Does Twenty20 cricket differ so much from the traditional form of the game that it could be considered a new product?

Another example of sports having to modify their range of product offerings has been seen in junior sports. For many years, juniors played the adult form of the game, complete with all the rules and traditions associated with that particular sport. As research began to show that this was not providing a satisfactory sport environment for juniors, many sports were modified to make them more attractive to juniors. In essence, sports have been modified to encourage more success in game elements, increasing the likelihood of juniors continuing to participate. Although sports initially did not see this as a marketing-related issue, this has now changed. The long-term fortunes of a sport, from both an elite performance and an ongoing interest and spectatorship perspective, are founded on the success of its junior programs. Market-development and product-development strategies have therefore assumed a heightened level of importance, with sports carefully considering their range of sport offerings for juniors in various age groups.

Product diversification

The final category of product diversification requires a firm to develop an entirely new product for a new market. This can be achieved internally through a strong research and development function, or via the external acquisition of a new firm with a new range of product offerings. In terms of the core sport product, this strategy is not common in Australian sport, although there are examples of professional clubs purchasing assets such as hotels and social clubs with a view to diversifying income opportunities. Sporting organisations in the main do not seek to buy other sporting organisations, although it remains an option. Internationally, for example, English Premier League clubs and European soccer clubs have been scrambling to acquire a share of the soccer action in China, as the world expects the economic boom in China to also impact on professional sport and soccer. In 2005, for example, Spanish soccer giants Real Madrid purchased a 25 per cent stake in Chinese Super League club Beijing Guaon for 200 million yuan (A$27 million) and Sheffield United acquired a 90 per cent controlling stake in Chengdu Blades Football Club in 2006. This is an example of product diversification in sport—in this case, acquiring a related (in terms of sport) product, but in a new market. The marketing objectives could include increased brand recognition for the English and European clubs by building an additional fan base in China, as well as economic benefits through merchandising and a larger television market. The product/market expansion grid provides a framework for the sport marketer to consider the balance of product offerings. This balance of product offerings should reflect the marketing mission, which in turn should mirror the overall mission, goals and objectives of the organisation.

Generic strategies

As indicated earlier, Porter (1985) describes three generic strategies that firms can use as an alternative framework to achieve competitive advantage:

- cost leadership
- differentiation, and
- focus.

Both the cost leadership and differentiation strategies aim to seek a competitive advantage in a broad range of markets. The focus strategy aims to seek a competitive advantage by using either a cost leadership or differentiation strategy in a narrow or niche market segment. Cost leadership is perhaps the simplest of the three options. The organisation's principal objective is to distribute its products to the widest possible market at a lower cost than that of its competitors. Achieving lower cost may be the result of internal economies of scale, innovative technologies or lower distribution costs. In the end, it is the consumer who decides whether the cost differential is significant enough to warrant the purchase of a product over those of competitors.

Differentiation is typically more expensive. It involves an advantage based on distinctive product attributes. Products may, for instance, offer benefits that others do not, or they might be new and innovative products that are not currently available. Again, differentiation is seeking to establish its product prominence in as wide a market as possible. In sport, cost leadership strategies are difficult to achieve. In a sporting league, the clubs generally compete on equal terms in terms of cost. Standardised prices for attendance and membership reduce the significance of cost as a source of competitive advantage, although increasingly—in the AFL, for instance—there is movement away from strict standardisation of ticket cost. This has largely been driven by improving facilities and a move to fully seated stadia, which have provided clubs with the opportunity to increase ticket sales revenues by selling the best seats at premium rates. The capacity to extract premium prices provides important extra revenue for the clubs. As will be examined in Chapter 6, clubs and leagues cannot always achieve full cost recovery on ticket prices. If full cost recovery (in terms of covering event costs) were an objective, most sports would become too expensive for regular attendance.

A differentiation strategy provides scope for application in the sport setting. Although all the clubs in a league appear to be the same in terms of production, they do offer distinct brand images. These are, of course, the clubs themselves—with their distinctive colours, heritage and traditions, with which supporters identify with a good degree of emotional intensity. On a macro level, each sport is a differentiated product in its own right, with each offering similar benefits to consumers. The choice for consumers, in terms of physical activity, competing or spectating, comes down to which of the myriad sports available offers the best outlet to satisfy their needs and wants. This is equally applicable for juniors when they (or their parents) are choosing the sports in which they wish to participate. Some sports—such as cricket, golf, softball, swimming and netball—offer the challenge of special skill development without any excessive body contact. Football codes, basketball and wrestling offer a different range of skills, to be mastered in the context of body contact. The challenge for the sport marketer is to accentuate the differentiated product benefits to potential participants, and this sometimes means changing the fundamental rules and traditions of a sport. Although this is obviously an option, sport managers and marketers need to consider the impact of proposed changes carefully before implementation.

Summary

This chapter introduced the SSMPP and reviewed the first four steps in this process. These four steps constitute the data collection and review phase of the planning process. Organisation-wide data are required to place into context the role that marketing strategy plays in ensuring that a sport creates a sustainable competitive advantage.

In the first instance, a sporting organisation needs to review the external environmental factors impinging on its existence. These factors are best described as the set of societal influences that encroach on all organisations, which include government legislation, economic environment, technology, political forces, and social and demographic trends. A more direct form of analysis involves a review of industry characteristics specific to a sport. Porter's five-forces model provides sport managers with a structured framework to scan the competitive environment, and is the precursor to a review of the internal capabilities of a sporting organisation. SWOT analysis was described in this chapter as a useful tool to assist with this internal examination.

Review of the external and internal environments is an important precursor to determining the best strategies to create a competitive advantage. In essence, marketing personnel are responsible for developing an array of product offerings that assist an organisation to achieve a competitive advantage. In predominantly single-product organisations such as those in sport, marketing's contribution to creating a competitive advantage is considerable.

In many ways, sport and marketing are now more comfortable with each other. For many years, most sport administrators did not believe that the role of marketing was important. However, as the sport landscape became increasingly competitive, sport managers began to adjust their thinking. Most large sporting entities have now created marketing departments, and many smaller sporting organisations are beginning to employ marketing specialists to manage the contribution of marketing in the planning process. As indicated in Chapter 1, sport organisations have been guilty of complacency in the past in relation to marketing and promoting their sport. This is clearly changing, as exemplified by the case study at the end of this chapter.

This chapter discussed the steps in the SSMPP and specifically outlined four of the eight steps shown in Figure 2.1. Such is the significance of understanding the sport consumer, conducting market research and defining market segments that it is incorporated in Part II of this book. Part III examines in detail the sport marketing mix variables that combine to form the nucleus of a core marketing strategy—a strategy based on the environmental scanning and data intelligence phase described in Steps 1–4 of the SSMPP in this chapter.

CASE STUDY

ARU report confirms code on wane

Rugby Union is suffering from the poorest 'brand health' of the major football codes, with declining television ratings and crowd figures underlining a general malaise in the game. The gloomy view of Rugby's current place in the sporting landscape has been backed up by market research commissioned by the Australian Rugby Union (ARU) and obtained by *The Australian*.

The ARU's 'brand health' tracking for the April–June quarter confirms Australian Rugby's popularity is on the wane and that passion has gone out of the game. Of the four football codes and cricket, Rugby Union was the least entertaining, innovative, grassroots-orientated and social. Only 4 per cent more (29 per cent to 25 per cent) rated Rugby more exciting than cricket. The Brand Health Index (BHI) comprises four areas—salience (advertising recall), equity (brand image statements), engagement (interest, viewership/attendance) and passion (preference, passion statements). Engagement makes up 50 per cent of the BHI, while equity and passion comprise 20 per cent and salience 10 per cent. The BHI is calculated on a score out of 100 built from a series of attributes and questions. Key questions were asked of all sporting codes to allow for comparison. According to an ARU update to the state unions, overall interest in sport has decreased, possibly because of a large decrease in cricket's appeal and lots of negative media reports.

Rugby League and Australian Rules had low scores on equity, but high scores on salience and passion. Soccer and Rugby Union had low scores on salience, while Rugby Union was also low on passion. Cricket had the highest engagement score. 'Rugby's brand equity is diluted by both soccer and cricket with no one attribute being owned by Rugby,' the ARU said. Bluntly put, consumers are not passionate about Rugby. They favour AFL and NRL, which tend to be more tribal. Disconcertingly, even our passionates are turning away. 'So overall, Rugby has the poorest health, but the main areas of disadvantage are in passion and salience versus other sports.'

The low BHI for Rugby was driven by the low percentage of Australians indicating Rugby Union as their favourite sports code. One in four indicated Rugby was their favourite or second-favourite sport. Rugby was regarded as 'exclusive and hard to follow'. There was a need to educate viewers on how to follow the game and understand the laws, penalties and referee gestures. While interest in all sports was down, there was a possibility of fans migrating from other sports to Rugby when general interest picked up again.

Television audiences and crowds for Test, Super 14 and club Rugby had declined. Overall crowd numbers at Test matches have fallen from 617 555 in 2006 to 386 287 this year [2009], while attendances at Super 14 matches have dropped from 115 317 to 75 393 in the same period. 'TV ratings for inbounds have remained fairly constant versus previous year, Tri-Nations witnessed the greatest decline in audiences,' the ARU said. 'Watching Rugby is one of the easier engagement activities, yet we've been losing eyeballs for Tests since 2006 and for the first time Super Rugby in 2009.' The evidence suggests Rugby's core message is not getting through to general sports fans, which is a big problem because this is the market the ARU needs to grow the game. Over the last three years, awareness of Rugby Union advertising among sports enthusiasts has declined by 13 per cent.

TABLE 2.2

Code in crisis: Ranking of Rugby of attribute v competitive set — general population (1=high, 5=low)

Attribute in order of strength	Rugby Union	Rugby League	AFL	Soccer	Cricket
International	3	4	5	1	2
National pride	2	5	4	3	1
World class	3	4	5	1	2
Tradition and heritage	3	4	2	5	1
Entertaining	5	2	1	4	3
Exciting	4*	2	1	4	5
Sportsmanship and fair play	2	5	3	3	1
Big event	4	5	3	4	2
Hard to understand the rules (negative impact)	1	3	2	1	5
Socialising	5	3	2	44	1
Grassroots oriented	5	3	1	2	4
Strong life values	3	5	2	4	1
Innovative	5	4	1	3	2

* Only 4 per cent additional people rate Rugby as more exciting than cricket (29 vs 25 per cent).

Source: ARU Brand Health Tracking, conducted by Colmar Brunton Mar–Jun 2009

The ARU told the states of the need to 're-engage this segment' of the market. The downward trend has also continued in Rugby membership and national participation. Overall membership of the ARU and state unions fell 14 per cent from 32 837 to 28 027 over the past year. Participation rates dropped 2 per cent from 193 382 in 2006 to 183 810 in 2008. The ARU will use these results to create a marketing strategy for next year. The ARU said the purpose of the marketing will be 'to build and maintain Rugby fan commitment to the code in a winning and losing season, now and in the future'. '[By] leveraging Rugby's rich tradition and heritage we will rekindle the relevance of rugby among the evolving Australian sporting fan,' it said.

Source: Harris (2009, p. 35).

Questions

1. How is the strategic marketing planning process relevant to the results described in the case study?
2. What were the challenges confronting the ARU, based on these results?
3. What competitive forces exist? Describe the impact of these forces.
4. What was the significance of 'engagement' as it relates to these results?
5. What is the potential importance of engagement for the ARU as it seeks to devise marketing strategies for Rugby Union? You may wish to read Chapter 11 to help you answer this question.
6. Based on this case study, and other information contained in this chapter in relation to Rugby Union, how would you draft a strategic sport marketing plan for the ARU?

3

Understanding the sport consumer

Stage 1—Identification of marketing opportunities

Step 1—Analyse external environment (forces, competition, publics)

Step 2—Analyse organisation (mission, objectives, SWOT)

Step 3—Examine market research and marketing information systems

Step 4—Determine marketing mission and objectives

▼

Stage 2—Strategy determination

▼

Stage 3—Strategy implemention, evaluation and adjustment

CHAPTER OBJECTIVES

Chapter 3 is the first of two chapters relating to understanding the sport consumer. It describes how sport consumer decision-making occurs and how this process relates to the development of sport involvement. The chapter details various personal, psychological and environmental factors that make the sport consumption decision-making process unique from other consumer scenarios. It concludes with a discussion of how diverse involvement levels among consumer bases influence the development of marketing strategies.

After studying this chapter you should be able to:

- describe the major phases in the sport consumption decision-making process
- describe how sport consumer involvement develops
- identify key external and internal inputs in the sport consumption process
- understand how involvement level influences sport consumption and the subsequent development of marketing campaigns.

HEADLINE STORY

Understanding consumer behaviour

According to the Australian Bureau of Statistics (2010), almost half (43 per cent) of the Australian population over the age of 15 attended at least one sporting event in 2009–10. This figure was down 1.1 per cent on the previous (2006) survey, suggesting that 455 200 fewer people attended a sporting event. Table 3.1 compares the 2006 figures with those of 2010, and provides the percentage change in attendance rate. Despite a nationwide decrease in attendance, some sports witnessed an increase. Australian Rules football remained the most popular spectator sport from 2006 to 2010, with an increase in attendance of over 300 000 spectators. Soccer witnessed the largest percentage increase in attendance with over 378 000 more spectators. Table 3.1 illustrate variance in attendance patterns between the two survey periods.

TABLE 3.1

Comparison between 2005–06 and 2009–10 sporting event attendance

Sport[a]	2005–06	2009–10	Attendance rate % change
Australian Rules football	2 526 700	2 831 800	+.04
Horse racing	2 003 700	1 940 30	−1.40
Rugby League	1 486 400	1 563 300	+.04
Motor sports	1 485 200	1 423 000	−1.20
Soccer (outdoor)	560 700	938 800	+1.90
Cricket (outdoor)	730 700	678 700	−0.07
Rugby Union	682 000	575 500	−1.00
Harness racing	444 200	412 100	−0.04
Tennis (indoor and outdoor)	267 900	293 700	0
Dog racing	224 800	281 400	+0.02
Total spectators[b]	7 096 700	7 551 200	−1.10

[a] The top 10 ranked sports for Australia in terms of total attendances in 2009–10.
[b] Includes attendance at all sports, not just those listed above.
Source: Australian Bureau of Statistics (2010).

As Table 3.1 shows, sport attendance and diversity of choice are very important to a large percentage of the Australian public. Today, Australians can choose to invest their leisure time in following any number of sport teams or events, as well as a number of competing leisure interests. Hence it is becoming increasingly important to ascertain why fans turn up to sporting events, week in and week out. Is it for team loyalty, stadium preference, clashes between traditional rivals, star appeal or reasons we have yet to discern? More importantly, why does attendance at sporting events seem to be decreasing? There has been an increasing amount of research on the sport-consumption process, with sport marketers now better prepared than at any stage in the past to make informed decisions based on their understanding of the consumer. Increasingly, sport marketers understand the decision-making process and what distinctive reasons influence individuals' choice of attending one type of sporting event over another. These reasons may be person-specific, psychological, or social and environmental. Furthermore, they may be largely experiential. Hence, choosing to attend a sporting event is an ongoing process. It should never be questioned that the better we know and understand our consumers, the more prepared we will be to deliver a satisfactory product or service, and ultimately the whole sport experience.

Sport consumer behaviour

The study of sport consumer behaviour emerged from a variety of academic disciplines to specifically focus on understanding sport-consumption activities. Sport consumer researchers have utilised theories from marketing, psychology, sociology, economics and communication to examine sport consumption in its many forms and contexts. This examination covers a wide range of personal, psychological and environmental factors that influence sport consumer behaviour, with increasing attention being given to this area in the sport-marketing literature. Sport consumer behaviour research strives to better develop sport marketing practices to increase and sustain consumer demand for sport products and services. Given the social, economic, political and health benefits of sport, the challenge for sport marketers is to understand the complexity of human behaviour to identify key elements of the decision-making process and develop marketing actions to enhance the sport-consumption experience.

The study of human behaviour is important for understanding sport consumers, and adopting an interdisciplinary approach has a broad appeal to sport marketers. One important principle of psychology is that each individual is different, and therefore each individual has a unique personality, as well as different perceptions, life experiences, capabilities and interests—and, importantly, different attitudes, beliefs and values. However, individuals also gravitate toward shared experiences with other individuals with whom they share a common interest in sport. Hence sport consumption has sociological principles, as it is undertaken individually as well as in groups. Participant sports such as running and golf involve individual activity that may also occur in the presence of others, through informal recreation and organised events. Recreational sport leagues depend upon a 'team' of people to compete against another team. Attendance at professional sporting contests is embedded in the context of large crowds, and the interactions between spectators form a large part of the sport experience. Consequently, sport marketers are interested in determining how individuals and groups interact to shape the sport experience.

Sport marketers use consumer research to determine how to position the sport experience using the marketing mix. A better understanding of their consumers through such research helps sporting organisations to not only determine price, promotion, place and product, but also identify how a sport experience provides the opportunity to achieve desirable outcomes. Using this knowledge, sporting organisations are best placed to develop effective marketing strategies that communicate these positive features. In general, the study of sport consumer behaviour examines attitudes and behaviours of the individual relative to the sport experience (Funk, Mahony and Havitz, 2003). A definition that adopts an interdisciplinary approach therefore has been offered by sport scholars.

Sport consumer behaviour can be defined as the process through which individuals select, purchase, use and dispose of sport-related products and services (Funk, 2008). This definition views sport consumer behaviour as a holistic process that describes how individuals devote available resources of time and money toward sport consumption activities—before, during and after the experience. This definition also informs the development of a sport marketing approach that positions the sport experience to better provide benefits and satisfy needs through the sport-marketing exchange process. As a result, the role of decision-making is fundamental to understanding sport consumer behaviour.

The sport consumption decision-making process

The sport consumption decision-making process is complex, but it can be simplified into three sequential phases. The three general phases are presented in Figure 3.1, and are labelled inputs, processes and outputs (Schiffman and Kanuk, 2000). The input phase represents a number of external forces that individually or collectively influence the second phase. These external inputs can come from marketing actions of a sporting organisation utilising the marketing mix to help the consumer make a decision. Inputs can also be socio-cultural influences of family, friends, media, social class issues, and commercial and informal sources. A more detailed discussion of inputs relevant to sport consumer behaviour is provided in the 'Inputs' section of this chapter.

The second phase, labelled 'processes', is a collection of unique and related internal processes that serve as the foundational phase of sport consumer decision-making. A common term for this phase is the 'black box', as it represents a number of unobservable cognitive processes that shape an individual's evaluation of any external stimuli (such as content, situation or object). This evaluation stems from an individual recognising a need or want, an information search, evaluation of alternatives and the experience of using a number of cognitive processes, including motivation, perception, learning,

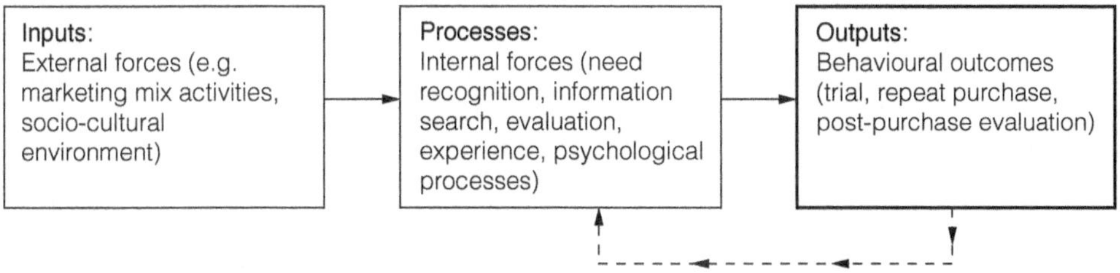

FIGURE 3.1 Consumption decision-making process

personality, memory and attitudes. Collectively, the evaluative process is the internal mechanism that determines the relative meaning and influence of inputs and leads to the third phase.

The third phase is labelled 'outputs', and represents post-decision behavioural outcomes as well as an internal feedback loop. Behavioural outcomes represent a type of behaviour (for example, trial, repeat purchase) that subsequently leads to a post-experience evaluation of the sport-consumption activity. The outcome of this evaluation subsequently leads back to the processes phase, as depicted by the dotted arrow in Figure 3.1. In other words, this feedback loop operates as a new input to influence subsequent processing and future decision-making. As a result, sport consumer decision-making is based upon not only external inputs but also internal inputs generated from evaluations of the experience in the output phase.

The following six steps are presented to further illustrate how the sport consumption decision-making process unfolds. To exemplify this process, Pat's decision to attend Australia's premier tennis event, the Australian Open, is used. The Australian Open is held each January in Melbourne, Victoria.

FIGURE 3.2
The consumer's decision-making process

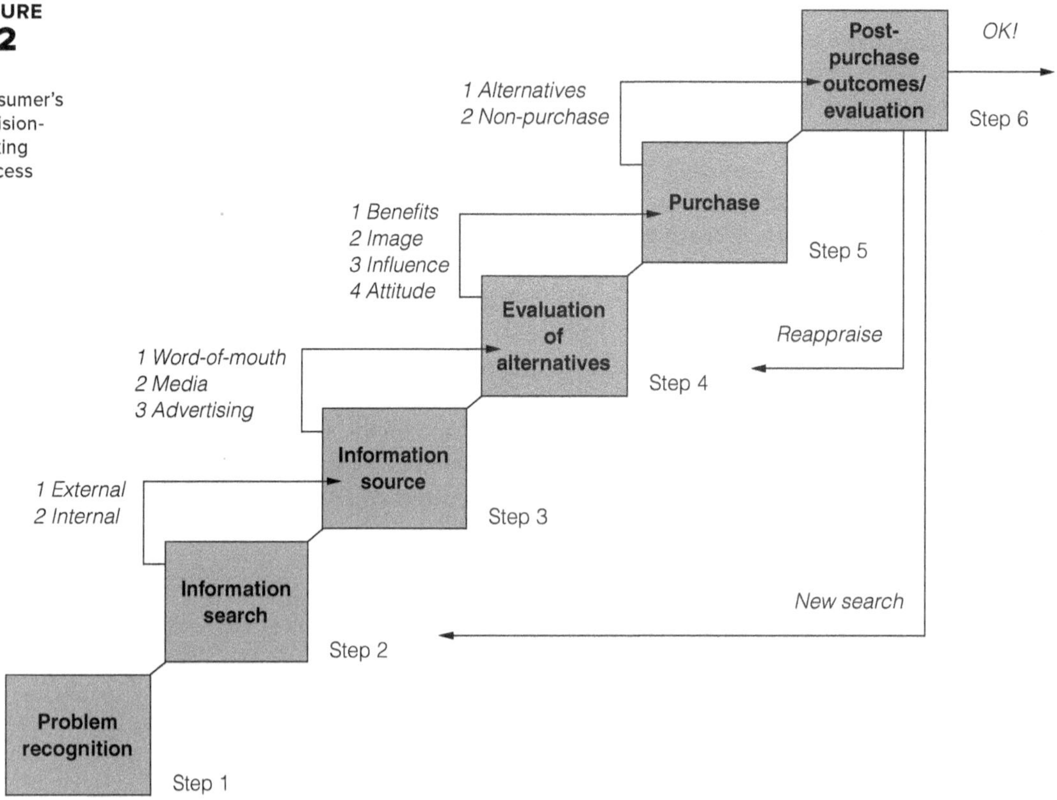

Step 1: Problem recognition

Problem recognition is usually a result of the depletion of existing goods or services that create a need or want. There are a number of ways in which a problem may be recognised. For example, Pat is feeling bored while sitting in his apartment. He also believes there are very few entertainment options in late January. Pat feels attending a movie is less appealing because the cinema does not allow the opportunity to chat with friends. He has begun to hang out with a new group of friends from the sport marketing course at university. This new reference group provides a shared interest in sport that is appealing, and Pat wants to spend time with these friends. In addition, the amount of television and newspaper advertising devoted to the Australian Open suggests attending an outdoor event may be a lot of fun. The recognition of a problem for Pat creates a desire to find a new form of entertainment that will accommodate particular social needs. This recognition leads to the search for the information required to make a decision.

Step 2: Information search

The information search can take one of two forms: a recall of stored knowledge in memory, or a seeking of additional information. Some products and services are bought solely on the basis of an internal search (recalled memory), and are usually related to habitual or routine decision-making. Here, the evaluation of alternatives is limited and based on what is remembered. Pat is aware of a range of entertainment options available—such as the movies, going out to dinner, the theatre or clubs, or attending a sporting event. Through an external search, he is seeking information not contained in the memory. The adoption of an external search is usually a response to two factors: recognising that there is a risk involved in making the purchase decision (price and negative consequences of poor choice); and believing that this type of search will greatly increase the chances of making a correct choice. For example, Pat may search for information on current events in Melbourne and see what his friends feel like doing. This leads Pat to source the information. At this stage, general information about the range of entertainment options available is collected and complemented by more specific information about a specific product or specific service characteristics (Can I go with my friends? Can I chat during the event?).

Step 3: Information source

Some sources of information are more powerful than others. For the sport marketer, it is important to identify which information sources are most useful when promoting sales. For example, a major source of information is via 'word of mouth', through family, friends and work colleagues. Pat's parents go to the theatre on a regular basis, so that might not be the coolest option for his group of friends. Another source of information is formal and informal media channels, which can include internet sites, magazine and newspaper articles, product reviews and television coverage of events. In the sport industry, the widespread media coverage received by most sport professional organisations and events allows for great opportunities to present sporting experiences as the preferred entertainment option to customers. Pat certainly sees a lot of information about tennis and the Open in the papers, online, on mass transit and on television during the event.

Finally, information can be obtained through promotional media, which include myriad forms of advertising. Pat recalls seeing Australian Open content and stories trending on Yahoo News and Twitter over the last week, and while having coffee he read an insert in the last edition of *Inside Sport*. It can be seen that the information that is available, combined with the source of the information, will allow sport organisation to position the experience favourably while potential consumers are evaluating the alternatives available to them.

Step 4: Evaluation of alternatives

The evaluation of alternatives is affected by the belief held about a certain product or service, as well as the purchaser's attitude towards it and the intention to buy. An evaluation of alternatives is conducted according to a set of selection criteria. These criteria can include attributes and benefits sought, the image of the product or service, trust in the company or brand, and the importance weighting of the range of product or service attributes according to the individual as well as the group. For Pat, the theatre is for old people; during the movies one is not supposed to talk; and going out for dinner is not that exciting. Conversely, going to a sporting event offers scope to address all these issues. But Melbourne can be very hot in January, so it might be better to attend either indoor events or night matches at an outdoor venue. Here, the Australian Open is very much part of the considered set of entertainment options. Pat believes Centre Court tickets are a bit expensive and really does not know how much fun it will be to sit in the one place all day. Perhaps Pat and his friends will just buy the ground pass so they can move around more after it cools down in the evening. Then Pat does not have to worry about buying a ticket in advance. Only after evaluation does the decision to buy take place. Pat has now decided that attending the Australian Open will satisfy the range of needs and wants identified during the problem-recognition stage.

Step 5: Purchase

The decision to purchase a particular product or service can best be described as:

Choice = Intention + Unanticipated circumstances.

Having made the decision to purchase the ground pass, Pat proceeds to the arena with that intent in mind. However, at the last moment Pat may find that the event is sold out, friends could cancel or the event may be postponed. Here a decision has to be made as to whether to consume an alternative offering or to wait for the selected item to become available. Everyone in the city must have turned up today, as all the ground passes are gone. However, it does not matter too much, as Pat is on holidays. He decides to buy a ticket for tomorrow, just to be sure. Future product consumption is the result of post-purchase outcomes and evaluation.

Step 6: Post-purchase outcomes/evaluation

Invariably there are three major outcomes possible during this stage:

- First, the consumer is entirely satisfied with the purchase and no further information is required. Pat feels attending the Open was the most fun he had ever had at a sporting event. It was great entertainment for an affordable price. Pat got to see some star players, and he had a great time with his friends.

- Second, the consumer is not entirely satisfied with the decision and may need to reappraise the alternatives gathered through the initial information search—or may seek out new information. Pat feels the day was a bit ordinary and would probably not rush back unless a large group of friends was going. There were too many people, all the good matches were on Centre Court and the price of food and drinks was a bit over the top.
- Third, the consumer is totally dissatisfied with the experience, and may decide that the solution to the initial problem of being bored was not provided by the sport experience, and may look outside this context in the future for satisfaction. Pat feels the Open was no fun. 'Perhaps I should just spend my summer at the beach!'

Involvement and decision-making

The process by which individuals arrive at the decision to buy or experience a particular sport product or service does not necessarily imply that each step in the process is always followed. Depending on the type and nature of the purchase/experience, an individual may devote a significant amount of time and effort to the decision-making process, or may make a snap or 'spur-of-the-moment' decision. The latter usually occurs when the adverse consequence of a poor choice is minimal or the purchase has become habitual behaviour. If a person purchases a ground pass each year for the early rounds of the Australian Open, then the purchase has become habitual, with the outcome of the experience essentially known in advance.

The preceding example illustrates how the sport consumption decision-making process follows a sequence, but is also dynamic and complex. To better understand this process in sport, a framework was developed for sport consumer research that integrates the decision-making process with sport involvement. This framework is called the Psychological Continuum Model (PCM) (Funk and James, 2001, 2006) (see Figure 3.3 below), and it suggests that inputs and outputs play different roles in the consumer decision-making process, depending upon an individual's psychological connection to the sport object or experience. This connection can be viewed as involvement. In other words, the relative influence of external and internal inputs is based upon the level of involvement. For example, Pat's existing connection to tennis or the Open event can influence the decision-making process. The following section provides a discussion of the PCM framework.

A model of sport consumer behaviour

Funk, Haugtvedt and Howard (2000) explored the nexus between sport marketing and consumer behaviour. Delving into the social psychology literature, they determined that understanding attitude formation enables the sport marketer to better determine factors that contribute to consumer behaviour. Funk and James (2001) extended this perspective by proposing the PCM, a framework to organise literature from various academic disciplines to understand sport consumer behaviour. The PCM uses a vertical framework to characterise various psychological connections that individuals form with sport objects. These progress along four general stages of awareness, attraction, attachment and allegiance. The framework explains the role of attitude formation and change that directs behaviours across a variety of sport-consumption activities. The framework is instructive in understanding how psychological involvement with a sport object develops progressively.

The PCM was revised to clarify movement within the vertical framework, and the role of decision-making as discussed in the previous section was integrated. Funk and James (2006) introduced a series of inputs, processes and outputs aligned with different stages in order to better explain how the psychological connection progressively forms. Subsequently, Funk (2008) integrated the sport consumption decision-making process into the hierarchical PCM framework to illustrate how individuals form stronger psychological connections to sport objects and experiences. It is useful to note that the PCM concentrates on decision-making that forms different psychological connections and this has implications for behavioural activity.

The PCM is considered theoretically sound for understanding active (participant) and passive (spectator) forms of sport consumer behaviour. Previously, scholars have used the framework to examine sport spectators, recreational participants, sport tourists, sport volunteers and internet consumers in Australia, China, Greece, Japan and the United States. The PCM framework has been revised to highlight key inputs and outcomes aligned to a continuum of hierarchical stages (Beaton, Funk and Alexandris, 2009). Furthermore, a segmentation tool has been developed to effectively place sport participants (Beaton, Funk and Alexandris, 2009; Funk, Beaton and Pritchard, 2011) and sport spectators (Doyle, Kunkel and Funk, 2013) into the four PCM stages. Figure 3.3 illustrates the revised PCM framework.

Figure 3.3 should be examined as a vertical illustration, beginning at the bottom with the awareness stage and proceeding upwards through progressive stages of attraction to attachment to allegiance. It may be helpful to imagine a four-storey building with an elevator or lift to understand the developmental progression of these stages. Each floor or stage represents a unique psychological connection that a person forms with a sport object (for example, sport, league, team, player, event or recreational activity). As the individual progresses upwards to a higher stage, the psychological connection becomes incrementally stronger. A useful example of this stage-based progression is illustrated in Figure 3.3 in terms of how an individual becomes increasingly involved with the Brisbane Lions, a professional AFL franchise.

PCM stages

Awareness

The ground floor is the awareness stage, where an individual enters the PCM elevator. Awareness reflects the statement 'I know about the Brisbane Lions', indicating that an initial connection with the team has formed. The awareness stage has key inputs consisting of socialising agents, cultural influences and the situational environment in which the team operates. The psychological connection of awareness creates attitudinal outcomes of knowledge and realisation that the team exists, and is characterised either by no behavioural outcomes or by behaviour that is unplanned or random. These awareness outcomes subsequently serve as internal inputs for the attraction stage.

Inputs/antecedents	Stage	Outcomes/characteristics
• Attachment outcomes • Value congruence • Identification	**Allegiance** *I live for the Lions*	• **Attitudinal**: Commitment, biased thinking • **Behaviour**: Consistent, repetitive and complex
• Attraction outcomes • Personal meaning and importance • Self-concept	**Attachment** *I am a Lions fan*	• **Attitudinal**: Stronger, assign emotional, functional and symbolic meaning • **Behaviour**: Frequent, expected and expressive
• Awareness outcomes • Hedonic and dispositional needs • Self-efficacy and perceived control	**Attraction** *I like the Lions*	• **Attitudinal**: Positive affect; linking attractive attributes and benefits • **Behaviour**: Trial, infrequent and evaluative
• Socialising agents • Cultural influences • Situational environment	**Awareness** *I know about the Lions*	• **Attitudinal**: Knowledge and realisation of sport object • **Behaviour**: None, unplanned or random

FIGURE 3.3 Psychological Continuum Model

Attraction

The attraction stage is reflected by the statement 'I like the Brisbane Lions', indicating that movement upwards has occurred within the PCM. The attraction stage has key inputs related to hedonic motives and dispositional needs, self-efficacy and perceived behavioural control. The attraction stage represents the formation of a psychological connection that has attitudinal outcomes of positive affect in terms of whether the Lions provide opportunities to satisfy needs and enable the individual to receive desirable benefits. Behavioural outcomes are related to trial, infrequent and evaluative behaviour related to the team. Although the connection in the attraction stage is stronger than in awareness, it is still relatively weak and unstable. The attitudinal and behavioural outcomes of attraction subsequently feed back and provide inputs for the attachment stage.

Attachment

The attachment stage is reflected by the statement 'I am a Brisbane Lions fan', and suggests that the psychological connection with the team has moved upward. Key inputs for this stage are the personal meaning and importance placed by an individual on the Lions, which indicate that the team is becoming part of the self-concept. Attitudinal outcomes for this stage include a stronger and more established attitude toward the team, whereby the individual now places functional, emotional and symbolic meaning on the Lions. Behavioural outcomes are reflected by team-related behaviour that is frequent, expected and expressive. The attitudinal and behavioural outcomes of attachment subsequently feed back and provide inputs for the allegiance stage.

Allegiance

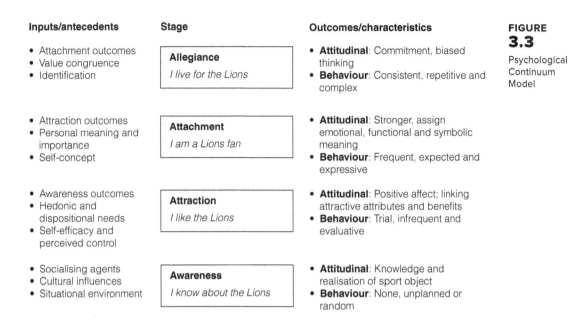

The final stage, allegiance, is reflected by the statement 'I live for the Brisbane Lions', and represents the strongest psychological connection to the team within the vertical continuum. Key inputs for allegiance are identification and value congruence, illustrating that the team is aligned with important values and self-identity. Attitudinal outcomes for allegiance are commitment (loyalty, devotion) and biased thinking that influences the way an individual processes information and situations related to the team. Behavioural outcomes of allegiance are consistent over time, repetitive and complex (that is, breadth and depth of consumption activities).

Models such as the PCM are instructive for the sport marketer as they allow for tracking of sport consumers, both upward and downward. As Mullin, Hardy and Sutton (2000, 2007) suggest, models of consumer behaviour should represent a process rather than a prescriptive formula. In other words, the sport-consumption experience evokes varied levels of psychological involvement, and an understanding of the process that creates different connections therefore assists marketing activities.

The PCM framework is unique in that it has the ability to account for internal processes that shape upward and downward movement within stages, and is alternatively called the Psychological Connection Model due to its stage-based focus on developmental progression. For example, the PCM recognises that a person may move upward or downward, or stay at a certain stage. Although a person may not skip a stage, the amount of time spent within a specific stage or the speed of movement between stages depends upon inputs and outputs. Hence individuals may have unique trajectories in terms of movement based on the decision-making process that governs the operation of the PCM framework. In addition, the existing segmentation tool derived from the PCM accounts for the unique connection to help investigate each stage (e.g. see Beaton, Funk and Alexandris, 2009; Doyle et al., 2013).

In summary, the sport decision-making process is the internal mechanism that controls movement between stages. Movement is based on the processing of external and internal inputs as well as attitudinal and behavioural outcomes that work independently and collectively to form various psychological connections. As a result, the inputs, processes and outputs sequence leads to the formation of the psychological connection and directs the type and frequency of behaviour. Decision-making represents the internal mechanism that controls movement of the PCM elevator between the four stages of awareness, attraction, attachment and allegiance. Given the important of inputs within the PCM, the next section provides a discussion of inputs relevant for sport marketers.

Inputs

Inputs in the PCM framework represent various internal and external forces that shape movement. Internal forces can be person-specific factors (such as demographics or personality) and psychological factors (for example, motives and needs) that promote a person's desire for a sport experience. External forces represent environmental factors (such as weather, culture or transport), which are often utilitarian and represent the functional and tangible attributes of a sport product or service that an individual desires. Both internal and external forces play a part in constructing the context from which the decision to purchase or engage in a behaviour is made (the consumption context). These inputs work individually and collectively to influence an evaluation that ultimately produces the level of psychological connection and directs behaviour.

The inputs are important for sport marketing in terms of positioning the sport experience for different consumers. Sport marketing activities for the awareness and attraction stages focus mainly on education and promotion. Hence marketing activities should communicate functional attributes and intangible benefits (for example, price, star athletes, venue, socialisation, escape) to new and casual spectators and participants. However, as the individual moves upwards to the attachment and allegiance stages, the evaluation is based more on the collective meaning of inputs, and the strength of this meaning is tied to the self-concept and important values (the functional, emotional and symbolic meaning of the sport team). Sport-marketing activities focus on using the marketing mix in conjunction with relationship-marketing strategies to strengthen the functional, symbolic and emotional meaning of a product and service. Within the PCM framework, sport consumer behaviour is viewed as the product of personal, psychological and environmental inputs, and a discussion of these inputs is now provided to highlight their role in the sport-consumption decision-making process. After this discussion, Sportview 3.1 provides an example of these inputs for a new professional sporting team.

Psychological inputs

Psychological inputs are internal to the consumer. Psychographics can be used to help identify psychological inputs. These are the set of beliefs and feelings held in relation to perceived outcomes a particular sport-consumption experience provides. Psychological inputs are the intrinsic motivators to consume and create a desire to seek out a sport-consumption experience to achieve positive outcomes. In general, motives to consume reflect desires to satisfy internal needs and wants, or receive intangible and tangible benefits through acquisition of a sport experience. Sport motives can be classified into push or pull motives. Push motives stem from an internal desire to eliminate an unpleasant state and reduce tension brought on by a recognised need or want. Pull motives represent a potential pathway (that is, a specific sport experience) that provides the opportunity to receive a desirable outcome to satisfy the need and/or want. For example, push motives are what initially compelled Pat to get off the couch and do something. The pull motives directed Pat to consider and then attend the Australian Open.

Sport consumer researchers have uncovered a number of push and pull motives that initiate goal-directed sport consumer behaviour. Sport spectator research has identified a number of discrete motives, including eustress, self-esteem, escape, entertainment, economic (gambling), aesthetic, group affiliation, family, vicarious achievement, acquisition of knowledge, drama, physical attraction, physical skills of players, social interaction, marquee player, specific team, head coach, entertainment value, success, players as role models, service quality, use of technology, management practices, community pride, logo design, promotions, price, desire for fantasy, flow, camaraderie, performance evaluation and celebrity attraction.

The two most widely used motive scales in sport consumer research are the Sport Interest Inventory (SII) (Funk, Mahoney and Ridinger, 2002) and the Motivation Scale for Sport Consumption (MSSC) (Trail and James, 2001). Sport participant research has identified discrete motives, including risk-taking, stress reduction, aggression, affiliation, social facilitation, self-esteem, competition, achievement, skill mastery, aesthetics, value development, self-actualisation, challenge, enjoyment, strength and endurance, positive health, weight management, ill-health avoidance, appearance, stress management, social affiliation and health pressures (Funk et al., 2011; McDonald, Milne and Hong, 2002), as well as sport tourism-related motives of getting away from everyday demands, facilitation of social interaction, the prestige of visiting and reporting upon a destination others want to visit, relaxation, or resting physically and emotionally while on vacation, desire to experience the culture of a foreign destination, desire for knowledge and to explore, and desire to learn specific aspects of a foreign culture (Funk, Toohey and Bruun, 2007).

Sport consumer researchers have developed a number of survey tools to measure a wide range of psychological motives specific to spectators. However, sport marketing professionals are more comfortable using a survey that is short and easy to administer in the real world. Funk et al. (2009) provided a solution by developing a survey tool to measure five main psychological motives that describe the benefits that sport consumers desire from a sport experience. The authors suggest that socialisation, performance, excitement, esteem and diversion are the main psychological benefits sought from a sport experience (spectator or participant context); these benefits are labelled with the acronym SPEED, and are commonly referred to as motives. They are listed below, together with an explanation for each motive.

- **Social interaction**: This represents a desire for sociability, as individuals are motivated to seek a sport event experience due to opportunities for the enhancement of human relationships through external interaction with other spectators, participants, friends and family.
- **Performance:** This represents a desire for aesthetic and physical pleasure, as individuals are motivated to seek a sport event experience due to opportunities to enjoy the grace, skill and artistry of athletic and physiological movement.
- **Excitement:** This represents a desire for intellectual stimulation, as individuals are motivated to seek a sport event experience due to opportunities for mental action and exploration from the atmospheric conditions created by the uncertainty of participation and competition, and the spectacle of associated activities.
- **Esteem:** This represents a desire for competency, as individuals are motivated to seek a sport event experience due to opportunities for achievement and challenge that produce a sense of mastery and heighten a sense of personal and collective self-esteem.
- **Diversion:** This represents a desire for mental well-being, as individuals are motivated to seek a sport event experience due to opportunities to escape and remove themselves from daily work and life routines, which create stress.

The SPEED motives represent a useful tool for examining psychological inputs. These inputs represent the core psychological benefits an individual receives from engaging in a sport-consumption activity. From a marketing perspective, these benefits should be taken into account when constructing marketing content to communicate the benefits of consuming a sport product or service. It is advisable for marketing professionals to augment these five benefits with sport-specific measures on their survey tools to provide more detailed information and a more accurate level of analysis.

Personal inputs

Personal inputs represent person-specific factors or dispositional characteristics that influence the sport-consumption decision-making process. Demographics can be used to understand personal inputs. Sport consumption can allow for the expression of important individual characteristics. An important consideration in the pursuit of any sport- or consumption-related activity is an individual's physical characteristics. Individual factors related to gender, body, personality characteristics and ethnicity influence the evaluation of a sport object.

Female participation in sport and exercise tends to be motivated more by socialisation, enjoyment and body-related concerns. In contrast, male participation is driven more by competition and ego-related concerns. Dietz-Uhler et al. (2000) determined that women were more likely to think of themselves as sport fans if they attended events with family and friends, while men more usually considered themselves fans if they played the sport. Ridinger and Funk (2006) observed a number of differences and similarities among spectators attending female and male collegiate basketball games. For example, female spectators (regardless of team gender) rated motives such as pride in the university, attendance affordability, socialisation opportunities, influence of family and/or friends and diversion as more attractive than did male spectators.

Body composition, physical conditioning and personality characteristics are important personal inputs. An individual weighing 65 kilograms may find contact or strength sports less enjoyable than sports or activities in which lightness is an attribute. Likewise, potential consumers who are physically fit may participate in endurance events such as triathlons and marathons. Sport experiences allow for the expression of important individual traits. Hawkins, Best and Coney (1992: 307) suggest that 'consumers tend to purchase products that most closely match their own [personality] or that strengthen an area they feel deficient in'. In most cases, personalities are individual, constant and enduring. They can change, of course, but this is usually due to the impact of a major life event. The two most common approaches to understanding personality are individual learning theories and social learning theories, more commonly referred to as trait and state theories of personality.

Individual learning theory argues that personality traits are usually formed in the early stages of an individual's development, and remain relatively constant into and through adulthood. The most common traits are extraversion, openness, agreeableness and conscientiousness, with noticeable characteristics of being reserved, quiet, shy, extroverted, relaxed or confident. This explains why certain individuals prefer cricket to football, bushwalking to boxing, or BMX to basketball, based on their individual personality characteristics.

Providing a different perspective, social learning theory argues that environment is an extremely important determinant of human behaviour. In such cases, the personality of the individual may alter, depending on the situation. For example, Mahony, Madrigal and Howard (1999) observed that high self-monitors used public association with athletic teams to enhance self-representation within a group. An introvert in one instance can be an extrovert in the next, whereas an assertive, aggressive individual can very quickly become timid when faced with a particular fear or phobia. Bungy jumping is a good example: A usually shy person may suddenly gain bravado and confidence in the moments before the leap.

Based on the diverse personal characteristics of individuals in sport marketing, it is necessary to cater for all personality types. For every fan who wants to stand in the outer among 'like-minded supporters' and cheer him or herself hoarse for a favourite team or athlete, there is another fan who wants to watch the action unfold while seated and in a less emotionally charged environment. For every consumer who wants the latest, brightest and most expensive athletic apparel, there is another who is more than comfortable in a nondescript tracksuit and functional footwear. Thus it is important that the product or service offerings provided fit the consumer's personality and vice versa. An understanding of basic personality types ensures that as wide a range of consumers as possible is being catered for in the marketplace.

Ethnicity is another personal input capable of shaping the evaluation of a sport object. Armstrong's (2001) study of the participation of black women in sport and fitness, and the implication for sport marketing, posited that, as a natural progression from the acknowledgement of women as viable sport consumers, ethnic consumers should be the focus of increased awareness. McCarthy (1998) had already examined marketing sport in the Hispanic community, but Armstrong's study was unique, as she segmented sport marketing along the lines of both gender and ethnicity. Armstrong (2001: 18) concludes that 'marketing strategies designed for the mainstream market may not be effective in reaching ethnically diverse sections of the population'.

Arguably, in a country as multicultural as Australia, it makes sense to explore strategies for marketing to ethnically diverse groups. Moreover, a sport fan who is a recent immigrant to Australia will most probably follow a sport that resonates with their nationality before sampling more indigenous offerings. The ethnic association of many of the A-League football (soccer) teams provides an opportunity for the sport fan to bridge the gap between the old and new sport experience.

Direct experience is an important personal input. Direct experience relates to an individual's prior exposure to, and use of, the product or service. Past experience influences the internal mechanism on which future decisions to consume are based. The role of direct personal experience is a key predictor of loyalty for professional sport teams. Creating positive experiences in the initial stages of awareness and attraction is an important and necessary step in upward movement. Fans of the Collingwood Football Club, Sydney Football Club and Canterbury Bulldogs continue to watch their teams play because their past experience as fans has enabled certain wants and needs to be satisfied. If prior exposure had been less than satisfactory, spectators would have explored alternative avenues to fulfil their needs, wants and expectations. Past experience contributes to the incremental development of the psychological connection and, for fans of many teams who are at the allegiance stage, past experience contributes to developing a connective bond that is rarely broken.

This discussion of personal and psychological inputs has illustrated their potential role in the consumer decision-making process. These internal inputs can create different needs and desire for intangible benefits through acquisition that influences the evaluation of a sport-consumption activity. However, these inputs and the resulting evaluation must

TABLE 3.2 Internal and external inputs

Internal inputs		External inputs	
• Gender • Age • Ethnicity • Culture • Direct experience • Knowledge and exploration • Learning styles and ability • Body characteristics • Physical ability • Physical conditioning • Life-cycle stage • Personality type • Cultural learning • Finances • Residential status • Family structure • Religion • Language	• Socialisation • Performance • Entertainment • Esteem • Diversion • Stress reduction and management • Aggression • Social affiliation • Competition • Skill mastery • Self-actualisation • Challenge • Strength and endurance • Positive health • Weight management • Ill-health avoidance • Appearance • Health pressures • Involvement • Attitudes • Motivation	• Family • Price • Heritage and culture • Safety and security • Style of play • Subculture • Management practices • Special events • Promotions • Price discounts • Nostalgia/tradition • Marquee athletes • Community pride • Customer service • Wholesome environment • Sport knowledge • Entertainment value • Geographic location • Event/team success • Mass media	• Parking • Food service • Venue • Cleanliness • Crowding effect • Crowd control • Access to technology • Destination attributes • Merchandise design • Charity/cause • Athlete role model • Peers • Organisations and institutions • Economics • Climate • Mobile devices • Constraints • Religion • Activity type • Politics

also consider environmental factors. Table 3.2 provides a comprehensive list of internal and external inputs.

Environmental inputs

Environmental inputs are external to the actual consumer. Having recognised that internal needs and benefits are desired, the individual explores potential solutions to the problem via attractive attributes of a sport experience. Funk and James (2004) suggest that while dispositional needs push an individual to engage in sport consumption, social situational factors (labelled endearing features) pull an individual towards a specific sport situation. Endearing features provide the environmental context or pathway to satisfy needs, wants and received benefits. Hence personal and psychological inputs create the push while environmental inputs provide the pull that directs the individual towards engaging in sport-consumption activities.

Family is a particularly influential environmental factor. In many instances, successive generations follow the same codes, leagues, clubs and leisure pursuits. Nevertheless, there is anecdotal evidence on every sports field and at every venue of the impact of family on the decision to be a sport participant or spectator. If one family member plays golf, netball, soccer or volleyball, there is a higher possibility that children or siblings of the same gender (in gender-specific sports) will adopt that activity. In Australian V8 motor racing, the Richards father-and-son combination is legendary. Similarly, while Tommy Smith is regarded as one of the greatest horse trainers Australia has produced, his daughter, Gai Waterhouse, has built a similar profile in this very competitive industry. There is little doubt that if a parent is an avid fan of the National Rugby League (NRL) or the Australian Football League (AFL), it would be rare for a family member to support an alternative code of football. Even more significantly, a family divided by club loyalties—Carlton vs Collingwood, Manchester United vs Arsenal or Parramatta vs Canterbury—would be the source of interesting dinner-table conversations whenever the opposing teams met.

Peers are also an important environmental factor. The behaviour and choices of companions often stimulate an individual to develop similar interests and behaviours. If a particular group is heavily involved in the consumption of basketball through playing, watching and reading, the pressure to conform to the group is strong. Individuals can either conform to the behaviour of the group or seek other groups whose interests are more in keeping with their own personal preferences.

Other significant environmental factors may include clubs with which an individual is affiliated, or schools and universities attended. The values and beliefs of Scouts and Guides organisations, or the local Surf Lifesaving Club, will be incorporated into the individual's set of beliefs and influence the decision-making process. Similarly, a private school that provides a variety of extracurricular sport activities, such as rowing, skiing and mountain climbing, offers very different possibilities from a state-funded, inner-urban high school that is cramped for space and perhaps lacking the level of resources to purchase large-scale capital equipment. In such instances, the focus may be on other areas of the curriculum, such as music, drama or visual arts, creating an environment that provides a very different set of experiences.

An individual's geographical location is also an important environmental influence. The sport offerings of country or coastal schools and universities can be very different from those of inner-city schools. Differences in sport participation between Gold Coast and Hobart residents would be expected to exist, based on climatic differences. The work of Doyle et al. (2013) also suggests that spectator sport consumption differs on the basis of location and the preference for certain sports over others that can be observed in Australia (e.g. AFL is the dominant sport in Victoria, NRL is the dominant sport in Queensland). In addition, international travel has become cheaper and faster, enabling more people to attend international events.

Economic considerations also exist as an environmental determinant to sport-consumer behaviour. Many Australians believe that they live in an egalitarian society, but differences based on class—predominantly linked to economic factors—do exist. While individual wealth will enable the purchase of the equipment to undertake a particular sport or activity, membership may be restricted for a variety of reasons. It may be easier to join a local golf club than the Royal Sydney or Royal Melbourne, even though the same equipment will serve at all venues. Moreover, unless you are a prime minister or parliamentarian, the wait to join the Royal Canberra Golf Club may be very long indeed.

Mass media and marketing are also recognised as important environmental factors that influence decision-making. Products, events and media provide information to the consumer in a manner that it is believed will encourage the consumer to buy. An incident on a sporting field may be downplayed by the organisation concerned, as it does not want adverse publicity, which could result in reduced attendance or a lessening of participation. Conversely, the media may play up the event, in the belief that graphic pictures or salacious commentary will sell additional newspapers or that television and internet consumers will view additional content of the provider. In most cases, media sources suggest that they are engaging in responsible journalism by presenting the product in total. Equally, the ongoing discussion associated with an incident may prove a boon to talkback radio, online fan forums and discussion-type sport shows.

The use of the internet and the emergence of new media technologies have become an increasingly important environmental input. Technological advancements mean that individuals can follow any number of sport offerings without physical attendance. Internet sites continue to play a key role in providing individuals with sport-related content and information, with social media platforms being adopted widely. Research has shown that social networking sites can influence interactive processes and heighten experiences of interaction and involvement, as many individuals have integrated social networking sites into their daily practices. According to Filo and Funk (2012), new media technologies alter traditional sport consumption activities by reducing geographic boundaries, as an individual can follow a team, player, league or event from any place in the connected world. In addition, the volume, speed and type of content delivered through the vast array of platforms, including Facebook, Twitter, blogs and YouTube, allow individuals to interact with and engage in various forms of sport consumption. These platforms are proving to be particularly engaging in that they enable individuals to personally connect with sport offerings at multiple levels, including individual athletes, sporting teams, sport leagues and governing bodies.

Political, religious, cultural and service groups are influential inputs. Often, these groups use sport to place their organisation in a positive light, or to piggyback on the popularity of a particular sport or activity. A local Rotary club's support of a community fun run is conceptually not very different from the entry of various church groups into a debate concerning the sporting use of religious holidays. In such instances, both groups are trying to establish a positive community profile. By linking themselves to sport and leisure, they are endeavouring to position themselves as a similar product for consumption purposes.

An interesting aspect of our political leaders has been their willingness to be seen at a variety of sporting events, to be photographed wearing a particular team's jersey or to stand in the winner's circle with the victors. It is an attempt on the part of politicians to be seen as 'the person in the street'. Here, sport is being used as a fundamental link or lure to encourage the individual to consume a particular ideology. Although most politicians in Australia align themselves to one or other sport code or team, the connection is usually transient at best. Yet there is no doubt that former Prime Minister John Howard remains one of the nation's great sport fans. Whether at the 2000 Olympics, where he was a regular attendee at all sports—not just the high-profile ones—attending Rugby League or Union games or watching perhaps his greatest sporting passion, cricket, his unabashed zeal for viewing sporting contests is legendary. Former Australian Test captain Mark Taylor referred to Howard as a 'cricket tragic', and it has been suggested—perhaps apocryphally—that if he had a choice between being prime minister or batting first wicket down for Australia, he might take the latter.

Climate and construction issues also play important roles. Issues such as global warming, pollution, rainforest destruction, over-population, urban sprawl and the general degradation of land and ocean are at the forefront of public consciousness. However, while society's relationship with the physical environment is usually viewed from a negative perspective, judiciously utilised changes in technology have the potential to provide the modern sport consumer with great benefits. Computer technologies and land management have allowed golf courses and resorts to exist side by side with rainforests and sensitive wetlands; sensible urban planning and council by-laws have allowed the establishment of new stadia or facilities that are sympathetic to local architecture and demographics; and government legislation has been enacted to protect both the rights of individual consumers and the collective good. It is important that the views of all categories of consumers—whether long-term, new, emerging or potential—be taken into account when sport promotion takes place.

Constraints as inputs

There are a number of situational and individual constraints that serve as inputs. Such inputs can serve a negative role and create 'obstacles' or 'barriers' that prevent sport-consumption activity. In other words, inputs can facilitate as well as constrain movement within the PCM elevator (for example, no movement, downward movement, slow movement). Lepisto and Hannaford (1980) identify five barriers to repeat purchase behaviour: marketing constraints, which depict the failed fit between product and consumer; cultural constraints, which act as prevailing cultural norms and values that might inhibit patronage; social constraints, which are the influence of reference groups and social expectations on action; personal constraints, which stem from the consumer's lifestyle, or pattern of living or use; and finally structural constraints, which curtail patronage as a result of certain physical, temporal or spatial challenges.

Within sport consumer research, Pritchard, Funk and Alexandris (2009) report that individuals without constraints consistently attend more games and use media more frequently compared with individuals who have internal and external constraints. External constraints represent environmental inputs such as financial (for example, the cost of tickets and concessions); schedule conflict, work and social obligations; limited access (to tickets and good seats); travel (parking and transportation to the stadium); and diminished appeal (weather or visiting team). Internal constraints represent personal and psychological inputs, including physical (being tired, poor health) and low priority (no personal interest and family priorities). Within Rugby Union, environmental inputs of weather, competition, lack of player quality and rain on match day also have been reported as reducing attendance (Owen and Weatherston, 2004). Sportview 3.1 explores psychological, personal and environmental inputs as factors that may lead an individual to support a new sporting team.

SPORTVIEW 3.1

New sporting teams

Over the past decade, a number of new sporting teams have been introduced to the Australian sport marketplace. In the last five years, all of the country's 'Big 4' football codes (NRL, AFL,

A-League, Super 15) have welcomed new franchises into their competitions, with many other sporting competitions also opting to expand. New teams are introduced to existing leagues or created for the purposes of establishing a brand new league. For example, the AFL introduced teams into the previously unrepresented and non-traditional regions of the Gold Coast and Western Sydney in 2011 and 2012 respectively. Elsewhere, eight new teams were created to form Twenty20 cricket's Big Bash League. Consequently, new sporting team introduction is generally born from a strategic effort by leagues to increase their market share and push into non-traditional and new regions. However, these goals are hard to achieve, and in many cases new teams have not been able to remain viable and have folded (e.g. A-League's North Queensland Fury and Gold Coast United). Given that Australians already have a wide array of sporting teams and other leisure pursuits to follow, new teams face unique challenges in building sustainable fan bases. Therefore, it is important that new teams place increased importance on satisfying the psychological, personal and environmental inputs discussed in this chapter.

Psychological inputs may be satisfied fairly easily by new teams, as they provide people residing in their communities with a new form of entertainment, an additional outlet for diversion and an important catalyst for social interactions. New teams represent novelty, given their lack of history, and provide individuals with a chance to experience top-level sport in their local community. Additionally, new teams provide an added outlet for an individual to escape the daily pressures of their life and an attractive avenue in which to invest leisure time. Perhaps most importantly, new teams facilitate increased opportunities to develop existing interpersonal relationships and meet new people who hold similar interests.

Personal inputs, such as the tendency for certain cultural groups to prefer a particular sport, may also be satisfied by new sport team introduction. Regions such as Western Sydney are home to an ever-increasing number of individuals from many differing cultural backgrounds. Existing sport offerings available to these individuals, such as Rugby League and AFL, are scarcely available outside of Australia, and may appear confusing or overly physical to individuals who have not grown up playing these sports. These individuals may prefer sports such as football (soccer), given its worldwide popularity and simple rules. In this case, the introduction of the A-League's Western Sydney Wanderers provides an opportunity for these residents to follow a sport they have directly experienced and that suits their interests.

Environmental inputs, such as an individual's geographical access to a particular sport, may be satisfied by new sport team introduction. For example, the Gold Coast is a region that typically attracts large numbers of tourists and relocated residents from Australia's southern and western states—locations where AFL is the dominant sport. The inclusion of the Gold Coast Suns allowed these individuals the chance to follow their favourite sport while also giving other individuals yet to be exposed to AFL a chance to engage with the sport.

In summary, new sporting teams provide an interesting outlet for leagues to achieve their goals. In order for new teams to remain viable, they must capitalise on the existing psychological, personal and environmental inputs that drive sport consumption.

In summary, sport consumption activity is a product of external and internal inputs that influence the decision-making process. These inputs can be classified into three general categories: psychological, personal and environmental. Collectively, the processing of these inputs influences the developmental progression of sport involvement within the PCM framework, and corresponds to stage-based attitudes and behaviour. The next section provides further discussion of how involvement can influence sport consumers.

Involvement in the decision-making process

The amount of effort devoted to a purchase decision can vary considerably, depending on the product and the consumer's level of involvement. For example, the purchase of new laces for running shoes requires little involvement compared with the original purchase of the running shoes, which requires a far more protracted process. The cost of a club membership to the Lions has to be weighed against a series of competing forces for disposable income, yet an individual may make the decision to attend a single game at the last moment. The club membership and expensive running shoes are high-involvement purchases; the single game and shoelaces are low-involvement purchases. Hence the consideration of price represents an environmental input that influences the decision-making process. However, this process is also influenced by the level of involvement: how devoted a person is towards a sport team or whether they want performance laces to accomplish a fast time in a running event. As mentioned previously, advancements by sport management researchers now enable sport marketers to segment sport participants and spectators into the PCM stages based on their dynamic involvement with the sport or team.

The role of sport involvement in consumer research has been well documented. In terms of the decision-making process, the level of sport involvement operates as an internal input. Hence sport involvement generally directs attention to initially considering a sport experience or product, while price, place and other inputs direct the consideration of alternatives within the decision-making process.

High-involvement purchases

High-involvement purchases make full and extended use of the decision-making process. Any number of internal and external inputs will be considered. Expensive, complex and high-risk purchases often fall into this category. In these cases, the consumer will invariably undertake a thorough information search, and carefully and selectively examine comparable attributes and benefits. The consumer may assess value for money, although cost may not be the major factor where special features, status or functionality are required. Finally, time will be allocated to the decision-making process, and the positives and negatives of the purchase will be weighed up. Once a tentative decision to buy has been made, affirmation may be sought from an external source such as an expert in the field or a product review or from a trusted friend. Yachts, golf clubs, snow skis and club membership may fall into this category.

Sport-marketing strategies aimed at consumers with high involvement should adopt an approach designed to increase greater elaboration of marketing communication. Funk and Pritchard (2006) report that committed (highly involved) sport fans put forth more mental effort to read and evaluate newspaper articles about a favourite professional sport team than non-committed (low involved) individuals. This research illustrates how high involvement has the ability to cue internal processing that prompts cognitive effort related to information search activity, elaborates information received and influences evaluation of alternatives. As a result, highly involved individuals will exert greater mental effort in processing a persuasive message as well as evaluating the applicability and credibility of the information. This may include the provision of maximum technical information or personal support for the service or product's use, and reinforcing the wisdom of the purchase choice. For example, marketing content used to advertise a marathon event should utilise race-specific information that includes detailed race information, including characteristics of the course, climate conditions and technical aspects of the timing systems utilised for the event. As with any advertising, the appropriate market segment should be considered in creating the content.

Sport-marketing strategies can also leverage high involvement with a sporting club, league or sporting event to attract corporate partners. Sport sponsorship is a communication vehicle used by corporations to increase the threshold of purchasing products and services such as cars, banks, insurance and mobile phones, which often require long-term commitment through contracts. For example, in 2013 the Brisbane Lions had major partners such as Vero, National Storage and Hyundai. In addition, Toyota was the premier partner for the AFL. The Melbourne Marathon had Medibank as its naming-rights sponsor. For sponsors, using sport in their sponsorship communications mix means the threshold of purchasing high-involvement products should theoretically be lowered by offering the qualities of attractiveness, recognisability and credibility. Hence the corporate partner can manage the decision-making process of a high-involvement purchase by linking the product or service with a sporting organisation (team, player or event) to which an individual is attached or to which they have allegiance within the PCM.

Low-involvement purchases

Low-involvement purchases occur when the product or service to be consumed is socially or psychologically unimportant, and there is limited risk. Hence information is acquired passively, and the decision to act is made with limited effort and evaluation. The level of prior experience with the product is low, and the consequences of poor choice are minimal. The sport industry competes with various entertainment alternatives for market share in a general market. As a result, the majority of individuals living in that market fit a low-involvement consumer profile (Robertson, 1976). For example, most individuals living in Sydney and surrounding suburbs are likely to be aware of the professional sporting teams that play in the city, and may even watch a game on TV or follow the news periodically, but do not purchase club membership or attend matches (that is, most individuals are in the awareness and attraction stages). These low-involved consumers will focus primarily on general product-level evaluations of a sport experience, and may not link or consider the SPEED benefits as unique attributes of the specific sport context.

The use of advertising and the role of the media among the less involved is important. In establishing an advertising strategy aimed at consumers exhibiting low involvement in the purchase process, sport marketers need to provide repetitive content and information, encourage familiarity, offer a variety of inducements, create attention-grabbing point-of-purchase (POP) displays and, if possible, distribute through multiple channels.

The substantial media exposure sport receives, and its link to sponsorship revenue, raise concerns about how a sport franchise is viewed by the general public. Funk and Pritchard (2006) found that negative publicity creates a threat to a sport organisation's low-involvement market base by affecting not only attendance but also sponsorship. Building strong relationships with local media is critical, and sport organisations should take a proactive stance to media relations (Nichols et al., 2002).

Sport marketing strategies can also leverage corporate sponsorship opportunities for the general public. Sport sponsorship provides the opportunity to market products that require a less-involved decision-making process. Sport selectively targets and segments audiences for sponsors, thus the connection between the sponsor's product and the sport creates a quick evaluation situation. The Brisbane Lions have Coca-Cola Zero for non-alcoholic beverage, Carlton Draught for alcoholic beverage, Four'N Twenty as the official pie and Skins for compression gear. The AFL has Hungry Jack's and Weet-Bix. The Melbourne Marathon has Asics for its shoe and apparel partner, while The Coffee Club provides a food and beverage association. Based on these examples, the sporting team or event provides a strategic platform to market low-involvement products for itself and others.

Summary

Understanding the sport consumer is not a simple task. Sport consumers' decision-making is a dynamic and complex process. Comprehending the complexity of this process is one of the more intricate tasks facing the sport marketer—indeed, it unquestionably has become a critical part of the marketing-management strategy. Although it is not always possible to fully understand how this process takes place, attention to the unique characteristics of specific consumers, coupled with a broad awareness of key inputs and outputs that influence how decisions are reached, will provide the sport marketer with a foundation on which marketing strategies can be developed. The PCM provides the sport marketer with a framework to understand the psychological, personal and environmental factors that influence consumer decision-making. The PCM framework also provides a basic guide to understanding how an existing level of involvement is important in the decision to initially buy or consume a sport product or service, as well as subsequent repeat behaviour.

CASE STUDY

AFL expansion—the Gold Coast Suns

By Jason Doyle

The Australian sports marketplace represents an increasingly competitive landscape, one that is complex in its design. Sport is a deeply entrenched way of life for most Australians, who have a vast selection of sports they can choose in which to participate and/or follow as spectators. From the spectator perspective, Australia is also the only country whereby four codes—Australian Rules football (AFL), Rugby League (NRL), Rugby Union (Super 15) and soccer (A-League)—compete for the title of 'football'. Usually, the code referred to simply as 'football' is their personal favourite—typically determined by where a person lives or their cultural background. Although each code enjoys some popularity across the nation, the AFL and NRL are traditionally seen as Australia's two most popular spectator sports. While the AFL enjoys a dominant following in the southern (Victoria, South Australia, Tasmania) and central/western (Western Australia, Northern Territory) states, the NRL remains the sport of choice for the majority in Queensland and New South Wales.

In an attempt to increase market share, the AFL has bolstered its presence in both Queensland and New South Wales in recent years. Introducing new teams to these regions represents a strategic approach designed to increase overall exposure to the game, and create rivalries with the existing AFL teams available to sport consumers. This approach saw the Gold Coast Suns become the second Queensland team (joining the Brisbane Lions) and the Greater Western Sydney Giants (GWS) introduced as New South Wales' second AFL team (alongside the Sydney Swans).

Along with the challenges traditionally faced by new teams entering a congested sport marketplace, the Gold Coast Suns had to overcome additional barriers stemming from the team's geographic location. First, the sport of choice for Gold Coasters has traditionally been Rugby League, with AFL capturing a smaller market. Second, although the Gold Coast is Australia's sixth largest city and one of the country's fastest growing areas, it has typically struggled to support professional sport franchises, with various Rugby League, soccer, basketball and baseball teams unable to avoid collapse. For these reasons, many people were sceptical of the team's longevity when the Suns entered the AFL competition in 2011.

The Gold Coast Suns experienced a tough inaugural season, which resulted in them finishing last on the ladder with a record of three wins and nineteen losses. Despite the lack of on-field success, the club was successful in signing up 14 064 members, and enjoyed a healthy home-crowd average of 19 169. Off-field successes such as awards for community engagement and providing a superior game experience were also highlights for the club. The 2012 season saw the club again win only three matches, finishing just ahead of newcomers GWS, who recorded two wins. In a sign that the novelty of the new team may have been wearing off, both member numbers (11 204) and average home-crowd figures (13 645) dropped from the 2011 benchmarks. These decreases meant that fewer people went to the stadium to support the team and less revenue was generated through ticket sales and other mediums.

The above case highlights the strategic decision-making behind introducing new sporting teams, and outlines the challenges that can arise in managing these franchises.

Questions

1. Imagine you are the marketing manager of the Gold Coast Suns. What strategies would you develop to engage fans using psychological, personal and environmental factors?
2. Apart from being more competitive on the field, how can the Gold Coast Suns improve their crowd and member numbers?
3. Are the psychological, personal and environmental factors the same in choosing to attend a Gold Coast Suns game versus attending a Gold Coast Titans (NRL) game? If not, what are some differences?

4

Market research: Segmentation, target markets and positioning

Stage 1—Identification of marketing opportunities

Step 1—Analyse external environment (forces, competition, publics)

Step 2—Analyse organisation (mission, objectives, SWOT)

Step 3—Examine market research and marketing information systems

Step 4—Determine marketing mission and objectives

▼

Stage 2—Strategy determination

▼

Stage 3—Strategy implemention, evaluation and adjustment

CHAPTER OBJECTIVES

Chapter 4 examines the development of marketing research and its use in segmentation, the selection of target markets and positioning. It demonstrates how marketing missions are created, objectives are established and target markets are selected. It also highlights how positioning is used to effectively locate a product or service within that target market.

After studying this chapter you should be able to:

- create a basic marketing information system
- articulate the components of small-scale market research
- comprehend the market segmentation process
- understand the rationale for the selection of target markets
- appreciate the concept of positioning.

HEADLINE STORY

Market research at work: Twenty20 cricket

Twenty20 Cricket originated in the United Kingdom in 2003. The game involves both teams having a single innings and batting for no more than 20 overs. An average game is completed in roughly three hours, putting the game on par with other popular spectator sports such as AFL, NRL, Rugby Union and Soccer. Twenty20 cricket is a product of market research, and was created to provide both game attendees and at-home viewers with a lively and entertaining version of cricket. Focus groups were conducted with individuals who did not consider themselves fans of cricket, who were asked to explain what could persuade them to watch cricket. The overwhelming response was that cricket was long and boring.

Twenty20 is a shorter version of the traditional form of cricket, and serves as a product extension. Twenty20 delivers fast-paced, exciting cricket, accessible to millions of fans who dislike the slower pace of the longer versions of the game. Long-time cricket fans are divided on the game. Michael Holding, a former West Indies fast bowler, described the game as 'rubbish', adding: 'There is nothing good about Twenty20 cricket'. In addition, many contend that some of the skills required for Test cricket (such as taking wickets, defence and overall concentration) are de-emphasised, or even eliminated, by Twenty20 cricket.

Despite these criticisms, Twenty20 has brought new energy to the sport, as shown by the enthusiastic fans who have packed stadia to see matches. Twenty20 has introduced the sport of cricket to an audience that otherwise never would have shown an interest, and continues to enjoy popularity and attention. In terms of drawing interest and spectators, it has been incredibly successful. The first matches in England drew an average of more than 5000 spectators, and attendance continues to increase steadily. The game has spread all over the world, to Pakistan, South Africa, Sri Lanka, Australia, New Zealand, the West Indies and India, and most Test-playing nations now have a Twenty20 domestic cup competition.

Australia's first Twenty20 game was played at the Western Australian Cricket Ground (WACA) in Perth on 12 January 2005, between the Western Warriors and the Victorian Bushrangers. The game attracted a sell-out crowd of 20 000. The popularity of this new form of cricket continued when, on 5 January 2007, the Queensland Bulls played the New South Wales Blues at the Gabba in Brisbane, in front of an unexpectedly large crowd of 27 653. Pre-match ticket sales were 11 000 and the extra day-of-game ticket demand of 16 000 caused disruption and confusion, leading the Gabba staff to open gates and grant many fans free entry. In February 2008, over 84 000 spectators attended a match between Australia and India at the Melbourne Cricket Ground. In February 2013, at ANZ Stadium in Sydney, the KFC Twenty20 International between Australia and India drew a record crowd of nearly 60 000. The development and emergence of Twenty20 cricket demonstrates the positive influence market research can have on major sport decision-making and sport consumer behaviour.

Information is power: the power to make informed decisions. Sport market research consists of activities designed to make good business decisions. These activities attempt to match the needs and wants of consumers with sport products, services and experiences to build and sustain volume. Developing a marketing approach that strategically positions the marketing mix requires an understanding of the sport consumer. Chapter 3's study of sport consumer behaviour provides the necessary foundation from which to develop a successful market research strategy.

Market research and strategy

There is little doubt that in order to make informed decisions, organisations need information—and lots of it. Mullin, Hardy and Sutton (2000: 99) suggest that:

> the most critical factor in marketing success is the marketers' ability to collect accurate and timely information about consumers and potential consumers and to use this data to create marketing plans that are specifically targeted to meet the needs of the specific consumer groups.

However, the collection of this material is only a starting point for the construction of a marketing information system (MIS). Once compiled, this information must be integrated, analysed and used to guide the direction of the organisation. Time spent on its assembly, maintenance and development can be the most effective marketing tool at an organisation's disposal.

Developing marketing information systems

An MIS is an 'ongoing, organised set of procedures and methods designed to generate, analyse, disseminate, store and later retrieve information for use in decision making' (Stanton, Miller and Layton, 1995: 48). Nevertheless, it is also acknowledged that for the MIS to be successful, the data should be of high quality, used in a realistic manner and adopted as a source of decision-making by the organisation. Figure 4.1 provides a basic design for the construction of an effective MIS. In this diagram, the population is divided into non-consumers and consumers, and relevant information is obtained using appropriate data-collection methods of internal and external data sources. This information is then collated and integrated, and serves as input for the data bank and analytics that lead to decision-making. The MIS represents an information resource to develop marketing strategies, along with mechanisms for monitoring effectiveness.

The current need for ongoing market research and the establishment of increasingly sophisticated MIS are the result of a dynamic, constantly changing sport environment. With less time for deliberation, increased accountability, growing consumer expectations, financial cost and the ever-expanding scope of marketing activities, sporting organisations need rapid access to reliable information that will result in clear, appropriate decision-making. Fortunately for sport organisations and managers, the quantity and quality of available information are constantly expanding.

How such information is used is the real key to organisational success. Matthews (2002) reports that an additional two golf courses were being added 'to what was becoming a crammed precinct on the Mornington Peninsula in Victoria'. However, the director of the Melbourne-based golf club properties was not concerned with the over-supply, stating that 'market research shows it's viable and we have had lots of talks with

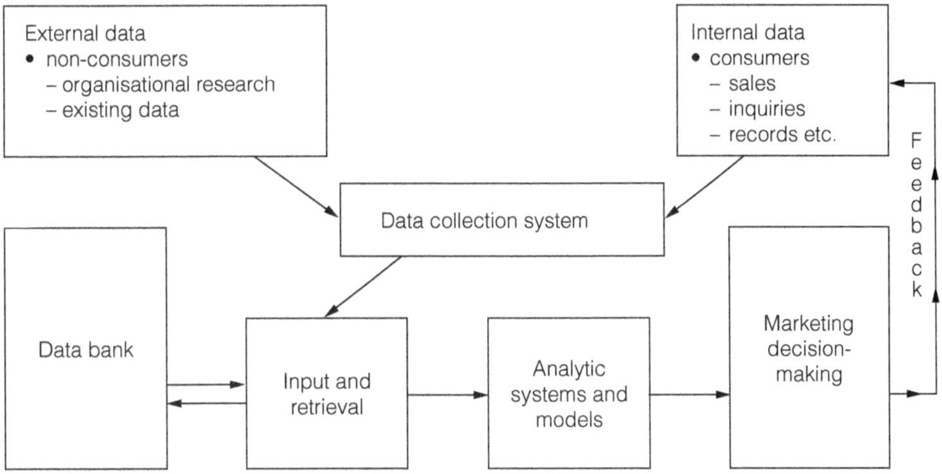

FIGURE 4.1 A basic design for a Marketing Information System

Tourism Victoria. The predictions are that this will become a mecca for golfers.' (2002: 75) In order to develop an extensive MIS, sport marketers need to collect information from four sources: general market data; data on individual consumers; data on competitors; and their participants.

General market data include all the information that relates to the broad environment in which the sport organisation operates. Within its area of operation—most commonly referred to as its critical trading radius—the organisation needs to establish size, demographics, the consumer habits of residents and workers, the ways in which individuals choose to spend their leisure time and any specific trends that will affect the sport—positively or negatively. This information is particularly important for sport leagues hoping to expand nationally and internationally in order to be successful. A comprehensive profile of sport consumers in the new market for the sport is needed to have any hope of success. For example, sport codes are continually expanding into new markets or reorganising their existing offerings (for example, Australian Rules football, National Rugby League, Super Rugby). In terms of expansion, the Gold Coast Titans and the Gold Coast Suns believed that there was a potential NRL and AFL base of supporters in Southern Queensland beyond the current fans for the Brisbane Broncos and Brisbane Lions. In 2011, Super Rugby expanded to fifteen franchises with teams in Australia, New Zealand and South Africa. The Greater Western Sydney AFL club began plans in 2012 with the hope that interest in AFL would emerge in the western suburbs of Sydney, which historically are a hotbed for Rugby League. Such expansion decisions should be gauged not only from potential consumer demand, but also the number of potential corporate sponsors and media outlets that can support a professional sport or sporting event.

A second source of information should be individual consumers, regarding their attitudes and behaviours related to a specific sport product or service. Once individual consumer data have been collected and entered on the appropriate database (for example,

Excel or SPSS), the sport marketer has a multitude of information available with which to establish marketing strategies. Name, address, email, phone number, gender, age, occupation or student type, purchase patterns and payment methods are a small representation of the type of information that can easily be collected by sporting organisations. This information can be collected from registration at sporting events, ticket sales, membership forms and social media. More detailed information can be collected using survey instruments (online and paper-based), with inducements to get spectators, fans and participants to supply names, email addresses, postal addresses and phone numbers. Information collected through these surveys can also be used to determine the specific motives for consumption, satisfaction with service delivery, behavioural intentions and level of involvement with a sport or team using the Psychological Continuum Model to develop divergent marketing communication strategies (Doyle et al., 2013).

The third and fourth sources of information for sporting organisations relate to competitors and their participants. It is critical that sporting organisations are not only aware of who their competitors are, but also know the consumers of a rival's products or services. For example, running, biking, swimming and triathlon events may attract similar participants. A number of sports and sporting events can successfully operate in the same area when their consumers are dissimilar. Basketball, tennis, soccer and netball appear to be quite different in their support bases. Therefore, apart from observing general promotional strategies, these sports would best be served by focusing on information that is internal to the organisation and sport-specific. Nevertheless, if a sport is jockeying for position in the marketplace, competitor pricing, promotion, and product breadth and depth need to be noted. This is particularly important when junior competitions and leagues are involved. Juniors will invariably gravitate to those sports that provide them with opportunities at the local level.

Data sources for a marketing information system

There are two major sources of data for any MIS: external and internal. External data may be primary or secondary, and have been collected by the sporting organisation or an external agency. Internal data include all the information—such as basic enquiries—that the organisation collects during the day-to-day operation of its business.

External secondary data

Numerous sources of secondary data can be used by sporting organisations to assist in the formation of a strategic marketing plan. The most obvious starting point is government agencies, such as the Australian Bureau of Statistics (ABS). The *Participation in Sport and Physical Activities* and *Spectator Attendance at Sporting Events* reports are two potential information sources. These ABS statistics show various demographic characteristics of persons involved in sport during a twelve-month period. For example, from April 2011 to March 2012, 1.7 million (60 per cent) of Australian children aged 5 to 14 years participated in at least one organised sport outside of school hours. During the same period, nearly two-thirds of Australians aged 15 years and over (65 per cent, or 11.7 million people) participated in sport and physical recreation. During the period

2009–10, more males attended a sporting event (50 per cent) than females (37 per cent). As discussed in Chapter 3, the highest attendance rates at sporting events were reported for AFL, followed by horse racing, Rugby League and motor sports. These are just two sources that provide basic information that is potentially useful for a number of sporting bodies. Such information is readily accessible on the ABS website at <www.abs.gov.au>.

Libraries and chambers of commerce are other useful sources of information, especially at the local level. Data relating to trends and uses of local events and facilities should be held there, as well as the various municipal rules and regulations governing the conduct of sport events. Larger community libraries, along with those attached to institutes of higher education, often contain much of the government or commercial data that have been collected in relation to sport. Chambers of commerce will hold data relating to the income and expenditure patterns of local industry, which can assist sport marketers in establishing profiles that may match their organisation.

An increasing amount of data is being gathered in various research units in Australian universities as well as by the Australian Sports Commission. While much of this information is proprietary, some of the findings are being presented at conferences and appearing in academic journals. Likewise, a growing number of sport marketing academics are being used as market research consultants, and are bringing an ever-increasing repository of skills and knowledge to their task.

Advertising media are constantly engaged in the collection of secondary data. While it may not be specific to the focus of the sport marketer, information relating to demographics and psychographics may be useful for sponsorship or advertising. This is particularly the case when the characteristics of the media information match a particular sport organisation's own data. The Australian advertising industry uses OzTAM data, which is the official source of television audience measurement. OzTAM manages and markets television ratings data for television viewing in Sydney, Melbourne, Brisbane, Adelaide and Perth, across all television households and nationally for all subscription television households. OzTAM uses a small sample of monitored households that can be extrapolated to the general population. Regional areas are serviced by commercial television networks and Nielsen Media Research Australia.

A final source of secondary data is private organisations such as Sweeney and Roy Morgan. Brian Sweeney and Associates surveys over 7000 Australians annually in rural and metropolitan Australia. Its publication, the *Sweeney Sports & Entertainment Report*, covers 27 sports and examines sports participation, attendance, television viewing, radio listening, newspapers, the internet and mobile devices. Sweeney also assesses sponsorship awareness levels of selected sports, sport-related spending, sport events and club followings, sport involvement and lifestyle characteristics, and interest in the Olympics. In 2013, Sweeney reported that Pat Rafter was Australia's favourite athlete, and released a top-ten list of most familiar athletes (see Table 4.1).

Similarly, Roy Morgan Research—most commonly associated with the Morgan Gallup Poll—has established a variety of services and products that can provide sporting organisations with significant data. Roy Morgan surveys over 50 000 Australians and 22 000 business decision-makers annually to provide information on media measurement, financial behaviour, voting intention and consumer confidence. The collection of such data provides wide-ranging information on consumer behaviour, and as such can be an

TABLE 4.1
Top ten athletes by familiarity

Athlete	% familiar with
Ian Thorpe	73
Cathy Freeman	72
Shane Warne	72
Ricky Ponting	68
Lleyton Hewitt	66
Pat Rafter	63
Greg Norman	63
Glen McGrath	63
Steve Waugh	59
Casey Stoner	56

invaluable secondary source for the sport marketer. For example, in 2012 Morgan revealed that Australia's largest concentration of Australian Rules football fans (38 per cent) live in Victoria, with 61 per cent of all Victorians supporting an AFL team. In addition, 22 per cent of all AFL supporters have played a sport in a given three-month period, and 63 per cent are likely to have attended a professional sports event. Furthermore, football fans appear to enjoy financial competition, with 45 per cent more likely than the average Australian to have placed a bet, 49 per cent more likely to attend horse races and 24 per cent to have visited a casino. Sport marketers requiring more detailed and specific information can also hire university academics to conduct sport research, as well as engaging small boutique consulting firms specialising in building and managing customers in the sports, arts and charity industries.

Primary data

Primary data may be internal or external, and are a product of collection methods and purpose. The most common type of internal data are collected from social media, enquiries, emails, websites, letters and telephone calls. These may be in the form of interest, complaints or praise. Accounts, credit card purchases and general sales can also provide a wealth of information, indicating consumer trends in relation to a sporting organisation's product or service. Promotions and sweepstakes that require a consumer to provide personal information for a chance to win a prize are a useful means of collecting primary data. Other sources of internal information can include an organisation's employees, contractors, suppliers and sponsors. All can offer the sport marketer useful advice, and any such comments should be heeded. However, there is little doubt that the best data available to the sport marketer are those that are purpose-driven by the organisation. In this way, direct answers to specific questions can be obtained about the habits and consumption patterns of sport participants and consumers. Moreover, the collection of primary data through market research is not difficult. All that is required is access to the information source, time, energy and good questions.

Marketing research in sporting organisations

In essence, market research in sporting organisations seeks to answer six questions about consumers in relation to their consumption of the product, service or experience. Initially, sporting organisations need to know WHO their consumers are, but this is only the tip of the iceberg. WHY they choose the particular sport product or service, and WHEN and WHERE that consumption takes place, are equally important. WHAT that consumption entails in terms of pre- and post-event activities and HOW the product is used are also critical in terms of establishing a complete consumer profile. Mixed-methods research designs, which include both quantitative (WHO, WHEN and WHERE) and qualitative (WHY and HOW) data-collection phases are particularly effective for developing such understandings. The potential use of sport marketing research generally can have numerous outcomes. Fundamentally, research attempts to collect information to make informed marketing decisions to build and sustain volume through the sport-exchange process. It can enhance the flow of communication between the organisation and the customer. It can facilitate the creation of promotional strategies or the development of sponsorship proposals. It should assist in general decision-making and programming. In no particular order, the information requested generally falls into the categories of general and sport-specific.

General information

Usually, the general information requested focuses on demographics, psychographics and product usage. Demographics are personal characteristics such as gender, age, occupation, income, household size, education level, place of residence and methods of transport. Psychographic information conveys data on attitudes, interest and opinions regarding social, political, economic and environmental topics. Behavioural information includes data on how many times in a given period a person visits a particular establishment (such as the gym, a stadium or a website), the number and type of vehicles in the household, and the various electronic items they use. This last issue is becoming more and more important as sporting organisations endeavour to ascertain how many of their consumers not only use personal computers but also have access to the internet and use mobile devices. With many sporting organisations establishing interactive home pages and active social media presences, new opportunities for establishing enhanced databases are plentiful. Through these media, professional sport franchises, sporting events and community recreation programs can communicate with members and users on a regular basis via technology.

An equally important general question relates to where consumers get their information. Frequency and type of newspapers read, websites visited, radio stations listened to, television stations and programs viewed, and magazines read—both general and specific—are crucial factors in determining promotional strategies. Sport consumers are now using technology to access information through blogs, social networks (e.g. Facebook, YouTube) and micro blogs (e.g. Twitter). Sport fans access information on TV (53 per cent), online (19 per cent), using smartphones or tablets (12 per cent) and via social networks (10 per cent). Each week, the average Australian sport fan spends three hours consuming sport on TV, 1.7 hours using mobile devices and one hour via print media (Global Sports Media Consumption Report, 2012). Word of mouth remains an important source of information for sport consumers, and a market research strategy needs to be developed to manage this.

Sport-specific information

Sport- or activity-specific questions often relate to attendance patterns, influences to buy or consume, and levels of satisfaction with various aspects of the sport or sporting event. This information relates to personal, psychological and environmental inputs, discussed in Chapter 3 as part of the sport-consumption decision-making process. In relation to attendance, organisations need to be aware of both the depth and the breadth of product or service use. Obviously, years of membership or season ticket-holding are examples of depth, but the range of single-match buyback programs, offering incentives to members who do not attend a particular match to place their seat/ticket back in the pool for general sale, is an increasingly popular example of the latter.

Likewise, organisations need to know what influences the consumer's decision to buy a particular product when faced with the diverse and ever-expanding range of options in the sport and entertainment marketplace. Sport-specific information provides an understanding of how participating and playing sport satisfies individual needs and provides benefits. Finally, organisations need to be apprised of the customers' levels of satisfaction—that is, their perceptions of the range and quality of the merchandise and concessions sold, of the scope and type of services offered, and of the way in which the organisation conducts its business. By asking such questions of sport consumers, organisations can establish comprehensive profiles of their customers, which in turn allow the organisation to strategically market its products or services in a diverse marketplace. As Huggins (1992: 40) notes:

> the principal focus of the marketing function in sport is not so much to be skilful in making sport fans or participants do what suits the interest of sport as to be skilful in conceiving or doing what suits the interest of the fans or participants without changing the sport itself.

The marketing mission

Before identifying the components of the market research process, it is useful to consider the benefit of determining the marketing mission. In many ways, the mission of the whole organisation will also assist managers in setting a direction for their respective departments, one of which can be the marketing department. Cheverton (2000) suggests that good mission statements actually guide the organisation with some consistency through the marketing decision-making process in a way that minimises conjecture or misunderstanding. Moreover, he argues that there are five key aspects to a mission statement: (1) acknowledging the business the organisation is in; (2) knowing the aspirational position; (3) being aware of the core competencies that are needed to guide the organisation toward that vision; (4) knowing which consumers or target market will best assist in reaching the position; and (5) understanding how an organisation knows when it has arrived. In other words, what are the measurements of success?

Baker (2000) concludes that the mission statement is more than just a strategic plan: it is the 'cultural glue' that enables a collective engagement in the marketing process. This approach is most appropriate to the sport-marketing environment. There is no doubting the importance of strategy in sport marketing, but given that sport organisations are diverse organisations, the overarching mission or vision is the focal point around which such diverse units can congregate.

The Australian Sports Commission (ASC) had a very simple mission: 'to enrich the lives of all Australians through Sport'. This mission (which has now been changed) was to be achieved through the development and maintenance of an effective national sports infrastructure, increased sport participation and enhanced sport performance. The ASC worked towards this mission by developing a national policy framework, coordinating and contributing to the national delivery network, and focusing on the development and dissemination of quality services, programs and products.

Inherent in such strategic plans, stated visions or marketing missions are the objectives by which the desired outcomes might be realised. Once again in keeping with this text, such objectives are strategic in that they carefully clarify the manner in which the organisation reaches its stated goal. There are numerous types of organisational objective, but they fall mostly into two major categories: sales and communication. Furthermore, there are a number of acronyms in existence (such as SMART = Specific, Measurable, Achievable, Realistic, and Timely) that guide the objectives-construction process. But the fundamental underpinning in the selection and creation of strategic objectives remains their evaluative benefit.

The success of the marketing mission is determined via the ongoing monitoring and evaluation of the stated objectives. The ongoing scrutiny of results against the framework of organisational objectives is necessary because of their basically organic nature. Organisational objectives will change as intermediate goals are obtained, or with the realisation that a structured strategy is not delivering the desired results—or if an external trigger necessitates an internal change. Quality market research further enables the sport organisation to collect the information that is necessary to keep the organisation on the right strategic course.

The market research process

Sport organisations can no longer rely solely on general sport market research to inform decision-making. Sport organisations can conduct their own market research, engage a specialist to assist in questionnaire construction, data analysis or interpretation, or contract a consultant to deliver product-specific information. Organisational decisions should be based on the needs and expectations of the consumer, and the only way in which this can be ascertained is to ask. While the phrase 'use it or lose it' is a sport cliché, when applied to market research there is no more appropriate sentiment.

The market research process principally consists of five distinct phases. In order to guide the complete process, and to achieve maximum results with limited resources and time, the first step in the process is to clearly define the research problem and set a number of measurable objectives. The research problem and objectives often are a direct derivative of the marketing mission of the organisation—for example, increase new participation for a marathon event by 20 per cent or increase membership renewals by 10 per cent. The second step in the process is to develop a research methodology—that is, to determine which data sources are needed (primary or secondary), and which methods of data collection (see below) are best used in the context of the research. The third step then involves the research planning and data collection, who collects the data, when and where. When all data are collected, they need to be analysed. Data analysis, as the fourth step in the process, can involve the crunching of quantitative data (for example, from questionnaires) with the help of statistical analysis software programs or the interpretation of more qualitative research data (such as that obtained from interviews). The final step in the research process is the presentation of the findings in a report so that the research objectives are achieved and the research problem is answered most effectively.

Funk, Mahony and Havitz (2003) suggest a seven-step sequence to help sport marketing professionals present their findings in a marketing report. This sequence is designed to expedite the research process by helping to determine the type of information required for a report. Step 1 determines how findings presented in the report will be implemented within the organisation; Step 2 test-markets the contents of the final report on key stakeholders; Step 3 specifies the information requirements needed to create the content; Step 4 determines the kind of information needed to carry out the analysis; Step 5 searches for existing secondary data, or finds out if none exist; Step 6 designs a plan to collect primary research data; and Step 7 actually conducts the primary research. Primary research depends upon information that utilises some form of data-collection method.

Data-collection methods

Surveys

The personal survey remains a useful research method, as it allows the sport marketer to source first-hand information on the purchasing and consumption patterns of sport consumers. These data can be collected at the event, by going door to door in a defined geographical area, at a shopping centre (mall intercepts), via direct mail or the telephone (telemarketing) and increasingly through the use of technology with online surveys. As discussed in Chapter 3, sport consumer behaviour researchers have developed a number of survey tools useful to collect information from spectators and participants. Most sport organisations that are serious about providing services to their constituency regularly engage in this type of research. Moreover, a serious sport organisation is not just a professional or semi-professional franchise. Local clubs, events and groups can often use the survey format to gain consumer and participant feedback. Obviously, the more professional an organisation is and the larger its stakeholder base, the more sophisticated the survey and its accompanying tools of analysis will become. Nevertheless, the underlying philosophy remains constant, and that is the collection of quality information that will assist in decision-making and in guiding the running of a successful club. Typically, surveys collect quantitative data but may also be augmented with open-ended questions, which allow respondents to add comment on issues not identified in the included quantitative questioning.

Focus groups

A focus group is a small group of interested individuals assembled to talk about the issues that an organisation and its consumers believe are important. Focus groups gather rich qualitative data, which usually provide detailed information concerning sport consumer behaviour. For example, a sport team may invite eight existing club members in for a one-hour discussion before a game to explore current and potential benefits and levels of membership for next year. Usually the size of the focus group is fewer than ten, which provides everyone present with an opportunity to contribute. This method encourages individuals to engage freely in dialogue with each other, with the data collector in this instance prompting, guiding and recording. Trends and issues emanating from focus groups are often the catalyst for more structured, follow-up research. Professional sport teams and sport event organisations often use focus groups to assist in the creation and refinement of marketing strategy, as well as collecting operational information.

Observation

Seeing is believing. Although not always undertaken in a formal manner, the observation technique should be used by the sport marketer on an ongoing basis. This can entail walking through the stands at a game or among participants at a race meeting. Technology can also be used to monitor behaviour during an event. From Bill Veeck with baseball during the 1940s, to Kerry Packer and World Series Cricket in the 1970s, to Michael Wrubleski and the National Basketball League (NBL) in the 1990s, to Lamar Hunt with the Kansas City Chiefs in the 2000s, good sport owners and marketers have recognised the value of getting out and both talking to the spectators and watching their behaviour. This simple act can inform sport marketers about which aspects of their marketing strategies are having the desired result and which need some work. During observation, many sport marketers will single out and interview a spectator or participant at the event on any number of topics. Ideally, the observation will lead to the focus group, which could lead to the structured survey, which should then lead to action based on rigorous data collection.

Experimentation

Experimentation can be useful to the sport marketer in specific circumstances. Here, the researcher or industry professional manipulates one marketing mix variable while holding all the others constant. Changing the venue, price, time or day of event, or altering uniforms, are just a few of the variables that professional sport clubs manipulate during a pre-season competition in order to gauge reaction to such changes. If the changes prove popular, they may be adopted for the regular season. If not, the previous modus operandi is utilised. This type of research is particularly useful for evaluating the persuasive impact of media, advertising and internet content on the general public and consumers (Filo and Funk, 2005; Funk and Pritchard, 2006).

Research design

The research design should be of sufficient scope to provide all necessary information, but short enough to encourage participation in the process. For example, qualitative approaches using focus groups, interviews and observations are useful for developing new and in-depth information that can be used to modify one or more elements of the marketing mix (for example, ticket and membership prices, advertising content and location). Quantitative approaches are useful for assessing whether modification to the marketing mix is a good idea, or to measure the success of implemented changes. Mullin, Hardy and Sutton (2000) suggest that the sport marketer needs to have a feel for the kind of answers expected. While it could be argued that this may introduce bias into the project design, most research is initiated through some type of intuitive process. Although types of research design are as varied as the sports products and services being researched, there are a number of basic principles that should be adhered to:

- Sport marketers should ask only questions to which they need to know the answer. If responses to perceived personal questions, such as income levels, are not needed, they should not be asked for, as incorrect responses can bias results.
- For ease of analysis, questions should be closed, mutually exclusive and free of ambiguity.
- While questions should be thematically linked, each response should provide a unique piece of information. This approach means that a questionnaire or survey can be reduced to sections, which can then be used and manipulated as a stand-alone instrument.

Segmenting the sport market

On any given weekend, Australian sport attracts millions of spectators and participants, who become involved for myriad reasons. Stanton, Miller and Layton (1995) suggest that market segmentation is the process of dividing the total, heterogeneous market for a product or service into several segments, each of which tends to be homogeneous in all similar aspects. Segmentation creates a smaller group of consumers from the overall customer base of a sport organisation who share a common interest. In other words, certain segments of consumers share similar personal, psychological and environmental reasons for their involvement. In an attempt to encourage such groups to initiate or maintain their involvement in the sport or activity, different marketing strategies must be developed that are specifically aimed or targeted at such groups or market segments.

Market segmentation is a consumer-oriented philosophy, and endeavours to satisfy as many needs and wants in the marketplace as possible. Moreover, by segmenting the marketplace, an organisation can more judiciously allocate marketing resources, which should result in greater returns on the investment, or 'more bang for the buck'. Mullin, Hardy and Sutton (2000) further suggest that segmentation is central to an understanding of consumers, as it recognises differences in consumer behaviour which directly inform marketing strategies. Consequently, the task facing sport marketers is to first determine how consumers use sport products or services to meet individual needs and provide benefits, and then to determine which factors are common. This allows the sport marketer to categorise or group customers according to the type of people they are, the way they use the product or service, and finally their expectations of it.

Although the segmentation possibilities are endless, there are a number of broad-based variables that provide an effective starting point for a segmentation strategy. Commonly, consumers are segmented on the basis of demographics, psychographics

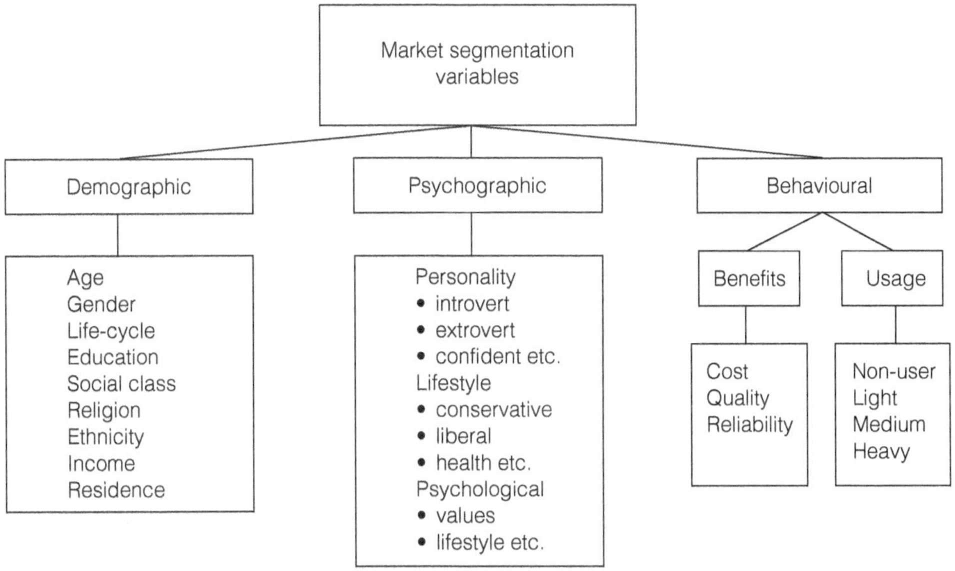

FIGURE 4.2 Market segmentation variables

and behaviour towards the product. This psychographic category is further divided into the benefits wanted from the product and product usage, or how the product is used. Figure 4.2 represents such variables schematically.

The market-segmentation process

Demographic segmentation

Demographic segmentation is the most common form, with important demographic determinants being gender, age, religion, income, occupation, education level, marital status, geography and life-cycle stage. The shifting demographic in society from Baby Boomers to Generations X and Y to the new 'E' Generation impacts the demand for sport products and services. All demographic variables are potentially important, especially when considering an individual's life-cycle. Traditional life-cycle stages include singles, married couples with and without children, 'DINKs', 'empty nesters' and elderly singles. However, single parents, older childless couples and young families increasingly are representing alternative stages in the life-cycle. The life-cycle stage has considerable impact on the amount of time and financial resources that can be devoted to sport consumption. Stages in the life-cycle directly affect consumer behaviour, and it is essential for sport marketers to provide mechanisms that encourage customers to remain loyal from childhood to the senior years.

Geographic issues such as regions, city size, the urban–rural dichotomy and climate can also influence strategic sport marketing. While it may appear safe to assume that spectator expectations in country and regional areas are quite different from expectations in the city, even the cities cannot be treated as homogeneous for the sport marketer. While ease of event access, parking and travel time are often important to the suburban commuter, public transport and additional entertainment possibilities may be far more important to the inner-city dweller.

Psychographic segmentation

While demographic information can inform the sport marketer about who the consumers are, this information alone does not explain why they consume. To partially answer this question, consumers need to be further categorised according to psychographics. Psychographics divide the market into segments based on attitudes, lifestyles or values. Psychographics can be more important than demographics in the consumer decision-making process; however, they can be more difficult to quantify. Psychographic segmentation is generally based on the attitudes, interest and opinions that guide behaviour. This approach attempts to explain consumer behaviour in terms of needs satisfied from a sport product or service. For example, strategies to differentiate fitness gym clients can be 'fitness-driven' segments motivated exclusively by fitness reason versus the 'health-conscious social' segment, seeking activities that are healthy but provide more social facilitation.

Psychographic segments can also be derived from an individual's desire for risk-taking, stress-reduction, aggression, self-esteem, competition, achievement and skill mastery. Other psychographic segments can be developed on the basis of core values, personality type and lifestyles (for example, outer-directed, inner-directed and need-driven, socially aware, visible achievement, traditional family life, young and optimistic) (Mullin, Hardy and Sutton, 2000; Stanton, Miller and Layton, 1995), attributes associated with a sport team brand (for example, star player, head coach, sport types, logo design, community pride and managerial decisions) (Gladden and Funk, 2002) or sport league brand (for example, competitive balance, rivalry, stadium atmosphere) (Kunkel, Funk and Hill, 2013), sportscape aspects and customer satisfaction (Hill and Green, 2001). Psychographic segments are particularly useful for benefit-segmentation approaches.

Benefit segmentation

Benefit segmentation refers to the benefits attributed to the consumption of the product. Stotlar (1993) comments that benefit segmentation is based on the unique benefits of a product or service that motivate a consumer to purchase it. Different consumers can expect different benefits from the same product or service. An important feature of this concept is that the consumer is purchasing the benefit of experience, not the physical product or service. A person may choose to attend a basketball game not because they like the sport, but because a friend is going. Here, the benefit inherent in going to the game is the opportunity for social interaction. If the friend were going to the zoo, the idea of attending the basketball game would be moot. In this instance, the chance for social interaction is just one benefit that the sport promoter provides. Similar benefit-segmentation strategies can focus on the entertainment aspect of the event or the opportunity to escape from the rigours of the daily grind and indulge in a sport activity, to be involved in the production and presentation of an event or activity, or simply to be seen at an event. These benefits are highlighted in discussion of the SPEED motives in Chapter 3. Benefit segments can be created from a desire for socialisation, performance, entertainment, esteem and diversion from participating in or watching a sporting event.

The purchase of sporting equipment and apparel can also be segmented according to benefit. An athlete may buy an electrolyte-replacement drink not because they are thirsty or like the taste, but because they believe that it will replace essential elements the body has lost during intensive exercise. Hence the athlete is purchasing the benefit—a more rapid recovery—rather than the product—a sport drink. Another example of benefit segmentation in sport relates to the purchase of the potential benefits of athletic footwear. Some individuals will purchase a running shoe because it offers a wide toe box, controls supination and provides arch support and stability. Others will purchase the same shoe because it looks fashionable, glows in the dark and a celebrity sport star wears the same shoe.

Sportview 4.1 provides an overview of effective market segmentation in the extreme sports context.

SPORTVIEW 4.1

Market segmentation—extreme sports

Perhaps no sport industry uses market segmentation, and particularly psychographic segmentation, more effectively than extreme sports. Extreme sports encompass the high-risk, high-adrenalin activities that provide participants with a chance of injury or danger. These activities include mountaineering, snowboarding, surfing and canyoning, all of which are attracting a consistently increasing body of participants. As the market continues to grow, the equipment and media offerings available to these consumers expand. State-of-the-art 'extreme' equipment such as gloves, sunglasses, helmets, T-shirts, sandshoes, protective padding, bikes, karabiners and surf wax are all on sale in a variety of styles and models. In addition, a variety of publications exist promoting each sport, and each reflects the language and risk inherent in the activities. *On The Edge*, *Thrasher*, *Slam*, *Rip Tide*, *Powder Hound* and *Ballistic* are a few examples of magazines that cover various extreme sports and—as is apparent from their respective titles—reflect the image and lifestyle of the different activities.

Extreme sports are currently thriving because of an understanding and awareness of the different demographics and psychographics drawn to the activities, as well as the benefits sought by participants. While predominantly youth oriented, extreme sports are not exclusively targeting Generation Y. Extreme sport tourism packages are now tailored for singles and honeymooners, as well as middle-aged couples and divorcees. In terms of psychographics, extreme sports flourish by marketing the attitude, lifestyle and values inherent to their activities. Accordingly, risk-taking, achievement, extroversion, non-conformity, fun and excitement are crucial elements promoted as part of the extreme sport experience. Doug Spong, founder and CEO of the Gold Coast-based Cult Industries Surfwear label, openly talks about how the key to his organisation's success is 'all a matter of cracking the "psychographic" of a very tribal market'. With regard to benefit segmentation, similar benefits sought through mainstream sport consumption relate to extreme sports, including socialisation, entertainment, esteem and diversion. Extreme sports represent a booming sector of the sport industry that relies heavily on effective market segmentation utilising demographics, psychographics and benefits.

Behavioural segmentation

Understanding behavioural patterns is critical in sport marketing. Generally, it is much easier and cheaper to get a customer to repurchase a product or service than get a customer to initially try a product. Behavioural segmentation refers to frequency and complexity of product usage. Usage segmentation can be the frequency in terms of repetition for using a product or service (that is, how many times a consumer participates in or watches a sporting event). The complexity of usage represents the different types of behaviour related to the product or service. For a sport team, does a person attend a sporting event, purchase licensed merchandise, wear team-logoed clothing, pay for memberships and subscriptions, or watch games via TV, radio or internet broadcast? Hence behavioural segmentation can have depth (frequency) and breadth (complexity).

In attempting to define the consumer in respect to usage patterns, broad categories including non-user, light user, medium user and heavy user are established. While it is often desirable to encourage consumers to elevate their level of consumption, this is not always possible or even desirable. For example, Spolestra (1991) believes that in terms of the consumption of professional sport, the season ticket or membership is not for everyone. The notion of perceived constraints is important, and whether it is due to a lack of finance, time or even interest, consumers often find that attending every game is not possible. Hence he argues that the concept of seat-sharing—whether corporate or with friends—results in maximum use of a particular seat. By adopting an approach called full-menu marketing, the organisation provides numerous packages that allow fans to consume at a level at which they are comfortable. Here the market has been segmented based on usage patterns.

Multiple segmentation

The establishment of a segmentation strategy depends on a number of features, such as the size, reachability and receptiveness of the target market. As such, multiple segment strategies are often developed, which enable the sport marketer to construct different yet coordinated strategies for delivering a product or service. The combination of various benefit segments with demographic segments is an instructive approach for sport marketing professionals. For example, Chapter 3 briefly discussed behavioural usage patterns based on the level of involvement: awareness, attraction, attachment and allegiance within the PCM framework; frequency and complexity of behaviour increasing with the stage of involvement. This has been supported in spectator sport for consumers of sport teams and sport leagues (Doyle et al., 2013). Combining multiple segments provides new insight into the demand, and allows for customisation of products and services to unique consumer groups. Other examples of sport spectator segments are illustrated below.

World Series Cricket supporters might include:

- the purist, who understands the nuances of the game, and has a history of active participation in the sport
- the sport enthusiast, who follows a wider range of activities
- the follower, who—while unlikely to attend matches—avidly follows the game via the media, and
- the entertainment-seeker, who seeks action and excitement.

Each segment is important for distinct reasons. While purists are perceived as essential for Test-match cricket longevity, enthusiasts are important for their current level of interest. Similarly, while followers are important because of their desire for cricket information, entertainment seekers provide for an important transition into the female and youth market. These segments are certainly appropriate, given the popularity of the new Twenty20 matches in Australia and England.

Similar segments can be created for team sports. Team-sports spectators might include:

- the passionate partisan, who displays undiminished loyalty to a team over time and identifies closely with winning and losing
- the champ follower, whose loyalty is essentially a function of team success
- the reclusive partisan, who displays strong identification that does not necessarily translate into actual support
- the theatregoer, who seeks a close encounter and wishes to be entertained, and
- the aficionado, whose loyalty is to the game rather than the team.

In many instances—especially related to sport consumer behaviour in the context of seasonal sport competitions—the passionate partisan is an important target market. Each of the other target markets requires a different marketing strategy, aimed at the specific orientation of potential consumers held by the market. As we saw with the product market grid discussed in Chapter 2, each distinct market segment may require a separate product offering or variation. The establishment and maintenance of, and ongoing addition to, an organisation's MIS will assist sporting organisations to become increasingly discerning and creative in their target market-segmentation strategies. Hence segmentation strategies basically provide the ability to customise the marketing mix to keep pace with the shifting demand for sport products and services. When we decide that a particular market segment will be the focus, we have selected a target market.

Target market selection

The selection of the appropriate target market follows the process of segmentation. Having identified the segmentation variables and developed profiles, the next step is to identify the attractiveness of each of the segments. To enable the sport marketer to identify attractiveness, market segments must be substantial enough to justify consideration; their size and attractiveness in terms of financial resources must be measurable; the sport organisation must have access to the segments, and must have the resources enabling the organisation to approach the segments; and the segments must enable differentiation from other segments. When these criteria are fulfilled, the sport marketer can assess the segment's size and growth potential, its structural attractiveness and whether the segment offers scope to achieve the organisation's strategic objectives and generate vital resources. Based on this information, the sport marketer is in a position to select a (number of) target market(s). Target market-selection strategies include the selection of a single segment, a number of unrelated segments, a number of segments that are selected on the ability of the sport organisation to deliver a particular product (such as football spectator services), a number of segments that are based on the ability of the sport organisation to serve a particular market (for example, the Melbourne metropolitan football market) very well, or a full market coverage strategy, targeting the market as a whole.

The growth of snowboarding since the 1980s serves as an interesting example for understanding segmentation. Capitalising on the popularity of skateboarding and surfing, and the growth in extreme sports, snowboard promoters identified a target market of people who were young, had discretionary income, eschewed the normal alpine skiing activities of their parents and wanted to be seen at the leading edge of a new recreational activity. While initially the alpine industry examined ways to ban the sport from many resort areas, snowboarding quickly gained a foothold and debuted as an Olympic sport in 1998. A sport once considered fringe is now at the forefront of winter activity. Moreover, resorts that had previously turned their back on this particular segment now aggressively market to this segment, and establish areas on the slopes where snowboarders can pursue their sport to the full. Some resorts even try to position their location as the place for snowboarding. Hence it can reasonably be concluded that snowboarding—initially positioned as a cult activity with a clearly defined non-mainstream target market—rapidly progressed through stages of development (which included alpine resorts endeavouring to position themselves as snowboard-friendly) to a point where it is now a mainstream sport.

Positioning

The final piece in the puzzle of preparing a marketing action is the identification of positioning strategies for segments. This process involves the customisation of the marketing mix for selected target markets. In this process, it is important to remember that the key to successful positioning lies in the sport marketer's ability to differentiate the product offering from segment competitors. Whatever is different in the offering of the sport organisation needs to be important and distinctive for the consumers to consider the (alternative) offering. For example, positioning can focus on bundling benefits that consumers seek in consuming the product; quality or price can be used to set the offering apart from others; or the image of the product or organisation can sway consumers to purchase a trendy 'brand' rather than a non-branded product.

Companies that provide products and services to a broad spectrum of consumers often target sport. Hence sport consumers represent a diverse but identifiable segment within the general population to which to customise the marketing mix. Soft drinks, fast food, telecommunication, mobile devices, insurance and banking are examples of products that are omnipresent in the sports environment. Furthermore, codes, teams and athletes are often used to promote various products and services. The National Rugby League has partnered with Wild Turkey Bourbon as the official spirit of the league, securing the naming rights for the NRL's Saturday games. The AFL's Melbourne Demons promote Tourism Northern Territory through the media, on polo shirts and on signage around the MCG. Bernard Tomic promotes Yonex and Nike equipment and apparel during matches. Manufacturers believe that using athletes to market their products makes them stand out in a cluttered environment. Chapter 13 examines this concept at length.

Ries and Trout (1986: 5) suggest that 'the basic approach of positioning is not to create something new and different, but to manipulate what's already in the mind'. In other words, positioning is really about what the marketer does in the mind of the consumer. In reality, there are probably two ways in which sport can be positioned in the mind of the consumer. As Ries and Trout indicate, the best option is to be first; but if you can't be first, be different. When it comes to sport, marketers and promoters constantly try to effectively position their product or service in the mind of an increasingly discerning consumer. Furthermore, given that consumer preferences are in a constant state of flux, the positioning process demands creativity, responsiveness and perspicacity.

Given that the sport marketplace is so dynamic and constantly in a state of change, sport marketers must not only recognise change, but be strategically ready to respond to it quickly. Moreover, the speed at which change occurs will only increase in the future, and sporting organisations—already sensitive to market share (if mergers and franchise relocations are any indication)—will need to be increasingly creative in their segmentation strategy. Defining product position and its application is considered in more detail in Chapter 5.

Summary

Sport market research consists of activities designed to collect information to make informed decisions. Ongoing data collection is essential for the adaptation of an organisation to a volatile and changing marketplace. Moreover, such data need to be collected in a systematic and ongoing manner, and stored in a marketing information system (MIS). The MIS should not only allow for ready accessibility but also enable ongoing decision-making and strategy selection. The major sources of information for an MIS include both external and internal data. External data may be classified as primary or secondary, and includes data that have been collected by the sporting organisation or an external agency. It should be understood, however, that while some general market and sport market research may have universal applicability, the sporting organisation cannot do better than collect its own data.

Market research in sporting organisations seeks to answer the questions of who, when, where, what, how and why. While the survey is the most popular mechanism for gathering sport-related data, mall or shopping centre intercepts, focus groups, observation and even experimentation are becoming increasingly popular methods. Collected data should explore general market conditions, individual consumers and competitors. Internal data consist of information that the organisation collects during the conduct of its business. A major advantage of solid market research is that it allows the sport marketer to divide the total market into several segments. Commonly, consumers are segmented on the basis of demographics, psychographics and behaviour. The psychographic category is further divided into the benefits wanted from the product and product usage. Finally, it should be remembered that the sport marketplace is in a constant state of change. Sport marketers must place themselves in a position to not just respond to change but even anticipate it.

CASE STUDY

The positioning and challenges of an underdog league brand—the case of the A-League

By Thilo Kunkel

Background

The Australian market is a very competitive sport consumer market. Four 'football' codes, each represented by a league—Australian Rules football (AFL), football/soccer (A-League), Rugby League (NRL) and Rugby Union (Super 15)—compete with each other for consumers. Hence proper league brand positioning is crucial for the competitiveness of the league. While the AFL, NRL and Super 15 are established leagues, the A-League was introduced in 2005 as a successor of the defunct National Soccer League (NSL). In the NSL, supporting a team was determined by nationality and ethnicity. These ethnic links limited the appeal of the NSL to an audience without ethnic backgrounds, which initiated the rebranding and repositioning of the league so they could compete with AFL, NRL and Super 15.

Positioning

Football/soccer underwent drastic repositioning in 2004. The positioning strategy was to rebrand former soccer to football to eliminate the ethnic connections associated with soccer in Australia and to appeal to a broad Australian audience. The governing body of all levels of football, the Australian Soccer Association (ASA), was renamed Football Federation Australia (FFA) and the A-League replaced the NSL in 2005. The first marketing campaign used the slogan 'Football, but not as you know it', highlighting the shift towards the global game of football. The A-League started as an eight-team competition, which was based on a one-team-per-city policy to leverage fans' involvement with their home city.

Initial success and expansion

In the first three seasons, the A-League was successful in generating solid attendance figures. Average attendances increased from 10 956 in the 2005–06 season to 14 608 in the 2007–08 season. This was accompanied by a noticeable shift in the fan culture, which was no longer related to the ethnic roots of the teams. These early successes led to a decision to expand the league. The A-League expanded with the addition of Gold Coast United and the North Queensland Fury in the 2009–10 season. While this expansion strategy extended the league's reach, average attendance figures decreased to an all-time low of 8393 in the 2010–11 season.

The decline of the league

Two main factors contributed to the decrease of average attendance figures of the A-League. First, the new teams were situated in markets that were not ideal for expansion. The North Queensland Fury was based in Townsville, which has a population of under 200 000 potential fans and a reputation as an 'NRL town'. Similarly, Gold Coast United was based in a 'NRL town' with a reputation for being a 'graveyard' for professional sport teams, because the

Gold Coast has numerous entertainment attractions, such as beaches, mountains and theme parks. Second, FFA focused its attention on bidding for the FIFA World Cup 2018/22, and neglected the A-League. The governing body invested heavily (money and time) in developing a competitive bid to host the FIFA World Cup in Australia. Thus these resources were not available to promote the league and the teams within it (FIFA, 2010).

The rationalisation of the league

As a result of the decline of the A-League, teams were struggling with financial instability and some team owners were not able to cover the costs. FFA took over the licence of North Queensland Fury and financially supported five other teams. However, at the end of the 2010/11 season, FFA decided to revoke the licence of North Queensland Fury because they needed to redirect resources to invest in league-wide marketing and promotions and could not justify the team's existence at the expense of other teams. Similarly, at the end of the 2011–12 season, FFA decided to revoke the licence of Gold Coast United because the team did not act in accordance to its franchise contract when the club decided to close parts of the stadium to reduce costs. Considering that leagues and teams are connected through their brand architecture (Kunkel, Funk and Hill, 2013), revoking the licences of these two teams alienated fans of the league in both the Townsville and Gold Coast geographic areas. Furthermore, it was an indication of the instability of the league, and reflected negatively on the brand image of the league. Therefore, the A-League needed to counter this downwards trend.

Market research, consumer segmentation and the recovery of the league

After the failed bid to host the FIFA World Cup 2018/22, FFA turned its focus back towards the A-League in two main areas. First, FFA conducted market research and gathered primary data through online surveys. A link was placed on the official web page of the league, inviting visitors to the web page to participate in research and provide their feedback. Based on the findings of the research, consumers were segmented and FFA decided to focus its A-League marketing efforts on one specific consumer segment: a core group of 18–34-year-old males who were classified as avid fans of the sport of football. To attract this market segment, the league launched a marketing campaign with the slogan 'We are football', focusing on fans and their connection with the sport to promote positive brand associations to consumers (Kunkel, Funk and King, in press).

Second, FFA collected internal primary data through Australia-wide football club memberships and external secondary data from television stations and the ABS to guide strategic expansion decisions. Data indicated that Melbourne and Sydney were most suitable for expansion, because these two cities are Australia's two biggest consumer markets and both have a high percentage of individuals who immigrated from parts of the world where football is the most-followed sport. Consequently, FFA expanded the A-League with the Melbourne Heart and the Western Sydney Wanderers in these two markets. Additionally, the A-League increased its media exposure, especially through social media sites, to adhere to fans' requests for more access to information. As a result, the A-League began to recover, with average attendances at the league's games increasing to 12 321 during the 2012–13 season.

Lessons learned from this case

There are three main lessons that can be learned from the case of the A-League. First, sport brand positioning needs to be implemented strategically. The positioning of the league brand to align with the global game of football helped to overcome negative aspects associated with the league. Second, sport brand positioning and marketing need to consider the target market and develop customised marketing towards core target market segments. To identify these core segments, market research from many different sources is necessary. Third, sport brand positioning needs to have a long-term focus. Key decisions that have a strong influence on fans—such as league expansions—need to be made with an understanding of fan behaviour and a long-term vision of how the sport is positioned in mind.

Sources: All attendance figures were calculated based on information from <www.ultimatealeague.com>. For further insight on the brand relationship between leagues and teams as perceived by fans, please see Kunkel, Funk and Hill (2013) and Kunkel, Funk and King (in press).

Questions

1. How did market research help the A-League to recover?
2. What were the data-collection methods used by FFA?
3. What three other methods of data collection FFA could have employed to develop consumer segments?
4. If you were the marketing manager of the A-League, which method of data collection would you employ to identify consumers' 'psychographics'?
5. If you were the marketing manager of the A-League, which consumer segment would you target next?

Part III

Strategy determination

Stage 1—Identification of marketing opportunities

▼

Stage 2—Strategy determination

Step 5—Determine core marketing strategy

Marketing and service mix—sport product

▼

Stage 3—Strategy implemention, evaluation and adjustment

5

The sport product

CHAPTER OBJECTIVES

Chapter 5 introduces the first variable in the marketing mix: the sport product. This chapter also moves to Stage 2 of the strategic sport-marketing planning process (SSMPP): strategy determination. During this stage, marketing mix variables are reviewed and combined in such a way as to determine the core marketing strategy. It is important to first identify and understand the product and its attributes. Key tools to assist in determining the core marketing strategy are introduced, including perceptual mapping and the product life-cycle.

After studying this chapter, you should be able to:

- identify the difference between core and product extensions in sport
- describe the characteristics of a service
- understand why sport is classified as a service product
- identify the dimensions of quality service
- understand the strategic importance of product positioning
- understand the strategic significance of the product life-cycle.

HEADLINE STORY

NBL story a tough one to sell

Basketball is arguably the second-most popular sport in the world. But Australian basketball's elite professional competition, the NBL, has waxed and waned in terms of success since its establishment in 1979. Kristina Keneally, the recently appointed CEO of Basketball Australia, was at pains during the 2012 NBL and WNBL season launch to promote the ongoing growth of the NBL. Ward (2012: 13) observed of Keneally's remarks that the 'inconvenient past truths are getting in the way. In her opening remarks at Basketball Australia's first-ever joint season launch of its men's and women's national leagues at Federation Square yesterday, Keneally promoted the continued growth of crowds in both leagues, NBL.TV—the league's new online television channel and the return of London Olympic flag-bearer Lauren Jackson to the WNBL this season.' Keneally highlighted the new deal, which will see NBL fans able to watch every NBL and WNBL game live on the internet at a cost of $79. This stage-setting announcement was contrasted by Olympic basketballer and Adelaide 36s player Adam Gibson reflecting on starting afresh with his fourth NBL team, illustrating how his three former clubs had folded. On the same day, Keneally stated that 'she supported the push to bring an NBA team to Australia, but only if it means more than a one-off showpiece game. Keneally said staging an NBA event in Australia would be good for basketball, but it needed to be more substantial than a one-off appearance. "I'm not opposed to bringing two NBA teams here to play, but the question I ask is what does that achieve for basketball longer term?"' (Gould, 2012: 78)

Keneally's concern for the longer term development of the basketball product, and specifically the NBL, is warranted, and provides a nice introduction to this chapter, which is focused on the sport product. While it might be good for the NBA product to expand into new markets, it remains unclear how such a strategy would benefit the basketball product in Australia. A one-off promotion of the world's premier basketball competition must have some benefits, but how can the NBA's appearance in Australia be maximised to leverage a longer term impact, particularly given the difficulties the NBL has experienced in recent years in re-establishing itself as a viable professional sport league. Keneally's selling of the merits of live internet coverage masks a more telling problem: the lack of free-to-air television coverage for the NBL, which not only impacts revenues, but significantly affects the promotion of the basketball product throughout Australia.

The purpose of this chapter is to examine the place of the sport product in the marketing mix, and illustrate the importance of service provision of the sport product. As can be seen from the headline story, the sport product comes in many sizes, shapes and configurations, complicating the capacity to apply standard solutions.

The sport product

Kotler et al. (2006: 386) describe a product as being 'anything that can be offered to a market for attention, acquisition, use or consumption that might satisfy a want or a need'.

Moreover, a product is a problem-solver in that it is purchased because of the benefits provided. Essentially, consumers buy benefits, not the product.

Quality is another feature of perceived product benefits. Perreault and McCarthy (2002: 249) define quality, from a marketing perspective, as 'the ability of a product to satisfy a consumer's needs or requirements'. As the authors point out, this definition focuses on the consumer's view of what quality may mean, or of a product's suitability for some specific purpose. In sport, the product is easily discernible; however, the quality of the core product is something over which the sport marketer has no control. This is a distinctly unique aspect of sport and sport marketing. For this reason, it is important to recognise a broader definition of the product than simply the game.

Mullin (1985a) identifies the playing of the game as the core product, and all the related activities—such as food and beverages, merchandise, half-time entertainment, video screens and the facility itself—as product extensions. For example, the Australian Tennis Open and the Melbourne Park facility, and all the services provided within and during the tournament, are crucial in measuring the overall success of the event. Ultimately, once players have agreed to play in the Australian Open, there is little organisers can do to ensure quality matches. Even matches receiving 'top billing', such as Federer vs Djokovic or Azarenka vs Sharapova, do not always guarantee quality contests. The quality of the supporting product extensions, however, *can* be guaranteed. It is at this point that similarities are observed between the importance of quality service provision and quality product extensions. Most product extensions possess an element of service provision, and hence quality is important. As a consequence, product extensions have the capacity to ensure that spectators at the tennis have an enjoyable day, irrespective of the on-court results.

The importance of winning, team loyalty and emotion are critical ingredients in professional sport. How important, for example, is on-field success in terms of team loyalty, and what is the impact of winning on the emotional attachment of sports fans? These questions have been the subject of research in recent years, and exemplify how the sport product has its own unique features that warrant deeper investigation in terms of marketing implications. Gladden, Irwin and Sutton (2001: 298), for example, state 'that 2000 to 2010 will be the decade in which team management activities evolve from a focus on winning as a means of realizing short-terms profits to a focus on strategic management of the team brand as a means of realizing long-term appreciation in franchise value'. Traditionally, the value of a sport brand (team) has relied on its winning percentage, which is usually reflected in its image. However, in a business in which ultimately only one team can be the 'winner' each year, our thinking about how we position our team for long-term financial viability and a resource-rich environment to provide a competitive edge on the field is challenged. There is evidence of this change in thinking within the AFL. Prominent AFL clubs Collingwood, Essendon and the West Coast Eagles have, in recent years, focused on building brand recognition to reduce their reliance on winning as the basis for revenue generation. The move to a national competition during the 1990s also provided a vehicle for these clubs to position their brand nationally, in order to leverage sources of revenue beyond their respective states.

What, then, is branding? 'Branding means the use of a name, term, symbol, or design—or a combination of these—to identify a product.' (Perreault and McCarthy,

2002: 260). The Collingwood and Essendon football clubs represent a brand within the AFL competition, as do the Melbourne Storm and the Newcastle Knights in the NRL. Brands are important to their owners/members, as they help consumers to recognise a company's products. If brand recognition and acceptance are high, the potential for high brand loyalty exists. In sport, teams and clubs such as the Melbourne Storm are examples of a brand, and it is through team and club loyalty that prominent brand recognition is achieved. Typically, there are four forms of brand development, two of which are more directly relevant to the sport product:

- *Line extensions*: existing brand names extended to new forms, sizes and flavours of an existing product category—for example, Coca-Cola's versions of its soft drinks: regular, diet, caffeine, caffeine free and Zero Coke. In sport, Test cricket, one-day cricket and Twenty20 cricket, or indoor volleyball and beach volleyball, could be considered line extensions.
- *Brand extensions*: existing brand names extended to new product categories—for example, Sony uses its company name to cover such different products as its televisions, DVD and Blu-ray players, cameras, laptop computers, radios, Bluetooth audio and data projectors. In sport, AFL Shops, AFL World, AFL Auctions and AFL Travel are all examples of brand extensions.

The issue of branding is considered in more detail in Chapter 16, where the role and purpose of promotional licensing are reviewed. Developing highly recognisable brands as trademarks and logos is an important source of revenue and promotion for sporting organisations and athletes. These trademarks form the basis of merchandise and licensing programs; these represent an important form of product extensions, the significance of which is noted in Sportview 5.1 and the focus on the Toronto Blue Jays baseball club. Sportview 5.1 raises the vexed question of the value of winning versus the value of building brand equity through a sound marketing strategy. Perhaps you might like to do some research to ascertain how the Blue Jays' brand equity project is progressing.

SPORTVIEW 5.1

Brand new

It is no surprise that otherwise sane adults paint their faces in their favourite team's colours or plaster their cars with team logos—in much the same way livestock owners brand their cattle. After all, the word 'brand' comes from the Old Norse word '*brandr*', meaning 'to burn'. It is part of the tribal experience of sports—my team against your team—and explains why clubs such as the New York Yankees and Detroit Red Wings hang on to their popular logos for decades. But what to do if fans find your logo tired and passé? If you're baseball's Toronto Blue Jays, you take a quarter-million dollar gamble and change it. But if there were any lingering doubts that sports is more business than play, team CEO Paul Godfrey's unveiling of the new Jays logo—a stylised (and angry-looking) blue jay next to three-dimensional metallic letters spelling out 'Jays' in graphite and silver with black-and-blue edging—should dispel them.

It's a no-nonsense logo, in keeping with the new approach of these fowl-ballers—including relatively new owner Rogers Communications Inc. (which also owns Canadian Business), second-season general manager J.P. Ricciardi and a bunch of young players. The Jays on and off the field, says Lisa Novak, senior vice-president of business affairs, no longer resemble their past soft, cartoon-like image. So two years ago the team turned to Toronto design firm Brandid to come up with an edgier emblem—something the firm knows a little bit about, having created the macabre Grim Reaper logo for the Toronto Phantoms indoor football club (RIP 2002). Shunning the current fad for retro sports brands, Brandid went contemporary. 'They wanted a little more energy, to make the mark a little hipper and a little younger,' says vice-president and creative director Randy Redford.

It took the firm eighteen months of research, conceptualising and bouncing marks off Jays management and focus groups to finish the design. And, while the $250 000 to $300 000 cost (some of that deferred by clothiers Roots and Majestic Athletic) seems steep, consider this: all-star first baseman Carlos Delgado makes that playing just two games. Sceptics point out that the new Jays logo is the third used by the team in seven years, and figure it's a cash grab. But licensing revenues are actually shared by all 30 Major League Baseball teams, so the Jays are left with a more nebulous trickle-down effect. Still, can a new logo light a fire under erstwhile fans? 'It's been ten seasons since the Jays' days of glory, and they can't offer the steak any more, so they keep on trying to sell a different sizzle,' says Howard Bloom, publisher of *SportsBusinessNews.com*. 'It makes no sense, adds little value to the product and creates confusion in the marketplace—all classic marketing mistakes.' Of course, marketing is an inexact science at the best of times, even more so in sports. 'In our business, it's difficult if not impossible to measure direct success, because no matter what we do on the business and marketing side, 90 per cent of the equation is how you perform in the field,' says Novak. Instead, the Jays see it as part of a long-term investment in building brand equity. In the short term, Novak hopes to see a few more tickets and shirts sold as proof that the Jays are heading in the right direction.

Source: Excerpt from Holloway (2003: 79). Copyright Rogers Publishing Limited. Reprinted with permission.

This section has stressed the importance of quality service provision in product extensions, so it is appropriate now to consider in more detail how and why sport is a service product.

Sport as a service

Sport is an important contributor to the service economy. Its contribution is contained within the broader classification of 'Cultural and Recreational Services', which consists of motion pictures, radio and television services, libraries, museums and the arts, sport and recreation, and gambling services. The sport and physical education sector employs approximately 95 000 people (ABS, 2012). In terms of gross value added (contribution of an industry to the overall production of goods and services in an economy), average annual growth for the cultural and recreational services sector between 2000–01 and

2004–05 was 18.6 per cent—fourth behind finance and insurance, the retail trade, and health and community services (ABS, 2007).

Major sporting events such as the Australian Open, Formula One Grand Prix, Melbourne Spring Racing Carnival and an Ashes Test series and One-day Internationals (ODIs) have the capacity to add to the strong performances indicated in the tourism-related, cultural and recreational service activities. The number and magnitude of sporting events in Australia have seen the evolution of sports tourism as a niche classification within tourism, which ultimately contributes to service sector output across a number of areas, including accommodation, cafes, restaurants and transport. For example, the 2006–07 Ashes Test series and One-day Internationals:

- generated $317 million in direct expenditure within the Australian economy
- created an additional 793 annual average time jobs during 2006–07
- contributed $54 million in Gross Domestic Product
- attracted 813 000 spectators to the five Test matches and 425 000 to fourteen ODIs, generating ticket sales of $18.66 million for the Test series and $11.6 million for the ODIs
- attracted 37 000 international visitors, with approximately 64 per cent of them coming specifically for the Ashes series (URS Australasia, 2007: ES-1).

Interestingly, the Ashes series and ODIs produced a greater economic impact than the 2002 Formula One Grand Prix and the Australian Tennis Open. However, economic impact was not greater than the 2003 World Rugby Cup and 2006 Melbourne Spring Racing Carnival (URS Australasia, 2007). Regardless of their respective contributions, major sporting events make significant economic contributions, not to mention the other intangible factors that contribute to community spirit, well-being and sociability as a consequence of attending, debating and engaging with major events.

Service defined

Why is sport considered a service? This section will answer this question by discussing the characteristics that distinguish a good from a service. A common theme of authors writing on sport marketing (Mullin, 1980, 1985a, 1985b; Mullin, Hardy and Sutton, 2000; Shilbury, 1989, 1991; Sutton and Parrett, 1992) has been their agreement about how the unique characteristics of sport as a product require marketing personnel to adopt different strategies from those traditionally espoused. Although many of these writings are devoid of specific references to services marketing, the discussions pertaining to these unique characteristics align sport with the attributes of a service.

Zeithaml, Bitner and Gremler (2009) summarise the characteristics distinguishing a good from a service. This summary helps in describing sport as a service:

- *Intangibility.* Services cannot be seen, tasted, felt or smelled before they are bought. Services are performances rather than objects. For example, is it possible to describe what product benefits people take home with them after playing sport? Or the benefits derived from watching a game of basketball? There is no tangible take-home product in this example.

- *Simultaneous production and consumption*. Services are simultaneously produced and consumed. The product cannot be put on the shelf and bought by the consumer. The consumer must be present during production. For example, consider getting a haircut, attending a sporting contest or visiting a physiotherapist. You need to attend during the process.
- *Heterogeneity*. Services are potentially variable in their performance. Services can vary greatly depending on who performs them. Many different employees can come into contact with the consumer; therefore, consistency becomes an issue. Few sporting contests are the same from one week to the next, and the consistency of service delivery by people working at such an event can also vary.
- *Perishability*. Services cannot be stored. Hotel rooms not occupied, airline seats not purchased or tickets to a sporting contest not sold cannot be reclaimed. They represent lost revenue, indicating the importance of understanding that services are time-dependent.

Perhaps the most significant difference between a good and a service is the simultaneous production and consumption of a product. The implications of this for marketing are examined specifically in Chapter 7, when the convergence of the marketing and operations functions is considered in relation to the 'place' of the facility in the marketing mix, and expanded in Chapter 8 in relation to service quality and customer satisfaction. A *service*, then, is predominantly any activity or benefit that is intangible and does not result in ownership.

Both spectators and participants take from the game a series of experiences, none of which is physically tangible. Students of sport marketing should be careful not to confuse some of the tangible products that can be bought as a consequence of the game or sport (product extensions) with the game or sport itself (core product). Without the sport, the merchandise would not exist.

Classification of services

When classifying services, we need to determine the extent to which the customer must be present. To assist in making this determination, Lovelock (1991) uses a four-way classification scheme, involving:

- tangible actions to people's bodies
- tangible actions to goods and other physical possessions
- intangible actions directed at people's minds, and
- intangible actions directed at intangible assets.

Table 5.1 illustrates Lovelock's (1991) schematic with examples. Considering the classification used in Table 5.1, where would sport be placed? This is an interesting question, as the answer might depend on whether we are being specific about physical participation or attendance. Physical participation could be classified as a people-based service directed at people's bodies. Attendance at sporting events could more accurately be classified as a people-based service directed at people's minds (and their hearts!). The context of participation in sport is important in framing marketing strategies. The most obvious example is the formation of marketing strategies aimed at attracting players to

TABLE 5.1 Understanding the nature of the service act

What is the nature of the service act?	Who or what is the direct recipient of the service? People	Possessions
Tangible actions	*Services directed at people's bodies* Health care Passenger transportation Beauty salons Exercise clinics Restaurants Haircutting	*Services directed at goods and other physical possessions* Freight transportation Industrial equipment repair Janitorial services Laundry and dry cleaning Landscaping/lawncare Veterinary care
Intangible actions	*Services directed at people's minds* Education Broadcasting Information services Theatres Museums	*Services directed at intangible assets* Banking Legal services Accounting Securities Insurance

Source: Lovelock (1991: 26). Reprinted with the permission of Prentice Hall, Inc. Upper Saddle River, NJ

participate in a competition or sport, and the marketing strategies required to attract people to attend a sporting event. In either case, it is necessary to ask why such a classification scheme is important.

Lovelock (1991: 27) notes the following, which helps to answer this question:

1 Does the customer need to be physically present:
(a) throughout the service
(b) only to initiate or terminate the service transaction
(c) not at all?
2 Does the customer need to be mentally present during service delivery? Can mental presence be maintained across physical distances via mail or electronic communications?
3 In what way is the target of the service act 'modified' by receipt of the service, and how does the customer benefit from these 'modifications'?

If, as is the case in sport, customers need to be present to play or watch a live event, they must enter the service factory, returning us to the importance of simultaneous production and consumption. When spectators or participants enter the sport factory, this has an obvious implication for the sport marketer. The sport factory is best known as the facility, and the implications for managing the customer in the sport factory or facility will be investigated specifically in Chapter 7. However, the major implication of the consumer entering the sport factory or facility is that sport spectatorship in particular is a service experience.

In sport, it is hard to overcome the winning (I had a good day/night) or losing (I had a bad day/night) syndrome. Although this special range of emotions will never be removed from the sport product, their importance can be diminished by ensuring that the quality of service is very good. Again, the importance of the product extensions through quality service provision is highlighted. Slowly, sporting organisations are beginning to recognise the need to plan for service quality.

Service and technology

An important trend in society generally has been the rapid escalation of technology, and specifically the use of the internet, in shaping the service experience. Interaction with a firm or sporting organisation can often be solely mediated via technology as a fan seeks to purchase a ticket to a sports event, buy merchandise, or simply seek information on fixtures, events and game times. All these interactions are important 'moments of truth' in the service experience for consumers, in the same way as a customer might interact with a member of staff to purchase a ticket. Perhaps one of the most important influences of the internet on the customer experiences is the ease through which fans can find information and research 'facts' about their favourite sports team. Knowledge is a powerful force in the hands of the informed consumer.

Embedded in the technology explosion is the need for sophisticated customer relationship-management systems that seek to aid service staff to provide streamlined and more efficient systems. Immediate access to customer information assists staff to provide a more relevant service experience. For example, in the merchandise area, such a system can quickly provide the sales employee with a detailed history of past purchases for a specific customer, and may shape likely advice on the merchandise the customer is likely to purchase.

In more recent times, the internet has facilitated a range of instant modes of communications, all of which can be the source of engagement with a sports team or organisation, but they can also become an extension of the service concept. Facebook, Twitter and fantasy sport simulations are all examples of ways in which sport organisations can enhance engagement with fans, and at the same time broaden the range of service experiences with fans. Understanding how these range of services fit within the overall product extension portfolio is important, as is understanding how the internet shapes the potential for the development of future product extensions. The role of social media as a product extension in the context of service is developed further in Chapters 8 and 12.

Service quality

Service quality research has become prominent in the marketing literature during the past 30 years. Much work has been conducted to identify the key attributes of quality service. These attributes have been developed from the perspective of the consumer. Extensive research using focus group interviews, conducted by Parasuraman, Zeithaml and Berry (1985) during the 1980s, originally identified ten dimensions of service quality. In subsequent work, Lovelock, Wirtz and Chew (2009: 369) note that Parasuraman, Zeithaml and Berry found a high degree of 'correlation between some of the variables, and eventually combined several of these variables and so combined them into five broad dimensions'. Parasuraman, Zeithaml and Berry (1985: 46) note that, 'regardless of the type of service, consumers used basically similar criteria in evaluating service quality'. These criteria are shown in Table 5.2.

Figure 5.1 illustrates the application of the original ten dimensions in relation to the way the consumer views quality: 'Perceived service quality is the result of the consumer's

TABLE 5.2
Dimensions of service quality

Dimension	Description	Questions
Tangibles	Appearance of physical facilities, equipment, personnel and communication materials	Is the stadium attractive? Are the stadium service personnel dressed appropriately?
Reliability	Ability to perform the promised service dependably and accurately	Is my experience in the stadium consistent, in terms of service personnel, food and beverages?
Responsiveness	Willingness to help customers and provide prompt service	Does my team respond to my needs as a member for quality seats in my price category, and assist me with questions about my team?
Assurance • Credibility • Security • Competence • Courtesy	Trustworthiness, believability, honesty of the service provider Freedom from danger, risk or doubt Possession of the skills and knowledge required to perform the service Politeness, respect, consideration and friendliness of contact personnel	Does the stadium/team have a good reputation? Is the stadium safe, particularly at night when leaving the carpark? Can the stadium personnel process my ticketing requests promptly? Do the ticket personnel or seat ushers have a pleasant demeanour?
Empathy • Access • Communication • Understanding the customer	Approachability and ease of contact Keeping customers informed in language they can understand and listening to them Trustworthiness, believability, honesty of service provider Making the effort to know customers and their needs	How easy is it to approach stadium personnel when I have a problem? When I have a complaint, how willing is the membership department to listen to my complaint? Does someone in the club recognise me as a member? Do they understand my seating and game-day needs?

Source: Adapted from Lovelock, Wirtz and Chew (2009).

comparison of expected service with perceived service' (Parasuraman, Zeithaml and Berry, 1985: 47). Figure 5.1 illustrates how word of mouth, personal needs, past experience and external communications build up a level of expected service quality. Word of mouth is a particularly strong source of pre-consumption information that determines the likelihood of purchase.

The lack of tangible clues creates difficulties for consumers in making decisions about service product purchase. In relation to purchasing a good, it is often possible to try out the product before purchase, or at least to see it in action. This would be the case with the purchase of a car or computer. As services are time-dependent, it is often not possible to try out the product before purchase. Consumer recommendation about a service is a powerful influence in pre-purchase decisions. Similarly, past experience with a service provides the same opportunity to develop perceptions about the quality of the service being considered. Finally, external communications—via advertising—create levels of expectations about service quality.

The gap that ultimately exists between 'expected' service and 'perceived' service is a result of the four factors consumers bring to product consumption. Companies should ensure that they do not promise more than they can actually deliver, as unrealistic

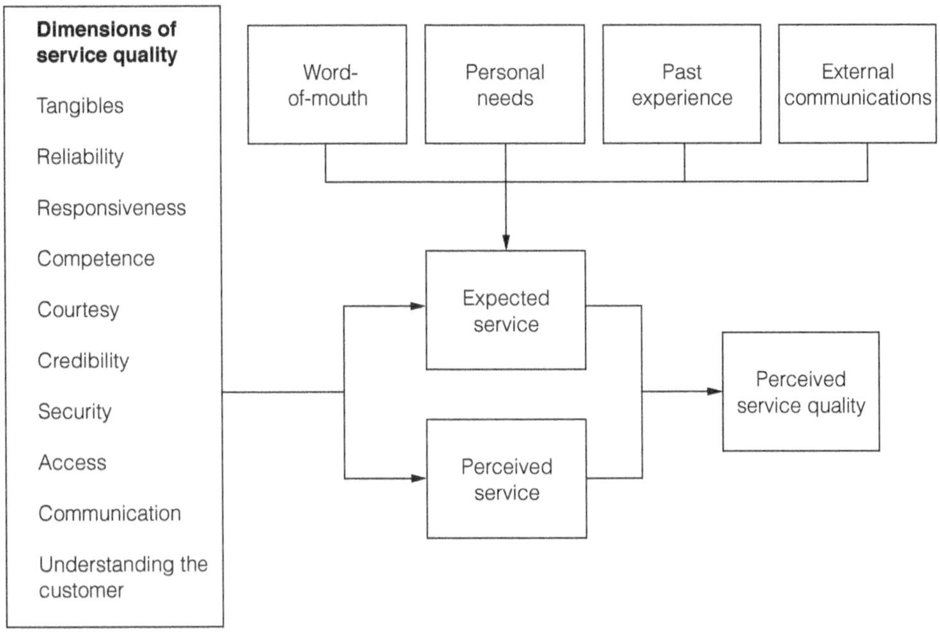

FIGURE 5.1 Customer assessment of service quality

Source: Zeithaml et al. (1990, p. 23) Reprinted with permission of The Free Press, an imprint of Simon & Schuster Adult Publishing Group, copyright 1990, The Free Press.

expectations created by a company can negatively affect the level of perceived quality, when in reality the level of service quality was good. By implication, a firm needs to understand customer expectations as well as to have an intimate knowledge of the product's attributes, which are the genesis of the expected service levels and product positioning.

Positioning the sport product

Positioning the sport product in the marketplace is strategically important, as it plays a pivotal role in marketing strategy. Product positioning links the market research and market segmentation phases described in Chapter 4. In essence, positioning is the perceived fit between a particular product and the target market. To a large extent, the success of a product within a chosen market depends on how effectively it has been positioned. The sport product—like any other product—is subject to the same range of preferences and perceptions by consumers.

Defining position

Use of a perceptual map to define positioning is helpful. The perceptual map is formed by asking consumers to rank certain product attributes. In much the same way as attitude is measured, key attributes of the sport product are identified. In a hypothetical example, two simple bipolar scales measure the level of excitement of the sport and expense, or

FIGURE 5.2
Mapping the perceptions of the sport product

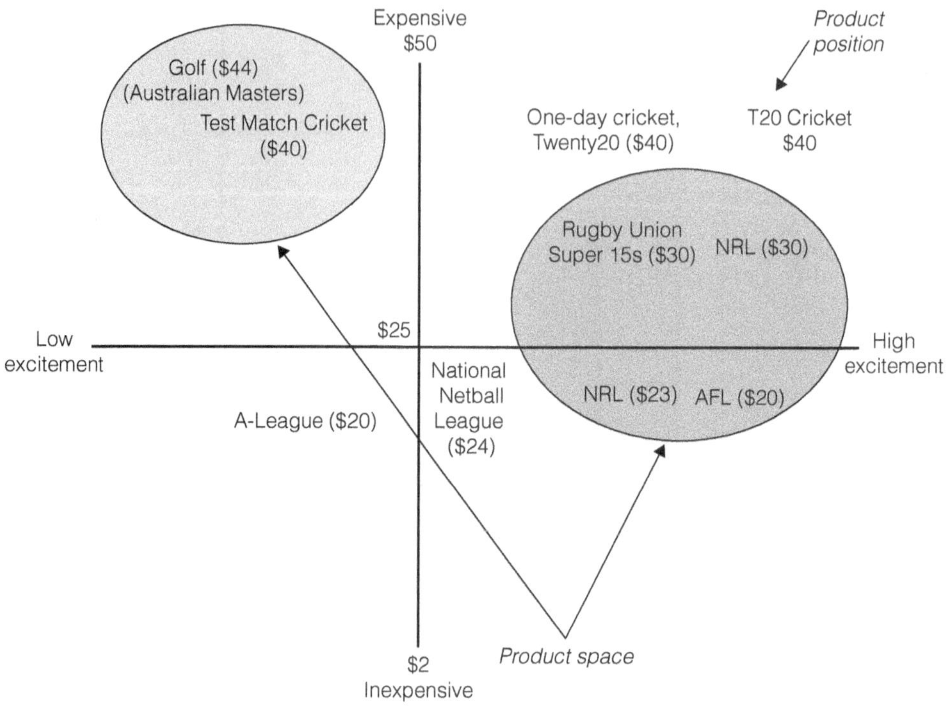

the cost to attend. The two attributes are put together to form a two-dimensional diagram, as is illustrated in Figure 5.2.

Location of the product in a product space is called a position, and is a crucial step in defining the market that a product is targeting. In the example shown in Figure 5.2, only sport products are considered. This is important, as the sports chosen here include the major professional sports played in Australia. An astute marketer would realise that the sport product should be positioned within a larger competitive frame than just sport, as professional sport is part of the much larger entertainment industry. However, to ensure that this example does not become too complex, it has been restricted to just sport entertainment. Costs for entry to the sports shown in Figure 5.2 are based on 2012–13 ticket prices. It is also important to note that, under normal circumstances, the market researcher would ask the sport consumer about the attributes used in this perceptual map. Spectators would be asked, for example, to rate the excitement level of Rugby League or cricket or basketball. Moreover, the ticket prices used are the basic general admission prices. It is recognised that a wide variety of ticket prices are available for ground entry, ranging from general admission to specific categories of seats—all priced according to the premium nature of the seating. On top of this, there are various membership seating packages as well as corporate packages.

Figure 5.2 highlights the intense competition that exists for the consumer's disposable income during the winter season. The Australian Football League (AFL), for example, is seeking a segment of spectators looking for high levels of excitement at moderate to low cost. Rugby League, through the National Rugby League (NRL) competition, is a direct competitor and thus a substitute for the AFL, given that both games are played during the winter. The genuine likelihood of substitution, of course, assumes that both codes are played in the same market. In Sydney, Melbourne and Brisbane, this is the case. In Melbourne, the National Basketball League (NBL) also appears to be a major competitor to the AFL. Figure 5.2 shows that the product attributes of the AFL and NBL are similar, as is demonstrated by the product space both occupy, although the NBL—in trying to distance itself from the AFL—moved from a winter to a summer season in 1998. Now the NBL season commences in September at the tail end of the football codes' season. The bulk of the season is completed after the football season, and before the major programming commences for cricket.

Establishing position

Establishment of a desired position in the marketplace is a priority for the sport marketer. This can be achieved in two ways: by physical design and through advertising.

Physical design refers to the rule changes and modifications that can be made to render a sport more attractive to certain segments of the market. Cricket is the best example of this. The three forms of the game shown in Figure 5.2 exemplify the way in which a sport has been modified to capture different segments of the market.

Establishing a product position through advertising is being done more and more by sport marketers. The most notable campaign aimed at repositioning a sport was the former New South Wales Rugby League's (NSWRL) advertisements featuring Tina Turner. In 1989, the NSWRL embarked on an advertising campaign aimed at presenting Rugby League as a glamorous, racy and exciting game. This was necessary, as the league was emerging from a period where the game was beset by image problems such as excessive on-field violence and a struggling image at both club and league levels. The 'What you get is what you see' and 'Simply the best' campaigns were extremely effective in creating a new and different image for the game. In effect, the game was being repositioned to broaden its appeal, which had been predominantly to the blue-collar male market. Between 1983 and 1990, when the league embarked on its turnaround strategy, attendances doubled and television ratings rose by 70 per cent, indicating some success in broadening the appeal of the game. This is also indicative of the phases through which products pass in varying stages of their life-cycle.

Product development

Kotler et al. (2006: 294) note that 'a company has to be good at developing new products. It must also manage them in the face of changing tastes, technologies and competition.' Every product, including sport products, seems to pass through a life-cycle. Typically, this follows a consistent pattern: the product is conceived or born, and develops through several phases of maturity before dying as new and improved products emerge. In sport, it is also true that various sports oscillate within this described life-cycle.

There are some differences, however. In general, it is unusual for a sport to die. It is possible to trace the history of many sports worldwide, and to note how the majority have stood the test of time. Not all sports have always been successful, but they have continued to exist and experience varying levels of success. Rather than the actual sport dying, sporting competitions, events, tournaments and clubs or teams tend to disappear or require marketing strategies designed to extend their life-cycle. Relocation of teams, rule changes, mergers and the provision of new facilities all constitute ways in which various forms of the sport product endeavour to avoid decline. The other major difference is that sporting organisations do not release new products often, in the same way that the car and computer industries do. The sport product is again seen to be reasonably stable.

The NRL, like the AFL, is an example of a sport that has had to rejuvenate its products. Expanding to form national competitions was one way in which this was achieved. In Rugby League, the previously described Tina Turner advertising campaign was an integral part of relaunching a sport that was losing market share or, in product life-cycle terms, was in decline. Other strategies included expanding the competition to Queensland, the ACT, Victoria and, for a brief period, Western Australia. Within Sydney itself, some clubs were closed or relocated to overcome changing or declining inner-city populations. For example, the Balmain Tigers survived 87 years on the dedication of its fans and working-class traditions. As the demographic profile of the Balmain region changed, the club was forced to look elsewhere to maintain the necessary financial infrastructure to continue participating in the league. The club's name was changed to the Sydney Tigers, broadening its appeal, and it relocated to a new facility in Parramatta.

The product life-cycle curve

Figure 5.3 illustrates the product life cycle (PLC). The typical PLC curve is S-shaped and characterised by four different phases:

1 *Introduction* is a period of slow sales growth. Profits are non-existent at this stage because of the heavy expenses of introducing the product to the market.
2 *Growth* is a period of rapid market acceptance and increasing profits.
3 *Maturity* is a slow period of sales growth because the product has been accepted by most potential buyers. Profits stabilise or decline because of increased marketing designed to defend the product against competition.
4 *Decline* is the period when sales show a strong downward drift and profits erode.

In the late 1970s and early 1980s, a number of traditional Australian sports entered the decline phase of the PLC. Cricket, the Victorian Football League (VFL) and the NSWRL all struggled as Australians' appetite for sport and leisure options began to diversify. A subsequent surge in interest in individual sport and recreational activities such as jogging, triathlon, aerobics and cycling saw the profits and previous market dominance of these sports begin to erode. Also in 1979, the NBL was formed, capitalising on the trend towards the professionalisation of sporting competitions. The NBL entry was indicative of the heightened intensity of competition that has emerged in the professional sport sector.

The NBL presents an interesting example of the way in which the PLC can be used to assess the phases of development of a product. The case study at the end of this chapter explains in more detail the progress made by the NBL since its inception in 1979. What can be understood from this information is that by 1995 the NBL had reached the

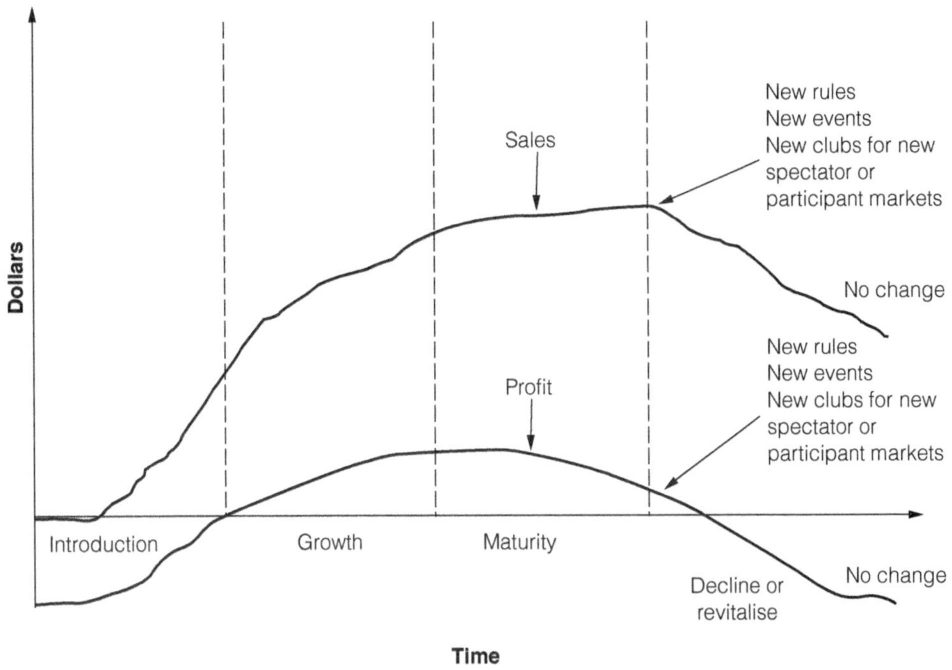

FIGURE 5.3 Product life cycle

maturity stage. Attendances and level of support seemed to have plateaued. This was not a special feature of the 1995 season, but a trend that had become apparent during the 1993 and 1994 seasons. Attendances had peaked at about 80 per cent of stadium capacity, sponsor interest had levelled, and the NBL was still experiencing problems in attracting good television ratings.

The challenge for the NBL was what to do to arrest the decline. One solution examined during 1996 was to change the playing season, moving it to the summer. Not only would this provide the impetus to relaunch the NBL as a summer game; it would, as shown in the perceptual map, have the capacity to alter its direct competitors, including the capacity to obtain more television time. Moving to summer would see the intense competition provided by the AFL, NRL and Super 15s reduced, at the risk of moving into cricket's competitive space.

The A-League would become a relevant competitor, but the A-League does not have the same product intensity as the AFL, NRL or Super 15s. Cricket—particularly one-day cricket—does have sufficient competitive intensity to create difficulties for the NBL. Programming of cricket is not as intense or as weekend-oriented as that of the AFL and NRL. In winter, the AFL usually schedules matches on Friday night, early and late Saturday afternoon, Saturday, Saturday night and Sunday afternoon. This creates difficulties for basketball in terms of both television audience and live attendance. Cricket has fewer matches, and these tend to be concentrated in one major city on any given weekend. The opportunity to rejuvenate the NBL was therefore presented through the season change that ultimately took effect in the summer of 1998.

Stages of the product life-cycle

It is worth returning to the stages of the PLC shown in Figure 5.3 for further examination.

Introduction

The introductory stage is characterised by the need to communicate the existence of the product to potential consumers. This can be very expensive, and accounts for the high start-up costs for a new product. The principal objective in this stage is to build awareness. Returning to the NBL example, building awareness of the new competition in 1979 was the primary objective for competition organisers. Successfully achieving this goal was inhibited, however, as basketball was not a traditional sport in Australia. Typically during the introductory stage, profitability is low or negative and sales are near zero. Attracting 190 000 spectators in the first year of the NBL competition compared with just over a million in 1995 illustrates the initial difficulties of developing a market segment for basketball. The other important consideration in this introductory stage was identifying the channels through which the NBL was distributed. Each club in the league was based in a major capital city or regional centre, with the intention of developing product awareness in that city or region. The most difficult phase of developing product awareness was trying to build team loyalty and team rivalry.

Growth

As product awareness began to build for basketball, it moved into the next stage of the PLC: the growth stage. The NBL attendances grew to 242 022 by 1984 and to just over 800 000 by 1990. In this period, considerable growth was achieved as many clubs moved to larger playing facilities. During the growth stage, the range of product offerings tends to widen, and refinements are made to the way in which the product is offered. The NBL found it necessary to provide large, comfortable facilities as well as quality product extensions. It was through product extensions that the NBL made its greatest change to product offerings. Merchandise and licensing programs emerged, associated television programming appeared, and basketball began to identify and open up new market segments. To overcome the high cost of enticing new consumers to NBL games, the clubs began to recognise the importance of retaining their members and loyal supporters. This marked the transition from the growth to the maturity stage. The clubs themselves became the most important marketing vehicles for basketball. Brand loyalty via individual clubs became important, and club memberships began to stabilise post-1990.

Maturity and revitalisation

The mature stage is characterised by a plateau in sales—in the NBL's case, sales in the form of attendance, memberships, sponsorships and merchandise. As has already been discussed in this section, action needs to be taken to extend the PLC. This returns us to the reasons why the NBL was considering a change of season, to recycle or extend the capacity of the NBL to capture market share. Given that the NBL is a relatively new sport product in Australia, it will be worth seeing what other action the NBL takes to extend the PLC of basketball.

Variations from the PLC curve

The PLC is a useful tool for the sport marketer to assist in strategy development for sports, and sporting leagues and associations. The S-curve indicated in Figure 5.3 can be misleading, however. Not all products progress incrementally through the stages of the life-cycle described, making it harder to discern the stage of the PLC at which a product can be classified. Another complication is the time taken to progress through the stages of the PLC. It is very hard to predict how long it will take a product to move from an introductory stage to maturity. Indeed, the NBL has been caught in this situation of taking at least two years to identify maturity, and a subsequent levelling off of interest.

Figure 5.4 illustrates some of the more common variations from the normal S-curve shown in Figure 5.3. The first curve (a) shows a product that has a long introduction stage because it is adopted slowly by consumers. The second curve (b) illustrates products such as one-day cricket, which are rapidly accepted and have a shorter introductory stage. The third curve (c) represents 'fad' products that typically have a rapid rise and rapid fall. The fourth curve (d) shows a product that has been frequently revitalised, going through stages of decline followed by growth. The Olympic Games provide a good example of the fourth curve, as this event has ebbed and flowed in terms of growth and popularity over the past 100 years. At present, the Olympic movement could be described as being in a growth phase, although as recently as 1980, leading up to the 1984 Los Angeles Games, it was in a state of decline. Los Angeles proved to be the catalyst that provided the necessary revitalisation for the Olympic movement.

Like all the models presented in this book, the PLC provides the sport marketer with a framework on which to base decision-making. There will always be variations on the models and theories discussed. However, it is incumbent on the sport manager to temper theory with the peculiar nature and development of each product.

Sport and television

Earlier in this chapter, we discussed the benefits provided by a product as being vital to the consumer's decision to purchase. In sport, television and increasingly iTV (internet TV) has emerged as an important substitute for attendance at the live event. Another question is whether sport on television or iTV is the same product as the live event. The exposure and promotional benefits to be gained by a sport from televising its games or events have been central to most sport-marketing strategies in the professional sport sector.

At issue also has been the revenue aspect of televising sporting contests versus the live game. That is, consumers have the choice either to attend the event or stay at home and watch it on television. For sports where consumers may decide to stay home and

FIGURE 5.4 Variations from the PLC S-curve

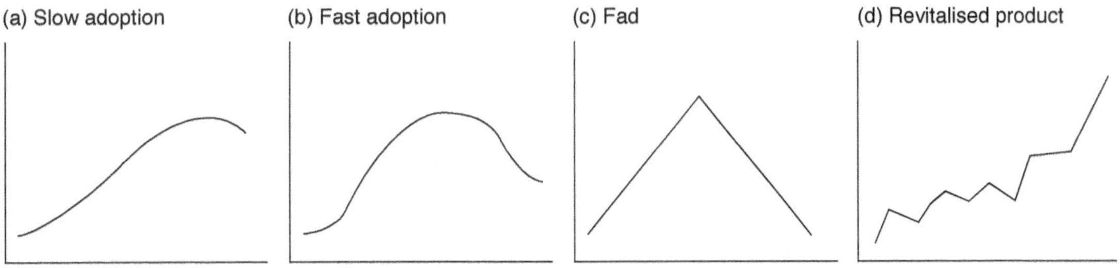

watch the event on television, this choice represents direct lost revenue. It is, however, also revenue that may find its way back to the sport indirectly, in the form of television rights as a consequence of high program ratings. Alternatively, the short-term lost revenue may result in a long-term revenue gain as the consumer is enticed to attend future games because the televised game was entertaining and enjoyable. The relationship between television and sport has always been prickly, as the balance between live coverage, delayed coverage and 'blacking out' home markets has created tension between respective sports and the television networks. Other tensions are observed in the form of scheduling, as television looks to the most favourable programming options to maximise its investment via television rights.

In this book, we consider the televised form of sport to be different from attendance at the live event. In other words, the benefits offered by watching the game on television are different from those gained by attending. Television offers different features, including commentary, slow-motion replays, live interviews and, depending on the sport, close-up action, which can sometimes detract from observing the build-up to the central action.

The television–sport relationship is considered in greater detail in Chapter 11. Specifically, Chapter 11 will examine why television has become such an important component of the economics and marketing of professional sport. Television is also discussed in Chapter 7 in relation to its role in distributing the sport product.

Summary

This chapter defined and described sport as a product. A product is anything that satisfies a need or want, and is acquired to do so. In relation to sport, two important concepts have implications for sport marketing. The first is the core product, defined as the actual game, over which the sport marketer has no control. The sport marketer must be very careful not to over-promise in terms of how good the game will be or how well specific athletes may perform. The second concept is the importance of product extensions to the overall marketing effort. It is here that the marketer can ensure that acceptable levels of quality are achieved. Discussion in this chapter also focused on the importance of delivering quality service. The dimensions of quality service were discussed, and the areas requiring attention in the delivery of product extensions indicated. These include anything that affects spectators' attendance and enjoyment of an event.

Issues of strategy were also considered when discussing product positioning and the product life-cycle. In both cases, these techniques allow the marketer to assess the relative standing of a product in relation to competitors and the phases of product growth. The perceptual map was used to illustrate the concept of product space and the way in which this defines direct and indirect competitors. Perceptual mapping also highlights the importance of key product attributes and their ability to entice consumers to purchase or attend games. Level of excitement was used as an example of a key product attribute. In this example, it was possible to determine the direct competitors of the NBL and other sports. The NBL was also used to illustrate the application of product life-cycle analysis, which revealed some interesting challenges confronting the NBL in its quest to arrest the plateau in the fortunes of its competition.

Finally, the importance of television to sport was noted. A distinction was made between the television product and the live product. It was posited that televised sport is a different product from the one viewed live. Different benefits are offered, so a different range of options is considered in the pre-purchase process.

CASE STUDY

The NBL—product development

A substantial drop in attendance figures forced the NBL to review its marketing strategies in a bid to generate more excitement and momentum in the early part of the 1993 season. After ten rounds, the NBL—which trumpeted a sensational growth in attendances throughout the 1980s and early 1990s—was down by almost 270 000 fans (Brown 1993: 6).

The ten-team NBL competition commenced in 1979 as an outlet to provide a regular opportunity for its elite players to play top-line basketball. It also quickly became the promotional vehicle for basketball in Australia. The gate for the first season was 196 000 for all home and away games. By 1995, as shown in Table 5.3, attendances had risen to 1 097 678 from 201 games played across the country. An average of 5461 fans attended games in 1995. From 1979 to 1984, average attendances grew 82 per cent, to 355 828 spectators, but in the five years to 1988 they jumped 130 per cent, clearly demonstrating the sport's appeal, and in the five years to 1993 they rose to just over one million. The 1993–95 seasons show that growth then slowed and that the NBL in terms of attendances had plateaued.

The success of the NBL in capturing the public's imagination in the 1980s can be traced to several reasons. It was a highly entertaining game, played in a comfortable, warm stadium, enjoyed by men and women, and revered by children. Hype generated by the NBL was also fostered by enormous goodwill from the print and radio media. There was no question that this most American of sports had taken off in Australia, but to continue to grow it needed television to play a more significant role (Brown 1992). The Seven Network, which held the rights to televise basketball in Sydney and Melbourne prior to 1992, was reluctant to give basketball a greater profile. Channel Ten took up the rights to televise the NBL in 1992 on the promise that the NBL would be shown in prime time. As the 1992 season unfolded, the Ten Network realised that NBL programming was suffering from low ratings. The only exception to this was Perth. Following the break for the 1992 Olympic Games, the Ten Network removed the NBL from prime-time television.

Television remains a source of frustration for the NBL. In 1995, the NBL made the following observations in relation to television and its impact on product development:

> With television we found ourselves in a difficult situation. In order to make television work, the NBL will have to become much more flexible in its scheduling (playing in non-competitive days and times), consider changing the time of year we play, clean up the court clutter (to increase NBL branding and strengthen television advertising). All of these strategies may have a cost to the clubs. This cost will not be initially met by television rights revenue. But without making some or all of these changes, television rights revenue may never reach the level to be able to finance the changes. Almost

every aspect of the NBL/Club business now comes back to creating success on television. Marketing, merchandising, attendance, rights money and sponsorship levels all point to television needing improving. The television ratings are a mystery. Our worst rating performance in recent history comes at a time when a new ARM Quantum survey shows that basketball has increased its stranglehold on the youth in this country. Basketball ranks as the top sport played by boys (10–17) at 59%, 12 points above the next team sport, cricket (47%). For girls, basketball ranks third at 31%, behind swimming (52%) and netball (36%). There are more mysteries in the result of the survey that indicates what the youth market are watching on television. Basketball is way out in front at 50%, ahead of cricket at 38%—significantly improving its position since the last youth monitor three years ago. Finally, in the 10–17-year group, basketball is the best attended sport at 22%, ahead of rugby league at 17%. (NBL 1995)

TABLE 5.3

NBL attendance 1984–2007

Year	Attendance	Average	No. of games
1984	242 022	1158	209
1985	317 372	1697	187
1986	394 685	2088	189
1987	483 467	2518	192
1988	563 493	3232	166
1989	662 493	3897	170
1990	887 443	4551	195
1991	825 645	4256	194
1992	945 117	5463	173
1993	1 083 490	5445	199
1994	1 127 033	5692	198
1995	1 097 678	5461	201
1996	1 019 988	5075	201
1997	896 349	5064	177
1998	771 364	4408	175
1998–99	645 073	4511	143*
1999–00	714 017	4636	154*
2000–01	814 918	4738	172
2001–02	840 074	4641	181
2002–03	749 207	4162	180
2003–04	724 108	3432	211
2004–05	698 465	3735	187
2005–06	653 710	3495	187
2006–07	518 457	3367	154*

* Does not include playoffs.

Source: NBL (1997, 2007).

In 1996, the NBL made the decision to move the NBL season from its traditional winter season to a summer season. This necessitated a transition—or interim—season, from January to July 1998. The new summer season commenced in October 1998. The rationale for the change, according to the NBL (2000), was first, to improve television arrangements; second, to increase media coverage through reduced clutter (less AFL media) and third, maintain sponsorship, although it was recognised that reduced attendance might result from the change. Although the interim season had a negative impact in terms of club mergers and further erosion of the fan supporter base, television coverage improved—albeit mainly through pay TV channel Fox Sports supported by ABC coverage. Attendances grew 8 per cent in the first full summer season, compared with a 5 per cent decline in the interim season. The second summer season allowed the NBL to experiment with innovative fixturing, such as the pre-season blitz, double-headers, an open-air game at Rod Laver Arena, Melbourne Park, as well as promoting local derbies. Attendances also rose by approximately 14 per cent, with average weekly television audiences of about 580 000.

By the 2002 season, however, the NBL and its teams were experiencing difficulties. Dampney (2002: 101) notes that 'two clubs appointed administrators, no naming rights sponsor, no free-to-air television rights—no national basketball League?' Both the Victorian Titans and Sydney Kings appointed administrators in 2002, although a consortium—including former Australian Boomer Shane Heal and Bob Turner, a founding member of the NBL in Australia—eventually bought the Sydney Kings. The Victorian Titans' future was less certain in mid-2002. Leading into the 2002–03 season, the eleven teams in the NBL competition were facing a series of collective challenges:

> The rebirth of Australian basketball features a returning 35-year-old legend, small crowds, tight budgets and a team—or possibly two—based more than 6000 kilometres from Sydney. It sounds like a peculiar recipe for success, but in the post-boom period of the National Basketball League, it may be a necessary reality. Low television revenues, a lack of big names (or an inability to effectively market them), competition from other sports and a failure to capitalise on gains made previously, has changed the NBL, whose preparation for 2006–07 has included the unprecedented addition of a Singapore-based club and another Melbourne team, the South Dragons, whose big signing is the once-retired Shane Heal. It has also been marked by the demise of yet another club, the Hunter Pirates. (Sygall, 2006)

As Sygall notes, the NBL has been struggling to find the right formula to relaunch basketball. In 2004, the NBL secured Philips as its major sponsor and Fox Sports as its broadcaster, which stemmed the tide to some extent. On the eve of the 30th NBL season in 2007–08, the NBL competition had grown to thirteen teams, two of which were based outside Australia. In 2003–04, the New Zealand Breakers were the first non-Australian-based team to enter the competition, followed by the Singapore Slingers in 2006–07. The long-term goal is to have two teams located in Asia, with television revenues an obvious lure. Meanwhile, the 2007–08 season commenced with the addition of a thirteenth team, the Gold Coast Blazers, and the NBL having lost its sponsor. The Philips sponsorship was estimated to be worth in excess of $1 million per year, and its loss is an obvious blow to the

NBL. However, on the eve of the new season, the NBL announced HUMMER, a division of General Motors, as its naming rights sponsor. One of the world's fastest growing truck brands, the mid-size H3 SUV HUMMER, was launched in Australia in 2007. In relation to television, the Fox Sports broadcasting deal is due to expire at the end of the 2007–08 season. As Dampney queried in 2002: 'Is all hope lost for a game once labeled the world's fastest growing participation sport?' The NBL's woes continued in the lead-up to the 2008–09 season with both the Sydney Kings and Singapore Slingers withdrawing from the competition. Product development continued to be a major issue confronting the NBL.

With the NBL boss, Chuck Harmison, admitting in 2008 that the NBL competition was in an embarrassing state with two major clubs struggling for survival, it was clear that the NBL had reached its lowest point in 30 years (Heming and Coomber, 2008). Key city clubs the Brisbane Bullets and the Sydney Kings were on the verge of having their licences terminated. Moreover, the lack of free-to-air television coverage added to the NBL's woes. Given the state of the NBL in 2008, major changes were required to revamp the league. As part of a sweeping reform program designed to revamp the NBL, the NBL and Basketball Australia (BA) merged their operations, so that the NBL would become a functional division within BA. As part of this governance change, a review of the NBL was instituted. Such was the state of the NBL that Clark (2008) noted speculation that the 2008–09 season would be scrapped. Ultimately, the review recommended an eight-team competition with a focus on one team per major state. The prospect of a New Zealand team was also raised. No change was recommended to the summer season, and overall the review that led to the re-launch of the NBL in season 2009–10 saw the NBL look similar in structure to the previous years. A one-year pay TV broadcast deal with Fox Sports was secured on the eve of the 2008–09 season, guaranteeing one live game per week.

In 2010, the NBL was able to secure a five-year deal with the Ten Network, which followed immediately after announcing the rebirth of the Sydney Kings as part of the revival plan for the NBL. The Sydney market was critical to securing a free-to-air television deal. The new five-year free-to-air TV deal included an agreement to broadcast two games live on either One HD or Ten, increasing to five live games in the final year of the contract. In September 2010, iiNet was announced as the NBL's naming rights sponsor for three years, followed in 2011 by Virgin Airlines renewing its second-tier sponsorship of the league. Slowly, the NBL was re-establishing itself as a viable competition. With television and sponsorship locked in, the NBL set out some important targets as part of its determination to rebound. In *Transition 2015*, the NBL noted that it aimed to increase:

- income from $3.9 million last season (2011) to $7.6 million
- attendances by 290 000
- average broadcast audience per game by 200 per cent
- sponsorship income from $1.163 million last season to $3.7 million, and
- club membership (season tickets) from a base of 14 860 in 2010–11 to 23 950 in 2014–15.

Two annual theme rounds would also be created, bringing the total to eight per year in 2014–15 (Sporting Pulse, 2011). In addition, the NBL expressed a desire to re-establish a team in Brisbane—a goal that had not been achieved by the 2012–13 season.

Unfortunately, the string of positive announcements was disrupted when the Ten Network announced in 2012 that it was cutting its commitment to sport broadcasting in response to cost-cutting measures. Tensions were already on the rise between the network and the NBL, as Ten had moved to exercise a 'near-live' clause (Ward, 2012) in the agreement to broadcast three games each round on a delayed basis from 10.30 p.m.; in the case of Perth, this meant some matches being broadcast after midnight. By season 2012–13, the NBL was an eight-team competition following the withdrawal of the Gold Coast Blaze due to financial difficulties. In the nine-team 2011–12 season, with 135 games played, a total of 578 389 spectators attended games at an average of 4284 spectators per game (Wikipedia, 2013c). In the 2012–13 season, average attendances remained steady at around 4000, and TV ratings were rather low. Table 5.4 provides a snapshot of games played during the 2012–13 season, illustrating the issues with the televised product.

TABLE 5.4

Snapshot of television audience and attendance, 2012–13 season

Game	Television audience	Attendance
NZ Breakers vs Perth Wildcats	28 150	4 000
Sydney Kings vs Melbourne Tigers	49 000	4 386
Melbourne Tigers vs Perth Wildcats	81 000	5 256
Melbourne Tigers vs Wollongong Hawks	18 000	2 774
Adelaide 36s v Perth Wildcats	60 000	3 696
Townsville Crocs vs Cairns Taipans	28 000	3 485
NZ Breakers vs Townsville Crocs	21 410	7 489
Perth Wildcats vs Melbourne Tigers	NA	12 336

Source: Difabrizio Report (2013); Wikipedia (2013d).

The NBL All Stars game was also reintroduced in 2012 as part of the revitalisation of the league, and overall re-launching of the NBL. This game attracted 38 000 viewers and approximately 4500 spectators. In a sign of the times, coupled with the NBL's difficulties with free-to-air live broadcasts of games, NBL fans can now see every game live through NBL.TV, which is a form of iTV. At a cost of $79, NBL fans can watch every game on all digital platforms. BA CEO Kristina Keneally said NBL.TV 'was a landmark development in the sport and would be owned by the league'. She further stated that: 'New media and digital broadcasting are already having a huge impact on the media landscape, and basketball fans rightly expect broad access to high-quality live programming in this space . . . and that NBL.TV could become a money maker for the league.' (Ward, 2012: 18). Time will tell whether this is the case, and whether the NBL's efforts in recent years to revamp and revitalise its competition will successfully reposition the NBL product.

Questions

1 What were the reasons for the decline in demand for the NBL?
2 How is the NBL a good example of the theory of the product life-cycle?
3 In product life-cycle terms, at what stage would you place the NBL?
4 What were the competitive positioning implications of moving the NBL season out of the winter to a summer season? Has it been successful?
5 Describe the product positioning of the NBL. Using your research skills, identify potential sports and allied products that might occupy a similar product space on a perceptual map. What competitive threats do these sports represent?
6 How would you position the NBL for future success?

Stage 1—Identification of marketing opportunities

▼

Stage 2—Strategy determination

Step 5—Determine core marketing strategy

Marketing and service mix—sport product, pricing

▼

Stage 3—Strategy implemention, evaluation and adjustment

6

Pricing strategies

CHAPTER OBJECTIVES

Chapter 6 introduces price as one of the marketing mix variables. Pricing strategies are discussed in this chapter in relation to overall organisational and marketing goals. Pricing as a process is defined as setting or adjusting a price charged to a customer in exchange for a good or a service. The techniques used to determine price, as well as the role of price in the marketing mix, form the basis of the chapter. However, through the headline story and one of the sportviews, the macro-perspective of achieving positive overall outcomes is discussed too. As will be shown, the 'big picture' cost–benefit analysis should always be the overriding measure of pricing effectiveness.

After studying this chapter, you should be able to:

- distinguish between factors that influence the pricing process
- see pricing in the context of organisational strategy
- determine demand and supply relations and the price sensitivity of markets
- apply a strategic pricing approach in setting or adjusting the price of sport products.

HEADLINE STORY

The relative 'price' of hosting major sporting events

If you believe the protestations of the 'Save Albert Park' group, the committee that has vehemently campaigned against the location of the Australian Formula One Grand Prix at the Albert Park circuit in Melbourne, a city would be unwise and irresponsible to consider attracting and hosting an international sporting event. Noise and air pollution, the destruction of inner-city parklands, restricted access to public property, significant expenditure of public monies, grossly over-stated economic benefits for the local community and political opposition all await the city that hosts hallmark events. On the other hand, the socio-economic conservationists are continually overwhelmed by the mass public and political appeal forged by hallmark events. In addition to the economic stimulus, research on hallmark events tends to reveal that their social impact is often positive, providing a normative glue fastening parochial sport fans and even the less frequently interested sport theatregoers with a vast bonding of collective identity and vicarious experience. Indeed, studies have for a long time suggested that the outcomes of most cost–benefit analysis are positive—that is, the benefits (such as, in Melbourne's case, the exposure of the city and revenues from tourism) outweigh the costs (such as air and noise pollution and the redevelopment of parklands). However, even the economic impact is increasingly being scrutinised.

Consider the following quote by Tourism Victoria (2011)—a key beneficiary of Melbourne hosting major events—about the benefits of government-supported major events:

> Comperio Research analyzed television broadcasts of the 2009 Grand Prix across a sample size of 82 countries including the key markets of China, New Zealand, the United Kingdom and the USA. In total, these countries generated 444 television broadcast hours with extensive coverage across free-to-air television and a combined television audience of over 270 million. Comperio Research monitored a sample of 43 hours of dedicated television coverage of the event. From this, it is estimated that the 2009 Grand Prix returned a media or advertising-equivalent value to Victoria of $35.6 million.

Furthermore, this position is supported by Brendan McClements, CEO of the Victorian Major Events Company (Pearson, 2007), who states:

> Destination branding through events is a powerful and proven tool to create greater awareness and visitation for a destination and hence provide economic benefits to the host city. Brand analysis and research reports indicate that destination branding opportunities offered by major events can be most effectively leveraged as part of a broader tourism leveraging strategy.

Despite these positive benefits, there are increased calls to terminate the Formula One Grand Prix when the contract expires in 2015. Proponents of this position cite the increased operating deficit that is subsidised by Victorian state taxpayers as their principal motive. In recent years, Victorian taxpayers have subsidised the Australian Grand Prix to the value of A$56.65 million (2012), up from A$40.23 million (2010) and A$34.63 million in 2007 (Australian Grand Prix Corporation, 2011, 2012). Further pressure is added to the situation from new economies looking to host the event to promote their country and pressure from the president and CEO of Formula One, Bernie Ecclestone, to hold the Australian race at night, which would require further taxpayer investment in infrastructure. With attendance figures remaining relatively stagnant (and disputed) at around 300 000 since 2006, and the contract to host the event expiring in 2015, the $1 million question remains: is the event worth the relative price to the host city (Westerbeek and Smith, 2001)?

As a process, pricing can simply be defined as setting or adjusting a price charged to a customer in exchange for a good or service. Pricing a product or a range of products properly is of utmost importance to an organisation. The level of pricing determines how many customers are inclined to buy the organisation's products. At the end of the day, the price multiplied by the number of products sold must at least cover the costs of production. This is, however, a simplified version of reality, which will be elaborated on later in this chapter.

In Chapter 5, it was shown that the sport product is made up of different components: the core product and product extensions. Although the core product may be the main attraction for customers in terms of potential income, product extensions make up a considerable part of the overall revenue for sporting organisations. This is one reason why, for example, the Australian Football League does not price its core product (tickets to attend a football match) at a higher level. The core spectator product is priced relative to the product extensions (such as sponsorship services and television rights)—or, in other words, the total product mix. Throughout this chapter, examples of this 'big picture perspective' will be given in relation to hosting major sporting events and city marketing.

In this chapter, the pricing process will be examined from a strategic perspective. After presenting a strategic pricing model, the different steps of this model will then be discussed.

The strategic pricing process in sport

The importance of recovering the costs of production through setting the right price is highlighted in the above headline story. However, cost of production is only one of the variables that needs to be taken into consideration when setting or adjusting price. The strategic pricing process incorporates both internal characteristics of the organisation and its products (for example, goals and objectives) and external characteristics (such as competitors' pricing behaviour). This will enable the marketer to create a pricing strategy beyond the short-term future of the organisation. Figure 6.1 describes the strategic pricing process for sporting organisations.

Step 1: Determine pricing goal(s)

Although there exists a subtle difference between introducing a product then setting a price and adjusting the price of an existing product, the pricing goal must be determined for both. It is vital to recognise the influence that price has on customers' perceptions of the product. A relatively high-priced product will often be perceived as a high-quality

FIGURE 6.1

The strategic pricing process in sport

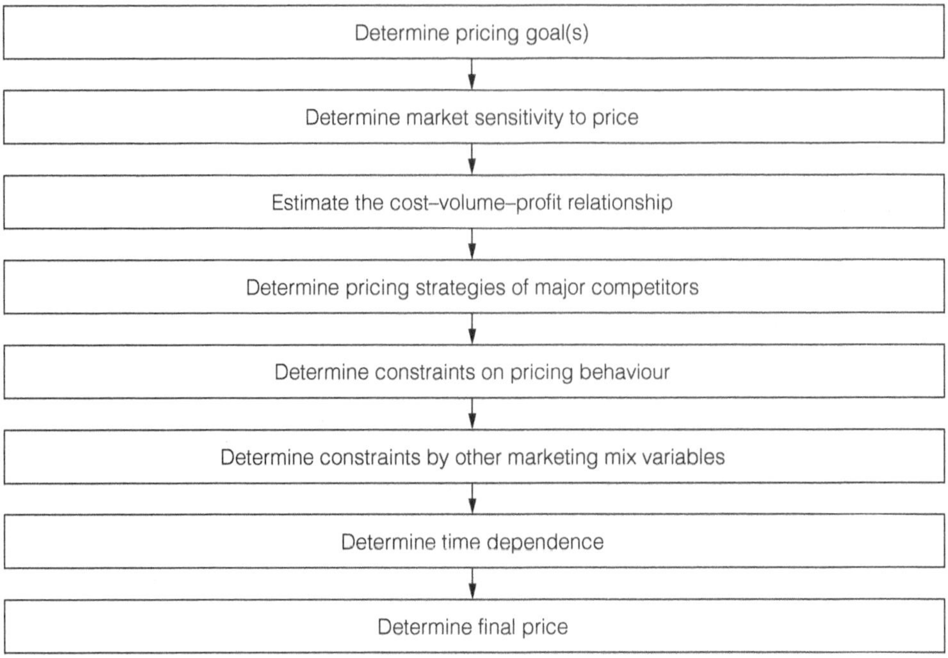

product. Pricing, in other words, has a strong impact on the positioning of the product. Determining the pricing goals should be a direct derivative of the organisation's reason for being (that is, its mission) and the resulting marketing goals. Marketing goals of different organisations and derived pricing goals are shown in Table 6.1.

Maximum shareholder value

Private enterprises and privately owned sport franchises often pursue goals designed to maximise shareholder value. In order to do this, pricing goals would include maximising profit, maximising sales growth or maximising revenue:

- *Maximising profit* is often seen as a short-term goal, concentrating on current financial performance and assuming little influence from competitors (that is, to undercut the set price).

TABLE 6.1

Marketing goals and derived pricing goals

Marketing goals	Derived pricing goals
Maximise shareholder value	Maximising profit Maximising sales growth Maximising revenue
Be the most innovative in the business	Market skimming
Deliver the highest quality products	Premium price
Be accessible to all members of the community	Full cost recovery Partial cost recovery

- *Maximising sales growth* is a long-term pricing goal. Although profits could be higher, the organisation aims to sell its products at a lower price to as many customers as possible. The goal is to obtain a large share of the market and reap the subsequent long-term benefits.
- *Maximising revenue* can be the pricing goal of, for example, the organisers of Wimbledon. With an infrastructure (buildings, equipment and personnel) in place, every extra customer adds to the revenue of the organisation. The organisation itself is incurring little extra cost by providing services to that one extra visitor, and this makes selling the extra tickets—such as ground passes—extremely attractive.

Most innovation

If an organisation aims to be an innovative company, the pricing goal may be to skim the market. Nike, as an athletic footwear manufacturer, establishes a price high enough for a small segment of the market to buy its products. As soon as competitors introduce similar products, Nike lowers the price to sell to the segment below the 'early adopters'. Nike skims the market by receiving the maximum price from the different segments of the market. Nike can adopt this strategy because it ensures that it is the first to introduce a new, trendy, high-quality product.

Highest-quality products

If an organisation aims to deliver the highest-quality products, a premium pricing strategy may be an alternative pricing goal. In order to communicate the high quality of the product (for example, a world title boxing contest), a correspondingly high price is set. Customers valuing the high-quality features of the product will pay the premium price, and the organisation will achieve an above-average return.

Community accessibility

Not-for-profit organisations, government organisations and many sporting organisations often set pricing goals such as partial or full cost recovery. Public hospitals, for example, may set prices in order to recover their costs because they do not need to make a profit, their main goal being to serve the community. National sport-governing bodies can price their products in order to break even, incorporating funding from the federal government (partial cost recovery). The London Olympic Games Organising Committee proposed a stated community goal regarding its pricing strategy, summarised as 'Everybody's Games'. This goal saw that half of the eight million tickets for the 2012 London Olympics sold at £20 in order to create 'shared value' between local 'Londoners' and revenues for the Olympic Games (Bertini and Gourville 2012) . Setting or adjusting the price depends not only on the goals of the organisation but also on the other elements of the pricing process. This will become clear in the following sections.

Step 2: Determine market sensitivity to price

How sensitive customers are to a change in price is important in determining a range within which the final price may be set. It is also vital to know the estimated size of the market and how it is segmented. In this section, it is assumed that this information is available. The concepts of demand and supply, price elasticity and non-price factors are important in determining market sensitivity to price. Given the marketing focus of this book, we start by discussing the concept of demand.

Demand

The quantity demanded of the product by potential customers depends on the price assigned to the product. In general terms, the higher the price of a product, the lower the quantity demanded. Figure 6.2(a) shows that, for a certain product, a demand curve can be drawn demonstrating the linear relationship with the price. The quantity demanded also depends on the prices of other factors, such as product (substitutes and complements), income of customers, expectations of future prices and the size of the population.

Substitutes are products that can be used in place of another product (e.g. spectator tickets to a football match and a basketball match). If the price of a product (football tickets) rises, the quantity demanded of the substitute (basketball tickets) is likely to rise as well, because consumers may elect to purchase the cheaper substitute.

Complements are products used in conjunction with another product (e.g. golf clubs and a golf course membership). If the price of a product (golf course membership) falls, the quantity demanded of this product and its complement (golf clubs) will rise.

Generally, when the income of customers rises, demand for most goods will also rise. Expectations of higher prices in the future may prompt customers to buy now, and hence demand will rise. In general, the larger the population, the greater the demand will be for products.

Supply

When a product is providing attractive returns to producers, more organisations will be inclined to supply the product to the market than when the price is relatively low. In general terms, the higher the price of a product, the greater the quantity supplied. Figure 6.2(a) shows that, for a certain product, a supply curve can be drawn demonstrating a linear relationship with the price. The quantity supplied also depends on resource prices, technology, the number of sellers and expectations about future prices.

In general, when resource prices rise, the quantity supplied will fall. Similarly, technological improvements and increasing efficiency will result in a rise in the quantity supplied because a greater quantity can be produced at the same cost. The more sellers there are, the greater the quantity supplied. Expectations about future prices are a more complicated issue. When a sporting goods firm expects the prices of tennis racquets to rise after the final at Wimbledon, it may choose to hold back the racquets in stock in order to sell them at a higher price. Racquet manufacturers, however, may decide to increase production and supply more racquets to the market.

Market equilibrium

Figure 6.2(a) shows that, at the point where demand equals supply, the market is in equilibrium (E). This point represents the price that the market is prepared to pay, given the quantity supplied. Figure 6.2(b) shows that at a price of $120 there will be a supply of 120 000 racquets, but a demand for only 80 000. There will be an excess supply of 40 000 racquets. Figure 6.2(c) shows that the reverse will occur at a price lower than the equilibrium price (e.g. $80). Therefore, in that situation there will be an excess demand of 40 000 racquets.

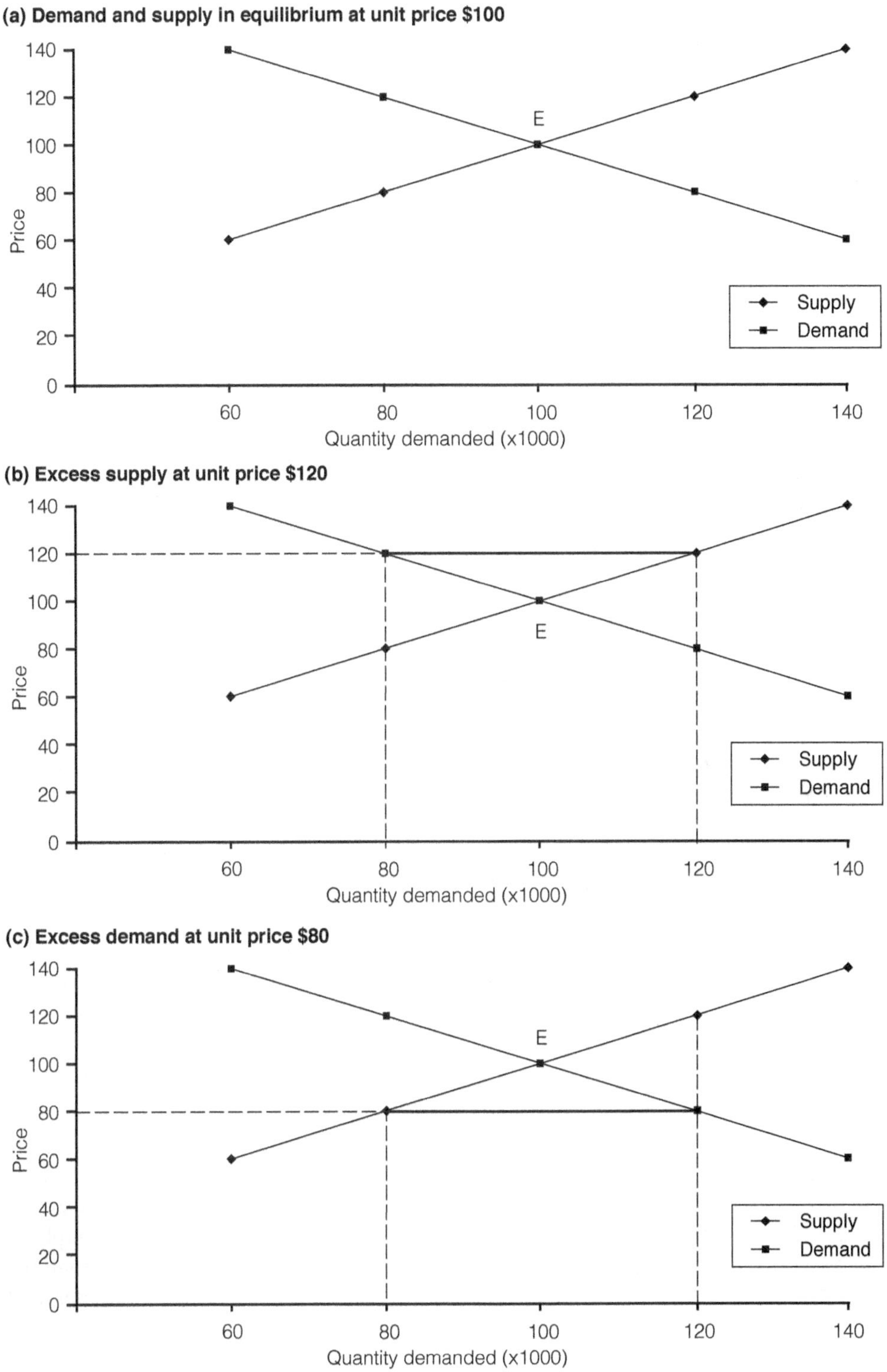

FIGURE 6.2
Demand, supply and market equilibrium

If the demand for tennis racquets after the Wimbledon final rises, the demand curve will move to the right. This will result in a rise in the quantity supplied (that is, a movement along the supply curve) because the price will go up to establish a new equilibrium. Let us assume that people keep demanding the new quantity. With this increase in demand, new producers will be lured to the market because of the higher price, supply will go up and the supply curve will move to the right. This again will result in a fall in price. Equilibrium will return to the point where it is not attractive enough for new suppliers to enter the market. At the end of this process, the only change will be that the total quantity supplied has risen. It goes beyond the scope of this book to further elaborate on demand and supply issues.

Price elasticity of demand

We have now explored the influence that price can have on the quantity of products supplied and demanded. What we do not know is how sensitive a customer is to a change in price. Will a rise or fall in the price of a product result in a great or small change in the quantity traded? Price elasticity of demand is a measure projecting this relationship. It is calculated as the absolute value of the change (%) in the quantity demanded, divided by the change (%) in price. The absolute value can range between 0 and infinity. A value between 0 and 1 represents inelastic demand; a value greater than 1 represents elastic demand; a value of exactly 1 is called unit elastic demand.

Figure 6.3(a) shows that inelastic demand occurs where the fall (%) in the quantity demanded is less than the rise (%) in price. In other words, the organisation will benefit from raising the price because the number of customers lost will be less than the gain in revenue. For example, the number of customers will not vary greatly when the price of tickets for the final of the World Cup is raised.

Figure 6.3(b) shows that if the fall (%) in the quantity demanded equals the rise (%) in price, the elasticity of demand is 1 (unit elastic demand). This means that total revenue will not change.

FIGURE 6.3 Price elasticity of demand

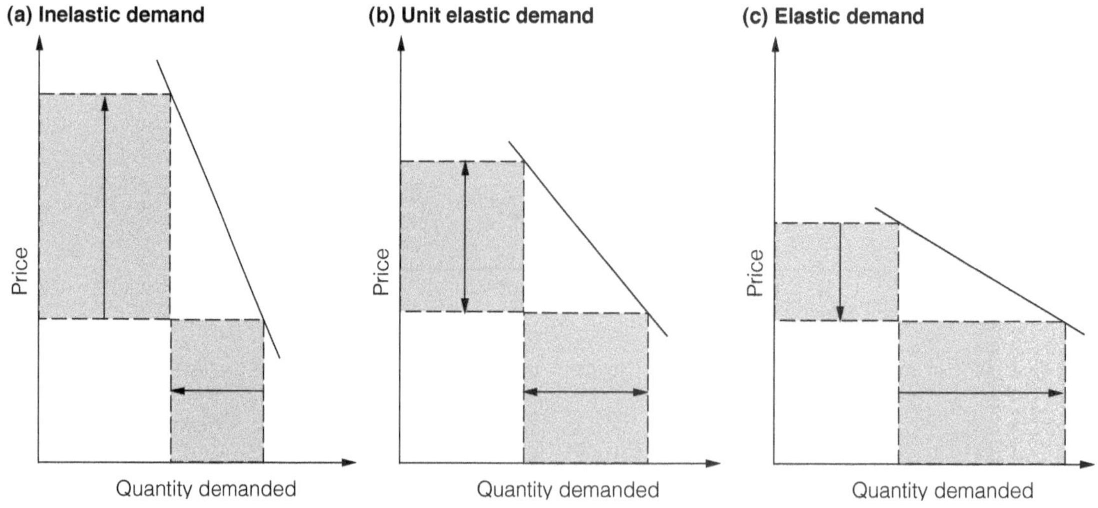

In Figure 6.3(c) it is shown that if the fall (%) in the quantity demanded exceeds the rise (%) in price, demand is considered to be elastic. In this case, the organisation will benefit from reducing the price because the gain in number of customers will be greater than the loss in revenue. For example, the number of customers will vary greatly (that is, rise) when the price of a golf course membership is lowered.

Factors determining elasticity

The size of the elasticity of demand is mainly determined by three variables:

- the substitutability of the product
- the amount of time since the price change, and
- the proportion of customer income spent on the product.

The more substitutes there are available for a product, the easier it is for a customer to replace one product with another when the price rises, hence the higher the price elasticity. A range of professional sports are playing in the metropolitan area of Melbourne less than a kilometre apart. A rise in the admission price for one sport will force customers to search for cheaper alternatives. A substantial price rise will result in an even more substantial loss of customers. However, existing customers of a basketball club, for example, will not immediately be able to go to a football club because they may have purchased long-term memberships.

The longer the time since the price change, the more opportunities customers will have had to find alternatives, hence the greater the elasticity of demand. The higher the proportion of customer income spent on club membership, the higher the elasticity of demand. If expenditure represents a large part of an individual's income, every extra dollar on top of that expenditure will be scrutinised and can make the customer decide not to purchase. If, however, a very rich person has to make the same decision, money spent on membership represents only a small portion of total income, and a price rise will not greatly affect the decision to buy. This last example shows that price elasticity of demand can differ not only between products but also between consumer groups, and provides the marketer with the opportunity to differentiate between customer segments. Different issues related to price elasticity of demand are explored in an historical review of pricing in the sport of Australian Rules football. Although the information presented in Sportview 6.1 reflects on the first few years of the new national AFL competition, it is interesting to observe that the AFL has continued to keep its prices of admission much lower than in other Western economies during the first decade of the new millennium.

SPORTVIEW 6.1

Supply, demand, price and substitutability in the Australian Football League

In the late 1980s, the game of Australian Rules football was struggling due to declining attendances, a federated power base largely located in Victoria and unequal distribution of player talent. These factors led Fuller and Stewart (1996) to describe the decline of Australian

Rules football at the time as 'indicating football was becoming proportionately a less popular form of entertainment'. In response to this decline, an independent Australian Football League (AFL) commission was created, which departed from the traditional federated model that oversaw the sport's decline within Australian society after World War II. The initial decisions made by the AFL commission were to hold down ticket price rises in the late 1980s, the construction of the new Great Southern Stand at the Melbourne Cricket Ground, the player draft from 1986 and the continued program of ground rationalisation—major factors in boosting game attendances. Furthermore, supply was increased from an eleven-team Victorian-based competition to an eighteen-team national competition. The nationalisation of AFL occurred in two types of markets: traditional AFL markets (Western Australia and South Australia) and non-traditional AFL markets (Queensland and New South Wales), where Rugby League was considered the predominant sport.

In traditional AFL markets, there was excess demand due to a high interest in Australian Rules football, a lack of supply of teams in the national competition (AFL) and low/no substitutability with other elite football codes such as Rugby League during the period of AFL nationalisation. Thus, when supply was increased via the introduction of new AFL franchises (West Coast Eagles, 1987; Adelaide Crows, 1991; Fremantle Dockers, 1995; Port Adelaide Power, 1997), demand also increased. On average, new franchise teams in these markets had a 23 per cent higher attendance at their home and away games than the league average in their first year in the AFL.

In non-traditional AFL markets, there was little pre-existing demand, a lack of supply of teams in the national competition and high substitutability with other elite football codes—particularly Rugby League and Rugby Union—during the period of AFL nationalisation. Thus, when supply was increased via the introduction of a new AFL franchise (Sydney Swans, 1982; Brisbane Bears, 1987; Gold Coast Suns, 2011; Greater Western Sydney, 2012), the initial demand (in home and away attendance) of the AFL product in non-traditional AFL markets was 50 per cent lower than in traditional AFL states.

Although new supply does not always meet demand in expansion markets with established substitutes, the introduction of Australian Rules football into non-traditional markets does have commercial benefits for the AFL. In 2011, the AFL signed an A$1.253 billion, five-year broadcasting rights deal with Seven-West and Foxtel. An influential factor in the increase in value of this deal compared with the previous deal was the AFL's new presence in New South Wales and Queensland.

Despite this, challenges remain for new franchises such as the Gold Coast Suns and Greater Western Sydney, as the substitutability of their football product is high, there is a low initial demand to attend games and inherent difficulties exist with regard to pricing due to relatively low price elasticity that comes from diverse membership categories. The challenge now is to establish what (pricing) strategies these new franchises can adopt to increase their demand through sponsors and attendances, with a fixed supply of games at their home stadiums.

Source: AFL Tables (2013); excerpts from Henderson (1996: 5). Copyright *The Australian*. Ian Henderson is Economics Correspondent at *The Australian*. Reprinted with the permission of *The Australian* and the author.

Non-price factors

Non-price factors influence buying situations and reduce the importance of price in the buying process. Non-price factors include an intangible perception of a product or the influence of socialisation agents, resulting in a perceived value being shaped. In other words, some customers may be willing to pay a higher-than-average market price (premium price) to receive product benefits. Other customers may be willing to forgo these benefits in return for a lower-than-average market price. For marketers, it is therefore important to understand key product attributes in order to enhance the perceived value and hence charge a premium price. In sport, a consumer may place a final value on an entry ticket contingent upon a number of variables that influence their enjoyment, such as an event's or product's attractiveness, its uniqueness or the fact that the event involves an opportunity to share the experience with friends or colleagues.

In the sport industry, non-price factors are very important. The rules of demand and supply, and price elasticity, can be applied to sport's core product and extensions. In addition, different combinations of core and extensions can enhance the perceived value of the total product, justifying extra expenditure for customers. The core product cannot be remixed, but in combination with different product extensions the perceived value of the total package can be increased (for example, the AFL's mobile application in partnership with Telstra).

Furthermore, the more important the product is to the consumer, the less important price will become. For example, a $100 repair on a $2000 bicycle will enable a cyclist to ride the bicycle again. The perceived value of the $100 expenditure is likely to be higher than that of another $100 expenditure on something less important (such as a television repair) to the cyclist.

If the marketer is able to enhance the perceived value of the product, customers will become less sensitive to price (that is, elasticity will decrease) and the organisation will benefit from raising price. This applies also to the reverse situation. If the marketer is able to filter out the product attributes less valued by customers (for example, cushioned seats or undercover seats in a sport stadium), customers will become more sensitive to price (that is, elasticity will increase) and the organisation will benefit from lowering the price.

It is clear from these examples that different segments of customers are targeted as part of the pricing strategy. The next section shows the impact of the cost–volume–profit relationship.

Step 3: Estimate the cost–volume–profit relationship

Cost–volume–profit analysis, also called break-even analysis, examines the interaction of factors influencing the level of profits. These factors, as identified by Anderson and Sollenberger (1992), are:

- selling prices
- volume of sales
- unit variable cost
- total fixed cost, and
- sales mix.

The first four factors are discussed in this section, with sales mix left to the section on constraints by other marketing mix variables (product mix).

In general terms, the total costs of production represent the minimum financial figure (that is, the break-even point) that needs to be recovered from sales in order to at least break even (total costs = total revenue). Total costs are made up of a fixed cost and a variable cost component. Fixed costs are the costs that an organisation has to incur in order to operate (for example, costs of plant and equipment, taxes, insurance), regardless of the level of production. Variable costs fluctuate in direct proportion to changes in the activity of the organisation. The cost of direct materials like leather for shoes is a good example. Pertaining to the goals of the organisation, the break-even point may vary. For an organisation with a partial cost-recovery goal, this point is relatively lower than for a full cost-recovery organisation. Both organisations, however, need to be able to ascertain their cost of production, enabling the organisation to arrive at a minimum price for its products by dividing the cost of production by the (estimated) number of products sold.

For a large athletic footwear manufacturer, total costs are made up of a fixed and variable component. In order to produce 10 000 pairs of shoes a day, for example, a certain infrastructure needs to be evident. Plant, equipment and labour are needed in order to start operations and represent the fixed costs of operations, which are independent of the output level. Raw material to manufacture the shoes is the major component of the variable costs, which vary with the output of the plant. Although certain levels of production will be more efficient, in this example it is assumed that the variable cost per unit of production is the same. In Figure 6.4, a break-even chart is shown.

FIGURE 6.4 The break-even chart

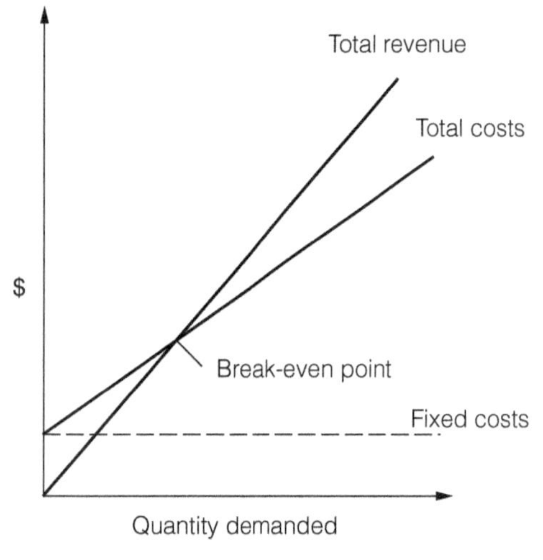

It can be derived from Figure 6.4 that the higher the total costs, the smaller the average fixed cost in each unit of production (for example, pairs of shoes). In other words, the fixed cost component will decrease with volume of production. If a factory with building costs of $10 million produces 100 million pairs of shoes over its productive lifetime (for example, ten years), the fixed cost component in every pair of shoes is $0.10. The relationship between total fixed costs, price and unit variable cost can be shown in the break-even formula:

$$\text{Break-even point (pairs of shoes)} = \frac{\text{Total fixed costs}}{\text{Unit price} - \text{Unit variable cost}}$$

The formula shows that, with a variation in the unit price, the amount of shoes sold to break even varies. This relationship is shown in Table 6.2. When we turn our attention to service products—and many sport products *are* service products—the unit variable costs in the break-even formula are much harder to determine. Many costs are both

TABLE 6.2 The relationship between unit price and break-even point

Unit price	Break-even point (pairs of shoes)	Unit variable cost	Total fixed costs (per year)
10	2 000 000	5	10 million
100	105 264	5	10 million
200	51 282	5	10 million

fixed and shared across different services. In a large stadium, the building, its equipment (for example, indoor courts, tennis nets, computers) and labour (a majority of which is often multi-skilled in order to deliver different services) are all needed to provide the total mix of services offered by the facility. The variable costs per unit are hard to determine. What, for example, are the variable costs of providing basketball spectator services when one extra ticket is sold? Most costs have to be incurred, irrespective of the number of customers on the day or over a longer period.

We can state that most costs are fixed. This is why it is very attractive to entice that one extra customer: with little to no extra (variable) cost, the revenue from one extra customer is almost pure profit. This explains why, in the health and fitness industry, competition is based primarily on price. An organisation has to incur little extra cost in order to gain a substantial increase in revenue.

This also indicates the importance of managing the non-price factors in the sport industry. Because we know that most costs are fixed, it becomes a matter of sophisticated marketing to enhance the perceived value of the sport product. This should lead to sufficient and sustainable market share to at least cover the costs of operation.

Step 4: Determine pricing strategies of major competitors

As in any strategic-planning effort of an organisation, it is important to monitor competitor behaviour and adjust actions accordingly. The first questions that need to be answered are: Who are the major (potential) competitors? Do they operate in the same market (for example, an amateur soccer team and a professional basketball team) or even in the same segment of the market (for example, an inner-city golf course and a working-class outer suburban golf course)? Organisations can then determine when to respond to price changes by competitors.

The next step is to determine how competitors are positioned in terms of their relative prices, providing an organisation with an indication of the competitive price range for which the product is on offer. It would also be very useful to know which strategies of competing firms are successful.

Finally, if an organisation is able to find out what the probable responses of competitors would be to a price change, different pricing scenarios can be developed in order to make the appropriate choice.

Step 5: Determine constraints on pricing behaviour

Laws and regulations are the most obvious constraints on pricing behaviour. Most of these are a direct result of government intervention in regulating the market behaviour of organisations. Some cases of price fixing (that is, agreement between organisations about price) can be regarded as disadvantageous for the public, and are therefore forbidden by law. In order to keep government-owned facilities accessible to all members of the community, local government can set a maximum price level (ceiling). Even when a management company is hired to manage the local pool, local government can constrain it in its pricing strategies. Regulatory organisations, like national sport organisations, can set membership fees for members, clubs and associations in order to optimise participation levels.

Social responsibility constraints can also affect the pricing behaviour of organisations. If, for example, the local professional soccer club feels that disabled members of the local community should be able to enjoy a game of soccer, it will have to adjust its facility in terms of access and seating arrangements. This will have a direct impact on the fixed-cost component of the total costs of the club, and it may decide to set different unit (for example, admission) prices to recover those costs. The pricing strategy of this club will be different from that of a club focusing solely on profit maximisation. Legal and social responsibility constraints therefore limit the pricing range for the product.

Step 6: Determine constraints of other marketing mix variables

The variables of the marketing mix—product (mix), place (dependence) and promotion (mix)—all affect each other.

Product mix

Prices in supermarkets are based on the overall mix of products rather than the individual products. Some products are priced at an attractive level (for example, soft drinks during summer) in order to entice customers to do the rest of their shopping in the same supermarket. A strategy adopted by expansion clubs in the AFL in Sportview 6.1 demonstrates the importance of looking at the overall product mix before pricing individual products. The AFL's admission prices are low compared with other sporting codes—particularly in new markets where there is a high substitutability of the AFL product by Rugby League and Rugby Union. These prices attract larger crowds, enhancing the atmosphere for attractive television coverage; as a consequence, they have an impact on the attractiveness of the total product for television sponsors. The AFL can offset the loss of income from gate receipts against the increase in income from television, sponsor contracts and other in-stadium purchases.

Place dependence

A majority of sport products are produced and consumed in a facility specifically designed to produce those sport products. The capacity of the facility limits the number of customers that can be serviced at a certain point in time, and consequently the maximum total income. The location of the facility determines the catchment area of potential customers, and hence partly determines the profile of the customer. In general terms, dependence on the place of distribution further limits the possible pricing range of the products of the organisation. Place dependence is discussed in more detail in Chapter 7. Sportview 6.2 also includes some elements of place dependence—that is, dependence on a number of geographic regions (cities) of distribution.

SPORTVIEW 6.2

Hallmark sporting events can make (but also lose) money

The commercial turning point for hallmark sporting events occurred more than three decades ago. It is widely recognised that the 1984 Los Angeles Olympic Games created a turnaround in attitudes towards embarking on the colossal task of organising mega-events such as the Olympics and soccer's World Cup and Euro Championships. The Los Angeles Games demonstrated that when astute business ideas are applied to selling spectator sport products, money can be made. Over the past three decades, it has been the vast injections of money that have made the world of big events go round. It is the positive economic impact of events on the hosting communities that has been the critical (political) justification for investing heavily in bidding and building for the event. Hallmark events have the propensity to deliver immense economic development to a region as an outcome of the combined encouragement of government, business and visitor spending.

The economic benefits of hallmark events are typically expected to outweigh their costs. In economic terms, this is because large-scale events have a high cost–benefit ratio. In other words, their capacity to generate exports, stimulate domestic spending, improve capital utilisation, develop and regenerate infrastructure, mobilise government involvement, marshal commercial sponsorship, assemble community supporters and drive consumable manufacturing is irreplaceable, and seldom achieved via any other program or activity.

Nevertheless, despite the anticipated benefits of hosting hallmark sporting events, the exponential increase in their funding, and often the need for underwriting by the local government, has driven the need for more rigorous justification of investments. As government authorities provide the lynchpin infrastructure for the events, they also assume the burden for justifying the community rewards in expending public monies. Thus, to invest in hallmark events for communal benefits, there has been a greater need to validate spending by measuring the event's contribution to the economy.

The 2006 World Cup in Germany had a significant impact on all 32 participating countries. It was estimated that competing nations netted a total £13 billion (A$20.6 billion) boost to their economies. Television audiences were estimated to be in excess of three billion worldwide and foreign visitations were to exceed one million with three million tickets available for sale. The event organisers argued that an additional 60 000 jobs had been created.

According to the Department for Culture, Media and Sport (Thornton, Gough and Martin, 2012), the 2012 Olympic Games in London was 'considered a national success in terms of organisation, medal haul, national engagement and as a summer of celebration'. More specifically, the authors cite a national increase in sports participation of 2.6 per cent between 2005 and 2012; a net impact of £7.3 billion (A$11.56 billion) and 160 000 job years of gross value added to the UK economy; as well as 10 000 new homes built in the low socio-economic area of East London, of which 40 per cent had been designated as 'affordable housing'. Given that the UK government's Public Spending Funding Package was valued at £9.3 billion (A$14.75 billion), it appears the net economic legacy of London 2012 will be around a £2 billion (A$3.17 billion) loss (Robertson, 2012). Olympic Games such as London, Athens, Sydney,

Moscow and Montreal are good case studies to demonstrate that hallmark sporting events such as the Olympic Games can lose money as easily as they can make money—as did previous games in Beijing, Atlanta, Barcelona, Seoul and Los Angeles (Rishe 2011).

Source: Adapted from Westerbeek and Smith (2001: 24) and *Sunday Times* (2006).

Promotion mix

The promotion mix (that is, the means by which communication with the target markets will take place) can be constructed after product, price and place information is available. A low price strategy often needs an intensive promotional effort in order to sell as many units as possible. If the tools for intensive promotion are not available due to limited funds, the organisation will be limited in pursuing a low price strategy. The promotion mix is constraining the pricing strategy. A pricing strategy never stands on its own, as it needs to be backed by adequate promotional efforts.

One of the characteristics of services is that they cannot be stored, as services are time-dependent.

Step 7: Determine time-dependence

A spectator at the Olympic Games witnesses the production of the sport product at the same time they consume the product. The customer is therefore part of the production process. When the Games are over, nobody will ever be able to consume this (past) product again. Dependence on the time of consumption makes it imperative for the Games organising committee to sell as many tickets as possible, because the tickets for today's event cannot be sold the next day.

Time-dependence makes sport suitable for price discrimination. This implies that different groups of customers pay different prices for basically the same product. In the case of a health and fitness club, part of the peak demand (i.e. full utilisation of capacity) between 5.00 p.m. and 7.00 p.m. can be moved to a low-demand timeslot by offering the same product at a lower price during an off-peak time. Senior citizens and parents with home duties, for example, may be able to take advantage of this offer. Pre-selling tickets to the Olympic Games is another example of price discrimination. By offering the same tickets at a lower price, the organising committee fills up seating capacity with customers who are able to plan and purchase in advance.

Step 8: Determine final price

Throughout this chapter, it has been shown that many factors affect the pricing process of a certain product. Figure 6.5 summarises these factors, and shows how the possible pricing range of the product narrows down after taking the influence of these various factors into consideration.

Final price determination is based on cost, competition, demand or a combination of all three. Most of the time, one method provides the basis for decision-making, although the others often contribute. As shown in this chapter, cost-based price determination proves to be more difficult for service-based sport products. The break-even

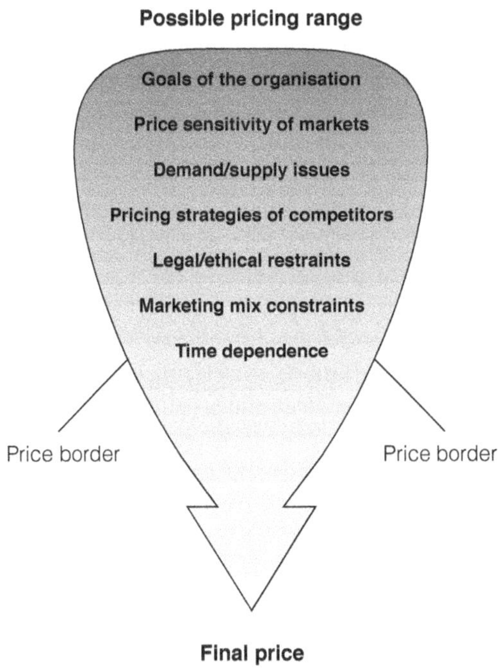

FIGURE 6.5 The possible pricing range

analysis has been presented as a cost-based approach. Many providers in the health and fitness industry will base their pricing on competition. In this industry, it is important to fill the capacity of the facility, and thus to attract those few extra customers from direct competitors. It is likely that the larger spectator sport organisations base their pricing on demand. In this method, the value of the product to the buyer is estimated. Westerbeek and Turner (1996: 394) found that:

> together with an increase in televisual appeal and hence income, the AFL was able to devise strategies in which demand characteristics of their markets (like elasticity of demand) could be used to optimise net income. Mass attendance at games was deemed more important than maximum profit from gate receipts. By undercharging at the gate [it was found that demand was inelastic at the current pricing level], income from TV and sponsorship could be raised, leading to greater total income rather than maximising gate receipts.

In this chapter's opening example, the state government of Victoria and the bidding organisation (then the Melbourne Major Events Company, which is now known as the Victorian Major Events Company) will have estimated the value of the television product to the broadcast network, the sponsor product to the sponsors, and the economic, social and cultural value of the Grand Prix event to the host community. It can be concluded that, ultimately, the AFL based its pricing strategy on the perceived value of its total product mix. Along similar lines, the price charged by the Grand Prix organisers for tickets makes up only a small component of the overall pricing equation. The final price charged by Grand Prix organisers includes a significant tax contribution by the local residents of Melbourne and Victoria, not to mention a range of environmental costs. Overall, the 'final price' paid for the right to host the event is a function of the range of benefits—both tangible (economic) and intangible (social and cultural)—that the event is able to generate.

Summary

In this chapter, price as one of the variables of the marketing mix was discussed in the context of setting or adjusting the price of a sport product. In order to arrive at a final price, a strategic pricing model was introduced. To enable the sport marketer to set appropriate prices, it is important to set pricing goals in concert with the overall organisational and marketing goals. Then the sensitivity of markets to changes in price can be determined and, as a consequence, the elasticity of demand established. This information, combined with marketing data such as the size of the market and the number of competitors, is used to estimate cost–volume–profit relationships, leading to the creation of a break-even chart with an emphasis on a cost-based pricing strategy. When the organisation is able to base its pricing on the demand in the market—in other words, when this is powerful enough to lead the way in setting price—the emphasis will be on demand-based pricing. It may, however, be more important to find out about the pricing strategies of competitors and to determine constraints (legal, social, other marketing mix variables) on pricing behaviour in the industry. This can lead to a competitor-based pricing strategy. When taking into consideration the time-dependence of many sport products, a combination of cost-based, demand-based and competitor-based pricing will often be exercised in setting the final price or adjusting the current price.

CASE STUDY

Pricing valued membership packages at the Greater Western Sydney Giants

By Lynley Ingerson and Jonathan Robertson

The Greater Western Sydney (GWS) Giants is the Australian Football League's (AFL) eighteenth team, and its newest expansion club. In their inaugural AFL season of 2012 the GWS finished eighteenth with only two wins. The GWS Giants and Gold Coast Suns are the result of the AFL's desire to have an AFL game played every week in two of Australia's most populous states: Queensland and New South Wales. Traditionally, both states have heavily followed Rugby Union and Rugby League; however the AFL is keen to increase its presence in these geographic areas. A key part of this expansion is to increase the club's membership base, in GWS's inaugural year the membership was 10 241 and in 2013 head coach Kevin Sheedy was hoping to increase this to 15 000.

As the newest team in a national competition, the GWS Giants have generated significant public interest backed by the support of the AFL—which wholly owns the club—via the recruitment of high-profile rugby league player Israel Falou (who increased the public interest in AFL in Western Sydney in his two years before again changing sport to Rugby Union), senior coach Kevin Sheedy and up-and-coming players in the national draft. Adding to the interest was the construction of a new boutique facility, Skoda Stadium, at the Sydney Showgrounds and a training camp at Blacktown.

The case of GWS Giants membership is also relevant, as public opinion views every AFL member gained in Western Sydney as one taken from either Rugby League or soccer—the AFL's main domestic competitors for spectators. In its bid to reach 15 000 members, the club offers a range of products for members and spectators in three categories: ultimate, giant and reserve. Table 6.3 identifies the various packages and prices.

TABLE 6.3

Membership Packages for Individual and Family Memberships

Class	Ultimate $A	Giant $A	Reserve $A
Adult	430	290	175
Concession	300	203	120
Junior (under 13 years)	129	75	45
Family (2 adults + 2 juniors)	989	655	395
Pet Membership	N/A	N/A	25

The new Skoda Stadium was opened after an upgrade and refurbishment in May 2012. With a seating capacity of 25 000, this boutique stadium offers a complete viewer experience in terms of design, function and comfort, such as the largest stadium video screen in the Southern Hemisphere and unique fan zones, members' bars and facilities. As shown in Sportsview 6.1, the GWS Giants operate in a market where there is excess supply; therefore a new state-of-the-art facility, an up-and-coming team full of the best talent and proximity of the stadium to public transport present an ideal opportunity to grow their membership base and begin to build long-term loyalty for their members through tiered membership packages.

When the demand for the sports product is greater than the supply, then prestige pricing can be established. In the case of the GWS Giants, supply is greater than demand, and the marketing department must develop suitable packages at a desirable price to stimulate demand. The GWS Giants club believes its successes both on and off the field are aligned to its pursuit of quality and excellence, and this presents the club with membership (packaging) opportunities to reflect these values. The selection of appropriate pricing strategies is essential in this competitive marketplace. They must reflect the organisation's overall objectives, the consumer's perception of value, and the type and quality of product being offered.

Questions

1 How would you describe the current pricing strategies used by the GWS Giants?
2 Consider the GWS Giants' new stadium. What pricing objectives could you develop for the team to reflect its 'new place'?
3 How would you make sure the price set is not too high or too low?
4 How can the new objectives support other elements of the GWS Giants' marketing mix?
5 Develop a pricing strategy for a range of membership (individual and corporate) packages for the GWS Giants, including a timeline for launching memberships for the new season—for example, how long before kicking off the new season do you need to put the new pricing strategy in place?

Stage 1—Identification of marketing opportunities

▼

Stage 2—Strategy determination

Step 5—Determine core marketing strategy

Marketing and service mix—sport product, pricing, **place (physical evidence, people, process)**

▼

Stage 3—Strategy implemention, evaluation and adjustment

7

The place of the sport facility

CHAPTER OBJECTIVES

Chapter 7 introduces the facility as the most important means by which sport services are distributed. Place as an element of the marketing mix is discussed in terms of preparing for and delivering quality service to visitors to the facility. Where to focus attention in relation to preparation for the sporting contest (planning and physical evidence) and actual delivery (people and process) are the central concepts discussed in this chapter. The practice of blueprinting is introduced to assist in this analysis. The chapter also examines different channels of distribution in sport.

After studying this chapter, you should be able to:

- identify the critical elements of the sportscape model
- identify and apply the four variable components of place
- create a blueprint of how a sport product is delivered
- identify the marketing channels through which sport products can be delivered.

HEADLINE STORY

Venues for now and the future

The regeneration of East London was a central component of the legacy of the 2012 Olympic Games. East London suffered from long-standing problems of multiple deprivation, and as a result was historically one of the poorest parts of the United Kingdom, struggling to keep pace with many of the socio-economic advances experienced elsewhere in London. The Games provided a unique opportunity to tackle these issues, and as such the focus was placed on:

- ensuring that the Olympic Park could be developed after the Games as one of the principal drivers of regeneration in East London, maximising the investment in venues, infrastructure, utilities and the environment
- securing a socio-economic legacy from the Games in the host boroughs so that, 'within 20 years, the communities which host the 2012 Olympic and Paralympic Games will enjoy the same social and economic chances as their neighbours across London' (Thornton et al., 2012).

When London successfully bid for the event in Singapore in 2005, the bid was based on a vision to 'Inspire a Generation', and as such was heavily based on sustainability and legacy themes. For London and the United Kingdom, the Olympics served as a tool to reach an aspirational future as much as being a global hallmark event.

The central legacy pillar in this bid was the transformation of East London. The 2.5 square kilometre area was traditionally one of the poorest areas in the United Kingdom, and was known for its 'derelict, polluted and inaccessible land' (Thornton et al., 2012). Adopting a strategic approach, the Olympic Delivery Authority (ODA), in partnership with its stakeholders, demolished 200 buildings, created 100 hectares of 'green space' and built 10 000 new homes—of which 4000 were to be allocated as affordable housing for the local community—as well as a new utilities network and 30 bridges and connections into East London.

To complement the physical transformation of the area, the Olympic Park facilities were designed with a focus on sustained future use. By adopting learnings from previous Olympic Games in Beijing and Sydney, the London Olympics was the first games to define and measure its carbon footprint. To achieve this, the ODA emphasised both the materials used for construction and the construction process itself. Over 63 per cent of materials were transported to the site via rail or water, in preference to carbon-intensive road transport, and almost all the materials (98 per cent) from the Olympic Park demolition were reused or recycled. In addition to utilising the least carbon-intensive materials feasibly possible, the ODA adopted sustainable design through using natural lighting throughout its facilities, reducing the need for heating and cooling in venues through low ceilings and partitioning the venues, and via innovative design of the Games' 25 temporary facilities. Combined, these efforts led to significant reduction in the carbon footprint of the Olympic Games venues (47 per cent) and non-essential comfort cooling (82 per cent) (LOCOG, 2012). Post-Games, East London's new sporting infrastructure, urban renewal and shopping districts are likely to be further utilised and developed to become a significant public space for London into the future—a significant departure from an area that was known for its run-down buildings and polluted soil.

In Chapter 1, place as an element of the marketing mix was described as distributing the product to the right place at the right time to allow ease of purchase. A unique characteristic of the sport distribution system was described, in that sports generally do not physically distribute their product. Most sport products are simultaneously produced, delivered and consumed at the one location, at one point in time. The exceptions are sporting goods and broadcast sport. Given this characteristic of the sport-distribution system, the sport venue or facility becomes the most important element in the distribution strategy of the sporting organisation. In other words, the place variable in the marketing mix is the sport facility.

By manipulating the elements of the marketing mix into varying combinations, different marketing strategies can be created. For one group of customers, the sport marketer will use the place variable differently from another group of customers. To be able to do this, it is necessary to identify the variable components of the marketing mix element of place. It is no coincidence that the last three of these variable elements of place are also elements of the services marketing mix. The variable components of place are:

- facility planning
- physical evidence
- process, and
- people.

The variable components are presented in Figure 7.1 and are discussed in more detail in following sections of this chapter. The variables are presented in the sequence shown in Figure 7.1 because decisions made at a higher level (such as facility planning) dictate decisions at the lower levels.

After identifying the different variable components of place, bringing them together in an integrated fashion becomes the primary task of the sport marketer, which will be the topic of the next section. Where and when to interfere and exert influence can be mapped out in a blueprint, or overview, of the sport service-delivery system. The chapter finishes with a discussion of more traditional distribution systems, mainly used to distribute sporting goods but, as a conceptual model, also applicable to sport service products.

Sport as a service product is briefly discussed in Chapter 5, and is covered more extensively in Chapter 8. But in order to fully appreciate the variable components of the

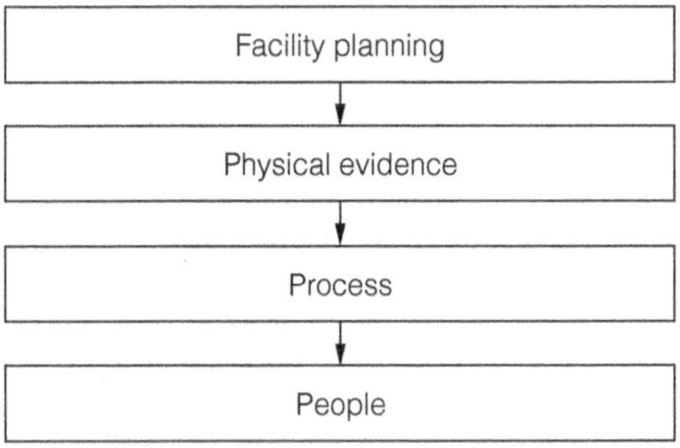

FIGURE 7.1 Variable components of place

(sport) place, a closer look at what makes up the sport facility—or 'sportscape'—is justified. We can indeed define the service environment in and around the stadium as the 'sportscape'. A considerable amount of research has been conducted into the influence of the fixed elements of the servicescape—that is, those elements that remain the same from game to game (Wakefield and Sloan, 1995; Wakefield and Blodgett, 1994, 1996; Wakefield, Blodgett and Sloan, 1996; Lambrecht, Kaefer and Ramenofsky, 2009; Green and Hill, 2012). These elements include layout accessibility, facility aesthetics, seating comfort, electronic equipment and displays, and facility cleanliness.

The Wakefield and Blodgett (1996) study found that layout accessibility, facility aesthetics, seating comfort, electronic equipment and displays, and facility cleanliness all have a significant influence on how sport fans perceive the quality of the stadium. In turn, the higher this perceived quality of the sportscape is, the higher the sport fan's satisfaction with the sportscape will be. If sport fans are more satisfied, they are likely to stay in the stadium for a longer period (and spend more money!); also, they are likely to return more often. These relationships between the sport fan's behavioural intentions and the sportscape are presented in Figure 7.2.

Now that we have established the importance of the inanimate and permanent structure that is the sport facility, and its impact on sport fans' response to the distribution of sport products, it is time to introduce the first variable element of place. The case study looking at the London Olympic Games at the start of this chapter further serves as an example of the first important consideration pertaining to planning the sport distribution system: facility planning.

Facility planning

Planning of facilities for mega-events like the Olympic Games, or facilities for a professional basketball club or the local sport club, should all involve a long-term perspective of the prospective usage of the facility. With production and consumption of the sport products taking place in the facility, both current and future provision need to be taken into consideration. It is extremely costly to redevelop and redesign existing facilities. Figure 7.2 also shows that those elements that directly derive from how we plan for the development of the facility affect the purchase behaviour of sport fans. In

FIGURE 7.2 Sportscape model

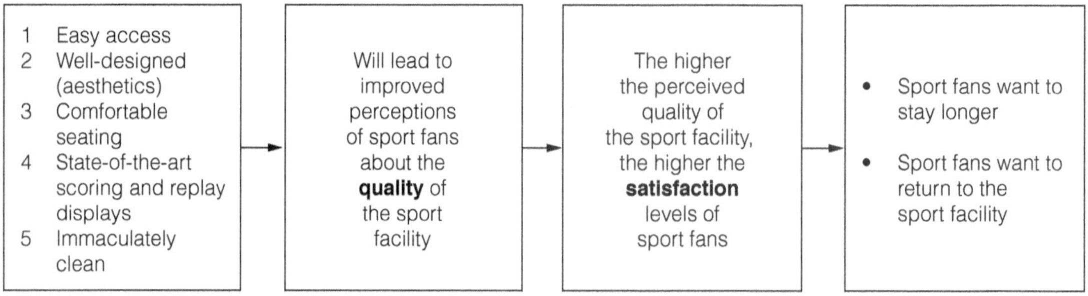

Source: Adapted from Wakefield and Blodgett (1996: 46)

that regard, does the sport facility as it currently is significantly determine opportunities and limitations for sport product provision? For example, due to its size and design, the Olympic Park soccer stadium in Melbourne is not able to host a cricket or Australian Rules football match. The physical conditions of Olympic Park (poor drainage, flooding and limited seating) meant the facility was below standard for staging elite events. As a result, the state government of Victoria, in conjunction with the Melbourne and Olympic Parks Trust, redeveloped Olympic Park at a cost of A$268 million to build AAMI Park, a purpose-built rectangular stadium. The stadium is perceived to be the 'missing link in Melbourne's sport infrastructure' (Melbourne and Olympic Parks, 2007). It will host elite-level competition, primarily for soccer, Rugby Union and Rugby League, and have a seating capacity of 31 000. The Amsterdam Arena in the Netherlands, on the other hand, can host soccer matches at any time of the year. Opened in 1996, it is the world's first 'real grass' soccer stadium with a retractable roof. Excessive rainfall is not a potential limitation. Since the opening of the arena, other sport providers have followed suit. For example, Etihad Stadium in Melbourne has a retractable roof, allowing for soccer, 'indoor' cricket and AFL matches through its unique Australian design. It must be noted that the Amsterdam Arena in particular has had problems ensuring that the 'real grass' playing surface is of sufficient quality (due to limited daylight exposure) to play premier league soccer matches. This just shows that when you plan to solve one problem, another may arise.

Many sporting arenas around the world were originally developed and built to host sporting events and enable a certain number of spectators to watch the game. Few of the older arenas, however, were built to host guests in corporate boxes. With many sporting organisations dependent on corporate dollars, an old stadium can become a severe competitive disadvantage. In other words, the ability to cater for a range of sport products is highly dependent on the planning and design of the sport facility. The state of Victoria in Australia proudly communicates its building of a wide range of international standard stadiums and sport facilities for horse-racing, tennis, football (all codes), basketball, cricket, netball and the Commonwealth Games, with the intention of attracting more sports fans and revenues to the city. Sportview 7.1 further discusses the importance of the sport facility and its physical environment.

SPORTVIEW 7.1

The importance of the sportscape for repeat sport participation in fitness centres

In the case of leisure services, it is more than just the perceived quality of the service rendered (such as whether a meal was delivered in a timely fashion) that influences whether consumers are satisfied with the service experience. For example, the purpose of going to an amusement park, a theatre or a sporting event would seem to be for the excitement and stimulation of the experience. This kind of situation differs from a trip to the dry-cleaner, in which the customer is not likely to have any expectation of emotional arousal.

Because the sport product is generally purchased and consumed simultaneously, and typically requires direct human contact, customers and employees interact with each other within the organisation's physical facility. Ideally, therefore, the organisation's environment should support the needs and preferences of both service employees and customers simultaneously. Even before purchase, consumers commonly look for cues about the organisation's capabilities and quality. The physical environment is rich in such cues, and may be very influential in communicating the organisation's image and purpose to its customers.

Based on Bitner's (1992) concept of the servicescape, Wakefield and Sloan (1995) suggest that sports facilities themselves may have a substantial effect on the customer's satisfaction with the service experience, and hence can play an important role in determining whether the customer will re-patronise the service-providing sporting organisation. The important aspects of the sportscape are the spatial layout and functionality of the facility, and the elements related to aesthetic appeal.

Wakefield and Blodgett (1994) tested the importance of the servicescape on Major League Baseball (MLB) consumers. The effect of the servicescape has been gaining increased attention from owners of MLB teams, as rising attendance and increased fan satisfaction have accompanied new stadiums in Baltimore, Cleveland, Texas, Toronto and Chicago. MLB stadiums provide a good setting in which to explore both the layout and functionality aspects of the servicescape, as well as its aesthetic appeal. The ways in which seats, aisles, hallways and walkways, food-service lines, restrooms, and entrances and exits are designed and arranged influence fan comfort, while the external environment, the architectural design, facility upkeep and cleanliness, use of decorative banners and signs, and personnel appearance all influence the ambience of the place.

Wakefield and Blodgett (1994) exposed potential customers to two different servicescapes: one old, low-quality servicescape stadium and one new, high-quality servicescape stadium. They found that the old stadium was being perceived as a significantly lower quality servicescape compared with the new one.

Respondents who perceived the servicescape to be of high quality reported higher levels of satisfaction with the servicescape, and hence were more willing to attend future games. Respondents who perceived the servicescape to be of high quality also experienced greater levels of excitement, and hence satisfaction with the servicescape. It was also found that respondents who felt crowded were less excited about the servicescape and perceived the servicescape to be of lower quality.

The results of the study may have direct implications for those who have investments in stadium projects. A return in increased gate receipts might be expected owing to new stadiums or renovations. Spectators are likely to be more excited and more satisfied when in a high-quality stadium, and therefore more likely to return. Consistently fielding a winning team is increasingly expensive and difficult, owing to uncontrollables such as player injuries and changes in competitors' performances. Thus another basic recommendation coming from this study is that owners/managers should be sure that the controllable aspects of the servicescape are properly managed to maximise stadium capacity.

Source: Adjusted from Bitner (1992: 57–71); and Wakefield and Blodgett (1994: 66–76).

Based on extensive market research, economic trend analysis and environmental scanning, the sport marketer can determine current demand and predict future customer needs. This should lead to market information on which specialists such as the architect and the engineer can base their sport facility planning and construction. If the sport marketer can influence facility location, design and construction decisions, the place variable will be optimised in terms of facility opportunities. It should be noted, though, that many sport marketers have to work with existing sport facilities. Nevertheless, identification of the service provision opportunities and limitations of the facility remains a task to be performed by the sport marketer in order to move on to the next step: supplying physical evidence.

Physical evidence

As described in Chapter 1, the sport product itself is intangible and subjective, making it harder for the sport marketer to sell the sport product as a commodity, standardised in quality and physical shape. Legg and Baker (1987) identify three major areas of concern that customers face when purchasing services:

- understanding the service offering
- identifying the evoked set of potential service providers, and
- evaluating the service before, during and after purchase.

Stated differently, it is hard for the customer to judge the quality of the product and then compare it with other products (providers) to arrive at a final purchase decision. If the sport marketer is able to make the sport product more tangible for the customer prior to purchase, the customer is more likely to buy it. Physical representation, if unique and attractive, can 'tangilise' the facility, giving it brand identity and inducing strong mental images (Mittal, 2002). Hence the sport marketer has to provide the sport product with physical evidence.

Physical evidence should support the quality characteristics of the product, because the majority of customers will judge the product on its quality. Physical evidence can be enhanced by optimising:

- sport facility design
- 'virtual' walkthroughs of the facility
- online marketing and social media groupings/discussions, linking participants to a venue
- promotional material and advertising, and
- service provision (discussed below).

The sport facility

The sport facility is the most tangible and visible physical evidence sport marketers can have for their products. The name of the facility can be displayed and marketed as the place where exciting events occur. The FA Cup at Wembley, the Australian Football League (AFL) Grand Final at the Melbourne Cricket Ground and the National Basketball Association (NBA) playoffs at Madison Square Garden are all examples of events growing in their perceived quality in combination with the respective venues. Who would get excited about the FA Cup at Queenstown football ground, the AFL Grand Final at Bendigo football oval or the NBA playoffs at Pinola basketball stadium?

High-tech scoreboards showing instant replays and the provision of sports trivia enhance the tangibility of the event (and hence the perceived quality of the sportscape, as shown in Figure 7.2). In addition, banners, photographs or statues of sporting heroes can decorate the outside and inner walkways of the facility. Portraits of all past Australian Open tennis champions decorate the inside walkways of Melbourne Park. Video or television screens and trophy exhibitions can show the famous moments of success of the teams playing in the facility. The museum at Barcelona Football Club's Nou Camp stadium in Spain installed a continuous video display of Ronald Koeman's winning goal in the final of the 1992 European Club championships at Wembley Football Stadium. In 2006, the images of winning the Champions League for the first time were added. The European Cup stands next to the 8.5 metre video display to further provide physical evidence. More recently, the application of games technology with content management has added a new dimension in displaying digital interactive multimedia to any output screen around the facility, further enhancing the ability to involve the public in the active imagery of sport organisation history.

Promotion

Because of the intangibility of the sport product, promotion is another way to add to the physical evidence. Adding this physical evidence is not specific to distribution through the facility, and examples are therefore not necessarily facility-linked. Through either advertising or promotions, distributed among potential customers or distributed by direct mail to selected markets, the quality image and brand name of a sporting organisation can be enhanced. Legg and Baker (1987) suggest that advertisements should be vivid, using relevant tangible objects, concrete language and/or dramatisations. Photographs of past events, listings of services and explanations of different product offerings will materialise intangible services offered by the organisation. Media channels are another important consideration. Satisfied customers prepared to participate in these promotions can be used to endorse the different products, communicating their satisfaction. Celebrities, including athlete celebrities, can also be used in this process as an influential and forceful communication channel. This type of promotion is explored in Chapter 13. In 2006, the NFL Miami Dolphins introduced hand-held video technology into the stadium for their fans. This enabled each fan to view network broadcasts of Dolphins games and fantasy statistics while at the stadium. The intention of management was clearly 'to improve the fan experience' (Dolphin Stadium 2006), but in the process another avenue for the promotion of the sport organisation was opened up. Furthermore, with the development of fourth generation (4G) mobile technology and a trend for major sports facilities such as Real Madrid's Santiago Bernabeu to increase their wireless network capability, the second screen (mobile, tablet, laptop) is becoming a personalised 'fan experience' complement for live scores, replays and statistics for spectators at the live event.

Irrespective of the media channel used, the sporting organisation should try to link pictorial (posters, merchandise, advertisements) and written (brochures, flyers, advertisements) physical evidence to the name of the organisation. Licensing strategies (team merchandise) used by the Los Angeles Lakers, Cricket Australia (CA) and Manchester United Football Club are excellent examples of sporting organisations adding to their physical evidence and making money with their marketing promotions. These organisations also show that the fit between the name of the organisation and physical evidence is very important when considering a licensing and merchandising strategy. This topic is discussed in Chapter 16.

Process

So far, only the variables that can be manipulated when preparing for the customer to come to the facility to buy and consume the product have been discussed. Purchase and consumption involve the process by which the sporting organisation actually distributes the product to the customer. Sport marketers heavily involved in this sport service-delivery process can influence and optimise the contacts between the customer and the sporting organisation. Shilbury (1994: 31) notes that 'the facility is of paramount importance because it represents the convergence of the marketing and operations functions'.

The marketing function

Grönroos (1990) distinguishes between the marketing department and the marketing function of an organisation. In traditional consumer goods marketing, the marketing department is the unit responsible for planning and implementing marketing activities. Deciding on how to market a can of beans is almost the sole responsibility of the marketing department of the manufacturer; the retailer has only to put it on the shelf and sell it.

In an emerging service economy, however, marketing activities (delivering the service as opposed to selling the beans) cannot be taken care of solely by the marketing department. Contacts between the service provider (for example, the basketball club) and the customer are so important in terms of overall customer satisfaction that marketing activities have to be carried out by the whole organisation, not only the marketing department. Ushers and food and beverage sellers are producing and delivering parts of the overall service package and can be identified as 'part-time marketers'. They belong to what Grönroos (1990: 177) defines as the marketing function, 'including all resources and activities that have a direct or even indirect impact on the establishment, maintenance, and strengthening of customer relationships, irrespective of where in the organisation they are'.

Sport servuction model

The process by which the overall package of services is planned, produced and delivered to the customer can best be explained with the help of the sport servuction model shown in Figure 7.3. This model will be explained further by using service delivery at a basketball match as an example. The term 'servuction' refers to the visible production and delivery of the service experience.

The sport servuction system model portrays the invisible and visible parts of the organisation. In the invisible part, facility management and the two basketball clubs'

FIGURE
7.3
The sport servuction system

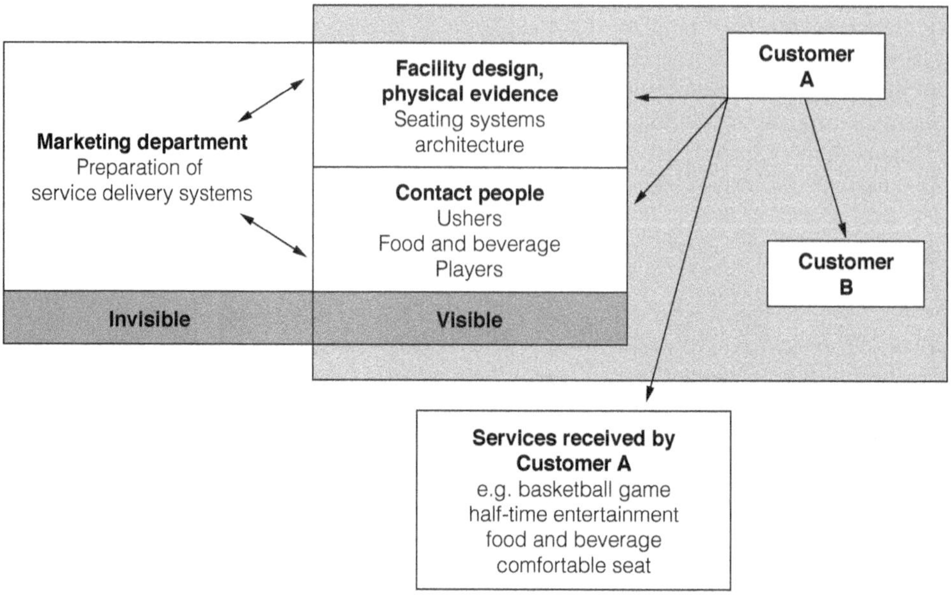

Source: Adjusted from Langeard et al. (1981). Reprinted with permission of the publisher.

managements combine to organise and plan for game night. This can be classified as the traditional marketing department role. The visible part of the organisation consists of the facility itself, the inanimate environment (physical evidence) and the service providers (contact people). The importance of the inanimate environment was described earlier in this chapter. Contact people—ticket sellers, ushers, and food and beverage sellers, but also the basketball players—provide the different services to the customers. This accumulation of services represents the customer's overall perception of their interaction with other customers, facility staff and players.

It is in the invisible part of the organisation that managers put together the service-delivery process. Questions about issues like where merchandising stands are located, how many ticket sellers and ushers are needed, how ticket sellers and ushers are expected to approach customers and how many food and beverage stands will be operated are asked in the cause of optimising the service-delivery process. Later in this chapter, the sport service-delivery system is blueprinted based on the sport servuction system model. First, however, it is necessary to include people as the final variable component of place.

People

Staff are responsible for the delivery of the product, and as a consequence are the main distinguishing quality factor in the consumption process. The outcome of the basketball game cannot be guaranteed; therefore, consistency in service delivery is of the utmost importance in determining the customer's overall perception of the quality of the sport product. In Chapter 8, five criteria that customers use to evaluate service quality are discussed further. These are:

- tangibles
- reliability
- responsiveness
- assurance, and
- empathy.

These five criteria show the importance of marketing function personnel in the delivery of quality service. Apart from tangibles (partly personnel) and security, all the criteria are fully dependent on the training, skills and abilities of people in delivering high levels of service quality. The selection and training of human resources for service delivery in sport are tasks in which the sport marketer should have strong involvement. The level of training, skills and abilities of potential employees of the sporting organisation become 'people variables' that will make the difference between mediocre and excellent service provision.

Blueprinting the sport service delivery system

Having identified the four variable components of the marketing mix element place, and knowing how one component can be varied independently from the other components, the sport marketer can start looking at how to combine the different components in an integrated fashion. By identifying operations (service preparation and service delivery) within the physical design of the sport facility, it is possible to create an overview or blueprint of the sport service delivery system. The blueprinted sport service delivery system will incorporate the four variable components of place. It is now up to the sport marketer to create the right mix of what is to be produced and consumed in the system.

Figure 7.4 displays a blueprint of the sport service delivery system for a basketball match. It follows the flow of customers through the facility and identifies different parts of the sport facility where interactions between the customer and facility personnel take place. The accumulation of these interactions contributes to the overall service experience of the customer.

Facility planning and physical evidence directly affect all visible operations. The design of the facility determines how easy it is for customers to move between their seats, restrooms, and food and beverage stands. Physical evidence such as signage not only tells customers where to go and what is going on in the facility during their visit, but can also be used to advertise or communicate upcoming events. Poster and video displays of past events can increase the customers' perception of being in a place where the product is basketball entertainment.

Facility planning has an equally important influence on invisible operations. How monitoring, maintenance and television operations take place is highly dependent on provisions made in the design and construction of the facility.

Figure 7.3 showed that the planning and preparation of the service-delivery system took place in the marketing department (an invisible part of the organisation). This involved process and people issues, such as how to approach customers, how to supply them with information or food, how many employees would be needed on game night

FIGURE 7.4

Blueprint of the sport service delivery system of a basketball game

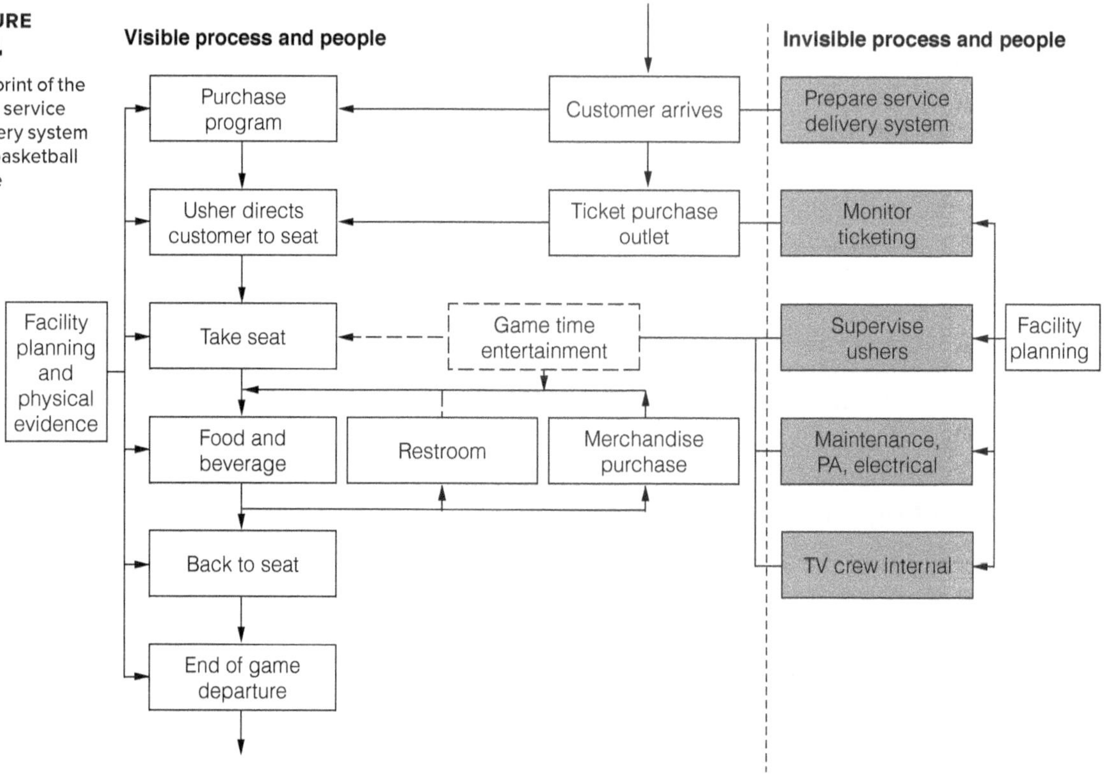

and for which functions (ushers, food and beverage sellers, ticket sellers), and how often and when to clean restrooms. With larger crowds, parking issues and crowd flow to and from the facility become important.

The blueprint tracks the customer from entering the facility to exiting the facility, and maps all possible interactions with the sporting organisation and its personnel. The blueprint identifies where the sport marketer can influence and vary the different components of place. A blueprint is therefore a vital instrument for the sport marketer in optimising the service experience. It is, however, only a start. As described at the beginning of this chapter, the actual delivery of service is the key to success.

In the final section of this chapter, traditional marketing channels are discussed—again using the basketball example to relate these channels to the distribution of sport products.

Marketing channels for sporting goods and services

It was noted earlier that most sport service providers deliver the sport product to the customer directly. The organisations involved in the process of making the product available for consumption or use are jointly called a marketing channel. The marketing channel performs different functions in order to enable producer and customer to exchange goods or services. Boyd, Walker and Larréché (1998) identify the following functions of marketing channels:

- transportation and storage
- communication of information via advertising
- personal selling
- sales promotion
- feedback (marketing research)
- financing, and
- services such as installation and repair.

A trade-off between costs and benefits will decide whether channel intermediaries are necessary to perform some of these channel functions. Figure 7.5 shows different marketing channels for sport products.

Channels A and B are the most important marketing channels for sport products. The majority of sport service products will be delivered through those channels, as discussed earlier in this chapter. Channel A shows the delivery of the sport product through the sport facility. Because the facility usually is owned and operated by a third party, the facility provider is the channel intermediary. Channel B shows the distribution of televised sport and distribution through a facility provider. Both the television station and the facility owner are channel intermediaries at the same level in the channel. They depend on each other to get the product to the consumer.

Channels C and D are more applicable to sporting goods. Manufacturers of sporting goods will often use wholesale organisations, or even agents (persons selling to wholesale organisations), to channel their product from the manufacturing plant to the retailer

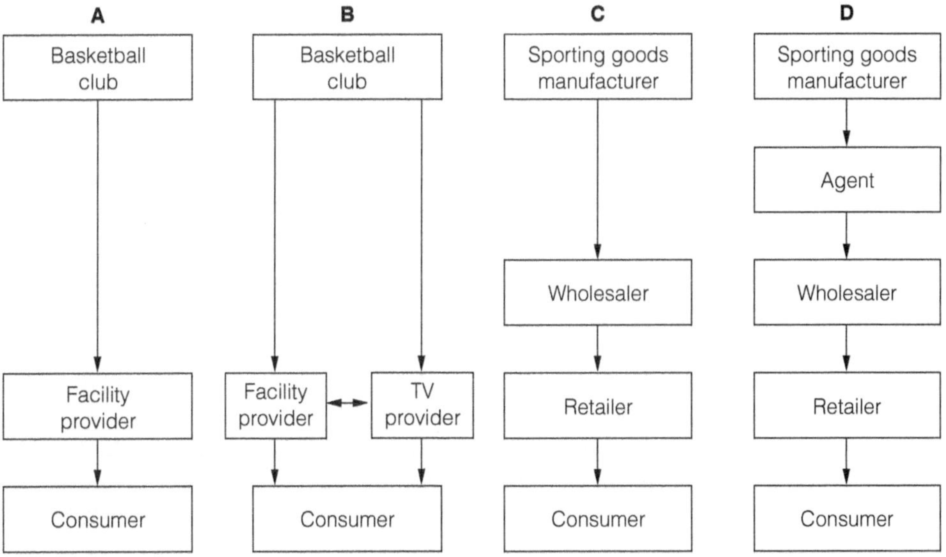

FIGURE 7.5 Marketing channels for sport products

and ultimately to the final consumer. Manufacturing organisations use other organisations in the marketing channel to concentrate on what they do best—namely, manufacturing. Overall costs will become too big for the manufacturing organisation if it has to fulfil all marketing channel functions (for example, marketing and sales to the final consumers of the product). The manufacturing organisation therefore hires other organisations to perform those functions.

The longer a marketing channel, the less control an organisation has over delivery of the product to the final consumer. Because actual service delivery is critical to consumer satisfaction, sport service organisations should aim to keep their marketing channels as short as possible, as shown in channels A and B.

In the headline story, the organising committees of the London Olympic Games have used all described marketing channels to distribute the variety of sport products. Olympic sport events were distributed through newly built facilities or existing/renovated government-owned facilities. Some events were not shown on television (channel A). The majority of events, however, were broadcast throughout the world on television (channel B). Huge amounts of licensed Olympics merchandise were produced by many different manufacturers around the world, using channel C or D as their means of distribution. After the Games, ownership of the facilities and actual users were largely separated, and the distribution of sport products now predominantly takes place through channels A and B. Both before and during the distribution process, facility planning, physical evidence, process and people are all place variables to consider in the short and long term. Quality service delivery both during and after the Games was, and will continue to be, of the utmost importance.

Summary

This chapter described and explained the unique characteristics of the sport-distribution system. Identifying sport products primarily as service products, it was explained how layout accessibility, facility aesthetics, seating comfort, electronic equipment and displays, and facility cleanliness all have a significant influence on how sport fans perceive the quality of the stadium. In turn, the perceived quality of the sportscape affects the sport fan's satisfaction with the sportscape. And if sport fans are more satisfied, they are likely to stay in the stadium for a longer period, spend more money and return to the stadium more often.

Following the importance of the inanimate stadium, the chapter continued by discussing the four variables of place: facility planning, physical evidence, process and people. Sport product delivery can be enhanced by planning and designing the facility to suit customer and management needs. Providing physical evidence to the intangible sport service product can enhance distribution of the sport product and the actual service delivery process, and the people involved in this process are crucial to the success of the sporting organisation. Where and when to intervene, and how to influence the service-delivery process, were highlighted by introducing the blueprint, or an overview of the sport service delivery system. The chapter finished with a discussion of distribution systems, or marketing channels, used to distribute sport products.

CASE STUDY

The future of the sportplace—build it and they will come . . . ?

As observed by Westerbeek and Smith (2003): the issue of stadium capacity is a double-edged sword. On the one hand stadia with limited capacity will lead to occupants not profiting from maximising their gate receipts. On the other hand, too large stadia contribute to increased operational costs, lack of atmosphere and consequently, lack of support from the fans, impacting on other business areas of the club like sponsorship, corporate hospitality and TV revenue.

Although the trend in international sport business is for the importance of gate receipts as a component of the overall revenue picture to decline, a comparison of six European football leagues shows how important this income stream still is.

FIGURE 7.6

Income (% of total) from ticket sales in six major Football leagues in Europe

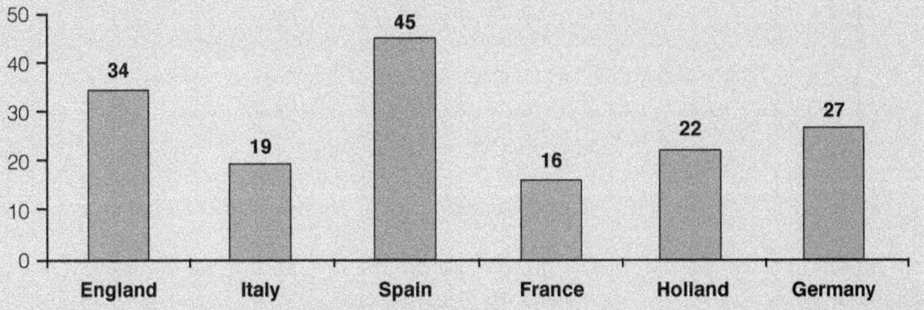

Sources: Boon (1999, 2001).

The multi-purpose requirement

Most modern-day stadia cannot afford to be built for single-sport usage. According to Rod Sheard, senior principal at sport architects HOK, 'stadia need to be future proofed by building a critical mass of other facilities that will ensure the project's economic survival in another 20 years' time' (Menary, 2001: 46). As a result of the changing functionality of sporting arenas, the current (fourth) generation of stadia incorporate facilities such as office space, hotels, restaurants, retail arcades, exhibition pavilions, television studios, business centres, health and fitness areas, and late-night activity options such as bars and nightclubs.

The corporate push

Traditionally, the cost structure of building new stadia has been based on the standard 'cost per seat'. Over the past two decades, the corporate push has seen an increase in costs for new stadia. In the early 2000s—depending on the standard of quality required, which largely relates to the type of league the club is playing in, and the type of customers it wants to target—stadium construction costs started as low as US$700 (A$726) per seat. According to Colin Fearns, director of Birse, the contractor building Leicester City's new stadium, you can get a nice stadium, including executive suites, for about US$1120 (A$1162) per seat (Menary, 2001), which is very reasonable compared with the US$1750 (A$1815) per seat costs of the Bolton Wanderers Reebok stadium. Nothing exemplifies the corporate push more than the difference between the new (opened 2009) and old (opened 1923) New York Yankees stadium. Nicknamed 'The House that Ruth Built', in reference to famed baseballer Babe Ruth, the new stadium is exactly the same field dimensions as the old; however, the reconstruction cost of US$1.7 billion (A$1.76 billion), equates to an amazing US$33 806 (A$35 077) per seat! The new home of the New York Yankees has a capacity of 50 287 people (6599 fewer than the previous stadium); more private luxury suites (nineteen compared with 56); 'party' suites (none compared with 410); concession stands (298 compared with 444) and has seen the doubling in size of, and upgrade to, a high-definition scoreboard. On top of this, corporate sponsors Delta, Audi and Jim Beam have their own lounge areas, and there is a Hard Rock Café in the stadium. The fact is that average income from corporate seats can amount to US$40,500 (A$42 022) per season, whereas the average income from a regular attendee will probably not exceed US$1620 (A$1680) per seat per season (New York Yankees, 2012). This explains why so many sport organisations devote more space to developing their corporate facilities. With this increased preoccupation with building, and hence catering for corporate hospitality, comes the impact on attendance patterns at matches. Not only is the corporate dollar an increasingly important source of revenue for facility operators, but the space in the stadium devoted to corporate facilities, the architectural building style and multiple relationships with other stadium stakeholders also require a reassessment of the facility's positioning strategies. In other words, the facility operators need to reassess their target markets.

Back to the future?

The sheer importance of investing in sport's 'hardware' infrastructure becomes clear when looking at the long-term stadium investment figures from England's Premier League. Jones (2012) reports that in the five years leading up to 2010–11 season, some £570 million (A$904.3 million) was invested by English clubs in upgrading existing stadiums or building new ones. Interestingly, despite this considerable investment on upgrading facilities, no new stadium projects have been undertaken by English clubs in the past five years, reflecting a difficult economic climate for major new stadia construction and spiralling player wage and transfer costs. Despite this, cumulative investment by English clubs in their stadia now stands at over £3.0 billion since 1992–93 with over 30 new stadia built during this period. Premier League average attendance dropped 2 per cent to 34 628 while capacity utilisation increased 3 per cent to 93 per cent for the 2011–12 season, compared with the year before.

In the United States, recent stadium development projects have turned back the clock. At least on the field, there seems to be a push towards re-establishing single-purpose stadia—particularly in soccer and baseball. Off-the-field multi-purpose space allocation (office space, restaurants, retail, etc.) does, however, remain the norm. Baseball teams in particular have recognised the value of the past, and have embarked on redeveloping existing ballparks or building new ones that reflect the history and tradition of the game, ensuring that the architecture blends in with the early 1900s inner-city buildings yet incorporating the latest technology that the modern-day fan requires to enjoy the game to the fullest—better views, in-seat interactive video screens, multiple replay screens in the stadium, comfortable seats, automated payment systems at concession stands and interactive games for the kids prior to, during and after the match. You may even want fries with that!

Sources: Boon (1999, 2001); Jones (2012); Menary (2001); New York Yankees (2012); Westerbeek and Smith (2003).

Questions

1 How do the variables 'facility planning' and 'physical evidence' apply to the different sections of this case study?
2 How do the variables 'people' and 'process' apply to the different sections of this case study?
3 Can you think of other standards that may replace 'cost per seat' as a better way to account for facility construction costs? Justify your answer.
4 Given the different distribution channels presented in Figure 7.5, can you suggest the most likely (future) distribution channel for spectator sport? You may want to consider the strategic distribution principle of 'vertical integration'.

8

Customer satisfaction and service quality

Stage 1—Identification of marketing opportunities

▼

Stage 2—Strategy determination

Step 5—Determine core marketing strategy

Marketing and service mix—sport product, pricing, place (physical evidence, people, process), **customer satisfaction**

▼

Stage 3—Strategy implemention, evaluation and adjustment

CHAPTER OBJECTIVES

Chapter 8 introduces customer satisfaction and service quality, two constructs central to customer retention and building loyalty, and therefore important to organisational success. The chapter details why sport organisations should provide high-quality service to consumers (both spectators and participants), focusing on the importance of both core and peripheral aspects of the sport product that consumers evaluate. It describes a relational approach to customer management and defines service quality and satisfaction, providing information on how to model and apply both. The chapter concludes by looking at the management and measurement of satisfaction and service quality in organisations, considering the centrality of customer expectations and best practice aspects to measurement.

After studying this chapter, you should be able to:

- recognise the importance of relationship marketing in developing an approach to service quality and satisfaction
- understand the sport service and recognise its varied aspects that customers evaluate
- understand the processes by which satisfaction and service quality are derived and the centrality of customer expectations to them, and
- understand measurement practices for customer satisfaction and service quality.

HEADLINE STORY

Money back and satisfaction guaranteed as sport promotions

One of the original and most innovative sport marketers was American Bill Veeck, a leader in sports promotion in the 1960s. His view was that the sport experience for consumers should have a focus on three areas: the fans, the game and the periphery, with the over-arching idea that to be satisfied, consumers should be immersed in conversation about the game and the sport experience. As well as a winning team—something over which marketers have little control—he argued that the game itself had to be attractively packaged and aggressively promoted, and that the comfort and satisfaction of the fan should be paramount. As part of this, he offered 'the money back guarantee' (Veeck and Linn, 1962), adding to his events a range of resources and product extensions to add value to the experience.

Decades later, many marketers—including those in sport—continue to develop the 'money back' concept as a sales promotion to attract consumers. In 2012, the Phoenix Suns of the National Basketball Association (NBA) held a 'Satisfaction Guaranteed Night', where consumers could acquire a refund on the purchase price of the game ticket if the experience did not satisfy. The Suns promoted the opportunity to see 'edge-of-your-seat action live . . . and if you're not completely satisfied with the experience, we'll give you your money back' (NBA, 2012). Customers—many of whom may have been first-time attendees trialling the Suns' match experience— could send in a copy of their ticket after the event to claim their refund, and were invited to tell the team what they did not enjoy about the game. In a very different 'money back' concept in 2012, the Gold Coast Titans of Australia's National Rugby League (NRL) announced a 'home-win guarantee'. Promoted by the team as a world first, fans would receive free entry to the next game if the team lost a designated early season game against the Melbourne Storm, with the promotion underwritten by team sponsor iSelect.

Sources: NBA (2012); Pierce (2012).

As described in the headline story, Bill Veeck's idea was one that conceptualised the importance of satisfaction in early forms of the sport entertainment product. Customer satisfaction was an important dimension of Veeck's vision, where the creation of product and service encounters within sport would lead to short- and long-term benefits for organisations. His promotional mechanism sought to motivate consumers towards trial or purchase, with the 'money back guarantee' limiting the perceived risk of consumers in doing so. Both the Suns and Titans examples shown above rely on the organisation delivering a satisfying experience—one through a range of potentially controllable factors, the other through the performance of the team. However, while running such a promotion for a one-off game or event can have benefits, should consumers not be satisfied, the organisation will lose money and potentially more. In short, be it a one-off experience or something offered on an ongoing basis, it is not economically nor operationally feasible for any sport organisation to have large portions of a crowd or consumer base dissatisfied, either in the short or long term.

The impact on organisations of losing customers through product or service 'churn' is well documented, as is the expense of attracting new customers to replace those who leave or switch brands. In countering these situations, service quality and customer satisfaction play a key role in understanding and retaining customers, as well as generating other positive post-purchase behaviours. Today, most sport marketers recognise the importance of satisfying spectators and participants, and providing experiences of high quality. This has developed as sport organisations have become more professional, and given more consideration to the service environment and perceptions of customers. In turn, this has encouraged acceptance that relationships with customers and delivery of service quality and customer satisfaction can provide a competitive advantage for organisations.

The sport experience—through either spectating or participating—has become increasingly complex, and the market for many products or services has grown more competitive. Substitutes such as other entertainment, cultural or arts offerings can deliver fulfilment for needs like excitement, escape and social interaction, so it is as important as ever for sporting organisations to develop a firm understanding of what generates quality perceptions and ultimately satisfaction. More satisfied consumers mean higher levels of renewal or continuing sales, but can also channel other benefits, including fewer complaints, more positive word-of-mouth promotion, the buying of additional products, less attention paid to competitors, reduced transaction costs and lower marketing expenses. The wider contribution of satisfaction and satisfied consumers can therefore be presented in terms of profitability, marketability and sustainability for a range of sporting organisations.

Defining sport services

A sport product is defined as 'any bundle or combination of qualities, processes, and capabilities that a buyer expects will deliver wanted satisfaction' (Mullin, Hardy and Sutton, 2000: 12). While consumer value and benefit from sport products contain both tangible and intangible elements, the offering can be classified as a sport service if the core benefit source is more intangible than tangible (Berry and Parasuraman, 1991). Given this definition, professional and amateur sports teams, health and fitness centres, and facilities are among examples of sport-related services (Stotlar, 1993).

The sport servuction model in Chapter 7 demonstrates a range of factors that contribute to satisfying experiences for sport consumers. These can include the inanimate environment, contact personnel and other customers. The model also includes 'invisible' aspects such as the organisation, its processes and its systems, including marketing departments. These broad aspects that drive satisfaction (for example, the facility, organisational processes, communications and other consumers) are much the same for a vast array of sport experiences, ranging from spectators at a professional football game to participants in an aerobics class or a social netball tournament.

As well as being multi-dimensional in the factors that influence fulfilment and satisfaction, many forms of sport consumption are complex combinations of aesthetic, emotional, identification and hedonic benefits (McDonald, Karg and Vocino, 2013). Therefore, many sport services and consumption activities are high in 'experience qualities' (Zeithaml, 1991), with consumers becoming heavily involved in their consumption as a result. Such cases present additional complexity for organisations, that need to be aware of this multi-faceted consumption and seek to manage the 'experience' rather than just the event.

Within the broad dimensions of the sport 'experience' are core products (that is, the game or sport itself) and the wider product extensions that make up the overall sport service experience. Marketing theory suggests that customer satisfaction and service quality result from both dimensions, with overall evaluations strongly influenced by the extensions or peripheral components. Until recently, little was known about dimensions in sport that most strongly influenced customer evaluations, but Australian research using season ticket-holders indicates that product extensions contribute strongly to customer satisfaction (McDonald, Karg and Vocino, 2013; van Leeuwen, 2001). The dominant role played by product extensions in a spectator's satisfaction is good news for sporting organisations, as they are often the components that fall under the control of sport marketers. To revisit the opening story, the Phoenix Suns have greater control over the satisfaction assessments of their consumers, given that they can ensure the quality of—and hence manipulate customer satisfaction arising from—such service aspects as ticket purchase, entry, merchandise, concessions and entertainment. This is different from the lack of control that Titans marketers have over the core product (the game itself), which will determine the short-term success of their promotion.

A relational approach to customers (and the role of satisfaction)

Similar to all industries, sporting organisations have broadened their focus from internal product development and performance to include greater attention on external stakeholders, including attitudes towards the products consumed (Grönroos, 1992). Functions of this altered approach are a long-term focus and a more involved view of the customer, which can be framed within a relationship marketing approach. Relationship marketing refers to efforts within marketing where the buyer and seller attempt to provide a more collectively satisfying exchange. From the organisational side, it seeks to go beyond single transactions with customers (Grönroos, 1992), and attempts to create richer relationships with greater personalisation, interaction and eventual loyalty. Principles of relationship management can assist in driving better understanding of consumers, help in the development of products and lead to consumer loyalty and related behaviours in the short and long term.

Relationship marketing is relevant where alternatives exist for customers, and where purchase may be periodic and continuing. One example is subscription markets, which are becoming more common in sport (and other marketing domains). These play a role in developing purchase relationships, enabling attachment and involvement with a brand, and can enhance switching barriers through contracts or fixed purchase periods. Utilities, phone and internet provision are examples of services that are often consumed as subscriptions, while it has become more common to find subscription products aligned to both spectator and participation forms of sport—in line with the tenets of relationship marketing.

The offering of a season ticket package or sporting club membership is a common subscription practice for professional sport clubs, with around one in 34 Australians a member of one of the collective eighteen AFL clubs in the 2012 season (Karg, Dwyer and McDonald, 2012). In each case, ticket packages can vary in price and offer different levels of game access, seating location and benefits like club communications and merchandise. Such products are becoming more common in sport and are moving beyond teams, with ticket packages or membership available for events like the Australian Open tennis tournament, while they are also used to build loyalty with products that provide more remote consumer experiences. An example here is the GreenEdge professional cycling team, which offers memberships to subscribers, despite their team's races taking place both in Australia and overseas, and rarely in the same place consistently. As such, without the core product offering (the sport event), memberships are still used to drive additional loyalty and commitment despite inconsistent physical examples of consumption.

Memberships as a form of subscription are replicated by various other arts and leisure organisations (e.g. theatre companies, zoos, art galleries, gyms) and at lower level or local sporting clubs where consumers might participate by playing for a team. Likewise, health and fitness clubs offer memberships for users that share some of the same characteristics.

With the exception of one-off events or purchases, there appear to be few sport services that would not benefit from a relationship marketing approach, whether they distinctly offer subscription products or not. So how do service quality and satisfaction play a role in building customer relationships? Traditional customer relationship management (CRM) theory proposes that the management and monitoring of customer expectations, followed by delivering service quality that successfully meets or exceeds such needs, are vital to long-term success (Grönroos, 1990). 'The most widely accepted framework is that customer perceptions of service quality (performance) impacts upon customer satisfaction which impacts upon future behaviour (e.g. loyalty, future purchase intention, word of mouth).' (McDonald, Karg and Vocino, 2013: 43).

Overall, a theoretical and practical evolution is occurring towards service quality and satisfaction as methods of developing and enhancing relationships with customers. Creating satisfying and high-quality experiences is important, alongside the adage that it is cheaper or easier for a business to keep existing customers rather than find new ones. While business growth ultimately can be achieved through either method, it seems logical that marketers should attempt to balance 'offensive marketing' that targets new customers and increasing purchase frequency with 'defensive marketing' concentrated on reducing turnover, managing dissatisfaction and increasing loyalty through increasing both customer satisfaction and the switching barriers relevant to consumption (Fornicatell and Wernerfelt, 1987).

Defining and differentiating service quality and customer satisfaction

As both service quality and customer satisfaction are attitudes or types of consumer evaluations, and therefore related constructs, they are often referred to in an interchangeable way. Differentiation between the two is important, though, and is most easily defined by satisfaction being experience dependent, while service quality is not experience driven, but rather led and formed by consumer perceptions. Distinctly, then, perceptions of service quality can result without actual experience of the product. As an example, individuals must experience a sport product to be either satisfied or dissatisfied with it, but no experience is necessary to develop perceptions of quality. Therefore, satisfaction can be posited as a higher order construct, depending on the perceptions of service quality, and specifically on consumer expectations prior to the consumption experience.

Service quality is defined in terms of a judgement about how excellent a sport service or service component is (Lovelock, Patterson and Walker, 2001; Parasuraman, Zeithaml and Berry, 1988). The more closely the spectator's or participant's perception approximates excellence, the higher their evaluation of service quality will be. Parasuraman, Zeithaml and Berry (1988: 13) suggest that service quality is an 'abstract and elusive construct because of three features unique to services: intangibility, heterogeneity, and inseparability of production and consumption'. Adding to their complexity, services are 'dominated by experience qualities, attributes that can be meaningfully evaluated only after purchase and during production-consumption' (Berry and Parasuraman 1991: 7). Therefore, customers do not evaluate service quality purely on the outcome, but also consider the process of the service that is delivered (Zeithaml, Bitner and Gremler, 1990).

Alternately, satisfaction is an overall evaluation occurring post-consumption, as opposed to service quality, which is a multi-dimensional appraisal of aspects of the product offering (Iacobucci, Ostrom and Grayson, 1995). Within this, research demonstrates that sport customers evaluate a virtual plethora of service components, with customers' summary or overall satisfaction and perception of quality being a function of many different, 'smaller' evaluations. Customer satisfaction is defined in terms of fulfilment in accordance with Oliver (2010: 8), who defines satisfaction as 'a judgement that a product or service feature, or the product or service itself, provided, (or is providing) a pleasurable level of consumption-related fulfilment, including levels of under- or over-fulfilment'. Satisfaction is said to occur as inevitably as purchase and consumption (Oliver, 2010), and can be viewed as an end state of the overall consumption experience, or a reflection of the attitudinal processes that contribute to satisfaction. In line with earlier distinctions, service quality can then be presented as an antecedent to satisfaction, with satisfaction moderating the relationship between service quality and future consumer intentions (Taylor and Baker, 1994).

SPORTVIEW 8.1

An appeal to the fans—uncovering quality improvements

On 19 December 2011, David Balfour, General Manager of the Sydney Blue Sox, a team in the Australian Baseball League, sent a letter to all members or season ticket-holders of the club. Fourteen games into the season, he noted that 12 per cent of members were yet to attend one game, and that it was 'quite disturbing that on any given day or night for regular season games, we have averaged less than 32% of the members attending'. Balfour continued: 'We really appreciate your support, but please understand the big picture about getting the stadium to look full. We have even received comments from our players on needing to address the issue of filling the stadium.'

The Blue Sox were faced with a situation where, despite improving their selling of tickets, they were unable to attract members to come to multiple games or become consistent attendees at matches. This was having an impact on the atmosphere at the ground, and on perceptions of the team, the league and the sport of baseball. After all, if members were not going to attend, how would games attract casual fans of the team?

The response to the letter through social media, blogs and forums provided multiple avenues of feedback. Some were supportive, suggesting that members should do more to support the team by coming to games while groups of members urged non-attendees to use available ticket resale avenues or give tickets away so seats could at least be used. Others provided different forms of feedback, leading to the discovery of a raft of service quality issues that were of concern to consumers. Some of these were from members, or those who had attended games, providing views on the experience. Other people—who freely admitted that they did not attend Blue Sox games—weighed in with their own ideas, at the same time providing valuable insight into perceptions of service at the games.

While perhaps not the expected response of the General Manager, the letter did generate considerable insights for the team—albeit largely through informal and public channels. Elements such as poor facilities, the need for more dynamic environments, poor selection and high prices of food and beer ('Baseball is a sport built around food!') and better integrating aspects of the 'baseball culture' to develop the Blue Sox fan experience were all prominent comments. What was clear was that members and the wider fan-base had low perceptions of many of the product extensions, which were particularly relevant to the sport of baseball.

Service quality

Despite a strong history of service quality research, there remains limited agreement on its conceptualisation (Cronin and Taylor, 1992; Rust and Oliver, 1994), such that 'there is no universal, parsimonious, or all-encompassing definition or model of quality' (Reeves and Bednar, 1994: 436). Most commonly, service quality is viewed as the customer's perceptions of excellence defined by impressions of service levels provided (Berry, Parasuraman and Zeithaml, 1988). Quality, then, is 'a reflection of the degree and direction of discrepancy between consumers' perceptions and expectations' (Parasuraman, Zeithaml and Berry, 1985: 1).

The concept of quality in marketing was first considered in the manufacturing sector, where quality originally looked solely at the end-product (that is, the finished good). Later, the focus would transition to broader production processes and then further to provide a starting point for understanding service quality. Admittedly, the concepts were not immediately transferable to service organisations, given differences such as inseparable production and consumption, and variation in service delivered across consumption periods. A focus on process in services would eventually become prominent, despite service quality remaining more complex to achieve than in manufacturing.

Adding to this complexity, sport organisations do not control the core sport product, which has resulted in marketers focusing more on delivering product extensions relevant to the sport product. In doing so, much more can be done to shape the experience of a consumer. For example, while a marketer of a professional sporting team cannot guarantee that a particular team will win or lose, they can develop processes and encourage outcomes of higher perceived quality of extensions such as entertainment, entry to the stadium or facility, ticketing, service and merchandise. Delivering these elements seeks in some ways to provide a 'barrier' to on-field performance, and provide a high-quality experience regardless of what happens on the field.

Modelling service quality

Service quality is a matter of perception (that is, the individual customer's perception), and two people who experience the same service may thus have very different perceptions of its quality. This is particularly so in the context of sport, where two customers—whether players or spectators—are barracking or playing for opposing teams. Further, an individual's perception of service quality may vary from one experience to the next, due to a range of factors that often are beyond the organisation's control, such as the customer's mood, loyalty, past experiences or who they are sharing the experience with.

For sport marketers to increase perceived quality of their services, a vital starting point is understanding how service quality is constructed by a consumer. Gaps within the service quality framework (Parasuraman, Zeithaml and Berry, 1985) assist with articulating how service quality develops for consumers (see Figure 8.1). Gaps exist among the expectations and perceptions of customers, management and employees. The

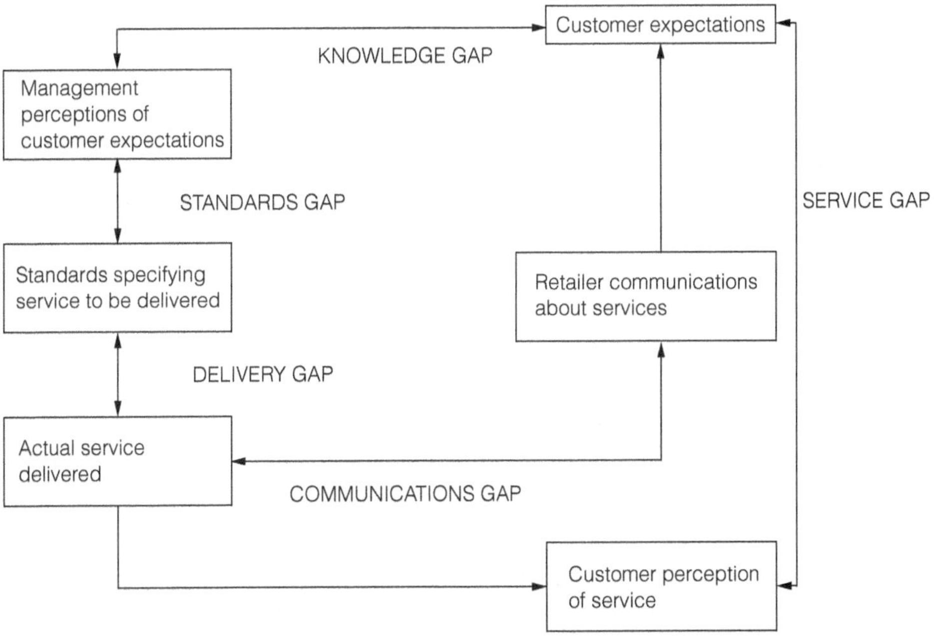

FIGURE 8.1 Conceptual model of service quality

Source: Hoffman and Bateson (1997). Reprinted with permission of South-Western College Publishing, a division of Cengage.

overarching service gap—between what customers expect and what they perceive they actually have—is a function of four other gaps described below.

- The *knowledge gap* exists between customer expectations of service and management perceptions of these expectations. It occurs when what management believes customers expect is different from what customers actually do expect (for example, a manager of a community sport centre might believe that players expect hour-long games of netball when they would instead prefer the opportunity to play shorter but more numerous games).
- The *standards gap* exists between management's perceptions of customer expectations and the organisation's service specifications. This gap occurs where there are insufficient resources to deliver what customers expect, or when management is apathetic to providing expected service levels (for example, a marketing manager of a professional basketball team may be aware that season ticket-holders expect more interaction with players, but may not see this as a priority or regard it as too difficult, given numerous other commitments of the players).
- The *delivery gap* exists between an organisation's service quality specifications and actual service delivery. It generally arises as a result of a lack of willingness or ability of the service personnel (for example, even if an aquatic centre's service charter may stipulate that service staff should be friendly and helpful to customers at all times, its staff may either be unwilling to fulfil this commitment to customers or simply not have the service or interpersonal skills to do so).
- The *communications gap* exists between perceptions of actual service delivery and external communications about the service. It occurs where an organisation over-promises in its advertising and other communications (for example, a professional sport club's advertisements promising its supporters a win at the next home game).

It is important that marketers are familiar with these potential gaps and how they contribute to spectators and participants getting what they expect. Expectations, whether driven by communications, service charters or past experiences, will impact consumers' evaluations of service quality. Sport marketers will be able to improve the quality of services by identifying and then closing each of the knowledge, standards, delivery and communication gaps. More on understanding and measuring consumers' attitudes and these gaps is provided in the following section.

Measuring service quality: SERVQUAL and applications to sport

The original tool to measure service quality is known as SERVQUAL, which has been adapted to a number of different contexts since its initial development. SERVQUAL is an instrument incorporating five service-quality dimensions, and is the most well-known and used tool for assessing service quality across a range of industries (Parasuraman, Zeithaml and Berry, 1988: 23). The five components (comprising 22 statements in total) are:

- tangibles—physical facilities, equipment and appearance of personnel
- reliability—ability to perform the promised service dependably and accurately
- responsiveness—willingness to help customers and provide prompt services

- assurance—knowledge and courtesy of employees and their ability to inspire trust and confidence, and
- empathy—caring, individualised attention that the firm provides its customers.

Use of SERVQUAL involves a series of questions around measuring: (1) expectations of excellence within a particular industry; and (2) consumer perceptions of the subject organisation. This is in line with the knowledge, standards, delivery and communications gaps described above, where expectations and perceptions are paramount in understanding gaps of managerial concern. For each of the SERVQUAL statements, both expectations and perceptions are asked, and then compared to assess where service gaps exist. Expectations and perceptions are measured on a multiple-point scale and compared to determine 'gap scores' for each of the five dimensions. SERVQUAL therefore allows assessment of service quality at the micro-level (for example, physical facilities or equipment), semi-global level (that is, tangibles or reliability) or the overall or macro-level (for instance, an holistic view of a sport service).

It was acknowledged by the original authors that, given the breath and variance of service experiences across industries, SERVQUAL should be modified and applied to new contexts. In line with this, a significant number of sport-based studies have developed frameworks of service quality in sport through adoption and modification of SERVQUAL.

For example, fitness centres and public recreation facilities have provided a basis for application of SERVQUAL dimensions (Chelladurai and Chang, 2000). The Service Attributes of Fitness Services (SAFS), Service Quality of Sport Centers (QUESC) and Service Quality Assessment Scale (SQAS) are among those measures that have identified dimensions of service quality in sport and fitness centres (Chelladurai, 1987; Kim and Kim, 1995; Lam, Zhang and Jensen, 2005). Aspects such as atmosphere, staff attitude, reliability, information, programming, price, convenience and facilities were all found to be important considerations.

Sport participation has also been a focus of research that has replicated core dimensions of the original SERVQUAL (Howat et al., 1996). The Service Quality of Sports Participants (SSQPS) scale looked at the range of programs, service interactions and results (physical and social change), as well as the delivery environment (Ko and Pastore, 2001). Scales have also been adapted specifically to outdoor activities or schools programs. In the case of the latter, elements such as cost, skills of staff, planning or organisational elements, social relations and communication were among those found to be important assessable areas.

Spectators have likewise been a setting with perceived quality elements found to include access, parking, aesthetics and cleanliness of facilities, quality of scoreboard, comfort, cost, concessions, service, crowd control, convenience and anti-smoking policy (Kelley and Turley, 2001; Wakefield and Sloan, 1995). More specifically, McDonald, Sutton and Milne (1995) developed TEAMQUAL by applying SERVQUAL dimensions focusing on service encounters in professional team sport. Similarly, Theodorakis et al. (2001) and other authors utilised the SPORTSERV tool to measure spectator service-quality perceptions in professional sports. The instrument included measurement of access (parking), reliability (delivering on promises), responsiveness (staff service), tangibles (stadium), and security and safety. Most recently, this scale was further developed using the five 'process' dimensions from the original SPORTSERV, combined with two 'outcome'-related dimensions of team performance (that is, players performed well) and game quality (that is, competitiveness of the game) (Theodorakis et al., 2013).

Overall, SERVQUAL has provided a useful base for application to various areas of sport services, including fitness centres, participation programs and spectating contexts. In many cases, these have largely been derived from the original SERVQUAL components, with unique applications to each service quality context. Their application has sought to deliver meaningful insight for managers around consumer perceptions of quality, weighted against expectations of what the service was expected to deliver.

Satisfaction

As noted earlier, there are important distinctions between service quality and satisfaction, including ongoing attention on how customer satisfaction and service quality are linked to customer service and wider aspects of relationship and service marketing. Service quality can be viewed as an antecedent of customer satisfaction, in that it influences but not fully predicts satisfaction levels (Theodorakis et al., 2013). Further, satisfaction was developed as requiring an experience of the product, as opposed to service quality being perception led.

As an overall measure, satisfaction represents a desirable end-state of consumption, and can facilitate a sense of achievement and reaffirmation of the decision-making competence of a consumer (Oliver, 2010). Satisfaction occurs as an inevitable result of purchasing or consuming a good or service, with variants of satisfaction including 'interim' and overall 'end-state' forms—that is, attitudes can be assessed both during and at the conclusion of a consumption experience (Oliver, 2010). Considering sport, and a complete consumption experience, dimensions or 'variants' may include satisfaction with events or elements during consumption (waiting in line, seat comfort, noise and surrounds), satisfaction with the final outcomes (enjoyment, entertainment, emotions) and satisfaction with the level of satisfaction received (inadequate, adequate, excessive). As such, the level of satisfaction can be viewed either in terms of singular event(s) leading to an outcome, or as a collective impression (Oliver, 2010).

Unless a good or service represents a one-off or isolated purchase, satisfaction should be viewed as an important measure, considering that ongoing customer interactions are a prerequisite to organisation success. Satisfaction has a viable link to primary variables like profitability and market share (Anderson and Mittal, 2000; Kotler, 2000) and secondary impacts like word of mouth and decreased complaints. While it is known that attitudes correlate with repurchase in the case of satisfied customers, dissatisfaction can result in negative word of mouth, complaining or other dysfunctional behaviours. Therefore, understanding what drives satisfaction for a range of products or services is important. In modelling satisfaction, it is known that different aspects can represent differing levels of importance, even where overall satisfaction is delivered equally. Additionally, it has been shown that the importance of various attributes can alter as a result of experience and expectations changing over time (Mittal and Kamakura, 2001).

Role of expectations and 'disconfirmation' in satisfaction

In understanding how satisfaction is determined, the 'disconfirmation of expectations' (Oliver, 2010) paradigm remains the dominant theoretical framework (McDonald, Karg and Vocino, 2013). A judgement of fulfilment under this model requires an outcome and a comparison point (Oliver, 2010), and denotes that customers: (1) form certain expectations of product performance; (2) observe or experience the performance; and (3) form perceptions of that performance. Note that where service quality considers expectations and perceptions, the Oliver (2010) model includes experience as a distinct part of the process. These experience-dependent *perceptions* of performance will be compared with the customers' originally held *expectations* (Churchill and Surprenant, 1982; Oliver, 2010). Together with customer satisfaction, these three determinants (expectations, perceived performance and disconfirmation) form the 'disconfirmation of expectations model' (DEM) depicted in Figure 8.2.

The DEM and subsequent interactions and rationalisation of performance versus expectations can produce three outcomes: negative disconfirmation (performance falls short of expectations); zero disconfirmation (or confirmation with what was expected); or positive disconfirmation—which can result in a highly satisfied consumer. Therefore, expectations can be met, they can be exceeded (resulting in consumer delight) or the experience can fall short of expectations.

Measuring satisfaction in sport services

Specific to sport, there has been an increasing amount of work dedicated to satisfaction with services, particularly spectator services. For example, perceptions of the servicescape or sport facility have been assessed in terms of their impact on satisfaction and re-

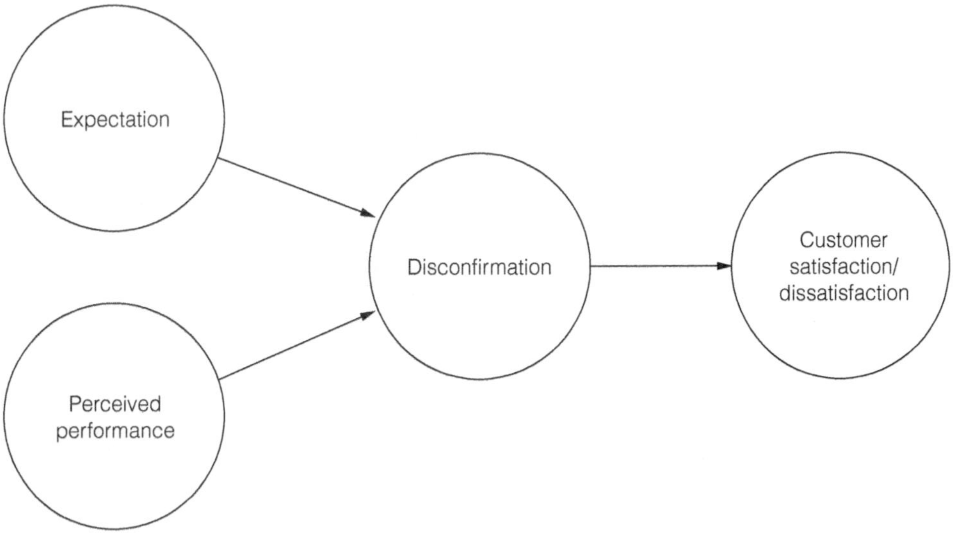

FIGURE 8.2 Disconfirmation of expectations model (DEM) of customer satisfaction

patronage (Madrigal, 1995; Wakefield and Blodgett, 1994). Further building on the DEM—and adding to the complexity of measuring satisfaction—it has been suggested that a range of factors can moderate the satisfaction relationship. Specifically, van Leeuwen, Quick and Daniel (2002) propose that unique aspects of sport—such as club identification and the win/lose phenomenon—should be considered, given that those who are more committed, and those fans whose teams experience on-field success, could logically be more satisfied. Additionally, van Leeuwen, Quick and Daniel (2002) note that both core service dimensions (that is, the game) and peripheral service dimensions or 'product extensions' such as parking, concessions and half-time entertainment (Mullin, Hardy and Sutton, 2000) are valuable additions to any consideration of what drives overall satisfaction.

Recent work has also considered the relational consumer, such as the season ticket-holder. Here, the assessment seeks to move beyond the single consumption experience towards understanding and building satisfying relationships with consumers through a range of product extensions delivered in addition to the match-day component. Using frameworks from sport (Beccarini and Ferrand, 2006; van Leeuwen, Quick and Daniel, 2002) and other industries such as the arts (Garbarino and Johnson, 1999), McDonald and Shaw (2005) and later McDonald, Karg and Vocino (2013) developed a comprehensive set of service-based club-performance measures that can be demonstrated to affect seasonal ticket-holders' satisfaction within a sporting context. The framework (presented in the case study at the end of this chapter) tests the importance of, and level of delivery for, a number of components relating to the season ticket-holder product, including ticketing, service, communications, administration, personal involvement and home ground. As well as satisfaction with each element, overall levels of satisfaction with the holistic season ticket-holder are measured and assessed, with the tool shown to be robust enough to handle significant changes in variables such as on-field performance.

Managing and measuring service quality and satisfaction in organisations

Developing high levels of customer satisfaction and retention requires management of three distinct processes: 'designing the service product, designing the service environment, and delivering the service' (Rust and Oliver, 1994: 3). Given the importance of satisfaction to direct outcomes and organisational goals, steps to measure and manage satisfaction present as actionable areas for sport organisations in both participant and spectator forms of sport.

It should be clear, given the models of service quality and satisfaction presented above, that a sport customer's expectations play an important role in their evaluations of quality and satisfaction. The management of expectations represents a key area that organisations need to understand—particularly given that disconfirmation of expectations processes strongly influence evaluations of quality and satisfaction. Multiple types of expectations are considered by consumers, with each impacting service quality and customer satisfaction, and as such it is important for sport marketers to understand the influence they have over such expectations. So where do expectations come from, and what can organisations do to influence them?

Consumers' expectations are determined by myriad characteristics, some of which can be influenced by organisations. Communication or information provided by the sport organisation is a common method, meaning the communication used in various promotions may shape the setting of expectations as part of the consumption process. Promising a 'market-leading sport experience', 'world class sightlines within a stadium' or '24-hour delivery of a sport product' may be features of advertising that attract consumers, but organisations must also realise how this influences the expectations customers develop. Similar to promotions, other marketing 'Ps' can guide how consumers may set expectations for a service. For example, the place or physical environment, inclusive of the facility, or the price attributed to a service will play a role in shaping expectations of how it will perform and what value it will deliver. Additionally, there are other external or environmental inputs that will influence expectations. These may include comparisons consumers make to similar or substitutable products of which they are aware, or that they have consumed, or the influences of networks of family and friends on their experiences with or perceptions of the service.

Given the central role of expectations to service quality and customer satisfaction, and the influence that sporting organisations can exert on their expectations, it is essential that sport marketers learn to manage what customers expect from them. Sport marketers must not promise more than their organisations can realistically deliver. Management and reaffirmation of expectations can be undertaken through programs or communications, with the creation of induction programs and communications one example of such action (see Sportview 8.2).

SPORTVIEW 8.2

Managing expectations of new consumers

The ability to retain consumers and convert them into loyal long-term supporters has been shown to be key to business success. However, figures from major Australian and US professional sports teams suggest that 35 per cent or more of first-year season ticket-holders will 'churn' or not renew their ticket. Such behaviours—particularly when teams have limited numbers of consumers from which to draw—can create significant hurdles to growing season ticket-holder bases. Even in high-demand cases where waiting lists exist, season ticket-holders have been shown to churn at high rates, even if customers have spent many years waiting for the chance to acquire tickets.

As in many industries, the non-renewal rate slows significantly once a season ticket-holder has been a constant customer for a few years, meaning positive first-year experiences are vital for retaining consumers, and for growing season ticket-holder bases over the long term. For many of this first-year group, a core reason for churn is the lack of satisfaction with the purchase decision, or a lack of perceived value—which in many cases is driven by unrealistic expectations of what a season ticket will offer.

When looking in from the outside as a casual buyer or attendee, research has shown that consumers can have very different expectations from what may actually eventuate post-purchase. For example, season ticket-holders may think that their purchase will allow them automatic allocation of premium seating, access to free tickets for family and friends, the ability to meet players or attend functions, devoted account managers on hand for enquiry-handling or free merchandise. While many of these may not be unrealistic expectations, or they could be met for very small season ticket-holder bases, delivering these benefits for season ticket-holder bases that exceed 40 000 or 50 000 people can be very difficult. Additionally, it is common for first-time season ticket-holders to have a lack of accurate knowledge about aspects such as the cost of parking and concessions, and ticket resale or allocation policies that can add significantly to the financial outlay of season ticket-holder ownership. Therefore, the first-year experience will be one that, even if delivered impeccably by the team or club, may have aspects that do not meet the first-timer's expectations.

Many better managed professional teams across a range of sports now undertake sophisticated research to better understand, and ultimately manage, season ticket-holder expectations. One outcome of this process has been specific induction and communication programs to assist in the integration of first-time season ticket-holders into the consumer base. Such induction programs provide first-year members with a specific contact person within the organisation, better information on activities and match-day access, functions specifically for first-year members to meet and socialise, and specific actions where the club contacts first-year season ticket-holders over the season to check in on their progress and experience to date. Each of these activities represent basic service actions—relevant to professional sport teams as well as other subscription organisations—to better integrate and manage expectations so consumers will have more positive experiences and perceptions when the next purchase decision arrives.

As well as assisting the development of realistic expectations for services, the measurement of satisfaction presents as a complex issue for organisations. Given that satisfaction can be assessed at various levels, it is reasonable to use satisfaction on specific areas of a product or service, as well as the interpretation of overall measures. There are multiple ways in which organisations can gather and interpret information to understand satisfaction levels, including indirect and direct measurement of consumer attitudes.

Indirect methods of customer satisfaction measurement can include tracking and monitoring customer complaints, sales records, profits and rates of customer retention. Importantly, though, many of these are not solely dependent on consumers' satisfaction. Increasingly, there are other information sources—ranging from suggestion boxes and feedback mechanisms to monitoring social media and online forums that provide mass volumes of consumer feedback that can help inform both the level and cause of satisfaction.

Likewise, direct measures of customer satisfaction can be undertaken using research. Methods may include qualitative approaches such as interviews or focus groups, or rely on quantitative methods such as surveys or questionnaires. In the latter, respondents indicate a level of satisfaction based on a multiple-point scale. Given that many consumers have similar experiences in service-based interactions, often longer scales (seven- or eleven-point scales) are more appropriate for satisfaction research. Within such an investigation, consumers will be asked to note how satisfied they were/are with an aspect or an overall level of satisfaction, where '0' or '1' = very dissatisfied and '7' or '10' = very satisfied. As above, the process can be applied at multiple levels, focusing on specific services aspects, a combination of core product elements and extensions, or a more holistic offering such as the experience with a fitness centre membership or season ticket-holder with a professional sport club. In such examples of holistic service measurement, there may be a range of service dimensions with which consumers might be satisfied or dissatisfied that impact on overall satisfaction to varying degrees.

As well as satisfaction levels, it is important to understand *why* consumers are satisfied or dissatisfied. This can be done using statistical investigation and modelling to determine the strongest drivers of overall satisfaction, but can also be achieved by asking participants to identify exactly what was satisfying or dissatisfying about their experience. Such a process can assist in capturing ideas about what aspects of the service were poorly delivered or can assist with developing improvements. Given the high level of identification associated with sport services and products, consumers are often very forthcoming in providing customer satisfaction researchers with this sort of valuable information. However, while large-scale surveying and data collection provide reliable information on which to develop satisfaction data, the interpretation of results can be more complex.

A considerable amount of data suggests that the majority of respondents report being satisfied (Peterson and Wilson, 1992) and, given that customer satisfaction is measured by degrees ranging from dissatisfied through to very satisfied, and is a function of prior expectations, there are no firm metrics or levels of satisfaction that are 'acceptable'. Indeed, such levels may differ from year to year, from consumer to consumer and across products and industries. Therefore, interpretation of data can be difficult. For example, a season ticket-holder base or fitness centre membership segment may provide an overall satisfaction rating of 8 out of 10, or 75 per cent may indicate they are highly satisfied, with interpretation of such data vastly aided by wider collation and interpretation of sources. As such, a need for longitudinal or comparative data by which to make comparisons can add value. Here, if a sport facility scores higher on satisfaction or quality scores the year following investments made to improve the facility, the change in data or scores provides a more direct comparison and interpretation of those improvements. Likewise, benchmarking data such as industry averages can provide valuable information for teams or facilities that offer comparable services.

Measurement can also be made more difficult given the 'halo' effects that influence attitudes such as service quality and satisfaction. A halo effect is defined as 'a marked tendency to think of a person (or event) in general as rather good or rather inferior and colour the judgements of the specific performance dimensions by this general feeling' (Thorndike, 1920: 20). Relevant to sport, there is evidence that high team identification of spectators or fans, or the impact and feelings provided by winning teams, can greatly influence the level of satisfaction experienced by season ticket-holders. Here, the involvement or 'winning feeling' presents as a halo factor that can influence (positively or negatively) other specific performance dimensions of the service. In line with a halo effect, these impacts are seen to influence more strongly those elements perceived as closest to the 'core product' (that is, perceptions of on-field performance, involvement and team administration), as opposed to other product extensions such as communications or home ground (Karg, McDonald and Shaw, 2008).

In the context of spectator sport, Madrigal (1995) found that the affective components of basking in reflected glory (BIRGing), or an individual's inclination to 'share the glory of a successful other with whom they are in some way associated' (Cialdini et al., 1976: 366), together with enjoyment, disconfirmation of expectations, team identification and quality of opponent, contributed to customer satisfaction with university basketball games. Additionally, Lapidus and Schilbrowsky (1996) conclude that the quality and results of basketball games affects the perceived quality and satisfaction of peripheral services under the pretence of the halo effect. As the title of their article suggests, the hot dogs did taste better when the home team won! That is, specific aspects and the overall service was perceived as better when the team or on-court product was satisfying. Such influences have implications for collecting and interpreting satisfaction data, as well as its measurement.

Outside of quantitative measures to assess customer satisfaction, marketers are advised to seek additional qualitative information, including why consumers evaluate the service in the way they do, and how the service might be improved. Those cases where consumers are not satisfied present opportunities for remedies and action. Such detail allows organisations to work to improve specific areas, and to respond to complaints. The ability to identify and communicate back to consumers the changes that are made can also communicate positive word-of-mouth or similar opportunities where the organisation is showing a proactive approach to consumers and marketing. Complaint-inducement can be derived from survey, phone, email and even social media mechanisms. Handling of complaints well has positive implications for sport organisations, as well as the satisfaction of their customers within the realm of relationship marketing. Well-handled complaints can shape evaluations positively (Bitner, Booms and Tetreault, 1990) where spectators who are initially dissatisfied can develop enhanced levels with future or remaining aspects of the service, leading to higher levels of retained customers.

Finally, while certainly proven, the strength of the relationship between satisfaction and positive behaviours or loyalty can be over-estimated. For example, an over-reliance on satisfaction while not being aware of other reasons for purchase or churn away from a product can impact the projections and actions that managers make. Indeed, many consumers who perceive high quality, or who are highly satisfied, may still churn given the lack of availability of a service, or changes to personal circumstance such as financial, geographic or lifestyle changes. As such, while high levels of service quality and satisfaction are certainly desirable, it is important for marketers to constantly be aware of how products are perceived and positioned for consumers.

Summary

This chapter has explored service quality and satisfaction. The importance of developing a relational approach to service management framed the chapter, with the provision of high-quality and satisfying sport services linked to organisational success through a number of positive consequences for the sport organisation. Customer satisfaction and service quality were described as distinct types of evaluation. It was noted that these evaluations can be of the overall spectator or participant service, as well as of individual aspects or components.

A number of factors need to be managed successfully in order for customers to enjoy the sport experience, and thus evaluate it positively. Due to the uncontrollability of the core product, sport marketers must realise that they have minimal influence over perceptions of quality and feelings of satisfaction arising from the game or sport experience itself. As such, sport organisations must focus on ensuring that the product extensions are of the highest possible standard.

Service quality was modelled in accord with the work of Parasuraman, Zeithaml and Berry (1985), who conceptualised it in terms of a number of 'gaps' (that is, service, knowledge, standards, delivery, communications) between the expectations and perceptions of customers, management and employees. The traditional SERVQUAL was shown to be applied to multiple sport service types, inclusive of participation and spectator formats. Satisfaction was presented as a desirable interim or end-state form, with variants including satisfaction with events or elements during consumption, satisfaction with the final outcomes and satisfaction with the level of satisfaction received. The processes by which customers arrive at their satisfaction judgements were modelled with experience-led perceptions leading to confirmed or disconfirmed expectations of the sport service in accordance with the DEM.

Management and measurement of service and satisfaction closed the chapter. Sport marketers must understand those factors that influence the expectations held by spectators and participants, and learn to manage them successfully. Through identifying, understanding and managing expectations, sport organisations will be better placed to provide high-quality and thus satisfying sport services, which in turn may provide them with a competitive advantage and related benefits. It was recommended that sport marketers collect and collate multiple data forms to aid understanding, and ask their customers not only how satisfied they are and how high they perceive the quality of the spectator or participant service to be, but also why they perceive the service the way they do. This combined approach enables sport marketers to identify the things their organisation is doing particularly well, together with those things that need improving. When measuring customer satisfaction and service quality, proactive actions and responses can provide opportunities to turn around poor levels or cases of customer satisfaction and service quality, leading to improved and sustainable business outcomes.

CASE STUDY

Keeping AFL members satisfied

by Heath McDonald

Over 700 000 memberships (or season tickets) for AFL clubs are now sold each year. The revenue generated is vital to the ongoing viability of clubs, and having a strong membership base also enhances prospects for sponsorship and media revenue. Despite the importance of membership revenue to clubs, the management of membership services had not been a priority for most clubs as they made the transition towards becoming fully professional in the 1990s.

Over the last 20 years, however, member numbers have increased so rapidly that clubs have had to rethink their approach to customer service and service quality. In 1987, there were fourteen clubs in the AFL with a total of 71 000 members. On average, that represents an increase per club from just over 5000 members in 1987 to around 39 000 in 2012.

The rapid growth in member numbers raised a range of problems for clubs, as it would for any organisation. On the practical front, managing a database of 40 000 members is far more complex and time-consuming than running one for 5000. Significant investment in infrastructure, such as software, database and phone systems, was needed. Additionally, the 'member experience' changes as a function of increased member numbers. Where once it may have been possible to mingle freely with players after games, with tens of thousands of members, such casual arrangements are no longer possible. Membership departments in AFL clubs typically were staffed by only one manager and several part-time or volunteer staff, making service improvements difficult.

As a result, it became clear to clubs that, as their membership numbers grew, their practices must be updated and focused more on providing a consistently high-quality service. The problem was that AFL clubs had very little information about why members joined clubs, what they wanted from their memberships and member perceptions of the quality of services currently being provided. In order to ensure that they offered the right things, in the right way, research was needed.

Since 2004, AFL clubs have systematically been researching member perceptions of service quality and satisfaction with membership products. In 2012, fifteen clubs participated in large-scale surveying of members. The survey aimed to identify the level of member satisfaction with membership services, and provide guidance to the clubs on how that satisfaction level could be managed. In total, over 35 000 responses were received—an average of over 2300 per club. For the purpose of comparison, 1500 members from each club were randomly selected and combined into one database, so that the results were not unduly influenced by clubs with larger response levels. Table 8.1 shows the overall results of that combined sample, highlighting member satisfaction with their membership service.

TABLE 8.1 Scores and importance of drivers to overall satisfaction

	Average score (measured on 0–10 scale)	Strength of driver to overall satisfaction (%)
Membership arrangements	8.0	31
Service to members	7.9	14
Marketing/communications	7.9	4
On-field performance	6.2	10
Personal involvement	6.9	15
Club administration	7.4	10
Home ground	8.1	16
Overall satisfaction	7.7	

Two major components of member satisfaction were measured in this research: the perceived performance of services, and the importance of those services to overall satisfaction. Satisfaction was measured on a ten-point scale, and covered six main areas of the membership product identified as being important to members in qualitative research. These areas include:

- membership arrangements and ticketing (seating, packages offered, ease of purchase, etc.);
- service to members (enquiry handling, speed of service, helpfulness of staff, complaint handling, etc.)
- club communications (magazine content, email updates, social networking, etc.)
- on-field performance (number of games won, level of match quality, etc.)
- personal involvement (voting rights, club functions, social opportunities, recognition of members, etc.)
- club administration (board performance, financial performance, promotion, etc.), and
- home ground (facilities, atmosphere, feeling of home ground, etc.).

Overall, with an average satisfaction rating of 7.7 on a ten-point scale, we would conclude that AFL club members were satisfied with the membership services they received in 2012. Satisfaction scores ranged between clubs from a high of 8.8 out of 10 to a low of 6.6 out of 10. The variations within particular components were predictably different. For example, the minimum and maximum satisfaction scores achieved by clubs for elements such as on-field performance varied significantly, whereas home ground and communications—where club activities or facilities are more uniform—produced more similar results.

Also shown in Table 8.1 is the relative importance of each aspect of the membership product to overall satisfaction. This was determined using regression analysis. The results show that, on average, perceptions of membership arrangements contributed 31 per cent towards overall member satisfaction, making it the most important factor when members assessed performance. Home ground and personal involvement were the next most important contributors to satisfaction, at 16 and 15 per cent respectively. These results can be interpreted as saying that ticketing is twice as important as on-field performance in determining overall satisfaction with membership packages.

It was noted that importance levels vary between clubs as well. For some clubs, communications were not important at all, while in others they contributed strongly towards overall satisfaction. This variation results from members' past experiences and expectations. For example, if members expected to have regular communications from the club and that did not occur, then communications were likely to have a stronger impact on satisfaction than if they had been delivered as expected.

The results are surprising in that they suggest that winning (on-field performance) is less important than providing good service quality and making members feel involved. This is good news for clubs, which can be assured that if they manage the service components of their membership offering well, their membership numbers should not rise and fall dramatically with on-field results. Members, it seems, can still be satisfied with the membership product even if the results of the games don't please them.

Questions

1 Based on this research, what are the areas on which you would recommend that club membership managers focus? Give some specific recommendations of actions they could undertake to improve member satisfaction.
2 Why is on-field performance not the most important thing to club members when they determine how satisfied they are with their annual club membership?
3 How else could an AFL club measure the quality of the service it is offering its members?
4 Each year, up to 20 per cent of AFL club members do not renew. What relationship would you expect between service quality, member satisfaction and member renewal? Why would a satisfied club member not renew?

Stage 1—Identification of marketing opportunities

▼

Stage 2—Strategy determination

Step 5—Determine core marketing strategy

Marketing and service mix—sport product, pricing, place (physical evidence, people, process), customer satisfaction

Promotion mix

Step 6—Determine tactics and performance benchmarks

▼

Stage 3—Strategy implemention, evaluation and adjustment

9

The sport promotion mix

CHAPTER OBJECTIVES

Chapter 9 introduces sport promotions as tools used in an integrated manner to achieve communications objectives and stimulate demand. It begins by defining communications and providing a model of communication that underpins the promotions process. It then considers the development of promotions, including trends influencing the current promotions landscape. The importance of an integrated mix is then discussed before the components of the sport promotions mix are introduced. Traditional elements include advertising, public relations and publicity, and sales promotions. Direct marketing, interactive marketing and promotional licensing are also included. This chapter concludes with a focus on selecting and developing a sport promotions mix.

After studying this chapter, you should be able to:

- understand the definition of promotions and the nature of promotions as communication tools
- explain the communication process, aims of promotion and process models describing cognitive, affective and behavioural stages
- understand the importance of a structured, integrated approach to promotions use
- recognise components of the promotion mix and give examples of each
- establish procedures and articulate the process for selecting and planning a promotions mix
- understand standards to assess the suitability of a promotions mix.

HEADLINE STORY

World Series Cricket to dress-up parties—the changing face of cricket promotion

The case of promoting one-day, 50-over international cricket to Australian audiences highlights changes in the communicated messages over differing time periods, as well as different promotional mix options available to organisations. In 1977, Australian cricket underwent a major evolution when World Series Cricket was created and positioned as an alternative to the game's traditional longer formats. In the process, it attracted the best athletes in the sport, but also brought about stylistic changes in the game's production and presentation. The sport was repackaged as a television spectacle to captivate the home viewer with multiple camera angles, coloured uniforms, on-screen graphics and various auditory devices introduced to elevate the entertainment appeal of the game. Sport fans in general—not just cricket devotees—were targeted and captivated.

The transformation of a sport that had once been restricted to white clothing and games that could span days into a colourful, prime-time spectacle was complemented by an advertising campaign, 'C'mon Aussie', a hit on radio at the time; it remains an iconic campaign in Australian sport marketing. The overall strategy comprised a wide range of promotion activities surrounding the stars of the game and the spectacle of the new format. Promotion strategies were implemented at the ground, on television, on radio, in newspapers and magazines, and in department stores and supermarkets across the country. Through its promotional strategy, World Series Cricket communicated a message that emphasised excitement, glamour, aggression, superstars and non-stop entertainment. It used cricketers as its focal point across the campaign (in the song and imagery), and promoted the 50-over format as a new and exciting age for the sport.

Fast-forward 35 years and the cricket landscape is much changed. One-day cricket is under threat from the popularity of even shorter forms of the game, exemplified by the T20 format, a shorter, faster, more high-powered version of cricket. With the cricket calendar now comprising multiple cricket products—Test, one-day and T20—Cricket Australia realised that there was a need for an innovative approach to promotion. The resulting campaign was 'Summer's Biggest Dress-Up Party', which focused on the Australian summer themes of barbecues and backyard sport. Distinct from the 1977 campaign, its central theme is the off-field spectacle: fun, music, colour and social interaction within the crowd. The television campaign does not show match highlights and barely features athletes competing in the series. Instead, it emphasises a house party with young and enthusiastic guests, DJs, drinks and a few recognisable players warming up for a backyard game for good measure.

In short, the campaign sends a very different message from that relating to the original 50-over product. There is now a clear, defined communication of the social experience of the event, and a movement away from the sport and its athletes as its core. Cricket Australia states that the positioning seeks to communicate a 'fantastic way to spend a glorious summer's day with friends', responding to fans' insights that the format and event was 'as much about what happens in the crowd as on the pitch' (Cricket Australia, 2012). Like its 1977 version, the campaign seeks to extend the appeal beyond core cricket consumers to those driven by social and entertainment motives.

As in the earlier campaign, an integrated, multi-channel promotional mix is central. This includes mass media TV and radio advertising, supported by print and outdoor placements and a large social media campaign encouraging Facebook communication and content-sharing, competitions and sales promotions through social networking and a range of online and digital advertising. Proactive public relations were used in the launch of the concept to achieve cross-generational coverage, supported by direct marketing campaigns using established databases to communicate with existing fans of the sport.

The agency responsible for the brief stated that the campaign seeks to capture energy and excitement, 'featuring a pumping house party at a suburban home, filled with people wearing colourful costumes from all walks of life and a world-class game in the backyard' (Cricket Australia, 2012). While both promotional approaches were multi-faceted and integrated in their approach, two clear trends emerge from the comparison: the amendment to the core messaging and positioning (sport vs entertainment); and the increase in options used within the promotional marketing mix.

Sources: Cricket Australia (2012); Haigh (2013).

Defining promotions

Promotion is the way sport marketers communicate with potential consumers to achieve communications objectives such as informing, reminding and persuading. Promotional campaigns like those in the cricket examples above commonly utilise many integrated tools to contribute to awareness, image, consideration or sales goals that ultimately contribute to organisational success and sustainability.

Promotional goals can focus on a wide range of outcomes, from encouraging consumers to become aware of product or service offerings, to communicating features and benefits of new or enhanced products, to articulating competitive advantages. Further, promotion can reinforce the position of a brand or organisation, it can make customers aware of important information, such as distribution channels, or it can be used to help develop favourable opinions with the intention of stimulating consumers to purchase or use a product or service.

As such, promotions must communicate a distinct and clear ability to fulfil customer needs, with a view to ultimately creating demand for consumption within a market. A *promotional strategy* is defined as an integrated program of communication activities to present an organisation and its products or services to customers (Belch et al., 2011). This may be focused on creating generic demand for a particular product category (for example, an industry-wide focus on communicating health and fitness benefits) or brand demand relevant to a more specific organisational unit (for example, a specific club, program or association). Additionally, a manufacturer may promote an element of a product, which may stimulate demand for that component, and may indirectly stimulate demand for a particular brand. For example, Lycra manufacturers promote the attributes of Lycra, which indirectly stimulates demand for products made using the fabric, such as fitness and cycling apparel.

Irrespective of the type of demand, the audience targeted by the promotion strategy invariably remains the same. Current and future customers, stockholders, the public at large and special-interest groups are all existing or potential consumers. However, responses to promotion strategies will vary based on myriad consumer behavioural factors (discussed in Chapter 3) and models of response to messages. Given such differences, sport promoters need to tailor marketing strategies in order to attract specific consumer groups. This is done by fully comprehending the stages of promotion strategy development, and then manipulating the promotion mix to suit target segments.

There are many kinds of promotional activities that can be used simultaneously as part of a promotions or integrated marketing communications (IMC) mix. Well-planned and executed promotional strategies should comprise a range of 'seller-initiated efforts' that can access channels to inform and persuade (Ray, 1982). The controlled and integrated nature of a promotional strategy requires careful consideration of aspects such as alignment with wider marketing objectives, message and strategic integration, as well as timeframes, cost or budgets, and quality of message and creative elements.

It is important from the outset to differentiate between the wider marketing strategy and the promotional strategy. The latter is only one of many of the 'Ps' of marketing, and is limited to the communication strategies inherent within a wider marketing strategy. Marketing objectives of a sport organisation may include increasing market share, participation or revenue. While promotional objectives should be aligned, they should be focused on specific communications objectives that can help deliver these broader, higher level outcomes. Although promotion is impacted by price, place and product, the aim of promotions—to inform, persuade and remind—should clearly demonstrate its use as a communications tool within the wider strategic marketing mix.

Communications model

In order for promotional strategies to have their desired impact, they must successfully transfer messages through a communication process. An understanding of how a message is transmitted and the processes by which the consumer receives and processes communication is required in order to adequately develop relevant strategies. Communication is said to have taken place once information processing has occurred—that is, once an individual attends to a message and attributes importance to it (Cravens, 2010).

The key components in the communications process are the *source*, the *message*, the *channel* and the *receiver*. The communications process begins with the sender or source, which may be an organisation or individual. Once the context has been established, any resulting message is encoded by its source and decoded by its receiver. Messages do not always need to be verbal, as non-verbal cues are often just as prevalent. The use of visual scenes containing previous elite performance or competition to promote an upcoming event is an example of a non-verbal message.

The message or content is executed and communicated via a channel. Channels can be any kind of media, ranging from personal, customised communications delivered face to face or through digital means such as email; or physical forms, such as a letters, brochures or sales tools. In this sense, the communication can take the form of a one-to-one or one-to-many interaction. Considering message, often the more effective sport promotions use simple, non-confronting, unambiguous messages to highlight a service or product. Adidas's 'Impossible is Nothing' is an example of this. Likewise, Football Federation Australia's 'We Are Football' provides a basic but powerful message around which to centre fan communications campaigns.

The final message—the receiver's perception following decoding—may then be shared or transmitted further. While the complexity in communication arises in the encoding and decoding processes, the components remain the same for a variety of communication examples. In a traditional advertising context, the message may be delivered to the consumer through radio, television, billboards and print media. As a further extension, an original recipient of a message may also become a source—for example, if the recipient was to share the message within their own network. The message can be transmitted and received by individuals or networks in the same manner, either through word of mouth or via digital means (for example, through social networks). Thus messages originating from trustworthy sources—whether they are brands or individuals (friends or endorsing athletes)—can play a big role in the success of the communication and its reception.

Consumers are often faced with highly cluttered markets, and are exposed to multiple brands, products and messages each day, or even each hour. The greatest inhibitor or source of interference to successful message conveyance is *noise*. Noise can be physical, psychological or simply an unintended interpretation or decoding of a message. There is therefore a need for targeted placement, as well as for clear, consistent, reinforced messages that will be received in the best possible way by consumers.

SPORTVIEW 9.1

Endorsements—athletes as communication sources

Endorsements are an increasingly common form of promoting products and services through leveraging the popularity of a sportsperson or athlete. Similar to sponsorship and product placement, an athlete is retained as the spokesperson or 'face' of a brand. The process seeks to gain attention and awareness, and to transfer the goodwill and image of the individual to the brand itself. As such, fit or congruence between the two parties—either in the product or brand traits—is sought.

As an example, the vitamin and supplement brand Swisse has been endorsed in Australia by a range of athletes and personalities, past and present. Specific products from the organisation's 170-product range have been aligned with a relevant athlete, with mass media advertising used to leverage the endorsement strategy. The campaign helped Swisse to become the most recalled advertised brand in Nielsen consumer surveys taken around the time of the London 2012 Olympics.

In this case, the athlete is a communication source, and delivers a message that seeks to raise awareness, detail the product benefits and encourage consideration and purchase.

Once the message is developed, TV, radio, home shopping networks, print media, launches and interviews may be used to convey the message, which is received and interpreted by consumers.

The use of an athlete to convey messages about the product seeks to create a more memorable communications experience, ideally leveraging the source's credibility and value as a brand ambassador. But what are the characteristics that drive this connection? Organisations need to consider the choice of athletes carefully, as the arrangement can quickly turn negative if the athlete is involved in a scandal or exhibits poor behaviour. Commonly, organisations use the dimensions of awareness, likeability, trust and appeal to consider how an athlete may influence brand affinity, consumer behaviour and purchase intent.

The primary desired outcome of communications is to produce a favourable change in attitudes and behaviour. There are several communication response models that explicate progress through a number of affective, cognitive and behavioural stages in processing; these are relevant as a foundation for understanding how messages are developed and decisions made regarding the selection of promotional elements. Perhaps the most prominent is the AIDA (awareness, interest, desire, action) model. In this instance, the promotion aims to get the consumer's attention, create an interest in and desire to purchase the product or service, and stimulate action by engaging in an exchange process—usually involving actual purchase. A hierarchy of effects model, commonly applied to the understanding of sponsorship, uses a similar process. Here, typically over a period of time and with supporting activities, sponsorship between a brand—for example, a bank—and a sports organisation—for example, a professional football team—seeks to first generate awareness and knowledge of the parties and the relationship. From here, the sponsor (the bank) seeks to leverage the goodwill that the consumer (the fan) has for the sponsee (the team) in order to progress liking, preference and conviction before consideration towards positive behaviour, such as consumption or usage. Other examples include innovation-adoption and information-processing models (Belch et al., 2011). All of these models seek to describe the way in which consumers progress from awareness through varied levels of consideration to positive actions.

Towards a strategic, integrated promotional mix

Sport promotions represent the most visible component of the sport marketing mix, in many cases presenting to markets the end-results of a process of strategy and planning around how the organisation wishes to communicate with consumers. The promotional process and the elements used to communicate can vary, depending on the target market; the stage of the product life-cycle; the message or marketing goals of a company at a certain time; the positioning strategy the brand wishes to adopt; and the budget and timeframe. The complexity of planning and executing promotional strategy emerges from this, with potentially variant messages required for different groups of consumers and target markets.

Accordingly, promotional mixes must embrace strategic and planned communications that play a fundamental role in generating interest and achieving marketing and organisational goals, rather than take the form of a series of attention-grabbing or entertaining activities. The high-profile role played by sport in consumers' lives, and the level of media attention that sport garners, are advantages in achieving this aim. However, while a high profile is an advantage for reach and exposure, there is a need to leverage such benefits to create conversations, share information, generate interest and ultimately drive action towards purchase and usage of sport products and services.

The use of sport promotions dates back to the 1800s (Mullin, Hardy and Sutton, 2007) while later, in the 1940s and 1950s, American sports marketing entrepreneur Bill Veeck became known for unique and innovative marketing actions to help generate sales (see Veeck and Lin, 1962). In Australia, the comparatively late professionalisation of sports meant that a more strategic and concentrated adoption by sport organisations of promotional strategies did not take place until the 1970s. This was a time characterised by major shifts and innovations in sport products, with the introduction of night games, more TV and fan-friendly conditions, media and corporate brands leveraging the popularity of sport, and a focus on leveraging highly marketable personalities. From this age arose some of the more iconic Australian sport marketing campaigns, including those for World Series Cricket in the late 1970s ('C'mon Aussie', see headline story above) and later for National Rugby League ('Simply the Best') and Australian Rules ('Unbelievable').

Since this time, there have been a number of important developments and trends in marketing theory and in the sport environment that have impacted the ways in which promotional mixes are designed and operationalised. Organisations and marketing managers now face demands for greater accountability and objectivity; further, there has been a shift in power from manufacturers to retailers (including online retailers), which have sought greater involvement as distribution partners. Developments in communications and marketing theory have led to a greater focus on relationship marketing as opposed to stimulating transactional activities. Additionally, there has been support for strategic and integrated suites of activities that are complementary and synergistic. In line with this, marketing communications have shifted away from a reliance on mass media advertising spend, and have embraced a wider range of existing tools and components—some of which have proved to be more measurable, interactive, customisable and effective.

New technologies have also added a stream of possibilities in direct, online or digitalised communication formats. In the digitalised context, the growth and development of direct and interactive marketing, along with the use of customer relationship management (CRM) platforms and databases, have provided organisations with more personal and focused approaches to generating sales and achieving other marketing goals within an established market. Such techniques also provide scope for a greater use of segmentation tools and better developed relationship marketing initiatives. Finally, the rapid growth of the internet has seen the advent of a number of digital or new media, which are increasingly being used by organisations. Some of these include the use of websites, e-commerce, internet advertising or forms of social media or content development (see Chapter 12). It is, in fact, rare to see a modern campaign, promotion or piece of communication from a sport organisation that does not include a digital component.

Overall, these changes have both increased the promotional options available for marketing managers and elevated the focus on integrated promotional campaigns to deliver consistent, reinforced messages using diverse tools.

Tools for promotion

As a result of the processes of commercialisation and professionalisation, sport has become a source of entertainment, an occupation and a lifestyle; in addition, sport must continue to generate revenue and reach levels of profitability in order to guarantee the sustainability of organisations. Marketers are faced with an increasingly cluttered marketplace, as well as a need to deliver accountability, while consumers have more options and modes of consumption. As such, sport organisations' scarce marketing budgets, variety of goals and wide-ranging stakeholders have increased the reliance on promotion and communication as vital tools with which to communicate effectively with stakeholder groups and customers.

In recent years, the variety of promotional mix variables has diversified. In line with this, a promotional strategy is now best conceived of as an IMC mix. The use and terminology of IMC encourages a comprehensive, strategic approach to the communications process, such that promotional campaigns rarely feature only one component; rather, they tend to be a cohesive, synergistic mix of communication actions.

The use of IMC reinforces the view that a modern promotion mix is more than just a mass advertising approach; it integrates a number of interrelated activities that exhibit consistency of message and alignment with objectives of the organisation, and that use various forms of communication. Additionally, target audiences are likely to be channel-agnostic—meaning that they do not rely solely on any single channel (for example, print, online, offline, mobile, social) for communications. As such, organisations wishing to both enforce consistent messages and reach a wide range of markets should use a mix of tools.

The focus now turns to introducing the various communications or promotions tools available to sport marketers. In some cases, this discussion is supported by a specific chapter within this text, listed in brackets:

- advertising (Chapter 10)
- public relations and publicity (Chapter 15)
- sales promotions
- personal selling
- direct marketing
- interactive marketing and new media (Chapter 12), and
- promotional licensing (Chapter 16).

Advertising

Advertising represents the obvious form of sport and event promotion, and is defined as a form of one-way communication where a marketer pays someone else to have their product, brand or organisation identified. In its traditional form, it is a non-customised, one-to-many, mass media promotion tool (that is, all consumers receive the same message), the success of which is heavily reliant on brand identification, clarity of message, visual or audio stimulants, and generating impact and reach through media decisions about placement.

Common examples of advertising include television commercials, magazine and newspaper advertisements, radio spots, posters, internet and website pop-ups or static adverts, digital or virtual advertising and outdoor advertisements, such as on billboards and public transport. Traditionally, TV or other media have garnered the largest share of advertising spend; however, as a promotional tool and revenue stream, internet and online advertising now generate the largest growth rates.

While the sport organisation, event or brand may choose to advertise its products or services through any of these means, venues and websites also provide opportunities for sport organisations to generate revenue through the sale of advertising opportunities. Specific to sport, some of these include advertising opportunities through scoreboards, signage, the playing field, programs, equipment, ticketing and other digital communication forms such as fan forums and social networking sites. An expanded analysis of the role of advertising in sport marketing is presented in Chapter 10.

Public relations and publicity

Public relations (PR) relates to the determining of various publics' attitudes and interests, and the subsequent implementation of media and communication strategies to disseminate core information and announcements related to organisational activities. Ultimately, it seeks to draw attention to, or shape attitudes and perceptions towards, a person, product, organisation or event. Some of these objectives may be to raise awareness, inform and educate, develop understanding or trust, or assist in motivating consumers or incentivising purchase. While marketing and PR traditionally have been distinct in their structure and operations, increasingly PR is a fully integrated element of the communications strategies of organisations—particularly where PR has brand or marketing related objectives.

Importantly, PR can be both proactive and reactive in nature. For example, a small organisation may seek to develop a profile or awareness of an upcoming event by creating a newsworthy angle that will attract media outlets to carry the story. Alternatively, an organisation may seek to react to positive or negative news about competitors, or to react to issues or situations—such as player misbehaviour, or other prominent stories surrounding a team, player or event.

The process of conducting and integrating PR into the promotional mix involves:

- developing an understanding of public attitudes about the organisation and its products
- establishing a PR plan
- detailing the tools and strategies for implementation, and
- developing and executing the PR program.

Particularly in this latter sense, publicity is closely aligned to PR, as it involves the generation of news about people, products or services through the broadcast, online or print media. The best example of this is the amount of copy, space and time given to sport and related activities in the media—for example, a major sporting event such as the Grand Prix, which permeates sport and other news and cultural domains. Although more immediate, publicity objectives are also more short term, and can often be generated by sources outside the control of the organisation.

PR has the advantages of being viewed as more credible and cost-effective than advertising, and is able to overcome the clutter associated with other media and advertising by communicating through different channels (that is, away from paid messages). The outgoing messages can be controlled and directed by the organisation concerned, targeted to a specific market and measured reasonably effectively through public perceptions and reactions. Likewise, publicity has the advantage of being free—or at least more cost-effective; however, while the message from the organisation—for example, through press releases or statements—can be controlled, ultimately the organisation cannot control the time and placement of the story, or the slant a particular journalist or writer may place on it. Public relations and the need for publicity are discussed in Chapter 15.

Sales promotions

A sales promotion is a short-term activity with the primary objective of providing an enticement or incentive to purchase, or of stimulating a short-term or immediate increase in sales. Consumer-focused promotions include samples, coupons, premiums, contests, sweepstakes, refunds and rebates, bonus packs, price-offs, loyalty programs and event marketing. They can involve the creation of value through either price or non-price approaches.

Sales promotions based on price can include two-for-one deals, group or packaged discounts or free product trials. Often these are directed towards children, which influences family attendance and consumption, or other segments of new or casual users. For example, sport teams or leagues may reduce game ticket prices for games later in the season or for those that have lower demand in order to attract new fans or people who only attend sporadically. Such a strategy seeks to communicate affordability and added perceived value, while giving the organisation opportunities to use other strategies within the game experience to convert such fans into relational customers.

The use of giveaways—such as caps, drink bottles, posters or sport memorabilia—is an example of non-price promotions, where additional value is offered to attendees. Other examples of sales promotions include the chance to enter a draw or win a prize, which can double as at-ground entertainment. For example, it is common for a lucky attendee to have a chance to win cash or prizes by hitting a crossbar from the penalty spot, kicking a goal or making a half-court shot.

In these instances, integration becomes possible as a brand or sponsor may partner the promotion. For example, in US collegiate basketball, a particular sponsor will cover a student's tuition if they can make a half-court shot at half time. Additionally, sales promotions can be activated by non-sport brands and products—that is, a case of marketing through sport. A successful example here is provided in the case of the David Boon talking dolls that were given away with purchases of a brand of beer, Victoria Bitter, during one Australian cricket summer. The doll was digitally integrated with cricket broadcasts over the summer, and would spontaneously come to life and speak.

This award-winning concept had the impact of stimulating additional incentives to purchase, and generated a short-term sales spike for Victoria Bitter in a key sales period (summer). Sales returned to par in subsequent parts of the year, demonstrating that sales promotions' primary effectiveness is as short-term transactional tools that require more attention to turn product trials into sustainable revenue or sales sources.

While sales promotions are most commonly used to target consumers as an incentive, bonus or additional value-add to buy the sport product, they can also be relevant for retailers or trade partners within the distribution network. This makes sales promotions effective tools at multiple points of the marketing distribution channel. Trade-oriented promotions include contests and dealer incentives, trade allowances, provision of point-of-purchase displays, training programs, trade shows and cooperative advertising. In fact, sales promotions—particularly for sporting goods—often need the assistance of retail or distribution partners to be effective. For example, a two-for-one purchase of a good such as shoes or packs of tennis balls needs to be activated in store or at the point of purchase, requiring the support of retail partners.

SPORTVIEW 9.2

A promotion a day—baseball promotions in the United States

Consider the job of marketers for Major League Baseball (MLB) clubs. Each team plays over 160 games in a regular season, with 80 or more home games each year. Even when factoring in the most loyal fan bases and attendees, it becomes necessary to focus attention on a wide range of fan segments to generate crowds for each game. As such, a creative range of sales promotions becomes a key tool to deliver additional value and incentives that keep bringing fans to ballparks. Looking at many team schedules, each home game is highlighted by a specific promotional event; the event may be linked to giveaways or special offers for a certain number of attendees; it may celebrate a historic figure, anniversary or cultural heritage; or it may be targeted at a specific fan group or sponsor.

Additionally, at minor league levels of baseball, there is a similar need to use promotions for the same outcomes. Here, the quality of play at the game may be lower and the teams have lower pools from which to draw fans, given that teams in many cases reside in smaller markets. The challenge of developing creativity in promotions at this level has been met by teams' marketers, resulting in some innovative concepts. Among them have been 'Cash Drop Night', where money was dropped on to the field for consumers to grab, and 'Second Chance Night', which allowed traffic violators or those with fines to purchase two-for-one tickets. This night also included free entry for probation officers, and mug-shots and holding cells as part of entertainment. Finally, 'George Costanza night' was held in honour of an episode of the TV show *Seinfeld*, in which a character does everything the opposite to the way he would normally, with great success. As a tribute, everything at a particular game was done backwards. This included use of the scoreboard, fans being rewarded rather than paying for parking, tiers of seating prices being inverted, players wearing opposite home and away uniforms and the night concluding with players asking for fans' autographs.

In all the cases above, from sponsor-engaged nights to other themed events, the characteristics of sales promotions are visible and consistent. Organisations seek to induce short-term responses or impacts on sales by temporarily offering additional value or incentives.

Source: Pumerantz (2012)

In both the consumer and trade sense, sales promotions are a good example of an integrated form of promotion in that they generally are supported through other areas of the promotions mix. Here, advertising, personal selling, public relations and publicity may form part of the process of building awareness and distributing coupons or physical vouchers that facilitate sales. This represents one of the advantages of sales promotions: measurability of the investment made in sales promotions through the inbuilt ability to track respondents and their resultant behaviour. By recording the number of vouchers or coupons used, or the number of times a promotional code is entered, organisations can track customer response, and ideally determine future promotions for customers. As such, while sales promotions are generally temporary in nature, measurement can provide evidence of developed long-term customer relationships as a result of introductory approaches.

Personal selling

Personal selling involves selling through individual and personal communication, usually over the phone, face to face or through an internet portal. It is explained as a systematic process of identifying prospects and needs, determining and communicating a strategy, and evaluation (Evans and Berman, 1987).

Personal selling to consumers is most relevant in certain circumstances and for certain forms or types of goods and services—for example, where product purchase is a complex or highly involved decision, or where features may require demonstration, trial or a greater level of information of than delivered in advertising. Personal selling is also appropriate in situations where aspects of the product can be customised, or where price is flexible or negotiated. Some examples of appropriate uses of personal selling may be the purchase of expensive equipment such as golf clubs where trial is important, or high-involvement products such as season tickets (which require both consumers' money and time), where there may be a need to explain benefits to new consumer or acquisition targets.

While personal selling is an important aspect of promotion, it is often linked with other IMC activities to maximise its impact—for example, it can be combined with advertising campaigns or PR to generate leads, initial awareness or interest. The direct and interpersonal communication aspects of personal selling often make it a resource-heavy component of promotion. Developing trust and effective relationships can require much time and effort; however, this can be offset by the benefits of direct and immediate interpersonal communication, which enable the customisation of the marketing message and provides immediate feedback on the sales target, as well as on the product and service. For example, a telemarketer selling a product can adapt the sales message to suit the motivations of the consumer, or can adjust the positioning of product benefits or communications to better handle objections.

In the context of sport, personal selling is also commonly associated with business-to-business activities, such as sponsorship, corporate hospitality, and trade or licensing arrangements. In particular, sponsorship—as a mutually beneficial partnership—is heavily reliant on face-to-face presentation and communication, both at the selling and negotiation stages, as well as in servicing and renegotiation. Examples can be found in corporations such as Toyota and Telstra, and their relationships with the AFL, NRL and Cricket Australia. Such organisations make significant investments in sport, and are engaged in often very complex relationships, requiring a high level of negotiation and personal communication.

As personal selling usually is stimulated through accessing an existing dataset, a base of knowledge exists about consumption patterns. Therefore, there are opportunities to upgrade or up-sell to existing consumers, or to target lapsed ones. In some cases, the outcome may not always be sales, but in line with communications objectives, personal communication with a consumer may initiate interest or increase consideration. Additionally, personal communication can assist a data-collection process to acquire information about positive and negative experiences, guide future intentions and barriers to purchase, understand motivations for disengagement or become aware of service issues—all useful insights with which to frame future marketing strategies.

Direct marketing

Direct opportunities to sell to consumers may be through personal selling scenarios, but can also take the form of direct marketing through other media. Direct marketing is defined as one-to-one communication of a personalised message to a consumer, with the purpose of eliciting a direct response or sale. As opposed to mass media advertising, such as television advertisements or billboards, after identifying the consumer as a relevant part of a target market, the message is directed towards that specific consumer. It therefore removes the third party from the communication process, directly communicating messages to consumers and allowing detailed and customised interaction to communicate information about products and services that may satisfy identified consumer needs.

The media by which direct marketing approaches are communicated are not channel defined, and are more diverse than in past decades, largely as a result of changes to marketing theory and improved technology and database capacities. Previously, door-to-door or telemarketing (overlapping with personal selling) and direct mail campaigns, using physical brochures and mail order, represented the dominant forms of direct marketing. These were complemented with home shopping channels, and text or short message services (SMS). Today, direct marketing also involves a suite of activities, including database communications and email marketing, direct-response advertisements, and the use of internet and broadcast platforms, such as websites and social media.

While the channels that support digital marketing are constantly evolving, the principles or conceptual approach of direct marketing practice remain the same. It is defined by communications that are personalised, data or research led and highly measurable (Direct Marketing Association, 2011; McCarthy, 2011a) and seek to elicit a direct response (Kotler and Armstrong, 2010). Direct marketing has seen a recent surge in growth in its share of marketing spend, given the importance of digital platforms and its high return on investment.

In the case of direct marketing, email approaches can be facilitated through customer relationship management (CRM) platforms. Such tools, commonly used to manage customers, are now essential for modern organisations to record, track and communicate with their customers, and to generate database-led promotions. Such databases provide past consumption and behavioural data to complement segmentation, and can be combined with interfaces that produce and distribute high volumes of automated communications that are delivered via email or other platforms. Thus targeted approaches can be made to consumers to generate activation or reactivation, retention and promotion.

Most commonly, CRM programs have been embraced by organisations with regular users or buyers—for example, fitness centres, teams and associations—to manage their member bases. However, the use of database or CRM platforms should not be limited to subscription services, and should represent both transactional and relationship customers. Additionally, direct marketing should be seen as only one function of CRM, with service, support, measurement, planning and tracking also highly relevant. Further, CRM can seek to better understand consumer bases to appease and support sponsors, help conduct and record survey responses and feedback, and help develop and facilitate rewards and loyalty programs.

SPORTVIEW 9.3

Database and direct marketing outcomes

Given advances in databases, supporting platforms and the storage of digital information, a strategic approach to CRM has been shown to advance direct marketing approaches for sport teams, as well as furthering a range of other business outcomes. Through tracking consumer history, demographics and actions, various useful metrics—purchasing habits, attendance, TV consumption and merchandise purchase—can be captured. Even specific data tracking the time that consumers enter the stadium, the concessions bought and social media activity can be collated as part of a consumer's data record.

Analysis of such data can aid understanding of fan and member bases, and allow for identification of tangible and measurable benefits arising from planning and managerial action. For communications, rich data can be used to identify and target specific segments, which can be relevant to create more appropriate commercial messages. As opposed to broadcast media, direct marketing based on past consumer behaviour is more likely to elicit a positive response. CRM data can also aid sponsorship leverage. For example, UK Rugby Club Harlequins has developed a well-populated database of consumer insights that current sponsors such as Emirates can use to develop specific promotions (Harman, 2012). Such a database is likewise attractive in selling to new or potential sponsors, who can gain an accurate understanding of a customer base and potential opportunities.

Such programs can also be integrated with loyalty programs where consumer activities toward a brand are aggregated and rewarded. Major League Soccer (MLS) team Philadelphia Union presents a good example of a rewards program: consumers gain points for game attendance (points vary based on attractiveness and demand of the opposing team), as well as receiving bonuses for home wins and early entrance. TV consumption (tracked through entering a code online) and purchase of concessions and merchandise also attract points, with the program seeking to encourage more consistent and deeper levels of loyalty and behaviour (Philadelphia Union, 2013). Reward points can be exchanged for unique and engaging experiences such as meet-the-team events, opportunities to play a game on the home ground, event invites, seating upgrades, tours and discounts.

While the implementation of systems can mean an initial resource commitment, and upkeep and analysis requires data acumen, there are significant trade-offs in delivering more appropriate communications, such as positive outcomes for a range of stakeholders and facilitation of tools to manage and encourage engagement and loyalty.

Interactive marketing and new media

There are various new and digital media that enable users or consumers to increasingly interact with an organisation. Sport organisations use their web presence for a variety of objectives, such as information provision, awareness and image, establishing communication, gaining feedback and generating sales and leads (Brown, 2003). New media and tools of engagement allow two-way connections and direct communications between organisations or brands and consumers, driven by tools such as social media, mobile applications, gamification (see Chapter 12) and website use.

While new forms of interactive media in sport can be used for a range of revenue and engagement means (developed further in Chapter 12), one specific promotional or communications process within interactive media is content marketing. This can be positioned as a hybrid of marketing and publishing (Clark, 2013), where entertainment and engagement are stimulated through the creation and distribution of content such as videos, photo albums, newsletters, e-books and audio material. Such activity aims to stimulate connection with a brand, and ultimately seeks to encourage feelings of community and foster positive consumer responses.

Particularly in the sport industry, where consumers are known to have high emotional connections, sports events, teams and products can effectively utilise content marketing strategies, balancing promotional messages with engaging content. Given that consumers now have more control, face greater levels of advertising clutter, and use and access more devices than previously, utilising targeted and relevant content to deliver communications can help brands find new opportunities for interacting with their target markets, which can lead to positive behavioural and attitudinal results.

Promotional licensing

Promotional licensing is the 'act of granting a second party permission to use a mark, name, symbol or likeness' (Irwin, Sutton and McCarthy, 2002: 242). It is defined by a partnership, and driven by marketing and promotional goals between licensors and licensees with regard to the contractual right to use the name or logo of a sporting organisation. The partnership seeks dual benefits in provision of exposure, revenue for the organisation and its licensing agent, and opportunities to leverage and build the brand equity of the sport. Licensing strategies as a form of promotion date back to the 1920s, with major growth seen in the late 1990s. Globally, licensed product revenue accounts for approximately 15 per cent of all sport revenue, with the segment's worth estimated to reach around $20 billion in 2015. Seventy-one per cent of merchandise revenue is generated in North America (PricewaterhouseCoopers, 2011).

The success of licensing is dependent on the equity of a sporting brand as well as fan identification and emotional attachment. As discussed in Chapter 3, one aspect of psychological attachment defined by Funk and James (2004) is the 'sign'. This refers to the behaviour of sport consumers in identifying with their favourite teams through display of merchandise and clothing. Clothes such as caps, shirts, jackets, scarves, and key-rings are examples of 'signs', but the array of licensing products is extremely diverse, with supermarkets, service stations and markets often providing consumers with options to purchase licensed products. For example, organisations such as the AFL can have hundreds or thousands of licensed products, requiring the management of several complex contracts and partnerships. Licensing programs provide substantial opportunities and risks for both the licensee and the licensor, so need to be managed carefully. Key elements of licensing are discussed at length in Chapter 16.

The promotions process

This section introduces the process used to develop a promotions, or IMC, mix. The development of strategic promotional programs requires a systematic *promotions process*, which involves the identification of aims or objectives, the selection and development of tools to be used and the assessment of these tools. Given that multiple, integrated elements of a promotional mix are deployed, it is necessary to use various media outlets and organisational resources to produce and implement the required strategy. For example, in a large sporting organisation, a senior or general manager may oversee and approve the development of a promotional plan that includes elements of advertising, public relations and new media. In implementing this campaign, the resources of multiple sub-functions of the organisation, including marketing, brand, IT and media staff, may be required. Additionally, external organisations, such as advertising or digital agencies, may also perform the required activities. This complexity requires careful and detailed planning and activation.

Undertaking successful promotions processes requires a comprehensive, strategic approach combining people, funds and communications strategies. While promotions is only a single 'P' of the marketing mix, and represents only one part of the strategic marketing mix, it still comprises defined development, implementation and measurement stages. Figure 9.1 shows the promotional planning process, including situation analysis, objective development, program development and an evaluative measurement loop.

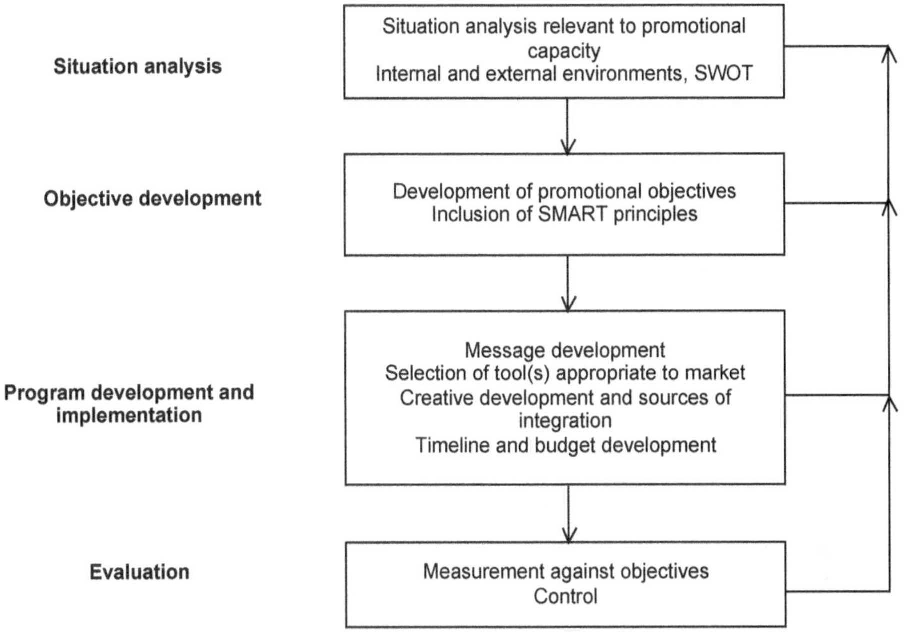

FIGURE 9.1 Promotions process framework

Situation analysis

Building on the work done as part of the situation analysis for the overall marketing plan, the promotional process requires an understanding of the internal and external factors that allow an organisation to leverage its internal capacities within its market. These stages, covered in detail in Chapter 2, include a review of the internal and external environments and marketing plan to determine the strengths, weaknesses, opportunities and threats that may be particularly relevant to the organisation's promotional efforts. Some examples might include identification of financial and skill-based resources and gaps within the organisation or marketing team; consumer insights relevant to message and communication planning; particular technologies or existing partnerships that may be leveraged for promotional gain; identification of current promotional efforts; and any successful or non-successful impacts of past programs.

Objective development

The processes of setting objectives are vital to the strategic development of a promotional campaign. Objective setting represents specific statements about what the IMC program attempts to accomplish at a given point in time. While promotional or IMC goals should reflect the broader organisational marketing goals of an organisation, promotional objectives are much more focused and narrow than higher-level marketing and organisational objectives. Promotional objectives traditionally focus on stimulating interest, awareness and purchase (Mullin, Hardy and Sutton, 2007) through communicating, informing and reminding consumers of benefits of products or services. They should be linked to a particular target market or markets, they should state clearly what the IMC program should accomplish in terms of communication strategies, and they should include measurable targets.

Program development

The development of the IMC program includes the tasks, schedules and responsibilities that 'operationalise' the plan or bring it to action. The strategy for the creative elements and the key message are both decided at this point, and choices are made about the platforms to be used, which media will be included, the timing of activities and how the components will be integrated. Equally important are the creation of synergies across the promotional mix, and the timing and resource allocation to optimise the impact of communications. Program development overall seeks to connect promotional objectives with the promotions mix, including development of action and implementation charts, project timelines and budgets that operationalise the steps required to achieve communication goals.

Resource allocation and budget spend committed to the plan are also developed at this point. The establishment of budgets and levels of investment will differ between organisations undertaking promotion plans. There are many approaches that can be applied to the setting and allocation of budgets and to deciding how much money to spend on promotion. Each of the methods is generally determined by a combination of external concerns, such as what competitors do, and internal projections or targets within an organisation, such as the desired return on investment, sales targets or increases to sales expected as a result of the plan.

Evaluation and measurement

Measurement remains one of the more complex and difficult stages of the promotional process, but it is vital in assessing the quality of promotional plans, their implementation and their effectiveness. Measurement and tracking of success can assist in avoiding poor decisions, enable adjustments to promotional strategy, increase efficiency and provide feedback on objectives that have been achieved. It is important that measurement is linked to the specific objectives of the plan, and vital to have specific key performance indicators that can be used to indicate whether a particular initiative has been successful.

Studies have suggested that managers agree on the importance of measurement but are not satisfied with or confident about either their organisations' approaches to it or their capacity to demonstrate business impact from IMC activities (Belch et al., 2011). Measurement can often be costly—particularly when it involves collating consumer attitudes—and there can be time limitations that make measurement difficult. Adding to the complexity of measurement is the combination of multiple components that are often used as part of the promotions mix. In this sense, it can be difficult to isolate or separate the specific impact of a single activity. For example, if a mix of promotions is undertaken, which sales increase can be attributed to advertising, as opposed to publicity or PR campaigns? Some aspects are easier to measure than others. For example, tracking measures in digital marketing activities, such as direct email campaigns through CRM databases, are relatively easy to collate and evaluate. In a non-digital context, while readership and TV viewing measures may assist in calculating the reach of a publication or advertising slot, it is more difficult to measure the direct sales impact of such initiatives.

Considerations for the IMC/promotions mix

A number of considerations are integral to a well-developed promotions or IMC campaign. In its construction, it is important that the campaign is part of a wider strategic process. This was discussed at a marketing strategy level in the opening chapters of this book, and includes capitalising on the assets and resources of an organisation and consideration of competitors and the environment. When focusing on the promotional mix, goals and objectives need to be consistent with the strategic direction and the overall marketing and positioning strategies of the organisation in order to transmit consistent messages and communications. These objectives should be focused on specific target market(s) and include measurable targets.

Promotional elements can effectively be combined to complement one another, as some tools or combinations of tools are more suitable for communicating with specific targets. Likewise, some messages are best transmitted through particular channels. Simultaneous use of components should be encouraged, but it is vital that the elements are consistent, complementary and ideally synergistic. Integration between the elements of a promotions strategy is therefore essential, meaning a) the various components used to communicate with target markets should be consistent in the message they communicate, and b) brand or product positioning is aligned with organisational positioning. During implementation, multiple functions, departments or spokespeople may be used; for this reason, there is a need for organisational-level integration and cooperation in order to maintain consistency of message and creative approach.

Summary

Given the importance of the marketing function, the sport marketer not only needs to be fully conversant with the components of the promotions mix, but also needs appropriate skills to develop and operationalise a comprehensive promotional campaign relevant to a given situation and its objectives. To this end, the establishment of promotion or IMC programs, while complex and challenging, is an important, creative and rewarding task. The carefully planned deployment of advertising, public relations and publicity, sales promotion and personal selling, as well as direct marketing, interactive marketing and promotional licensing, is crucial to the success of any sport organisation. Use of a greater range of such tools is now encouraged as part of a shift away from mass media as the dominant promotional category, and more emphasis is now placed on direct and interactive marketing tools. The presentation of a promotions framework to conclude this chapter was structured around developing communications objectives consistent with broader marketing plans, and the strategic selection of tools that are integrated and can deliver consistent messages to enable organisational outcomes.

CASE STUDY

Applying the promotions mix to fan development strategies

Fan development has become a popular term for sport marketers in the last decade, increasingly being used by teams and organisations to articulate, plan and measure elevations towards more loyal and consistent segments of customers. The broad aim of fan development is for an organisation to understand its market size and the behaviours of current consumers, and to develop activities for users or attendees with varying levels of commitment and consumption. As well as data and insights, segmentation tools exist that comprise attitudinal or behaviour variables to help determine groups or segments. Examples may include elements of the Psychological Continuum Model (Funk and James, 2004) from Chapter 3 and the Attendance Frequency Escalator (Mullin, 1985a) shown below.

Conceptually, such frameworks can be applied not just to the sport spectator, but to varying products and users such as health and fitness participants who may indulge in their activity of choice from levels of infrequently to daily. However, fan development in many professional team markets has evolved towards a much more complex approach than these previous frameworks represent. For example, the Mullin framework conceptualises groups of non-aware, aware, indirect or media consumers as well as consumers of varying levels of consumption. It provides a base for fan development, but is limited given that modern fan development approaches are about much more than just encouraging attendance and seek to incorporate a range of additional experiences and engagement mechanisms. Additionally, given new consumption modes, large groups of consumers may be heavily committed, but may do the majority of their consumption through media sources, generating segments of media-dominant consumers not represented by previous behavioural frameworks. So, while suggested movement up the escalator remains conceptually relevant, knowledge of how fans connect and consume sport team products can be combined with club-specific data to allow much more specific targeting and strategies.

When applied to professional teams, fan development seeks to widen the number of consumers who are engaged at each level, requiring the elevating of involvement levels of existing consumers, while at the same time introducing new consumers to products and services. The fan development approach is in line with a focus on developing transactional consumers into relationship customers, and seeks to create greater loyalty, connection and attachment while contributing to the long-term goals of a team through growth and sustainability. A white paper by Gilt Edge (n.d.) suggests:

> Not placing an emphasis on fan development is simply misguided. Equally, assuming that fan development will just happen organically with winning, or conversely cannot happen unless the Team wins, is also misguided. The single most important factor in determining the asset value of a franchise is the existence of a large and passionate local fan base.

Fan development for a professional sport organisation may refer to a wide range of promotional activities, inclusive of those that drive sales and communication outcomes. They may include, but are not limited to:

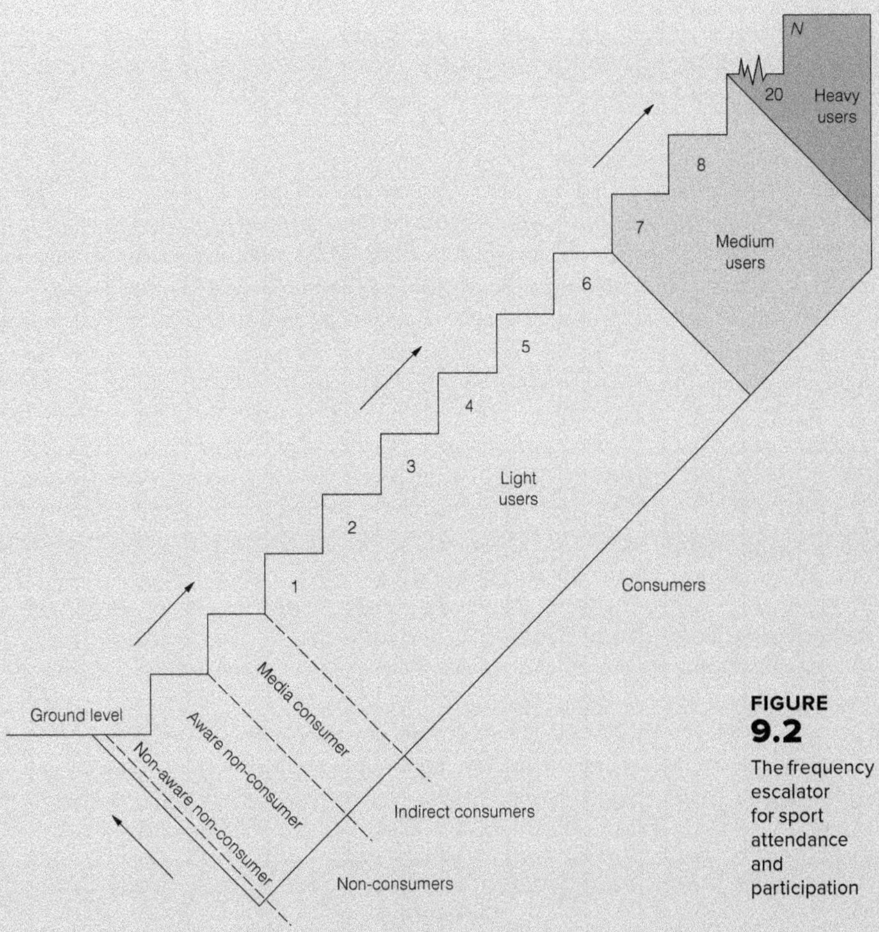

FIGURE 9.2 The frequency escalator for sport attendance and participation

Source: Mullin (1985a: 163). Reprinted with permission of Michie, Charlottesville, VA, in conjunction with LEXIS-NEXIS.

- increasing attendances and ticket revenue through sales promotions sampling and product trial
- building awareness and experiences of products and services such as attendance and membership or season tickets
- focusing on enhancing the customer experience at games
- seeking to develop deeper connections through communications and interactivity via digital or content marketing strategies
- introducing the sport to new players and increasing the fan base by developing and executing grass-roots programs, and
- direct engagement with communities through activities such as family days, festivals and team events.

While the above list may seem broad, organisations may also seek to identify particular segments and develop specific strategies or actions for them. For example, Sydney FC sought to engage a multicultural or culturally and linguistically diverse (CALD) segment of potential fans and media influencers. Promotions included ticket promotions, customised editorial and advertisements, community press conferences and events, and provision of game hospitality for CALD media journalists (Red Elephant, 2011). Outcomes of the activities included increased awareness in target communities, attendances and ticket revenue from community groups, direct engagement with communities and the establishment of relationships with media partners representing 32 ethnic or culturally diverse communities (Red Elephant, 2011).

Grassroots programs are also seen as a way to develop young fans. Soccer and basketball are two sports in Australia with huge participation bases whose national leagues and teams have—for various reasons—comparatively poorer followings. Leveraging activities to convert participation to attendance is one option, while growing participation in the sport itself is another. In the NHL, the Los Angeles Kings Fan Development Department 'promotes the sport of hockey on a grassroots level through developmental programs such as camps, clinics and other events that stress the fundamentals of recreational hockey in the community' (LA Kings, 2013). Using the team brand and exclusive opportunities with players and facilities, they develop activities for new and established hockey fans that aim to develop 'skill sets of local players and coaches, [while] introducing the sport to new players and increasing the fan base of the Kings' (LA Kings, 2013).

Regardless of the approach or dimensions implemented, fan development activities—inclusive of those linked to promotion—should be carried out as part of a planned, strategic structure, and should be led by a firm understanding of a market, and segments within it specific to that team or organisation. Other keys of fan development strategies include a strong brand identity, an organisational culture where fan development is central, efficient and effective data-management systems, and a focus on providing match and non-match engagement inclusive of unique and memorable experiences (Gilt Edge, n.d.).

Questions

1 Summarise the concept of fan development. What are specific short- and long-term benefits for organisations undertaking such strategies?
2 What information might marketers require: (a) prior to the development of a fan development strategy and (b) after its execution, in order to assess the effectiveness of the activities?
3 Choose a professional team with which you are familiar. How would you develop and describe a range of segments they may target in fan development activities?
4 Choose a segment or segments. How would you design a program of activities that incorporates as many elements of the promotions mix from this chapter as possible?
5 What might some SMART objectives of such a campaign be?

Stage 1—Identification of marketing opportunities

▼

Stage 2—Strategy determination

Step 5—Determine core marketing strategy

Marketing and service mix—sport product, pricing, place (physical evidence, people, process), customer satisfaction

Promotion mix, advertising

Step 6—Determine tactics and performance benchmarks

▼

Stage 3—Strategy implemention, evaluation and adjustment

10

Advertising

CHAPTER OBJECTIVES

Chapter 10 introduces advertising as a component of the sport promotions mix. Advertising is a non-personal paid message aimed at creating awareness about a product or idea. This chapter examines some of the ways in which advertising is used in sport to promote sporting contests and events. The creative techniques used to develop ideas and communicate them are described, and types of advertising and media options, as well as principles for selecting an advertising mix, are discussed.

After studying this chapter, you should be able to:

- articulate the concepts related to advertising
- understand decisions related to creative strategy and development of a message
- recognise the media options available to marketers and the message capabilities of various media
- establish procedures and strategies for selecting the appropriate media mix
- develop mechanisms for measuring advertising effectiveness
- acknowledge the ongoing potential in advertising for ambush marketing.

HEADLINE STORY

Buying a part of the game: Super Bowl advertising campaigns

One of the most sought-after advertising properties each year in the United States is a slot during the NFL Super Bowl. Costing around $3.8 million for a 30-second spot in 2013, the Super Bowl is one of the most expensive advertising options, but reaches an annual audience of over 100 million people. In addition to this, the opportunity to leverage the prestige and attention that Super Bowl advertisers draw in the lead-up to the event adds to the attractiveness of this option.

The advertising or media spend is only one aspect of an advertiser's spend, though, given that marketers need to produce the advertising content—including messages and creative—that seeks to attract attention, appeal and likeability and ultimately create sales for a brand. Remembering that the media spend of $3.8 million only covers the 30-second on-air slot, and not the creative, production or development costs of the advertisement and campaign, the need to fully leverage the event is paramount to produce return on such a substantial investment.

The success to be had by advertisers is highlighted by the case of Mercedes-Benz, whose 2013 advertising spot featured celebrities such as pop star Usher, supermodel Kate Upton and actor Willem Dafoe. Mercedes-Benz spent heavily, outlaying a reported eight-figure sum for advertising time during the game (Vranica, 2013). However, the company claims it has easily recouped the investment, citing a return on investment figure that is double their spend, with resultant benefits drawn largely from publicity from media outlets, mentions in major publications and newspapers in the United States and abroad, and coverage across TV news and entertainment programs. It is now common for advertisers to hire public relations firms to help promote and support their Super Bowl spots and wider campaigns, with Mercedes-Benz no exception. As well as internal departments, it had two outside PR firms working on generating media attention (Vranica, 2013).

As part of this wider approach, Super Bowl advertisements now form part of an overall campaign, with online and web videos, content marketing, social media campaigns and publicity used to build a lead-in to and continuation of the feature advertisement played during the game. Commonly, brands release 'teasers' or versions of their ads on the internet well before the game to maximise their coverage. Overall, Super Bowl advertising has transitioned beyond a single prime-time advertisement to evolve into increasingly integrated productions incorporating television, press, content marketing and social media.

Source: Vranica (2013).

Given the breadth of promotional options now available, competition is stronger than ever for share of marketing spend. Advertising, though, maintains its attractiveness, something particularly illustrated by the continuing growth of popular sport properties such as the NFL Super Bowl. Having said that, advertising is no longer the independently used tool it once was, and is more commonly—as the Super Bowl example shows—

integrated with a range of promotional tools to form more holistic marketing communication strategies. Likewise, advertising is no longer defined by mass media spend, or by the television, radio, print and outdoor media that have formed the major share of advertising in previous decades. As this chapter will show, various digital opportunities now exist that can be included in the suite of advertising options.

Advertising is defined as a 'paid form of non-personal communication about an organisation, product, service or idea by an identified sponsor' (Belch et al., 2011: 5). It differs from other promotional media, given the control the advertiser has over the message and its placement. While advertising can take many forms, it is basically constructed around a message that is designed to build audiences and promote sales. However, Ries and Ries (2009) argue that the purpose of advertising is not to build a brand; rather, it should be used as a protective or defensive strategy once that brand has been built through other media.

Irrespective of context, the foundation of successful advertising is the ability to communicate, making creativity and clarity of message vitally important. Gifford (2007) states that sports form a large part of today's society, with advertising playing a prominent role in sport through many varied forms. She supports this assertion with what she believes are ten amazing sport ads that cut across both competitive and non-competitive sport. From the Tennis Masters in China, to Nike shoe boxes, to soccer games in men's rooms or cycling in the United Kingdom, these pieces of advertising are excellent examples of the creativity required to stand out in a cluttered advertising marketplace.

Through these examples, we see sport provides a range of properties—both within stadiums and through specific communications properties—that can add value to advertisers and brands. From venue signage to program inserts, from scoreboard placements to athlete apparel and spectator merchandise, the potential for companies to use the many facets of sport as a vehicle to advertise or promote products or services is endless. Moreover, the audience at such events is clearly captive and segmentable. This is particularly relevant in the example of television advertising. In the age of DVRs and recorded or downloaded programming, there are few formats of programming that maintain their premium value when consumed live. Sport remains one of these. For example, it is much more likely that consumers will watch a sporting game or event live—inclusive of advertising—than a sitcom or movie, which they may be happier to record and watch at their own convenience. The willingness of organisations to use sport to communicate messages to consumers is evidenced by Sportview 10.1; however, as also evidenced, advertising needs to form part of a broader communication strategy.

SPORTVIEW 10.1

Sport fields and advertising

It has long been argued that sport venues are the perfect vehicle for promotional advertising. The array of opportunities for advertisement at such locations is vast, including signage, equipment and on-field opportunities, as well as various leverage or activation opportunities to support or extend campaigns, which are becoming increasingly popular to support advertising.

Lynch and Dunn (2003) used a Brisbane cricket ground to survey spectator recall of SunSmart skin cancer-prevention advertising. The location of this research was entirely appropriate, given that it has been determined that sunburn is often most prevalent during passive recreational activity, which clearly includes sport spectatorship. The major purpose of the research was to determine the efficacy of the choice of medium—in this case, the sport arena, to inform an at-risk population.

A total of 231 cricket spectators were surveyed over five days during the cricket season, and asked a series of questions related to their recall of scoreboard advertising. Factored into the research was the respondent's personal behaviour around sun protection, from appropriate apparel and eyewear to the use of a sunscreen. The research indicated that recall was higher among those who were already engaging in sunburn-minimisation techniques. However, it was also apparent that, for those for whom the message would be most beneficial—people who use minimal sunburn protection strategies—recall was limited.

This research demonstrates that venue advertising, important as it is, needs to be part of a broader promotional or sponsorship campaign if it is to actively influence public behaviour.

Source: Adapted from Lynch and Dunn (2003).

The advertising management process

O'Hara and Weese (1994: 9) established a framework to 'better communicate product and service offerings to target groups'. Entitled the 'advertising management process', the five-step program incorporates research, campaign planning (including advertising strategy, objectives, budget and key message), creative development, media planning and, finally, implementation and evaluation. The process is illustrated schematically in Figure 10.1.

The process represents a simple yet effective way of establishing sports advertising strategy, linking the five components of advertising management in a sequential manner.

FIGURE 10.1 The advertising management process

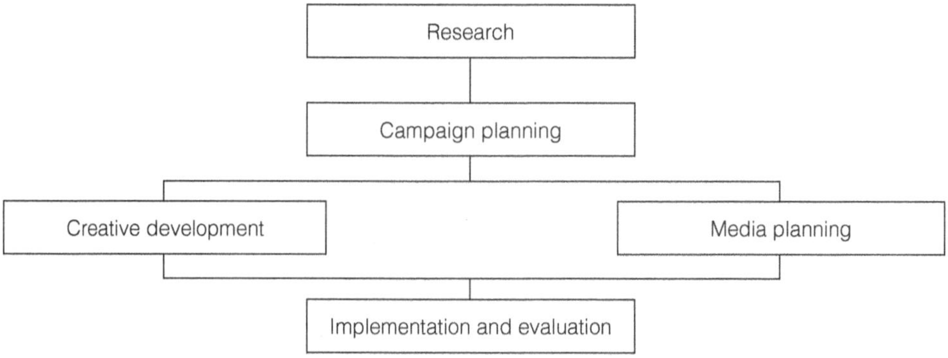

Source: O'Hara and Weese (1994:11).

Following the data collection or research, a campaign is planned around a major theme. At this time, how that theme will be creatively developed, and how it will be produced and presented for different media are established simultaneously. During implementation, an evaluative mechanism is established to ascertain the effectiveness (or lack thereof) of the campaign. The stages from campaign planning to implementation and measurement will be the focus of this chapter, and form the structure for the following sections.

Advertising strategy

Following the research stage, the next step is to consider the advertising strategy (O'Hara and Weese, 1994). This can comprise the following issues at an introductory stage:

- Has the target audience been identified, and can it be described?
- What part does advertising play in relation to the totality of the promotional or integrated marketing communications strategy and what other tools will be used?
- Are the objectives sales or communication related, and how does this affect both the media and creative strategy to be used?
- Have instruments for monitoring and evaluating effectiveness been established, and are they in place?
- What is the advertising budget?

It is important that the answers to all these questions are known before an advertising campaign is embarked upon.

Both the size of the community and the size of special-interest groups or target audiences in the market can affect advertising strategy. Despite any benefits that one advertising medium may have over another, a mix of several media is often the best strategy. Even the use of just two media, such as print and radio together, can result in an interaction that makes each more effective. Similarly, the integration of advertising with other promotional elements (as in the Super Bowl example in the headline story) can lead to synergistic benefits.

The major issue facing a sport marketer's use of advertising is whether to stress reach or frequency. Reach refers to the identification of potential consumers, while frequency relates to the number of exposures required to access the consumer. Both are critical to a successful advertising strategy. When determining reach, the advertiser must decide which consumers are being targeted. When determining frequency, the advertiser must decide how many exposures are necessary to reach the prospective consumer. Here factors such as price, stage in the product life-cycle, purchase frequency and competitors' advertising need to be addressed. It should be remembered that it takes a number of exposures to communicate a specific message, as there are always communication barriers to overcome.

Reach should be stressed over frequency when a product is being introduced or when it has a large target market. Frequency should be stressed over reach when products are frequently bought and brand switching may take place, as well as when the target market is relatively small or when the message is difficult to explain, and repetition is required to communicate and solidify the advertising idea in the mind of the consumer.

Advertising objectives

O'Hara and Weese (1994) contend that advertising must create exposure, generate processing and lead to long-term communication effects such as attitude and awareness, and ideally lead consumers toward behavioural changes. Quite simply, the purpose of advertising is to influence consumers to respond positively to products or services. While this can best be achieved by establishing advertising campaigns that are linked to prior experience and are strategically focused, there are no fail-safe mechanisms to ensure success, given that every campaign is different.

Likewise, advertising objectives can differ across campaigns, products and markets, but should be either sales or communication related. *Communication objectives* endeavour to provide messages that are understood by consumers about the product or service as a result of the campaign. This type of advertising is used predominantly when a change of image is desired, or there is an attempt to build or strengthen a message or positioning within a particular demographic. It may also be appropriate if an organisation wishes to generate community goodwill or there is a need to counter a competitive campaign thrust. Advantages of adopting an advertising strategy based on communication objectives are that they encourage the identification of process goals and require that the campaign be evaluated in terms of those goals. Communication goals are also less likely than sales objectives to be affected by other variables such as price or availability, making measurement more pertinent. One disadvantage of communication objectives is that attitudes sought from the campaign may be unrelated to purchase intention or later behaviours. It could be argued that, given that the fundamental basis of advertising is to communicate, objectives should be communication linked.

Sales objectives indicate a target level of sales to be achieved as a result of the campaign. Advertising of this type is used when the desire is to encourage membership, audience or product consumption. The obvious advantage of this type of advertising is that sales are a result of purchase behaviour, which is the ultimate goal of the advertiser. The main disadvantage of basing a campaign purely on sales objectives is that the number of sales alone rarely provides much in the way of decision-making guidance. Additionally, advertising often has a lagging effect on sales; hence past, not present, advertising may influence current sales. Finally, changes in competitive decisions may cause changes in current sales.

When determining advertising objectives, the issue of timeframe is critical. On some occasions, sport marketers are limited in scope because the event, product or service—like a major event or tournament—is a 'one-off' experience. Conversely, advertising may be part of a long-range communication plan, with various steps along the way. Here, advertising strategies can build on or lead into previous campaigns. Timeframes can also influence the advertising media to be used, as some can be used with little advance notice while others require lead time. In general, for immediacy, nothing is better than television, while for mass distribution, newspapers and digital forms on high-traffic websites are excellent.

Advertising budget

The development and distribution of the budget for advertising can play a large role in the quality, prominence and ultimately the impact of advertising. In determining how the advertising budget should be allocated, a decision first needs to be made about whether the budget strategy should be massed or distributed.

When adopting a massed strategy, the advertising budget is used heavily at the beginning of a campaign and falls away as the weeks pass. The percentage of advertising recall is initially high, but then drops off quite quickly. This is an appropriate strategy to adopt for annual events, the commencement of seasonal or holiday activities such as snow skiing, or the introduction of a new product or model into the marketplace.

With a distributed campaign, the advertising budget is used evenly throughout the year for a pre-defined period. The percentage of recall is initially low, but recall elevates with repeated weekly exposure. Activities such as professional sports, which are constant, result in a playoff period and have a limited off-season, mainly use a distributed advertising budget. It should be remembered that all advertising campaigns have time limits in terms of their effectiveness. However, eventual advertising wear-out can be delayed by introducing variations on the theme or message. The time will come, however, when the advertising campaign has no effect—or, more significantly, a negative impact—on sport consumption.

Irrespective of whether a massed, distributed or combination advertising strategy is adopted, the advertising budget should be determined by the importance of the campaign, which in turn should be based on expected returns from the investment. While some types of advertising are cost-intensive, others are labour-intensive, and available resources need to be taken into account when establishing strategy. Radio, television, newspaper, magazine and supplements, outdoor advertising, direct mail, posters and premiums or giveaways are cost-intensive, in that they require more in terms of money than staff time. Conversely, press releases, contact with special-interest groups, personal contact with business and community leaders, speakers, personal appearances, special-event stations, involvement in community events and promotional stunts are labour-intensive, in that they require more in terms of staff time than money.

Message strategy

Once the advertising strategy is set, inclusive of the objectives and budget, work can begin on the development of the message, inclusive of the creative and media strategy. Here, three questions can be used to develop and deliver an advertising platform: 'What to say?' (the message); 'How to say it?' (the creative); and 'Where to say it?' (the choice of media).

The development of the message should constitute the first part of this process. Here, there are various tools such as copy platforms (Belch et al., 2011) and message strategy statements (Schultz and Schultz, 2004) that can assist in the development of clear and concise message descriptions. This forces the marketer to consider a range of key criteria, and develop within them a statement that summarises the major communication or selling idea that should be the focus of the advertising effort. Some of these criteria—for example, consideration of objectives and research findings—may form part of prior stages of the advertising process. Others may include the target market, consideration of the product or service, its positioning and key benefits or differentiating characteristics. Based on these criteria, a message strategy may be generic or brand specific, focus on unique selling points, be pre-emptive, target an affective or emotional response, or seek to highlight specific positioning or brand image traits (Fraser, 1983).

As part of this, and before making decisions about the appropriate media to be used, sport marketers need to understand the relationship between advertising and the phases of the product life-cycle discussed in Chapter 5. During the goods or services introductory phase, advertising should be informative. Here, the advertisement should provide all the salient information about the product. This may include special features, relevant technical specifications, pictorial or illustrative representations, place of purchase and/or consumption, and even price. Basically, the sport promoter is stating what the goods or services are and where they can be obtained. During the growth and maturity phases, advertising should be persuasive in nature. Consumers should be reminded of the benefits and/or the desirable attributes that can be gained by consuming the product.

Creative strategy

Once the key message is defined, the work of developing and shaping the message creatively, and planning its communication, can begin. As well as establishing the creative approach, an organisation must also set its media strategy—which determines the best media for the message. This will be in part a function of responses to the following questions:

- What is the purpose of the advertising?
- Who is it aimed at?
- What is promised?
- How will it be delivered?
- What will be the 'personality' or the essence of the product?

In considering media and creative strategy, this is not a sequential process, given that an organisation must know the format of the advertising (magazine or outdoor) before it can produce or develop the creative content. Similarly, an idea of the media alternatives to be used can help develop the creative direction of the advertising. For the purposes of this chapter, mechanisms for establishing a creative strategy will be noted before potential media strategy is examined.

The task of the creative strategy is to develop message ideas and execute them effectively. Effective message ideas should be based on consumer research findings, fit the overall marketing strategy, be appropriate for the target market, be simple or basic (limited to one major point per message), and be developed so they are most resistant to counter-attack. It should be remembered that if an organisation's unique selling proposition (USP) is price, it is very easy for competitors to attack in the marketplace. While creativity is usually situation- or even person-specific, and hence highly individual, there are a number of more general creative approaches or techniques that organisations can utilise or combine to develop advertising strategies. These include:

- *Straight sell advertising.* This is reliant on factual material or clarity around presentation of features and benefits of a product or service. It focuses on the rational traits of a product, and seeks to provide clear articulation of usage and benefits.
- *Demonstration advertising.* This shows the product in use, and is applicable when potential consumers are unfamiliar with the product or how to use it. While the obvious example is the raft of celebrity-endorsed home fitness equipment that appears during late-night 'infomercials', it also has applicability to sporting events. Demonstration of games or activities can both inform and persuade consumers, especially if associated with lifestyle.
- *Technical evidence advertising.* This form of advertising is similar to demonstration sells, but is reliant on scientific evidence or tests to showcase a particular attribute of a product or service. For example, sport performance drinks such as Gatorade or Powerade may highlight laboratory-proven attributes of recovery or replenishment of vital fluids that make the product advantageous to users.
- *Comparison advertising.* This form of advertising can distinguish and position a brand against competitors. This could be done on many platforms, ranging from longevity of the product to cost. Providing a point of comparison allows clear enforcement of product positioning as better value, or more suitable for a consumer's needs.
- *Testimonial advertising.* This involves an actual user of the product serving as a spokesperson. Past athletes are often used to promote sport and related products by organisations that believe former champions strike a chord with older market segments. This, in turn, may encourage them to consume the current offering, which may be a sport or non-sport product. During the 2002 football World Cup, Brazilian soccer star Pele—at the time, arguably the world's most famous athlete—appeared nightly in a television advertisement extolling the virtues of treatment for erectile dysfunction. Likewise, a number of Australian sport stars became advocates for various products of the Swisse vitamins range, and were promoted in the lead-up to the 2012 Olympics.
- *Imagery based advertising.* This can be used to elicit powerful emotional responses to sport products or services. For example, slow-motion footage or action highlights can be used to provide a concentrated selling pitch for events or games. When combined with music and graphics, the power of such imagery—particularly given the emotional nature of sport—can have strong effects.
- *Slice-of-life advertising.* This uses some aspect of daily life as a part of the advertisement. The intent behind this approach is to communicate messages and images to consumers, to which they can relate. This approach is probably most appropriate when it connects fans with their past—usually their youth. While this belief is a fundamental underpinning of Major League Baseball (MLB) in North America, it has real relevance in most sport settings—especially cricket in Australia. This is the case when cricket advertisements feature children in backyards hitting 'sixes' over the neighbour's fence, or highlight traditional 'pick-up' games comprising both athletes and kids in the yard or on the beach. When brands then embed that activity as a television advertisement into a Test match in front of 80 000 people at the MCG, consumers readily see the connection between the two.

- *Lifestyle advertising.* This operates on the basic tenet that the use of a product or service will result in the user accessing a particular lifestyle. Although this type of advertising has obvious relevance for the health and fitness industry, sport events such as horse racing have adopted this type of advertising in recent years in an attempt to entice groups to the track. In an increasingly hectic environment, sports that can incorporate traits related to family or social lifestyle in their advertising may find themselves well placed in the sport marketplace.
- *Announcement advertising.* This provides information about a new brand, product, package, design or formula. The most common examples of this type of advertising happen when sports apparel companies introduce new models on to the market. In most cases, the release is accompanied by a new advertising campaign. Sporting organisations use announcement advertising to inform their consumers of changes about which they need to be aware to ensure their enjoyment of the event. Event timing, parking conditions, public transport facilities and member information related to event entrance are just a few of the instances that warrant announcement advertising.
- *Imitation or symbolic association advertising.* This attempts to associate attractive personal qualities with ownership or use of a product. Such an approach is often connected to celebrity endorsement. Here, the advertisement suggests that adoption of a particular product or service will infuse the consumer with desirable traits. Gatorade famously tapped successfully into this advertising vein in the early 1990s, when it ran the iconic 'I want to be like Mike' advertisements.

Media alternatives

Before establishing guidelines that help decide the advertising strategies and media to be used, it is necessary to make a number of general observations about key advertising media.

- *Newspapers* are current and relatively inexpensive, and therefore reach a mass audience. In deciding to advertise using newspapers, sport marketers need to provide copy that is eye-catching and succinct. It is also important to be aware of the sections the target audience reads, which can differ across newspapers. As well as sport, general interest and business sections of daily newspapers are increasingly becoming a repository for sport advertising.
- *Magazines* invite leisure readership, as they invariably lie around the house or business for an extended period. Similarly, the one issue is often read—or at least browsed through—by potentially quite different consumer groups. Here, appearance and layout designs are of paramount importance. Sport-specific magazines such as *Inside Sport* or *Sports Illustrated* provide obvious examples of sport advertising.
- *Digital advertising* on the internet has become a major source of information and opportunities for organisations and brands. Increasingly, sporting organisations are turning to the internet to conduct their business, with websites established by myriad sport organisations to inform, entertain and otherwise engage their consumer base. Social media and blogs provide new extensions of the web advertising experience.

Advantages of the internet include the ability of a site to link to other sites for further information, as well as increasing opportunities for customisation and measurement. There is no doubt that this expanding technology is providing information to organisations on a scale previously not possible. Increasingly, as newspapers and magazines take virtual and interactive forms, digital advertising within these forms is becoming increasingly prominent.

- *Outdoor advertising*, in the form of billboards or fence signage, involves the presentation of an uncomplicated message. Usually just a logo or a few words dominate, which the advertiser hopes will trigger recognition of a much more complicated message. Signage advertising for major sporting events, such as the Australian Open tennis, the Formula One Grand Prix and the Melbourne Cup, regularly appears at the appropriate time on central business district buildings and freeway billboards. Such displays usually feature the major slogan or logo, event date and ticket availability, or a similar call to action. This information is then reinforced and elaborated through other media.
- *Brochures, flyers and posters* usually combine the features of billboards plus newspaper and magazine advertising. The advantage of this type of advertising is that it can segment the market very well.
- *Radio advertising* relies on recall in a heavily cluttered marketplace, so frequency is critical. Radio's advertising advantage lies in the fact that, given its lack of visual images, the imagination of the listener may be stimulated by suggestive advertising. As a result, event promoters can create advertising around the sounds of the ski slope, the beach and summer or the city, while at the same time creating an element of mystery.
- *Television advertising* also exists in an extremely cluttered marketplace, although there is little doubt that television advertising reaches the largest possible audience. Moreover, the use of visuals plus sound provides the most effective mechanism for presenting specific information. One problem facing television advertisers is how to stand out in an increasingly crowded marketplace, with humour, shock, celebrity advertising or music usually a feature used to capture the viewer's initial attention. The relationship between sport, advertising and television is discussed at length in Chapter 11.
- *Stadium signage* is a further form that may present opportunities. Increasingly, electronic signage is replacing static boards, providing increased visibility and customisability. One advantage here is the ability to capture and extend sport viewers' attention, with individuals already engaged with the programming (and related brand) on television or at the event. An example is the use by Liverpool Football Club to promote ticket sales to its Australian tour using the electronic signage at their Anfield home ground during the first half of 2013. Other English Premier League clubs use this medium to promote merchandise, corporate hospitality or sponsors' products, including those of gambling companies and airlines.
- *Virtual advertising* is an innovative medium. Used with success in only a few markets until recently, it provides for real-time video insertions into television broadcasts to produce dynamic or static versions of two- or three-dimensional images. These are

created by placing coverage over a camera face to overlay existing signs on primary locations, usually a sporting ground. This practice uniquely provides the opportunity to display one advertiser's message at the stadium and a different message to viewers at home, or the ability to customise messages to a market or even a particular household. See Sportview 10.2 for an NRL example of virtual advertising.

- *Product placement* within television and movies is another increasingly common form of communication that is seen as more credible than advertising. In a related manner, *athlete or celebrity endorsements* provide another avenue to communicate a message. Here, a trusted or likeable source is used to communicate a message, or is featured in advertising.
- *Gaming advertising* placement within video games represents a variant of the above product placement, with millions of gamers across sport video games and virtual life interactions providing a market for advertisers. With many gamers connected to the internet in real time, opportunities to update and customise messages exist in such forums.

SPORTVIEW 10.2

The NRL confronts a new world of virtual advertising

In the 2010 lead-up to the Rugby League State of Origin series (one of Australian television's highest rating sport programs), rain had fallen steadily and threatened an important part of the match planning. As Tabakoff (2013) describes it

> National Rugby League officials were in a flap. Their concerns were not that the game would not proceed; rather, they were worried that the promotional field signage for the major sponsor of the series at the time could not be painted on the field in time for the match.

NRL general manager of commercial and marketing Paul Kind noted that the sponsors 'were paying a significant fee to have [signage] delivered to a three million-plus audience nationally, but it was pouring'. The fears of NRL officials were well founded, with only one of the eight contracted signs being visible for the start of the match. In the NRL's collective mind, it was this moment that prompted the sport's move to pursue superimposed 'virtual signage' on to its football fields (Tabakoff, 2013). Nearly three years later, Channel Nine became the first NRL match with virtual signage for the full game, featuring logos of Victoria Bitter, Telstra and Holden branded across the field. Only one sign was directly painted on the field: that of the competition title and sponsor.

The technology to produce the images on NRL grounds fits within the head of the camera, and vastly improves the quality of on-field imagery (compared with painted signage). With over $4 million generated from sponsor signage annually (Tabakoff, 2013), the investment towards innovation for the NRL is a worthwhile one, particularly at multi-sport venues where over-used turf can impact the clarity and effectiveness of traditional brand signage.

Source: Tabakoff (2013).

Timing and cost

Two additional factors that need to be considered, irrespective of the media alternatives, are timing and cost. The dual questions related to timing are how soon the advertising goals need to be achieved, and how the advertising mix is established to gain optimal support and recognition. Cost is usually determined as cost-per-thousand, or CPM. Here, it needs to be ascertained how much it will cost to make impressions on 1000 people. The formula is:

$$\text{CPM} = \frac{\text{Cost}}{\text{Reach}} \times 1000$$

For example, if a radio commercial costs $2000 and is estimated to reach 175 000 listeners, the CPM is $11.43.

Media selection

Media selection depends on many of the factors previously discussed in this chapter. Elements such as budget, sales or communication objectives and target audience are, in the main, internal to the organisation. However, there are also a number of qualitative and quantitative media factors that need to be considered.

While television advertising can be strong in terms of its total population reach, uniform coverage, emotional stimulation and the ability to use slice-of-life and humour all mean it is rather weak with respect to up-scale selectivity, positioning and the predictability of audience levels. Marginal sports such as polo would be better advertised in other media, such as magazines, whereas television is a perfect outlet for the traditional and more popular summer and winter sports.

Radio's advertising strength lies in its young adult selectivity, its CPM and its ability to exploit time-of-day factors and opportunities to stimulate the imagination. The downside of radio is its lack of uniform coverage, its lack of depth in demographics and its inability to conduct product demonstrations or exploit attention-seeking devices. Demographic-specific activities that have been appropriated by identifiable consumer markets would be well served by using radio. An upcoming skateboard exhibition, surfing contest or harness race meeting could better be served by advertising on a niche-market radio station than on television.

The potency of newspaper advertising lies in its capacity to select local markets, to exploit day-of-week factors, and to convey detail and information. The downside of newspaper advertising relates to its lack of national coverage (except for national newspapers), its general inability to negotiate rates and its inadequate ability to intrude. For sport marketers, newspapers are best used to provide fixture information and updates.

Magazine advertising is appropriate if market selectivity, frequency control, advertisement positioning and prestige of the medium are important. It is difficult to stimulate emotion or imagination, negotiate rates, use slice-of-life or, once again, be intrusive when using this medium. Noting magazines' strength, sport advertisers would be well served by advertising in their sport-specific magazine(s).

Finally, online or digital forms of advertising (websites, social media and networking, gaming) represent the fast growing component of advertising, and have advantages through their levels of customisability and measurability that are not offered by some other platforms. However, advertising clutter remains an issue in this medium, with adequately targeted and attention-grabbing copy remaining important criteria for successful advertising within these media.

Measuring advertising effectiveness

The components of a successful testing program for advertising are many and varied. The successful advertising campaign must not only be clear and objective, and aid in the decision-making process; it must also offer good value, and be valid and reliable as well as practical and defensible. Finally, it should produce understandable and measurable results.

The sport marketer should expect that the organisation's advertising will be both seen and heard, communicate messages and/or create impressions, associate brands with images and both be persuasive and sell. To ensure that this is the case, the organisation needs to engage in copy testing. This action has the potential to minimise risks and marketing mistakes, maximise budget efficiency, and move the product or service ahead in the marketplace.

The two major testing programs are recall and recognition. Recall requires respondents to remember a particular advertisement (unaided) or an advertisement within a product category (aided). Recognition involves showing the respondents the advertisement. Chapter 13 develops the concepts of recognition and recall in detail.

The current industry trend in advertisement testing uses the recall method. The philosophy behind this method is that if people can remember a commercial, its intended message and the brand name, there is a better chance that persuasion will occur and the brand will sell. The most common recall-testing method used in television is the day-after recall (DAR) interview, which is conducted within 24 hours of the advertisement's display. This interview establishes respondent type, programs viewed, whether or not the respondent recalls the advertisement and the components recalled. As an example, and with respect to print media, the Starch Readership Test also examines recall. Less than 17 per cent related recall is regarded as low, and anything above 32 per cent as high. It should be ascertained through additional questioning what respondents were doing during the advertising period and what media they were attending to.

To perform well in a test of recall, a commercial must cut through the clutter of the medium and the apathy of viewers and gain attention, which in turn maximises the audience for the message to follow. This has tended to lead to loud and flamboyant commercials. The ARU, NRL and A-League have adopted stunning visuals, usually augmented by music, to advertise their respective products.

Although there is no guaranteed formula for success, effective advertisements usually exhibit the following traits:

- They identify the brand early and are clear and convincing.
- They are simple, yet interesting and involving.
- They adopt audio and visual reinforcement wherever possible.
- They link the brand to the image created.

Some other aspects for advertising campaigns to consider are that they should be consistent with other marketing communication elements that are used, be appropriate for the target market, be appropriate for the media in which they are used, and be honest and tasteful. Once an advertising campaign has been tested, the results obtained can give rise to different courses of action. An organisation may:

- give an unreserved green light to the campaign
- alter the media mix
- alter timing based on demographic information, or
- if the advertisement is not communicating the intended message to the correct demographics, decide to start the process again.

Ambush marketing through advertising

The logic and strategies behind ambush marketing are discussed in Chapter 14; however, in terms of advertising, ambush marketing has long been the bane of legitimate sports promoters and advertisers worldwide. Chadwick and Burton (2011: 710) suggest that the 'efforts made by unassociated brands to capitalize on the financial benefits and media value provided by sport has increased [with] the need for marketers, sponsors, and officials to acknowledge, understand, and defend against ambushing magnified by the staggering growth of sponsorship investment'. There have been countless documented cases of unauthorised advertising activity, many revolving around well-known sports companies and soft drinks. Major events such as the FIFA World Cups and Olympic Games, for example, often provide the vehicle for such activity, with London 2012 no exception (see Sportview 10.3).

Kent and Campbell (2007: 118) suggest that 'ambush marketing represents the set of activities that companies use to create the impression of an association with a sport or event', and that in doing so the ambush marketer 'is attempting to exploit the commercial potential of a property, without supplying any financial support for the right to do so'.

However, it is not just mega-events that provide an environment for ambush marketing. In the past, both the AFL and Cricket Australia have sought to ban aerial advertising from venues across the country where Ashes Test series or grand final games were being played. Cricket officials were trying to protect the rights of their sponsors, and were seeking state government support to establish restricted air space around the venues. Likewise, the Victorian government has banned all aerial advertising during the AFL Finals series at the AFL's request. While fines of up to $250 000 await those who attempt to flout the law, there is little doubt that, regardless of the sport or event, if there are large crowds in attendance, ambush marketers will use all means available to advertise their products or services.

SPORTVIEW 10.3

Fun with 'London'—ambush marketing and the Olympic Games

Alongside the 2012 London Olympics, Nike launched a campaign showing athletes 'finding their greatness' in various 'London' locations around the world. The film showed various locations sharing the name of the British capital, including East London in South Africa, Little London in Jamaica, London, Ohio in the United States and London Gym, a health club. However, Nike was not an official sponsor of the games and was seeking to capitalise on the games through ambush marketing, and thus impact the effectiveness of official sportswear sponsor, Adidas.

While not able to directly reference the host city version of London, the 'Find Your Greatness' campaign sought to inspire individuals' personal achievements. Featured through traditional advertising media, as well as prominently executed through social and digital channels, the advertising included vision of 'weekend sportsmen, children and amateurs avidly participating in different sports to the subliminal message that greatness isn't reserved to the chosen few and the bright lights of the Olympics' (*Marketing Magazine*, 2012). As per the advertisement's voiceover: 'Greatness is not in one special place and it is not in one special person. Greatness is wherever somebody is trying to find it.'

Nike was certainly not the only organisation to challenge the IOC and LOCOG branding and sponsorship rules, with small businesses including London butchers and florists feeling the wrath of the IOC's heavy ambush marketing-protection policies in place during the 2012 event. The Nike campaign continued the prominent ambush marketing battles between itself and Adidas that have been a feature of past Olympics and FIFA World Cup events. In this case, creativity meant Nike avoided a reprimand from the IOC, while its well-designed media placement produced a competitive edge over its rival in London 2012 marketing.

Sources: Marketing Magazine (2012); Miller (2012).

Summary

Sport advertising is now a multi-billion dollar industry, and has as its prime purpose the influencing of consumers to respond positively to products or services. The foundation of successful advertising is the ability to communicate, and this can take place through various media using vastly different strategies. Newspapers are current and relatively inexpensive, and they reach a mass audience, while magazines invite leisure readership. Radio can bring the imagination into play, while television unquestionably reaches the largest possible audience. Outdoor advertising involves the presentation of an uncomplicated message, while brochures, flyers and posters effectively segment the market. Digital and internet forms increasingly are being used to provide information and content, adding customisation and measurement aspects that provide an advantage over other formats. Two additional factors that need to be considered, irrespective of the media alternatives, are timing and cost.

Media selection depends on elements such as objectives (that is, whether they are sales or communication objectives), budget and target audience. However, a number of qualitative and quantitative media factors need to be considered. The successful advertising campaign must not only be clear and aid in the decision-making process; it must also offer good value, be valid and reliable as well as practical and defensible, and produce understandable results.

Advertising services is different from advertising goods. However, through advertising to employees, realising the value of word-of-mouth, providing tangible clues, making the service comprehensible, ensuring continuity in advertising themes and images and, most importantly, promising only that which can be delivered with total certainty, the potential impact of intangibles on service can be reduced and, to a lesser extent, controlled.

Recognising that creativity in advertising is very much a matter of individual choice and perception, this chapter has focused on the strategies that can be adopted to inform the creative underpinnings of sport advertising. A thorough understanding of the objectives of, and the budget allocated to, a sport advertising campaign will in part dictate the type of campaign to be run and the media to be used. Once these decisions have been made, the creative component can be established within a well-defined structure. A clear indication of the effectiveness of the strategies can be obtained through ongoing monitoring of the advertising campaign. In all cases, however, sport organisations need to be vigilant in relation to ambush marketing and employ strategies to protect their sponsors accordingly.

CASE STUDY

The rising case for socially responsible advertising—promoting alcohol, gambling and fast food to sport consumers

In the 1990s, the banning of tobacco advertising, and later tobacco sponsorship, was a prominent stance taken by governments, policy-makers and health advocates that would have an impact on sports organisations and broadcasters. Until this time, tobacco manufacturers had been strong supporters of sports, ranging from motor racing to cricket, with the influence of this legislation limiting the ability of organisations to garner financial resources from organisations in this industry.

Into the 2010s, a range of other product classes, including alcohol, gambling and fast food, face criticism of their role in promoting unhealthy behaviours and social issues, in part through their leverage of sport-focused advertising. The next decade will provide an interesting situation for potential regulation or bans that may hinder the ongoing ability of organisations in these industries to advertise and sponsor forms of sport programming, events, leagues and teams.

Alcohol advertising and sponsorship presents as the next category to face heavy scrutiny. Professor Greg Kolt, a biomedical and health science expert at the University of Western Sydney, has drawn a comparison between alcohol advertising in sport and tobacco advertising, noting that there has 'always been a link made between alcohol and sport . . . [highlighting detrimental effects] in the same way as there was previously between cigarettes and sport'. Dr Kerry O'Brien from the University of Manchester says advertising during sporting events has much more to do with youth binge drinking than the behaviour of role models and sport stars. Dr O'Brien states: 'We continue to criticise individual sports stars for their poor behaviour, particularly when it comes to drinking, however it doesn't actually appear that sport stars' drinking patterns . . . are actually having an influence on young people.' Rather, Dr O'Brien says there is a consistent pattern with alcohol advertising through sporting events and alcohol consumption, citing that alcohol companies spend about 80 per cent of their advertising budget on sport. He says: 'They [alcohol brands] know that sport is a great avenue for marketing their products and it does influence young people.'

Alcohol sponsorship has also been criticised within the mega-event sector. When Heineken was named the official beer of the London 2012 Olympics, the deal faced criticism from medical authorities in Britain. Sir Ian Gilmore, special adviser to the Royal College of Physicians on alcohol, was quoted as saying: 'When any major sporting event has an official alcohol supplier, it sends out completely the wrong messages to young people, making it seem as though no major event is complete without alcohol.' An initial step towards harnessing alcohol companies' involvement has been the Australian government's GoodSports program in 2012. It offered national sport organisations in Australia compensation in return for not accepting sponsorship and advertising dollars from alcohol companies. Rather, those organisations who signed up to the program chose to share the 'Be the Influence' message, focused on responsible drinking and drinking behaviour.

Similarly, experts suggest that increasingly prominent gambling advertising and promotion during sports broadcasts should be put in the same category as alcohol and smoking, and restricted. Recent federal parliamentary inquiries into gambling reform in Australia have considered the promotion of live odds and gambling advertising in sport. Experts such as Australian Psychological Society spokeswoman Heather Gridley have told the hearings that the proliferation of gambling advertising in sport has the effect of normalising it, with increased exposure to gambling advertising a risk factor for developing gambling problems. She suggests that 'gambling advertising during sporting matches and related broadcasting should be seriously restricted, if not banned'. In 2013, the coalition of Major Professional and Participation Sports, which represents the AFL, Rugby Union, Rugby League, netball, soccer and tennis, signed a code restricting live odd promotions during sports broadcasts. It bans promotion of live odds by commentators, but still allows paid and clearly identified forms of advertising and sponsorship.

Michael Valenzuela, a senior research fellow in the Faculty of Medicine at the University of New South Wales, adds that fast food advertising and sponsorship that are prominent in sport are doing enormous harm in the obesity battle. With obesity the leading cause of premature death and illness in Australia, and 55 per cent of the population either overweight or obese, healthy weight is now a minority position. For highly influential groups such as children, the figures were just as worrying, with 25 per cent either overweight or obese—a figure that has more than doubled in the past quarter of a century. He states that 'fast-food advertising during prime time and children's TV is contributing to this state of affairs. Certainly, there are several factors weighing on this complex issue, but the bottom line is energy imbalance. Children are consuming far too many calories than they are burning in their day-to-day activities.' He argues that solutions must confront both sides of the equation, and calls for regulation of fast-food advertising as one part of a coordinated response.

Well-known brands McDonald's, Hungry Jack's and KFC are high-profile commercial partners of Australian sport properties and global events, with signage and numerous advertisements encouraging consumption of such brands and products. As well as domestically, the Olympics commercial arrangements with McDonald's came under fire leading up to the 2012 games. Terence Stephenson, a spokesman for the Academy of Royal Medical Colleges, was quoted as saying: 'It's very sad that an event that celebrates the very best of athletic achievements should be sponsored by companies contributing to the obesity problem and unhealthy habits.'

While such advertisers may argue that children are not their specific target market, Professor Simone Pettigrew of the University of Western Australia's Health Promotion Evaluation Unit has found evidence that such partnerships are having a result on young consumers. Three-quarters of children in her study could align a sponsor with the relevant sport, with more than half correctly matching a fast-food chain with an AFL team. She concluded that there is 'support for the argument that sports sponsorship effectively reaches child audiences', even if not their solely targeted market. Professor Pettigrew continues:

> There is potential for children to become confused if healthy lifestyle messages or imagery are promoted by the marketers of unhealthy products. Limiting children's exposure to sponsorship messages of companies promoting unhealthy food and drinks are an important element of public policy efforts to reduce child obesity.

The collective contributions of these industries—often mega-brands themselves or backed by large parent companies—provide substantial financial backing to sport events or properties. However, while sport and sports stars 'represent fitness, athleticism, excellence and teamwork—all worthy traits' (Valenzuela, 2011), organisations entering commercial deals to sell products that may contribute to social and health issues related to alcohol, gambling and obesity may need to negotiate future regulation of these products in much the same way as the tobacco industry has.

Sources: Australian Associated Press (2013d); Pettigrew (2013); Roberts (2010); *The Guardian* (2012); Valenzuela (2011).

Questions

1 List the stakeholders related to this issue. What are some of the sport properties that are supported by organisations in these industries and what would be the broader impact for identified stakeholders if there was a ban on broader product categories?

2 Undertake some research to consider how other countries and sport organisations currently handle advertising in these industries. What policies and legislation govern alcohol, gaming or fast-food advertising within sport in other countries?

3 Outside of an outright ban on advertising of alcohol, gambling and fast food, what restrictions could effectively be placed on sport organisations and broadcasters?

4 What differences exist between tobacco, alcohol, fast-food and gambling products that might support legislation or authorities treating them differently from each other?

11

Sport and television

Stage 1—Identification of marketing opportunities

▼

Stage 2—Strategy determination

Step 5—Determine core marketing strategy

Marketing and service mix—sport product, pricing, place (physical evidence, people, process), customer satisfaction

Promotion mix—sales promotion, advertising, **television**

Step 6—Determine tactics and performance benchmarks

▼

Stage 3—Strategy implemention, evaluation and adjustment

CHAPTER OBJECTIVES

This chapter examines the television–sport nexus. Specifically, it describes how television generates its principal source of revenue through advertising, and how this revenue determines the level of television rights paid to sporting organisations. This chapter also describes how program popularity is measured, and looks at the link between this system of measurement and how advertisers assess the value of their advertising investment. Pay television is also discussed.

After studying this chapter, you should be able to:

- identify the nature of the sport–business–television relationship
- understand the commercial basis on which television operates
- identify why sport programming is so attractive to television networks
- understand and apply the terminology used to measure television audiences
- recognise issues associated with determining advertising effectiveness
- explain the dimension that pay television brings to the sport–television relationship
- convert advertising revenues to the relative worth of sport television rights
- recognise the impact of digital technologies on television broadcasting and the implications for fan engagement.

HEADLINE STORY

TV deal great fillip for code

> Television's love of live sport has another happy union to announce, with Football Federation Australia (FFA) set to trumpet a four-year, $160 million broadcast rights deal with Fox Sports and SBS, beginning on 1 July 2013. Soccer is the third code to cash in on TV's need for live action, following last year's AFL contract for $1.25 billion (over five years) and this year's $1.02 billion NRL deal. It is understood Fox Sports will pay about $32 million a year and SBS $7 million to broadcast the A-League's five games a week, including one free-to-air game on SBS, together with World Cup qualifiers. FFA's current seven-year deal is $19 million a year, meaning soccer has doubled its broadcasting revenue. TV ratings for soccer have risen this season from an average of 65 000 viewers a game to 95 000. A-League ratings are still small compared with NRL and AFL. The new deal allows SBS, which has paid $25 million for all quadrennial FIFA World Cup tournaments until 2022, more than just a four-week window every four years. It can now pitch to advertisers its year-round coverage, produce preview and review shows and cement a relationship with FFA and FIFA. (Masters, 2012, p. 17)

In an unprecedented rush to secure the television rights to a succession of major events, Australian broadcasters understand the importance of major sporting events to the mix of programming, and their capacity to sell advertising inventory during these events. For the broadcaster, it is simply good business. Each broadcaster anticipates recouping its investment through strong advertising and sponsorship sales during major events such as the Soccer World Cup, Wimbledon, the US Open (golf), Tri-Nations Rugby Union and the Commonwealth Games. The World Cup in particular provides four weeks of premier programming, during which the networks are able to sell advertising inventory at peak rates.

The Sydney 2000 Olympic Games—like all recent Olympic Games—relied on substantial revenues from broadcast rights. For example, the International Olympic Committee (IOC) (2002a) reports that Sydney 2000 generated US$1.3 billion (A$1.35 billion) from the sale of its television rights worldwide. The Sydney Olympic Organising Committee was allocated US$800 million (A$832.5 million), the International Agency Against Doping US$25 million (A$26 million), the IOC itself retained US$130.9 million (A$136.2 million), international federations received a share of US$189.7 million (A$197.4 million) and National Olympic Committees shared US$185.9 million (A$193.5 million). Television coverage garnered during Sydney 2000 included 220 countries that televised the event, a global (unduplicated) audience of 3.7 billion, global coverage of 27 600 hours and total viewer hours estimated at 36.1 billion viewers (IOC, 2002a). By contrast, Salt Lake City in 2002 attracted 2.1 billion viewers with 160 countries televising the Winter Olympics, and total viewer hours were estimated at 13.1 billion (IOC, 2002b). Finally, for the networks, programming of this profile provides the opportunity for pre-emptive promotion of forthcoming station programs to a large and captive audience. In essence, the networks capitalised on the opportunity to boost the ratings of future programs, further enhancing the value of major sports event programming.

Television and sport marketing

The purpose of this chapter is to explore the sport–television relationship. Clearly it is a business relationship, and one that has grown in importance throughout the world. For many sports, including the National Basketball Association (NBA) and National Football League (NFL) in the United States, cricket and the Australian Football League (AFL) in Australia, and soccer, golf and tennis worldwide, television rights provide a substantial source of revenue. (A summary of some of the world's major professional sport television rights is provided in Appendix 11.1.) Television networks now demand more from their right to broadcast than in their previous passive business partnerships with various sports. To ensure that networks maximise their revenue and profits, program directors and television executives are increasingly influencing the scheduling of games and events. The balance between playing at times conducive to optimum athletic performance and playing at times best suited to optimum ratings is one aspect of the sport–television relationship that creates tension. This tension has the potential to upset the mutually beneficial relationship currently in existence.

Figure 11.1 displays the principal players in the sport television business. Fundamentally, the business of the commercial television industry is the sale of airtime to advertisers. The price at which commercial TV airtime is sold is a function of a number of factors, the most important of which are the number of television viewers, and the price and availability of advertising space on suitable alternative media. Commercial television uses programming to influence the size and profile of its viewing audience, which is measured by independent ratings (ANZ McCaughan, 1993: 9):

> The principal profit equation for commercial television is to ensure that the revenue generating capacity of a schedule of programming sufficiently exceeds both its cost

FIGURE 11.1 The sport–business–television relationship

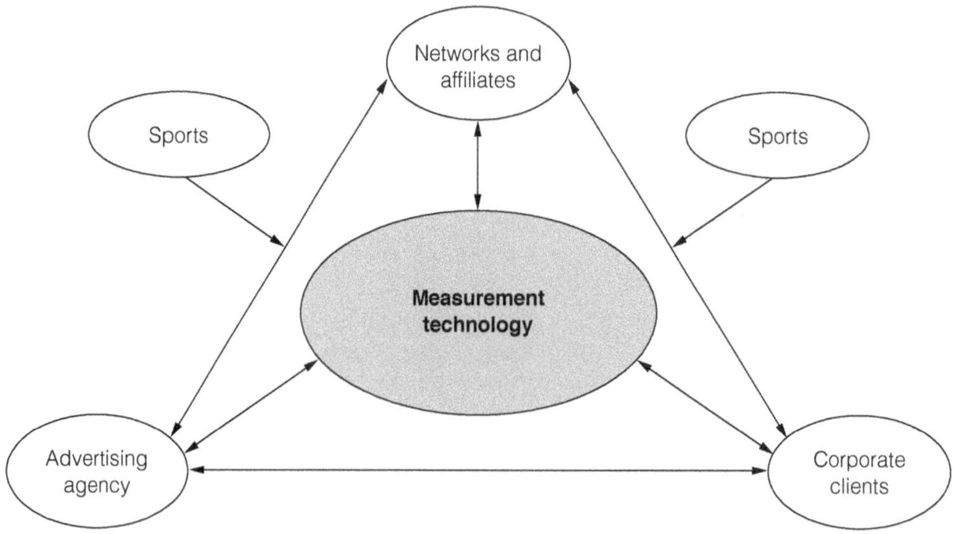

of production or acquisition as well as associated overheads, to produce a reasonable return on investment for the broadcaster.

To achieve a reasonable return on investment, the networks rely on programming that has the ability to capture and captivate an audience. The series of relationships shown in Figure 11.1 is driven by the middle circle—the system of measuring the number of people watching specific programs. The currency used to measure the success of television programming is a rating point. These rating points, as is shown later in this chapter, determine the success or failure of programs and, as a consequence, network profitability.

The advertising agency shown in Figure 11.1 acts as a broker, or 'middleman', between corporate clients purchasing advertising time and the networks. In general, advertising agencies form buying groups, allowing them to obtain discounts on advertising rates from the networks. These discounts are obtained due to the high volume of advertising inventory purchased by the advertising agency—a volume that corporations individually cannot match. Corporate clients at times also negotiate directly with networks, although this is less common because of the ability of the advertising agency to negotiate more favourable rates due to the volume of inventory being purchased.

Advertising agencies also offer expertise in recommending the most efficient forms of advertising or media buys for a particular product. A media buy refers to the range of advertising spots purchased across a variety of networks and programs. In its broadest sense, a media buy also includes other avenues for advertising, such as radio, newspapers, magazines, outdoor billboards and online inventory such as Facebook, LinkedIn and the web generally. A spot refers to the purchase of advertising inventory on television, usually in the form of a fifteen-, 30- or 60-second placement of an advertisement during a program. The costs to purchase these spots during sport programming are considered later in this chapter.

Sport programming

The importance and significance of the sport–television relationship are indicated by the rapid increase in sport programming in Australia that has occurred since the inception of television in 1956. In Sydney in 1958, just over twelve hours of sport programming went to air during the week commencing 1 September. Ten years later, during the week commencing 31 August, four stations showed a total of 22 hours of sport programming. Channels Seven and Nine covered Australian Rules and Rugby League, with ten one-hour boxing and wrestling programs also shown. By 1978, during the week commencing 2 September, 33 hours of sport programming were shown in Sydney, and by 1988 five channels had shown 43 hours of sport during the week beginning 15 August (Jarratt, 1988). In Melbourne during the week beginning 26 May 1996, free-to-air sport programming had escalated to 79 hours. By 2002, in the week commencing 16 June, the five free-to-air networks showed just under 100 hours of sport programs. In addition, pay television providers offer three channels dedicated to 24 hours of sport programming. In September 2007, just under 90 hours of sport programming was shown on free-to-air channels, with at least three local pay television channels providing 24-hour sport programming plus ESPN. The increase from 1996 is largely, but not solely, attributable to the sustained number of major sports events noted in the opening to this chapter.

These results suggest—as did the headline story—that sport programming is a ratings winner. Networks would not schedule so much sport programming if it were not profitable to do so. Why, then, is sport programming so attractive? Klattell and Marcus (1988: 4) summarise the intrinsic value of sport programming to television:

> At its best, television sports is the finest programming television can offer. In many respects, sports may be the quintessential television program format, taking fullest advantage of the role TV plays in our daily lives. Sports on TV have visually attractive elements—splashy colours, attractive locations, motion and movement galore. They have expansive vistas, exquisite details, and larger-than-life images . . . There is drama, tension, suspense, raw emotion, real anger, unvarnished joy, and a host of other responses. Most of all you are watching real people compete for real, as unsure of the outcome as the viewer. In sports TV the 'bad guy' of the script often wins, unexpected things happen, virtue doesn't necessarily triumph, and goodness is not always rewarded.

The features of sport programming described by Klattell and Marcus underpin the reasons why sport is so attractive to television. They also explain why the networks are prepared to pay large fees to obtain the exclusive rights to broadcast a competition such as the AFL or cricket, or a major event such as the Olympic Games.

How is the IOC able to command these fees, and how do sports such as cricket, Rugby Union and tennis command significant revenues from the sale of these exclusive rights? Calculation of fees is based on the projected advertising sales and profit derived from the exclusive broadcasting of an event such as the Olympic Games. The value of advertising is determined by the system of measurement used to determine the popularity of programs—or, more specifically, how many people watch.

More than 20 years after Klattell and Marcus articulated why sport and television was such a good match, Ferguson and Idato (2012) reinforce the central role sport continues to play in free-to-air programming. Sportview 11.1 describes the 'storm of change' confronting the television industry, largely due to the impact of the internet and the redirection of advertising spends by the corporate sector. Other important trends impacting the sport–TV alliance are also noted, such as sporting teams developing their own in-house media capabilities.

SPORTVIEW 11.1

Storm of change—coming soon to TV

A decade ago, Australia's three commercial TV networks were described by one fund manager as 'fat bloated grubs' supported by huge cash flows and huge margins. The most protected sector in Australian business, television enjoys cheap access to broadband spectrum, tough anti-siphoning rules designed to prevent the pay TV industry from spoiling its exclusive control of sport, free spectrum to open up multi-channels and juicy TV licence rebates. But free-to-air television is approaching an evolutionary crossroads. One commercial network—Nine—was taken to the brink of collapse this week, and another—Ten—announced a result soaked in red ink and a program of job cuts. Coupled with the looming shadow of dramatic structural ownership changes across the industry, audience fragmentation, TV piracy and dwindling advertising revenues are conspiring to crush the traditional business model.

Next year is expected to be a watershed for the broadcast industry. For the first time, the amount of money spent on advertising over the internet will match the ad spend on free-to-air television. 'All washed up: traditional television is facing an unprecedented challenge from online viewing. Change is not just coming, it is coming fast. By 2014 online will overtake TV, which is the greatest change in the history of media,' says media buyer Harold Mitchell. To survive, networks 'will have to get hold of the digital dollars'.

Furthermore, the media consultants Commercial Economic Advisory Service of Australia and Aegis Media forecast that by 2015 digital advertising expenditure will hit 31.2 per cent and TV will be 26.3 per cent. The biggest threat TV faces is clearly the internet. Besides appealing to advertisers because it produces detailed information about who is watching and, more importantly, what else they do, it also appeals to viewers due to its easy availability and portability. It is this ease of availability that is wreaking havoc on the traditional business model.

The three macro-drivers of free-to-air TV were historically news, sport and movies. The first is gradually being lost to the internet. The last has lost its momentum because of a coterie of ad-free platforms, including pay TV (with pay-per-view), DVD and online. What is left in television's sights is exclusive sport. The reason is simple: live sport and live reality shows remain largely immune from 'time-shifted' viewing and illegal downloading, and they attract big audiences. But even premium sporting rights are proving to be a challenge. Deals such as Nine's $1 billion NRL rights tie-up and future deals for the Olympics require non-traditional partners, such as Foxtel, to create the breadth of delivery needed to justify the cost and meet expectations of multi-channel, multi-platform coverage. Complicating that balance of power is the fact that many sports teams and bodies are developing their own media businesses, stretching the 'exclusivity' of broadcast rights to generate content from which they can profit.

The AFL, for example, has launched its own media content unit, following a trend started by NBA basketball in the United States, which plans to allow audiences to download games directly. In Britain, football teams operate their own pay TV channels, such as Manchester United's MUTV. Mark Fennessy, CEO of production company Shine Australia, believes that model will eventually roll out in Australia. 'Every football club, every sports organisation, is looking to interact with a community,' he says. 'They want to know what your experience is, and what you prefer it to be.' Negotiations for the 2014 Winter and 2016 Summer Olympics begin soon, and Nine's $300 million cricket deal expires next March. With Seven keen to retain the ratings crown and Nine effectively given a second chance with a debt-free balance sheet, the industry anticipates a bloody fight.

Source: Ferguson and Idato (2012).

Measuring the television audience

The size and composition of television audiences are measured by ratings services. Ratings are collected by using the 'people meter', an electronic measuring device that records what programs are being watched. This device also has the capacity to record who is watching, which provides important demographic information to networks and advertisers.

Measurements made

The following terminology is used in relation to measuring television audiences.

Homes using television

Homes using television (HUT) is the number of homes where at least one television set is switched on at any point in time. For example, in 2011 there were 1.72 million households (HH) in Sydney and 1.63 million households in Melbourne (ABS, 2011a, 2011b). However, it is not enough to know the number of households in the five major cities of Sydney, Melbourne, Brisbane, Perth and Adelaide on which the metropolitan ratings figures are based, but how many of these homes have working televisions. Although a precise number of homes using television could not be found, the Australian Communications and Media Authority (ACMA) (2011) found that there were 18.7 million television sets in 8.4 million households across Australia. Only 100 000 of these households did not have a television. The penetration of pay TV—another important outlet for sport programming—into Australian households has plateaued at approximately 29 per cent, with about 34 per cent of the population having access to pay TV services. Foxtel is the main pay TV provider in Australia, with approximately 2.3 million subscribers (Department of Broadband, Communications and the Digital Economy, 2013).

Program ratings

Program ratings are the percentage of households that are tuned to a particular station at a particular time. An example showing top-rating shows in Australia for a specific week is provided in Table 11.1, with both the total people watching and the rating points for the five cities. OzTAM and the television networks are interested in the specific rating points for those programs, which are derived using the following formula:

$$\text{Rating} = \frac{\text{HH tuned to program}}{\text{Total HH}} \times 100 \quad \text{or} \quad \frac{\text{People tuned to program}}{\text{Total individuals}} \times 100$$

The top-rating program shown in Table 11.1 was the New South Wales vs Queensland State of Origin Rugby League match, which traditionally is a top-rating program. Overall, ratings of 14 appear low, but remember that this figure is derived by dividing the people watching by the five-city population of just over 14 million people. Note the variance in Table 11.1 in people watching from state to state, depending on the event and the other programs that feature in the top 20. The State of Origin telecast is a particular case in point. In the traditional Rugby League markets of Sydney and Brisbane, this match rated 45 and 27.3 respectively. Both are very strong local market ratings and confirm the appeal of this television product in these markets. The Melbourne market, the second largest in the country, was less interested in watching this program, and this was reflected in a low rating of 6.3. This example highlights the fact that ratings are market sensitive, as are advertising rates.

Audience share

Audience share is the percentage of the total viewing audience in a given period tuned to a particular station. This is an important figure because it considers the number of televisions actually in use and the total size of the potential audience. The number of televisions in use is likely to be fewer than the total number of households with televisions. Audience share is calculated by dividing the number of households watching a program by the number of households using televisions:

$$\text{Share} = \frac{\text{HH tuned to program}}{\text{HUT}} \times 100$$

Significantly, the percentage share is always higher than rating points, because the total number of households actually using televisions is lower than the actual number of households with a television. For example, an AFL semi-final between the West Coast Eagles and Collingwood was a high-rating football match on Seven. Table 11.2 displays the audience share, peak audience and average audience for this match, which was a gripping final in which the scores were tied at the final siren, necessitating ten minutes of extra time to determine a winner. Interestingly, Seven cites audience share data that show some impressive numbers—particularly in Melbourne, Perth and Adelaide. As the match extended well past 11.00 p.m. Melbourne time, the number of televisions in use waned as people not interested in the football went to bed, but the match likely held football viewers due to the tied score. These factors combine to present the impressive numbers shown in Table 11.2, underscoring the importance of sport managers, advertisers and television executives understanding exactly what data are being examined and what they mean.

Target audience rating points

Target audience rating points (TARPs) are the audience at a given point in time expressed as a percentage of the potential audience available. Table 11.3 illustrates the cumulative nature of TARPs in relation to a Friday-night NRL telecast. It shows the average Friday-night TARPs for the duration of the NRL season as well. Also shown are the various demographic groups typically used in the analysis by advertisers, networks, corporations and sporting organisations. Corporations are often more interested in the detailed demographic data, as these relate to the groups most likely to purchase the firm's product. In other words, if Coca-Cola advertised during the Rugby League telecast, the company might be more interested in the number of people in the 16–24 years age group watching Friday night matches, as this might represent an important buying group.

Gross rating points

Gross rating points (GRPs) are another cumulative measure representing the sum of TARPs for a given schedule, often referred to as total TARPs. Cumulative ratings such as GRPs and TARPs are usually calculated for a week or month and, as noted by

TABLE 11.1 Top 20 programs 10–16 June (total people)

Rank	Program	Channel	Five cities total 000s	Rating points	Sydney 000's	Melbourne 000's	Brisbane 000's	Adelaide 000's	Perth 000's
1	State of Origin rugby league NSW v QLD 2nd match	9	1961	**14.0**	915	261	725	36	24
2	Seven News—Sun	7	1684	**12.0**	429	470	337	168	280
3	Seven News	7	1612	**11.5**	425	434	295	206	252
4	It Takes Two	7	1604	**11.4**	464	527	248	173	191
5	60 Minutes	9	1540	**11.0**	388	495	266	172	219
6	Seven News—Sat	7	1529	**10.9**	436	472	298	150	173
7	Today Tonight	7	1516	**10.8**	400	429	281	188	219
8	Desperate Housewives	7	1468	**10.4**	476	479	182	163	168
9	All Saints	7	1447	**10.3**	417	498	215	153	164
10	RPA Where are They Now?	9	1427	**10.2**	430	456	225	161	155
11	1 vs 100	9	1425	**10.1**	349	479	258	169	169
12	Grey's Anatomy	7	1390	**9.9**	441	428	185	107	228
13	Getaway	9	1383	**9.8**	409	414	255	143	162
14	National Nine News—Sunday	9	1373	**9.7**	426	433	198	201	115
15	My Name is Earl	7	1350	**9.6**	367	395	280	163	145
16	What's Good for You	9	1349	**9.6**	378	467	242	118	145
17	NCIS	TEN	1314	**9.4**	377	374	233	159	172
18	National Nine News	9	1282	**9.1**	353	409	260	155	106
19	The Rich List	7	1273	**9.0**	347	403	201	144	177
20	A Current Affair	9	1263	**8.9**	328	406	272	136	120

Source: Adapted from OzTAM. (2007)

Buzzard (1992: 40), are often 'used as a comparison to circulation figures in the print media. It measures the station's overall effectiveness, or the total number of different people who saw a program or commercial'. Reach is a measure of the number of different people watching, and frequency is the number of times a person or household watches the same program, commercial or station. A total television buy of 240 GRPs could be calculated as follows:

$$\frac{\text{GRPs}}{240} = \frac{\text{Reach}}{80} \times \frac{\text{Frequency}}{3}$$

	Peak audience	Average audience	Audience share (%)
Sydney	239 000	156 000	33
Melbourne	853 000	762 000	73
Brisbane	158 000	115 000	36
Adelaide	284 000	223 000	64
Perth	449 000	380 000	74
Network	1 983 000	1 636 000	

Source: Seven Network (2007).

TABLE 11.2 West Coast Eagles vs Collingwood, semi-final, 2007

	TCN-9 Sydney		QTQ-9 Brisbane	
	Average homes rating		Average homes rating	
	6.30–7.30 p.m. 24 weeks		5.30–7.30 p.m. 24 weeks	
		TARPs %		TARPs %
Total households	245975	17.30	138161	16.20
Total individuals	417851	10.00	215880	9.30
All people 18+	351661	11.00	190478	10.90
Men 18+	203278	12.90	105428	12.30
Men 16–24	25269	9.30	9189	6.00
Men 16–39	89929	11.30	39533	9.50
Men 18–39	83136	11.30	36851	9.60
Men 40–54	59805	13.60	36613	14.90
Men 55–64	30251	16.00	14043	13.10
Men 65+	30086	14.30	17921	14.80
Women 18+	148383	9.10	85049	9.50
Women 16–24	13911	5.30	6757	4.50
Women 16–39	64616	8.30	31965	7.60
Women 40–54	34106	7.80	27463	10.90
Women 55–64	18842	10.30	10934	10.40
Women 65+	33039	11.90	16861	11.00
Ppl AB	70846	9.70	31553	9.40
GB	157342	11.00	88095	10.30

Source: GTV Nine (2002).

TABLE 11.3 Friday night NRL average ratings

Average audience

Average audience is the estimated audience over a stated period, usually fifteen minutes. This figure is usually expressed in thousands. Examples are given in Tables 11.2 and 11.3.

People meters

The method used to collect ratings data has changed during the past 20 years. Up until 1991, the diary was used. This required randomly selected households to fill in their viewing patterns during a two-week period, usually referred to as the ratings period. At the end of the two weeks, the diaries were collected and analysed to determine program ratings. The method by which this information was collected, collated and interpreted was rather slow and cumbersome, compared with the use of the people meter.

In 1989, the first trials began with ACNielsen's people meter. The most significant change as a result of using the people meter was that data could be collected for 52 weeks of the year, thereby removing the tendency of networks to schedule major programs during known ratings periods. A major advantage of the people-meter technology is its capacity to download the results of the previous day's viewing by 9.00 a.m. the next day, providing television executives with immediate feedback on the success of their programs. In 2002, ACNielsen's people-meter service was replaced in the metropolitan area by OzTAM, which is a joint venture between the three main commercial broadcasters in Australia. OzTAM subsequently appointed the AGB Group as the ratings provider—the agency responsible for data collection. In 2004, the AGB Group merged with the Nielsen Media Group to form AGB Nielsen Media Research, and this group is responsible for the supply of television audience measurement services and managing the TV ratings panels from which ratings data are collected. So what is the people meter, and how does it work?

The people meter is a small eight-button unit placed on top of the television set. Each member of the household is assigned a button number, and their names are printed above their assigned button number. There is a set of red and green lights on the front of the unit to indicate whether selected people are in the viewing audience. Green indicates viewing; red indicates no viewing. Household members indicate their viewing by pushing their assigned button on either the people meter or the remote control, changing their light from red to green. There is a button labelled 'OK' that must be pressed when all viewing entries have been made. When a household member leaves the room, that person must again press a button to indicate no viewing and press the 'OK' button to signify a change in audience. When visitors come into the room, they must indicate their presence by pushing a visitor button on the unit placed on the television. Visitors will be asked their sex and age.

Data collected from people meters are downloaded to a central computer, and it is from here that the various rating figures are generated. As can be seen from the need for visitors to input their basic demographic information, detailed reports are possible for every program. Indeed, detailed reports are possible for every minute of the day for every program. Typically, data are reported in fifteen-minute blocks.

People meters are an improvement on the diary system, where the accuracy of data reported by households was often suspect. Household members often forgot to complete the diary daily, relying on their memory to fill it in at a later date. Of course, people meters rely on household members diligently turning their green and red lights on and off as they cycle in and out of watching television.

The other major weakness of the people meter is that it cannot detect whether household members are actually watching television, even though they are recorded as being in the room. Remember, this is important because the advertisers assume that people recorded as being in the room actually watch the program and register or acknowledge the advertisements shown.

Finally, the diverse ways in which a television screen is now used (for example, for DVDs, Blu-ray, video games, time-shifted viewing, use as a PC, teletext, etc.), together with the increasing number of television sets in a household and increasing platforms such as multi-digital and pay TV channels, and more remote controls per household, is providing a more dynamic and challenging environment within which to provide accurate audience measurement. In response, from 2009 OzTAM commenced measuring 'playback' or 'time-shifted' viewing—in other words, programs that had been recorded and watched within seven days of the originally scheduled program. Moreover, 10 per cent of panel homes also have both their TV sets and their PCs metered for viewing of television. Smartphones, inevitably, will be next. What, then, is a panel home and how is an audience sample determined?

Audience sampling

People meters—often referred to as Unitam devices in Australia—are not installed in every house using a television. This would be too costly and time-consuming. To obtain reliable data, a random sample of the population is taken. The objective of the sample is to install meters in a random, representative and projectable sample of households for the defined market. In 2012, OzTAM increased the number of 'panel' homes from 3035 to 3500 metropolitan households randomly selected, including 900 from Sydney, 900 from Melbourne, 700 from Brisbane, and 500 each from Adelaide and Perth. In addition, 1413 homes form part of the sample for subscription pay television. These 3500 homes determine the success and failure of free-to-air television programs, and in turn the value of advertising. Regional television ratings data are collected by a separate entity known as RegionalTAM, which is a joint venture owned by the five free-to-air regional commercial networks. Nielsen Television Audience Measurement is also responsible for regional data collection. To ensure a valid sample, there must be a genuine representation of the population within each city or regional area. Factors taken into account include postcode, size of household, number of television sets, age of the grocery buyer, presence of children and claimed reception of TV stations . Households not eligible for the sample include:

- non-private dwellings—hospitals, prisons, schools, etc.
- households without a television
- households of people working in the television, market research or advertising industries
- households moving within the next three months, and
- households occupied for less than nine months a year.

Advertising during sport programming

Super Bowl XLVII (2013) advertising inventory was sold at an average of US$3.8 million (A$3.95 million) for a 30-second spot, up 7 per cent on 2012. Some marketers were buying 60-second spots at US$7.5 million (A$7.8 million) (James, 2013). Experts, however, differ in their views about the value of premium cost to advertise during the Super Bowl, although it would appear that some experts see increased value for Super Bowl advertising. Sportview 11.2 illustrates the potential value of Super Bowl advertising in an increasingly fragmented TV market, compounded by the clutter of social media. The Super Bowl remains the premier televised sporting event capable of generating record ratings through a massive audience.

SPORTVIEW 11.2

Super Bowl advertising's new game

In some respects, the Super Bowl used to be a fairly simple event for marketers. A brand team would purchase a spot, aim to develop a high-impact commercial, run it and hope that all worked well. Apple's '1984' spot is a perfect example of this approach; Apple secured space, developed a remarkable piece of advertising and ran it. Things all worked out well.

While developing a good spot is still important, Super Bowl advertising has changed fundamentally; it is now far more complex and challenging than ever before. One reason why the challenge of Super Bowl advertising has changed is that the Super Bowl has become far more unique in today's competitive landscape. Whereas most shows are seeing fragmented viewership, Super Bowl viewership continues to climb; the 2010 Super Bowl passed the finale of *M*A*S*H* to become the most watched show ever. The 2011 Super Bowl set a new record, and the 2012 Super Bowl set yet another record. At the same time, threats assail viewership in many other media properties. People are more distracted than ever, with smartphones and personal computers fighting for attention during commercial breaks. The explosion of cable channels has further fragmented audiences. Online video platforms such as Hulu and YouTube are eroding traditional media outlets. The second reason the challenge of Super Bowl advertising is changing is due to the rise of social media platforms. Facebook and Twitter give people an opportunity to communicate broadly and engage with other people and with brands. These factors together have transformed the Super Bowl for marketers in three notable ways.

First, the Super Bowl is more important than ever. For advertisers, the Super Bowl is now the single biggest marketing event of the year. It is the one time marketers can be certain to reach a large portion of the US population. As a result, it is impossible to rival the Super Bowl if you are trying to launch a new brand, build an established brand or defend a strong brand.

Second, the Super Bowl has gone from being a one-time event to being the high point of an extended campaign. Marketers appear to be focusing more intensely on the weeks leading up the Super Bowl. Doritos begins its Super Bowl marketing effort early in the fall. Many advertisers announce their plans before the holidays. And virtually every Super Bowl advertiser will see additional attention for their spots on YouTube and elsewhere after the spot has aired.

Third, social media appears to be becoming a critical part of the DNA of Super Bowl advertising. Some of the most innovative social media programs come from Super Bowl advertisers. Companies support contests, ask for advertising suggestions and encourage chatter on Twitter and YouTube.

The overall impact is that the stakes have increased for Super Bowl advertisers. Effectively, using the Super Bowl is now about managing an entire multimedia campaign, not just one spot. Done well, a strong Super Bowl effort can propel a brand forward. Chrysler, Honda, M&Ms and Samsung have all moved ahead sparked by a strong Super Bowl campaign. A botched Super Bowl ad, however, can damage brands and careers. With all the moving parts, fielding a Super Bowl spot is more difficult than ever, but the opportunity for those who do it well is bigger than ever too.

Source: Rucker and Calkins (2013).

By contrast, the AFL Grand Final—one of the biggest TV-watching days of the year in Australia—was able to sell national 30-second spots in 2012 for $100 000, with Whalley (2012) estimating that the Seven Network would reap more than $10 million revenue from this event. The 2007 Rugby World Cup was also an attractive television product. Peak 30-second spot rates for pool games involving Australia were valued at $20 000, decreasing to $19 000 for qualifying/semi-final matches and increasing to $25 000 for the final. As the sale of advertising inventory must be costed well in advance of the World Cup, the 'value' of each 30-second spot in the qualifying and semi-finals and the final is difficult to capture. Clearly, the value of these spots increases if Australia plays in any of the early finals matches and the final. The uncertainty of the sport product is clearly evident. One of the features of the sport product is its capacity to attract peak audiences during non-peak times. The World Cup has this potential, as does cricket, which typically attracts the same number of people during the day as normal evening peak programming.

An example of the strategy used to sell advertising inventory by the networks is seen in Figure 11.2. Some of the sales data for an Australian Formula One Grand Prix in Melbourne are shown, along with sample ratings data telecast schedules, the cost of television sponsorships of the event and the cost of 30-second spot packages. National sponsorships of such sporting events usually offer more to the corporation than traditional spot advertising. In this example, television sponsorship benefits included:

- specially produced opening and closing and internal billboards
- promotion—sponsor received logo association with telecast promotion
- ten 30-second spots spread through all telecasts on all Nine Network stations, and
- placement—4 × 30 seconds on Saturday and 6 × 30 seconds on Sunday.

Sponsoring an event like the Grand Prix is obviously more expensive than simply purchasing a series of 30-second spots, as is indicated in Figure 11.2. Most coverage of major sporting events includes television sponsorship opportunities. Sales of advertising time and television sponsorships are the precursors to determining the worth of television rights purchased by networks. It is important for sport managers to value the potential revenue to networks from televising their sport.

Advertising effectiveness

Nakra (1991: 217) notes that:

> commercial avoidance and audience erosion are two interrelated problems that marketing executives and media planners have been aware of for more than 30 years. With the rapid advancement of technology the problem of 'zapping' has become even more predominant.

Zapping involves viewers rapidly changing channels in order to avoid commercials. It also involves video-recorded programs, where viewers simply fast-forward past the advertisements. Zapping therefore represents a fundamental challenge to the basis of the television advertising formula, which assumes—as indicated earlier in this chapter—that viewers recorded as watching a program also watch and acknowledge advertisements. A difference can exist between exposure to the program and exposure to the commercial messages. It is likely that further advances in technology will improve the ability of the viewer to zap commercials.

Central to this issue of zapping is the cost-effectiveness of advertising. The best-known method for establishing the cost-efficiencies between program buys is cost per thousand (CPM). This method has been widely used to show 'audience or target size counts, which may or may not accurately represent the number of people viewing the program, segments of it, or the commercials' (Lloyd and Clancy, 1991: 34). Lloyd and Clancy posit three questions in relation to their suggestion for the use of a measure known as cost per thousand involved (CPMI):

1 Do individual programs differ in their ability to involve viewers?
2 Just how closely related are CPM and CPMI for the same set of programs?
3 In other words, would media planners and buyers make the same or different media buys if the decision were based on CPM versus CPMI?

The answers to these questions are based on the extent to which the media environment affects, tempers or moderates the nature of the advertising response. Two hypotheses have emerged from research investigating these questions. The first asserts that the more involved viewers are in a program, and the more they like it and are engaged by it, the weaker will be the advertising response. Proponents of this hypothesis maintain that commercial breaks represent an unnecessarily intrusive element in an otherwise enjoyable viewing experience. As a consequence, the advertisements are filtered out, perceived negatively or simply avoided. The second hypothesis adopts the opposite view: it suggests that characteristics of the program, as subjectively perceived by the involved viewer, produce efforts to minimise surrounding distractions and cause an enhanced orientation towards the program and source of the stimulus (Lloyd and Clancy, 1991). Enhanced involvement prompts the viewer to remain activated, producing a more positive impact on advertising effectiveness. Implications of these hypotheses are:

- to develop appropriate ratings indexes to determine program involvement, and
- to factor these indexes into CPMI measures.

The Formula One Series will hit Melbourne in February–March for the 1st round of the FIA Formula One Championship at Albert Park.

11 Formula One teams, 22 Formula One drivers, and hundreds of thousands of fans will flock to the Albert Park circuit.

The 2002 Qantas Australian Grand Prix will be held from 28 February to 3 March and promises to be one of the most tightly fought championship contests in years.

Nine's *Wide World of Sports* cameras will be on hand to provide a comprehensive coverage of the weekend's racing, coverage that has earned the FOA award for best telecast worldwide, five times.

Once Melbourne has been decided, the circuit will continue on its journey around the world in 16 different countries. Monaco, Imola, Magny Cours, Spa Francorchamps and Monza are just a few of the exotic locations.

The Nine Network will take you along for the ride as we buckle up for another year of high-octane action, only on the *Wide World of Sports.*

Average rating for Sunday, 3 March 2001

	TCN-9 Sydney		GTV-9 Melbourne		QTQ-9 Brisbane		NWS-9 Adelaide		STW-9 Perth	
	000's	TARP %	000's	TARP %	000's	TARP %	000's	TARP %	000's	TARP %
Homes	176588	12.40	364228	27.10	146578	17.20	89936	18.10	67925	12.60
All people	272337	6.50	612924	15.90	203600	8.80	144993	11.40	94880	6.40
Child 5-12	18961	4.40	42009	10.40	12992	5.20	11954	9.30	2099	1.30
Teens 13-17	7843	2.90	38280	15.30	386	0.20	4388	5.20	4066	3.70
All people 18+	231590	7.20	514019	17.30	184453	10.50	122276	12.50	88051	7.80
Men 18+	157875	10.00	289191	19.90	114696	13.40	75920	16.00	56182	10.10
Men 18-24	25197	11.70	20129	9.80	10542	8.80	6584	10.60	4289	5.20
Men 25-39	56911	10.90	123888	26.60	41294	15.70	22337	16.30	23097	13.50
Men 40-54	37629	8.50	91303	22.90	30292	12.30	22901	16.80	15527	9.60
Men 55-60	21371	11.30	26302	15.20	18483	17.30	10622	17.70	7708	11.20
Men 65+	16767	8.00	27569	13.30	14083	11.60	13477	16.70	5561	7.70
Women 18+	73715	4.50	224827	14.80	69757	7.80	46356	9.20	31868	5.60
Women 18-24	10624	5.10	13318	6.70	6823	5.70	3650	6.10	4913	6.20
Women 25-39	26448	5.10	86936	18.50	16942	6.30	15960	11.80	10848	6.50
Women 40-54	14716	3.40	50399	12.40	18105	7.20	16044	11.40	10363	6.30
Women 55-60	8801	4.80	47051	26.90	11619	11.00	4576	7.40	2251	3.40
Women 65+	13126	4.70	27123	10.00	16268	10.60	6125	5.70	3497	3.70
Grocery buyers	97867	6.90	220274	16.30	80321	9.40	59531	12.00	40363	7.50
SE AB	54389	7.50	88841	14.70	18420	5.50	20261	11.90	11281	5.00

FIGURE 11.2
Wide World of Sports telecast guide for the Australian Formula One Grand Prix, Melbourne, 2001

2002 telecast schedule

	Saturday, 2 March 2002	Sunday, 3 March 2002
TCN-9 Sydney	12.30pm–4.00pm	10.30am–4.30pm
GTV-9 Melbourne	12.30pm–4.00pm	10.30am–4.30pm
QTQ-9 Brisbane	11.30am–3.00pm	9.30am–3.30pm
NWS-9 Adelaide	12.00pm–3.30pm	10.00am–4.00pm
STW-9 Perth	9.30am–1.00pm	7.30am–1.30pm

Television sponsorship

National sponsorship of the telecasts of the Melbourne Grand Prix is available and provides association with this unique sporting event. Sponsorship benefits include:

- Billboards—opening, closing and internal.
- Promotion—sponsors will receive logo association with telecast promotion.
- Spot package—10 × 30 seconds per network station.
- Placement—Saturday 4 × 30 seconds
  Sunday 6 × 30 seconds

*Only sponsors receive airtime in actual race—2 × 30 seconds

The price of this national sponsorship is:

TCN-9 Sydney	$ 40 000
GTV-9 Melbourne	$ 95 000
QTQ-9 Brisbane	$ 25 000
NWS-9 Adelaide	$ 25 000
STW-9 Perth	$ 20 000
Network	$205 000

Spot packages

Spots can be purchased through all telecasts on all stations or in any specific telecast on individual stations or in any combination.

	Saturday, 2 March 2002	Sunday, 3 March 2002
TCN-9 Sydney	$2500	$4000
GTV-9 Melbourne	$6000	$10 000
QTQ-9 Brisbane	$1000	$2200
NWS-9 Adelaide	$1000	$2200
STW-9 Perth	$600	$2000
NETWORK	$11 100	$20 400

Source: GTV Nine Network (2002).

At present, no research is available indicating the level of involvement that sport programming generates. However, sport programming for cricket, for example—where only one short commercial can be shown between overs—may have an advantage in ensuring that viewers watch and acknowledge the commercial (that is, do not zap). Australian Rules football may also have a similar advantage, as commercials are shown after a goal is scored and typically last just 30 seconds before play recommences. Sports such as golf, basketball and car racing may provide viewers with the opportunity to leave the room, knowing that a series of four to five commercials will be shown. This also raises the question of advertisement placing in programs. Typically, first-in and last-out commercials are considered more valuable, as viewers see the first before leaving the room and the last when returning after the commercial break. Interestingly, networks often use the first or last advertisement for their own station program promotion purposes.

All of these factors impinge on the effectiveness of advertising during sport programming. Not a lot of research has been conducted on sport programming to shed more light on the answers to the questions raised in this section. There is little doubt, however, that these issues form the basis on which networks set advertising rates and, as a consequence, the amount in television rights they are prepared to pay sporting organisations.

Pay television

Another player has recently entered the sport–business–television relationship. Pay television was introduced to Australia in 1995. It is slowly becoming available worldwide, contributing to the globalised economy and in particular the familiarity of sport.

The business basis on which pay TV is predicated is fundamentally different from that of the free-to-air networks described in this chapter. So far, we have described how free-to-air networks rely on advertising as their primary source of revenue and profit. Free-to-air networks are in the business of reaching the widest possible audience, hence the term 'broadcasting'. Free-to-air television is popular, and generally taken for granted as an everyday part of life. Pay television, on the other hand, requires the payment of subscription fees to receive programming. The basic operating premise on which pay TV exists is known as narrowcasting, and its revenue base is sourced from subscription fees. Unlike the free-to-air networks, advertising is not the predominant revenue source on pay TV.

Pay TV in Australia at present is not as freely accessible as the free-to-air networks. It is assumed that this market will expand over time. Initially, advertising on pay TV was banned for a period of five years, although in mid-1997 advertising became legal, diversifying revenue opportunities and more closely aligning pay television with the free-to-air networks. Logically, this will intensify competition for advertising revenue in the television industry.

Legislation governing the introduction of pay TV in Australia prohibits major sporting events being shown solely on pay TV. For example, the AFL Grand Final, the Melbourne Cup, major golf and tennis events and the Olympic Games are subject to anti-siphoning laws designed to ensure that the majority of the population retains the ability to see these sporting events. Pay TV represents further opportunities for sports, with their marketing, promotion and revenue-generating strategies. The sport channels, in concert with the movie channels, are pay TV's greatest strength in terms of attracting subscribers. The opportunity therefore presents itself to an increasing range of sports to obtain some exposure via pay television.

In terms of extracting rights revenue from pay TV operators, the same principle applies as for free-to-air operators: to determine how much revenue the sport contributes to the network. The difference is that it is not so easy to calculate this contribution. Free-to-air networks, as shown earlier in this chapter, can simply calculate the total advertising time in dollar terms, thereby determining how much direct value sport programming represents. It is more difficult to determine how many subscribers subscribe solely or predominantly because a specific sport is shown on a pay TV channel. In some cases, major sports such as cricket, the AFL and Rugby League clearly add to the likelihood that subscriptions will grow due to their availability on a pay TV channel.

Fundamentally, sports not already receiving extensive free-to-air coverage will want to obtain exposure on pay television. In the end, for some of these sports the benefits may be the exposure via programming rather than any financial gains via television rights for exclusive coverage. This highlights the important role of television in the overall marketing and promotion of sport. Some sports, as demonstrated in this chapter, have the capacity to gain financially from television broadcasts; others do not. For some sports, the opportunity to gain exposure through programming without receiving any financial incentive is another important consideration when developing promotion mix decisions. It is also possible that some sports will have to pay to have their sport shown on either pay TV or free-to-air television. In this case, the decision to spend money will come from the promotion mix budget. Television is therefore an important consideration when framing promotion mix decisions.

Another question that arises is what sport managers need to do to enhance the attractiveness of a sport for television. There is no easy answer to this question. Some sports have used rule changes to make the game more attractive; others have changed the uniforms worn by players to make them more appealing; still other sports have simply paid for airtime until their sport has become well recognised and people want to watch it on a regular basis. Whether it is pay TV or free-to-air television, the formula does not change. Television executives will want to know how much revenue and subsequent profit the sport will attract for the network before they agree to show it on television. It is possible that pay TV offers slightly greater opportunities in the early years as there will be pressure to fill programming—particularly on all-sport channels. One thing is certain: the complexity of the sport–business–television relationship is intensifying in terms of attracting revenue sources and viewers. What has not changed is that programming is designed to capture a market of viewers, to either expose them to advertising or to get them to subscribe to a pay TV operator's range of channels.

Digital television

Fancy using your television to order a pizza, enter a competition or change the narration on a documentary? Digital television promises such features, but Australians are far from being able to take up the advantages. Not so in Britain, where 39 per cent of the population has access to interactive TV—compared with 35 per cent who use the internet—allowing them to control which court they watch during Wimbledon, for example, or to order food while watching a Pizza Hut ad (Hickman, 2002: 6). By early 2012, Ofcom (2012), the independent regulator and competition authority for UK communications industries, stated that 96.2 per cent of homes had digital TV. By comparison, penetration of digital TV in Australia had reached 82 per cent (Department of Broadband, Communications and the Digital Economy, 2012).

This is the brave new world confronting the television executive, and ultimately the sports consumer and sport marketer. Imagine being able to choose your preferred match and court at Wimbledon, or the golf hole or players you, the sport fan, would actually like to watch during a golf tournament. This may be possible with the onset of digital television during the next decade. The implications for sport broadcasting are significant. Digital television's introduction to Australia has commenced—albeit in a rather uncertain environment, as it relates to standards and protocols for the delivery of digital services. Nevertheless, high-definition television services are becoming increasingly affordable and available, and with them the potential for interactivity, such as that described by Hickman.

Although pay TV has brought a greater number of channels to consumers worldwide, this is nothing compared with the capacity of digital television, which has the potential to unblock the content bottleneck through the provision of hundreds of channels. In the traditional analogue format, delivery was restricted by television's large usage of spectra or frequencies available to broadcast. Digital transmission is expected to improve quality and allow interactivity, and consequently greater control by sports consumers of the type of programs watched and the cameras and angles used. At the heart of this technological revolution is bandwidth:

> Bandwidth refers to the capacity to distribute content . . . Digitized information can be made to take up much less space than analog signals. In a process known as compression, unnecessary information can be removed from video signals. (Todreas, 1999: 79)

The opportunities to arise from technological developments such as digital television need to be considered carefully by sport marketing managers. The implications extend beyond the value of television rights to sporting organisations, but also to where the control starts and stops for the provision of services to sports consumers, and the extent to which consumers can actively engage with the sport product via the television. Recent issues surrounding virtual advertising—essentially made possible by digital technology—highlight the complexities new technologies create for sport managers and television executives. For example, virtual advertising can be incorporated into a telecast without disrupting the view to the spectators. However, these images can be set to block out existing ground signage, which would cause some obvious problems (individual corporations pay for the right to display ground signs knowing that television will pick up these signs as part of the broadcast).

Our understanding of interactive TV has evolved beyond the examples noted above. As Andrew Fisher, the CEO of Shazam, describes in Sportview 11.3, the use of various devices such as tablets and smartphones is expanding the means by which viewers can engage with TV. Significantly, these trends broaden interactivity and engagement beyond the traditional 'red' button that allowed some form of interactivity. Already, we are witnessing Twitter interactivity with TV programs as an example of bypassing the red button.

SPORTVIEW 11.3

Interactive TV and the 'second-screen' experience

A decade ago, when viewers tuned into their favourite television program, they never imagined that they could do more than simply watch the latest shows and talk about them with their friends and co-workers the next day. Today, as our lifestyles grow increasingly digital, the passive act of watching television is steadily becoming far more interactive, with viewers multi-tasking on their mobile devices while watching television. This is known as the 'second-screen' phenomenon, where the mobile becomes an interactive part of regular TV viewership. You only need to look at how busy Twitter feeds become when high-profile programming such as the Brits or BAFTAs are broadcast to see that watching TV is becoming an ever more interactive experience these days.

Interactive TV isn't exactly a new invention, but until recently it wasn't an activity readily adopted by most viewers. One of the main reasons for this has been that there simply hasn't been a convenient way to encourage most people to interact with television programming. Until recently, the premise of interacting with TV meant that you had to have special gadgetry to do it—or, in the case of the 'red button' feature here in the United Kingdom, that it would interrupt the viewing of other people who may be in the room at the time. Even using a PC or laptop while watching is awkward, as it requires people watching at home to launch a browser window, then remember and type specific URLs for the show or the brand campaign in question. It's no wonder, then, that interactive TV didn't really take off until smartphones and tablets became more ingrained in people's daily lives.

Nowadays, with the use of mobiles and increasingly tablets, the opportunities for interactive television are greater than ever. The main reason for this is that mobile apps are available for almost every possible need from being your alarm clock, to helping you check bus and train timetables, to providing information from news to weather to restaurant reviews. Smartphone and mobile usage is rapidly taking over as a standard way of life—in fact, within the next three years mobile access to the internet will surpass that of computers. When you look at these findings together, you have more than a trend—you have a tsunami that points to mobile devices, be they phone or tablet, as the ideal candidates to revolutionise interactive television. Viewers can now literally use their mobiles to interact with what they're watching, whether it's to get more information about the shows they love or order products they want to buy in the moment.

Currently, our mobile devices provide us with a variety of ways to take advantage of the second-screen experience. They range from simple social check-ins where people tell their friends what they are watching, to using 'super-fan' apps developed for particular shows such as *The X Factor*, which provide special mobile features and games related to that one program.

However, the check-in apps are struggling to reach scale and maintain repeat usage from those who try it, suggesting that simply checking in is not compelling enough. And the network and show-specific apps are good for a specific group of people who watch a specific show, but the typical viewer of a typical show is not going to take the time to find and download numerous show apps. At Shazam, we believe that what people are really looking for in their second-screen experience is a rich offering that includes access to exclusive content and offers, as well as social features.

So what's in it for consumers is pretty easy to understand—but why should broadcasters and advertisers invest in this technology? We believe the second screen enables them to extend engagement and encourage people to get more involved.

Shazam is a media discovery company. What we mean by this is that we have a technology that allows us to listen to any content—whether it's a song, TV show or advert—and identify what it is as well as give users additional information about it. Shazam is known by many for our mobile phone app, which more than 200 million people worldwide use to tag songs. Now, we're expanding to include television, as well, so that people can use the app to discover and share more content that they love. When viewers take the time to use Shazam with a show, they can interact with it in their own time—either during the broadcast or maybe the next day building a stronger bond with the program. For advertisers, second-screen engagement can take a 30-second advert into two, three, even five minutes of engagement with a brand, giving people more information and a more personal interaction.

All signs point to mobile technology being the cornerstone of interactive television. Building what that interaction looks like and what will drive engagement—both from the app perspective as well as that of the show or brand—is developing at an increasingly rapid pace. Mobile has revolutionised the very act of watching television itself, opening up many possibilities for the future of television programming, advertising and fans alike, but this is just the start.

Source: Fisher (2012).

Summary

This chapter attempted to demystify the sport–business–television relationship. Television rights to sporting events are one of the most visible and talked-about components of sport marketing, and the networks of the world pay exorbitant sums for the exclusive rights to broadcast sporting events such as the Olympic Games and World Cup soccer. These sums merely recognise the number of people watching such events. Sporting events at varying levels—some worldwide, some nationally—deliver audiences to advertisers via programming, which in turn delivers revenues to sport in the form of rights fees and profits to television networks through the sale of advertising inventory.

The people meter is the electronic device used to measure the success of television programs. It collects ratings, which measure how many people with televisions are watching a particular program. Audience share and TARPs also measure the success of television programs, providing detailed and specific information about who is watching. It is not enough simply to identify how many people with televisions are watching a program; it is also important to know the demographic profile of these viewers. Advertising rates are based on ratings figures, and the income derived from advertising determines what fees can be paid for the exclusive broadcast rights to sporting events.

Some sporting organisations have been slow to awaken to the value of their product. In marketing terms, many sports have not maximised their revenue opportunities through television, primarily due to failing to understand how the worth of television rights is calculated. As the sport sector professionalises, this is changing, as evidenced in the escalation of rights fees during the past decade.

The other major marketing benefit to be gained from television is exposure and consumer engagement. Indirectly, televised sport has the potential to attract viewers to the live event, thereby contributing to the revenue generated via gate receipts. In many ways, this is a vicious circle. Televised sporting events can contribute to reduced attendances, explaining why sport programming is often 'blacked out' in the city where the event is being staged. Television is therefore an important consideration when framing marketing and promotion mix decisions. In recent years, promotion mix decisions have expanded to account for the increasing importance of social media, technology and interactivity through television. As discussed in the next chapter, which examines social media and associated technologies, the way in which interactivity was originally conceptualised through digital TV has expanded to fan engagement. The TV has become more than just a TV, providing the capacity for viewers to interact with TV programming. This presents the opportunity for sport marketers to develop strategies to actively engage with sports fans through sport programming. This new form of engagement, as outlined in Chapter 1, captures current challenges in applying marketing theory to engage technologically active fans through the use of smartphones, tablets, Twitter, online fantasy sports and the internet generally.

Pay television contributes to the exposure sporting organisations may gain from television. The relatively recent introduction of pay TV to Australia has meant exposure for sports not normally shown on television. Pay TV is beginning to offer reasonable exposure because the subscriber base is growing steadily. Therefore, only the major professional sports have demonstrated the capacity to attract revenue from pay TV providers. Over a period of time, however, it might also offer some revenue-generating potential for smaller sports. This chapter showed that the principal source of revenue for pay TV operators comes from individual household subscriptions; however, pay TV operators are also allowed to show advertisements, thereby diversifying their sources of revenue. This revenue source is not anticipated to be large in the short term, but will create some discomfort for the free-to-air networks.

The various business relationships described in this chapter are neither mysterious nor surprising once the commercial basis on which television operates is understood. What is interesting is the complex set of relationships developing between sport and television as both endeavour to maximise the revenues and profits from their respective product offerings.

CASE STUDY

OzTAM and ACNielsen TV ratings services

> It is not surprising that Australia's big advertisers and media buyers are feeling exasperated. With the close of the first official television ratings week of 2001 on Saturday, 17 February, the audience measurement figures have created nothing but confusion and bad feeling between the metropolitan commercial networks and the advertisers who pay about $2.5 billion to them each year. (*Business Review Weekly*, 2001)

The reason for the conflict can be traced to the three commercial networks' decision to jointly form a company to undertake the important task of measuring audiences watching television programs. OzTAM, jointly owned by Nine, Seven and Ten, is responsible for providing to the networks daily measurements garnered from service provider Australian Television Research (ATR). The decision to form OzTAM meant that ACNielsen, the company previously responsible for data collection and reporting, was replaced, although it maintained responsibility for regional television audience measurement.

The source of the conflict between the advertisers and networks was a result of measurement discrepancies reported by both OzTAM and ACNielsen. The latter continued to report its rating results after the contract had expired. Meade (2001: 8) reports, for example, that

> ratings figures from OzTAM reveal the Nine Network medical drama *ER* to be the no. 1 program for last week, with a total of 1.8 million viewers nationally. Nine's other hit show, *Friends*, came ninth with 1.6 million viewers. But ACNielsen data for the same week has the US sitcom taking out the top position with 1.9 million viewers.

With so much advertising money contingent on ratings points, a few points' variance can be costly for both network and advertiser. Bryden-Brown (2001) confirms the industry-wide criticism confronted by OzTAM due to the acute differences in ratings data between OzTAM and ACNielsen.

The reason there is so much difference between OzTAM and ACNielsen is the size of the sample and its location. As it is too costly and impractical to measure the viewing habits of every household with a television, the measurement agencies employ a sample of the five major cities in Australia, the formation of which is based on statistically accepted procedures. However, there remains the potential for sample bias and sample error. The importance of obtaining an accurate and objective sample lay at the heart of the dispute between advertisers and networks, and between the networks themselves. Independent New Zealand auditor Professor Peter Danaher, who was recruited by OzTAM and ACNielsen to analyse and explain the reasons for the differences between television ratings data (Meade, 2001), notes that:

> Since both ATR and ACN operate a sample of homes, the ratings they report are subject to usual sampling errors. For the Sydney market ATR has about 1900 panellists, while ACN has about 1400 panellists. For samples of this size the respective maximum sampling errors are 2.3% and 2.7%. Therefore, all rating comparisons must be put into the perspective of an expected sampling error band of the order 2 to 3 per cent. That is, two ratings are significantly different only if they differ by more than 3 rating points. For the smaller panels in Brisbane, Adelaide and Perth, this tolerance level is up to 3 to 4 rating points. (OzTAM, 2001)

Wilmoth (2001: 2) reports that Danaher found that the 'weighting' system used by Australian Television Research, the company that collects ratings for OzTAM, meant a greater proportion of young people's viewing habits had been recorded. It found that the disproportionate weighting in OzTAM's audience sample clearly needed attention—especially in Melbourne, where over half the survey groups were badly under- or over-represented. The report, covering the period 18 March to 7 April, found that on 30 March one panellist had a 'weight' of 20 000 people and that this accounted for half a rating point, which was estimated to be worth approximately $12.5 million in advertising revenue (Wilmoth, 2001). Danaher also found that about 85 per cent of the ratings reported by OzTAM and ACNielsen were within the statistical tolerance expected of a sample survey. Other important issues included the number of age categories used, establishing the correct proportion of single-person homes, and thus finding the right balance of older people, younger people and homes with children. Also, the length of time people have been on the panel and panel fatigue can influence results. The people meter system relies on the diligence of panellists to register their viewing by pushing the buttons that control the people meter.

Finding the right statistical balance will always be a challenge for whatever company is responsible for collecting and interpreting television ratings data. As long as it is too costly to measure all households, it will remain important to accurately and independently measure television audiences. The agency responsible for measurement is also an issue.

Tensions between the networks in the early stages of OzTAM's entry to the market created an interesting situation, as each network was a part-owner of the company responsible for reporting audience measurement. The Nine Network, in particular, was strident in its criticism of the new measurement systems, with Schulze (2001: 3) observing that: 'Nine Network chief executive David Leckie must be thinking it's better the devil you know.' Nine was the initial loser in the new system, with Wilmoth (2001: 2) noting that: 'When OzTAM first published its ratings in January [2001], the Seven Network took the lead from Nine for the first time in many years, causing alarm at Kerry Packer's TV stations.'

With half a rating point worth approximately $12.5 million per annum to a network, it is no wonder that the Nine Network was concerned about the system responsible for knocking it off its perch as the number 1 network in Australia—albeit temporarily.

Questions

1. Why is OzTAM a joint venture of the three Australian commercial networks? Comment on the ethical dimensions of the three networks' decision to jointly organise for the supply of television audience measurement.
2. Why is the sample error important in understanding rating measures? How do the differing sample sizes used by ACNielsen and ATR affect sample error?
3. Why is it important to attain a representative sample from various demographic groups? Explain, using specific television shows you watch or know about, how the under- or over-representation affects the sale of advertising inventory for television programs.
4. How would you explain why the ACNielsen and ATR systems produced different ratings data?
5. What is panellist fatigue? How might panellist fatigue affect ratings measurement?

APPENDIX 11.1 Worldwide television rights

US professional sports

NFL	$US million	Network	Baseball	$US million	Network
1978–81	646.0	ABC, CBS, NBC	1980–83	46.0	ABC, NBC, USA
1982–86	210.0	ABC, CBS, NBC	1984–89	183	ABC, NBC
1987–89	1 430.0	ABC, CBS, NBC	1990–93	365.0	CBS, ESPN
1990–93	3 650.0	ABC, CBS, NBC,ESPN, TNT	1994	85.0	The Baseball Network (joint venture ABC, NBC), ESPN
1994–97	4 388.0	ABC, Fox, NBC, ESPN, TNT	1996–2002	2 331.0	Fox, NBC, ESPN
1998–2005	17 600.0	Fox, CBS, ABC, ESPN	2003–08	3 300.0	Fox, ESPN
2006–13	22 400.0	CBS, Fox, NBC, ESPN, The NFL Network	2009–13	NA	Fox, TBS, ESPN
2014–22	39 000.0	Fox, NBC, CBS, ESPN	2014–22	12 400.0	Fox, TBS, ESPN
NBA	**$US million**	**Network**	**NHL (in USA)**	**$US million**	**Network**
1982–86	27.0	CBS, TBS, USA	1987–88	8.0	ESPN
1986–90	66.0	CBS, TBS	1988–89	15.9	SportsChannel
1990–94	219.0	NBC, Turner	1989–90	16.8	SportsChannel
1994/95—1997/98	1 292.0	NBC, Turner	1990–92	23.3	SportsChannel
1998/99—2001/02	2 640.0	NBC, TNT,	1992–94	29.5	ESPN
2002/03—2007/08	4 600.0	ESPN, ABC (Walt Disney Co.), TNT, TBS America Online (AOL Time Warner)	1994/95—1998/99	216.5	Fox, ESPN
2007/08—2015/16	7 400.0	ESPN, ABC, TNT	2006–2010/11	750.0	Comcast/Versus
			2011/2012—2020/21	2 000.0	Comcast/NBC

NA=Not available

Source: *USA Today* (1994); Hirsley (1998); Zbar (2002); Mermigas (2002); Wikipedia (2007, 2013a, 2013b); Cohen (2007); Flint (2011); L. McCarthy (2011); Lee (2012)

Olympic Games

USA Summer	US$ million	Venue	Network	USA Winter	US$ million	Venue	Network
1980	85.0	Moscow	NBC	1980	15.5	Lake Placid	ABC
1984	225.6	Los Angeles	ABC	1984	91.6	Sarajevo	ABC
1988	300.0	Seoul	NBC	1988	309.0	Calgary	ABC
1992	401.0	Barcelona	NBC	1992	243.0	Albertville	CBS
1996	456.0*	Atlanta	NBC	1994	295.0	Lillehammer	CBS
2000	705.0	Sydney	NBC	1998	375.0	Nagarno	CBS
2004	793.0*	Athens	NBC	2002	545.0*	Salt Lake City	NBC
2008	894.0*	Beijing	NBC	2006	613.0*	Turin	NBC
2012	1320.0*	London	NBC	2010	880.0*	Vancouver	NBC
2016	4 400.0#	Rio	NBC	2014		Sochi	NBC
2020		Yet to be named	NBC	2016		Yet to be named	NBC
Australia Summer	**US$ million**	**Venue**	**Network**	**Australia Winter**	**US$ million**	**Venue**	**Network**
1984	10.6	Los Angeles	10	1984	1.0	Sarajevo	7
1988	7.4	Seoul	10	1988	1.1	Calgary	7
1992	34.0	Barcelona	7	1992	8.5	Albertville	9
1996	30.0	Atlanta	7	1994	5.0	Lillehammer	9
2000	45.0	Sydney	7	1998	9.3	Nagano	7
2004	50.5	Athens	7	2002	11.8	Salt Lake City	7
2008	63.8	Beijing	7	2006	14.8	Turin	7
2012	81.2	London	9, Foxtel	2010	18.8	Vancouver	9, Foxtel
2016		Rio		2014		Sochi	10

NBC paid US$4.4 billion for the rights to four Olympic Games, two Summer Games and two Winter Games. Two of the Games venues had not been selected at the time of preparing this edition of this text.

* Includes profit-sharing.

Source: International Olympic Committee (1996, 2011); Steffens (2007).

12

Sport and new media

Stage 1—Identification of marketing opportunities

▼

Stage 2—Strategy determination

Step 5—Determine core marketing strategy

Marketing and service mix—sport product, pricing, place (physical evidence, people, process), customer satisfaction

Promotion mix—sales promotion, advertising, television, internet, **sponsorship**

Step 6—Determine tactics and performance benchmarks

▼

Stage 3—Strategy implemention, evaluation and adjustment

CHAPTER OBJECTIVES

This chapter examines the impact of 'new media' on sport marketing. New media are having a profound impact on how we communicate in all areas of life, and sport is no exception. Sport marketers who are able to understand and leverage new media opportunities can help develop a competitive advantage through the use of digital technologies. In this chapter, you will be introduced to the concepts of new media and digital communication, and the way in which the relationship between sport, content and technology is evolving. A range of options for incorporating new media into the promotional mix for sport organisations are provided.

After studying this chapter, you should be able to:

- define the terms 'new media' and 'digital', and understand the characteristics of each
- appreciate how new media challenge notions of control and distribution
- be able to articulate components such as interactivity, consumer engagement and Web 2.0, which are features of new media use
- develop an awareness and provide examples of new media opportunities, including those through social networking, broadcast and content extensions, fantasy sport, online communities and fan forums, and e-commerce
- be aware of how new media impacts consumers and what the implications are for sport organisations
- describe how new media can be incorporated as part of the sport marketing framework.

HEADLINE STORY

'Media-dominant' consumption

Building on the use of traditional media channels, the last decade has seen increased options for sport organisations to share messages and engage new markets through emerging communication modes (Santomier and Shuart, 2008). While consumers have long made choices about how they consume sport—be it live or through media broadcasts—complementary and competitive consumption forms supported through new media add to the complex range of options among which modern sport consumers must choose. This means that the decision of whether to consume games live at the stadium, or elsewhere via media broadcasts or in digital form, is becoming increasingly difficult—even for highly committed fans.

For many sports, commercial growth is aligned with the increasing popularity of media and new media. Major League Baseball (MLB), the National Football League (NFL), the English Premier League (EPL) and Australian leagues, including the Australian Football League (AFL) and the National Rugby League (NRL), are among those that have recently signed record rights deals, seeing broadcasting further emerge as a critical revenue stream (Deloitte, 2013). These escalating levels of media consumption and broadcaster spend continue 'to indicate attendance is becoming less central to an organisation's profitability' (Pritchard and Funk, 2006: 316). This creates a paradox for organisations, as they need to balance the delivery of broadcast ratings for advertisers and broadcast partners, but must also ensure that attendance—which provides the required atmosphere in the stadium—remains an important financial driver.

Additionally, the globalisation of sport and the ability of 'non-local' fans to access sport from other markets are assisting these trends. For example, North America, Africa and Asia have become important commercial markets for EPL clubs, and Australians now see more NFL and NBA content through TV and internet than they did in earlier decades. In both the North American and Australian markets, trends of higher broadcast ratings and stagnant or slightly declining attendance figures are noted in recent football seasons. In 2012, an ESPN poll of North American fans showed less than one-third (29 per cent) of fans preferred to be at a live game than to watch it at home. In the same poll fifteen years earlier, 54 per cent preferred the live experience (Rovell, 2012). Even among the most avid groups of fans—season ticket-holders—it has been shown that increasing volumes of fans are migrating towards a media dominant form of consumption (Karg, McDonald and Leckie, 2012), in part because of the additional interactivity offered by new media.

NFL team owner Stephen Ross stated that the biggest challenge of any sports team was 'knowing that the fan experience at home, watching it on TV, is probably a better experience today than it is going there live' (Rovell, 2012). There are many reasons for the increased attractiveness of media consumption and digital products. These include improved quality of sport broadcasts (through high-definition transmission, camera angles and close-ups), greater availability—including more 'live against the gate' broadcasts—and the integration of interactive elements (such as social media, fantasy sport and gaming), which some consumers feel allow the home experience to exceed that on offer in the stadium. These features are supplemented by the added comfort and convenience of home and more flexible products, such as view-on-demand, customised channels and increasing control over replays and telecast components. Compared with the escalating costs of the live sport experience, and often a lack of wi-fi connectivity at the stadium (impacting device use and access to digital content), there are justifiable reasons why a segment of media-dominant consumers is emerging.

While the stadium experience is by no means dead, it is important to recognise the changing consumption patterns that are occurring, as well as the differences in the way that sport is consumed. New and digital media tools now represent normal operating activities for sport organisations to create added engagement and interactivity with consumers. In many ways, the impact of technology presents challenges for the sport industry that mirror those faced by the music and publishing industries as a result of downloading, or those faced by the retail industry as a result of online shopping. These challenges force organisations to reconsider their consumers' trends, adapt their organisations and, ultimately, shape their product offering to meet consumers' new expectations.

While driving consumption decisions, new forms of media represent great opportunities for sport organisations. This chapter seeks to demonstrate how consumption options are changing and the impact that changing preferences have on sport products and organisations. In all industries, organisations that are early adopters of technology and innovation can generate competitive advantages; hence an understanding of the application of new media to sport is imperative.

Media refer to any instrument or means of communicating information with the general public through organisations, including television and radio broadcasters, newspapers and magazines. The media traditionally have played a key role in the success of sport, with the relationship being a symbiotic one: sport is reliant on the reach and profile provided by media, while the media leverage the substantive popularity of sport to generate readership and advertising revenue, and therefore sell products.

More recently, new media has evolved as a broad term that presents as a complementary, emergent part of the communications mix. Specifically, the term 'new media' refers to the use of technologically developed or digital platforms to transmit or deliver information. Such information can be accessed on demand, in real time, and is increasingly participatory, interactive and unregulated.

In many ways, new media can be considered a complement or extension to existing ideas in sport marketing. While many of the principles of communication remain the same, new media offer tools and processes that are fundamentally and philosophically different. For example, advertising conducted in traditional mass media platforms is now replicated as a prominent part of a web or e-commerce strategy. Likewise, teams and organisations still aim to engage and communicate with fans to build loyalty and ultimately sales, but now have social networking and e-communications platforms to assist in delivering more direct and customisable messages.

In these examples, the objectives for communication and underpinning concepts remain the same, but the emergence of digital outlets creates greater possibilities and efficiencies. Given the emergence of technological platforms, there are now multiple conceptual and operational differences in the relationship between sport and the media. These include the focus on interactivity and participation; immediacy in speed of communication; the ability to reduce geographic distance; the ability to distribute far greater amounts of content; interconnectivity of content; and changes in the level of control an organisation may have (Neuman, 1991).

Impact of technology

There are a number of technological developments that have impacted the generation of digital content as well as the way it is delivered. Gephart (2004) suggests new media are communication technologies that allow computer processing and digitalisation of information, that are reliant on (tele)communications networks and that enable connectivity. To accommodate high levels of content and usage, the broadband and internet capabilities on which we rely as consumers are constantly upgrading. For example, in Australia the National Broadband Network (NBN) promises high-speed broadband through optic fibre connected to 93 per cent of homes and businesses. Such coverage will support technologies and enable applications and devices that need reliable internet performance with high speed and capacity (Department of Broadband, Communications and the Digital Economy, 2011). The implications of this added capacity extend beyond households and businesses to stadia and other venues, where fans are expecting to be connected and engaged, often through wi-fi or data networks that require substantial resources.

Likewise, the hardware or physical devices and equipment that make up new media technologies, such as mobile phones and smartphones, tablets, laptop computers, gaming consoles and other multimedia devices, continue to evolve. Mobile communications now allow consumers to access information and content—seemingly without limit or boundary—through wireless communication systems. More than ten billion mobile devices are forecast to be in use by 2016, with 71 per cent of mobile data traffic in video format. The choice and sophistication of internet-driven platforms, applications and systems software that enable technology to function are therefore important and developing considerations.

Defining digital

New media are characterised by the application of digital or computer technology to mass communications. While digitalisation traditionally refers to numerical representations, in the new media definitions it has arguably taken on a wider consideration, merging with communications, systems and computer-led terminology. Through digitalisation, technology is applied and prominent in acquiring, processing, distributing and storing information. Within new media, the creation and distribution of digital content can be automated, represented and measured numerically, and transferred, stored and shared in multiple file or delivery formats (Manovich, 2001).

In our context of sport marketing, we consider *digitalised content* primarily as new and enhanced methods of engagement, promotion and communication. Distinct from the 'one-to-many' model of traditional mass media, new media allow communication to occur within a 'many-to-many' framework. Although new media can still take on a one-to-many approach (for example, a team interacting directly with its fan base), new media can also be positioned as digital technologies that are tools of collaborative consumer engagement. This suggests shifts in organisations' operations, control of information, experience and resources required for communications (Shapiro, 1999, cited in Croteau and Hoynes, 2003: 322).

SPORTVIEW 12.1

Approach to a digital future—the rise of AFL Media

Over the 2012 pre-season, the AFL launched AFL Media, a functional unit comprising over 100 people. Employing a team of journalists, editors and digital content specialists, it produces and distributes news, press conferences, features, video content and statistical analysis, as well as housing other assets like the weekly match-day program, the AFL Record and a fantasy sport offering through the AFL.com.au site. AFL Media is also a production arm, providing outsourced services for other sport organisations, and includes AFL Films and AFL Photos.

While many organisations have made structural and strategic shifts to incorporate new media into their business model, the AFL has made the most significant changes within its market, effectively setting up an 'in-house' media company to produce content for the league and its clubs. The inaugural year produced good results on key indicators, with the revamped AFL.com.au attracting over 3.5 million unique visitors over a million video views every week, and recording more than 1.4 million downloads for AFL mobile and tablet apps (Stensholt, 2012). Return on the estimated $5 million investment was expected within two years (Stensholt, 2012), causing leading media buyer Harold Mitchell to suggest that the AFL 'is going to be one of the biggest media companies in Australia'.

However, the approach sees AFL Media now in competition with traditional media platforms and brands for digital readership and market share of consumers. AFL CEO Andrew Demetriou was quoted as saying 'we are trying to control as much as we can control and not deal with as many third parties', representing a major shift in the previously symbiotic relationship between sport and media organisations. There were concerns AFL Media's journalists, editors and producers would get preferential treatment or receive exclusive information compared with other print, radio or TV journalists. Others expressed apprehension that AFL Media may 'water down' coverage of important or negative issues in order to protect the AFL brand. This potential conflict has necessitated a balancing of unique, engaging content production with a transparent approach that protects existing relationships and the organisation's credibility.

Dimensions and characteristics of new media

Traditionally, sport has relied on mass media to distribute content and information to consumers. Under this relationship, the organisation or rights-holder would provide content to a broadcaster or media source, who would distribute the content in exchange for a financial return to the sport organisation or rights-holder. New media have challenged these established distribution channels for sport marketers and organisations. The nature of new media strategy for consumers also changes, with a greater focus now placed on interactivity and participation. The key aspects of the new media and content relationship—distribution, content and interactivity—are now introduced.

Distribution

Sportview 12.1 demonstrates the AFL's increased range of distribution options. By becoming a producer of content, the AFL offers more options for consumers, through a mix of traditional media as well as its own channels (AFL.com.au). While the AFL, along with other high-profile sports in Australia—such as Rugby League and soccer—have recently signed medium-term (five-year-plus) deals committing their games and competitions to traditional free-to-air (FTA) and pay television (as well as various Internet Protocol Television, or IPTV, and mobile rights platforms), the possibility of wholly sport-owned channels featuring live match telecasts presents as a very real possibility in the not-so-distant future.

The situation of the AFL mirrors global examples where sport organisations are becoming more directly involved in providing content and communicating with consumers. MLB, the NBA and the NFL operate their own distribution outlets, allowing consumers to access content that includes games, highlights, interviews and news directly through the sport organisation. In this sense, organisations are using disintermediation processes, 'cutting out the middleman', and are providing more flexible and cost-effective solutions accessible to large audiences, including those in non-local markets.

These approaches represent strategic shifts for organisations, which are shortening their distribution channel and becoming direct providers of content. In current or recent deals, new media platforms still only form a part of overall broadcast approaches, with all major sports still engaged in an ongoing relationship with traditional TV networks or media channels. Although a sport organisation undoubtedly sees new media approaches and ownership of distribution channels as beneficial, there are still some aspects of consideration that emerge.

For example, the production and distribution of content require large resource commitments, which the sport organisations must provide or have access to. Either substantial in-house investment or outsourcing of services is required to produce news articles, interviews, radio shows and, foreseeably in the future, content of matches and games. Further, there is a need to generate revenue from these channels in order for new media platforms and business models to be feasible. While in the past a sport organisation would receive a rights fee from a media company or television network, revenue must now be generated either through a subscription platform or through an advertising model, again creating a complex business model and requiring investment in human and physical resources to manage the process.

Content

New media also develop new challenges around controlling published content through official and unofficial means. In traditional media—mainly through communication with journalists or press and media releases—there were opportunities to direct the timing and nature of stories published in the media. While there were no guarantees the story would go to press in the context intended, monitoring and management of one-to-many communications through traditional media outlets was easier to achieve than it is today.

The speed and openness of the new media landscape, combined with the proliferation of sources (from mass media to individual bloggers), make it increasingly difficult to monitor, let alone control, the media messages to which consumers have access. This presents an interesting complex for sport organisations. User control and content sharing present opportunities for interactivity—a key component of Web 2.0 and new media (discussed below)—yet instant blogging and forums present potential for negative sentiment or inaccurate information to be shared, which could damage a sports brand.

In the opposite manner, content produced in-house provides a different but related complexity. Many organisations produce content for their own websites—news articles, stories, videos and highlights—with the aim of generating awareness, interest and engagement, and developing a readership; these organisations then look to commercialise the site in some way. As Sportview 12.1 shows, it is questionable whether leagues and organisations would publicise negative stories and if so, in what manner. Similarly, non-rights holding media outlets can only broadcast minimal amounts of coverage—perhaps limited to 30 or 60 seconds of content in news telecasts. As such, the only extensive coverage accessible to sport fans may be produced by the league or central organising body itself, under new media frameworks. With the organisation producing its own content, and consumers accessing news and opinion direct from the organisation (as opposed to independent media), there is a need to promote transparency—given that the league is increasingly at risk of losing the credibility associated with traditional media.

Extending the discussion on sport organisations' control, there have been instances of rights-holders looking to gain greater control of media messages by restricting traditional media outlets' ability to access and report on their events. An Australian cricket tour of India in 2013 highlights an example of rights-holders and accreditation issues. While there was a pay TV broadcast and various online news services (such as ESPN-owned CricInfo), only a limited number of radio and press outlets had received accreditation from the Board of Control for Cricket in India (BCCI) to cover the series. In a farcical situation (partly in protest), national papers in Australia used cartoons, Lego and hand-drawn images to depict play in the absence of photos captured under accreditation in India (Leys, 2013).

Interactivity and engagement

Part of the change brought by new media is an increased focus on producing a more customised and collaborative environment, where users are more involved with the production and sharing of content. *Interactivity* has multiple dimensions, including user control, responsiveness, real-time connectedness and personalisation or customisation. Within new media environments, social presence and networks, empowerment and engagement are influenced by the interactivity of communications, making this an important consideration for marketers.

In early editions of digital media or internet communications, websites were limited to static presentation of information with little interactive content. At this stage, websites were a collection of pages where users could read, gather and consume information, but little else. The shift towards interactivity is aligned with the philosophy of Web 2.0, a reference to generational changes in the way web technologies are used and implemented.

The modern rendition of digital media, under the preface of Web 2.0, facilitates a much greater focus on engagement and collaboration than is possible in mass media communications. Internet-driven media have transitioned from static information to participatory and interactive content encouraged by social networking sites, user-centred design, blogs and forms, video-sharing sites, interactive applications and gamification. Each of these elements can be used as tools for consumer engagement through encouraging consumer interaction with each other or with the organisation.

Within the domain of interactivity, service-dominant (S-D) logic (Vargo and Lusch, 2008) recognises the role of networks and interactions in value creation. In this domain, consumers work with each other and with organisations to create value, often encouraged by the choices they make to shape their experience and the social integration and communication inherent in new media. In many ways, the digital components integrated into sport marketing embrace the role of consumers as advocates and value creators. As well as better products and higher engagement, successful co-creation can lower (marketing) costs and produce more loyal and satisfied customers (Auh et al., 2007)

Many of the benefits of co-creation are activated by the engagement of consumers. Consumer engagement is defined as a customer's physical, cognitive and emotional presence within their affiliation with a subject (Bowden, 2009; Brodie et al., 2013), with the term increasingly being used to describe virtual or digital interactions and relationships between consumers and organisations. Engagement sits within the domain of relationship marketing (Vivek, Beatty and Morgan, 2012), with engaged consumers exhibiting enhanced consumer loyalty, satisfaction, empowerment, trust and commitment.

In this sense, new media present both an operational shift and a philosophical change in the role and function of media usage. The emergent tools and activities used to leverage interactivity towards outcomes for organisations and consumers are discussed in the remainder of this chapter.

New media and sport marketing

With the internet providing more sources of interaction, commerce and flexibility around popular goods and services, sport has a key role to play in the digital economy. The digital economy is defined as the 'global network of economic and social activities that are enabled by platforms such as the internet, mobile and sensor networks' (Department of Broadband, Communications and the Digital Economy, 2011).

The next sections address some examples of digital technology that have underpinned new media strategies for sport organisations. It is important to realise that many of these areas or objectives, such as communication, engagement, viewership and revenue generation, were in existence prior to the convergence or advent of new media, but that there have been considerable increases in the reach, access and popularity now provided. For example, organisations have always sought to communicate with consumers through advertising and information-sharing, but now have more cost-effective, customisable and direct means to do so through online advertising, e-communications and social media.

Examples of how sport organisations effectively use new media to engage consumers include social media, broadcast and content complements (including second-screen and mobile interaction), fantasy sport, fan forums and e-commerce. Each of these is examined below. The key characteristics of new media, including real-time interactivity, volume of content, customisability, user control and implications for sport organisations, are detailed within each format.

Social media and networking

Given the increasing value attributed to digital media and its role in relationship marketing initiatives, new forms of information-sharing and interaction continue to be prevalent for organisations. *Social media* are defined as 'internet-based applications that build on the ideological and technological foundations of Web 2.0, and that allow the creation and exchange of user-generated content' (Kaplan and Haenlein, 2010: 61). As part of the focus on digital content within an integrated communications mix, organisations are committing increasing attention and resources to social media.

While social media encompass multiple formats, the dominant category is *social networking* (Hutton and Fosdick, 2011), where 'companies or individuals . . . communicate, collaborate or be in community with each other' (Klososky, 2012: 42). Video (for example, YouTube) and photo and video sharing sites (for example, Instagram) have considerable presence, but it is the growth of Facebook and micro-blogging platform Twitter that have been most central. Facebook and Twitter represent forums for two-way communication to link fans directly to a brand (Wallace, Wilson and Miloch, 2011), and exist as online media networks (Kujath, 2011), with user-generated content and interactivity being central features. The popularity of these platforms to stimulate direct, authentic communication between fans and athletes (Pegoraro, 2010) and between fans and organisations is highlighted by an ESPN Consumer Insights study suggesting that 55 per cent of Twitter users and 40 per cent of Facebook users access these platforms for sports-related purposes (ESPN, 2011). Social networking is also used by journalists (Sheffer and Schultz, 2010) and media organisations to disseminate messages and content.

Through social media, organisations are seeking to communicate in new ways and to exploit opportunities for consumer engagement through cost-effective channels. The use of social media allows for the removal of barriers to high-profile individuals: A-League and AFL fans are invited to sessions where they can 'tweet' or post live questions to the CEO or coach, and audio-visual forums such as Google Hangout have also been used to connect fans with athletes. In such cases, social media provide professional teams with opportunities to use social media to 'gain maximum leverage in strengthening and building long-term relationships' (Williams and Chinn, 2010: 435).

Effective social networking between organisations and consumers also allows organisations to share news, build awareness about products and leverage existing commercial or promotional campaigns—for example, merchandise sales, ticket deals or sponsors' promotions. Given the immediate and two-way nature of social media communication, organisations can also respond to and address crises, gather feedback from fan bases and gauge sentiment from influential consumers. Content analysis has shown that the social networking posts of Australian teams have dramatically increased in volume in recent years, and can be classified under five categories (developed from Hambrick et al., 2010): interactivity; information-sharing; promotional; fanship; and diversion—with the latter two being low utilised categories. Results from Australian football clubs showed differences across the content for each medium, with Facebook used more for promotion while Twitter involved much more interactivity (Karg, Davis and Gaarenstroon, 2012).

While social media can be an effective tool when used independently, their value is also evident as a part of a wider integrated communication mix, through their capacity to extend and leverage advertising, sales promotions, events, sponsorship and sales-related campaigns. The Super Bowl in 2013 provided an excellent example of this, with key advertisers leveraging social media to support traditional mass media campaigns. Some advertisers also used a break in play, caused by a power shortage, to bring further attention to their brands through the use of additional promotions and creative communication activities using social media (Kosner, 2013).

Despite being a relatively new means of communication, the opportunities provided by social media are quickly becoming an important component of marketing strategy, particularly when used as a participatory tool rather than in a promotional manner. For example, fan communities can be enhanced and made more favourable when users can upload and review content, establish social connections and communicate with fellow users. This open and public environment has the effect of 'loosening the social restrictions found in many other sport environments' (Hambrick and Mahoney, 2011: 164). The value created by social media also helps facilitate online or Electronic Word of Mouth (EWOM) (Kunz et al., 2011), as consumers become creators of content and 'join the conversation'. Such interactions fit the tenets of S-D logic, where users play an active role in creating value extracted from participation in activities.

Given the popularity of social media, it has become almost essential for organisations to build and maintain a social media presence. Large brands such as Barcelona FC and Manchester United FC have quickly built followings in the tens of millions, finding a way to engage with large, global fan bases that it previously had been difficult to identify and establish interaction with. The Ultimate Fighting Championship (UFC) is an example of an organisation for which social media play a key role in the suite of engagement activities for a wide fan base. Even smaller events and local organisations can actively engage their fan base or users in direct and cost-effective ways. Having said that, a social media presence can require substantial resource commitments as the follower base grows and becomes a core source of information and queries by fans.

While advantageous, there has been a need to clarify the most appropriate role for social media use in organisations (Kunz and Hackworth, 2011; Mangold and Faulds, 2009), and to develop management policies around their use. An over-reliance on social media can be misplaced, given that social media are still in an adoptive phase. For example, during the 2013 season, AFL clubs averaged over 28 000 Twitter and over 95 000 Facebook followers. While this represents large annual growth, these figures represent less than 20 per cent of the estimated national club supporter base (Karg, Davis and Gaarenstroon, 2012). It should therefore be realised that messages, while cost-effective and delivered in real time, will not reach entire markets on fan bases at current levels of uptake.

In relation to content, there are multiple cases of athletes and organisations making poor decisions around social media communications. Given the public and interactive nature of social media, organisations have little control over what is said about their brand, by fans or others on their official pages. Legal precedents regarding responsibility are developing, in which accountability for the content is attributed to the owner of the page, regardless of the source of the comment or posting. As such, a need for clear policy and triage charts to deal with issue- and risk-management are prominent considerations. Increasingly, organisations have needed to respond to potential risks through the development of policy and practice, with the 2012 London Olympics providing an example of a highly regulated social media environment. In the lead-up to and during the Games, the International Olympic Committee (IOC) sought to control the use and prevalence of social media by issuing Social Media, Blogging and Internet Guidelines (SMBIG), which restricted what athletes and teams could communicate. Largely, this action sought to protect the official sponsors of the Games from ambush marketing, but it also actively sought to control negative statements and sentiment about the Games to preserve their image.

Broadcasting and content extensions

As the internet develops as a primary component of sport content distribution, new media are prominent in providing alternate broadcast options for consumers. No longer does a team need to be covered on mainstream TV channels for fans to be educated and involved; nor do consumers need to be in the geographic market for that team. In addition to traditional channels, organisations increasingly are using internet platforms to distribute content. While professional sport organisations 'were often faced with limited broadcasting options (terrestrial or cable only) . . . now technology is presenting a number of new and innovative distribution systems' (Turner, 2012: 44). This has included a focus on internet-driven distribution through Internet Protocol Television (IPTV), and mobile channels delivered to computers and handheld devices such as tablets and smartphones.

Along with new devices, emerging platforms are used to deliver content. In 2011, Facebook broadcast a match between Ascot United and Wembley FC in the English FA Cup, while the UFC also uses Facebook to televise preliminary fights to a large audience. Likewise, YouTube is used as a direct-delivery channel by a number of sports, including the English Cricket Board to distribute live coverage of the 2013 Ashes series to non-traditional cricket markets, and NASCAR, which has tens of thousands of viewers and subscribers and attracts millions of video views annually.

As well as content accessible through social media, bespoke internet platforms for sport leagues and teams are becoming increasingly popular. The NBA League Pass in the United States is a well-established product, attracting both domestic and overseas fans. NBA games are shown into local and overseas markets through traditional media; however, the internet platform allows access to live and archived games, as well as other customisable content. Consumers can access content via mobile devices, watch multiple games simultaneously or watch condensed highlights packages of various lengths.

For smaller sports, opportunities exist for rights-holders to show products that might not generate sufficient demand to make them attractive to mainstream broadcasters. For example, in regions where rights have not been sold to television networks, agencies and rights-holders of large and small sports use new media platforms to deliver live streaming and video content to niche markets. In the lead-up to the 2014 FIFA World Cup, agency SPORTFIVE showed several qualifying matches in a range of markets accessible through multiple platforms, including YouTube, social networking sites and internet or smartphone applications (McCullagh, 2012). Likewise, national and state or regional sporting championships and events can be provided to niche or target markets using the same platforms, providing content and potentially generating revenue through platforms that are not served by commercial or traditional broadcasters for that sport.

There are a number of implications of the rise in alternate broadcast channels. While agencies may offer services and platforms to assist distribution channels, content needs to be produced in-house or with a production partner. The digitalised nature of televised or broadcast content has also brought issues of internet piracy, making it easy for consumers to access illegal or pirate feeds of channels. Despite these possible drawbacks, options to reach new audiences can mean cost-effective opportunities for sports to distribute content and generate revenue from online advertising and sponsorship.

Second-screen and content marketing

In addition to providing alternate broadcast channels, new media provide extensions where viewers can use multiple screens simultaneously to access additional complementary content to the broadcast. The use of additional electronic devices is known as 'second screening', and is becoming an increasingly prominent complement to media consumption. Second-screen behaviour and its interactivity are most effective in television programming such as sport, which delivers much of its value when consumed as a live product. Access is delivered through a secondary device (for example, a laptop computer, tablet or mobile phone), and facilitated by web browsers or mobile applications (or 'apps'). The functional purposes of apps span content, information such as statistics, gaming, location-based services and e-commerce.

The content that can be accessed by the consumer is varied, ranging from additional highlights, a choice of camera angles to support or customise viewing, statistics, news and behind-the-scenes interviews, all of which can be packaged and delivered on demand. Content may also provide sources of interactivity between consumers and the team or organisation, and between each other through chat pages, forums or social media. Social media in itself is a dominant example of second-screen engagement for sport, where even though sport's share of TV programming is only 1.3 per cent, 40 per cent of all TV-related tweets are sports related (Murphy, 2013).

The use and encouragement of second-screen viewing offers benefits for media companies and television networks that hold rights, as well as for non-rights holders. For example, Sky Sports in the United Kingdom has the rights to Formula One races and offers alternative content to the main programming through an app. However, there can also be considerable benefits for non-rights holders leveraging second-screen behaviour—for example, ESPN offers statistics, biographies, news, votes, competitions and interactive elements for many sports, including many for which they may not hold official rights.

The activity can be viewed as a form of content marketing, defined as a hybrid of publishing and promotions. Here, content can be shared by organisations and consumers, and seeks to build interest and engagement, and to complement other promotions or activities. As discussed in Chapter 9, content marketing's function is more aligned with communications, although the interactivity and user creation—either as a form of second screening or a primary media source—gives value to its consideration as an engagement tool. This is particularly so, given that it is often leveraged with social media, websites and apps, forums or e-commerce platforms, which play a key role in second screening.

Overall, second-screen activities allow opportunities for additional engagement with sponsors, organisations and teams, particularly during telecasts. Where sports and broadcasters once were responsible for developing the entire consumer experience, the level of interactivity means users are more commonly involved in creating experiences for themselves and each other. It can be argued that additional content may distract the consumer during breaks in play or divert attention away from advertising, but equally it may limit the channel-switching behaviour of consumers. Increasingly, if the consumer and relevant data can be identified, then personalised or customised messages or content can be provided, thus providing additional opportunities for commercialisation by advertisers and sponsors.

Fantasy sport

Fantasy sport is a consumer activity predominantly played online, where participants manage a fictional team of chosen or assigned players and make the decisions of a coach or manager. These fictional teams compile points based on the performance and statistics of the actual players. The points achieved by fictional teams are then used in competitions against other players. The first fantasy sport games date back to the 1960s and 1970s, in the form of 'rotisserie' leagues that were facilitated as paper-based games. The popularity of fantasy sport has grown alongside digital capacity and accessibility, enabling it to become a mainstream activity.

There are estimated to be over 35 million fantasy sport users in North America (Fantasy Sport Trade Association, 2011) and over one million in Australia (Karg and McDonald, 2011). In Australia, it has been slower to develop, generating a participation rate half that in North America (Karg, Dwyer and McDonald, 2012). All manner of sports now offer fantasy play, including football codes, basketball and baseball. However, fantasy play is no longer restricted to traditional team-based, statistic-heavy sports; golf, tennis, NASCAR, Mixed Martial Arts (MMA) competitions and horse racing have all begun to provide fantasy sport offerings in recent years. Even the sport of bass fishing has sought to capitalise on the popularity of the medium, with one competition offering its winner a US$1 million prize in 2009 (PR Newswire, 2009).

Fantasy sport has developed into a wildly popular complement to traditional forms of sport consumption, encouraging greater media consumption of games, news and statistics, and helping develop social networks between sport fans. The competitions are primarily run by sport organisations themselves, or managed by media organisations, which combine fantasy platforms with existing media products such as team and league news and statistics. Fantasy sports are evolving into an important dimension in the engagement of contemporary sport consumers, leveraging media-dominant consumers (Pritchard and Funk, 2006) and the 'increasingly empowered sports fan' (Roy and Goss, 2007: 104). Fantasy sport participants are avid consumers of sport and associated products and services (Dwyer, 2011; Dwyer and Drayer, 2010; Fisher, 2009), with players shown to spend a significant amount of time on the activity, motivated by surveillance, ownership, arousal, entertainment, escape, achievement, self-esteem and social interaction (Farquhar and Meeds, 2007; Spinda and Haridakis, 2008). Studies show that fantasy sport players score higher on attitudinal measures as well as behavioural measures such as game attendance, television viewing and secondary spending, when compared to non-fantasy sport players (Karg and McDonald, 2011; Nesbit and King 2010a, 2010b), and that experienced players show higher sport consumption patterns than those new to fantasy sport.

Therefore, research supports the notion of fantasy sport as a complementary, rather than competitive, mechanism for sport marketers. This is enforced by its ability to provide fans with additional engagement with their favourite sports outside of their own team, outside the stadium itself and even outside the period when games are played through the week. While the potential impact of fantasy sport as a primary revenue generator has not been fully leveraged (many competitions—particularly outside North America—do not charge entry fees), it represents a valuable tool to aid the building of knowledge and engagement for new markets and new segments of fans. Additionally, the high traffic and 'sticky' nature of fantasy sport, which sees players spending hours each week on the playing platform, offer game sponsorship and online advertising benefits that organisations and media companies can leverage.

SPORTVIEW 12.2

Engaging through new media—Ultimate Fighting Championship

The UFC is a rising sport with a cutting-edge approach to social media and digital marketing. Led by CEO Dana White, it is an organisation that is 'super aggressive when it comes to any form of social media'. In a recent interview with *Mashable*, White commented:

> It's literally how we operate now. I do everything through Twitter, YouTube or the Internet somehow . . . the power of the internet [is] the ability it gives us to talk directly to our fans. It's so powerful and information moves so fast for so many people. It's an exciting time for someone in a business like this because you can interact with so many people directly.

The UFC's digital multi-platform approach spans large and engaged Facebook and Twitter followings, live webcasts of preliminary events on websites and Facebook, video blogs, Pinterest, Spotify and YouTube; it also has a focus on content production and sixteen versions of the UFC website for different markets. All of the 400 or more contracted UFC fighters are active on Twitter, as are social media consultants—both daily and at events. White himself is constantly connected with the sports followers through participation in blogs, forums and social networking. In an interview with ESPN's Burns Ortiz, White said his role included during-event monitoring and communication:

> When we go live, the fans are always saying on the Internet, 'Oh, he's such an idiot. He's got the best seat in the house, and he's always on his phone or looking at the TV.' The reason for that is I'm watching the TV screen because I'm making sure that everything looks good on TV. I'm on my phone because I'm reading Twitter.

In doing so, White is familiar and up to date with issues that consumers and fans may be having with ticketing, TV or online coverage, and is able to direct resources to fix problems in real time.

The organisation provides an excellent and instructive example of a sport building a platform and raising its profile through innovative new media use. Without a free-to-air or pay-per-view television following, the UFC started as a website-led content business, and the initial lessons and growth from these interactions have shaped its continuing digital-driven approach. The online fan base now extends globally and numbers in the millions, complemented by events, a range of content-marketing activities, a successful reality TV show and on-demand pay-per-view events. White sees the boundaries of social media as unlimited, and states that the medium is fun and low cost. His *Mashable* interview gave an insight of business as usual into the future:

> We've always been online and ahead of the curve . . . Any new thing that comes out with the ability to enhance our show or my ability to communicate with fans and give people more behind-the-scenes access, you know we'll be all over it.

Sources: Burns Ortiz (2011, 2013); Laird (2012).

Online communities and fan forums

Online brand forums have long leveraged the benefits of communities where passionate and engaged users act as advocates, posting queries and information on a range of topics (Davis, 2012). Such activities give rise to marketing implications, and are increasingly being used by sport brands to cultivate interaction, real-time information and content-sharing. Forums may be 'firm-sponsored'—run by the organisation themselves in an official capacity—while other platforms may be unofficial, relying on fan-driven content and affording organisations little control over, or ability to moderate, interactions. Media organisations and news sites may also leverage other activities with forums—for example, CricInfo provides a range of scores, news and updates for cricket fans, merged with discussion platforms.

Online communities and fan forums provide a structure for internet communication among fans (Pitta and Fowler, 2005), leveraging the advantages of convenience, accessibility and near-instantaneous communication. Online communities and fan forums can be differentiated from other social media platforms through their generation of in-depth qualitative data (not limited by number of characters or length of post) (Davis, 2012) and their ability to offer multiple forms of one-way and two-way communication between marketers and consumers (Pitta and Fowler, 2005). The impact of such media on consumers can include increased attachment to brands and communities, higher brand recall, a greater consideration given to purchasing products and contributions to social capital outcomes (Davis, 2011, 2012). Further, these forums have the ability to generate useful feedback for organisations on satisfaction or dissatisfaction, future products and price sensitivity.

Within the sport context, many kinds of organisation have leveraged the benefits of forums and communities. Forums have been effective in bringing together sport supporters from different geographic areas (Joshi, 2007). In Australia, user-generated (i.e. unofficial) sports forum BigFooty.com has over 100 000 members with over 20 million posts on various topics, promoting lively discussion and social interaction. Nike has manufactured shoes from designs submitted from online forum participants, while other global brands such as Major League Baseball have combined these activities with various media to generate fan content. Here, innovative strategies use influential fans and bloggers to lead discussion and provide authentic material for the league and teams. As part of this, the MLB Fan Cave, located in New York City, mixes baseball with other cultural realms such as media, interactive technology and art, hiring 'Cave Dwellers', who compete to watch and report on every game of the season through a range of media (Major League Baseball, 2013).

While fan forums increasingly are being used within the sport industry to foster interactive communication and engagement between fans and organisations, their use can pose issues for management. Often, there is a mass of data produced that can be difficult to filter, and risks exist with relation to member conduct or comments over which the organisation has little control.

E-commerce, online advertising and interactive web elements

The role of e-commerce in sport is large and complex, swelled by the capability of the digital landscape to increase ease of information, purchase and delivery. Online sales in Australia will reach $37 billion in 2013, with further growth expected as the Australian government supports the production of a leading digital economy by 2020 (Department of Broadband, Communications and the Digital Economy, 2013). In line with this, digital internet spend by marketing managers continues to be a growth area, with 67 per cent planning to increase their online or digital marketing budgets (Econsultancy, 2013). As a starting point, the role of online communication and exchange can facilitate information concerning organisations and products, purchases, and the arrangement of distribution (Van den Poel and Leunis, 1999). This is no different in sport, with virtually all participants—including teams, facilities and manufacturers—using the reach of the internet for the sale of goods, apparel, merchandise and tickets.

E-commerce models have also been integrated with social media channels—for example, the New York Red Bulls use a bespoke Facebook app to sell tickets (Walsh, 2013). This is seen as an alternative to online ticket purchasing platforms, and one that can be integrated with greater fan connection and promotion. Online betting and gambling are another area undergoing growth, given improved access to sport and online platforms. Here, $1.6 billion is gambled per year on Australia's two largest football codes (AFL and NRL), a figure expected to double in the next five years (Kwek, 2013). The sale of goods through virtual means at the stadium is also more prominent with new technologies. The ability to buy food and have it delivered to seats, and to pre-purchase and collect concessions, is increasingly becoming a part of sport services strategy within the technology-led stadium experience. As well as business-to-consumer transactions, consumer-to-consumer sales have demonstrated profound growth, in part due to secondary ticket markets such as StubHub, and auction and sales sites such as eBay.

Online advertising can also be a prominent part of organisations' e-commerce strategy, as both a promotional mechanism and a generator of revenue. Sport organisations may choose to advertise their own products, such as merchandise, coaching camps or tickets to upcoming games, or sell advertising space to partners or sponsors, earning revenue under such a model. For many reasons, the attractiveness and effectiveness of online advertising are growing. First, online advertising has the capacity to allow advertisers to customise their messages to consumers though unique personalised advertisements developed on the basis of a consumer's data profile. For example, if an avid consumer is logged into a league website, the ability to access consumption data and provide that consumer with more relevant targeted advertising becomes an option that is more attractive for partners. Second, impact measurement through tracking becomes easier to evaluate through online means. Counts of website visitors and 'click through' to purchase can be undertaken, as can longer term analysis, representing inbuilt impact measurement that is not present in TV or other mass media advertising.

In order to support increasingly complex e-commerce models and integration, websites and databases have undergone significant development to generate capability. Modern sport sites now commonly have built-in consumer relationship management (CRM) platforms, and require approaches that consider search engine optimisation and analytics to understand consumer behaviour, and drive and attract traffic.

As well as measurement and curation of consumer data in CRM platforms, organisations are also taking steps to encourage and reward online consumer behaviours though loyalty programs and gamification. This involves integrating digital gaming-type features, or 'game mechanics', to help motivate consumers towards positive behaviours. Game mechanics are defined as 'actions, tactics and mechanisms used to create an engaging and compelling experience for the consumer' (Donato and Link, 2013: 40). By doing so, organisations place incentives within communication and sales channels to motivate consumers. Rewards might include various loyalty levels, leader boards, gifts, or virtual badges or icons as consumers progress through levels of commitment or engagement in virtual or physical consumption. Gamification can be applied to encourage consumers in purchase behaviour, consumption of advertising or other information, or their participation in research projects.

Implications for organisations

Many components of sport marketing now cumulate within the digital environment, and present differing degrees of evolutionary, sustaining and disruptive innovation. They improve and vary product offerings, and they change distribution platforms, partners and value chains, and the strategies and philosophies involved. Certainly, many of the core objectives that new media seek to achieve existed in some form before, but they have been enhanced in their production or delivery with the advent of new technologies. These objectives are vastly different now in both their operation and delivery, and in the way they are managed and prioritised by sport organisations.

Equally, not all aspects of new media described in this chapter are direct revenue-generating activities. Some aspects that have brought changes to broadcast delivery have been commercialised through subscription fees, while e-commerce creates sales channels, and online advertising its own revenue stream. However, aspects such as social networking as a form of communication—and even fantasy sport, as a free-to-play activity in many markets—represent engagement tools, which seek to extend levels of cognitive, affective and behavioural consumption through enhanced generation and sharing of content and involvement. It is here we see these engagement activities tied heavily to the ideas of co-creation of value and consumer experience, as well as with the interactivity aligned with Web 2.0.

While often low cost or resource efficient, the tools described in this chapter can stretch the existing resources and skills sets of sport organisations, and often require capital or start-up investment. The development and management of many new media tools can also fall outside the specialisation of many sport organisations' existing marketing functions, particularly for small organisations. For example, a complex digital media strategy may require the merging of teams or individuals, demanding cross-function integration across marketing, media, IT and sponsorship teams. Additionally, the content production and management of apps, websites or a CRM platform, and the subsequent maintenance of these, may require the engagement of external organisations. As such, new media implementation can often require high levels of knowledge and expertise to make full use of the potential benefits.

Additional resourcing may be required to counter the rise in engagement that consumers come to expect from an organisation. The need to monitor and reply to consumer bases commonly now extends outside of mail and email queries, with instantaneous or highly responsive social media engagement requiring around-the-clock resourcing. This is particularly the case for major events or leagues.

Physical or environment resource limitations are also applicable, given that many stadia or event locations continue to have poor connectivity. While improved facilities are a feature of new or upgraded stadia, the lack of access and reliability of networks or wi-fi can create an environment where consumers may not consistently be able to access many of the engagement tools to which they can easily gain access away from the stadium. As such, the argument from the headline story regarding media-dominant consumers enjoying a superior experience away from the stadium is brought into play, challenging sport marketers on many levels.

As with all promotional tools—whether objectives are revenue led or seek other marketing outcomes such as communication, awareness, consideration or engagement—it is important that the strategy and planned impact of new media investment is clear. Digital integration can deliver meaningful metrics for consumer activities and responses, and measurement in the digital environment should form part of a strategy to evaluate return on investment. Many of the tools (social media and online communities in particular) also provide a wealth of detailed qualitative input that can help determine consumer sentiment and can be used for research and development, as well as for process and product improvement.

Finally, it is important not to over-state the role and function of technology in sport marketing. Application of the tools described here must be done in a manner that contributes to an integrated communications platform, and is consistent with the brand, message and tone of other communications. Digitalisation, by its early definition, is about reduction to numeric components, and it is important that commodification of consumers does not take place. In this sense, consumers need to feel like more than just another number being sent content or automated approaches by technology. As the consumption of sport products is driven by emotion, loyalty and feelings of involvement, it is vital that organisations maintain a personality and retain the ability to communicate authentically and meaningfully with consumers, balancing commerce and promotion with interaction and participation as part of community.

Summary

Digital technology and its ability to complement existing promotions and provide additional value to partnerships and relationships have seen it emerge as a vital part of the marketing consideration for sport managers. The change is driven by embracing conceptual adaptations of relationship marketing and engagement, and technological philosophies toward Web 2.0 and the developing digital economy. New media have impacted the distribution and control surrounding content, and have fostered attention to interactivity and engagement that may either directly impact revenue or seek to assist in the attainment of other marketing or communications goals. Important factors that make the new media tools discussed here both unique and effective include the ability for personalisation or customisation, real-time interactions, responsiveness, connectedness, user control and measurability.

CASE STUDY

The website as a sport event portal

With a need to integrate multiple elements of digital strategy alongside the promotional mix, organisational websites take on an increasing presence as portals to the communications and digital offerings of an organisation. Ioakimidis (2010: 271) notes that modern websites leverage user interaction and empowerment, and are 'increasingly sophisticated, powerful and user-based medium[s] that offer marketing challenges and opportunities to business organisations including professional sport organisations'.

The Australian Open website provides an example of the changing nature of the website as a consumer interface. For over 20 years, IBM has worked with Tennis Australia as a technology partner to deliver engaging and connected experiences for millions of fans around the globe. In 1996, the platform was a basic, static site, hosting information such as news, draws and ticket information. In line with Web 1.0, consumers could read and learn, but there was little interaction outside of moving between pages. In 2013, the site is integrated with innovative cloud computing and big data solutions around social media polls and feeds, live weather updates, and links to online points of sale, live video, radio and a TV channel, live webstreams, and interactive fan centres and sponsor activities. Innovations including social media sentiment testing, digital replications of points, sophisticated statistics and advanced analytics that predict match winners also provide tools to optimise engagement both for those physically at the event and fans at home.

Tennis Australia's chief information officer, Samir Mahir, states that the aim of the technological approach is to deepen fans' engagement with and enjoyment of the event. While fans benefit from the consumer experience delivered by the technology, the event organisation also benefits and uses interactions to develop event strategies. Analytics is used through social media feeds to identify social media trends, topics and public opinions. Tracking social and website behaviour also allows the organisation to track and predict data demand, and allocate resources to ensure a high-quality experience of site usage.

Source: Yahoo (2013).

Questions

1 How could you summarise the benefits and opportunities for both Tennis Australia and fans of the Australian Open, based on the event's current approach to new media use?
2 Given that the Australian Open event lasts for only two weeks of the year, what are some of the new media components the Australian Open uses, or could use, to enhance year-round engagement in the sport and event?
3 Choose an organisation or event and review the components of its own website and digital strategy. Which new media tools discussed in this chapter are evident in the approach of your chosen organisation? To what extent do they encourage interactivity between the organisation and consumers, and between groups of consumers?

13

How to attract and implement sponsorship

Stage 1—Identification of marketing opportunities

▼

Stage 2—Strategy determination

Step 5—Determine core marketing strategy

Marketing and service mix—sport product, pricing, place (physical evidence, people, process), customer satisfaction

Promotion mix—sales promotion, advertising, television, internet, **sponsorship**

Step 6—Determine tactics and performance benchmarks

▼

Stage 3—Strategy implemention, evaluation and adjustment

CHAPTER OBJECTIVES

This chapter introduces the concept of sponsorship, one of the most visible elements of the sport promotion mix. Here, a framework for how to create win–win relationships is presented. Celebrity marketing is discussed as a special case of sport sponsorship, and the chapter concludes by overviewing some research trends that drive the future of sponsorship.

After studying this chapter, you should be able to:

- describe sponsorship as a distinctive element of the promotion mix
- create a win–win relationship between a sponsor and a sponsee
- identify some of the trends that drive the future of sport sponsorship
- describe the basics of implementing and leveraging a sponsorship arrangement.

HEADLINE STORY

Boosting sales, raising awareness or philanthropy?

> I was always very conscious of the fact that we weren't able to offer our sponsors anything specific in return for their support... The obvious way of raising money by doing deals was just not available to us. I wanted to make sure that the Sydney bid was never criticised if we lost; that no one could say we didn't look after the people who had given us money. So I worked hard at trying to give all our sponsors value for their money. (McGeoch and Korporaal, 1994: 114)

In these few lines, Rod McGeoch, chairman of the Sydney 2000 Olympics bid committee, succinctly describes the sponsorship dilemma. One organisation needs sponsorship to reach its goals; another expects to benefit from sponsoring an organisation or individual. How can sponsorship be made to work? When is the sponsor satisfied? Can the effectiveness of the sponsorship be measured? Is sponsorship more effective than, for example, advertising? These questions can be answered only if a clear understanding of the goals of the sponsoring organisation exists. Does it want to boost sales or raise awareness, or is the chief executive officer simply a philanthropic follower of the team or sporting code?

This chapter defines and discusses the concept of sponsorship from both the sponsor's and the sporting organisation's points of view. It is important to understand which other organisations are competing with sporting organisations for limited sponsorship dollars, so a brief overview of the market for sponsors is provided. Sponsorship as an integrative tool of the sport promotions mix is discussed when goals of sponsorship are considered, followed by a look at the advantages and disadvantages of sport sponsorship. The second part of the chapter presents a sponsorship framework, and discusses how to create win–win situations. These exist when all parties entering into an agreement benefit from it. Sponsoring individual athletes as an area of special interest in the sport industry is considered next. The benefits for both the sponsor and sponsee should be taken into consideration when aiming to create a balanced win–win situation. The third part of the chapter takes us beyond the basics of sponsorship. To take a really integrated marketing approach, sponsorship support activities and tie-in promotions need to be initiated.

What is sponsorship?

Historically, sponsorship has often been associated with charity and altruism. The *Penguin Pocket English Dictionary* still defines sponsorship as 'somebody who pays for a project or activity'. In today's (sport) business environment, however, nothing is further from the truth. As an important marketing tool for many organisations, sponsorship involves a reciprocal relationship. One party puts something in and the other party returns the favour. Sleight (1989: 4), in his pointed definition of sponsorship, acknowledges the importance of the reciprocal relationship. His definition is used in the remainder of this book:

> Sponsorship is a business relationship between a provider of funds, resources or services and an individual, event or organisation which offers in return some rights and association that may be used for commercial advantage.

In marketing, it is common to look at the different marketing tools—like sponsorship—from an applied point of view. In other words, how can we use this tool (that is, spend money, resources or services) to reach sales-related goals? This is the perspective of the sponsoring organisation. From the sporting organisation's point of view, the main goal of sponsorship is not sales related. Sporting organisations or athletes mainly use sponsorship to accumulate funds, resources or services. These are then used to run the operations of the organisation. We discuss the business relationship between sponsor and sponsee further later in this chapter. Application of the sponsorship tool is not limited to sporting organisations, as is shown in the next section.

The market for sponsors

A market, as a collection of buyers, consists of all those organisations and individuals in need of something. The collection of organisations and individuals in competition for sponsors (funds, resources or services) therefore makes up the market for sponsors. According to PricewaterhouseCoopers (2011), worldwide expenditure in this market needs to be considered in light of the global growth of sport sponsorship, growing in value from US$26.7 billion (A$28 billion) in 2006 to US$35 billion (A$36.8 billion) in 2010 and an estimated US$45.3 billion (A$47.6 billion) by 2015. Geographically in 2010, North America (34 per cent, US$11.9 billion) and Europe, the Middle East and Africa (EMEA) (34 per cent, US$11.9 billion) accounted for over two-thirds of the global sport sponsorship market, followed by the Asia-Pacific (28 per cent, US$9.8 billion) and South America (4 per cent, US$1.4 billion).

Although these figures are only estimates, it can be argued that this is a huge pool of potential funds for sporting organisations. There are two major trends that have to be taken into consideration before we arrive at a final conclusion about available funds: the move to big event sponsorship and the growing competition for sponsorship dollars.

According to the IOC around 92 per cent of the funding for an Olympic Games comes from sponsorship (45 per cent) and broadcast rights (47 per cent), with the remainder coming from ticketing (5 per cent) and licensing (3 per cent) (International Olympic Committee, 2012a). For London, total sponsorship was estimated (exact figures are protected on the basis of commercial sensitivity) to be around US$2.178 billion (A$2.3 billion). The IOC and London Organising Committee adopted a tiered approach to sponsoring the Games: there were eleven TOP sponsors (The Olympic Partner Program—sponsors with exclusive worldwide marketing rights to both summer and winter Games), which contributed an estimated US$100 million (A$105.1 million) per sponsor; seven 'tier one' sponsors, valued at US$64 million (A$67.26 million) each; seven 'supporters' valued at US$31 million (A$32.58 million) each and 28 'suppliers', whose sponsorship was valued at US$15 million (A$15.76 million) per sponsor (Rogers, 2012). Furthermore, despite a 23 per cent increase in the sponsorship value of TOP sponsors to US$866 million (A$910 million) for Beijing 2008, sponsorship again rose a further

10.5 per cent for London 2012 to an amazing US$957 million (A$1005.8 million) (International Olympic Committee, 2012a).

The Olympic Partner Program is a key source of funding for the IOC. Since its inception in 1985, it has generated more than US$3.5 billion (A$3.68 billion) in cash and kind services for the Olympic movement. Since it began at the 1988 Olympic Games, the TOP program has grown nearly 1000 per cent in the space of six Olympic cycles between the 1988 Seoul Olympics (US$96 million) and the London 2012 Olympics (US$957 million), and in many ways typifies the growing commercialisation and importance of sponsorship to major sporting events (International Olympic Committee, 2012a). An important aspect of this continued growth is the continued interest and competition from new corporations who want to enter into the program in an attempt to reach the global market. For example, in the information technology category Atos Origin replaced IBM in 2004; Lenovo tried to carve out a market niche for itself by becoming a TOP partner for the 2008 Beijing Games in the computer equipment category, while Panasonic (audio-visual) and Samsung (wireless communications) have maintained their Olympic affiliation and global market position since 1988, Westerbeek and Smith (2002) observe that: 'Sponsors will simply not spend such amounts of money without the committed support of major broadcasters to the event.' The *IOC Marketing Guide* (International Olympic Committee, 2012b) points out that the London 2012 Olympics were set to attract a global audience of 4.8 billion viewers across more than 200 countries and introduce the first ever live 3D coverage of the Olympic Games.

SportBusiness in Numbers (2007) reported a disproportionate amount of sponsorship spending in Australia as the majority went to sport (60 per cent), while cause-related activity (18 per cent), arts (12 per cent) and entertainment (8 per cent) made up the balance. In Australia, the biggest business sectors involved in sponsorship are financial services (30 per cent), telecommunications (13 per cent) and automotive (9 per cent), with an average spend of A$2.5 million per company annually (*SportBusiness in Numbers*, 2007).

Although expenditure on sponsorship is still growing, the increasing dominance of big sporting events and powerful sporting organisations, as well as increasing competition from organisations other than those in sport, are making it more difficult for many (smaller) sporting organisations to attract funds, resources or services through sponsorship. The relative distribution of the top five industries that sponsor sport worldwide is presented in Figure 13.1.

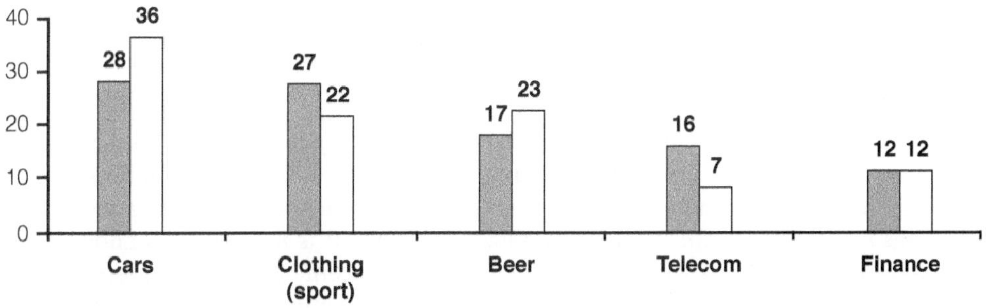

FIGURE 13.1 Relative comparison (%) of top five industries that sponsor sport in Australia and worldwide

Source: Adapted from *SportBusiness* (2000: 58); Sport and Recreation Victoria (2000: 5).

Of all the sponsorship deals in the top five, 30 per cent are finance industry related. The results from *SportBusiness in Numbers* (2007) show automotive industry support in Australia shifting significantly from top position in 2001 (36 per cent) to third in 2007 (9 per cent), and replaced by the financial services industry (30 per cent), which in the past was in fifth position (12 per cent).

Sponsorship goals: The right to associate . . .

Historically, the sponsorship tool can be seen as a derivative of either advertising or public relations, as elements of the promotion mix or as a combination of the two. Throughout the past decade, however, sponsorship has developed as an independent and important element of the promotion mix. In other words, sponsorship clearly stands apart from other promotion mix elements, to be considered as potentially the dominant promotional tool in a marketing communications program.

In Chapter 10, advertising was defined as a non-personal communication by an identified sponsor. From the sponsor's point of view, the difference between sponsorship and advertising is the actual message communicated, and how that message is communicated. In advertising, the content of the message and the moments of communication are determined by the paying organisation. When using sponsorship, however, the sponsor provides financial or material support for what are often independent organisations, individuals or activities. Less control can be exercised over the communication through these entities, and the timing of communication cannot be controlled. Although indirect (through the sponsored organisation), the actual message is often communicated at a more personal level (for example, to people visiting an event). These points are returned to when discussing the advantages and disadvantages of sport sponsorship.

Public relations goals such as 'earning understanding and acceptance' and 'creating goodwill' can be sponsorship goals as well. The fact that the organisation has to pay for the association with the sponsored organisation, and that communication takes place through an independent organisation, distinguishes sponsorship from pure public relations. The sponsored organisation is used as the means of communication, which in effect can make sponsorship a public relations tool.

A general goal of sponsorship is described by Wilmshurst (1993: 377). Elements of both advertising and public relations can be found in this goal, which reads:

> sponsorship is usually undertaken to encourage more favourable attitudes towards the sponsoring company or its products within a relevant target audience, such as consumers, trade customers, employees or the community in which it operates.

Earlier in this chapter, we described the difference in goal orientation between the sponsoring organisation (sponsor) and sponsored organisation (sponsee). Because the sporting organisation, most of the time, is the sponsee, neither advertising nor public relations goals seem to fit! In order to obtain sponsors, it is important to know about the sponsor's goals, but sponsee goals are often different. Research undertaken by S-Comm Australia and the Australian Sponsorship Marketing Association (ASMA) in 2006 identified the importance of benefits for the sponsor. A sponsoring organisation

TABLE 13.1 Sport sponsor and sponsee goals

Sponsor goals	Sponsee goals
Image creation or improvement	Obtaining *funds*
Business relationship marketing	Obtaining *resources* (goods)
Media relationship marketing	Obtaining *services*
Employee relationship marketing	Raising awareness
Community relationship marketing	Brand positioning
Business development	Raising credibility
Increasing sales	Image creation or improvement
Brand positioning	
Raising awareness	
Corporate responsibility	
Targeting new market segments	
Developing new distribution channels	

values 'category exclusivity' (8.7 per cent of responses) as the prime benefit of sponsorship, closely followed by 'media exposure' (8 per cent) as important to their commitment to sponsoring an organisation. Table 13.1 presents an overview of different sponsor and sponsee goals—goals that have to be matched when a sponsorship framework is created.

It can be argued that the sponsor goals listed in Table 13.1 need to be categorised—for example, under headings such as corporate, marketing and media objectives. Strategic, tactical and operational would be another possible categorisation, as would the distinction between direct (sales) and indirect (exposure) marketing objectives. The reality of the sponsorship opportunity, however, is that what is really bought by the sponsor—as outlined in our definition at the beginning of the chapter—is the right to 'associate'. In other words, the sponsor attempts to forge a connection between the sponsorship property (that is, the event or athlete) and the company or brand. The assumption is that a value transfer from the event or athlete to the company or brand occurs, in the process achieving sponsorship objectives. (We will further introduce this 'image transfer' concept later in this chapter when discussing celebrity marketing.) Perhaps the best way to describe sponsorship objectives is to use the 'buyer readiness sequence'—or AIDA (attention, interest, desire, action)—presented in Chapter 9, rather than categorising sponsorship objectives according to their functional or hierarchical intention. For example, a high-profile event can best be used to attract attention to a new brand, a high-profile athlete to generate further interest, a special niche event (for example, Xtreme Games) to create 'desire' to own the product and, finally, a community-based event to make people buy the product in a convenient and comfortable environment. In other words, sponsorship, when applied to different properties, can be used to achieve a wide range of objectives. (We use the AIDA model again in Chapter 14, when we discuss measuring the effect of sponsorship programs.)

Advantages and disadvantages of sport sponsorship

It was shown above that sponsorship has distinctly different characteristics from other elements of the promotion mix, such as advertising and public relations. Sponsorship in a sport context allows the sponsor to communicate more directly and intimately with their target market (in this case, the people interested in the sporting organisation and its products).

In Chapter 1, some unique characteristics of the sport product are listed, some of which are applicable when discussing the advantages of sport sponsorship. First, sport consumers tend to identify themselves personally with the sport, which creates opportunities for enhancing brand loyalty in products linked to the sport. Sport evokes personal attachment, and with this the sponsor can be linked to the excitement, energy and emotion of the sporting contest. In other words, sport has the potential to deliver a clear message. Sport has universal appeal and pervades all elements of life (geographically, demographically and socio-culturally). This characteristic presents the opportunity to cross difficult cultural and language borders in communication, enabling the sponsor to talk to a (global) mass audience. At the same time, the variety in sports available makes it possible to create distinct market segments with which it is then possible to communicate separately. The universal appeal and strong interest in sport give it a high level of media exposure, resulting in free publicity. This can make a sponsorship deal very cost-effective. Thousands of dollars of advertising expenditure can be saved when a sporting organisation or athlete attracts a lot of media attention. This makes many organisations want to be associated with sport. Also, because of the clear linkage of the sponsor to a sporting organisation or athlete, sponsorship stands out from the clutter—contrary to mainstream advertising, in which people are bombarded with hundreds of messages each day.

With so many advantages, why do organisations not simply spend their complete promotional budget on sponsorship? Well, there are some disadvantages to be considered before entering into a sponsorship agreement. In ambush marketing (discussed in Chapter 14), non-sponsors take advantage of the efforts of real sponsors in that they try to be associated with the sponsored organisation, event, product or athlete. Lack of control over media coverage is another disadvantage of sport sponsorship. Also, the media are sometimes reluctant to recognise the sponsor's name when reporting on events or the achievements of athletes. Achievements of teams or athletes are another area that cannot be controlled. A non-performing team or athlete will have direct influence on the perception the public holds of the sponsor. The implications of this for the sponsorship of individual athletes are considered later in this chapter.

Creating win–win situations

If both sponsor and sponsee have to benefit from a cooperation, certain goals of both need to be satisfied. The main question that sponsor and sponsee have to ask themselves is: How can we successfully reach our own goals by assisting the sponsor/sponsee to reach their goals? The sponsorship framework in which win–win situations are created is conceptually quite simple, and is presented in Figure 13.2.

The assumption in the framework is that certain benefits will satisfy certain goals. Those benefits can be delivered only by an entity other than the organisation. If two entities, both in search of benefits to satisfy their own goals, are able to deliver the benefits needed by the other entity, they can become engaged in an exchange of benefits.

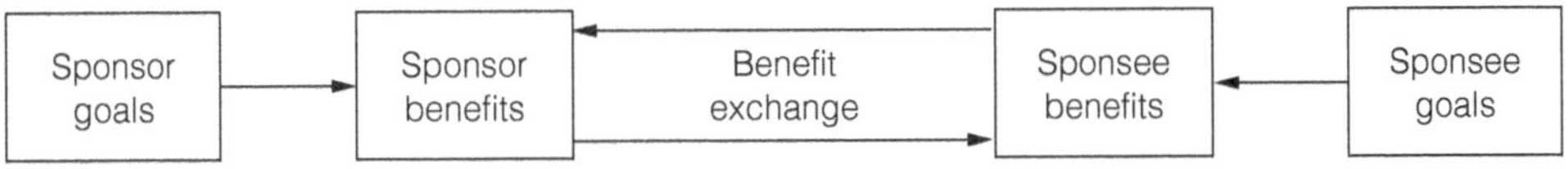

FIGURE 13.2 Sponsorship framework to create win–win situations

By exchanging benefits, both organisations 'benefit' from the cooperation; therefore, a win–win situation is created.

It must be noted, though, that in today's sporting environment it is often not enough to 'create' a win–win situation and leave it at that. It is rapidly becoming common practice for sponsor and sponsee executives to organise regular strategic planning meetings in order to maximise the effectiveness of the sponsorship. During these meetings, it is evaluated whether the goals of both the sponsor and sponsee are being reached, and whether any new insight and ideas can increase the effectiveness of the sponsorship. More and more, executives discuss new business opportunities beyond the scope of the (current) sponsorship through which the actual sponsorship can lead into a strategic alliance. A strategic alliance is a commitment and relationship between two organisations from which both organisations hope to benefit.

It is now time to examine the conceptual sponsorship framework in practice. Table 13.1 presented possible sponsor and sponsee goals. Table 13.2 expands on this to include the operationalised benefits needed to reach the listed goals, and provides an example. The goals of a sponsor (beer brewer Heineken) and a sponsee (a sporting organisation) are shown in bold type. The benefits needed by both organisations to reach their goals are shown in bold type as well. If both organisations are willing and able to provide the

TABLE 13.2 Exchanging benefits to satisfy goals of sponsor and sponsee

Sponsor goals	Sponsor benefits	Sponsee benefits	Sponsee goals
Image creation or improvement Business relationship marketing Media relationship marketing Employee relationship marketing Business development Increasing sales **Brand positioning** Raising awareness Corporate responsibility Targeting new market segments Developing new distribution channels	**Television exposure** **Print media exposure** Access to sporting organisation's mailouts Naming rights Logo use Signage **Advertising rights** Merchandising rights Product exclusivity Sampling opportunities Athlete use **Hospitality opportunities** Access to database (addresses etc.)	**Dollars** Goods **Services** Exposure Affiliation	**Obtaining funds** **Obtaining resources** (goods) **Obtaining services** (Raising awareness) (Brand positioning) (Raising credibility) (Image creation or improvement)

Heineken Beer Breweries' goal	Heineken Beer Breweries' benefits	Sports organisation benefits	Sporting organisation goals
Brand positioning	Television exposure Print media exposure Advertising rights Hospitality opportunities	$25 000 Fully created party for sporting organisation members	Obtaining funds Obtaining services

benefits needed by the other organisation, a win–win situation can be created. The example is summarised at the bottom of the table. In the context of the sponsor that we have chosen in the example, it is worth noting that Heineken spends 80 million Euros every three years as one of the main sponsors of the European Champions League! For that amount of money, it is vital to create a win–win situation.

A variety of issues need to be considered before a deal can be closed and a win–win situation created. How to write a sponsorship proposal and how to enhance the value of a sponsorship are covered in this chapter's case study. Sportview 13.1 provides an opportunity to explore a new sponsorship opportunity. Following the Sportview, we take a closer look at a typical sport industry sponsee: the individual athlete.

SPORTVIEW 13.1

An AFL event activation and sponsorship opportunity —AFL and Toyota

by Lynley Ingerson and Jonathan Robertson

Background

According to the Australian Football League (AFL) Chief Executive Officer (CEO), Toyota's sponsorship of the AFL is the 'largest sponsorship for any sport in Australia' (*SportBusiness*, 2011). Since taking over from Carlton and United Breweries in 2004, Toyota has been the AFL's primary naming rights sponsor—the deal was extended to the end of the 2014 season and is estimated to be worth $7.5 million a year (Wilson, 2012). As the AFL's premier partner, Toyota's deal with the AFL provides great coverage for Toyota throughout the season. Features of this deal include:

- naming rights—the 'Toyota' AFL season; the 'Toyota' AFL Grand Final
- advertising campaigns—the Toyota Legendary Moments campaign featuring past AFL stars
- community initiatives—a 'Good for Footy' program allowing local Toyota dealers to financially give back to the local community
- digital media—the Toyota AFL Dream Team, an online fantasy football game.

The ongoing sponsorship has created a win–win relationship for both the AFL and Toyota, although it is not without its difficulties. The Australian car market—particularly the family sedan market—is highly competitive, both for sales and sponsorship. Toyota also sponsors two teams (the Adelaide Crows and the West Coast Eagles); however, there is strong competition from Hyundai (Brisbane Lions, Carlton Blues); Lexus (Collingwood Magpies); Kia (Essendon Bombers); Ford (Geelong Cats—Australia's longest running sponsorship); Skoda (Greater Western Sydney Giants); Opel (Melbourne Demons); Mazda (North Melbourne Kangaroos); Jeep (Richmond Tigers); and Volkswagen (Sydney Swans). While none of these companies sponsors the AFL to the same degree as Toyota, the company has previously expressed concerns of infringement to its sponsorship from competitors such as naming rights of Hyundai at Brisbane; Holden hiring a blimp to fly over a football ground; and Geelong premiership captain Tom Harley refusing to mention Toyota after winning the 2008 premiership (Warner, 2010).

Task

In light of recent trends to shift to more environmentally friendly large family sedans in Australia due to rising fuel costs and environmental concerns, Toyota is planning to launch its new (fictional) family sedan 'The Dorado'. Toyota hopes to leverage its existing sponsorship with the AFL to introduce its new electric, four-door family sedan in the lead-up to the AFL's premier event—the Toyota AFL Grand Final. You have been appointed Toyota's new marketing communications manager and it is your responsibility to design a launch event for the 'Dorado' in the week leading up to the Toyota AFL Grand Final. Your strategy should include physical activation events and publicity objectives, and be supported by digital and social media activities. As an experienced marketing communications manager, you realise that it is important to include the following in the strategy for the launch event.

1 Identify the objectives of the event.
2 Identify the objectives of Toyota for this event.
3 Identify the objectives of the AFL for this event.
4 Outline three broad marketing strategies to support the objectives. These are likely to incorporate other elements of the marketing or promotional mix.
5 Create an activation plan which specifically outlines the promotional tools applied to the event that would communicate the 'Dorado' and Toyota's brand personality and enhance the relationship between Toyota and the AFL.

Sources: SportBusiness (2011); Warner (2010); Wilson (2012); <www.afl.com.au>, accessed 20 March 2013.

Sponsoring individual athletes and celebrity marketing

Belch and Belch (2007) suggest that, when communicating a message, the credibility and attractiveness of the source are of particular importance. Credibility and attractiveness are therefore the concepts to consider when organisations choose to use athletes as their source of communication. Consider this example:

> Roger Federer is arguably the greatest tennis player of the modern era. He held the world number 1 position for 237 consecutive weeks from 2004 to 2008, appeared in eighteen out of nineteen Grand Slam finals from 2005 to 2010 and has won seventeen Grand Slam titles—the most of any tennis player. His estimated net worth is over US$150 million, which has come largely from endorsement contracts, including Nike, Rolex, Wilson, Mercedes-Benz, Credit Suisse, Lindt, Moët & Chandon and Gillette, and career prize money. These endorsements saw Federer's earnings increase from US$29 million in 2006 to US$52 million in 2012 (Forbes.com, 2012a). As his manager, Tony Godsick, who is the vice president of IMG, explains: 'What makes him so attractive for all the big companies is the fact that he is Swiss. Switzerland is a small

country with which one associates loyalty, luxury, precision and perfection.' (Jaberg, 2011). Often described by the media as 'Mr Perfect', Federer has enjoyed longevity in an elite sport brand that is highly credible and attractive for global companies.

Credibility and attractiveness

The Gillette company launched a new program in 2007 known as 'Gillette Champions', which employed the ambassadorial talent of three 'credible' sports stars: Roger Federer (ranked number one in tennis since 2005–08), Tiger Woods (fourteen times Major Championship winner) and Thierry Henry (World Cup and Euro Championship winner in soccer). All three ambassadors were fully integrated into the Gillette brand programs, including global print and broadcasting advertising, consumer promotions, point-of-sale materials, online and public relations support (*Business Wire*, 2007). Each athlete was recognised globally, was successful in his chosen field and, more importantly, was highly respected. However, when it came time to renew the Gillette contract in 2011, only one 'champion' remained—Roger Federer. At the time, *Forbes* estimates Tiger Woods was still the highest-paid athlete in the world—by a long way—as he had been since 2002, and Thierry Henry had just moved into the commercially important US market at the New York Red Bulls football club. So why not renew Woods' and Henry's contracts? While many reasons exist (upcoming Olympic year in 2012, Henry's lower presence in the US market, etc.), the factors that contributed to this disassociation can be attributed to both athletes losing credibility and hence attractiveness. For Woods, the loss of credibility came due to off-course indiscretions in his personal life, while Henry was seen to lose credibility through a deliberate hand ball that cost Ireland a spot in the 2010 World Cup. Although Henry's incident was relatively small, his credibility as an elite sports property was undoubtedly negatively influenced by the media frenzy that followed. Why were Federer, Henry and Woods such attractive athletes, and why did Roger Federer continue to be so successful in conveying the message of so many companies? Why are they such powerful sources? Are there limitations to the credibility and attractiveness of sporting celebrities? To answer these questions, it is first necessary to elaborate on the concepts of credibility and attractiveness. A simplified model of the communication process, including these concepts, is presented in Figure 13.3. The model shows that when a source is credible and attractive, the message will become more powerful and will have a higher impact on the receiver of the message. This, in turn, will lead to a positive association with the source and message, eventually leading to a planned change in the perception, awareness or buying behaviour of the receiver. If the source is not credible and attractive, the opposite is more likely to happen.

FIGURE 13.3 The impact of source credibility and attractiveness on the message and receiver

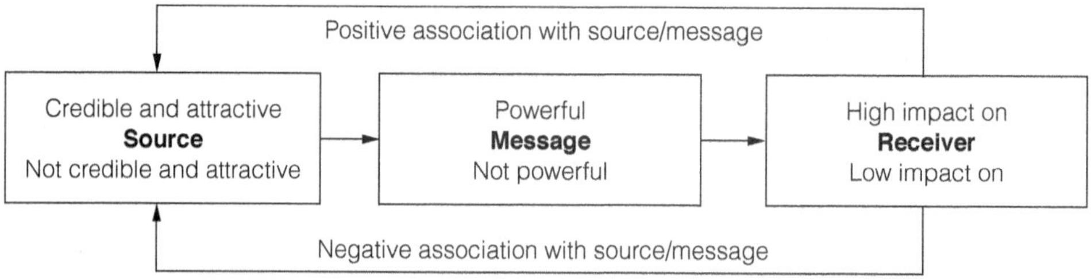

According to Belch and Belch (2007), a source is credible when it has expertise about the message. When cricketer Brett Lee endorses the sport drink Gatorade, he is a more credible source than golfer Adam Scott endorsing cricket shoes. It is more likely that, as a fast bowler, Lee has more expertise about the sport drink than Scott has about cricket shoes. A source also becomes more credible when it is trustworthy. Brazilian soccer star Neymar da Silva will probably be more honest and believable in supporting the well-being of the Amazon rainforest than in endorsing the benefits of being a member of the Turkish Automobile Club. Information from credible sources will influence the receiver in that the message communicated will become the opinion of the receiver. This opinion will have an influence on the (buying) behaviour of the receiver.

A source becomes more attractive when there is a similarity between the source and the receiver. The more similarities a person can (or wants to!) identify between the athlete and him or herself, the more likely that person is to be influenced by the message of the athlete. Many juniors aspire to 'bowl like Bing' (in reference to Brett Lee's nickname). Linking this message to drinking Gatorade, Lee successfully influences the buying behaviour of many cricket fans around the world. Likeability is another determinant of attractiveness. Sporting celebrities are admired for their performances, and become well known to the public, given the high visibility and hence media coverage of sport. Rather than a plain advertisement to launch the new Chevrolet Cruze Station Wagon and US-based Chevrolet brand into the UK market in 2013, Chevrolet controversially leveraged the Manchester United and Liverpool rivalry in the 'What are you #DrivenBy' campaign that used players from both teams to draw attention to Chevrolet's new product and message, in order to stand out in the very cluttered advertising media.

How important the attractiveness of an athlete is to organisations associated with that athlete is exemplified by golfer Tiger Woods. When the American PGA renegotiated its television contract, it agreed on a new four-year deal worth US$870 million (A$914 million), some US$90 million per annum up from the last deal. It has been argued that Tiger Woods singlehandedly is accountable for this rise, and the proof is in the pudding. Sport television ratings in 2000 in the United States showed the PGA tour to be up 22 per cent over the 1999 season. This increase is even more spectacular when compared with the 2000 ratings of the NFL (down 7.2 per cent), NASCAR (down 7.3 per cent), the NBA (down 11.9 per cent—Jordan was still in retirement) and the MLB (down 22.2 per cent) (Wilner, 2001). Conversely, when Tiger Woods was not on the PGA tour in the last half of the 2008 season, due to a knee injury, ratings fell by 47 per cent. The need for Tiger Woods to be part of the PGA tour was also exemplified in a Nielsen rating of the final day at the PGA championship (one of the four golf majors annually) from 1997 to 2012. Burke (2012) reported that on a rating scale of 15, for the six years in which Woods won the tournament, ratings averaged 7.2 while in the nine years he didn't, the ratings were a relatively low 4.8. In 2011, the PGA negotiated new contracts. Tim Finchem, the PGA tour commissioner, and network executives declined to disclose financial details, but it was made clear that CBS and NBC had entered into nine-year contracts that 'were increasing' from the previous five-year, US$2.95 billion (A$3.1 billion) contract arrangement. The focus of this contract—unlike previous contracts—was shifting toward young stars like Rory McIlroy and Keegan Bradley, and any 'fightback' from Tiger Woods would be perceived as a bonus (Mavo, 2013). Credibility and attractiveness, however, are influenced by other factors when using an athlete celebrity.

Considerations when using athlete celebrities

Using a single athlete, as opposed to a sporting organisation, team or event, brings with it advantages and disadvantages.

The single athlete can stand out in myriad advertising messages, especially when performance is high. However, this comes with associated risks of selecting a 'single' athlete. There is little higher performance from an athlete celebrity than Michael Jordan and his Nike sponsorship and association with the Air Jordan brand. However, in the 1984 NBA draft there were considered to be three exceptional talents: Hakeem Olajuwon, Sam Bowie and Michael Jordan. It is unimaginable in hindsight, but Jordan was taken at pick three behind the other two players. Jordan went on to be the highest performing NBA player of all time: a six-time NBA champion and finals Most Valuable Player (MVP), a five-time league MVP and a fourteen-time NBA All Star. In comparison, Olajuwon went on to have a very successful career while Bowie failed to reach any significant heights in his eleven-year career. It was Jordan's level of performance, marketability as a 'brand' and a little bit of luck from Nike (as Adidas was Jordan's first preference) that made the #3 selection in the 1984 draft one of the most successful celebrity partnerships of all time.

Another uncontrollable factor is the personality of the star athlete. Athletes who find it hard to control themselves when they lose, say things to the press they regret later or always seem to run into trouble are risky investments for organisations trying to build a consistent image or sell more products. While the performance and personality of athletes cannot be controlled, it can heavily influence their credibility—consider the above Tiger Woods and Thierry Henry examples.

Organisations also have to realise that young people are more likely than older people to be influenced by athlete celebrities. Therefore, the target publics with which organisations want to communicate by using athlete celebrities have to be selected carefully.

When using high-profile celebrities, organisations run the risk that the message or product they want endorsed will be overshadowed by the celebrity. Because high-profile celebrities are attractive to a mass audience, many organisations want them to endorse their messages. This can easily lead to over-exposure of the athletes, which will make the messages they communicate less credible. Over-exposure is noted when it becomes too obvious that the celebrities are being paid to endorse the message, and the public can become very sceptical. Sportview 13.2 gives examples of these considerations.

SPORTVIEW 13.2

A hole new ball game

by Jonathan Robertson

There are few sports celebrities that can consider themselves truly global. For a start, there are few 'global' sports that have high appeal in all economically significant countries. And, with the exception of football (and maybe basketball), truly 'global' sports are often individual sports such as tennis, golf, Formula One racing and boxing. Therefore, the pool of celebrity athletes for a global brand to leverage itself off often concentrates on around 20 to 30 athletes globally. Consider over the past 22 years that there have only been six celebrity athletes at the top of *Forbes*' highest paid athletes list from four sports: boxing (Floyd Mayweather, 2012; Mike Tyson, 1990, 1996; Evander Holyfield, 1991); basketball (Michael Jordan, 1992–95, 1998–99); Formula One (Michael Schumacher, 1999, 2000); and golf (Tiger Woods, 2002–2011) (*Forbes*, 2012b).

The heir apparent to this title seems to be Rory McIlroy from Northern Ireland, who signed a ten-year, $250 million contract with Nike in 2013 at the age of 23. This means that, without additional sponsorships, and excluding earnings from winning tournaments, the 2012 world number 1 golf player will receive a guaranteed $25 million per year until 2023. The move seems to be an investment in the future by Nike after a similar sponsorship with Tiger Woods saw him become the highest paid athlete globally for almost a decade from 2002.

The global popularity and individuality of golf as a sport help a brand such as Nike leverage itself, based on McIlroy's specific features. According to Mavo (2013), 'McIlroy's effortless talent, beaming smile, aw-shucks disposition, and celebrity girlfriend [tennis star Caroline Wozniacki] . . . it's undeniable that he represents the future of golf.' The 'celebrity couple' is a marketer's dream, as it can increase brand exposure and awareness across market segments that a male golfer may not be able to reach—such as the branding phenomenon between David Beckham and pop star Victoria Adams (of the Spice Girls).

It is likely that Nike views the move to bring McIlroy into its brand portfolio as a way to assure the succession from Tiger Woods. Tiger Woods for a long time was a sports marketer's dream—'a multiracial, Stanford-educated prodigy with the physique of an NFL wideout—riding an unprecedented wave of victories and, eventually, a ball with a Swoosh on it' (Mavo, 2013). However, with Woods' downfall due to off-field indiscretions, Nike's continuing association with the Tiger Woods brand and the rise of Rory McIlroy, the transition from brand Woods to brand McIlroy will be fascinating.

Source: Excerpts from Mavo (2013); *Forbes* (2012b).

The integrated marketing approach

Sponsorship support activities complement the sponsor's goals. Given the sponsorship framework, the sponsee can either supply support activities or participate in support activities in order to enhance the value of the sponsorship for the sponsor. An example of different sponsorship support activities is provided below. As a new Olympic sponsor, the Lenovo Group from China represents a growing name in information technology, and serves as a case example presented from the sponsor's point of view.

Sponsorship support activities

Initially, the way forward for Lenovo was challenging, as it decided to communicate its global brand solely through a public relations campaign. The purpose of the campaign was to create worldwide awareness of the Lenovo brand, emphasising its product's quality and innovation (a reputation only gained in China at this stage). It also aimed to further strengthen relationships with strategic partners, as it had taken over the successful and trusted IBM ThinkPad notebook product and needed to reassure channel partners globally of the company's credibility. As public relations is about utilising communication tools to create and maintain relationships with customers and other stakeholder groups, this 'stand-alone' strategy seemed to be the most logical approach.

The multifaceted communications program included a press release and a 'Welcome Lenovo' launch event. This was followed up by a 'Where's Lenovo?' press launch for a new product, adopting a more modern European setting rather than emphasising the company's Chinese origins. The program continued throughout 2005 with a series of activities such as a product review program, a press trip to China, a Chinese Embassy dinner (to maintain Chinese business culture links) and a media influencer program. In 2006, the program became geared towards customers with a 'So you think you know Lenovo?' campaign.

Event sponsorship is an effective means of supporting a public relations program, and Lenovo's next strategy was to phase in the negotiated TOP sponsorship with the International Olympic Committee as the major supplier of information technology for the Olympic Games. While the sponsorship contract alone would cost the company about US$50 million (A$52.5 million), an additional integrated marketing program supporting the sponsorship would cost about three times that amount. Lenovo's objectives for nominating as a TOP sponsor were to establish 'brand awareness, build unity among employees worldwide, and drive business with global customers' (<www.lenovo.com>, accessed 30 March 2013). Supporting activities began prior to the 2006 Turin Winter Olympics, with staff assisting with the installation, testing and training of computing equipment. Lenovo provided equipment, training and technical services for Beijing 2008. Additionally, there were internet lounges in the athletes' villages and Chinese Olympians Li Ting and Sun Tiantian (tennis) were used as brand ambassadors. Supporting advertising through global television and outdoor billboards further enhanced the public relations strategy. A global flagship retail store was positioned in Shanghai. Finally, strategic alliances with other TOP sponsors such as Visa and Coca-Cola, and media partner NBC, included joint advertising and point-of-sale promotions. However, perhaps Lenovo's greatest promotions coup was to be the successful designer of the Olympic torch 'Cloud of Promise', which travelled from Olympia in Greece to Beijing. This provided exposure to a brand destined to appeal to the global market in the future. Interestingly, it seems the profile of the organisation—as an up-and-coming organisation competing against established competitors—seems to be the profile for organisations that see Olympic TOP sponsorship as most beneficial. In 2007, largely based on the success of Lenovo, Taiwanese company ACER became the official Olympic TOP sponsor. However, following 2012, ACER exited the agreement, citing the presence of Samsung and Panasonic as fellow TOP partners as a major reason for the discontinuation.

Sponsoring (inter)nationally but making it work locally

Chavanat, Martinent and Ferrand (2009) confirm that sport sponsorship can be a very effective tool to enhance corporate brand image at the (inter)national level. They warn that to fully utilise international events in a local market, sponsors should consider two factors: building a sponsorship portfolio within the country and concentrating on activating the sponsorship. For example, at the 2006 FIFA World Cup, sports manufacturer Adidas sponsored the event (FIFA World Cup), the national team (France) and the star player (Zinedine Zidane). By creating this vertically integrated sponsorship portfolio, Adidas influenced purchase intentions of French consumers by creating a portfolio of brand images that increased consumer perceptions of the Adidas product. The second key aspect of sponsorship to capitalise on this increase purchase intent of a market is activation. The importance of activation can be described as follows: 'Sponsorship without activating is like buying an electronic device but not the batteries. Yet, even when sponsorship is activated, all too often the batteries are the wrong size.' (IEG 2006; Chavanat, Martinent and Ferrand, 2009). Activation strategies for this event could have included live sites to watch the French team play, in-store promotions and publicity events in the lead-up to the World Cup—all designed to develop relationships with local communities, target markets and eventually conversion of these relationships into sales.

An Olympic sponsor since 1986, Visa has gained a reputation as one of the most successful sponsors of sport in the world. The credit card business was extremely fragmented in terms of face-to-face communication with customers. Prior to the Salt Lake City Winter Games, Visa had 1.2 billion card-holders worldwide, who obtained their cards through one of 21 000 member financial institutions worth some US$2 trillion in business. As an Olympic sponsor, it aimed to create alliances with local partners in order to talk to (potential) customers, both on the Olympic site and through the various media outlets. In Salt Lake City, Visa created partnerships with the Salt Lake Visitors and Convention Bureau as early as 1996. It further aligned with the local Chamber of Commerce, Ski Utah, Park City, Deer Valley and the US ski team. Many banks historically have not been involved with the Olympic Games, yet Visa managed to convince twelve of the United States' largest banks to become active Olympic Visa marketers, representing 80 per cent of the financial market in the United States:

> Throughout the world, thousands of member banks [were] running marketing programs which utilise Olympic branding and messages. Millions of Visa cards now bear the famous five rings and the presence of Olympic branding at point of sale further cements the relationship. (Roberts, 2002: 22–3)

Large running events are becoming prime sponsorship opportunities for a variety of sponsors, given the long-term brand association that can be gained in addition to the participation and media coverage of the event day itself. The reason for this trend is that distance running events are unique in terms of the amount of training required in the lead-up to the event, and therefore opportunities to increase brand association. The case of the 2012 ING New York City Marathon provides an excellent insight into the sponsorship opportunities and risks associated with leveraging an event through social media. ING Bank has been the naming rights sponsor of the ING New York City Marathon (NYC Marathon) since 2003. The NYC Marathon is one of the world's largest and highest profile international marathons. As part of its activation in 2010–11 the NYC Marathon, in consultation with ING as its title sponsor, created a Facebook page and Twitter tag. This proved a successful relationship between event organisers and participants, with social media sites acting as a site for information dispersal, the establishment of running groups, training programs and integral publicity platforms for influencing brand image and association via online interaction.

However, social media's strength—online 'word-of-mouth' and mass publicity of an event/sponsor—can also be its Achilles' heel, as the 2012 event demonstrated. Six days prior to the 2012 event, New York was hit by Hurricane Sandy—the largest Atlantic hurricane ever. Initially, the event was re-branded as the 'Race to Recover'; however, public sentiment quickly turned and within two days the Twitter and Facebook sites became the focus of anger and vitriol toward event organisers (<www.facebook.com/ingnycm>, viewed 20 February 2013). Criticisms included the corporatising of the event (of which ING is the title sponsor), allocation of resources to the event instead of the relief effort, the event organiser's salary and the appropriateness of holding the event immediately after a natural disaster. As naming rights sponsor, ING was directly linked to the public relations and communications failure of that week, and suffered detrimental brand image association. As can be seen, the increase of social media can be a double-edged sword when an organisation allows itself to be part of communications that it cannot control.

The above examples show the importance of leveraging the sponsorship through support activities and tie-in promotions. If sponsorship is seen as a single, separate tool, the benefits resulting from it will be much less. Leveraging the sponsorship is as much in the interest of the sporting organisation as it is in that of the sponsor. An unsuccessful sponsorship deal is less likely to be renewed, leaving the sporting organisation without a sponsor. When the sporting organisation is able to supply or participate in support activities, sponsorship will more successfully operate as part of the total promotion and marketing plan. This ultimately will lead to a win–win situation.

To distinguish a win–win situation from a no-win situation, it is important for the sport marketer to measure the effectiveness of sponsorship—largely the topic of Chapter 14. Now we take a brief look at some of the current research trends in relation to sport sponsorship.

Current research trends in sport sponsorship

Since the beginnings of sponsor involvement in sport, there has been a focus on the return sponsors get from their financial investment—either in cash (the generation of direct sales) or through non-financial objectives (reputation, brand equity, exposure, etc.). Recent trends in sport sponsorship research have lent themselves to advances on both sides of this equation. The first side of this trend is the clarification of sponsor motivations and expectations of the relationship with the sponsee via outlining and distinguishing returns based either on investment and/or objectives. Despite appearing semantic, the distinction is critical, as return on investment (ROI) supposes that a measurable financial surplus is generated from the relationship that promotes advertising and sales generation. Return on objectives (ROO) supposes a commercial exchange in which the sponsor buys media objectives (exposure), marketing objectives (brand awareness/perception) or corporate objectives (client entertainment), which adds to the overall communication mix that in turn indirectly benefits sales (Karg, 2007).

In the latter case, the fulfilment of the agreed objectives forms the primary performance indicators of the sponsorship relationship rather than any direct financial return from such a relationship. The second side to this is the improvement in direct measurement of the value of the relationship through improving the accuracy-measurement and sponsorship-valuation tools, such as eye tracking, which values the sponsorship based on the visibility of the sponsor's logo with the time it appears on the screen to give a metric of 'exposure per 1000 viewers per 30 seconds' (Brueur and Rumpf, 2012). This type of technology, in combination with ever-increasing analytics from companies such as RepuCom—which measures and analyses metrics such as brand and asset exposure; strategy execution; cost per audience reach; cost per advertising spot; audience metrics; tonality and sentiment in social networks—and the value of the sponsor's media coverage, increases both the quantifiable return on the agreed objective-based or investment-based sponsorship agreement (RepuCom, 2013).

As discussed in Chapter 12, new media and digital communication are becoming vital trends for sports organisations. From companies to clubs and even individual athletes, sports organisations increasingly are utilising new media platforms like websites and social networking sites such as Twitter and Facebook to directly deliver a customised message to consumers and fans. Social media and networking allow sponsored properties to instantaneously reach a specific market segment with a targeted message at no additional cost outside of the original sponsorship agreement. For example, before a game, Brazilian footballer and Real Madrid champion Kaka might tweet a picture of himself in his Adidas boots to his 14 million followers. This action promotes image transfer and may assist the 'buyer readiness sequence' through increasing the interest and desire of Kaka's followers to purchase 'Kaka's Adidas shoes', not just 'the new shoes from Adidas'. Sport sponsorship trends are being influenced by further evolutions in digital communications, such as broadcasting and content extensions, the 'second screen' phenomenon, fantasy sport, online communities and fan forums, and the ability of organisations to monetise such relationships through e-commerce, online advertising and interactive web elements; these constitute a major trend in sport sponsorship research, as outlined in Chapter 12.

According to Pope and Voges (2000), consumers' intention to purchase can be derived from two predominant influences: first, a positive attitude towards the brand; and second, brand familiarity, which is obtained from brand exposure and prior use. Specifically, they report significant effects on purchase intention from the brand itself, the belief that the company sponsors sport, and from the general corporate image of the company. In addition to these factors, evidence points to the relevance of team support, as well as sponsor integrity and fit. In the near future, much of the research with regard to the effect of sponsorship will be combined with the increasing focus on managing the brands of organisations. As noted by Rein, Kotler and Shields (2006), this will require sport organisations to become more of a brand in their own right and less of a simple 'recipient' of sponsor dollars. Many of the issues in regard to measuring the effects of sponsorship will be dealt with in Chapter 14.

Another trend is the move from sponsoring the big, established sports to the new, exciting, up-and-coming sports. For example, extreme sports such as skateboarding, inline skating, surfing and snowboarding offer affordable sponsorship opportunities, especially when compared with the established global sports. The 'new' sports also boast a highly identified and segmented following. In other words, 'niche' sports offer excellent opportunities for sponsors to talk one on one with a target market, because the segmentation information that is available about the target market is much more specific than for the bigger sports' mass-market segments.

This extension of exploiting 'niche' market opportunities through sponsorship relates to another interesting trend, which can be described as the blurring of the line between sponsorship and corporate social responsibility. Where sport organisations have long been exempted from being looked at as corporate entities with corporate responsibilities, today both sport organisations and corporations are held accountable for their actions in society. This offers opportunities for sport as well, as sport products are naturally suited to provide social benefits for society at large, as explained by Smith and Westerbeek (2007). Davies (2002) makes the case for a more high-profile role for sport in tackling global and community challenges of health, peace, development and ethics. He argues that new expectations are emerging for corporate citizenship, from the activities of prominent organisations and institutions like the 2008 Beijing Olympics Organising Committee to the need for athletes to behave as role models. The power of sport as a communications medium confers upon it greater responsibilities for demonstrating corporate citizenship. Sport, Davies believes, should be a force for good in a troubled world.

The UN Inter-Agency Task Force on Sport for Development and Peace was formed to review activities involving sport within the United Nations, to promote more systematic and coherent use of sport in development and peace activities, to generate greater support for such activities among governments and sport-related organisations and to encourage the UN system to incorporate sport into its activities. Perhaps most importantly for the deployment of corporate social responsibility, the UN Task Force sought to promote the application of sport as a tool of development policy. One of the Task Force recommendations was a focus on communications-based activities using sport. These activities should include well-targeted advocacy and social mobilisation, as well as private-sector partnerships—particularly at national and local levels.

The range of possibilities for the deployment of corporate social responsibility through sport can be conflated to include sponsorships, financial contributions, philanthropy, gifts in kind, cause-related marketing, employee volunteering and partnership. This is where it can be observed that sponsorship, in the context of the definition presented in this chapter, only occupies a small space in the spectrum, which concerns activities that can be conducted to advance corporations' social responsibilities. For sport organisations to continue to receive corporate dollars, they not only need to be aware of this rapidly developing new paradigm, but also need to be on top of their social responsibilities to society to make sure that they can align these with the needs of potential corporate partners.

Summary

This chapter showed the strategic importance of sponsorship for sport organisations. For both sponsor and sponsee, sponsorship can be used to satisfy multiple goals, particularly advertising- and public relations-related goals for the sponsor, and fundraising-related goals for the sponsee. The relationship between the goals of sponsor and sponsee was shown in the sponsorship framework for how to create win–win situations. Relationships between sponsor and sponsee can even lead to a strategic alliance between the two organisations. Sponsorship as a tool of the promotion mix is still growing in popularity, because it is generally seen as a cost-effective way to achieve the sponsor's communication goals.

Because of the high visibility and attractiveness of sport as a communication medium, many sporting organisations tend to over-emphasise the importance of sponsorship as a potential source of income. Sporting organisations should be aware that this 'sponsorship myopia' can lead to an under-usage of the other elements of the marketing mix in developing a broad-based marketing program. From the sponsor's point of view, sponsorship alone will not satisfy the communication goals set. A comprehensive set of sponsorship support activities and tie-in promotions is required to optimise the sponsorship effort and make the sponsorship as successful as possible in the overall marketing effort.

Sponsoring individual athletes has distinct advantages and disadvantages. The sponsor–athlete relationship is similar to the sponsor–sporting organisation relationship in that both involve mutual commitment and obligations. Sponsorship-support activities need to be considered in both relationships. How we can measure the effectiveness of the sponsorship is further explored in Chapter 14.

CASE STUDY

Return on objectives—attracting and maintaining a major sponsor at a semi-professional basketball club through setting objectives

[This case study is purely fictional. The persons and organisations in the case are non-existent.]

In the lead-up to the 2014 season, Frank Smith—a long-time player at Nets District Basketball Club—had been at the club for twelve years when he was approached by the president, Sandra O'Conner, to sit on the board for the following season. Sandra, the president of the relatively successful district club for the last five years, was looking to fill the position of communications and sponsorship officer. The position had regrettably been left vacant by Michael Hessen, who could only focus on being treasurer due to increasing work commitments that season.

Knowing Frank's corporate expertise in the field of sponsorship and marketing, Sandra invited both Frank and Michael for a lunch meeting to discuss the history of sponsorship at the club, as well as challenges and opportunities moving forward.

Once seated and into their meal, Sandra invited Michael to provide an overview of his period as communications and sponsorship officer at the Nets. 'Well,' Michael said 'I began my affiliation with Nets when my children were in the second year at the club in 2005. As an accountant, the board approached me to be treasurer because I was good with numbers. I agreed to help them with the budget and raising funds through sponsorship from businesses in the district.'

'And how have you found the relationships with our community partners?' Frank asked. Michael exhaled deeply and flicked Sandra a defeated look. 'It has been really difficult, to be honest. For seven out of the nine years we have been able to get $5000–10 000 from a local business; however, only SportsDrink Inc.—our most recent sponsor—stayed with us for more than one season. However, at the end of last season they informed us that they would not be continuing the sponsorship for the upcoming season.' Sandra jumped into the conversation to explain: 'You see, Frank, as a not-for-profit community sports club, we need to get at least $5000 per season, otherwise we will struggle to pay our coaches, facilities and operational costs. We offer a standard major sponsor package that involves courtside and uniform signage, website links and newsletter links for our members, and two seats to each game for the company. A few months before each season, it was part of Michael's responsibilities to go out and sell this to businesses in the district and try to get a major sponsor for the following season.'

'I see,' said Frank. 'And what was the feedback from your previous sponsors?'

Michael explained: 'The relationships were difficult to maintain. While the financial support from our sponsors is vital for us as an organisation, our financial return on investment is not very high for our sponsors. Therefore, while they enjoy being associated with us, they often cannot justify the financial investment required to be a major sponsor.'

Frank nodded in understanding: 'This seems to be a common problem with a lot of smaller organisations that I have worked with. In particular, I have found that when highly skilled people come from a corporate background into a not-for-profit sports club they need to adapt to a different environment. For example, Michael you said you are an accountant and therefore return-on-investment makes sense to you. I would like the opportunity to broaden the discussion toward return-on-objectives, building relationships and tailoring sponsorship packages with local community partners.'

Sandra enthusiastically jumped in: 'That sounds great. We are having a board meeting next week to discuss the upcoming season. Would you be able to present your sponsorship strategy then?' Michael, Frank and Sandra agreed that this would be a good idea, and jointly worked on a sponsorship strategy to present to the board at the meeting the following week.

Suggested sponsorship strategy

The following week, Sandra, Michael and Frank joined the rest of the board at their first annual board meeting. After the group caught up on the happenings during the off-season, the meeting got underway. Sandra introduced Frank, and explained that they had previously met with Michael who would be handing over the communications and sponsorship role to Frank to focus on his role as treasurer. 'I have known Frank for a long time and believe he may be able to assist us with our ongoing sponsorship battle,' Sandra said. 'Frank, the floor is yours.'

Frank began: 'Good evening everyone, my name is Frank Smith and I would like to discuss with you two things: our sponsorship value proposition and our sponsor relationship strategy.' As I am new to the club, I have purposefully left the specifics of the proposal blank for us to fill in through discussion, although I feel the below strategy may be beneficial in attracting and maintaining long-term sponsors which Sandra and Michael had indicated has previously been difficult.

Value proposition: Return on objectives

'Previously our value proposition has been solely based on the loose idea of return-on-investment, which can be difficult to measure for our sponsors and often not specifically the objective of the investment by the sponsor. Sport sponsorship colleagues of mine, Terence and Norman (Zinger and O'Reilly, 2010: 287), suggest that small businesses will become involved in sport sponsorship for a number of reasons, including:

- community goodwill
- public awareness of the firm
- employee morale
- brand image
- product demonstration
- entertainment of key clients
- reaching new market segments
- blocking competition, and
- generating new sales.

'Therefore, I propose that as a board we design our value proposition based on offering a "return-on-objectives" to our sponsors. If one of the objectives is to incrementally increase sales through the sponsorship relationship, then return on investment may be one measure. However, I believe this should not be the sole focus of the value proposition.

Sponsorship proposal based on objectives

'Furthermore, once we know what our sponsors want, we need to construct a proposal that meets these objectives, including the following elements:

- executive summary
- organisation/event/athlete history and present situation—what is the organisation about?
- target audiences (for sponsor and sponsee)—who is the sponsor targeting?
- sponsorship track record—what is the organisation's sponsorship history?
- period of association for the proposed sponsorship—how long? Are there extension options?
- benefits on offer—what does the sponsor get out of the relationship?
- benefit valuation (capitalisation)—how much will the sponsor need to invest?
- packages—what is the total offer?
- sponsorship-activation activities—are there any publicity, advertising or marketing activities?
- ambush-prevention strategy—how is the organisation ensuring exclusivity?
- effectiveness measurement—what are the measures of effectiveness?

Questions

1 Given your knowledge of sponsorship after reading this chapter, can you detect any information explaining why the previous sponsor decided to cease the agreement?

2 Given your knowledge of creating win–win situations, how could these relationships have been improved?
3 Is there any difference between Frank and Michael's language around sponsor–sponsee relationships? Do you think this would make a difference in attracting sponsors?
4 Why do you think return on objectives is becoming a common term in sports sponsorship?
5 What examples and possibilities can you contribute in the context of your organisation for every heading in Frank's outline?

Stage 1—Identification of marketing opportunities

▼

Stage 2—Strategy determination

Step 5—Determine core marketing strategy

Marketing and service mix—sport product, pricing, place (physical evidence, people, process), customer satisfaction

Promotion mix—sales promotion, advertising, television, internet, **sponsorship**

Step 6—Determine tactics and performance benchmarks

▼

Stage 3—Strategy implemention, evaluation and adjustment

14

Measuring the effectiveness of sponsorship

CHAPTER OBJECTIVES

This chapter further explores the concept of sponsorship. While Chapter 13 examined the key success factors in attracting and implementing sponsorship, here we introduce the different methods that can be used to evaluate the effectiveness of sponsorship. It needs to be noted that the chapter is written from the perspective of the sponsor—that is, we consider the effect of sponsorship with regard to the goals set by the sport sponsor. Beyond effectiveness, we also explore the concepts of ambush marketing and location dependency of sponsorship. We have integrated an extended case study into this chapter, which means that the questions at the end of the chapter relate to all components of the case study presented throughout the chapter.

After studying this chapter, you should be able to:

- describe different methods of measuring sponsorship effectiveness
- understand the relationship between effectiveness measures, sponsorship objectives and the buyer-readiness continuum
- understand the principles that underpin ambush marketing tactics
- understand the relationship between 'exposure' and 'impact' with regard to the sponsorship property that is chosen by the sponsor.

HEADLINE STORY

Introducing the case study: We've signed the deal—but how do we make it work?

From the 2001–02 season, the English Premier League became known as the Barclaycard Premier League. Barclays Bank paid the league US$70 million for the privilege. As the title sponsor of the world's most prominent and successful domestic soccer competition, the relationship continued to develop. With the league being covered on television to over 212 territories, this investment may turn out to be one of the best sport sponsorship agreements of the decade. In the 2012 season, a three-year extension of the contract with Barclays, worth £40 million (A$65.3 million) a season, was agreed upon and the competition was renamed the Barclays Premier League.

Throughout this chapter, we introduce the different organisations that are involved in making the sponsorship work for Barclays, as part of a case study that is developed during the chapter.

When the complete sponsorship program is put into action, it is important for both sponsor and sponsee to measure its effectiveness. We show that sponsorship objectives cover the whole spectrum of the 'buyer-readiness continuum', a tool that demonstrates the stages through which consumers proceed before undertaking a transaction. As briefly discussed in Chapter 13, we recognise that sponsorship objectives can be categorised under headings such as corporate, marketing and media objectives, or as strategic, tactical and operational objectives. The real distinction is between direct (sales) and indirect (exposure) marketing objectives. We argue that the sponsorship opportunity is really about the right to 'associate': the forging of a connection between the event or athlete and the company or brand. This right to associate is then translated into potential communication outcomes, which can be plotted along the buyer-readiness continuum, or the 'attention–interest–desire–action' sequence. The relationship between objectives, buyer readiness and effectiveness measurement is visualised in a model in the second part of this chapter. Effectiveness can also be diminished by the practice of ambush marketing, a topic also discussed here.

SPORTVIEW 14.1

Case study part 1—the sponsor

Barclaycard, a fully owned subsidiary of Barclays Bank, announced its first title sponsorship of the Premier League only eight weeks before the start of the 2001–02 season. It surpassed companies like Budweiser, Coca-Cola and Vodafone in the betting stakes to become the new sponsor of the league. Sponsoring the title of the league has a distinct advantage over, for example, buying advertising time around football programming. It stands out from the clutter, and the association is with a 'living and breathing' entity. The credit card business has grown dramatically over the past decade, and Barclaycard as a market leader needed to step up to the international challenge. The principal company objective at the time was to double profit in the entire business every four years. The sponsorship of the Premier League has assisted the company to make the brand better and more widely recognised; in addition, by being associated with such an emotional product, the brand became more human, passionate, tangible and spirited. With the added growth of media exposure for the Premier League, this investment has proved very profitable. The Barclays Premier League is the world's most watched league: its 217 000 hours of coverage in 2012 was beamed into more than 720 million homes in 212 territories internationally, making the US$192 million (A$201.8 million) investment seem like money very well spent (Premier League Season Review, 2012).

By the way, much of the funds Barclays spent on sponsorship during the early 2000s came from a decreased expenditure on advertising, clearly indicating that sponsorship was perceived to be a superior means of marketing communication. That advertising space was rapidly filled by Coca-Cola, which bought the broadcast sponsorship of the ITV flagship program *The Premiership*. One could argue that Coca-Cola had obtained the perfect ambush position.

Source: Based on Gillis (2002b); Premier League Season Review (2012).

Measuring sponsorship effectiveness

As we have already indicated, how effective a sponsorship is or has been depends on the goals the sponsor and sponsee have set before they enter the sponsorship agreement. For example, Heineken invested more than A$10 million into Australian sport, including tennis, Rugby Union and golf. It had different goals when sponsoring the Australian Open tennis championships from those it had when sponsoring the Heineken Classic golf tournament. The goal at the tennis is global attention-related, whereas the goal at the golf is more related to direct sales—through, for example, business relationship marketing activities. But by 2005 the company no longer felt the need to 'paint the town green' with Heineken branding. It reassessed its strategic intentions, and chose to focus less on the big-ticket campaigns and adopt a more streamlined target market approach to its sponsorship programs in Australia (Australian Marketing Institute, 2005). As noted earlier, Heineken has concentrated its global sponsorship efforts on its association with the Champions League, in which it invests 80 million Euros every three years.

How the public perceives the association between sponsor and sponsee determines what can be measured as the effect of the sponsorship. If, for example, members of the public link the name of the sponsor only to the event and do not change their buying behaviour, it makes little sense to measure after-sponsorship sales. Poon and Prendergast (2006) suggest that sponsorship generally has been assessed by two distinctive categories of function-based and image-based similarity. *Function-based similarity* occurs when the sponsor's products are actually used in an event or by the sports entity. For example, Lenovo, Visa and Coca-Cola as TOP sponsors for the IOC had their products and services on show at the 2008 Beijing Olympics. *Image-based similarity* is when the compatibility between sponsors' and the sport's image is perceived by the consumer to be related. For example, the association between the Ford Motor Company and the Geelong Football Club (Ford runs a huge production plant in the City of Geelong) is built on a compatible image. Zinger and O'Reilly (2010) suggest that effective sponsorship measurement can be viewed on a continuum of sponsor–sponsee relationships, returns on sponsorship investment and the consumer response to sponsorship messages. The least effective relationship is termed 'patronage', where the sponsor sees their investment as almost a goodwill gesture, thus not expecting any return from their investment or any effect on the buyer readiness scale (attention, interest, decision, action). More effective sponsorship relationships—or fully functioning sponsorship—occur when there is a market exchange of cash or in-kind resources in return for the right to associate with a sports entity. Under this relationship, the sponsor expects a return on investment and/or objectives, and the progression of the customer through the buyer readiness sequence towards action.

In this section, it is assumed that the overall effectiveness of the sponsorship is based on the achievement of the sponsor's goals. Achievement of sponsee goals is partly met at the agreement of the sponsorship (i.e. receiving funds, goods or services). Other goals, like brand positioning, can be measured in a similar fashion to the sponsor's goals. For example, Kang and Stotlar (2011) indicated that decision managers in the Samsung sports marketing and sports sponsorship department valued 'enhancing brand equity', 'building corporate reputation', 'increasing sales' and improving the company's 'corporate social responsibility' as factors influencing the company's decision to become part of 'The Olympic Partner (TOP) Programme'. There has been a notable shift from a philanthropic offering to one where the sponsor expects a financial return on investment. Stotlar (2004) notes that any sponsorship decline in the United States may have been due to the economic recessions of 2001 and 2002, but more importantly that the transfer of value in the sponsorship exchange has not been measured effectively. Farrelly, Quester, and Burton (2006) point out that value is an intangible component, stemming from a variety of sources, and it is often difficult to always attribute value to specific elements of the sponsorship relationship. Notably, they claim the assessment of value is when it is realised. For example, the naming rights of a stadium or the financial contribution to staging an event bring immediate value to the sponsee, as funding ensures the progress of the sport entity's plans. On the other hand, for the sponsor, value is a delayed outcome as consumers' response to purchasing products or services, or recognising brand association, can take time.

Hansen and Scotwin (1995) identify four levels of measuring sponsorship effectiveness:

- exposure
- attention
- cognition, and
- behaviour.

As shown in the case study, exposure is the broadest measure of sponsorship effectiveness. It measures how many times (in seconds on television, or number of columns and photographs in print media) an organisation or brand is observable (Brueur and Rumpf, 2012). Television exposure, for example, is measured by multiplying seconds by the number of viewers; hence exposure is expressed in 'exposure per 1000 viewers in 30 seconds'. Often new techniques in sponsorship effectiveness use eye-tracking software to complement the above ratio by measuring the sponsor's 'exposure' (size of screen share) and 'exclusiveness' (lack of other sponsors in the same screen shot) (Brueur and Rumpf, 2012). This technique differentiates the value of sponsorships—for example, between a jersey sponsor (large exposure and exclusive position in frequent player close-ups during telecast) and ground signage (infrequent and small exposure in a cluttered space with other sponsors during telecast). Exposure value can be compared with advertising value by multiplying seconds (30) by advertising rates for 30-second commercials.

The resulting value presents the sponsor with the money figure that would have been paid had the sponsor invested the money in 30-second commercials. However, there are significant problems with these measures of effectiveness. For example, how do we know that viewing a 30-second commercial equals the value of viewing 30 seconds of scattered brand exposure throughout an event broadcast? This problem is compounded when one realises how hard it is to accurately measure the number of viewers. These problems relate to the fact that exposure is one thing, but what really matters is the impact of the exposure.

In other words, volume of exposure is only the start of measuring the effect of sponsorship. A better measure of impact is how much attention people pay to a brand or an organisation. Attention can be measured in terms of changes in recall or recognition by individual target-market members. Recall is the more powerful measure of effectiveness, in that research subjects are not aided in recalling sponsors' names. In recognition, subjects are asked to choose from a list of possible sponsors. The benchmark for attention measures has to be the recall or recognition measure before entering the sponsorship agreement. This may be achieved through pre-testing. Otherwise, changes in recall or recognition cannot be measured.

Cognitive effects also can be measured in individuals who are part of the target market(s) of the sponsor. The association between a car manufacturer and a car-racing event evokes a stronger cognitive effect than the association between a car manufacturer and a tennis event. The car manufacturer–car race link is logical, and requires little explanation. The car manufacturer–tennis event link is expected to evoke a more general association, and tries to link the image of the event to the image of the car. Both effects are often measured in associative tests. For example, given the Australian Open tennis championships, the question 'Which sponsors do you associate with this event?' can be asked. One can even consider using research techniques that compare attitudes people have about different brands, including the brands that compete with the sponsor. Tracking studies, where factors such as the brand image are researched over an extended period of time, also fit the category of measuring cognitive effects. Cognitive tests are better described as qualitative research techniques because they deliver information that allows the researcher to explain consumer behaviour, rather than the quantified measures that result from media monitoring. Cognitive research becomes more important towards the 'desire' and 'action' stages of buyer readiness.

The most direct measure of sponsorship effectiveness is buying behaviour. What are the effects of the sponsorship on attitudes towards buying, or even the direct sales figures or turnover of the organisation, or the sales figures of certain product lines? In this case, the benchmark for measurement has to be set before the sponsorship. However, as stated earlier, the delay between sponsorship activation and consumer buying response may be lengthy. Behavioural measurement of sponsorship has often been criticised because of the difficulties involved in isolating the effects of sponsorship on sales and turnover from those of other promotion mix tools. Experimental research designs or historical tracking of prior promotion and non-promotion impact may help the researcher to isolate the impact of sponsorship investment.

Measurement of sponsorship effectiveness is a difficult issue. How effectiveness is measured strongly depends on the goals of the sponsor, and even then many variables can influence effectiveness. One of the most important variables to influence sponsorship effectiveness is the choice of the sponsored object or sponsorship property.

SPORTVIEW 14.2

Case study part 2—the sponsorship research firms

IPSOS UK conducts sponsorship effectiveness research on behalf of all major brands in football. According to spokespersons for the organisation, there is still much confusion about the right approach to conducting useful research. Effectiveness research consists of both quantitative and qualitative approaches. In fact, IPSOS interviews some 20 000 individuals per annum, enabling it to both quantify and qualify the movement of perceptions and attitudes. IPSOS's director of sponsorship research, Mike Jackson, argues that effective sponsorship is underpinned by extensive pre-testing of what the sponsorship can do for the brand, which rights are obtained through the sponsorship, and how these rights can be exploited throughout the whole company. It took Barclays three months to achieve a desired level of association—one it would have expected to take at least two years. A majority of keen football fans, three months into the sponsorship, spontaneously associated Barclaycard as a leading brand within the premiership.

It is interesting to note that the research industry seems to develop along two distinct lines. One branch of the industry focuses on media evaluation, assessing the amount of exposure, whereas 'effectiveness' research aims to qualify the impact of exposure—impact that can, according to Jackson, be greatly improved if the sponsor realises that buying the rights is only the first step in the process of achieving an effective sponsorship.

Source: Based on Gillis (2002b).

The sponsorship properties: Events and athletes

It can be argued that there are literally hundreds of sponsorship opportunities, including sponsoring the name or title of an event or stadium, broadcast sponsorship, location sponsorship (for example, the fifteenth green), leader board sponsorship, corporate hospitality suites, athletic outfit sponsorship (for example, shoes, apparel)—the list goes on. It is largely up to the creativity of sport marketers to come up with new ways of packaging 'rights to associate with' for sponsors to buy and use. Irrespective of how this is done, the majority of sponsored properties in sport can be categorised as either events or athletes. As we noted earlier, what principally determines the success of the sponsorship is the amount of exposure received and the impact exposure has on the sponsorship objectives. Or, stated differently, generic global sport offers potentially greater exposure than local niche sport—hence the latter presents more affordable sponsorship opportunities. Again, it needs to be stated that, after picking the right property, success is largely determined by leveraging activities (impact) executed by the sponsor and its support agencies—also known as 'activation' of the sponsorship.

Sport research consultants Sweeney Sports undertake a significant analysis of the sport sponsorship market in Australia. According to the Sweeney Sports and Entertainment Report in 2013 (Proszenko, 2013), a quarterly survey of 7000 people, Australia's most popular athletes were Pat Rafter, Glenn McGrath, Cathy Freeman, Ricky Ponting and Ian Thorpe. In fact, at the time of the survey, seven of the most popular athletes had retired with the only current athletes in the top ten being swimmer Ian Thorpe (fifth), Australian cricket captain Michael Clarke (ninth) and Tour de France winner Cadel Evans (tenth). This indicates that successful athletes in Australia's sporting 'Golden Era' are maintaining their popularity in Australian culture while up-and-coming athletes are not capturing the hearts and minds of Australian consumers in the same way as their predecessors. Interestingly, the relationship between athlete and brand awareness is varying significantly between the most popular athletes and those just outside the top echelon of popularity. For example, although Libby Trickett was ranked the thirteenth most popular athlete in Australia at the time, and only 12 per cent of respondents could affiliate her with one of her sponsors, conversely 35 per cent of respondents could affiliate Ricky Ponting with one of his sponsors—in particular, Swisse Multivitamins.

Understanding which sports Australians are most interested in is also critical to potential sponsors. By understanding where the people go for sport entertainment, potential sponsors can be more effective in directing their sponsorship strategies. A Roy Morgan survey of more than 18 000 people in 2011 showed that cricket is the most viewed sport by Australians, with 42 per cent viewing it on television (Pesutto 2012). Researchers could attribute the level of popularity of cricket to the highly entertaining 2010 Ashes series between Australia and England, and the ICC Cricket World Cup occurring during the sample period. Cricket was closely followed by Australian Rules football at 41 per cent, tennis at 37 per cent, Rugby League at 34 per cent and the Melbourne Cup (horse-racing) at 33 per cent. When determining which sporting events and athletes to sponsor, it is important to consider the visibility of the sponsored entity. For example, cricket has only one male national side that would attract the majority of television coverage, while the Melbourne Cup and the majority of tennis viewership occur at particular times during the year (for example, the Australian Open in January) and in certain geographies (Melbourne). These factors allow sponsors to focus on reaching a target audience through event attendance or televised opportunities.

SPORTVIEW 14.3

Case study part 3—the sponsorship consultants

In order to capitalise on all opportunities that the football industry has on offer, Barclays employed Arena as its sponsorship consultants. Arena provided the link between the sponsorship and the football industry, and in the process offered Barclays access to an impressive network of football's stakeholders. It managed the Barclaycard Player of the Month award, which involved coordinating a comprehensive panel of experts who voted on a monthly basis. Every month, negotiations took place with the respective club of the 'Player of the Month' in order to maximise exposure and impact. For example, Arena always made sure the player was photographed with the trophy on Friday night so the papers could carry the picture in Saturday's lead-up to the round of football over the weekend. A Barclays director handed over the trophy and the broadcaster got a shot of the action to include in late-night reports. Next to this operational activity, Arena also provided top-end strategic branding advice. Sean Jefferson, the CEO of Arena, argued that his job was all about creating a new sub-brand. The Barclays Premier League did not exist before June 2001, so a lot of hard and smart work was required to go into building this brand for the benefit of the company as a whole. Ultimately, successful creation and leveraging of the sub-brand 'Barclays Premier League' needed to result in a new, revitalised brand image.

In the 2002 season, however, Jefferson was presented with a rather exciting operational problem. With the premiership race as close as it had been in years, five clubs were still in with a chance on the last day of the competition. With all challengers at home in the final weekend, Jefferson prepared a mobile 'Cup Presentation Unit' in a helicopter. Making the sponsorship work is hard yakka, right down to the wire!

Source: Gillis (2002b).

The SPONSEFFECT model

In both this chapter and Chapter 13, we have discussed the range of issues that are important in regard to attracting, implementing and measuring the effect of sponsorship. It has been noted that the formulation of specific sponsorship objectives is critical when selecting the right sponsorship entity, in turn affecting the different measures to be used when assessing the effectiveness of the sponsorship partnership. We have also argued that both objectives and effectiveness measures are strongly linked to the buyer-readiness sequence.

The practical value of the AIDA (attention, interest, desire, action) model lies in its strong focus on moving consumers from being unaware of a product to buying it. Ultimately, sponsorship is about only one thing: bringing as many customers to the sponsor's company and enabling them to buy as many products as possible—preferably many, many times over! In reality, the stages of attention, interest and desire are therefore quite awkward. We don't want consumers to be in those stages for too long. As can be observed from the model, it is much harder to define clear-cut objectives and sponsorship properties for the interest and desire stages than it is for the attention and action stages. It is thus very important to remember that the mid-stages of buyer readiness are transitory. An example of how sponsor objectives can vary in the mind of the consumer compared with a company's perception is shown in Sportview 14.4. As noted, sponsor objectives can be ambushed, incorrectly associated with events or even last much longer than believed possible!

SPORTVIEW 14.4

Sponsorship opportunity makes a cereal killing

by Lynley Ingerson

The widespread appeal of sport should make it easier for corporations to reach desired target markets through sponsorship. Problems occur when sponsoring organisations change their sponsorship focus or similar sponsors enter into the same or similar domain. For example, while Toyota was the official Australian sponsor of the 1992 Barcelona Olympics, General Motors was offering a new 'gold' car for every gold medallist at that Olympics, misleading consumers about who was the real car sponsor of the Olympic Games. While this is arguably a blatant example of ambush marketing, it does show how important it is for a sponsor to make sure their sponsorship program is not killed off before desired objectives are achieved.

Uncle Tobys had been the leader in the cereal and snack foods category of sponsorship since 1993, when measurements of sponsorship awareness were first carried out by reputable research organisation Sweeney Sports. Uncle Tobys' breakfast cereals and muesli bars are synonymous with sport. It was one of the first brands to show the association between nutrition and sport. Uncle Tobys' great ambassador was swimming legend Lisa Currie, who is credited with the longest sponsorship association of the time, from 1982 to 2003. Uncle Tobys also sponsored the Ironman and Ocean Man series, which has been directly attributed to its successful profile in the community. By 1997, Uncle Tobys was the most recognised sponsor by nearly 75 per cent of the population (Sweeney Sports, 2006). No other product category could penetrate its dominant position.

In 2001, Uncle Tobys made a strategic decision to withdraw its sponsorship from the Ironman series and direct its efforts to swimming and tennis. On paper, this would be seen as a strategically sound decision, as swimming had been recognised as the most popular sport of interest for Australians for much of the last decade of the twentieth century and Lisa Currie was universally popular. Tennis also had a resurgence in interest with the success of the Davis Cup team in 2003 and the international accomplishments of Lleyton Hewitt and Alicia Molik. By 2005, tennis was the third most watched sport on television. This shift of attention allowed close rival Kellogg's to enter the watersport market and take over Uncle Tobys' sponsorship of the Ironman series.

Despite the shift, Uncle Tobys' brand equity remained strong, and was still associated with the Ironman series until well after the agreement ceased. This example shows the power a brand can have if marketed well, and when there is a strong relationship between sponsor and sponsee. Interestingly, though, the Uncle Tobys brand was also associated with surf life saving, further testament to the residual power of the brand—and this is where an interesting issue surfaced. Surf life saving was actually sponsored by Kellogg's, yet consumers connected life saving with Uncle Tobys.

However, by 2006 Sweeney Sports reported that Uncle Tobys' rating was beginning to slip. For the first time since the 1990s, Uncle Tobys was no longer the number one brand, with the shift in interest moving from Uncle Tobys to leisurewear organisations Nike and Billabong, as well as the steady progress up the rankings for Kellogg's. Consumers were increasingly developing a penchant for a particular lifestyle rather than interest in fast-moving consumer goods. The change from a focused single-event strategy to a broad-based general sports sponsorship for tennis and swimming seemed to contribute to their decline. Added to this, swimming had a weakened position as an interest sport due to the retirement of Ian Thorpe. Tennis, while maintaining its position regarding television ratings, had fallen behind cricket and the AFL as the lack of international success was impacting on participation and media exposure (Sweeney Sports, 2006).

Sponsorship effectiveness is an essential element of a sponsorship relationship. For Uncle Tobys, the satisfaction of holding the number one interest position for a number of years, as well as being associated with sport activities such as life saving without a formal relationship, had given them value in sponsoring. However, as consumer choices change so does the perceived value of the sponsorship arrangement, and it is increasingly important for sponsor and sponsee to form a co-marketing alliance, aligning the brand with the sport more purposefully. Uncle Toby's must be mindful of Kellogg's growing potential in the marketplace and develop a more shared sense of strategic intent and responsibility with its sponsorship partners.

Source: Adapted from information from Sweeney Sports (2006).

All of these issues are summarised in the SPONSEFFECT model (Table 14.1). The model can be used by sponsors and sponsees to assist them in planning and executing sponsorship agreements. We briefly introduce the concept of ambush marketing here, because it may strongly influence the effectiveness of the sponsorship deal from the perspective of both sponsor and sponsee.

Ambush marketing

The Australian *Trade Practices Act 1974* (TPA) defines ambush marketing in an indirect manner under section 53 as follows:

> A corporation shall not, in trade or commerce, in connection with the supply or possible supply of goods or services or in connection with the promotion by any means of the supply or use of goods or services: (c) represent that goods or services have sponsorship, approval, performance characteristics, accessories, uses or benefits they do not have; (d) represent that the corporation has a sponsorship, approval or affiliation it does not have.

TABLE 14.1 The SPONSEFFECT model

Main sponsorship objectives	Buyer readiness stage	Main effectiveness measures	Most likely sponsored property*
• Image creation or improvement • Brand positioning • Raising awareness • Develop new distribution channels • Target new market segments • Community relationship marketing	**Attention**	• Audience numbers (on site, ratings) • Recall/recognition • Surveying (pre/post) • Media monitoring	• Global event • International event • International athlete
• Business development • Brand positioning • Image creation or improvement • Media relationship marketing • Community relationship marketing	**Interest**	• Attitudes • Recall/recognition • Number of enquiries • Preference testing • Surveying (pre/post)	• Global event • International event
• Business relationship marketing • Increasing sales • Brand positioning • Employee relationship marketing • Target new market segments	**Desire**	• Intentions to purchase • Brand preference • Brand image monitoring	• Regional event • Special (niche) event • Local event • National athlete • Local athlete
• Increasing sales • Employee relationship marketing • Business relationship marketing	**Action**	• Purchase from product sales tracking • Historical analysis of prior promotion impacts • Experimental designs	• Local application of all types of events • Local customisation of all types of athletes
• Relationship marketing	**Post-purchase**	• Repeat purchase • Attitudes • Brand preference • Comparative brands	• Continued sponsorship of those events and athletes that have proved successful

* It is recognised that potentially a wide range of events and athletes can be used to achieve the sponsorship objectives; however, we have chosen to list only a limited number of better suited entities.

Ambush marketing is a problem for the sponsor in that funds or services are invested in an association with a sporting organisation from which non-investing organisations reap the benefits. Ambush marketing is a problem for the sponsee in that the effectiveness of the sponsorship will diminish and a prolonged business relationship with the sponsor will be put in jeopardy. More and more, sponsors are demanding that sponsees take precautions to prevent ambush marketing. Australia lawmakers expanded on the TPA protection with event-specific legislation to ensure the rights of administrators and official sponsors were protected in both the 2000 Sydney Olympics and 2006 Melbourne Commonwealth Games. The new legislation prohibited inappropriate conduct in counterfeiting, aerial advertising, promotional leaflet distribution within the vicinity of sports venues, advertising on boats or the illegal use of event insignias (Mallesons Stephen Jacques, 2006).

In servicing the sponsor, sponsees should therefore take a proactive stance in preparing for potential 'ambushers'. A proactive strategy can consist of the following actions:

- identification of potential ambushers (these are often potential sponsors the sporting organisation did not sign up)
- identification of the commercial value of the sponsorship (which benefits the sponsee can deliver, and how potential ambushers can obtain these benefits without being involved as an official sponsor)
- detailed contracts (including exclusivity rights, detailed descriptions of what is being considered as conflicting signage/advertising, sponsor/sponsee obligations to prevent ambush marketing), and
- joint sponsor–sponsee counteract strategies (which determine how sponsor and sponsee will react in terms of public relations, advertising—for example, buying 'strategic' media time during potential 'ambush timeslots'—or public appearances when commenting on an ambusher's actions).

This is a limited and certainly not complete list of actions to prevent ambushers from taking advantage of a sponsorship relationship. Although ambush marketing can never be eliminated, solid preparation can assist sport marketers to service the sponsor to the best of their ability. It needs to be noted that ambush marketing, in the context of 'ethics' in sport marketing, increasingly is an activity that is viewed as unethical behaviour. As described at the end of Chapter 13, consumers are increasingly aware of and sensitive to 'corporate abusive practices', with ambushing being an obvious example. In the very near future, 'to ambush' may not be worth the effort. Behaving in a societally responsible manner may prove to be the best marketing medicine of all. Sportview 14.5 is an example of some historic ambush marketing during the 1988 Winter Olympics in Calgary, Canada, contrasted with recent moves by the IOC to implement 'ambush-prevention strategies'.

SPORTVIEW 14.5

Ambush marketing at the Olympics

The Olympic Games attract global interest and can deliver tremendous exposure. Billions of spectators watched the combined 1988 Summer and Winter Olympics, and many corporations would therefore like to benefit from the exposure of being associated directly or indirectly with the Olympic Games.

Research evaluating the effectiveness of sponsorship and ambush marketing at the 1988 Olympic Winter Games investigated the recall and recognition of official sponsors, ambushers and other organisations. The large drawing power of the Olympics was evidenced by the fact that 82 per cent of the people surveyed watched some part of the Olympic telecast. Of the respondents, 41.4 per cent were light viewers (watched one to four days), 27.2 per cent were moderate viewers (five to nine days) and 31.3 per cent were heavy viewers (ten to sixteen days).

Overall, 20 per cent of the respondents correctly recalled the official sponsors, with recall varying by product category: from 50 per cent correct for credit cards to 7 per cent for airlines. Recognition (choosing from a list with names) of sponsors was higher, with 39 per cent of respondents correctly recognising official sponsors. Recognition also varied by product category, from a high 59 per cent for fast foods to 25 per cent for hotels.

To determine the effect of viewing the Olympic telecast on consumer perceptions, the three viewer groups were used to analyse sponsor awareness. The ability to both recognise and recall sponsors varied directly with viewership: light viewers averaged 18.9 per cent correct recall; moderate viewers 33.5 per cent; and heavy viewers 37.5 per cent. For recognition, the numbers ranged from 37 per cent to 46 per cent to 52.2 per cent.

Twenty-two years later, when the Olympics returned to Canada (Vancouver) in 2010, a similar study was performed that investigated the interest in the event and the effect on purchase intent from ambush marketing (MacIntosh et al., 2012). The research found that the higher the levels of interest are in the Olympic Games, the stronger the negative attitudes towards ambush marketers and the higher the purchasing attitudes for official Olympic partners. Respondents with lower interest levels (who accounted for nearly 50 per cent of the sample) were more ambivalent about ambush marketing messages. MacIntosh et al. (2012) suggest that in order to leverage official Olympic sponsors and negate ambush marketers, official sponsors should increase on-the-ground marketing of their sponsorship (activation); continue to promote their position as official sponsors to differentiate themselves from ambush marketers; and show direct support for athletes, as consumers were more likely to support sponsors that were seen to directly support athletes.

Ambush marketers attempt to avoid the up-front high investment of sponsorship while gaining the glamour and benefits of an Olympic tie-in; their hope is that consumers will associate their products with the Olympic Games and thus weaken any major advantage of their competitors who paid for official sponsorship. To determine the effect that ambushers had on sponsorship awareness, the number of correct sponsor identifications were compared with the number of ambushers as sponsors. Seven product categories, each with one official sponsor and one major ambusher, were chosen. The results for recall and recognition were aggregated. Across the overall sample, an average of 2.57 official sponsors were correctly identified (out of a possible seven). In comparison, on average 1.43 ambushers were identified as official sponsors. Ambushers were significantly less recognised as official sponsors.

A closer look at these data by product category, however, leads to some interesting cautions for advertisers. In only four out of seven product categories studied were the correct official sponsors identified more than the non-sponsors (ambushers and others). In the other three cases, the sponsor was not number one when it came to sponsor identification; in two of these three cases, the official sponsors—while engaging in other promotional activities—were not major advertisers on the Olympic telecast; and in the third case (cars), the ambushers were engaged in very heavy advertising (Ford and Chrysler bought all available advertising time for domestic cars). This might indicate that to achieve any benefits from being a sponsor, it is necessary not only for a company to sponsor an event such as the Olympics but to heavily advertise the fact that they are official sponsors. Buying the right to be an 'official sponsor' may, in reality, only be buying a licence to spend more money!

Atlanta 1996 Olympic sponsors did everything within their power to combat the ambush strategies of competitors. But it seems that ambushers are always one step ahead of their 'official partner' competition. Nike, as the pre-eminent ambusher in Atlanta, achieved great exposure through building-high billboards and 'precinct theming', to the extent that parts of the inner city were transformed into Nike town suburbs. Although Nike was gladly accepted into the Olympic sponsorship family of Sydney 2000, when Reebok decided to discontinue its relationship with the five rings, the IOC had learned its lesson the hard way. The Salt Lake City Organising Committee (SLOC) installed a 'Brand Protection Program', obtaining a permit from city authorities to close all streets directly connected with the Salt Lake Ice Centre and the Olympic Medals Plaza. The streets of Salt Lake became an Olympic venue in their own right, 100 per cent controlled by SLOC. To prevent ambushers from using tall buildings as advertising banners, the SLOC launched a 'Cityscape Program'. Through negotiations with building owners, nominal fee contracts were drawn up allowing the SLOC to completely wrap the buildings in Games-related imagery. If space could not be leased, the contract stated that building owners would not lease the space to anybody for the duration of the Olympic Games. Life is becoming increasingly difficult for an ambusher!

Source: Excerpts from Sandler and Shani (1989: 9–14); based on Naidoo and Gardiner (2002).

Location dependency of sponsorship

In this final section, it is appropriate to reflect on the increasing specialisation in regard to sponsorship as a promotional tool. Here we would like to introduce the concept of 'location dependency' as a special characteristic of sport sponsorship. Westerbeek (2000) tested the hypothesis that 'revenue maximisation of tenants of sport facilities is dependent on geographical location of the facility (location of distribution)'. Revenue maximisation was operationalised pertaining to sponsorship. A survey instrument was sent to all sponsors of a Melbourne-based football club. Sponsors were grouped as location-dependent and location-independent, based on the location of their head office and the financial turnover achieved in the area around the sport facility. The survey collected information on three different steps in the sport-consumption process, including 'coming to the sport facility', 'being in and around the sport facility' and 'being serviced in the sport facility'. Indicative evidence was found in support of the general hypothesis. Smaller, low-spending sponsors with an important percentage of turnover in the area around the sport facility were less likely to move with the football club to a (remote) new facility. In relation to sponsors' objectives, it was found that objectives of location-dependent sponsors are directed more towards direct sales, whereas location-independent sponsors' objectives seem to be indirectly related to sales and more towards obtaining exposure.

In a follow-up study, Westerbeek and Smith (2002) found that location-dependent organisations had fewer employees, and spent less on sponsorship—and on sponsoring sport in particular—than their location-independent counterparts. Where location-dependent organisations predominantly operated in metropolitan or state territories, location-independent organisations operated largely on a domestic or international level. Location-dependent sponsors perceive issues in relation to 'location' of the sport facility (such as an attractive environment, close proximity to head office, distribution outlets and major residential areas) to be significantly more important than do location-independent sponsors. Location-independent sponsors perceive 'corporate exposure' issues (such as quality television coverage of the game, frequent telecasts from the stadium and excellent corporate hospitality facilities at the stadium) to be significantly more important than do location-dependent sponsors. The location dependency of sponsorship shows that the complexity of effectiveness measurement will only grow when sponsors become aware of how they would like to maximise their sponsorship investment.

Summary

In this chapter, we have extended our thinking about sponsorship as a concept. Whereas in Chapter 13 we predominantly looked mainly at the relationship between the sponsor and the sponsee, in this chapter we advanced that relationship to the audience that is most important to the sponsor—the (potential) customer. A range of measures that can be used to measure the effectiveness of sponsorship were introduced, discussed in direct relation to the sponsor's objectives, and placed in the buyer readiness continuum. Following the measures of effectiveness, it was argued that the amount of exposure and the potential impact of this exposure will make sponsors decide which sponsorship properties they can consider purchasing. Ultimately, sponsorship effectiveness is a combination of choosing a suitable sponsorship property, setting specific objectives that can be fitted to the buyer-readiness continuum, and linking this to the appropriate qualitative or quantitative effectiveness measures. In order to further protect the sponsorship rights, ambush marketing opportunities need to be detected in order to prepare for potential ambushers taking advantage of the sponsor's rights. Location dependency, as a special characteristic of sport sponsorship, was discussed as an example of the increasing complexity of the sponsorship effectiveness measurement environment. In the final part of the case study, it is shown that the public relations support function is paramount when aiming to maximise sponsorship benefits.

CASE STUDY

Bringing it all together—the PR consultants

Hitting the right tone with all the people involved in football—from the fans to the clubs and from the sponsors to the broadcasters—was the task at hand for Barclays' PR consultants Lexis, eight weeks from signing the contract in June to the start of the premiership in August. Because of the huge cultural significance of football in day-to-day life in the United Kingdom, you don't just sponsor the Premier League: you have to earn the right to sponsor it. Showing that you understand and respect the game, and the ways in which the game is being delivered to all its stakeholders, is the way to do this and requires constant creativity. At Lexis, the

Barclays team met every morning to have a brainstorming session on what was happening in football that day. Tim Adams, chairman of Lexis, said 'it is part of our job to act as an intermediary between the company and its outside audiences, creating campaign themes and spotting new opportunities'. Next to this strategic input, Lexis ran close to 3000 ticket competitions a year in order to sustain the sponsor's profile. In the end, Adams vehemently agreed that effectiveness research was also the key to PR success, stating that 'IPSOS research is a key measure of how we are performing and what comes through is that the sponsorship is working and the PR initiatives have a major part to play in that process'.

Source: Based on Gillis (2002b).

Questions

1 In your opinion, which five companies could take a genuine ambush approach in order to steal Barclays' glory as the official sponsor of the Premier League?
2 Over the three years of the initial sponsorship deal, which sponsorship objectives will be set for each of the years?
3 In the first year of any sponsorship deal, which stage of buyer readiness will dominate sponsorship planning? Justify your answer.
4 What do you think made Barclays decide to renew the sponsorship deal after successful completion of the three years of the contract?
5 If you were asked to measure the effectiveness of the sponsorship at the end of Year 3 of the renewed contract, and you were given the choice of three effectiveness measures, which would you choose? Justify your answer.

Stage 1—Identification of marketing opportunities

▼

Stage 2—Strategy determination

Step 5—Determine core marketing strategy

Marketing and service mix—sport product, pricing, place (physical evidence, people, process), customer satisfaction

Promotion mix—sales promotion, advertising, television, internet, sponsorship, **public relations and publicity**

Step 6—Determine tactics and performance benchmarks

▼

Stage 3—Strategy implemention, evaluation and adjustment

15 Public relations

CHAPTER OBJECTIVES

This chapter introduces public relations as an element of the sport promotion mix, and examines the public relations process, applied both proactively and reactively. The chapter notes how sporting organisations have been required to take a more active role in managing their public relations. How to execute a public relations program is discussed by examining the various stages of communicating with different media. Special attention is paid to publicity as an important component of the overall public relations strategy.

After studying this chapter, you should be able to:

- identify critical activities of the public relations process
- create an extensive list of sporting organisation publics
- distinguish between proactive and reactive public relations strategies
- link the public relations strategy to the promotion and marketing strategy
- develop a comprehensive set of public relations actions in order to generate publicity.

HEADLINE STORY

Introduction: 2013: 'Annus horribilis' for Australian sport public relations?

Although the term 'annus horribilis' is best remembered as the term Queen Elizabeth II used to describe 1992, a year of significant turmoil for the Royal family, the term may equally apply to Australian sport in 2013, if the first few months of the year were indicative of what would follow. While the following three issues will be individually highlighted within the 'Sportsviews', they are broadly outlined here.

The nation's premier football code, the Australian Football League (AFL), was forced to address alleged 'tanking' in a number of games by the Melbourne Football Club during 2011 in order to secure priority picks in the up-coming draft, and also had to address significant substance abuse issues, initially in relation to the Essendon club. However, as this story unfolded, it became apparent that this issue, coupled with the intrusion into sport of gambling and organised crime, had been the focus of an inquiry by the Australian Crime Commission (ACC). The ACC's ensuing report, *Organised Crime and Drugs in Sport* (ACC, 2013) suggested that the issue was not club or even code specific. The ACC 'identified significant integrity concerns with professional sports in Australia related to use of prohibited substances by athletes and increasing associations of concern between professional athletes and criminal identities' (ACC, 2013: 7).

While not as sinister, Australian swimming also addressed inherent concerns in 2013 that tested the faith of diehard supporters. Interestingly, this may be of greater public concern than the issues bedevilling the AFL, as elite swimming in Australia is funded via a taxpayer-supported system. Swimming has always been a focal point of Australian interest in the Olympic Games, and London 2012 was no exception. However, a less than stellar performance by the team, including the often-lauded relay squad, led to accusations, recriminations and two reviews of Australian swimming.

Finally, Ben Barba, the National Rugby League's (NRL) poster boy and winner of the code's highest individual honour, the 2012 Dally M medal, was stood down by his club, the Canterbury Bulldogs, on the eve of the 2013 season for 'personal reasons'. The *Sydney Morning Herald* (25 February 2013) cited 'behavioural issues related to a break up with his long term partner, gambling and alcohol issues' as the reasons behind his removal from the game.

Hence three of the most high-profile of Australian sports—swimming, Australian Rules football and Rugby League—were beset by issues that had the Australian sports-loving public questioning the integrity of sport and that forced commentators to legitimately ask how the administration of such sports could restore the faith and ensure the ongoing support of the Australian sports fan. The answer is obviously an effective public relations campaign, and the Sportsviews in this chapter will highlight the campaigns used by the respective organisations to address the issues and restore public faith.

Sporting organisations or athletes without problems are rare. Perhaps sporting organisations have more problems than other organisations, but it is more likely that the reason is their high visibility in society. This chapter deals with the management function of public relations, showing how public relations can be helpful in solving a crisis such as that described in the headline story. It is also shown that public relations can be used in a planned and positive way.

Public relations is one element of the promotion mix. Many people show considerable interest in the fortunes of sporting organisations and their athletes. A high level of interest results in high visibility, and therefore sporting organisations have relations with many publics. A public is a group of people who share an evaluation of specific problems or issues. This justifies special attention to public relations in the context of the sport industry. Being part of the promotion mix, public relations deals with communicating with the target audiences or, better, publics of the organisation. To understand better how, when and with whom to communicate, it is first necessary to define the concept.

Defining public relations

When defining public relations for the new millennium, McNamara (2012: 159) reverts to the definition established by the1978 World Assembly of Public Relations, which was endorsed at the time by 34 national public relations organisations. The definition emanating from the World Assembly was that public relations was 'the art and social science of analysing trends, predicting their consequences, counselling organisation leaders and implementing planned programs of action which serve both the organisation and public's interests'.

Obviously, numerous definitions have emerged since 1978, but fundamentally all bear the same characteristics. Effective communication, mutual understanding and beneficial outcomes for the organisation, stakeholders and publics are the fundamental concepts underpinning effective PR.

Smith (2009: 57) focuses on strategy, noting that 'PR is a management function that closely focuses on long term patterns of interaction between an organisation and all of its various publics, both supportive and non-supportive'. In conceptualising the process of public relations, Smith (2009: 111) articulates nine steps of public relations grouped into four phases. Phase 1 is formulative research, and this has three steps: the analysis of the situation, the organisation and the publics. Phase 2 is the strategy stage, and this is where the steps of goal/objective formulation, action and response strategies, and developing message strategies occur. The third phase is the tactical phase, both in terms of selecting communication tactics and implementing strategic plans. Evaluating the strategic plan via evaluative research is the final phase.

Wilcox et al. (2013: 7) also acknowledge the importance of strategy in their definition and suggest that PR is the 'strategic management of competition and conflict for the benefit of one's own organisation and where possible for the mutual benefit of the organisation and its stakeholders and publics.' Stoldt, Dittmore and Branvold (2012: 2) comment that 'sport public relations is a managerial communication based function designed to identify a sport organisation's key publics, evaluate its readership with those publics and foster desirable relationship between the sport organisation and those publics.'

Wilcox et al. (2013: 385) make the link between sport and the broader PR domain, acknowledging that

> sport PR employs the elements of any PR activity. Sport PR professionals need to be experts in relationship management, media relations, ethical and social responsibility, community relations, crisis communication, marketing communication, consumer [fan] relations, player relations and promotions, and international relations and more.

Consequently, if the basic premises of the above definitions and processes are acknowledged and observed by sporting organisations, the basis for a solid public relations strategy is established. This should result in effective proactive or reactive organisational public relations. Such thinking underpins the rest of this chapter.

Evaluating public attitudes

In Chapter 4, we discussed the process of marketing research. Marketing research techniques are also used in identifying and evaluating the attitudes that publics have towards the sporting organisation, its products and its employees (often the athletes). In order to communicate effectively, however, it is important not only to identify public attitudes, but also to convey these attitudes to the management of the organisation. Management can then adjust organisational strategies to more effectively influence public attitudes. For example, the negative perception sports consumers have of the relationship between racism and soccer is a worldwide phenomenon. Most readily observed at the international level, where nations, ideologies and ethnicities compete for supremacy (for example, following Euro 2012), Magowan (2012) reports that the Union of European Football Associations (UEFA) was told to take a stronger stance against racism after the Netherlands squad was taunted in Poland. Pollard (2013) highlights how racism was dividing fans within one club, Beitar Jerusalem in Israel.

Hardcore fans of the Jewish club were incensed that the club had signed two Muslim players, the last Israeli club to do so. The Australian reported that 'ultra-nationalist members held up a sign declaring "Beitar forever pure" to protest against their arrival' (Pollard, 2013: 8). In the following days, fans set fire to the club and destroyed much of its memorabilia in protest. Davies (2013), writing for BBC News in Jerusalem, suggests that an embarrassed management believed that 'at a time when they are actively trying to attract investors and sponsors, the "welcome" given by a minority of fans was completely counterproductive'. The club took immediate steps to correct the negative image by banning the ringleaders of the racist fans from home matches, while some were even arrested and charged with racist behaviour. Only time will tell whether the club's general manager, Itzik Kornfein, will be able to change the public perception of the club. Yet, in his determination to do so, he will use every public relations mechanism available to him.

Public relations objectives and their relationship to promotion and marketing objectives

Because public relations is part of the promotion mix, and the promotion mix is part of the marketing mix, it is obvious that marketing objectives are the basis for both promotion and public relations objectives. Hence, in general, the following broad public relations objectives can be formulated to support promotion and marketing objectives:

- earning understanding and acceptance for organisational activities
- explaining certain behaviour
- educating and informing publics
- raising awareness for the organisation or new products
- creating trust (in the organisation or its products), and
- creating goodwill.

These objectives show that most public relations objectives, and hence activities, will not be aimed directly at increasing sales or increasing memberships. Linked to the other marketing functions in the organisation, public relations becomes part of an integrated marketing approach, which should lead to a more efficient and effective achievement of overall marketing objectives. Take, for example, the 2010 World Cup in South Africa.

Curtin and Gaither (2012: 63) suggest a macro or Pan-African perspective was taken when communicating with a worldwide audience for the 2010 World Cup. It was important that a message of safety, tourist-friendliness and readiness was globally articulated. The authors argue that the country made three strategic decisions to spur its communication. First, 'it branded the World Cup as a celebration of African heritage and unity'; second, 'it wove South African culture into all visual and written communication in a deliberate attempt to weld South African symbols within African imagery', and finally, 'the country centralised its communication to ensure co-ordinated and consistent communication by the South African government, the International Marketing Council of South Africa and other private sector communities'.

While the sport fan's most lasting memory of the 2010 World Cup was probably not that Spain won a gripping final in extra time, but more likely the rise (or the sound) of the vuvuzela, there is little doubt that a successful integrated public relations campaign supported and delivered an equally successful World Cup for South Africa.

Public opinion

As discussed above, evaluating public attitudes has been defined as one of the critical activities of the public relations function. Seitel (1995: 52) defines an attitude as 'an evaluation people make about specific problems or issues'. A public, then, is a group of people who share an evaluation about specific problems or issues. When certain group attitudes become important and strong enough, they turn into opinions. Opinions about certain issues can lead to behaviour. It is the opinion of the larger public that influences the buying behaviour of target markets. Consider the following example that deals with one of the most 'successful' athletes of the past two decades, cyclist Lance Armstrong.

Alessandra Stanley (2013) of the *New York Times* said of Lance Armstrong:

> [T]here are other sport heroes . . . but Armstrong was a New World star in the European sport of cycling whose improbable comeback defied the odds and blunted the cynicism of the age: he was struck by testicular cancer at 25 and went on to beat Europe's best in the Tour de France seven years in a row. While he was not known

for his pleasing personality, his goodness seemed unimpeachable thanks to his foundation, Livestrong, one of the country's biggest cancer charities.

Armstrong's fall from grace was protracted, very public and extremely polarising. While it could be argued that professional cycling had long been considered an environment in which the taking of banned substances was necessary for success, Armstrong's ongoing denial of any wrongdoing, in the face of overwhelming evidence to the contrary, only exacerbated the public response when his admission of guilt eventually came. Following the admission, Armstrong lost sponsorship from numerous companies that included Nike, Oakley, Trek and Anheuser-Busch. For many, Armstrong became a sporting pariah, and this eventually led to him stepping down as chairman of Livestrong in an attempt to limit backlash against the foundation.

In an attempt to explain his behaviour, if not rebuild his brand, Armstrong conducted an interview with the queen of daytime television, Oprah Winfrey. Armstrong chose Winfrey for his *mea culpa*, as it was argued at the time that she would provide a more sympathetic environment and tone than a well-known investigative journalist. However, Harry Enten (2013) from *The Guardian* suggests that the interview was a public relations disaster. Enten argues that Armstrong should have maintained his innocent stance if he 'wanted to maintain his public standing'. He suggests that before the *Oprah* appearance, more Americans were 'with' Armstrong than against him, yet all the support vanished following the interview. Furthermore, it appears that his confession alienated most viewers. Enten concludes by stating that denial is a far more successful PR strategy, and that:

> Had he just continued lying history says that he still would have been able to convince many people, perhaps even the majority, that he was telling the truth. Armstrong painted himself into a corner by confessing: the problem for this American icon is that few, if any, now believe in his apologies.

Given that public opinion highly influences the buying behaviour of target markets, reinforcing existing positive public opinions and/or changing negative public opinions are the underlying aims of all public relations strategies. In the case of Lance Armstrong, the attempt to sway public opinion about the athlete had an adverse effect. While many other fallen athletes have rebuilt faith and positive public opinion, the attempt to rebuild the Lance Armstrong brand clearly failed. Armstrong's current ability to be a product spokesperson or an endorser is extremely limited. Arguably, it will be a very long time—if ever—before Armstrong can reconnect with a credible target market.

Publics of sporting organisations

In other chapters, the term 'target market' is used to define the group of people towards whom marketing activities are directed. Target market implies a focus on exchange between the sporting organisation and its customers. It was shown that publics have a much wider scope. Using situational theory, Gruning and Hunt (1984: 145) identified four types of publics of relevance to the sport environment. These are *latent publics*, or groups that do not recognise they are affected by an event but may do so at some future stage; *aware publics*, or groups that are aware of an issue or problem but choose not to act (but may do so eventually); *active publics*, or groups that choose to engage in action regarding the problem or issue; and *non-publics*, or groups that are not affected. In the Lance Armstrong example, a case can be made for the existence of all four publics. Closer to home, Sportview 15.1 also highlights—either directly or indirectly—a sporting organisation's publics.

SPORTVIEW 15.1

'If it looks like a tank, sounds like a tank and acts like a tank, it's a tank.' – Mark Robinson

In February 2013, the Melbourne Football Club was fined $500 000 for acting in a manner prejudicial to the interests of the AFL. The fine stemmed from activity that took place within the Melbourne Football Club during the 2009 season. It was alleged that Melbourne had 'tanked' in a number of games in 2009 to ensure priority draft picks for the following season. While the issue was examined at the time, and dismissed, it was brought to light again in 2012 when Brock McLean, a former player with the club, 'confirmed what had long been suspected—that the Demons had tanked in 2009' (Pierik, 2012). The 2013 investigation cleared the club of any wrongdoing, but in the process of clearing, the club instituted a $500 000 fine (the third largest financial sanction in AFL history) and suspended the former Melbourne Football Club manager, Chris Connolly, and former coach, Dean Bailey, for twelve months and sixteen rounds respectively.

Mark Robinson (2013), football writer for the *Herald Sun*, argued in his article: 'If it looks like a tank, sounds like a tank and acts like a tank, it's a tank.' He also said that 'the football fan in all of us should feel insulted and confused' (2013: 78) by the AFL's findings and decision. Robinson was articulating what many fans were silently wondering. How could players being rested or played out of position possibly be construed as doing everything to win a football match? And if the club were not guilty of tanking, why was it fined half a million dollars—and why was it happy enough to accept such a penalty?

To suggest that this was a public relations nightmare for the AFL is an understatement. AFL boss Andrew Demetriou defiantly suggested that tanking had 'never taken place in the AFL', and his deputy Gillon McLachlan stated that 'the Melbourne Football Club did not set out to deliberately lose matches in 2009' and that 'Dean Bailey did not coach on his merits or players didn't play to their utmost ability'. While football fans didn't doubt the latter assertion, it is difficult to comprehend how a player can perform to his utmost for the club if he is rested or played out of position. Moreover, fans can legitimately ask why, if Dean Bailey did coach on his merits in 2009, he was suspended for the first sixteen matches of the 2013 season. In the wash-up, Melbourne was happy with the fine, having threatened court action. Jon Ralph (2013: 76) suggests that Connolly 'could eventually be financially rewarded for being Melbourne's scapegoat', and Bailey can continue to work as an assistant coach at the Adelaide Crows but cannot have a match-day role or work with players during his sixteen-match ban.

The AFL has always been seen to be a credible sporting organisation, but public relations disasters such as this chip away at the fans' belief in the management of the code. Only time will tell whether the AFL learned from their handling of this issue and whether, when called to account in the future, it will treat the fans with more respect.

Often, public relations activities will go beyond direct communication with the target market, aiming to positively influence the wider public opinion. Brassington and Pettitt (2006) list the following publics that apply to most organisations:

- commercial—customers, suppliers, competitors
- authority—government, trade associations, regulatory entities
- financial—investors, shareholders
- media—print, visual, audio and internet
- internal—employees, unions, members, and
- general—community (local, broad), pressure groups.

When the publics of a sporting organisation are identified, and the sport marketer has knowledge of their opinions, the policies and procedures of the organisation can be linked to the public interest. However, even in the most stable of organisations, publics and publics' perceptions can change, and so can their desires and priorities. The constant review of the PR program is seen as a proactive strategy in sport organisations.

Linking policies and procedures to the public interest

How can an organisation create a fit between what it does and what its publics are interested in? If people are not interested in buying an organisation's products, can it at least make sure that they have a favourable perception of the organisation? These are questions that need to be answered when trying to act in a positive way as perceived by the publics. The organisation can do this in a planned, proactive way, but it is sometimes forced to do it in a reactive way. Examples of both are given in the following sections. How far an organisation can go in manipulating public opinion is discussed under the subject of ethics, then media relations are considered.

Proactive public relations: Why do we do the things we do?

Proactive public relations can be defined as a planned effort to influence public attitudes in order to create favourable opinions. Creating favourable opinions in order to boost sales, to enhance an image or to raise awareness for the organisation can all be the broad objectives of proactive public relations. The last part of the case study largely relates to proactive public relations, in which raising awareness for a new policy was the aim of the campaign. The product launch is another good example of proactive public relations. As an integrated part of the overall marketing efforts of an organisation, it supports the achievement of marketing objectives. Sport, however, is much more familiar with reactive public relations. Sportview 15.2 is an excellent example of reactive public relations.

SPORTVIEW 15.2

The Canterbury Bulldogs earn plaudits and respect

On the eve of the 2013 football season, Rugby League star Ben Barba was stood down by his club, the Canterbury Bulldogs, to allow him to deal with 'personal issues'. Barba was coming off a stellar 2012 Rugby League season, which saw him lead his side to the Grand Final and win the NRL's most coveted award, the Dally M player of the year. Seemingly all was laid out before the competition's leading player leading up to 2013—so much so, in fact, that he was to be the 'face' of Rugby League for the upcoming season. As the story broke on 25 February, popular thinking was that this was just another example of anti-social behaviour by another Rugby League player. However, rather than being a public relations disaster for the code, the handling of the situation by the player's club drew widespread admiration.

The collective wisdom among the sport writers covering the breaking story was that Barba had struggled to deal with the public spotlight in which he had found himself following his outstanding 2012 season. Although the exact nature and severity of Barba's problems was only speculated upon at the time, Jackson (2013) indicated that Barba was 'being stood down over behavioural issues relating to a break up with his long term partner'. The writer further suggested the Bulldogs were helping Barba to overcome gambling and alcohol issues, and that the player's time away from the game could be up to six months.

Canterbury chief executive Todd Greenberg believed that termination of Barba's contract would be of no value to the player, and that the club needed to provide Barba with the appropriate professional expertise and services to assist with his recovery. Hinds (2013), writing for the *Sydney Morning Herald*, argued that, 'by acting swiftly and of its own accord, the Bulldogs ensured the concern for Barba's welfare, and for those around him, was deemed to be more important than team performance'. He concluded by lauding the professional manner in which the Bulldogs dealt with Barba's increasingly erratic behaviour.

In this case, it must be acknowledged that the Canterbury Bulldogs, long regarded as the code's bad boys in terms of player behaviour, reacted in a timely, professional and concerned manner, and demonstrated a duty of care for the player. The process undertaken resulted in significant admiration for the stance taken by the club and, whereas the situation could have been viewed in a negative light and left Rugby League reeling again, the focus was taken off the athlete's behaviour and placed on to the club's appropriate and timely handling of the issue. This Sportview illustrates how reactive public relations in response to a crisis can have positive outcomes.

Reactive public relations: Why have we done the things we've done?

Reactive public relations actions are put in place when unplanned events occur that negatively influence the attitudes of the organisation's publics. Preventing the problem is always better than fixing it, but sometimes even careful planning does not prevent things from happening. Sporting organisations and their athletes receive high-level attention from the media, and hence are more likely than other organisations or persons to become involved in crisis situations. Just consider that, despite apparently rigorous drug-testing procedures and harsh penalties for drug cheats in the 2000 Olympics, the 'darling' of the athletics program, Marion Jones, managed to evade a positive drug test until 2007, when she eventually confessed to taking drugs prior to the 2000 event. Subsequently, she returned her medals and accepted a ban from competing for two years.

It can be argued that a crisis like a positive drug test or racial abuse might be expected and prepared for. During major events like the Olympic Games, national sporting bodies know that the chances of athletes being caught using banned drugs are much higher. How can a sporting organisation employ a proactive public relations strategy in preparing for a crisis situation? Sporting organisations cannot always prevent a crisis from happening, but anticipation and preparation will reduce the damage.

Ethics

Cameron et al. (2008: 204–5) believe that professionals have the burden of making ethical decisions that satisfy public interest, but are in agreement with the professional organisation's code of ethics and personal values while at the same time addressing the needs of the employer. They muse that 'the difficulty in ascertaining whether an act is ethical lies in the fact that individuals have different standing and perceptions of what is right or wrong'. They surmise that 'most ethical conflicts are not black or white but fall into the gray area'.

If one of the most important goals of the public relations function is to enhance public trust in an organisation, clearly the public relations professional must act in an honest and trustworthy manner. Linking the policies and procedures of the organisation to the public interest means that no other organisation or individual should be harmed by the actions of the organisation. Spreading unsubstantiated rumours about rival athletes or clubs in order to enhance one's own image is therefore unethical behaviour. Bribing the media to report favourably on important issues is also unethical behaviour. Much can be written about this topic. The bottom line is that, in the interest of the publics and the organisation, honest information and genuine procedures will benefit most in both the short and long run.

Media relations

Earlier in this chapter, it was shown that public opinion is one of the most important forces influencing the buying behaviour of publics of sporting organisations. It is the task of the sport marketer to influence public opinion in order to create a favourable image of the sporting organisation. In this decade of globalisation and booming communications technology—the media—communicating to a global mass audience is unequivocally the most powerful means of influencing public opinion. Lewis and Kitchen (2010: 189) suggest that 'the arrival of the new web paradigm may be an opportunity for sport PR managers to utilise expertise and knowledge of how the media is evolving to take a leadership role in the development of relationships based approaches'. In fact, Stoldt, Dittmore and Branvold (2012: 74) argue that 'organization websites are important platforms for the distribution of controlled messages to an organization's community' and, 'given the potential to [not only] deliver controlled messages to a mass audience [but to also] solicit feedback from a large number of people, its value as a PR tool is unmistakeable'.

In creating and maintaining favourable media relations, three actions are important to consider:

- form
- inform, and
- be informal.

Depending on the type of sporting organisation and its strategies, certain media channels are more important than others. Traditionally, the local tennis club will benefit more from local newspaper coverage and local radio, whereas a Grand Slam tennis tournament will need global television and newspaper coverage to satisfy sponsors' needs. However, in this day and age, micro-blogging using Twitter, establishing social communities through sites such as Facebook or creating event websites may be a good way to facilitate strong public relations.

That is why a comprehensive form of potential media outlets has to be put together. This form, or media database, will enable the sport marketer to inform the media. This is done through formal channels, but communication may also be successful if informal communication can be developed with media representatives.

Planning and executing a program of action

Once the sport marketer has identified the attitudes of the sporting organisation's publics, and thought of ways of linking their interests to the activities of the organisation, it is time to develop a program of action. With the media one of the sport marketer's most powerful means of communication, a large part of this section will be devoted to public relations communication through the media. To start this process, it is first necessary to know which media are available and how to get in contact with them.

Form—the media database

Helitzer (1996) lists three main sources that have to be included in the sporting organisation media database:

- the media that routinely cover sport
- personal contacts, and
- media directories.

These sources have to be categorised in a logical order—that is, the media outlets and contacts must be ordered according to the most relevant publics for individual sporting organisations. Contact persons and addresses are vital, and should be updated regularly. The different forms per media outlet can range from one or two contacts to several hundred.

Form—the communications plan

Planning communications is nothing more (and nothing less!) than putting together a plan of what to tell which media when. As previously discussed, proactive public relations communications should support the promotion and marketing goals of the sporting organisation. In relation to setting goals for the organisation, public relations action plans can be put together and, with the help of the database, distribution of information can be planned.

Inform—the media release

As a means of informing the media, media releases can be used for long-term proactive, short-term proactive and reactive public relations. Many organisations issue media releases on any topic of interest for one or more of their publics. The main goal of the media release is to inform the publics through the media in the way the organisation wants. Ideally, it will generate positive publicity for the sporting organisation or sportspersons.

A few standard rules apply to the format of media releases:

- Use a catchy and informative short title.
- Present the backbone information in the first paragraphs. Answer the questions who, what, when, where, why and how.
- Put facts first. Give accurate information. Use correct grammar.
- Include the name and address of a contact person.
- Use current media contacts and addresses when sending the press release.
- State the source of the press release, and date it.

The major causes of rejection of some press releases are:

- limited reader interest
- poor expression
- conflicts with media outlet policies
- difficulty distinguishing them from advertising
- material that is obviously faked or exaggerated
- apparent inaccuracies in the story, and
- duplication of material previously used.

If an issue is important enough to create widespread media attention, a press release can be used to announce a media conference.

Inform—the media conference

A media conference presents the sporting organisation with the opportunity to inform all present media at once. Also, when media representatives consider the issue of the conference important enough to attend, it is very likely that some kind of publicity will result. When the media attend, they often use the provided information. Conference organisers should realise that, besides printed publicity, photographs and audiovisual information will be collected by the media. This has implications for who the spokesperson will be, how they will dress, and how and where the names and logos of sponsors and the organisation will be displayed and presented.

Helitzer (1996: 179–81) states eleven reasons for sporting organisations to call a media conference:

- a major change in personnel
- a major change in the status of a star player
- an important event scheduled
- a major investigation (for example, into illegal drug use)
- a change in a major facility
- award presentations
- crisis developments
- post-game interviews

- the sport banquet speaker
- the introduction of a new product, and
- a new rule that is complex or controversial.

A media conference should be called only when the general public or specific publics of the sporting organisation are interested enough to be informed. One of the above reasons might be applicable to a sporting organisation. If, however, the people or issues involved are still insignificant to the public, the media will not show up and the unsuccessful press conference will only damage the reputation of the organisation.

Inform and informal—interviews

Both a media release and a media conference can serve as an invitation for interviews. Interviews are one-on-one contact opportunities in which disseminated information can best be controlled. The interviewee has the opportunity to tell only what he or she wants to tell. However, conducting and taking part in an interview are both skills in their own right. Poor preparation or failing to recognise an interviewer's leading questions can turn the opportunity into disaster for the organisation.

Helitzer (1996: 273) provides a list of the dos and don'ts of interviews:

- Don't permit off-the-record statements.
- Don't try to become a major part of the interview.
- Don't assume that every fact will be used.
- Don't complain if the result is not totally satisfactory.
- Do pick the best spokesperson.
- Do try to limit the subject to areas where your spokesperson is an authority.
- Do provide suggested quotes, anecdotes and statistics that can be used.
- Do rehearse fully!
- Do select the site where the spokesperson will be most comfortable.
- Do provide the press with full background.
- Do keep every promise to supply supplementary information.
- Do show your appreciation in a letter—it is even better than a call.

The interview presents the experienced sport marketer with an opportunity to use personal media contacts and disseminate information in an informal way. Informal contacts do not imply less care when supplying the information! The opportunity to talk informally to media representatives should not be turned into a disadvantage by accidentally releasing confidential information.

Form, inform and informal—publicity

Publicity, according to Belch and Belch (1998: 528), refers to 'the generation of news about a person, product, service [or organisation] that appears in broadcast or print media [at no cost to the organisation]'. Although not every public relations effort necessarily has to result in news appearing in broadcast or print media, it can be an effective and efficient means of public relations communication. As a sub-set of the overall public relations exercise, planning and executing a program of action (press release, press conference, interview) often lead to the generation of publicity. Mullin, Hardy and Sutton (1993: 260) state that:

> sport is the most interesting specimen examined by the media . . . and it prospered because it received at no cost reams of publicity in daily and Sunday papers . . . This coverage, for which any other business would have had to pay, was given freely because of its entertainment value and because a newspaper that contained information about sport would sell more copies, creating both higher circulation and higher advertising rates.

Publicity is generated when the information has news value. Because the sporting organisation does not pay for the publicity, content is very hard to control. Also, the release time and accuracy of information are hard to control. But because the sporting organisation is not the direct source of information (other than in advertising or sales promotions), positive publicity can become very powerful and credible. Negative publicity, however, has the opposite extreme effect. In an integrated public relations strategy, the content, timing and generation of publicity are as much as possible controlled in the proactive strategy, and as much as possible prepared for in the reactive strategy.

Reputation management

In recent times, an organisation's perceived reputation has become more closely associated with its public persona. A reputation is generally created as a result of the effectiveness of an organisation's interaction with its internal and external publics. It relates to the deeds that an organisation performs rather than what is said about them. Sport events and organisations can develop their reputation over time. For example, the reputation of the Olympic Games Opening and Closing Ceremonies has evolved, with each organising committee seeking to improve on the previous Games. Future organising committees know the strength of this reputation, and endeavour to make the next ceremony even better. Excellent reputation management can lead to significant competitive advantage (Brassington and Pettitt, 2006), and it is closely related to managing the brand of the organisation. People justify their perceptions about a sport organisation in a number of ways. Fombrun (2000) argues that there are six issues that relate to the reputation of an organisation:

- *emotional appeal*—respect, admiration and liking stakeholders have for the organisation
- *products and services*—level of quality, innovation, reliability and value offered
- *financial performance*—profitability, prospects and risk-management
- *vision and leadership*—management's ability to show strength and clarity
- *workplace environment*—the quality of employees and management, work conditions
- *social responsibility*—ethical practices, environment record, community involvement.

It is important in public relations activities to develop and maintain a distinctive reputation that is consistent with all publics, and that contributes to the organisation's identity. This can be achieved by focusing on a central theme. In the case presented in this chapter, this central theme is the fight that wrestling has on its hands after the IOC potentially removed it from the Olympic program. The PR battle has commenced, as described in the concluding case.

Advantages and disadvantages of public relations

At the beginning of this chapter, public relations was introduced as one element of the promotion mix. Public relations has some distinct advantages over other elements when applied under certain conditions. The most common advantages identified include the following:

- *Credibility*—contrary to advertising, the source of the public relations message is often not the organisation itself, which makes the message more credible to the receiver.
- *Excitement*—publicity addresses topical issues and that in itself generates a level of expectation. The Olympic Torch Relay creates excitement as it gains momentum travelling through a variety of countries from the preceding Olympics to the next Olympic location, culminating in lighting the flame to allow the Games to begin.
- *Cost*—apart from the public relations personnel cost, few other expenditures have to be incurred.
- *Avoidance of clutter*—because many public relations efforts lead to news generation, information will stand apart from, for example, advertising or sales promotions.
- *Lead generation*—for example, when Tiger Woods dropped that famously slow putt with the cameras zooming in on the Nike logo on the ball, sales of Nike golf balls went through the roof in the weeks following the event.
- *Ability to reach specific groups.*
- *Image building*—effective public relations programs lead to the development of a strong image, one that can resist negative publicity for a while. (Belch and Belch, 2007; Brassington and Pettitt, 2006).

The main disadvantage of public relations is the uncontrollability of publicity. When proactive or reactive public relations result in negative publicity, all potential public relations advantages turn into disadvantages. Publicity is about breaking news, and when athletes or officials report on alleged misdemeanours within the sport that are newsworthy (such as drug-taking), then the governing body needs to go into public relations mode to quell harmful implications the news may cause. Any good created through publicity can quickly be undone. Negative information will hit more powerfully, and it will cost more to repair the damage. The avoidance of clutter, lead-generation, ability to reach specific groups and excitement generated will now work against the organisation, damaging the positive reputation that was being built. The fallout from the following Sportview will be interesting to observe.

SPORTVIEW 15.3

'The team dynamic became like a schoolyard clamour for attention and influence'—Pippa Grange

In the lead-up to the 2012 London Olympic Games, the hype around the Australian swimming team—and especially its star, James Magnussen—was intense. At the 2011 World Swimming

Championships, Magnussen became the first Australian to win the coveted 100-metre sprint, and also led off the gold medal-winning relay team with an unofficial time of 47.49 that was the fastest ever by a swimmer not wearing a polyurethane suit. Magnussen was to lead the charge against the team's traditional swimming rivals, the United States. The Australians had finished second to the United States in the pool in the previous three Olympics, and there was nothing to suggest—publicly at least—that this event would be any different. Imagine the disappointment in Australia when the much-vaunted swim team could only manage one gold medal, and finished seventh on the medal table, only one place ahead of Tunisia; furthermore, the supposedly 'unbeatable' 4 x 100 men's relay, led by Magnussen, would finish out of the medal places. The swim team had always been an Olympic focal point for the Australian sport fan, so the lamentable performance by the team resulted in accusations, recriminations and shame. For a sport that gets significant funding from the public purse, it was a PR nightmare.

On 30 January 2013, Bluestone Edge provided a report to Swimming Australia entitled *A Review of Culture and Leadership in Australian Olympic Swimming* (Grange, 2013). The report concluded, among other things, that 'there was an undertone of divisions, now and then, us and them, men and women, the best and the rest'. Moreover, 'poor behaviour and disrespect within the team were not regulated or resisted strongly by other team members, and it was left unchecked or without consequence by staff and coaches on a number of occasions' (2013: 8). At the same time as the Bluestone report, the Australian Sports Commission released its own *Independent Review of Swimming*, which resulted in 35 recommendations to improve the design, delivery and administration of swimming's high performance programs. Paxinos (2013) referred to this as a 'second damning report'.

Both reports were critical of a number of processes within the governance and leadership of Australian swimming, and the word 'toxic' was regularly used by the media when referring to some of the report's more damning observations (Lane and Spits, 2013). In an attempt to limit the fallout from the reports, the members of the relay squad faced the media on Friday, 22 February, and admitted to a number of infractions which may have broken the team agreement (AAP, 2013b). In addition, head coach Leigh Nugent was called to account for his failure to act on what he knew about the team's behaviour (Balm, 2013). At the time of the writing of this Sportview, SAL had established an integrity panel to investigate the swimmers. The Australian sport fan awaits the findings of the panel with interest.

The performance and the fallout from the Australian swimming team's performance at the London Olympic Games was a public relations nightmare for SAL, the ASC and the AOC. It is unfortunate that the poor behaviour of a small group of individuals can tarnish the reputation of a larger team. However, given the general tendency of sport organisations to close ranks when faced with confrontation, and the media's habit of focusing on the salacious, it is difficult for sport fans to form more balanced views. Swimming Australia Ltd will need to engage in an extensive public relations campaign if it is ever to restore faith with the Australian swimming fan and consumer. The integrity commission is a small step in what will be a long journey.

Summary

This chapter described and discussed the promotion mix tool of public relations. This is an important tool for the sport marketer because of the high visibility and attractiveness of the sport product. Three critical activities were derived from a public relations definition in order to describe the main public relations activities:

- evaluating public attitudes
- identifying the policies and procedures of an individual or organisation with the public interest, and
- planning and executing a program of action.

It is important for the sport marketer to know how the sporting organisation's publics perceive the organisation and its product range. Knowledge of public opinion and how to influence opinion is vital in order to create proactive public relations strategies. Therefore, public attitudes need to be evaluated. Proactive strategies enable the sport marketer to 'control and adjust' public opinion, whereas reactive strategies always require changing negative public opinions. Prevention is a more effective approach than repairing damage. The added dimension of building organisational reputation through actions rather than words is a distinctive way to gain a competitive advantage in sport.

As a very influential public of many sporting organisations, relations with the media were considered, and the public relations tools of media releases, media conferences and interviews were introduced. There are basically three things that need to be considered when communicating with the media. The sport marketer has to know with whom to communicate, what information to supply and how to maintain excellent relationships with media representatives. In sport marketing, special attention needs to be given to the concept of publicity, as it is probably the most important means (and opportunity) of conveying information in the sport industry.

CASE STUDY

Wrestling on the mat—will it be forced to tap out?

This is a very simple case study, but the eventual outcome of the issue will have a profound effect not just on the sport of wrestling but on sport in general. Moreover, the result of the public relations campaign to reverse the decision will be known. However, the public relations principles applied will be universal to all sports that face similar issues of removal, relegation or non-registration. By analysing what worked (or didn't, depending on the outcome), students and potential PR practitioners will be better equipped to make key strategic decisions that will inform and influence eventual decision-making.

Background

On Tuesday, 12 February 2013, the International Olympic Committee announced that it was dropping wrestling from the 2020 Games. While not one of the more high-profile or glamour sports, wrestling has a long history with the Olympics. It not only has featured in every modern Olympic Games, but it also has its roots in the games of antiquity. It is as synonymous with the Olympic movement as athletics and archery. While not closing the door completely, wrestling joined 'seven other sports vying for one opening on the 2020 program: a combined bid from baseball/softball, karate, squash, roller sports, sport climbing, wakeboarding and wushu' (Dutt, 2013). Dutt comments that the decision to drop the sport was made via a secret ballot, and against the criteria of 'popularity, finances, ticket sales and governance'. The author also suggests 'frequent cases of doping involving wrestlers [had] also tarnished the sport's image'.

Response

The response from the wrestling fraternity was immediate from all corners of the globe. The outcry resulted in countries such as the United States and Iran uniting in their condemnation of the decision. Associated Press also noted that unlikely allies, the United States and Russia, had joined forces in an attempt to save the sport. Russia, and the Soviet Union, had won 77 gold medals in the sport (Australian Associated Press, 2013a).

Former Olympic gold medallist and now professional wrestler Kurt Angle, long considered one of the best in both amateur and professional wrestling, stated that 'the wrestling community is in a state of shock—we cannot sit back and allow this to happen. I will do whatever it takes and work with my company TNA WRESTLING and the competitive wrestling community to determine what we need to do to reverse this decision.' TNA also encouraged fans to use social media to voice support for the reinstatement of wrestling in the Olympic Games (TNA, 2013). However, the most significant response came from Raphael Martinetti, president of the International Wrestling Federation (FILA). At FILA's executive meeting in Thailand on 16 February, Martinetti resigned in protest at the IOC decision. Martinetti, from Switzerland, had held the presidency of FILA since 2002 (Australian Associated Press, 2013c). The IOC Executive met in May 2013 to choose the sports for inclusion, and a final vote took place at the IOC General Assembly in September 2013 in Argentina. At the time of writing of this case study, the outcome was as yet unknown.

Questions

1. Was the public relations campaign successful? Why or why not?
2. What role did the internet and social media play in the campaign?
3. What general lessons can sports learn from the preliminary decision to drop wrestling from the Olympic Games?
4. What public relations activities can sports such as wrestling undertake to minimise the need to engage in reactive public relations?
5. How do organisations such as the IOC use public relations to convince a wider sport community of the veracity of what at first glance may be an unpopular decision?

16

Promotional licensing

Stage 1—Identification of marketing opportunities

▼

Stage 2—Strategy determination

Step 5—Determine core marketing strategy

Marketing and service mix—sport product, pricing, place (physical evidence, people, process), customer satisfaction

Promotion mix—sales promotion, advertising, television, internet, sponsorship, public relations and publicity, **licensing**

Step 6—Determine tactics and performance benchmarks

▼

Stage 3—Strategy implemention, evaluation and adjustment

CHAPTER OBJECTIVES

This chapter deals with promotional licensing as an element of the sport promotion mix. Promotional licensing involves developing a relationship between a licensor and licensee with respect to the right to use the name or logo of the sporting organisation. Terms such as licensor, licensee, royalty and trademark are introduced. Related issues, including the role of licensing in raising revenues and branding, are also discussed.

After studying this chapter, you should be able to:

- understand the importance of the (registered) trademark
- identify the different steps in building a sport licensing program
- identify licensor and licensee goals
- describe the central role of branding in the sport licensing program.

HEADLINE STORY

Thorpedo thirst for more

What's in a name? This is a question tackled by many of sport's top stars, as agents and sponsors ponder the value of image and intellectual property rights. Ian Thorpe was recognised as Australia's most suitable sponsorship prospect from 1999 to 2006 (Sweeney Sports, 2005–06). His retirement from swimming in 2006 enabled him to capitalise on his brand 'style' and embark on a series of projects, which provided his own answer to the initial question. His name, logo and image featured on a raft of products ranging from food and beverages (Thorpedo Foods) to clothing (IT underwear, Adidas, Armani) and jewellery (Omega Speedmaster). These branded goods stood alongside an ambitious portfolio of projects such as television documentaries *Action Earth* and *Fish Out of Water* and the charitable Fountain of Youth Foundation. In addition, the swimming centre in Ultimo, Sydney has been refurbished and named the Ian Thorpe Aquatic Centre.

In 2010, Thorpe announced he was coming out of retirement in a bid to compete at the 2012 London Olympic Games. Despite not having success in the pool, Thorpe was able to take advantage of his brand equity and popularity within Australia (he was the fifth most popular athlete in 2012 according to Sweeney Sports), and Southeast Asia. Thorpe and IMG signed a strategic partnership to help leverage his brand internationally during the lead-up to the 2012 London Olympics. This relationship saw new sponsorship deals signed with Blackmores, Virgin Blue, Adidas and media company Play Up. The sponsorship deals largely focused on leveraging Thorpe's popularity in Japan, South Korea and China with sponsors' expansion plans into the region. While his sponsorship appeal as a swimmer has been reduced, he is a likeable and popular personality who is known globally. Despite his unsuccessful comeback, Thorpe's phenomenal early success in the pool linked perfectly to him being perceived as trustworthy, honest and charming—a good combination for pursuing a trademark licensing strategy, whether successful in the pool or not.

Although the income from licensed merchandise for sporting organisations worldwide has increased enormously over the past 20 years, it has never been easy to put together a solid licensing program. The second part of this chapter discusses how to build a sporting organisation's licensing program. The first part discusses the different elements of the licensing concept. The different parties involved and terminology employed are defined and, where possible, placed in a sport context.

Licensing as an activity involves a licence, a licensor and a licensee: 'A licence is first and foremost the granting of an intellectual property right from the licensor to the licensee.' (Wilkof, 1995: 5) This means that the intellectual property right of a licensor must be valuable enough for a licensee to use and pay a royalty, which is a fee paid for usage of the intellectual property, often calculated as a percentage of the sales of licensed products.

As implied in the title of this chapter, promotional licensing can be seen as an element of the promotion mix. In the context of the sport industry, it basically serves two purposes:

- promotion of the sporting organisation, and
- promotion of a third party or its products through use of the sporting organisation's name or logo.

In the latter case, the sporting organisation will derive royalty income from licensing the third party with the name or logo usage.

In the sport industry, we are most familiar with the usage of names and/or logos (as the licensed property) of sporting teams or organisations printed on apparel (such as baseball caps and t-shirts) or other merchandise (for example, pens, mugs, umbrellas). Names and logos of sporting organisations are intellectual properties, representing a certain or potential value. This value is built into the name or logo as a result of the organisation's sporting achievements and hence popularity, but also through (monetary) investment in the name or logo through the promotion efforts of the sporting organisation.

Not all sporting organisations, however, are in the position to license their name, logo or other properties to third parties. The name of the sporting organisation, or more broadly the brand, must be strong enough to generate interest and attention. Many sporting organisations set up licensing programs to receive royalties from the sale of licensed merchandise. However, without a strong brand name, this makes little sense. Potential licensees are interested only if the name or logo can generate extra interest in, and demand for, the products to which the name or logo is attached.

A sporting organisation without a strong brand name can still become involved in a licensing strategy. The main aim of the licensing strategy is to increase awareness of the sporting organisation, and indeed of its brand. The licensee, in turn, can use already strong sport brands in its own branding strategies, attaching the brand to newly introduced products or products with a questionable image. The Australian Football League (AFL), for example, links its brand name to the products of tens of companies. On those products, the AFL logo and an 'approved product' sign are printed.

Branding is discussed in the third part of this chapter. First, it is necessary to discuss the basis for licensing in the sport industry: trademark licensing.

Trademark licensing

Section 17 of the Australian *Trade Marks Act 1995* defines a trademark as 'a sign used, or intended to be used, to "distinguish" goods or services of the plaintiff from those of any other person'. A sign, then, includes the following or any combination of the following: any letter, word, name, signature, numeral, device (symbol or logo), brand, heading, label, ticket, aspect of packaging, shape, colour, sound or scent.

Trademark licensing is a multi-billion dollar industry, with the top ten global trademarks alone—Google (US$44.3 billion), Microsoft (US$42.8 billion), Walmart (US$36.2 billion), IBM (US$36.2 billion), Vodafone (US$30.7 billion), Bank of America (US$30.6 billion), GE (US$30.5 billion), Apple (US$29.5 billion), Wells Fargo (US$28.9 billion) and AT&T (US$28.9 billion)—worth US$338.6 billion (A$355.9 billion) alone in 2011, according to *Forbes* (Forbes.com, 2011). Trademark licensing is defined by Wilkof (1995: 1) as 'an arrangement by which one party consents to the use of its trade mark in accordance with specified terms and conditions'. It is used in many industries for different purposes, which can be appreciated by considering the following examples:

- the Calvin Klein clothing trademark being used to sell perfume (using the established brand/trademark to sell new products)
- Coca-Cola using an overseas franchisee to sell in new markets (using the established brand/trademark to sell in new markets)
- McDonald's using the Olympic rings to sell more hamburgers (using the established brand/trademark to boost sales), and
- licensing the Surf Life Saving logo to brand swimwear apparel and the Kmart retailer to build brand and trademark awareness and raise funds.

For a trademark to become the property of an organisation, it needs to be registered. When a trademark is registered, the owner will have the exclusive rights to:

- use the trademark, and
- authorise other persons to use the trademark (section 20(1)).

Registration of the trademark is of extreme importance to the sporting organisation. Without this registration, the original owner of the trademark has little legal protection when other organisations use the trademark in one way or another. Protecting the intellectual property rights (IPR) of Olympic symbols is one of the more significant imperatives for hosting the Olympic Games. This point is reinforced by the Australian Olympic Committee's (AOC) decision to seek additional protection for its insignia. The *Olympic Insignia Protection Act* 1987 (Cth) came into force in 1987 to enable the AOC to regulate the use of the Olympic symbol and other nominated Olympic designs. The Sydney Olympic Organising Committee for the Olympic Games (SOCOG) also sought added protection via the proclamation of the *Sydney 2000 Games (Indicia and Images) Protection Act 1996* (Cth) (repealed). Similar protection has now become the legislative norm for countries wishing to host Olympic Games. In the lead-up to the London 2012 Olympic Games, additional protection was awarded to protect all Olympic-related insignia, symbols and designs under the *London Olympic Games and Paralympic Games Act 2006 and the Olympic Symbol (Protection) Act 1995.*

Upon winning the right to host the 2008 Olympic Games, in 2002 the Chinese Olympic Committee (COC) and the Chinese government passed regulations protecting Olympic IPR with the *Protection of Olympic Symbols Regulations* (Mendel and Yijun, 2003). This was a positive step forward for Beijing authorities, as fake merchandising is a billion-dollar business, particularly in Southeast Asia. The counterfeiting situation in China made such legislation imperative in a country where Clark and Cheng (2007) estimate Chinese counterfeiting was costing American companies US$60 billion (A$63 billion) per year. As China is hoping to take advantage of the Olympic platform to showcase its capabilities to the world, it worked hard to police the counterfeit trade. In 2006, over 2000 trademark violations were summoned, with 4 per cent being in breach of the Olympic Symbols regulations (Clark and Cheng, 2007). It is also interesting to note the importance of sport in the general licensing business. It has been reported that sport is the second largest sector of licensing in the heartland of trademark licensing business, the United States and Canada, worth US$13.7 billion (A$14.4 billion) in annual retail sales in 2007. To put things in perspective, corporate trademarks and brands as the largest sector turn over US$16.7 billion (A$17.55 billion), and the largest (and in 2007 only!) growth is recorded in the sales of licensed video games and software (the sixth largest sector), worth US$4.6 billion (A$4.83 billion). Overall, one in every five pieces of licensed merchandise sold is an item related to sport (The Licensing Letter©, 2008).

The use of a trademark is important for an organisation in many ways. Some of the reasons are discussed in the next section.

Functions of a trademark

Wilkof (1995) identifies six different functions of trademarks. These developed over time, and hence the merchandising function incorporates elements of all other, earlier developed functions. The functions are:

- identification
- physical source
- anonymous source
- quality
- advertising, and
- merchandising.

Identification

The most obvious function of the trademark is to identify ownership, or who is responsible for producing the product. When the Dutch national team plays the Brazilians, for example, soccer consumers know that the 'orange' Dutch play the 'canary yellow' samba men from Brazil.

Physical source

Without being able to witness the production of certain products, the trademark can be seen as an acknowledgement of the physical source of the purchased goods. The trademark serves as a stamp of approval. When licensing trademarks, however, the licensee is not the actual source of the goods. T-shirts with National Basketball Association (NBA) logos printed on them are not produced by the NBA. Manufacturers are granted a licence to produce merchandise, and hence licensing seems incompatible with this function of the trademark. To reduce this incompatibility, it is important that the sporting organisation put in place stringent quality-control procedures to ensure that products will be of a quality that the 'physical source' organisation would deliver itself. For example, Adidas, as the exclusive apparel and uniform partner of the NBA, has exclusive rights to use the NBA trademark for the duration of the eleven-year agreement from 2006 to 2017.

Anonymous source

When the scope of production and marketing of an organisation expands, it becomes less likely that consumers of goods will know the actual name of the producer. The anonymous source function ensures that purchasers of goods or services with a given established trademark know that these goods or services emanate from a source that established those trademarks. In other words, the trademark products have proved their quality, validating their anonymous source. Large consumer good producers like Procter & Gamble and Unilever have hundreds of trademarks validating the 'anonymous source'. Sporting organisations are less likely to use this function of the trademark, although large entertainment companies involved in the sport industry actually do. For instance, sport properties such as the Mighty Ducks of Anaheim (National Hockey League) and the Anaheim Angels (Major League Baseball) are not only cartoon characters, they also are professional sporting franchises owned by the Disney Corporation. These sport properties are distributed through channels like ESPN, ESPN2 and ABC Sports, also owned by Disney. As well, Disney owns the names, logos and trademarks of all these organisational entities. In the case of the two professional teams—the Mighty Ducks of Anaheim and the Anaheim Angels—there are also licensing restrictions on the use of the logos and names placed by the National Hockey League (NHL) and Major League Baseball (MLB) as part of the franchise agreements.

Quality

Licensing of sport trademarks has become so popular because of the quality function of trademarks. If a trademark has the power to convey a quality perception, surely this perception can be transferred to products or entities linked to the trademark. From a legal perspective, this concept changed the position of licensing. Provided that the licensor establishes sufficient quality-control measures and procedures, it does not really matter whether the products emanate from the licensor (i.e. owner of the trademark) or another source. The quality level provided to the end consumer by the licensee should be similar to the quality level that would have existed if the product had been provided by the licensor.

Advertising

McDonald's using the Olympic rings, Kia Motors using Tennis Australia's logo and Nike using Manchester United's logo are all examples of trademark usage going beyond the creation of goodwill (as exemplified in the previous functions). Trademarks have become symbols with the power to sell goods and services. Although advertising can be criticised as an effort to manipulate the consumer's mind through slick, high-impact campaigns, it does serve as a way to mass-communicate the source and quality of a product through the trademark. It complements the source and quality functions. The positive perception that consumers have of Manchester United, Tennis Australia or the Olympic organisation is transferred to the associated organisations and products, stimulating these consumers to wear Nike products, drive a Kia vehicle or eat a McDonald's hamburger.

Merchandising

The trademark becomes a product in itself when it is not serving to sell other goods or services but rather serving to sell itself. Examples are the teenage fans of a rock band buying all possible merchandise with the name of the band on it, or football fans buying shirts, mugs, jackets and pens with the name of their team on them. The consumer wants to be identified with the trademark organisation. Which merchandise they buy is secondary. Often, the only criterion is that it is visible to others, showing the consumer's allegiance to the trademark organisation.

Quality control

Quality control is a vital and integral component of trademark licensing. We have shown that the legal position of licensing changed when the concept of quality control was included. As long as the licensor establishes sufficient quality-control measures and procedures, it does not really matter whether the products emanate from the licensor (that is, the owner of the trademark) or another source. The trademark identifies the source and distinguishes the products from those of others. The law loosely formulates standards for quality control in that the owner of the trademark should be capable of exercising control over the users of the trademark.

Wilkof (1995) distinguishes between two types of quality control: contractual and financial. Contractual control exists between two unrelated parties whose only mutual interest is the exploitation of the trademark. Financial control exists when two parties are related, in that one of them has an ownership relation to the other (for example, a holding or subsidiary relationship). Financial control is more stringent, as the aims of benefiting from the trademark are more likely to be in line with each other because of the ownership relationship between the organisations.

In the sport industry, contractual control is the most frequently used type of quality control. A contractual specification of quality-control terms and conditions should identify at least the following aspects of quality control:

- specification of standards
- inspection of products and methods of production, and
- supply of samples.

The trademark licensing agreement

The trademark licensing agreement sets out the broader relationship between the licensor and licensee. Ownership of the trademark, who can use the trademark as the licensee and how the trademark can be used (contractual—that is, quality control) are described first. Then the commercial and financial terms and conditions are described. Issues like how merchandise is going to be marketed and which royalties have to be paid by the licensee are described in this part of the agreement.

Sherman (1991: 330–1) describes several key areas that need to be addressed when preparing the trademark licensing agreement. In summary, the key areas are:

- scope of the territorial and product exclusivity
- assignability and sub-licensing rights
- definition of the property and the licensed products
- quality control and approval
- ownership of artwork and designs
- term-renewal rights and termination of the relationship
- initial licence and ongoing royalty fees
- performance criteria for the licensee
- liability insurance
- indemnification
- duty to pursue trademark and copyright infringement

- minimum advertising and promotional requirements
- accounting and record-keeping of the licensee
- inspection and audit rights of the licensor
- right of first refusal for expanded or revised characters and images
- limitations on the licensee's distribution to related or affiliated entities
- representations and warranties of the licensor with respect to its rights to the property
- availability of the licensor for technical and promotional assistance, and
- miscellaneous provisions, such as law to govern, inurement of goodwill, nature of the relationship notice and *force majeure*.

It goes beyond the scope of this text to specify further the contents of the trademark licensing agreement.

Before taking a closer look at building the sporting organisation's licensing program, we outline the trademark licensing agreement briefly from both the licensor's and the licensee's perspectives.

Licensor's and licensee's perspectives

The trademark licensing agreement from the licensor's perspective should serve one important goal. If the trademark is used by the licensee in any other manner than was intended by the licensor when entering the agreement, contractual arrangements must be in place to entitle the licensor to take action. Although this point is of obvious importance to the licensee as well, the focus of the licensee should be on the terms and conditions related to commercial and financial matters. This requires identifying the commercial possibilities of the trademark usage and how these may translate into a dollar figure. Sportview 16.1, adjusted from Schaaf (1995), exemplifies the licensor's and licensee's perspectives.

SPORTVIEW 16.1

The Rugby Union All Blacks/Wallabies/Springboks video game

Sport Excitement Video Games (a fictitious name) wants to create a game called *The All Blacks/Wallabies/Springboks Conquer the World*. The game will be marketed in New Zealand, Australia and South Africa. When sold in New Zealand, the game will be marketed as *The All Blacks Conquer the World*, in Australia as *The Wallabies Conquer the World* and in South Africa as *The Springboks Conquer the World*.

Sport Excitement has several licensing considerations. The company needs to develop the actual game, which includes writing the software code for graphical display, play options, opponents and voice enhancement features (the cost of this can go up to $400 000). Sport Excitement also needs to pay the New Zealand, Australian and South African national governing bodies of Rugby Union their licensing fees. In this case, all organisations have negotiated a minimum advance fee ($100 000) plus a percentage of sales royalty fee (4 per cent). On top of the licensing fees, Sport Excitement has to undertake the packaging, warehousing and shipping costs. Then it has to obtain the other necessary licences, from either the International Rugby Football Board (IRFB) or the Players Association, to feature identifiable teams and/or players other than the three already identified. Next, Sport Excitement has to decide which game platforms it will develop for (e.g. Xbox, PlayStation). Depending on which platform the manufacturer develops, the cartridges will add extra costs.

An analyst calculates the revenue streams and forecasts the potential return on investment. The net revenue per platform for an average game is $32 per game sold through, meaning purchased at a retail outlet such as Target. The All Blacks' royalty would likely be 4 per cent of that, less the advance. Therefore, if 100 000 units were sold through, the All Blacks' royalties would amount to:

$$100\,000 \text{ (units)} \times (0.04)(\$32) - \$100\,000 = \$28\,000$$

In this case, the sporting teams are not the catalyst for the game. The developer seeks a category and the teams are merely the well-known vehicles to differentiate the product. In the competitive video game development industry, the sophisticated marketplace will weed out poorly conceived games and they will fail in spite of a fabulous licensor. In this case, licensors will help to sell the products if those products are good.

Source: Adapted from Schaaf (1995).

How the general trademark licensing issues can be linked to a sporting organisation is explored in the next part of this chapter. Sportview 16.2 highlights some of the issues arising when using sport trademarks.

SPORTVIEW 16.2

Sport team logos are big business

Have you ever considered using the logo of your favourite professional sport team in a promotional campaign? Did you know it would cost you? Apparently not all marketing professionals realise that sport teams, like other companies that produce products or services, own protectable trademarks that others may not use unless they first obtain the trademark owner's permission and usually pay a licensing fee.

In a recent case, the Major League Baseball (MLB) successfully defended its trademark rights when it sued its former baseball card manufacturer, Upper Deck, for trademark infringement. Upper Deck (the licensee) had held the trademark rights to use the MLB (the licensor) logos on its trading cards for the previous 20 years. However, in 2009 the MLB decided to end this agreement and begin a new trademark licensing agreement with Upper Deck's competitor Topps. Instead of stopping production of cards that used the MLB logo in 2009, Upper Deck, without a current trademark agreement with the MLB, produced three new sets of trading cards. The trademark infringement was taken to a New York court and Upper Deck was ordered to pay the MLB an unspecified amount in damages (Craft, 2010).

Professional sport teams aggressively protect their trademark rights, which include the name and its logos. This is done by demanding licensing fees in other contexts. Recently, Major League Baseball has even cracked down on Little League and amateur adult teams that use Major League nicknames. Because Major League Baseball owns trademark rights in the names of all its teams when they are used in connection with baseball, it can legally require amateur teams using these names to wear only licensed apparel. This can add about $6 to the cost of each uniform.

Trademark licensing increased the marketing opportunities for many companies. Instead of diversifying directly into a new product line, a trademark proprietor could license an existing producer in another industry to manufacture a line of goods under the licensor's trademark. This became very common, for example, between perfume companies and apparel manufacturers. It is now also common between professional sport organisations, and apparel and novelty manufacturers.

The sport organisation must specify the products on which any licensee is permitted to use the trademark, as well as supervise and control the quality of those products. The public will benefit because it will receive a guarantee that the sport organisation stands behind the goods bearing its trademarks. What would happen if Major League Baseball ignored the Little Leaguers' use of its nicknames? Major League Baseball could lose its trademark rights, and that would mean the loss of millions of dollars a year in royalties from its extremely lucrative licensing business.

Professional sport organisations have much to lose if they do not adequately control the use of their trademarks. In addition, it is safe to say that many consumers want to know that the products they buy are both high quality and 'approved'.

Consider the value of the previous licensing contract that the MLB closed on behalf of its 30 teams. During the period 2005–09, the league earned an income of US$500 million (A$525.5 million), derived from its seven licensing partners. This was a 70 per cent increase on the previous deal, and also represented an era of growth for revenues from team merchandise—growth that has been sustained consistently since the 1998 season. The money was mainly generated from sales and royalties generated by seven prime partners: Majestic, Nike, New Era, Drew Pearson International, VF Imagewear, Twins Enterprises and Dynasty Apparel.

Source: Excerpts from Lans (1995: 6); Rovell (2003); Craft (2010).

Building the sporting organisation's licensing program

An operational protocol

Irwin and Stotlar (1993) investigated the operational protocol employed by six major US sporting organisations in their sport licensing programs. The six organisations were Major League Baseball (MLB), the National Football League (NFL), the National Basketball Association (NBA), the National Hockey League (NHL), the National Collegiate Athletic Association (NCAA) and the US Olympic Committee. Table 16.1 shows the different elements of this operational protocol—or, in other words, the activities

TABLE 16.1 Use of elements of an operational protocol for sport licensing programs

Operational element of program	Number of sporting organisations using the element (out of 6)
Program governance and leadership	
Internal licensing authority	5
Full-time principal licensing assignment	5
Direct report to central administrator	5
Licensing policy committee assembled	3
Professional licensing agency assistance	1
Program protection and enforcement	
Legal specialist consultation	6
Majority of logos registered as trademarks	6
Licensee application and screening process	6
Licence issuance and renewal procedures	6
Non-exclusive basic agreement	1
Execution of joint-use agreements	5
Execution of international licences	5
Product sample required for quality control	6
'Licensed product' identification required	6
Counterfeit logo detection procedures	6
Counterfeit logo reduction procedures	6
Program promotions and public relations	
Proactive recruitment of licensees	5
Proactive recruitment of retailers	4
Licensee/retailer public relations program	6
Advertising used to promote products/program	6
Licensing program information published	6
Revenue management	
Advance payment required	6
Uniform royalty charged on all products	2
Written royalty exemption policy	6
Royalty verifications routinely conducted	5
Royalty verifications conducted by specialist	5
Written royalty distribution policy	6

Source: Irwin and Stotlar (1993: 7–16). Reprinted with the permission of the publisher.

that need to be executed in sport licensing programs. The number of organisations (out of six) actually using the listed elements of the protocol are given. Table 16.1 presents a good overview of the operational activities that need to be considered when managing a sport licensing program. Before a sporting organisation can start managing a program, however, it has to be put together.

Key factors

Baghdikian (1996) has developed a model to assist the sport marketer in identifying the key factors (described below) that need to be considered when building a licensing program. The model is presented in Figure 16.1.

Organisational objectives

Like the other marketing tools discussed in this text, licensing should serve the broader purpose of achieving the marketing goals of the organisation, which in turn should

FIGURE 16.1
Building the sporting organisation's licensing program

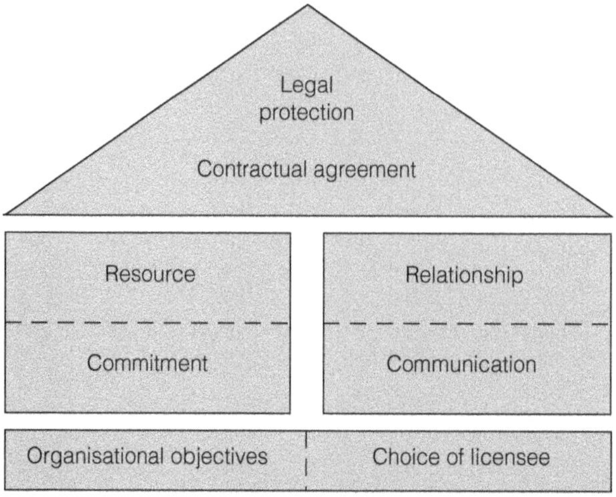

Source: Baghdikian (1996:39). Reprinted with the permission of the publisher.

support the achievement of overall strategic goals. In sport, licensing the organisation's trademark for merchandising purposes often aims to raise funds or to increase brand awareness. If these goals fit the marketing strategy, the organisation can pursue finding a licensee or licensees.

Choice of licensee

In light of the functions of the trademark and the organisational objectives, it is important to find the right licensee. Pertaining to the functions of the trademark, the potential licensee should be capable of satisfying the quality-control standards and should maintain the function of identifying the source of the products. From an organisational perspective, it is important for the sporting organisation to find reputable partners with an ability to deliver quality on time with regular payments.

Commitment

Rather than leaving the work to the licensee and simply 'licensing' it to use the sporting organisation's trademark, the sporting organisation should commit itself to doing the preliminary market research and financial analysis. Baghdikian (1996: 38) states that:

> the San Jose Sharks, during their first season, compiled the worst on-field record in the National Hockey League (NHL). However, due to the organisations spending 13 months on consumer research, and planning a name and design that would create an exciting image in the market, the Sharks outsold all other NHL team-licensed products.

Resource

In investigating sport and collegiate licensing programs, Irwin and Stotlar (1993: 15) conclude that 'with nearly half of all colleges assigning program administrators less than

10% of their time to licensing, the complex administrative tasks associated with a licensing program cannot effectively be addressed'. Although the resources invested in managing a sport licensing program might be high, the resulting benefits are likely to be proportionately higher than the investment.

Communication

Although the licensing agreement (including contractual agreements) should serve as the basis for business communication, regular and open channels of communication should be established. A clear understanding of both parties' goals, the early detection of problems and effective quality control are the results of open and frequent communication between licensor and licensee.

Relationship

The more formal business communication described above can be complemented by more informal communication (for example, between the two chief executive officers). An afternoon on the golf course with the aim of fostering personal relationships has often proved vital to the maintenance of business relationships.

Contractual agreement

The contract represents the written agreement that both licensor and licensee are legally obliged to fulfil. Examples of areas suggested by Sherman (1991) to be included in a contract were listed earlier in this chapter. The contract is the agreement to which the licensor and licensee can turn when they feel that one or the other party is not fulfilling the requirements of the agreement.

Legal protection

In Chapter 14, ambush marketing was described as a business marketing its goods or services in a way that suggests the business has a connection with a team, event or a competition where there is in fact no connection. The practice of ambush marketing is of particular interest when considering the power of trademarks. Without the law and legal advisers, the sporting organisation has little to protect it from organisations ambushing its trademarks and other properties. The specialised nature of licensing in general, contracts, interpretations of law and the management of licensing programs requires the support and advice of legally qualified experts. For example, the Nick Faldo Golf Company entered into a partnership with sports brand and business development consultancy WSM, which policed the licensing of his name (Gillis, 2002a). Figure 16.1 illustrates this by picturing legal protection as the 'roof' of the program.

Issues that can arise

The second part of this chapter has first provided a range of activities to be executed by sport licensing program managers, and then looked at the different steps that need to be taken when building the organisation's licensing program. Before we discuss branding in the context of the sport licensing process, Sportview 16.3 gives an insight into current issues related to building a sport licensing program.

SPORTVIEW 16.3

Using the established brand to build others

Although the market for licensed merchandise has experienced some difficult times, especially in the United States, the prospects for the future are bright—under the right conditions. Partly due to the experience of the last NBA lockout in 1997–98—where licensed merchandise sales dropped dramatically—key licensees of the NBA, such as Adidas, were rightfully concerned at the prospect of history repeating itself in the 2011 NBA lockout. Despite sixteen fewer games in the season, licensed merchandising increased—the opposite to what occurred in the previous lockout. Growth in the amount and value of licensed merchandise was mainly driven by three factors that were not as prevalent a decade earlier: online sales, globalisation and the performance of big-market teams. According to Sal LaRocca, the NBA's executive vice president of global merchandising, online sales of the newly formed 'Brooklyn Nets' increased an astounding 3034 per cent, the 'Jeremy Lin' phenomenon at the New York Knicks peaked consumer interest in China and commercially important big-market teams such as Chicago, New York, Oklahoma and Miami had strong regular season performances. In summarising the season, LaRocca said: 'We were using 1999 [the date of the prior NBA lockout] as a benchmark for re-entry . . . but I'm happy to say it was not an accurate benchmark.' (Lefton, 2012)

The Copyright Promotions Group (CPG), in its association with the 1999 World Cup Cricket event in England, is a good example of licensing in the context of a one-off event. Of the five product categories—apparel, toys and gifts, publishing, fast-moving consumer goods and promotions—60 per cent of revenue came from the apparel product category. The success of the CPG's licensing programs was based on its integral involvement in discussions that ranged from television rights to on-site sales of produce. This allowed the group to come up with the best licensing strategies that not only protected and leveraged the rights of (often exclusive) licensees, but provided the best possible value and return for the licensor as well. Even when fans are not able to attend the event or purchase memorabilia from event-specific merchandise stores, online shopping allows them to 'be part of the event' by ordering merchandise unique to the event (Westerbeek and Smith, 2003).

With the opportunities represented by the internet, online sales of licensed merchandise are now receiving a welcome boost. In particular, the market for soccer merchandise remains potentially very lucrative. Sales in relation to the Japan/South Korea World Cup generated in excess of US$1.5 billion (A$1.58 billion), some 20 per cent up from France 1998. The global opportunity presented to clubs such as Italian powerbrokers Juventus and Premier League giants Manchester United are there for the taking. Twenty per cent of the hits on the Juventus website are from Asia. The Asian opportunity consists of a potential two billion-person marketplace. The 'red devils' signed a new merchandising and licensing deal with Japan Sports Vision (JSV), the official World Cup distributor for Japan. JSV is a major client of Nike, and Nike in turn has signed a thirteen-year deal with Manchester United, reported to be worth US$427 million (A$448.8 million), to become an official sponsor and the official merchandise partner of the club. By the way, Nike and its swoosh—as a strong yet vulnerable brand (and symbol) in its own right—have taken the:

> unprecedented step of releasing a detailed report on its child labour policy. Its *Corporate Responsibility Report* offers an open assessment of the lobbyists' claims and details other ethical issues such as the effect of its activities on the environment and the company's involvement in local communities. Conscious of the impact even an isolated case can have on the image of the Nike brand—a commodity that has taken tens of millions of pounds to position. (Clarke, 2002: 26)

During the last decade of the twentieth century, European soccer clubs handled most of their licensing programs in-house. Because the scope of merchandising operations was mostly domestic, many clubs felt that spending scarce resources on an outside licensing agency could not be justified. However, this attitude is changing rapidly. In order to maximise profiting from the club's brand equity, more and more clubs are selecting licensing agents. Chris Protheroe, director of the Copyright Promotions Licensing Group, argues that 'if they keep their merchandising rights in-house they avoid paying agency commission but they will naturally incur overheads of manpower, design, legal advice and accounting expenses' (Wallace, 2002: 31). However, Edward Friedman of Zone Marketing thinks differently. He argues that 'licensing firms will never do as good a job as you can do yourself. A firm like Levi's, for example, wouldn't just hand everything over so why should football clubs? . . . You become only as good as the people who look after you.' (Wallace, 2002: 32)

However, the powerful governing body for European football, UEFA, still feels that more benefits can be derived by appointing an outside agency. UEFA commenced a long-term licensing deal with Warner Bros Consumer Products (WBCP) in 2010, with WBCP appointed as UEFA's exclusive worldwide licensing representative. Included in the deal are the European Football Championship 2012, UEFA's under-21 championships in 2011 and 2013, and the UEFA's Women's European Championship in 2013. Pilar Zulueta, senior vice president at WBCP, argues that, in the ongoing relationship with UEFA:

> It is our intention to bring football fans wherever they are a collection of official licensed products that is broad, creative, compelling and innovative in many aspects. We will look at selecting licensees and official retailers who are able to help deliver this. (UEFA, 2010).

Branding

The branding process

Chernatony and McDonald (1992: 18) define a successful brand as:

> an identifiable product, service, person or place augmented in such a way that the buyer or user perceives relevant unique added values which match their needs most closely. Furthermore its success results from being able to sustain these added values in the face of competition.

We can all associate with the practical application of the brand concept. Powerful brands are immediately associated with the product or service they represent. Coca-Cola is a soft drink, McDonald's sells hamburgers, Manchester United deals with soccer and the

Daytona 500 is about car racing. A brand represents the combination of the core product and the perceptions that consumers have about the product and its unique added values. Figure 16.2(a) shows what distinguishes a brand from the core product. In Figure 16.2(b), this is applied to a sport example.

Developing successful brands is important for organisations, because the brand can be used as a means to communicate with consumers. Branding, as the process of developing and sustaining successful brands, has strategic relevance for the marketing function. In other words, the full marketing mix is used in the strategic branding process. The marketer tries to position the brand 'in the mind' of the consumer. Consumers start perceiving the brand as the symbolic total of the packaging, design, recall advertising,

FIGURE 16.2 Conceptual models of brand

(a) **Brand = core product + perceived product**

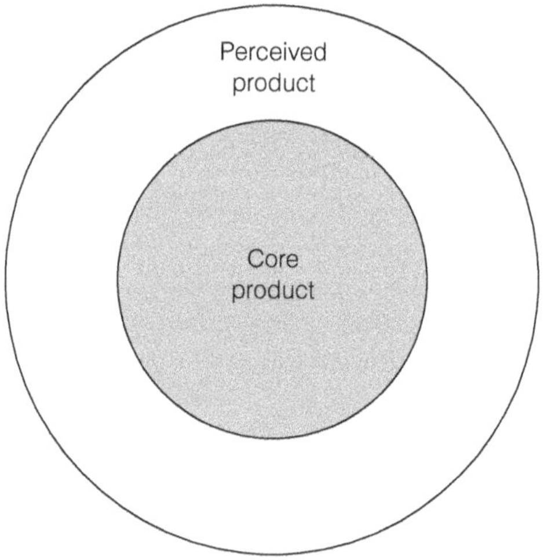

(b) **A sport brand**

quality of product, price paid, and store or outlet where the product can be bought. This total brand perception enables the marketer to link mental visions to the organisation's branded products—expressing, for example, a lifestyle, a personality or a feeling. Powerful brands differentiate themselves from similar products of competitors, and provide the opportunity to build long-term relationships with consumers, developing brand-loyal buyers. Brand equity, according to Gladden, Milne and Sutton (1998), is the combined tangible and intangible value of the brand, and can be broken down into four constituents: perceived quality (of the brand); brand awareness (recall, recognition); brand associations (in sport, often emotionally loaded); and brand loyalty (the ability of the brand to retain customers). In the sport industry, the antecedents to brand equity are team related (for example, success, star players), organisation related (such as reputation and tradition, overall entertainment package, service reputation) and market related (for instance, media coverage and reach, competitive forces).

Table 16.2 describes eight different ways of using a brand in practice. Irrespective of which usage is chosen from this list, adding value—as perceived by the consumer—is the critical activity in the branding process. The marketer can use the brand as a symbol of, for example, prestige, status, lifestyle or personality, and can position the symbol in such a way that it expresses physical and psychological comfort to the target market.

If the sport marketer chooses to build the registered trademark into a brand, licensing in many ways can assist in achieving branding objectives.

Branding and licensing

In the first part of this chapter, the relationship between the trademark of an organisation and the licensing process was explained. Trademark licensing, as an arrangement by which one party consents to the use of its trademark in accordance with specified terms and conditions, makes sense only if the trademark is in any way valuable to the potential licensee. The trademark can have value as an established brand, making it a powerful means of communication. If the trademark has the potential value of becoming an established brand, it has future earning power, making it an interesting investment.

TABLE 16.2 Different ways of using a brand in practice

Usage of brand	Why use it in that way
Brand as a sign of ownership	Buyer knows which organisation produced the product
Brand as a differentiating device	Buyer knows the product is different from comparable products
Brand as a functional device	Buyer knows why and how to use the product
Brand as a symbolic device	Brand communicates something about the buyer
Brand as a risk reducer	Brand communicates trust about the producer of the product
Brand as a shorthand device	Brand is a means to recall sufficient brand information from memory at a later purchasing time
Brand as a legal device	Trademark registration is legal protection from counterfeit production
Brand as a strategic device	Brand positioning is a means of ensuring a long-term future for the organisation

Source: Adjusted from Chernatony and McDonald (1992).

Sporting organisations can capitalise on this potential value by using other organisations to raise their own brand awareness.

The potential power of sport brands

In Chapter 13, we discussed the advantages of sport sponsorship. These advantages also explain why sport brands, or sport trademarks, are potentially powerful tools to add value. The advantages explaining the potential power of sport brands may be summarised as follows:

- Sport consumers tend to identify themselves personally with the sport, which creates opportunities for increasing brand loyalty in products linked to the sport.
- Sport evokes personal attachment, and with this the licensee can be linked to the excitement, energy and emotion of the sporting contest. In other words, sport has the potential to deliver a clear message.
- Sport has universal appeal and pervades all elements of life (geographically, demographically and socio-culturally). This characteristic presents the opportunity to cross difficult cultural and language borders in communication, enabling the licensee to talk to a global mass audience.
- The variety of sports available makes it possible to create distinct market segments with which to communicate separately.
- The universal appeal and high interest that sport has in society give sport high media exposure, resulting in free publicity. Free publicity can make a licensing deal very cost-effective.
- Because of the clear linkage of the licensee to the sporting organisation's trademark, the relationship stands out from the clutter—as opposed to advertising, in which people are bombarded with hundreds of 'sender unknown' messages each day.

The top four sports brands according to *Forbes* (2012b) are:

- athlete—Tiger Woods: US$38 million
- team—New York Yankees: US$363 million
- sport business—Nike: US$15.9 billion
- sport event—Super Bowl: US$470 million.

Earlier, this chapter presented some examples of how organisations use licensing and for which purposes. These purposes are repeated here in the context of the sport industry.

Using the sport brand to add value

Adding value, as the most important activity of creating powerful brands, can be done in many ways. It has been explained that branding is a strategic effort in that the marketer should use the whole marketing mix to build the brand. Using an established trademark or brand to add value to another brand is one means of applying the marketing mix. The Olympic sponsors are licensed to link the Olympic rings to their products. A variety of consumer goods licensees (e.g. Caltex, Sony, Qantas, Toyota) are licensed to use the AFL logo on their products. The potential licensees of Ian Thorpe's name in the headline story use the brand equity he has built over the years to add value to already existing brands or general products. The earlier mentioned Daytona 500 brand, according to

Forbes (Janoff, 2007), was the world's fourth most valuable sports event, with US$91 million in TV rights, sponsorships, ticket sales and licensing in 2007. The Super Bowl (US$379 million), the Olympics (US$176 million) and the FIFA World Cup (US$103 million) are numbers one to three. In 2008, the Daytona 500 celebrated its 50th anniversary. This sport event, in a unique partnership with supermarkets owned by the Kroger company, has collected over US$100 million in licensing income through selling the 50th anniversary logo in product exclusive categories to companies like Kellogg's, Unilever, ConAgra, General Mills, Nabisco and PepsiCo. The Retail Sports Marketing Company coordinated the marketing campaign among Kroger stores, NASCAR, the International Speedway Corporation (which owns the Daytona 500 track) and the marketers from the nearly 50 products that were branded with the 50th race logo. In-store promotions included point-of-purchase displays, circulars, in-store television ads, radio commercials, a dedicated website, in-store appearances by NASCAR drivers and NASCAR-Daytona 500 displays.

This example clearly shows what the added value is of using a highly regarded and popular sport brand on other products. It fulfils one of the following purposes:

- to sell in new products using the established brand/trademark
- to sell in new markets using the established brand/trademark
- to boost sales using the established brand/trademark, or
- to reinforce a particular image using the established brand/trademark.

The major aim of the sporting organisation in this process is to use its established brand/trademark to raise funds for the organisation. An extra bonus is the widespread attention given to its brand name through the promotional efforts of licensees. This is why careful selection of licensees is important, because the established sport brand should not be associated with a wrong or inferior product or organisation.

The branding process in a sporting organisation can be enhanced by using licensing as a means of raising brand awareness.

Using licensing to add value to the sport brand

If the sport brand is not established yet, but careful preparation and commitment have been put into preparing an appropriate and attractive brand name and symbols, licensing can be used as one way of informing consumers about the brand. The San Jose Sharks, used as an example earlier, increased their brand awareness and raised funds by offering a potentially profitable trademark to a selection of merchandise licensees. Using the marketing mix elements to integrate pricing, distribution and promotion of the merchandise, they successfully established the San Jose Sharks brand.

More specifically, licensing is used to license the unknown trademark to build brand/trademark awareness and raise funds.

The previous examples have shown that licensing plays a vital role in adding value to the licensor's, licensee's or both organisations' brands. The realisation that brands/trademarks are successful only if they add value to the product or the organisation, as perceived by the consumer, highlights the strategic importance of branding. Powerful brands can be developed only if the organisation views the branding process as integral to the marketing function, using all marketing mix elements to build powerful brands.

Summary

This chapter discussed the licensing of the sporting organisation's intellectual property (name and/or logo registered in a trademark) to a third party. It was shown that promotional licensing in the sport industry basically serves two purposes: promotion of the sporting organisation; and promotion of a third party or its products through use of the sporting organisation's name or logo. In the latter case, the major benefit derived by the sporting organisation is a royalty fee, often calculated as a percentage of sales of licensed products.

The importance of registering a trademark was shown by discussing the different functions of the trademark. Registration of the trademark is always important, because trademarks can become valuable organisational assets—namely brands. Through careful management, trademarks linked to products can be built into powerful brands. This was discussed in the last part of this chapter. A powerful sport brand is a valuable organisational asset because it has the power to represent multiple consumer perceptions. Consumers perceive a brand as a symbolic total of the organisation's product—in sport's case, the excitement, speed and action orientation of the core product and its star players. Sport brands therefore are capable of linking powerful messages to other products through licensing.

The second part of the chapter discussed the process of building a sporting organisation's licensing program. This process was summarised in Baghdikian's (1996) model, but three issues were highlighted as being of particular importance. Operational activities in managing the program were presented, the minimum contents of a licensing agreement (as identified by Sherman, 1991) were briefly summarised, and the importance of legal support and protection was emphasised. Promotional licensing is an expanding area in sport marketing, and offers many sporting organisations potential for future income or growth—especially in the rapidly developing global sport marketplace.

CASE STUDY

Setting up a sporting organisation's licensing program

[This case study was originally written by Eddie Baghdikian and is purely fictional. The organisations and persons in the case are non-existent.]

In June 2002, Juan Garcia, director of hockey development at the South American Hockey Federation (SAHF), was approached by ALEGG Interdomestic Pty Ltd with a proposal promising to generate substantial revenue for the SAHF with no financial outlay required. ALEGG was proposing a licensing agreement by which the SAHF logo would be used to brand a wide variety of merchandise, and these products would be marketed to SAHF members.

The role of the SAHF, as the central administrative body, is to manage, coordinate and unify the diverse facets of the sport of hockey in South America. This includes overseeing the development of grassroots programs, managing competitions and tournaments, and promoting hockey at all levels. As the representative body of all affiliated clubs and associations throughout South America, the SAHF ensures the commercial viability of hockey and seeks out and encourages sponsorship for hockey events on a national level. The core product of the SAHF is essentially the development of the game of hockey. Until the approach by ALEGG, the SAHF had never undertaken any product-extension strategies. ALEGG's proposal to enter into a licensing arrangement with the SAHF promised to develop and market a range of hockey merchandise and accessories aimed at SAHF members.

ALEGG was formed in late 2001 for the purpose of entering into licensing agreements with organisations such as the World Soccer Federation (FIFA) and other sporting bodies. Between them, its two directors and its South American general manager boasted more than 30 years' knowledge in the areas of manufacturing, importing, wholesaling, retailing and marketing in a very wide range of consumer items.

At the time of the approach to the SAHF, ALEGG informed Juan Garcia that, as of February 2002, the company had entered into a merchandise licensing agreement with FIFA. Juan did not believe that there was much of a market for SAHF-logoed products. He felt that there was no particular attraction or brand equity in the registered trademark of the organisation. However, with no financial outlay required, Juan also felt that he had nothing to lose if ALEGG thought that it could make the idea work.

The concept of a licensing program that to Juan represented no risk and no responsibility held considerable appeal, and so he and the SAHF ventured into the world of licensing.

The basis for the relationship

The negotiations began. Over the next four months, the SAHF and ALEGG discussed the basis for the relationship that would ultimately lead to drafting the licensing agreement.

ALEGG would develop a range of SAHF merchandise known as the SAHF Members' Collection. The range of licensed products would be entirely up to the SAHF. ALEGG would source the selected product line through its 'worldwide' manufacturing and supplier network, which was concentrated predominantly in the Southeast Asia region. All sourced products would be 'branded' as well as displaying the SAHF name and logo. The list of products included tracksuits, pens, key rings, cufflinks, playing cards, calendar posters, diaries, umbrellas, t-shirts, sports bags, calculators and hats.

ALEGG would primarily be responsible for the promotion and distribution of all agreed merchandise, including a SAHF Members' Collection brochure and other advertising material such as posters for all clubhouses. Coinciding with the marketing campaign, ALEGG would also have the entire range of goods made available at all major South American hockey competitions, and have a salesperson to service this area. The SAHF would not be responsible for holding and purchasing stock.

The SAHF agreed to assist in the promotion of the merchandise through:

- *South American Hockey News* (communications newsletter for members)
- advertising
- exposure at all SAHF events
- regular mailouts to all clubs
- a list of club secretaries to be provided to ALEGG, and
- mutually agreed general promotions.

So far, the negotiations for the SAHF's first licensing program were going along well.

Estimating the projected income from the marketing program was not as important to Juan as the ability to make money out of something requiring no financial expenditure and with a minimal amount of resources required. In addition, the program would lift the profile of the organisation in the marketplace through the promotion of the SAHF name and logo. These were the broad objectives Juan set for the licensing program. In ALEGG's final proposal, Juan was also told that anticipated income figures in the first formative year would be exceeded significantly in subsequent years, as the promotion programs gained momentum and the SAHF name and logo grew in recognition.

The licensing agreement

The 'exclusive licensing/marketing/manufacturing agreement' between the SAHF and ALEGG was drafted and arrived on Juan's desk. From this time onwards, the normal printed ALEGG letterhead was no longer used and communications were now with ALEGG's international marketing director and not the SAHF's usual ALEGG contact, the South American general manager—who seemed to have vanished.

ALEGG was to become the sole and exclusive producer, manufacturer, wholesaler and marketing representative of the SAHF. The agreement stated that the appointment of ALEGG was verbally formalised and agreed to on Thursday, 8 October 2002 in order to permit ALEGG to incur expenditure in time and money to set up the logistical, administrative and initial manufacturing and marketing requirements of the project. However, the three-year term of the agreement was to officially start on 1 January 2003, with a three-year option commencing on 1 January 2006, the three-year option being automatically renewable except for either party cancelling the agreement.

Cancellation of the agreement could be done only during the 30-day period in the month prior to the expiration of any three-year term of the agreement by giving eighteen months' notice in writing. Alternatively, cancellation could be effected, by the SAHF only, during the 30-day period in the month prior to the expiration of any three-year term of the agreement by giving 90 days' notice in writing and purchasing and paying the freight-on-board (FOB) price for all goods and/or services and/or work in stock and/or in progress for and on behalf of ALEGG in relation to ALEGG fulfilling its obligations and undertakings as part of the agreement. Payment then would have to be made prior to the expiration of the 90-day notice period. In fact, whether or not the SAHF or ALEGG breached any of the conditions of the contract and cancelled, the SAHF would still be obliged to pay the FOB price under the terms of the agreement.

Juan pondered this legal document. He did not like it in its present state. Even with his non-legal background and inexperience with licensing programs, he figured that there was no 'out' clause without a substantial penalty to pay. He read on that ALEGG would pay the SAHF a licensing fee equal to 15 per cent of the manufactured cost, paid at the end of each calendar month. ALEGG would also conduct the reconciliation and monitoring of all royalty payments.

Although there was the issue of the termination terms and conditions to resolve, the SAHF still thought that there was some scope for the program to work. Consequently, ALEGG was encouraged by the SAHF to review the contract and keep working with the SAHF, even though an agreement was never signed.

Disjointed proceedings

The SAHF did not hear directly from ALEGG for some time. During the period up to May 2003, Juan heard that ALEGG had only made a few approaches at different SAHF-affiliated clubs. At this point, Juan started to believe that the project had basically ended.

It was at this juncture that the SAHF changed its trading name to Hockey South America and embraced a new corporate logo. With the proliferation of initialled identities in the business world, the use of 'SAHF' was continuously being confused. The decision to adopt this new identity also brought the organisation in line with Hockey International, the controlling hockey body at the international level. Hockey South America, realising the importance of the role of marketing to its organisation and in line with the identity change, appointed a marketing and media officer in April 2003. This position, which reported to Juan, had as its primary objective the task of lifting the profile of the sport through the media and business world. Juan, who now was the director of development and marketing, decided to inform ALEGG of the changes.

On receiving the news, ALEGG advised Juan that it had more than US$400 000 of SAHF-logoed goods on order and approaching delivery, and further advised that the SAHF should consider not changing its name until 2004 to allow a stock rundown without financial loss to all parties concerned. In the same communication, ALEGG conveyed that in the last few months it had been gearing for sales, through the 2931 affiliated clubs, to the 1.1 million SAHF members.

The situation did not improve. The SAHF name change went ahead, and ALEGG kept struggling for credibility—without success. Juan rang FIFA to gauge the progress of FIFA's licensing agreement with ALEGG. He was told that FIFA was wanting to get out of the agreement. In September 2003, Juan wanted out too. The last twelve months spent in attempting to develop a suitable merchandising relationship with ALEGG was sufficient time. Juan did not see evidence of any prospect for progress, now or in the future. Hockey South America informed ALEGG in writing that it wished to terminate the proposed agreement and would deal with ALEGG only on a non-exclusive basis, as required by Hockey South America, the exclusive nature of the agreement also being part of the reason to terminate.

ALEGG had other ideas. It wanted to continue with the exclusive manufacturing and marketing licensing arrangement. It was committed to the three-year agreement with SAHF/Hockey South America. The subsequent meetings with ALEGG worried Juan. Present at these meetings was a person taking the minutes in shorthand. Anticipating the worst from an agreement that was not actually signed, and with no in-house expertise on these types of contracts, Juan sought legal advice.

In the meantime, ALEGG argued that the SAHF proposed to change its name to Hockey South America in or around July 2003, with little or no prior notice given. As a result, more capital investment and greater time allowance were now required. ALEGG also debated that it had outlaid in excess of $1.2 million in time and money, all with a view to completing at least the first three years of the program, with an intention to ensure success so that the relationship would go beyond this initial three-year period.

ALEGG was determined to represent itself as a dedicated organisation with the right intentions to implement the letter of agreement, and to represent SAHF/Hockey South America as the main cause of the current state of the project through its lack of cooperation, commitment and communication. Nevertheless, ALEGG continued to have dialogue with Hockey South America on the 'new' line of merchandise and the 'new' 2003–04 catalogue/brochure incorporating the Hockey South America logo. ALEGG also discussed new club member updates and marketing strategy, and looked forward to receiving Hockey South America's positive response and full support.

Essentially, the response from the solicitors advised Juan to adopt a 'wait and see' posture—meaning to await further approaches from ALEGG—hoping that, as a result of the lack of enthusiasm and support from Juan, the relationship would simply wither away. The solicitors also pointed out, however, that although Juan had not signed the proposed agreement with ALEGG, there could be an enforceable agreement based on negotiations and part-performance of the agreement.

Source: Written by E. Baghdikian and not previously published. Printed with the permission of the author.

Questions

1 What are the risks and rewards to an organisation of licensing its brands?
2 How well does the strategy of product extension, through licensing, fit the corporate objectives of the SAHF?
3 Identify the reasons why the licensing agreement between the SAHF and ALEGG failed.
4 What factors should Juan Garcia have considered in making his decision on whether or not to enter into the licensing agreement?
5 Juan felt that the SAHF logo had no inherent appeal or value. On what criteria should the marketer judge the equity in a brand and its suitability for licensing?

Part IV

Strategy implementation, evaluation and adjustment

Stage 1—Identification of marketing opportunities

▼

Stage 2—Strategy determination

▼

Stage 3—Strategy implemention, evaluation and adjustment

Step 7—Implement and coordinate marketing and service mix

Step 8—Coordinate marketing function (feedback, evaluation)

17

Coordinating and controlling marketing strategy

CHAPTER OBJECTIVES

This chapter summarises the important concepts introduced throughout this book. It does so by reviewing the role of the control function in coordinating and implementing the selected marketing strategies. Three forms of control are introduced—feed-forward, concurrent and feedback—and their role is discussed in relation to the key measures used to determine the success of the sport-marketing program. A short section reviewing careers in sport marketing is also included.

After studying this chapter, you should be able to:

- understand the importance of control in the marketing function
- identify the three types of control
- identify the primary measures of success
- comprehend the relationship between measures of success and the control process
- recognise the importance of coordinating and implementing marketing strategies
- identify possible career options in sport marketing.

HEADLINE STORY

Local Rugby League Registration and Fun Day

The Canberra Raiders have further strengthened their commitment to grassroots rugby league in the ACT region by throwing their support behind an exciting new initiative aimed at increasing the games registration numbers in the capital's centenary year. The Raiders, in conjunction with the Canberra Region Rugby League (CRRL) will host the Sportenary Local Rugby League Registration and Fun Day on Saturday, 2 February, at Northbourne Oval in Braddon, from 9.00 a.m. to noon. The Raiders' NRL squad (with the exception of the club's All Star representatives), will be in attendance in a bid to boost local Rugby League numbers to their highest levels yet. There will be stalls from eleven of Canberra's junior Rugby League clubs, with Raiders players to be stationed at each stall. In addition to registering junior players, there will also be a registration tent for any aspiring referees, to help boost numbers in the area of match officiating. There will be a carnival-type atmosphere on the day, with activities including a jumping castle, giant slide, pass-the-ball and Wii competitions with specially tailored skills sessions for any girls aged between twelve and fourteen who might be interested in playing. The first 50 players registered at each club will receive a special Raiders show bag (Canberra Raiders, 2013).

The Raiders' need to build community presence brings us to the last theme of this book: coordinating and implementing marketing strategies. The book has considered the marketing mix, and thus all the variables the sport marketer can manipulate to ensure that a sport is able to identify and sustain a competitive advantage. The Raiders' decision to strengthen their commitment to grassroots Rugby League in their region is an example of a range of marketing and promotion mix variables combining to form a marketing strategy. How these strategies are implemented is part of the management aspect of marketing.

This chapter reviews the range of functions necessary to implement strategies. It examines some of the control mechanisms available to the marketer to ensure that performance targets are met, and considers some of the more relevant measures used to gauge success in sport. Inherent in these measures is the question of game design and its contribution to the marketing process. Also, the place and importance of sponsorship are discussed in the context of overall strategy determination. Finally, the chapter revisits the question of sport-marketing planning, noting the importance of integrating all the components of the marketing mix in one overall strategy. Given that the strategy-determination process is the job of the sport marketer, it is important to review this role in sporting organisations. As part of this analysis, careers in sport marketing will be examined.

Controlling the sport marketing function

Boyd, Walker and Larréché (1998: 487) note that the control process 'consists essentially of setting standards, specifying and obtaining feedback data, evaluating it, and taking corrective action'. Setting standards is part of the marketing planning process discussed in Chapter 2. Marketing objectives established during this process will have identified the standards to be achieved. In sporting organisations, these objectives and standards differ from those of organisations solely concerned with profit and providing dividends to shareholders.

Sport is unique in this regard as there are often broader goals than simply maximising profits, as was discussed in Chapter 6. For example, in the dispute between the Australian Rugby League (ARL) and Superleague, the judge noted that the ARL board was 'motivated in large part by considerations other than the pursuit of profit. It is concerned with the preservation and enhancement of the traditions of the game.' (Burchett, 1996: 65)

Recognition of these broader considerations does not in any way lessen the importance of marketing to sport. In fact, the reality is quite the opposite, as sport—like most non-profit entities—often does not have access to financial resources to the same extent as for-profit entities. Sporting organisations rely on the ability of marketing programs to raise the revenue required to run the club, association or league. Several consistent themes have emerged during this book, which allude to the main measures of success in sporting organisations. Most of them are directly aligned with elements of the marketing mix. Establishing and benchmarking performance standards represent the first step towards controlling the marketing program.

Types of control

There are three types of organisational control:

- feed-forward
- concurrent, and
- feedback.

Feed-forward control takes place before production and operations begin, and commences during the strategic sport-marketing planning process (SSMPP). Determining the operating procedures and setting standards for the operation of a facility prior to a season commencing are examples of feed-forward control. As part of this review of operational procedures, appropriate staff training will be provided consistent with service-quality policies. This form of control ensures all inputs are of the highest quality for optimum spectator enjoyment.

Concurrent control occurs during the sporting fixture—in other words, while the plans are being carried out. Often in sport, this will be a major event or the weekly fixtures in a season. In the sport facility, monitoring the quality of service delivery exemplifies concurrent control. Supervisors will be responsible for checking that staff carry out their jobs in a manner consistent with the organisation's policy. In some cases, it is possible to fine-tune the activity as it occurs or to rectify problems immediately, which is an example of concurrent control. Concurrent control can also occur during a major event or a season when monitoring attendances. If these are lower than expected, advertising may need to be intensified or altered, or sales promotions implemented to return the organisation to a satisfactory level of performance. Determining acceptable levels of performance requires the identification of appropriate measures during the strategic sport-marketing planning process.

Feedback control focuses on the final performance measured against previously ordained standards or targets. As a consequence of this feedback, the marketing plan

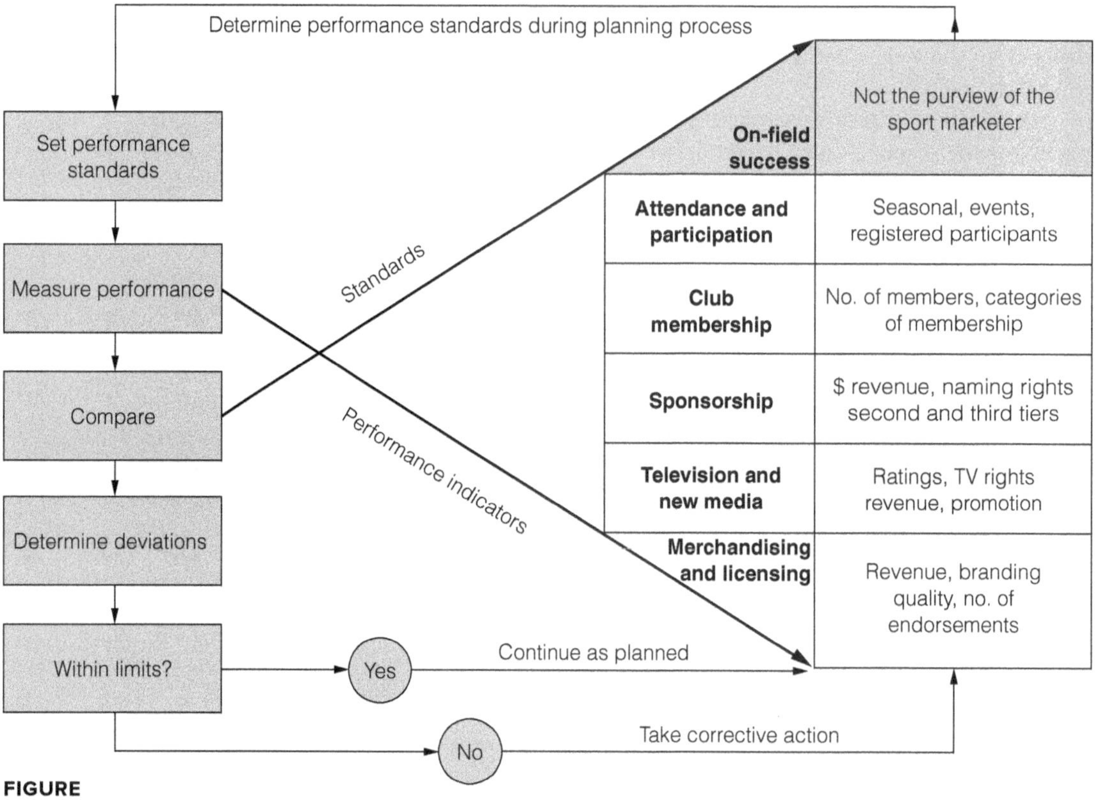

FIGURE 17.1
The control process and measures of success

can be reviewed and modified where necessary to ensure that the defined performance standards can be achieved during the next season or event.

Figure 17.1 displays the link between the stages of the control process and the measures typically used to ascertain success in a sporting organisation.

Measures of success

On-field success

On-field success is typically the most obvious and visible measure of success by which to assess the performance of sporting organisations. It is, however—as indicated in Chapter 1—an area over which the sport marketer has little control. Unlike most products, where the marketer has some input into design and packaging, the sport marketer has no control over the quality of the team selected. The selection and development of players are not the purview of the sport marketer. The sport marketer, however, is responsible for promoting the team based on its quality and its star athletes. Elements of this marketing effort will be seen in ticketing and games promotions, advertising, public relations and sponsorship strategies, all discussed in earlier chapters.

It has been stressed in this book that the sport marketer needs to ensure that over-promising is not a feature of the promotion mix. It could be argued, for example, that the head coach of the Australian swimming team at the 1996 Olympic Games over-promised in relation to the success of his athletes. Ultimately, the Australian swimming team performed well, but expectations were so high that the actual performance (in terms of medals) was seen to be relatively poor. What could have been a perfect situation on which to build future marketing strategies turned into an exercise in managing negative public relations.

On-field success, then, is an organisation-wide measure not specific to the efforts of marketing personnel. The derivatives of on-field or off-field success, however, are the purview of the sport marketer. These are now discussed.

Attendance and participation

Attendance and participation are two key measures of marketing performance. They are linked, as elite athletes serve as role models for those participating at lower levels of sporting competition. Known previously in Australia as the 'Norman factor', or globally as the 'Tiger Woods' factor, the effect that Tiger Woods has on golf participation and attendance when he visits to play in major golf tournaments is undisputed. Typically, attendances at the event and interest in golf both rise. Increased participation in a sport has the added benefit of contributing to increased attendances, as people's affinity with a sport grows with participation and they are therefore more likely to watch it—either live or on television.

Sporting organisations are therefore concerned with boosting the numbers of registered participants. Strategies designed to ensure participation have been discussed in this book. The introduction of modified rules for juniors has been the main strategy designed to attract juniors to play sport. These modified rules programs become integral parts of marketing strategy as all sports strive to capture a finite group of participants. Registration numbers are important measures of success, in particular of the success of marketing programs.

Attendance is another frequently cited measure of success for an association, club or league. Elements of the promotion mix, pricing policies, service quality and facility management have been important factors discussed in this book, contributing to the likely success of maximising attendances.

Club membership

Club membership, too, is an important measure. As discussed in Chapter 9, club members represent heavy attendance on the frequency attendance escalator, and are thus a significant source of revenue. More importantly, this revenue often comes well before the season, providing much-needed income during a period when no games are conducted to generate weekly revenues. Chapter 9 also highlighted the importance of ensuring loyalty for long-term members. Marketing programs should be designed to reward longevity and minimise defection—or season ticket-holders 'falling off' the frequency attendance escalator.

Sponsorship

Sponsorship is another key measure of success in the marketing program. In fact, sponsorship has been considered so important that many sports have developed unidimensional marketing programs aimed at attracting sponsorship revenue. In the long term, this myopic view is detrimental to the sporting organisation for two reasons:

- It negates the extent to which the sporting organisation can devise a full range of marketing-related benefits that can be provided to the sponsor.
- It concentrates the success of the marketing program on one objective.

Concentration on any one objective is potentially poor strategy. Sporting organisations need to diversify their range of marketing strategies to ensure that there is not an overreliance on any one area. For example, if sponsorship income falls well below anticipated projections, the overall success of the organisation will be threatened because no effort has been made to raise revenues by ensuring attendance, attracting members and selling merchandise. As Chapters 13 and 14 noted, sponsorship myopia is caused by the capacity of sport to attract sponsors seeking a relatively inexpensive way to promote their products. As some sporting organisations have the capacity to fulfil sponsor objectives easily, this adds to the potential to concentrate solely on sponsorship income at the expense of developing a broad-based marketing program, incorporating all elements of the marketing mix.

Television and new media

The importance of television to the marketing effort has been stressed throughout this book. Television has the capacity to provide significant streams of revenue, as well as to act as an important promotion vehicle for sports—even if no television revenue is forthcoming. Therefore, television as a measure of success is very important.

Sport marketers must carefully determine the role of television in their marketing plans. Questions to be answered in relation to setting marketing objectives include: Is the sport capable of attracting television rights revenue? If so, how much? If not, can some coverage be obtained to help promote the sport? Answers to these questions determine the marketing objectives set in relation to television, and thus the measures used to assess performance. Chapter 11 conveyed in detail the range of measures used to assess the success of sport programming and the subsequent advertising revenue that these programs can attract. Successful sport marketers need to have an intimate knowledge of how the television business operates to ensure that television revenues or promotions are successfully implemented in the overall marketing strategy.

Television's impact on sport is an important strategic issue for sport marketers. To what extent are sports required to modify their game to make it more attractive to television? Although the need to appease television can be a potential problem, in some instances it has also forced sports to modernise, and therefore present a more attractive product. Cricket, as discussed in this book, has been better off for the World Series Cricket revolution in 1977. The introduction of the one-day game, with a variety of new rules better suited to television, has brought an added dimension to playing standards through improved fielding, more creative batting and an array of tactics not seen previously. Twenty20 cricket is the latest form of the game to capture the imagination of spectators and television networks. It is not the purpose of this book to take one view as to whether television's impact on sport in relation to changing the game is either good or bad. Clearly, there are examples of such changes benefiting sport and others working to its detriment. This is an important issue and, rather than adopt an extreme position either way, sport marketers should carefully think through the implications of change. The sport marketer should conduct research, consult past and current players, and trial changes in just the way marketers do when preparing to introduce new products.

Chapter 12 introduced two other important elements of revenue-raising, promotion and communicating with sports fans. New media, or the digitisation of media based on rapidly advancing technologies, represent another medium of which sport marketing managers should be cognisant. As with anything new and still evolving, there are challenges for sport marketers in how they control the use of properties generated by sporting organisations, and manage new forms of communications through online communities increasingly familiar with 4G phone networks, broadband, blogging, social media and e-commerce transactions. These media will become central to sport-marketing planning generally, and fan engagement specifically—particularly as sport marketers develop a more sophisticated understanding of how they can capitalise on changing technologies and social media.

Merchandising and licensing

Merchandising and licensing are important marketing objectives. Promotional licensing was the subject of Chapter 16, where it was shown that sporting organisations license their logos and trademarks for two reasons:

- to create awareness of the sport, club or league, and
- to endorse product lines outside of sport as a means of generating additional revenue.

Revenue from licensing income becomes the main measure in determining the success of such a program. Clearly, this revenue can easily be measured.

Service quality

Another important, though less tangible, measure is service quality, which has been developed as an ongoing theme through this book. It was specifically discussed in Chapters 5, 7 and 8 as providing the basis for establishing a competitive advantage. It also indirectly affects everything that is concerned with attracting spectators, members and sponsors, contributing to the likelihood of repeat purchase. Strategically, it is significant because it has the capacity to even out the fluctuations in enjoyment governed by winning or losing. An enjoyable night at the basketball, for example, may to some extent offset the disappointment of losing.

This raises the critical question, in relation to this intangible area, of assessing how much participants and spectators enjoy the sport experience. Equally, this question relates to winning. Clubs, associations and leagues increasingly are realising that their marketing programs should be designed to build loyalty—loyalty that has the capacity to withstand periods of poor on-field performance. The reality of most sporting competitions is that it is in their own interest to ensure that winning is shared by all, and therefore mechanisms will be put in place to even out the competition. Clubs will experience periods during which they are successful and those when they perform poorly. Success on the field does not guarantee success off the field, but poor on-field performance almost certainly guarantees a poor off-field result based on the measures discussed above. Reducing the impact of these periods of poor on-field performance enhances the likelihood of achieving financial stability.

Financial stability

Despite an earlier statement in this chapter that profit is not the sole goal of sporting organisations, it has grown in importance over the past 25 years. Many sporting organisations once typified the extreme position, where debt could be freely incurred without considering the consequences. Fortunately, this culture is changing, reinforcing the importance of control in the implementation of marketing activities. Modern sporting organisations more readily understand the balance between on-field success and sound off-field success.

Most of the measures of success discussed in this section contribute to the income-generating potential of the organisation. The ability to rein in costs is the subject of broader texts in the management domain, covering the issue of control in more detail.

Coordinating and implementing marketing strategy

The framework for determining marketing strategy was discussed in Chapter 2. Coordination and implementation of this strategy are primarily the responsibility of the marketing department. Marketing implementation is the process that turns marketing strategies and plans into actions in order to fulfil strategic marketing objectives. Coordination cannot occur, however, without the support of the entire organisation. Marketing staff are often reliant, for example, on sport operations staff to allow star players to become involved in promotion activities. Typically, these star players are in high demand for such promotion activities, which often conflict with training and playing schedules.

Implementation is primarily about staff management, and in essence deals with the who, what, where and when of the marketing plan. The who, what, where and when activities are the result of the strategies determined—otherwise referred to as the what and why. Implementation is often difficult—more difficult than determining the strategies. It is easy to dream up a range of interesting and creative strategies; however, when it comes to actual implementation, it may be found that they are totally unrealistic or impractical. When setting SMART objectives, as discussed in Chapter 2, the 'R' for realistic is of paramount importance. Ultimately, it is the staff and their expertise that determine the ability of the organisation to coordinate the marketing strategy.

Added to the difficulties of coordinating marketing strategies is the relatively recent introduction of marketing personnel—even marketing departments—to sporting organisations. In fact, in some sporting organisations in Australia, a national development officer or state development officer is responsible for the marketing program, based on their responsibility for promoting and encouraging participation. In many sports, specialist sport-marketing staff are now employed. These positions could include, for example, a general manager of marketing, a sales manager, brand manager, digital or social media marketing manager, an events and sponsorship manager, an events assistant and sponsorship officer, a licensing manager and a marketing officer. Careers in sport marketing are beginning to flourish!

Careers in sport marketing

Professional sports in particular offer the greatest range of career options. The main focus of marketing staff is normally increasing revenues for the sport. Marketing staff employed in Australian Football League (AFL) clubs have multiplied markedly over the last 25 years. The Collingwood Football Club, for example, employs approximately 20 staff to service its commercial operations area, which includes staff responsible for digital media, commercial partnerships, membership and merchandise, sales, commercial business and media and public relations. All 20 staff are responsible for the implementation and coordination of all the club's various marketing activities. Also, their employment is indicative of the breadth and range of activities undertaken by the club. Sponsorship, media and public relations, sales of merchandise, overseeing licensing and merchandising, and servicing game-day functions cover the gamut of marketing mix variables discussed in this book.

Compare the size of the marketing staff at a professional sporting club with a traditional National Sporting Organisation (NSO), and it is clear that a gap is emerging between the true professional sports and many NSOs whose role is to cater to both its elite athletes and their development and build a foundation for participation. Swimming Australia, a traditional NSO with responsibilities for elite athlete development and mass participation, is organised around eight functional departments: high performance; community sport; finance; marketing and communications; sponsorship and events; facilities; strategic relations; and corporate services. Two of these departments are directly related to the marketing function, illustrating the growing prominence of marketing-related tasks. Softball Australia, by contrast, lists two employees with marketing-related jobs: membership and marketing coordinator and e-communications coordinator.

Slowly, evidence is emerging that marketing personnel are being employed in a greater variety of sporting organisations. The biggest hurdle to overcome in expanding an organisation's staff expertise has been the view that sport promotes itself, and therefore does not require marketing staff. This complacency has been responsible for the slow pace at which sport has embraced the need for marketing expertise. There is evidence of this changing.

Interestingly, the pace of change has become more urgent as sporting organisations realise the capacity of a skilled marketing team's potential to contribute to the full range of revenue-earning possibilities via marketing programs. It is true that in some instances it is necessary to spend money up front to ensure that revenue-earning potential is maximised. Advertising, public relations launches and staff training in terms of service delivery are examples of this. However, they are also the means of communicating with a public that is increasingly subject to an attractive range of recreation and leisure pursuits capable of detracting from interest in sport. The past 25 years in particular have seen a rapidly intensifying range of competitive forces within the recreation and leisure industry.

In many ways, this has been good for sport, as sports have been forced to professionalise their operations and modernise the way they deliver the overall sport package. The overall sport package remains the domain of all staff and board members associated with various sports, but the sport marketer's input to the package is growing rapidly.

Sport-marketing planning revisited

Central to this book has been the role of strategic marketing planning in sporting organisations. Figure 2.1 showed the steps involved in the process. Sport marketers should follow the steps shown until they become familiar with the process. It is possible to vary the steps at times, but in general the process remains unchanged for the different sporting organisations. What does change is the emphasis placed on the importance of various steps in the process. A summary of the strategic sport-marketing planning process (SSMPP) is provided in Figure 17.2. Sport marketers required to develop an SSMPP should use this framework to prepare their plan. This book has provided the added detail to help the sport marketer consider all necessary issues at each stage of the marketing plan.

Stage 1, 'identification of marketing opportunities', should remain fairly constant. As each organisation prepares to enter a new three- to five-year plan, a renewed analysis of the environment and review of the organisation's capabilities should be undertaken. Importantly, this review should recognise the changing forces driving competition in the sport and recreation industry. This book has already noted changes in the competitive

FIGURE 17.2 Summary of the strategic sport-marketing planning process

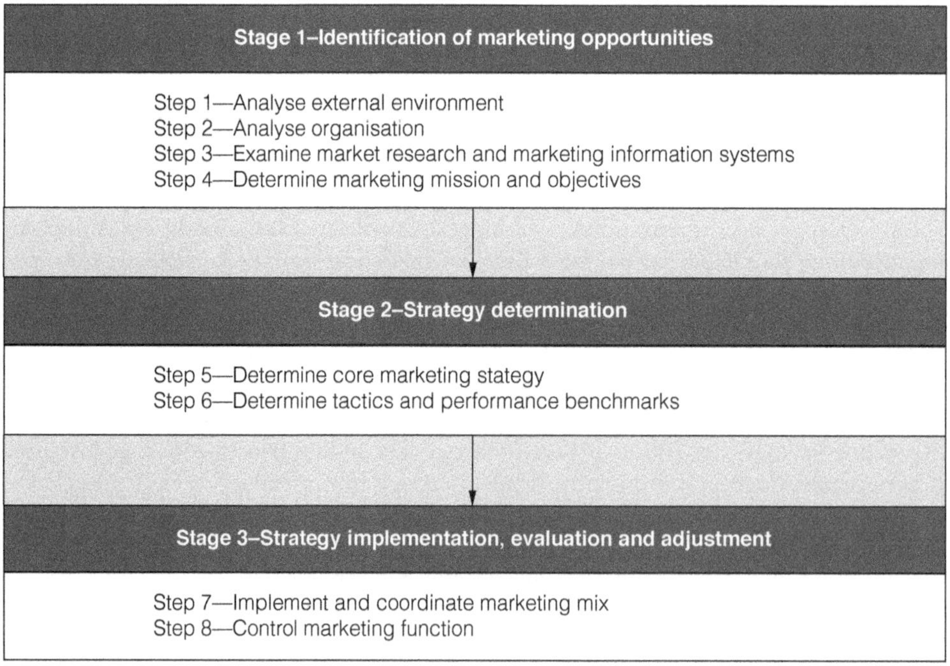

forces confronted by sporting organisations during the past 20 to 25 years. Decisions taken in regard to the overall analysis of the organisation filter down to the marketing mission and objectives set, to allow marketing activities to contribute to broader organisational goals. Most of these decisions are based on the market research and data available to accurately assess buying patterns and consumer behaviour in general. Understanding consumer behaviour in sport and market research and segmentation were covered in Part II of this book. In general, these stages remain constant components of the SSMPP.

Stage 2, 'strategy determination', represents the greatest detail provided in this book. This is because it is at this stage of determining the core marketing strategy that the range of marketing mix variables can be varied to suit the circumstances confronting an organisation. The reason for selecting the mix of variables also changes depending on whether a repositioning exercise is required, such as that described for the NBL in this book or the development of product offerings aimed at specific market segments. Stage 2 also represents the greatest unknown in terms of 'Have we chosen the right core marketing strategy?' There is no correct answer to this question. It can only be answered over time, and even this is subject to the ability of staff to implement marketing plans.

Stage 3, 'strategy implementation', consists of measuring performance based on standards determined earlier in the process and, where necessary, modifying or altering the way in which the core marketing strategy is implemented. Control, implementation and coordination, as discussed in this chapter, are crucial to the overall success of the marketing strategy. Implementation, like strategy determination, is an ongoing process. As one season or event rolls into the next, it becomes important for marketing personnel to step back every so often to assess progress and to ensure that strategies are not subject to rapid change based on short-term success. In particular, for seasonal sports it is important that week-by-week winning or losing does not unduly interfere with strategic marketing plans, usually prepared for three to five years. This is one of sport's greatest pitfalls: reacting to short-term poor on-field performance. It also represents the main difficulty confronted by the sport marketer: to market a product over which there is little control.

Implementation is also guided by the assumptions made during the planning process. Because all strategies and action plans are based on these assumptions about the future, they are subject to considerable risk. It is necessary for marketing managers to assess continually the assumption on which strategies were based. It is here that the beginning and end of the planning process meet. In fact, there is never an end, as the cycle continues in a feedback loop that sometimes blurs beginning and end. To some extent this is a good sign. It indicates that once the plan and associated strategies are formulated, they are not simply put on the shelf. Plans put into action are subject to contingency planning to correct assumptions that do not prove to be true. Therefore, the SSMPP is dynamic, rarely stagnant and laden with challenges to ensure that the full potential of marketing's contribution to the overall functioning of a sporting organisation is optimised. We wish you well with this challenge!

Bibliography

Anderson, E. and Mittal, V. (2000). 'Strengthening the satisfaction–profit chain', *Journal of Service Research*, 3(2), pp. 107–20.

Anderson, L.K. and Sollenberger, H.M. (1992). *Managerial Accounting*, 8th edn, South-Western Publishing, Cincinnati, OH.

Ansoff, H.I. (1957). 'Strategies for diversification', *Harvard Business Review*, September–October, pp. 113–24.

ANZ McCaughan (1993). *Broadcasting Bounces Back: A Financial Evaluation of Australian Commercial Metropolitan Television—Part 1, Industry Overview*, ANZ McCaughan, Melbourne.

Armstrong, K. (2001). 'Black women's participation in sport and fitness: Implications for sport marketing', *Sport Marketing Quarterly*, 10(1), pp. 9–18.

Auh, S., Bell, S., McLeod, C. and Shih, C. (2007). 'Co-production and customer loyalty in financial services', *Journal of Retailing*, 83(3), pp. 359–70.

Australian Associated Press (AAP) (2013a). 'Wrestling Federation president quits after Olympic omission', 16 February, <http://online.wsj.com/article/SB10001424127887324616604578308153849705218.html.mod=googlenews_wsj>, retrieved 19 February 2013.

——(2013b). 'Childish, stupid bunch of dopes', *The Herald Sun*, 23 February, pp. 4–5.

——(2013c). 'IOC boss, wrestling head to discuss sport's removal from Games', CBC Sports, Canada, 13 February, <www.cbc.ca/sports/story/2013/02/13/sp-ioc-olympics-wrestling-jacques-rogge.html>, retrieved 19 February 2013.

——(2013d). 'Ban gambling ads in sport: Expert', 5 March, <www.theage.com.au/national/ban-gambling-ads-in-sport-expert-20130305-2fj3i.html#ixzz2RxVCf5WL>, retrieved 23 April 2013.

Australian Bureau of Statistics (ABS) (2007). *Year Book Australia, 2007*, cat. no. 1301.0, AGPS, Canberra.

——(2011a). 2011 *Census Quickstats, Greater Melbourne*, <www.censusdata.abs.gov.au/census_services/getproduct/census/2011/quickstat/2GMEL>, retrieved 29 January 2013.

——(2011b). *2011 Census Quickstats, Greater Sydney*, <www.censusdata.abs.gov.au/census_services/getproduct/census/2011/quickstat/2GSYD>, retrieved 29 January 2013.

——(2012). *Year Book Australia, 2012*, cat. no. 1301.0, AGPS, Canberra.

Australian Communications and Media Authority (ACMA) (2011). *Television Sets in Australian Households 2011*, Commonwealth of Australia, Canberra.

Australian Crime Commission (ACC) (2013). *Organised Crime and Drugs in Sport: New Generation Performance and Image Enhancing Drugs and Organised Criminal Involvement in their use in Professional Sport*, ACC, Canberra, <www.crimecommission.gov.au/sites/default/files/files/organised-crime-and-drugs-in-sports-feb2013.pdf>, retrieved 19 February 2013.

Australian Football League Tables (2013). 'Attendances (1921–2013)', <www.stats.rleague.com/afl/crowds/summary.html>, retrieved 4 April 2013.

Australian Grand Prix Corporation (2011). *2011 Annual Report*, Australian Grand Prix Corporation, Melbourne.

——(2012). *2012 Annual Report*, Australian Grand Prix Corporation, Melbourne.

Australian Marketing Institute (2005). 'Heineken to paint the town green no more', <www.ami.org.au/amimu/0505May/0505_hospitality_gifts.htm>, retrieved 1 November 2007.

Baghdikian, E. (1996). 'Building the sports organisation's merchandise licensing program: The appropriateness, significance, and considerations', *Sport Marketing Quarterly*, 5(1), pp. 35–41.

Baker, M. (2000). *Marketing Strategy and Management*, 3rd edn, Macmillan, London.

Balm, T. (2013). 'Head coach backed despite keeping mum', *The Herald Sun*, 23 February, p. 4.

Beaton, A., Funk, D.C. and Alexandris, A. (2009). 'Operationalizing a theory of participation in physically active leisure', *Journal of Leisure Research*, 41, pp. 177–203.

Beccarini, C. and Ferrand, A. (2006). 'Factors affecting soccer club season ticket holders' satisfaction: The influence of club image and fans' motives', *European Sport Management Quarterly*, 6(1), pp. 12–26.

Belch, G.E. and Belch, M.A. (1998). *Introduction to Advertising and Promotion: An Integrated Marketing Communications Perspective*, 4th edn, Irwin, Homewood, IL.

——(2007) *Advertising and Promotion: An Integrated Marketing Communications Perspective*, 8th edn, McGraw-Hill/Irwin, New York.

Belch, G.E., Belch, M.A., Kerr, G. and Powell, I. (2011), *Advertising and Promotion: An Integrated Marketing Communications Perspective*, 2nd edn, McGraw-Hill, Sydney.

Berry, L. and Parasuraman, A. (1991). *Marketing Services: Competing Through Quality*, The Free Press, New York.

Berry, L., Parasuraman, A. and Zeithaml, V. (1988). 'The Service-Quality Puzzle', *Business Horizons*, September, pp. 35–43.

Bertini, M. and Gourville, J.T. (2012). 'Rethinking the way prices are set can expand the pie for everyone', *Harvard Business Review*, June, pp. 97–104.

Bitner, M.J. (1992). 'Servicescapes: The impact of physical surroundings on customers and employees', *Journal of Marketing*, 56(2), pp. 57–71.

Bitner, M.J., Booms, B.H. and Tetreault, M.S. (1990). 'The service encounter: Diagnosing favorable and unfavorable incidents', *Journal of Marketing*, 54, pp. 71–84.

Boon, G. (1999). *Deloitte & Touche Annual Review of Football Finance (1997–1998 Season)*, Deloitte & Touche, Manchester.

——(2001). *Deloitte & Touche Annual Review of Football Finance (1999–2000 Season)*, Deloitte & Touche, Manchester.

Bowden, J. (2009). 'The process of customer engagement: A conceptual framework', *Journal of Marketing Theory and Practice*, 17(1), pp. 63–74.

Boyd, H.W., Walker, O.C and Larréché, J.C. (1998). *Marketing Management: A Strategic Approach with a Global Orientation*, 3rd edn, McGraw-Hill, Irwin, Boston, MA.

Brassington, F. and Pettitt, S. (2006). *Principles of Marketing*, 4th edn, Pearson Education, Harlow.

Brodie, R., Ilic, A., Juric, B. and Hollebeek, L. (2013). 'Consumer engagement in a virtual brand community: An exploratory analysis', *Journal of Business Research*, 66(1), pp. 105–14.

Brown, M. (1992). 'The big gamble', *The Age, Green Guide*, 14 February, pp. 1–2.

——(1993). 'NBL rethinks its strategy as crowds fall', *Sunday Age, Sports Extra*, 27 June, p. 6.

——(2003). 'An analysis of online marketing in the sport industry: User activity, communication objectives, and perceived benefits', *Sport Marketing Quarterly*, 12(1), pp. 48–55.

Brueur, C., and Rumpf, C. (2012). 'The viewer's reception and processing of sponsorship information in sports telecasts', *Journal of Sport Management*, 26(6), pp. 521–32.

Bryden-Brown, S. (2001). 'OzTAM figures to get no respect', *The Australian*, 5 March, p. 3.

Burchett, J. (1996). *News Limited v Australian Rugby League Limited and Others*, NG 197 of 1995, Federal Court of Australia, Sydney.

Burke, M. (2012). 'When Tiger Woods wins, the game of golf does, too', <www.forbes.com/sites/monteburke/2012/06/04/when-tiger-woods-wins-the-game-of-golf-does-too>, retrieved 7 January 2013.

Burns Ortiz, M. (2011). 'Dana White leads UFC into social realm', *ESPN Playbook*, 6 June, p. 2, <http://sports.espn.go.com/espn/page2/story?page=burnsortiz/110606_ufc_dana_white>, retrieved 20 March 2013.

——(2013). 'Social media: Inside the UFC, Dana White', *ESPN Playbook*, 1 March, <http://espn.go.com/blog/playbook/trending/post/_/id/14717/social-media-inside-the-ufc-dana-white>, retrieved 20 March 2013.

Business Review Weekly (2001). 'Ratings war gets serious', 23 February, p. 16.

Business Wire (2007). 'Tiger Woods, Roger Federer and Thierry Henry are introduced as the faces of New Gillette Champions Program', <http://findarticles.com/p/articles/M1_MOEIN/is_2007_Feb_4/ai_n17167026>, retrieved 29 October 2007.

Buzzard, K. (1992). *Electronic Media Ratings: Turning Dollars into Sense*, Focal Press, Boston, MA.

Cameron, G., Wilcox, D., Reber, B. and Shin, J. (2008). *Public Relations Today: Managing Conflict*, Pearson, Boston, MA.

Canberra Raiders (2013). 'Local Rugby League registration and fun day', *Canberra Times*, 24 January, <www.raiders.com.au/news-display/Sportenary-Local-Rugby-League-Registration-and-Fun-Day/67524>, retrieved 25 February 2013.

Chadwick, S. and Burton, N. (2011). 'The evolving sophistication of ambush marketing: A typology of strategies', *Thunderbird International Business Review*, 53(6), pp. 709–19.

Chavanat, N., Martinent, G., and Ferrand, A. (2009). Sponsor and sponsees interactions: Effects on consumers' perceptions of brand image, brand attachment, and purchasing intention', *Journal of Sport Management*, 23, pp. 644–70.

Chelladurai, P. (1987). 'Multidimensionality and multiple perspectives of organizational effectiveness', *Journal of Sport Management*, 1(1), pp. 37–47.

Chelladurai, P. and Chang, K. (2000). 'Targets and standards of quality in sport services', *Sport Management Review*, 3(1), pp. 22–9.

Chernatony, de L. and McDonald, M.H.B. (1992). *Creating Powerful Brands*, Butterworth/Heinemann, Oxford.

Cheverton, P. (2000). *Key Marketing Skills*, Kogan Page, London.

Churchill, G.A. Jr and Surprenant, C. (1982). 'An investigation into the determinants of customer satisfaction', *Journal of Marketing Research*, 19, pp. 491–504.

Cialdini, R.B., Borden, R.J., Thorne, A., Walker, M.R., Freeman, S. and Sloan, L.R. (1976). 'Basking in reflected glory: Three (football) field studies', *Journal of Personality and Social Psychology*, 34, pp. 366–75.

Clark, G. and Cheng, W.G. (2007). 'China gets serious about fake Olympic merchandise', *International Herald Tribune*, 26 April, <www.iht.com/articles/2007/04/26/business/fakes.php>, retrieved 14 November 2007.

Clark, L. (2008). 'Basketball Australia and NBL merge', *The Age*, 24 June, <http://news.theage.com.au/sport/basketball-australia-and-nbl-merge-20080624-2w4w.html>, retrieved 27 March 2013.

——(2013). 'Content is King', *B&T Magazine*, 7 February, pp. 16–19.

Clarke, R. (2002). 'Wearing out the opposition', *SportBusiness International*, pp. 26–7.

Cockerill, M. (2011). 'Clever strategies help turn the A-League around', *Sydney Morning Herald*, 26 November, p. 13.

Cohen, R. (2007). 'NBA extends TV deals with ESPN/ABC, TNT', *USA Today* online, 27 June,

<http://usatoday30.usatoday.com/sports/basketball/2007-06-27-3096131424_x.htm>, retrieved 29 January 2013.

Coyne, K.P. (1986). 'Sustainable competitive advantage—what it is, what it isn't', *Business Horizons*, January–February, pp. 54–61.

Craft, J. (2010). 'Properties, licensees must cover all bases in rights agreement', *Sport Business Journal*, <www.sportsbusinessdaily.com/Corporate/SS-Sports-Group.aspx>, retrieved 15 January 2013.

Cravens, D.W. (2010). *Strategic Marketing*, 8th edn, McGraw-Hill, Columbus, OH.

Cricket Australia (2012). 'GPY&R and Cricket Australia have created an exciting new advertising campaign for the Commonwealth Bank Series, called Summer's Biggest "Dress-up" Party', 14 December, <www.cricket.com.au/news-list/2012/12/14/summers-biggest-dress-up-party-campaign>, retrieved 21 March 2013.

Cronin, J.J. and Taylor, S.A. (1992). 'Measuring service quality: A re-examination and extension', *Journal of Marketing*, 56, pp. 55–66.

Croteau, D. and Hoynes, W. (2003). *Media Society: Industries, Images and Audiences*, 3rd edn, Pine Forge Press, Thousand Oaks, CA.

Curtin, P.A. and Gaither, T.K. (2012). *Globalization and Public Relations in Post-colonial Nations*, Cambria Press, Amherst, NY.

Dampney, J. (2002). 'NBL's rocky road teams tighten belts', *Daily Telegraph*, 22 June, p. 101.

Davies, W. (2013). 'Beitar Jerusalem FC strive to shed racist reputation', BBC, 14 February, <www.bbc.co.uk/news/world-middle-east-21455750>, retrieved 19 February 2013.

Davies, R. (2002) 'Sport, Citizenship and Development: Challenges and Opportunities for Sports Sponsors', World Sports Forum, Lausanne, 23 September.Davis, P. (2011). 'Netnographic analysis of user generated online communities', Conference Proceedings, Australia and New Zealand Marketing Academy Conference, Perth.

——(2012). 'Online forums: The forgotten social media platform', *The Playbook*, 10 March, <http://theplaybook.com.au/sports-social-media/online-forums-the-forgotten-social-media-platform-2>, retrieved 20 March 2013.

Deloitte (2013). *Captains of industry: Football Money League*, Deloitte, London.

Department of Broadband, Communications and the Digital Economy (DBCDE) (2011). *National Digital Economy*, AGPS, Canberra.

——(2012). 'What's happening in each switchover area?' *Digital Tracker Report: Summary Report for Quarter 2, April to June 2012*, <www.digitalready.gov.au/Content/Documents/Digital-tracker-reports/PDF/Digital-Tracker-Q2-2012-Summary-Report.aspx>, retrieved 20 February 2013.

——(2013). 'Pay TV', <www.dbcde.gov.au/television/pay_tv>, retrieved 29 January 2013.

DeSensi, J.T. and Rosenberg, D. (2010). *Ethics and Morality in Sport Management*, 3rd edn, Fitness Information Technology, Morgantown, WV.

Dietz-Uhler, B., Harrick, E.A., End, C. and Jacquemotte, L. (2000). 'Sex differences in sport fan behavior and reasons for being a sport fan', *Journal of Sport Behavior*, 23(3), pp. 219–31.

Difabrizio Report (2013). 'NBL TV ratings 2012–13', <www.michaeldifabrizio.com/nbl-tv-ratings>, retrieved 27 March 2013.

Direct Marketing Association (2011). *Power of Direct Marketing Report*, DMA, New York.

Dolphin Stadium (2006). 'Miami Dolphins team up with Kangaroo TV on a full-year trial of NFL SUNDAY TICKET™ In-Stadium by DirecTV', <www.dolphinsstadium.com/content/pressrelease.aspx?id=64#>, retrieved 11 July 2007.

Donato, P. and Link, M. (2013). 'The gamification of marketing research', *Marketing News*, February, pp. 38–42.

Doyle, J.P., Filo, K., McDonald, H. and Funk, D.C. (2013). 'Exploring sport brand double jeopardy: The link between team market share and attitudinal loyalty', *Sport Management Review*, in press, advance online copy available at <http://dx.doi.org/10.1016/j.smr.2012.11.001>.

Doyle, J.P., Kunkel, T. and Funk, D.C. (2013). 'Sports spectator segmentation: Examining the differing psychological connections amongst spectators of leagues and teams', *International Journal of Sports Marketing and Sponsorship*, 14(2), pp. 95–111.

Dutt, Y. (2013). 'Wrestling's omission from the 2020 Olympics is a wake-up call for the sport', *The Times of India*. 14 February, <http://articles.timesofindia.indiatimes.com/2013-02-14/edit-page/37080065_1_olympic-sports-yogeshwar-dutt-wrestlers>, retrieved 19 February 2013.

Dwyer, B. (2011). 'The impact of attitudes and fantasy football involvement on intentions to watch NFL teams on television', *International Journal of Sport Communication*, 4, pp. 375–96.

Dwyer, B. and Drayer, J. (2010). 'Fantasy sport consumer segmentation: An investigation into the differing consumption modes of fantasy football participants', *Sport Marketing Quarterly*, 19, pp. 207–16.

The Economist. (2011). 'Glory at what price?', 18 September, <www.economist.com/blogs/gametheory/2011/09/rugby-world-cup>, retrieved 2 November 2012.

Econsultancy (2013). *State of Digital Marketing in Australia*, Econsultancy, Sydney.

Enten, H.J. (2013). 'Lance Armstrong's *Oprah* PR disaster: Poll shows confessing is for losers', *The Guardian*, 21 January, <www.guardian.co.uk/commentisfree/2013/jan/21/lance-armstrong-oprah-pr-disaster/print>, retrieved 19 February 2013.

ESPN (2011). 'Consumer Insights study: 55% of Twitter users say they use it for sports-related purposes; 40% of Facebook users said the same', Twitter post, <https://twitter.com/ESPNResearch/status/101321699336798210>, retrieved 11 August 2011.

——(2012a). 'German Bundesliga Stats: Team Attendance—2012–13', <http://soccernet.espn.go.com/stats/attendance/_/league/ger.1/german-bundesliga?cc=3436>, retrieved 10 January 2013.

——(2012b). 'South African Premiership Stats: Team Attendance—2012–13', <http://soccernet.espn.go.com/stats/attendance/_/league/rsa.1/south-african-premiership?cc=3436>, retrieved 10 January 2013.

Evans, J.R. and Berman, B. (1987). *Marketing*, Macmillan, New York.

Fantasy Sport Trade Association (2011). 'Fantasy sports participation sets all-time record, grows past 35 million players', *FSTA*, 10 June, <www.fsta.org/blog/fsta-press-release/fantasy-sports-participation-sets-all-time-record-grows-past-35-million-players>, retrieved 20 March 2013.

Farquhar, L.K. and Meeds, R. (2007). 'Types of fantasy sports users and their motivations', *Journal of Computer-Mediated Communication*, 12, pp. 1208–28.

Farrelly, F., Quester, P. and Burton, R. (2006). 'Changes in sponsorship value: Competencies and capabilities of successful sponsorship relationships', *Industrial Marketing Management*, 35, pp. 1016–26.

Ferguson, A. and Idato, M. (2012). 'Storm of change: Coming soon to TV', *The Saturday Age, Business Day*, 20 October, pp. 6–7.

FIFA (2010). 'Qatar World Cup 2022 Bid Presentation: Mr Hassan Abdullah Al Thawadi', Lausanne, Switzerland.

Filo, K. and Funk, D.C. (2005). 'Congruence between attractive product features and virtual content delivery for internet marketing communication', *Sport Marketing Quarterly*, 14, pp. 112–22.

——(2012). 'Leveraging e-strategies and the online environment', In M. Pritchard and J. Stinson (eds), *Leveraging Brands in Sport Business*, Routledge, New York.

Fisher, A. (2012). 'Interactive TV and the second screen "experience"', *Huffpost Tech, UK*, <www.huffingtonpost.co.uk/andrew-fisher/interactive-tv-and-the-se_b_1505886.html>, retrieved 20 February 2013.

Fisher, E. (2009). 'Fantasy players seen as big spenders in key consumer categories', *Street & Smith's SportsBusiness Daily*, 21 September, <www.sportsbusinessdaily.com/Daily/Issues/2009/09/Issue-6/Sponsorships-Advertising-Marketing/Fantasy-Players-Seen-As-Big-Spenders-In-Key-Consumer-Categories.aspx>, retrieved 19 December 2012.

Flint, J. (2011). 'NFL signs TV rights deals with Fox, NBC and CBS', *Los Angeles Times*, 15 December, <http://articles.latimes.com/2011/dec/15/business/la-fi-ct-nfl-deals-20111215>, retrieved 29 January 2013.

Fombrun, C. (2000). 'The value to be found in corporate reputation', *Financial Times*, 4 December, p. 2.

Forbes.com. (2011). 'The 10 Most Valuable Trademarks', *Forbes*, 15 June, <www.forbes.com/pictures/eidl45jl/the-10-most-valuable-trademarks-2>, retrieved 20 January 2012.

——(2012a). 'Roger Federer', *Forbes*, <www.forbes.com/profile/roger-federer>, n.d., retrieved 7 January 2013.

——(2012b). 'Forbes Fab 40: The most valuable brands in sports', *Forbes*, 17 October, <www.forbes.com/sites/mikeozanian/2012/10/17/the-forbes-fab-40-the-worlds-most-valuable-sports-brands-4>, retrieved 20 January 2013.

Fornicatell, C. and Wernerfelt, B. (1987). 'Defensive marketing strategy by customer complaint management: A theoretical analysis', *Journal of Marketing Research*, November, pp. 337–46.

Fraser, C. (1983). 'Creative strategy: A management perspective', *Journal of Advertising*, 12(4), pp. 36–41.

Frenkel, S. (2013). 'Racist supporters trash Israeli club Beitar Jerusalem for signing Muslim players', *The Times*, 12 February, <www.theaustralian.com.au/news/world/racist-supporters-trash-israeli-club-beitar-jerusalem-for-signing-muslim-players/story-fnb64oi6-1226575711077>, retrieved 19 February 2013.

Fuller, P. and Stewart, M. (1996), 'Attendance Patterns at Victorian and South Australian Football Games', *Economic Papers: A Journal of Applied Economics and Policy*, no. 15, p. 83–93.

Funk, D.C. (2008). *Consumer Behaviour for Sport & Events: Marketing Action*, Elsevier, Oxford.

Funk, D.C., Beaton, A.A. and Pritchard, M.P. (2011). 'The stage-based development of physically active leisure: A recreational golf context', *Journal of Leisure Research*, 43(2), pp. 268–89.

Funk, D.C. and Bruun, T. (2007). 'The role of socio-psychological and culture-education motives in marketing international sport tourism: A cross-cultural perspective', *Tourism Management*, 28, pp. 806–19.

Funk, D.C., Filo, K., Beaton, A., and Pritchard, M. (2009). 'Measuring motives for sport event attendance: Bridging the academic–practitioner divide', *Sport Marketing Quarterly*, 18, pp. 126–38.

Funk, D.C., Haugtvedt, C.P. and Howard, D.R. (2000). 'Contemporary attitude theory in sport: Theoretical considerations and implications', *Sport Management Review*, 3(2), pp. 124–44.

Funk, D. and James, J. (2001). 'The psychological continuum model: A conceptual framework for understanding individuals' psychological connection to sport', *Sport Management Review*, 4(2), pp. 119–50.

——(2004). 'The fan attitude network (FAN) model: Exploring attitude formation and change among sport consumers', *Sport Management Review*, 7(1), pp. 1–26.

——(2006). 'Consumer loyalty: The meaning of attachment in the development of sport team allegiance', *Journal of Sport Management*, 20, pp. 189–217.

Funk, D.C., Jordan, J., Ridinger, L. and Kaplanidou, K. (2011). 'Capacity of mass participant sport events for the development of activity commitment and future exercise intention', *Leisure Sciences*, 33, pp. 250–68.

Funk, D.C., Mahony, D.F. and Havitz, M. (2003). 'Sport consumer behavior: Assessment and direction', *Sport Marketing Quarterly*, 12, pp. 200–5.

Funk, D.C., Mahony, D.F. and Ridinger, L. (2002). 'Characterizing consumer motivation as individual difference factors: Augmenting the Sport Interest Inventory (SII) to explain level of spectator support', *Sport Marketing Quarterly*, 11, pp. 33–43.

Funk, D.C. and Pritchard, M. (2006). 'Sport publicity: Commitment's moderation of message effects', *Journal of Business Research*, 59, pp. 613–21.

Funk, D.C., Toohey, K. and Bruun, T. (2007). 'International sport event participation: Prior sport involvement; destination image; and travel motives', *European Sport Management Quarterly*, 7, pp. 227–48.
Garbarino, E. and Johnson, M.S. (1999). 'The different roles of satisfaction, trust, and commitment in customer relationships', *Journal of Marketing*, 63(2), pp. 70–87.
Gephart, R.P. Jr (2004). 'Sensemaking and new media at work', *The American Behavioral Scientist*, 8(4), pp. 479–95.
——(2002b). 'Delivering on the deal', *SportBusiness International*, March, pp. 58–9.
Gifford, A. (2007). 'Ten amazing sport ads that demand attention', *InventorSpot*, <http://inventorspot.com/articles/amazing_sports_ads_7472>, retrieved 23 April, 2013.
Gillis, R. (2002a). 'Being Nick Faldo', *SportBusiness International*, March, pp. 24–5.
——(2002b). 'Delivering on the deal', *SportBusiness International*, March, pp. 58–9.
Gilt Edge (n.d.) 'Fan development in major league soccer', Gilt Edge Soccer Marketing, <http://giltedgesoccer.com/wp-content/post-files/MLS-Fan-Development1.pdf>, retrieved 25 March 2013.
Gladden, J. and Funk, D.C. (2002). 'Developing an understanding of brand associations in team sport: Empirical evidence from consumers of professional sport', *Journal of Sport Management*, 16, pp. 54–81.
Gladden, J.M., Irwin, R.L. and Sutton, W.A. (2001). 'Managing North American major professional sport teams in the new millennium: A focus on building brand equity', *Journal of Sport Management*, 15(4), pp. 297–317.
Gladden, J., Milne, G.R. and Sutton, W. (1998). 'A conceptual framework for assessing brand equity in Division I college athletics', *Journal of Sport Management*, 12(1), pp. 1–19.
Global Sport Media Consumption Report (2012). 'Australia', <www.slideshare.net/DeclanGallagher/global-sports-media-consumption-report-2012-australia>, Retrieved 2 April 2013.
Gould, R. (2012). 'Push for NBA', *Herald Sun*, 21 September, p. 78.
Grange, P. (2013). *The Bluestone Review: A review of culture and leadership in Australian Olympic Swimming (Abridged version)*, Bluestone Edge, Melbourne.
Green, B.C. and Hill, B. (2012). 'Repeat participation as a function of program attractiveness, socializing opportunities, loyalty and the sportscape across three sport facility contexts', *Sport Management Review*, 14(4), pp. 485–99.
Grönroos, C. (1990). *Service Management and Marketing*, Lexington Books, Boston.
——(1992). 'Service management: A management focus for service competition', in C. Lovelock (ed.), *Managing Services: Marketing, Operations, and Human Resources*, Prentice Hall, Englewood Cliffs, NJ, pp. 9–16.
Growden, G. (2011). 'World Cup "costing" top teams', *The Age*, 29 September, p. 17.
Gruning, J. and Hunt, T. (1984). *Managing Public Relations*. Holt, Rinehart and Winston, Orlando, FL.
The Guardian (2012). 'UK doctors blast McDonald's' Olympic sponsorship', 1 May, <www.guardian.co.uk/world/feedarticle/10221106>, retrieved 23 April 2013.
Haigh, G. (2013). 'Cricket as a backdrop: It's an adman's party and I'll cry if I want to', *The Australian*, 12 January, <www.theaustralian.com.au/sport/opinion/cricket-as-a-backdrop-its-an-admans-party-and-ill-cry-if-i-want-to/story-fnb58rpk-1226552305955>, retrieved 21 March 2013.
Halbish, G. (1995). 'Developing professional sporting leagues', Keynote Address to the Sport Management and Marketing Conference, Sydney, August.
Hambrick, M. and Mahoney, T. (2011). '"It's incredible—trust me": Exploring the role of celebrity athletes as marketers in online social networks', *International Journal of Sport Management and Marketing*, 10(3/4), pp. 161–79.
Hambrick, M., Simmons, J., Greenhalgh, G. and Greenwell, C. (2010). 'Understanding professional athletes' use of Twitter: A content analysis of athlete tweets', *International Journal of Sport Communication*, 3, pp. 454–71.

Harman, L. (2012). 'Hitting the target', *SportBusiness International*, 185, pp. 14–15.
Hansen, F. and Scotwin, L. (1995). 'An experimental inquiry into sponsoring: What effects can be measured?', *Advertising, Sponsorship and Promotions: Understanding and Measuring the Effectiveness of Commercial Communication*, ESOMAR, Amsterdam, pp. 65–82.
Harris, B. (2009). 'ARU report confirms code on the wane', *The Australian*, 12 October, p. 35.
Hawkins, D.I., Best, R.J. and Coney, K.A. (1992). *Consumer Behavior: Implications for Marketing Strategy*, Irwin, Boston, MA.
Helitzer, M. (1996). *The Dream Job: Sports Publicity, Promotion and Marketing*, 2nd edn, University Sports Press, Athens, OH.
Heming, W. and Coomber, J. (2008). 'NBL boss says clubs struggling', *Sydney Morning Herald*, 27 May, <http://news.smh.com.au/sport/nbl-boss-says-clubs-struggling-20080527-2imw.html>, retrieved 27 March 2013.
Henderson, I. (1996). 'AFL kicks a goal on marketing strategy', *The Australian*, 23 July, p. 5.
Hickman, B. (2002). 'To get interactive, viewers must box clever', *The Australian*, 3 May, p. 6.
Hill, B. and Green, B.C. (2001). 'Repeat attendance as a function of involvement, loyalty, and the sportscape across three football contexts', *Sport Management Review*, 3(2), pp. 145–62.
Hinds, R. (2013). 'Dogs deserve a pat for benign intervention', *Sydney Morning Herald*, 25 February, <www.smh.com.au/rugby-league/league-news/dogs-deserve-a-pat-for-benign-intervention-20130225-2f1u9.html>, retrieved 25 February 2013.
Hirsley, M. (1998). 'ABC, ESPN gobble rest of NFL rights: Networks pay $17.6 billion for 8 years', *Chicago Tribune*, 14 January, p. 1.
Hoffman, K.D. and Bateson, J.E.G. (1997). *Essentials of Services Marketing*, The Dryden Press, Orlando, FL.
Hogan, J. (2012). 'Crowded Out: The crowds for 50-over internationals are diminishing', *The Age*, 19 February, p. 12.
Holloway, A. (2003). 'Brand New: The Toronto Blue Jays gamble on a younger, edgier logo', *Canadian Business*, 76(18), p. 79.
Howat, G., Absher, J., Crilley, G. and Milne, I. (1996). 'Measuring customer service quality in sports and leisure centres', *Managing Leisure*, 1, pp. 77–89.
Huggins, M.H. (1992). 'Marketing research: A must for every sport organisation', *Sport Marketing Quarterly*, 1(1), pp. 37–40.
Hutton, G. and Fosdick., M. (2011). 'The globalization of social media', *Journal of Advertising Research*, 51(4), pp. 564–70.
Iacobucci, D., Ostrom, A. and Grayson, K. (1995). 'Distinguishing service quality and customer satisfaction: The voice of the customer', *Journal of Consumer Psychology*, 4, pp. 277–303.
IEG (2006). 'Fully charged sponsorship: Strategic activation', paper presented at the 23rd Annual Sponsorship Conference, Chicago.
International Olympic Committee (IOC) (1996). 'Marketing matters', *The Olympic Marketing Newsletter*, 8.
——(2002a). 'Sydney 1997–2000 Games of the Olympiad: Facts and figures', <http://multimedia.olympic.org/pdf/en_report_180.pdf>, retrieved 28 June 2002.
——(2002b). 'Marketing matters', *The Olympic Newsletter*, 21 June.
——(2011). 'IOC awards US broadcast rights for 2014, 2016, 2018 and 2020 Olympic Games to NBCUniversal', <www.olympic.org/news/ioc-awards-us-broadcast-rights-for-2014-2016-2018-and-2020-olympic-games-to-nbcuniversal/130827>, retrieved 29 January 2013.
——(2012a). 'Revenue sources and distribution', <www.olympic.org/ioc-financing-revenue-sources-distribution?tab=sources>, retrieved 28 March 2013.
——(2012b). *IOC Marketing Media Guide*, IOC, London.
International Rugby Board (2009). 'Rugby World Cup: Financing the global game', <www.irb.

com/mm/document/newsmedia/0/090904webfinancingtheglobalgame_8964.pdf>, retrieved 2 November 2012.

——(2012). *RWC 2011 boost for all areas of the game*, 22 March, <www.rugbyworldcup.com/home/news/newsid=2061570.html>, retrieved 2 November 2012.

Ioakimidis, M. (2010). 'Online marketing of professional sport clubs: Engaging fans on a new playing field', *International Journal of Sports Marketing & Sponsorship*, 12, pp. 271–82.

Irwin, R.L. and Stotlar, D.K. (1993). 'Operational protocol analysis of sport and collegiate licensing programs', *Sport Marketing Quarterly*, 2(1), pp. 7–16.

Irwin, R.L., Sutton, W.A. and McCarthy, L.M. (2002). *Sport Promotion and Sales Management*, 3rd edn, Human Kinetics, Champaign, IL.

——(2008). *Sport Promotion and Sales Management*, 2nd ed., Human Kinetics, Champaign, IL.

Jaberg, S. (2011). 'How Federer hit the marketing jackpot', <www.swissinfo.ch/eng/Specials/Roger_Federer/Analysis/How_Federer_hit_the_marketing_jackpot.html?cid=29453650>, retrieved 7 January 2013.

Jackson, G. (2013). 'Ben Barba is ill and he needs help: Bulldogs poster boy may be out for six months', *Sydney Morning Herald*, 25 February, <www.smh.com.au/rugby-league/league-news/ben-barba-is-ill-and-he-needs-help-bulldogs-poster-boy-may-be-out-of-game-for-six-months-20130225-2f0w6.html>, retrieved 25 February 2013.

James, M. (2013). 'Super Bowl as conundrum: Do early releases spoil the show?' *Los Angeles Times*, 22 January, <www.latimes.com/entertainment/envelope/cotown/la-et-ct-super-bowl-ad-conundrum-20130121,0,2263573.story>, viewed 18 March 2013.

Janoff, B. (2007). 'Marketers seek gold at 50th Daytona 500', *Brandweek*, 25 June, p. 4.

Jarratt, P. (1988). 'A nation of Norms', *The Bulletin*, 4 October, pp. 56–8, 92.

Jones, D. (2012). *Annual Review of Football Finance 2012: New Rules, Narrow Margins*, Deloitte Sports Business Group, Manchester.

Joshi, S. (2007). 'Virtually there: Cricket, community, and commerce on the internet', *The International Journal of the History of Sport*, 24(9), pp. 1226–41.

Kang, K.J. and Stotlar, D. (2011). 'An investigation of factors influencing decision making for participation in the Olympic Partners Sponsorship: A case study of Samsung', *International Journal of Applied Sports Sciences*, 23(1), pp. 225–51.

Kaplan, A.M. and Haenlein, M. (2010). 'Users of the world, unite! The challenges and opportunities of social media', *Business Horizons*, 53(1), pp. 59–68.

Karg, A. (2007). 'Sport sponsorship management: Practices in objective setting and measurement', paper presented at the UNSW Honours Colloquium, University of New South Wales, Sydney.

Karg, A. and McDonald, H. (2011). 'Understanding experiences of fantasy sport participation', *Sport Management Review*, 14, pp. 327–46.

Karg, A., Davis, P. and Gaarenstroom, T. (2012). 'Social media for sport teams: Strategy and evidence of consumer segments', in *Conference Proceedings, Sport Management Association of Australian and New Zealand Conference (SMAANZ)*, SMAANZ, Sydney.

Karg, A., Dwyer, B. and McDonald, H. (2012). 'A whole new ball game? An international comparison of fantasy sport usage and outcomes', in *Conference Proceedings, North American Society for Sport Management*, NASSM, Seattle, WA.

Karg, A., McDonald, H. and Leckie, C. (2012). 'A comparison of media and live dominant sport consumers', in *Conference Proceedings, Australian and New Zealand Marketing Association Conference (ANZMAC)*, ANZMAC, Adelaide.

Karg, A., McDonald, H. and Shaw, R. (2008). 'A longitudinal analysis of the halo effect of team success on season ticket holder attitudes', in *Conference Proceedings, Sport Marketing Association Conference*, Gold Coast.

Kelley, S.W. and Turley, L.W. (2001). 'Consumer perceptions of service quality attributes at sporting events', *Journal of Sport Business Research*, 54(2), pp. 161–6.

Kent, A. and Campbell, R.M. Jr (2007). 'An introduction to freeloading: Campus area ambush marketing', *Sport Marketing Quarterly*, 16(2), pp. 118–22.

Kim, D. and Kim, S.Y. (1995). 'QUESC: An instrument for assessing the service quality of sport centers in Korea', *Journal of Sport Management*, 9, pp. 208–20.

Klattell, D.A. and Marcus, N. (1988). *Sports for Sale*, Oxford University Press, New York.

Klososky, S. (2012). 'Social technology: The next frontier', *Financial Executive*, 28(4), pp. 40–5.

Ko, Y.L. and Pastore, D.L. (2001). 'A multidimensional and hierarchical model of service quality in the participant sport industry (Scale Development of Service Quality in Participant Sport – SSQPS)', in *Conference Proceedings, American Alliance for Health, Physical Education, Recreation and Dance (AAHPERD) Conference*, AAHPERD, Cincinnati, OH.

Kosner, A.W. (2013). 'As power outage at Superdome shuts down Super Bowl, Twitter was the best explainer', *Forbes*, 3 February, <www.forbes.com/sites/anthonykosner/2013/02/03/power-outage-at-superdome-shuts-down-super-bowl-twitter-explains>, retrieved 25 March 2013.

Kotler, P. (2000), *Marketing Management*, 10th edn, Prentice-Hall, Upper Saddle River, NJ.

Kotler, P., Adam, S., Brown, L. and Armstrong, G. (2006). *Principles of Marketing*, 3rd edn, Pearson, Sydney.

Kotler, P. and Andreasen, A.R. (2003). *Strategic Marketing for Nonprofit Organisations*, 6th edn, Prentice-Hall, Upper Saddle River, NJ.

Kotler, P. and Armstrong, G. (2010). *Principles of Marketing*, 13th edn, Pearson, Sydney.

Kujath, C.L. (2011). 'Facebook and MySpace: Complement or substitute for face-to-face interaction?' *Cyberpsychology, Behaviour, and Social Networking*, 14, pp. 75–8.

Kunkel, T., Funk, D.C. and Hill, B. (2013). 'Brand architecture, drivers of consumer involvement, and brand loyalty with professional sport leagues and teams', *Journal of Sport Management*, 27(3), pp. 177–92.

Kunkel, T., Funk, D.C. and King, C. (in press). 'Developing a conceptual understanding of consumer-based league brand associations', *Journal of Sport Management*.

Kunz, M. and Hackworth, B.A. (2011). 'Are consumers following retailers to social networks?', *Academy of Marketing Studies Journal*, 15(2), pp. 1–22.

Kunz, B., Hackworth, B., Osborne, P. and High, D. (2011). 'Fans, friends, and followers: Social media in the retailers' marketing mix', *Journal of Applied Business and Economics*, 12(3), pp. 61–8.

Kwek, G. (2013). 'AFL leaves other codes in the dust', *Sydney Morning Herald*, 26 March, <www.smh.com.au/data-point/afl-leaves-other-codes-in-the-dust-20130326-2grkp.html#ixzz2OkwFVU9A>, retrieved 26 March 2013.

Laird, S. (2012). 'Dana White explains the UFC's social media choke hold', *Mashable*, 14 December, <http://mashable.com/2012/12/13/dana-white-ufc-q-and-a>, retrieved 20 March 2013.

LA Kings (2013). 'About LA Kings fan development', <http://kings.nhl.com/club/page.htm?id=41260>, retrieved 25 March 2013.

Lam, E.T.C., Zhang, J.J. and Jensen, B.E. (2005). 'Service Quality Assessment Scale (SQAS): An instrument for evaluating service quality of health–fitness clubs', *Measurement in Physical Education and Exercise Science*, 9(2), pp. 79–111.

Lambrecht, K.W., Kaefer, F. and Ramenofsky, S.D. (2009). 'Sportscape factors influencing attendance and satisfaction at a professional golf association tournament', *Sport Marketing Quarterly*, 18, pp. 165–72.

Lane, S and Spits, S. (2013). 'Review slams "toxic" culture', *Sydney Morning Herald*, 20 February, <www.smh.com.au/sport/swimming/review-slams-toxic-culture-in-swimming-20130219-2eoee.html>, retrieved 25 February 2013.

Langeard, E., Bateson, J., Lovelock, C. and Eiglier, P. (1981). *Services Marketing: New Insights from Consumers and Managers*, Report no. 81-104, Marketing Science Institute, Cambridge, Mass.

Lans, M.S. (1995). 'Sports team logos are big business', *Marketing News*, 29(12), p. 6.

Lapidus, R.S. and Schilbrowsky, J.A. (1996). 'Do the hot dogs taste better when the home team wins?', *Journal of Consumer Satisfaction, Dissatisfaction and Complaining Behaviour*, 9, pp. 1-11.

Lee, E. (2012). 'MLB said to get $6.6 billion from Fox, Turner for TV rights', *Bloomberg*, <www.bloomberg.com/news/2012-10-02/mlb-said-to-get-6-8-billion-from-fox-turner-to-renew-tv-rights.html>, retrieved 29 January 2013.

Lefton, T. (2012). 'NBA licensing revenue climbing', SportsBusiness Daily, 29 October, <http://m.sportsbusinessdaily.com/Journal/Issues/2012/10/29/Leagues-and-Governing-Bodies/NBA-licensing.aspx>, retrieved 15 January 2013.

Legg, D. and Baker, J. (1987). 'Advertising strategies for service firms', in C. Surprenant (ed.), *Add Value to Your Service*, American Marketing Association, Chicago, pp. 163-8.

Lepisto, L.R. and Hannaford, W.J. (1980). 'Purchase constraint analysis: An alternative perspective for marketers', *Journal of the Academy of Marketing Science*, 8(1), pp. 12-25.

Lewis, R. and Kitchen, P. (2010). 'New communication media for sport', in M. Hopwood, P. Kitchen and J. Skinner (eds), *Sport Public Relations and Communication*, Elsevier, Oxford, pp. 187-214.

Leys, N. (2013). 'Test of wills figures in Indian cricket brawl', *The Australian*, 18 March, <www.theaustralian.com.au/media/test-of-wills-figures-in-indian-cricket-brawl/story-e6frg996-1226599355169>, retrieved 20 March 2013.

The Licensing Letter© (2008). EPM Communications, Inc., <www.epmcom.com>, retrieved 20 February 2013.

Lloyd, D.C. and Clancy, K.J. (1991). 'CPMs versus CPMIs: Implications for media planning', *Journal of Advertising Research*, August/September, pp. 34-43.

London Organising Committee of the Olympic Games and Paralympic Games Limited (LOCOG) (2012). *London 2012 Post-Games Sustainability Report*, LOCOG, London.

Lovelock, C.H. (1991). *Services Marketing*, 2nd edn, Prentice-Hall, Englewood Cliffs, NJ.

Lovelock, C.H., Patterson, P.G. and Walker, R.H. (2001). *Services Marketing: An Asia-Pacific Perspective*, Pearson Education, Sydney.

Lovelock, C.H., Wirtz, J. and Chew, P. (2009). *Essentials of Services Marketing*, Prentice-Hall, Englewood Cliffs, NJ.

Lynch, B.M. and Dunn, J. (2003). 'Scoreboard advertising at sporting events as a health promotion medium', *Health Education Research: Theory and Practice*, 18(4), pp. 488-92.

MacIntosh, E., Nadeau, J., Seguin, B., O'Reilly, N., Bradish, C.L., and Legg, D. (2012). 'The role of mega-sports event interest in sponsorship and ambush marketing attitudes', *Sport Marketing Quarterly*, 21, 43-52.

MacKay, K.J. and Crompton, J.L. (1988). 'A conceptual model of consumer evaluation of recreation service quality', *Leisure Studies*, 7(1), pp. 40-9.

Madrigal, R. (1995). 'Cognitive and affective determinants of fan satisfaction with sporting event attendance', *Journal of Leisure Research*, 27, pp. 205-27.

Magowan, A. (2012). 'UEFA told to take a tougher line against racism in football', *BBC Sport*, 8 June, <www.bbc.co.uk/sport/0/football/18356761>, retrieved 25 February 2013.

Mahony, D.F., Madrigal, R. and Howard, D.R. (1999). 'The effect of individual levels of self-monitoring on loyalty to professional football teams', *International Journal of Sports Marketing & Sponsorship*, 1(2), pp. 146-67.

Major League Baseball (2013). 'About MLB Fan Cave', *MLB*, <http://mlb.mlb.com/fancave/about.jsp#fbid=iK9o_NU0dH5>, retrieved 20 March 2013.

Mallesons Stephen Jacques (2006). 'Sponsorship rights and ambush marketing—winning the race for public recognition', <http://mallesons.com//publications/2006/May/8409080x.htm>, retrieved 5 November 2007.

Mangold, W. and Faulds, D. (2009). 'Social media: The new hybrid element of the promotion mix', *Business Horizons*, 52(4), pp. 357–65.

Manovich, L. (2001). *The Language of New Media*, MIT Press, London.

——(2003). 'New media from Borges to HTML', in N. Wardrip-Fruin and N. Montfort (eds), *The New Media Reader*, Cambridge University Press, Cambridge, MA, pp. 13–25*Marketing Magazine* (2012). 'Nike gazumps Adidas in stunning Olympics ambush', 26 July, <www.marketingmag.com.au/news/nike-gazumps-adidas-in-stunning-olympics-ambush-17209/#.UX9hWHcmHIs>, retrieved 23 April 2013.

Masters, R. (2012). 'TV deal great fillip for code', *The Age*, 17 November, p. 17.

Matthews, B. (2002). 'More courses for new mecca', *Herald Sun* (Melbourne), 31 July, p. 75.

Mavo, K. (2013). 'Why golfer Rory McIlroy will never be Tiger Woods', *Bloomberg Businessweek*, 14 January, <www.businessweek.com/articles/2013-01-14/why-golfer-rory-mcilroy-will-never-be-tiger-woods>, retrieved 23 January 2013.

McCarthy, L. (1998). 'Marketing sport to Hispanic consumers', *Sport Marketing Quarterly*, 7(4), pp. 19–24.

McCarthy, L. (2011). 'NBC wins rights to Olympics through 2020; promises more live coverage', *USA Today*, 7 June, <http://content.usatoday.com/communities/gameon/post/2011/06/olympic-tv-decision-between-nbc-espn-and-fox-could-come-down-today/1>, retrieved 29 January 2013.

McCarthy, S. (2011a). 'The future of direct marketing looks bright', *B&T Magazine Australia*, p. 17.

McCullagh, K. (2012). 'New media, new money', *Sport Business International*, p. 16.

McDonald, H. (2010). 'The factors influencing churn rates among season ticket holders: An empirical analysis', *Journal of Sport Management*, 24 (6), 676–701.

McDonald, H., Karg, A.J. and Vocino, A. (2013). 'Measuring season ticket holder satisfaction: Rationale, scale development and longitudinal validation', *Sport Management Review*, 16(1), pp. 41–53.

McDonald, H.J. and Shaw, R.N. (2005). 'Satisfaction as a predictor of football club members' intentions', *International Journal of Sports Marketing and Sponsorship*, 7(1), pp. 81–8.

McDonald, M.A., Milne, G.R. and Hong, J. (2002). 'Motivational factors for evaluating sport spectators and participant markets', *Sport Marketing Quarterly*, 11(2), pp. 100–11.

McDonald, M.A., Sutton, W.A. and Milne, G.R. (1995). 'TEAMQUAL: Measuring service quality in professional team sports', *Sport Marketing Quarterly*, 4, pp. 9–15.

McGeoch, R. and Korporaal, G. (1994). *The Bid: How Australia Won the 2000 Games*, William Heinemann, Melbourne.

McNamara, J. (2012). *Public Relations: Theories Practices and Critiques*, Pearson, Sydney.

Meade, A. (2001). 'Outsider to test TV ratings agencies', *The Australian*, 20 March, p. 8.

Melbourne and Olympic Parks (2007). 'Melbourne rectangular stadium', <www.mopt.com.au/deskstopdefault.aspx/tabid-22//243_read247>, retrieved 1 October 2007.

Menary, S. (2001). 'Clubs profit from good groundwork', *Football Business International*, December, pp. 44–6.

Mendel, F. and Yijun, C. (2003). 'Protecting Olympic intellectual property', *China Law and Practice*, 17(4), pp. 33–4.

Mermigas, D. (2002). 'NBA passes over to Disney and AOL', *Electronic Media*, 21(4), p. 6.

Miller, M.J. (2012). 'London 2012 watch: Nike flips the bird to Olympics brand police', *brandchannel*, 25 July, <www.brandchannel.com/home/post/london-2012-nike-ambush-marketing-072512.aspx>, retrieved 23 April 2013.

Mittal, B. (2002). 'Services communications: From mindless tangibilisation to meaningful messages', *Journal of Services Marketing*, 16(5), pp. 424–31.

Mittal, V. and Kamakura, W.A. (2001). 'Satisfaction, repurchase intent, and repurchase behavior: Investigating the moderating effect of customer characteristics', *Journal of Marketing Research*, 38, pp. 131–42.

Mullin, B.J. (1980). 'Sport management: The nature and utility of the concept', *Arena Review*, 3(4), pp. 1–11.

——(1985a). 'Characteristics of sport marketing', in G. Lewis and H. Appenzellar (eds), *Successful Sport Management*, Michie, Charlottesville, VA, pp. 101–23.

——(1985b). 'Internal marketing—a more effective way to sell sport', in G. Lewis and H. Appenzellar (eds), *Successful Sport Management*, Michie, Charlottesville, VA, pp. 157–75.

Mullin, B.J., Hardy, S. and Sutton, W.A. (2007). *Sport Marketing*, 3rd edn, Human Kinetics, Champaign, IL.

——(2000). *Sport Marketing*, 2nd ed., Human Kinetics, Champaign, IL.

——(1993). *Sport Marketing*, Human Kinetics, Champaign, IL.

Murphy, S. (2013). 'Avid sports fans 52% more likely to own a tablet', *Mashable*, 23 January, <http://mashable.com/2013/01/22/sports-digital-technology>, retrieved 20 March 2013.

Naidoo, U. and Gardiner, S. (2002). 'Preventing ambush—innovative ideas from Salt Lake City 2002', *SportBusiness International*, March, p. 62.

Nakra, P. (1991). 'Zapping nonsense: Should television media planners lose sleep over it?', *International Journal of Advertising*, 10, pp. 217–22.

NBA (2012). 'Satisfaction guaranteed night', n.d., <www.nba.com/suns/guaranteed>, retrieved 20 April 2013.

National Basketball League (2000). *Chief Executive Annual Report*, NBL, Melbourne.

National Rugby League (2012). *The Game Plan 2013–2017*, NRL, Sydney.

Nesbit, T.M. and King, K.A. (2010a). 'The impact of fantasy football participation on NFL attendance', *Atlantic Economic Journal*, 38(1), pp. 95–108.

——(2010b). 'The impact of fantasy sports on television viewership', *Journal of Media Economics*, 23(1), pp. 24–41.

Neuman, W.R. (1991). *The Future of the Mass Audience*. Cambridge University Press, Cambridge.

New York Yankees (2012). 'Stadium comparison', <http://newyork.yankees.mlb.com/nyy/ballpark/new_stadium_comparison.jsp>, retrieved 15 December 2012.

Nielsen Research (2012). *State of the Media: 2012 Year in Sports*, Nielsen, New York.

Nichols, W., Moynahan, P., Hall, A. and Taylor, J. (2002). *Media Relations in Sport*, Fitness Information Technology, Morgantown, WV.

Ofcom (2012). 'Facts & figures', <http://media.ofcom.org.uk/facts>, retrieved 25 January 2013.

O'Hara, B. and Weese, W.J. (1994). 'Advertising theory applied to the intramural recreation sports environment', *Sport Marketing Quarterly*, 3(1), pp. 9–14.

Oliver, R.L. (2010). *Satisfaction: A Behavioral Perspective on the Consumer*, 2nd edn, M.E. Sharpe, Armonk, NY.

Owen, P.D. and Weatherston, C.R. (2004). 'Uncertainty of outcome, player quality and attendance at national provincial championship rugby union matches: An evaluation in light of the competition review', *Economic Papers*, 23, pp. 301–24.

OzTAM (2001). 'Comparison of OzTAM and ACNielsen TV ratings services', media release, 22 May.

Parasuraman, A., Zeithaml, V.A. and Berry, L.L. (1985). 'A conceptual model of service quality and its implications for future research', *Journal of Marketing*, 49, pp. 41–50.

——(1988). 'SERVQUAL: A multiple-item scale for measuring consumer perceptions of service quality', *Journal of Retailing*, 64, pp. 12–37.

Paxinos, S. (2013). 'Swimming hit by second damning report', *Sydney Morning Herald*, 19 February, <www.smh.com.au/sport/swimming/swimming-hit-by-second-damning-report-20130219-2eopl.html>, retrieved 25 February 2013.

Pearson, D. (2007). *State Investment in Major Events*, Victorian Auditor-General's Office, Melbourne.
Pegoraro, A. (2010). 'Look who's talking—athletes on Twitter: A case study', *International Journal of Sport Communication*, 3, pp. 501–14.
Perreault, W.D. and McCarthy, J.E. (2002). *Basic Marketing*, 14th edn, McGraw Hill, New York.
Pesutto, G. (2012). *Cricket and AFL Dominate Sports Watched on TV*, Roy Morgan Research, Melbourne.
Peterson, R.A. and Wilson, W.R. (1992). 'Measuring customer satisfaction: Fact and artifact', *Journal of the Academy of Marketing Science*, 20(1), pp. 61–71.
Pettigrew, S. (2013). 'Study shows kids influenced by sport ads for alcohol, fast food', *UWA News*, 17 January, <www.news.uwa.edu.au/201301175376/business-and-industry/study-shows-kids-influenced-sport-ads-alcohol-fast-food>, retrieved 23 April 2013.
Philadelphia Union (2013). *Season Ticket Cards & Loyalty Program*, <www.philadelphiaunion.com/tickets/season-ticket-cards-loyalty-program>, retrieved 25 March 2013
Pierce, P. (2012). 'Titans guarantee they will beat Melbourne Storm or give away free tickets', *FOX Sports*, 16 March, <www.foxsports.com.au/league/nrl-premiership/gold-coast-titans-guarantee-they-will-beat-melbourne-storm-or-give-away-free-tickets/story-fn2mcuj6-1226301202265#ixzz2MaLpMjBC>, retrieved 20 April 2013.
Pierik, J. (2012). 'Demons tanked: McLean', *The Age*, 31 July, <www.theage.com.au/afl/afl-news/demons-tanked-mclean-20120730-23akv.html>, retrieved 27 February 2013.
Pitta, D.A. and Fowler, D. (2005). 'Internet community forums: An untapped resource for consumer marketers', *Journal of Consumer Marketing*, 22(5), pp. 265–74.
Pollard, R. (2013). 'Not the goal: Israeli football racism divides fans', *The Australian*, 12 February, p. 8.
Poon, T.Y. and Prendergast, G. (2006). 'A new framework for evaluating sponsorship opportunities', *International Journal of Advertising*, 25(4), pp. 471–88.
Pope, N.K. and Voges, K. (2000). 'The impact of sport sponsorship activities, corporate image and prior use on consumer purchase intention', *Sport Marketing Quarterly*, 9(2), pp. 45–56.
Porter, M. (1980). *Competitive Strategy*, The Free Press, New York.
——(1985), *Competitive Advantage: Creating and Sustaining Superior Performance*, The Free Press, New York.
PR Newswire (2009). 'Fantasy Sports History: Reeling in a Fantasy Fishing $1 Million Payday', *PR Newswire*, 22 July, <www.prnewswire.com/news-releases/fantasy-sports-history-reeling-in-a-fantasy-fishing-1-million-payday-62258067.html>, retrieved 25 March 2013.
Premier League Season Review (2012). 'Premier League Season Review', <http://addison.ceros.com/premier-league/season-review-2011-12/page/1>, retrieved 12 January 2013.
PricewaterhouseCoopers (2011) 'Changing the game: Outlook for the global sports market', <www.pwc.com/en_GX/gx/hospitality-leisure/pdf/changing-the-game-outlook-for-the-global-sports-market-to-2015.pdf>, retrieved 25 March 2013.
Pritchard, M.P. and Funk, D.C. (2006). 'Symbiosis and substitution in spectator sport', *Journal of Sport Management*, 20, pp. 299–321.
Pritchard, M., Funk, D.C. and Alexandris, K. (2009). 'Barriers to repeat patronage: The impact of spectator constraints', *European Journal of Marketing*, 43, pp. 169–87.
Proszenko, A. (2013). 'Old hats out of the game still beat the young guns', *Sun-Herald*, 17 March, pp. 62–3.
Pumerantz, Z. (2012). 'The craziest promotions in sports history', bleacher report, 13 September, <http://bleacherreport.com/articles/1331719-the-craziest-promotions-in-sports-history>, retrieved 25 March 2013.
Ralph, J. (2013). 'Pay off may come later', *Herald Sun*, 20 February, p. 76.
Ray, M.L. (1982). *Advertising and Communication Management*, Prentice-Hall, Englewood Cliffs, NJ.
Red Elephant (2011). 'Marketing campaign to drive CALD community fan development and

attendances for Sydney FC', 29 September, <www.redelephantprojects.com/projects/marketing-campaign-to-drive-cald-community-fan-development-and-attendances-for-sydney-fc>, retrieved 25 March 2013.

Reeves, C. and Bednar, D. (1994). 'Defining quality: Alternatives and implications', *The Academy of Management Review*, 19(3), pp. 419–45.

Rein, I., Kotler, P. and Shields, B. (2006). *The Elusive Fan: Reinventing Sports in a Crowded Marketplace*, McGraw-Hill, New York.

RepuCom. (2013). 'RepuCom—media evaluation', <http://repucom.net/what-we-do/media-evaluation>, retrieved 2 April 2013.

Ridinger, L. and Funk, D.C. (2006). 'Looking at gender differences through the lens of sport spectators', *Sport Marketing Quarterly*, 15(3), pp. 155–66.

Ries, A. and Ries, L. (2009). *The Fall of Advertising and the Rise of PR*, Harper Collins, New York.

Ries, A. and Trout, J. (1986). *Positioning: The Battle for Your Mind*, Warner, New York.

Rishe, P. (2011). 'How does London's Olympics bill compare to previous games?' *SportsMoney*, <www.forbes.com/sites/sportsmoney/2011/08/05/how-does-londons-olympics-bill-compare-to-previous-games>, retrieved 15 January 2012.

Roberts, G. (2010). 'Ads, not sport stars, to blame for binge drinking', *ABC News*, 22 April, <www.abc.net.au/news/2010-04-22/ads-not-sport-stars-to-blame-for-binge-drinking/406948>, retrieved 23 April 2013.

Roberts, K. (2002). 'Visa playing its cards right', *SportBusiness International*, February, pp. 22–3.

Robertson, H. (2012). *London 2012 Olympic and Paralympic Games—Quarterly Report, June 2012*, Department for Culture, Media and Sport, London.

Robertson, T.S. (1976). 'Low commitment consumer behavior', *Journal of Advertising Research*, 16, pp. 19–24.

Robinson, M. (2013). 'If it looks like a tank, sounds like a tank and acts like a tank, it's a tank', *Herald Sun*, 20 February, p. 78.

Robinson, M. and Warner W. (2013). 'After seven-month investigation AFL says thanks … but NO TANKS', *Herald Sun*, 20 February, p. 80.

Rogers, S. (2012). 'London 2012 Olympic sponsors list: Who are they and what have they paid?', *London 2012 Olympics Data*, <www.guardian.co.uk/sport/datablog/2012/jul/19/london-2012-olympic-sponsors-list>, retrieved 28 March 2013.

Rovell, D. (2003). 'Seven licensees will pay the bulk of the fees', ESPN.go.com, 6 August, <http://espn.go.com/sportsbusiness/news/2003/0804/1590167.html>, retrieved 19 November 2007.

——(2012). 'Best seat in the house', *ESPN Outside the Lines*, 16 December, <http://espn.go.com/espn/otl/story/_/id/8636927/nfl-taking-note-many-fans-watching-games-tv-beats-going-stadiums?src=mobile>, retrieved 20 March 2013.

Roy, D.P. and Goss, B.D. (2007). 'A conceptual framework of influences of fantasy sports consumption', *Marketing Management Journal*, 17(2), pp. 96–108.

Rucker, D. and Calkins, T. (2013). 'Super Bowl advertising's new game', *Forbes*, 23 January, <www.forbes.com/sites/onmarketing/2013/01/23/super-bowl-advertisings-new-game>, retrieved 20 March 2013.

Rust, R.T. and Oliver, R.L. (1994). 'Service quality: Insights and managerial implications from the frontier', in R. Rust and R. Oliver (eds), *Service Quality: New Directions in Theory and Practice*, Sage, Thousand Oaks, CA.

Saltau, C. (2007). 'Twenty20 set to be in big league', *Sunday Age, Sport*, 9 September, p. 17.

Sandler, D.M. and Shani, D. (1989). 'Olympic sponsorship vs "ambush" marketing: Who gets the gold?', *Journal of Advertising Research*, August/September, pp. 9–14.

Santomier J. and Shuart, J. (2008). 'Sport and new media', *International Journal of Sport Management and Marketing*, 4(1), pp. 85–101.

Schaaf, P. (1995). *Sports Marketing: It's Not Just a Game Anymore*, Prometheus Books, Amherst, NY.

S-Comm & ASMA (2006). *Sponsorship Outlook 2006: Australian Sponsorship Industry Report*. Sydney.

Schiffman, L.G. and Kanuk, L.L. (2000). *Consumer Behavior*, 7th edn, Prentice-Hall, Upper Saddle River, NJ.

Schultz, D.E. and Schultz, H.F. (2004). *IMC Next Generation*, McGraw-Hill, New York.

Schulze, J. (2001). 'New ratings system shakes the networks', *The Age*, 12 February, p. 3.

Seitel, F.P. (1995). *The Practice of Public Relations*, Prentice-Hall, Englewood Cliffs, NJ.

Sheffer, M. and Schultz, B. (2010). 'Paradigm shift or passing fad? Twitter and sports journalism', *International Journal of Sport Communication*, 3, pp. 472–84.

Sherman, A.J. (1991). *Franchising and Licensing: Two Ways to Build Your Business*, American Management Association, New York.

Shilbury, D. (1989). 'Characteristics of sport marketing: Developing trends', *ACHPER National Journal*, Autumn, pp. 21–4.

——(1991). 'Marketing scores with game plan for sports', *Marketing*, July, pp. 18–22.

——(1994). 'Delivering quality service in professional sport', *Sport Marketing Quarterly*, 3(1), pp. 29–35.

Sleight, S. (1989). *Sponsorship: What It Is and How to Use It*, McGraw-Hill, Sydney.

Smith, A. and Westerbeek, H.M. (2007). 'Sport as a vehicle for deploying corporate social responsibility', *Journal of Corporate Citizenship*, 25, pp. 43–54.

Smith, R.D. (2009). *Strategic Planning for Public Relations*, 3rd edn, Routledge, New York.

Spinda, J.S.W. and Haridakis, P.M. (2008). 'Exploring the motives of fantasy sports: A uses-and-gratifications approach', in L.W. Hugenberg, P.M. Haridakis and A.C. Earnheardt (eds), *Sports Mania: Essays on Fandom and the Media in the 21st Century*, McFarland, Jefferson, NC, pp. 187–202.

Spolestra, J. (1991). *How to Sell the Last Seat in the House*, vol. 1, SRO Partners, Portland, OR.

Sport and Recreation Victoria (2000). *Sport and Recreation Business Information Series*, no. 3. p. 1.

SportBusiness (2000). 'Sportfacts', April, p. 58.

——(2011). 'Toyota extends AFL sponsorship deal', <www.sportbusiness.com/news/183887/toyota-extends-afl-sponsorship-deal>, retrieved 15 December 2012.

SportBusiness in Numbers (2007). 'In focus: The Australian sponsorship perspective', <www.scomm.com.au>, retrieved 1 June 2007.

Sporting Pulse (2011). 'NBL reveals four year transition plan', <http://sport.gameday.com.au/index.php?id=518&tx_ttnews%5Btt_news%5D=670&cHash=d11e621503>, retrieved 27 March 2013.

Stanley, A. (2013). 'Dispassionate end to a crumbled American romance', *New York Times*, 18 January, <www.nytimes.com/2013/01/18/arts/television/lance-armstrong-interview-with-oprah-winfrey-lacked-emotion.html>, retrieved 19 February 2013.

Stanton, W.J., Miller, K.E. and Layton, R. (1995). *Fundamentals of Marketing*, 3rd edn, McGraw-Hill, Sydney.

Steffens, M. (2007). 'Nine's $110m for ratings gold medal', *The Age, Business Day*, 15 October, p. 1.

Stensholt, J. (2012). 'AFL's $5m media division exceeds internal targets', *Australian Financial Review*, 10 December, <www.afr.com/p/lifestyle/sport/afl_media_division_exceeds_internal_1GJ3Bc3XHbYHXLP3mibQIO>, retrieved 20 March 2013.

Stoldt, G., Dittmore, S. and Branvold, S. (2012). *Sport Public Relations: Managing Stakeholder Communications*, 2nd edn, Human Kinetics, Champaign, IL.

Stotlar, D. (1993). *Successful Sport Marketing*, Brown & Benchmark, Dubuque, IA.

——(2004). 'Sponsorship evaluation: Moving from theory to practice', *Sport Marketing Quarterly*, 13(1), pp. 61–4.

Sunday Times (2006). 'Net wealth: The global impact of the World Cup', 6 November, p. 2.

Sutton, W.A. and Parrett, I. (1992). 'Marketing the core product in professional team sports in the United States', *Sport Marketing Quarterly*, 1(2), pp. 7–19.
Sweeney Sports (2005–06). 'Thorpe still the favourite as swimmers take plunge' and 'Bogut, cricketers do well', media releases, <www.sweeney research.com.au/newspdf/news_pdf_12.pdf>, retrieved 1 November 2007.
——(2006). 'Seven, Ten getting Rules at a peak', <www.sweeney research.com.au/sports_report.asp>, retrieved 12 January 2007.
Sygall, D. (2006). 'How the NBL is trying to rebound', *Sun-Herald*, 30 April, p. 88.
Tabakoff, N. (2013). 'NRL tackles new world of virtual advertising', *The Australian*, 22 April, <www.theaustralian.com.au/media/broadcast/nrl-tackles-new-world-of-virtual-advertising/story-fna045gd-1226625374885>, retrieved 23 April 2013.
Taylor, L. (1984). 'The marketing and sponsorship of sport in Australia', *Sports Coach*, 8(2), pp. 12–14.
Taylor, S.A. and Baker, T.L. (1994). 'An Assessment of the Relationship Between Service Quality and Customer Satisfaction in the Formation of Consumers' Purchase Intentions', *Journal of Retailing*, 70, pp. 163–78.
Theodorakis, N., Alexandris, K., Tsigilis, N. and Karvounis, S. (2013). 'Predicting spectators' behavioural intentions in professional football: The role of satisfaction and service quality', *Sport Management Review*, 16, pp. 85–96.
Theodorakis, N., Kambitsis, C., Laios, A. and Koustelios, A. (2001). 'Relationship between measures of service quality and satisfaction of spectators in professional sports', *Managing Service Quality*, 11(6), pp. 431–8.
Thorndike, E.L. (1920). 'A constant error in psychological rating', *Journal of Applied Psychology*, 4(1), pp. 25–9.
Thornton, G., Gough, D. and Martin, D. (2012). *Meta-Evaluation of the Impacts and Legacy of the London 2012 Olympic Games and Paralympic Games*, Department for Culture, Media and Sport, London.
TNA (2013). 'TNA IMPACT WRESTLING. Raises voice to save Olympic Wrestling', media release, 12 February, <http://finance.yahoo.com/news/tna-impact-wrestling-raises-voice-194400930.html>, retrieved 1 March 2013.
Todreas, T.M. (1999). *Value Creation and Branding in Television's Digital Age*, Quorum, Westport, CT.
Tourism Victoria (2011). *Formula One Australian Grand Prix: Benefits to Victoria*, Tourism Victoria, Melbourne.
Trail, G.T. and James, J.D. (2001). 'The Motivation Scale for Sport Consumption: Assessment of the scale's psychometric properties', *Journal of Sport Behavior*, 24(1), pp. 108–27.
Turner, P. (2012). 'Regulation of professional sport in a changing broadcasting environment: Australian club and sport broadcaster perspectives', *Sport Management Review*, 15(10), pp. 43–69.
UEFA (2010). 'UEFA appoints worldwide licensing representative', <www.uefa.com/uefa/events/marketing/news/newsid=1495401.html#uefa+appoints+worldwide+licensing+representative>, retrieved 15 January 2013.
URS Australasia (2007). *Economic Impact Analysis of 2007 Ashes Tour*, Cricket Australia/Tourism Australia/Department of Industry, Tourism and Resources, Melbourne.
USA Today (1994). 'TV pays the way', 21 October.
Valenzuela, M. (2011). 'C'mon Aussie, enough of the junk food ads during the cricket', *Sydney Morning Herald*, 3 February, <www.smh.com.au/opinion/society-and-culture/cmon-aussie-enough-of-the-junk-food-ads-during-the-cricket-20110202-1adri.html>, retrieved 23 April 2013.
Van den Poel, D. and Leunis, J. (1999). 'Consumer acceptance of the internet as a channel of distribution', *Journal of Business Research*, 45, pp. 249–56.

van Leeuwen, L. (2001). Determinants of customer satisfaction with the season ticket service of professional sport clubs, unpublished doctoral dissertation, University of Technology, Sydney.
van Leeuwen, L., Quick, S. and Daniel, K. (2002). 'The Sport Spectator Satisfaction Model: A conceptual framework for understanding the satisfaction of spectators', *Sport Management Review*, 5, pp. 99–128.
Vargo, S. and Lusch, R.F. (2008). 'Service-dominant logic: Continuing the evolution', *Journal of the Academy of Marketing Science*, 36, pp. 1–10.
Veeck, B. and Linn, E. (1962). *Veeck as in Wreck*, New American Library, New York.
——(2002). 'Hitting an all-time low', *Sydney Morning Herald*, 10 July, p. 35.
Vivek, S.D., Beatty, S.E. and Morgan, R.M. (2012), 'Consumer engagement: Exploring customer relationships beyond purchase', *Marketing Theory and Practice*, 20(2), pp. 122–46.
Vranica, S. (2013). 'Costly Super Bowl Ads Pay Publicity Dividend', *Wall Street Journal*, 3 February, <http://online.wsj.com/article/SB10001424127887324900204578282360008085752.html>, retrieved 23 April 2013.
Wakefield, K.L. and Blodgett, J.G. (1994). 'The importance of servicescapes in leisure service settings', *Journal of Services Marketing*, 8(3), pp. 66–76.
——(1996). 'The effect of the servicescape on customers' behavioral intentions in leisure service settings', *Journal of Services Marketing*, 10(6), pp. 45–61.
Wakefield, K.L., Blodgett, J.G. and Sloan, H.J. (1996). 'Measurement and management of the sportscape', *Journal of Sport Management*, 10(1), pp. 15–31.
Wakefield, K.L. and Sloan, H.J. (1995). 'The effects of team loyalty and selected stadium factors on spectator attendance', *Journal of Sport Management*, 9(2), pp. 153–72.
Wallace, T. (2002). 'Expanding the branding', *Football Business International*, March, pp. 31–2.
Wallace, L, Wilson, J. and Miloch, K. (2011). 'Sporting Facebook: A content analysis of NCAA organizational sport pages and Big 12 Conference athletic department pages', *International Journal of Sport Communication*, 4, pp. 422–44.
Walsh, S. (2013). 'New York Red Bulls first MLS club to sell tickets via Facebook', Digital Football. com, n.d, <http://digital-football.com/featured/new-york-red-bulls-to-sell-tickets-via-facebook>, retrieved 20 March 2013.
Ward, R. (2012). 'Ten, NBL stay in the picture despite cuts', *The Age*, 24 February, p. 18.
Warner, M. (2010). 'Sponsors collide head-on', *Courier-Mail*, <www.couriermail.com.au/sport/afl/sponsors-collide-head-on/story-e6frepf6-1225845736862>, retrieved 13 January 2013.
Westerbeek, H.M. (2000). 'Is sponsorship retention dependent on the geographic location of the sport facility?', *Journal of Marketing Communications*, 6(2), pp. 53–68.
Westerbeek, H.M. and Smith, A. (2001). 'Understanding the criteria for a winning bid strategy', in *The Future for Host Cities*, SportBusiness Group, London, p. 24.
——(2002). 'Location dependency and sport sponsors: A factor analytic study', *Sport Marketing Quarterly*, 11(3), pp. 151–61.
——(2003). *Sport Business in the Global Marketplace*, Palgrave Macmillan, London.
Westerbeek, H.M. and Turner, P. (1996). 'Market power of sport organisations: An Australian case study', in *Conference Proceedings, 4th International Conference on Sport Management (EASM)*, Montpellier, France.
Whalley, J. (2012). 'Football the jewel in the media crown as business hunt the big game', *Herald-Sun*, 29 September, <business/football-the-jewel-in-the-media-crown-as-businesses-hunt-the-big-game/story-fn7j19iv-1226483736110>, retrieved 17 August 2013.
Wikipedia (2007). 'NFL on television', <http://en.wikipedia.org/wiki/NFL_on_television>, retrieved 15 October 2007.
——(2013a). 'NFL on television', <http://en.wikipedia.org/wiki/NFL_on_television>, retrieved 29 January 2013.

——(2013b). 'NHL on Versus', <http://en.wikipedia.org/wiki/NHL_on_Versus>, retrieved 29 January 2013.

——(2013c). 'List of attendance figures at domestic professional sports leagues', <http://en.wikipedia.org/wiki/List_of_attendance_figures_at_domestic_professional_sports_leagues>, retrieved 27 March 2013.

——(2013d). '2012 NBL All-Star game', <http://en.wikipedia.org/wiki/2012-13_NBL_season#All-Star_Game>, retrieved 27 March 2013.

Wilcox, D., Cameron, G., Reber, B. and Shin, J. (2013). *Think Public Relations*, Pearson Education, Boston, MA.

Wilkof, N.J. (1995). *Trade Mark Licensing*, Sweet & Maxwell, London.

Williams, J. and Chinn, S. (2010). 'Meeting relationship-marketing goals through social media: A conceptual model for sport marketers', *International Journal of Sport Communication*, 3, pp. 422–37.

Wilmoth, P. (2001). 'TV ratings system favours the young', *The Age*, 23 May, p. 2.

Wilmshurst, J. (1993). *Below-the-Line Promotion*, Butterworth/Heinemann, Oxford.

Wilner, B. (2001). 'Tiger helps PGA pay $870m TV deal', *SportBusiness International*, September, p. 18.

Wilson, C. (2012). 'AFL sponsor deal brewing', *Sydney Morning Herald*, <www.smh.com.au/afl/afl-news/afl-sponsor-deal-brewing-20120426-1xo0s.html>, retrieved 14 January 2013.

Whalley, J. (2012). 'Football the jewel in the media crown as businesses hunt the big game', *Herald Sun*, 29 September, <www.heraldsun.com.au/business/football-the-jewel-in-the-media-crown-as-businesses-hunt-the-big-game/story-fn7j19iv-1226483736110>, retrieved 1 February 2013.

Yahoo (2013). 'IBM and the Australian Open mark 20 years of serving a winning advantage to tennis fans', *PR Newswire*, 15 January, <http://finance.yahoo.com/news/ibm-australian-open-mark-20-203000904.html>, retrieved 25 March 2013.

Zbar, J.D. (2002). 'Ball's bounce goes ESPN, TNT's way', *Advertising Age*, 73(23), p. S12.

Zeithaml, V.A. (1991). 'How consumer evaluation processes differ between goods and services', in C. Lovelock (ed.), *Services Marketing*, 2nd edn, Prentice-Hall, Upper Saddle River, NJ.

Zeithaml, V.A., Bitner, M. J., and Gremler, D.D. (2009). *Services Marketing: An Integrated Approach Across the Firm*, McGraw Hill, Boston.

——(1990). *Delivering Service Quality: Balancing Customer Perceptions and Expectations*, The Free Press, New York.

Zinger, J.T. and O'Reilly, N. (2010). 'An examination of sports sponsorship from a small business perspective', *International Journal of Sport Marketing and Sponsorship*, 11(4), pp. 283–302.

Index

7Ps of service marketing 7–8

A-League Football 24, 36, 37, 58, 63, 88–90, 107, 217
Academy of Royal Medical Colleges 215
accountability 181
ACER 276
AC Nielsen TV ratings 226, 239–40
acquisition-based strategies 6
active publics 306–7
Adidas 212, 274, 277, 279, 332
administration *see* management of sport products
advantages of sports sponsorship 267–8
advertising 197–215
  budget 202–3, 209
  cost 209
  creative strategy 204–6
  creativity 199
  data collection for 73
  definition 199
  distributed campaign 203
  during sports programs 227–9
  effectiveness, measuring 210–11, 230–3
  independent tool 198–9
  integration 199, 201, 203
  low-involvement purchases 65–6
  management process 200–1
  massed campaign 203
  media choices 206–8
  media selection 209–10
  message strategy 203–4
  objectives 202
  online advertising 206–7, 210, 257–8
  physical evidence and 143
  product positioning via 105
  promotion mix, in 182–3
  reach versus frequency 201
  socially responsible 213–15
  strategy 201
  television *see* television
  timeframe 202, 209
  trademarks and 324
  value adding 199
advertising agencies 218, 219
advocacy 280
Aegis Media 221
aerial advertising 211
AFL *see* Australian Football League
AFL Media 246
AGB Group 226
AIDA (awareness, interest, desire, action) model 180, 267, 292–3
alcohol sponsorship 214
allegiance stage 53–4
alternative products 47, 48, 49–50, 58, 64, 125
amateur athletics *see* local sports
ambush marketing 16, 211–12, 268, 294–8, 331
Amsterdam Arena 141
Anaheim Angels 324
announcement advertising 206
anonymous source, trademarks and 323–4
anti-siphoning laws 220–1, 233–4
apparel purchases 84
apps 26, 236–7, 246, 253–4, 257, 259
Arena 292
Armstrong, Lance 305–6
Ascot United 252
Asia-Pacific, sponsorship levels 264
athletes *see also* celebrities; names of athletes; players
  communication sources, as 179–80
  endorsements 179–80, 208, 271, 320
  popular 291, 320
  sponsorship of 271–5, 290–2
  top ten by familiarity 74
Atlanta Olympic Games 298
attachment stage 53
attendance figures
  AFL 45, 73
  Australian 45
  cricket 4–5, 69
  decrease 45–6
  frequency escalator 194–5
  measure of success 349
  NBL 112
  patterns 76

repeat 10
rugby union 42, 45, 62
technological advances, effect on 61
attention, measuring 288, 289
attitudes, market segmentation by 82
attraction stage 3
attractiveness 272–4
audience sampling 227
audience share *see* ratings points
Australian Baseball League 159–60
Australian Bureau of Statistics 45, 72
Australian Communications and Media Authority (ACMA) 222
Australian Crime Commission (ACC) 302
Australian Football League (AFL)
aerial advertising ban 211
AFL Media 246
ambush marketing 211
attendance levels 45, 73
brand loyalty 29
brand name 321
changes to game 11–12
competition for consumers 104–5
crisis management 307
customer satisfaction 171–3
event sponsorship 270–1
expansion 11–12, 62–3, 66–7, 134–5
family loyalties 59–60
Grand Final 229
intensity of competition 28–9
marketing staff 353
marketing strategy 125–6
'media-dominant' consumption 243–4
membership packages 134–6
membership satisfaction 171–3
membership services 171–3
popularity of 291
pricing strategies 119, 125–6
social media 251–2
substance abuse issues 302
supply, demand, price and substitutability 125–6
supporter statistics 75
'tanking' allegations 302, 307
television rights to 218, 219
turnover of 28
Australian Olympic Committee 322
Australian Psychological Society 214
Australian Rugby League 30, 347
Australian Rugby Union (ARU) 23, 24, 26, 31, 41–3
brand health 41–3
Australian Rules football *see* Australian Football League
Australian Sponsorship Marketing Association (ASMA) 266
Australian Sports Commission 26, 31–2, 73, 77, 316
Australian Television Research 239–40
Australian Tennis Open 48–51, 95, 98, 158, 207, 287
ticket packages/ membership 158
website 261
automotive industry sponsorship 266, 270–1
average audience 225
aware publics 306
Awareness, Interest, Desire, Action (AIDA) model 180, 267, 292–3
awareness stage 52
Bailey, Dean 307
Balfour, David 159
Balmain Tigers 106
bandwidth 235
Barba, Ben 302, 308–9
Barcelona FC 251
Barcelona Olympics 293
Barclaycard sponsorship 286–7, 290, 292, 299–300
bargaining power 27–8
barriers 62
baseball *see* Australian Baseball League; Major League Baseball (US)
basketball 40, 57, 60, 82, 94, 108, 112–13, 275 *see also* National Basketball League
Basketball Australia 94
basking in reflected glory 170
Beckham, David 275
behavioural information 75
sponsorship 288
behavioural segmentation 84
Beijing Olympics
registered trademarks 322
sponsorship for 264–5, 276, 288
Beitar Jerusalem 304
benefit segmentation approach 82–3
BigFooty.com 257
Billabong 294
billboards 179, 183, 187, 219, 276
BIRGing 170
blogosphere 15, 75, 206–7
Bloom, Howard 97
Blue Jays 96–7
blueprinting 147–8
Bluestone Edge 316
Board of Control of Cricket in India 14, 248
Bowie, Sam 274
Bowls Australia 6
boxing 275
Bradley, Keegan 273
Brand Health Index (BHI) 41

branding 95–6, 321, 333–7
brand demand 177–8
brand equity 320, 333, 335
brand extensions 96
brand value 336–7
building on 332–3
licensing and 335–6, 337
logos 96–7
process 333–5
recognition and 95–6
sports brands, power of 336–7
break-even analysis 127–9
Britain
interactive TV 235
Premier League 286–7, 292
broadband 245, 351
brochures 207
budget for advertising 202–3
buyer-readiness model 267, 286
buying behaviour *see* consumers

Calgary Olympics 296–8
Canada
trademark licensing 322
Canberra Raiders 346
Canberra Region Rugby League 346
Canterbury Bulldogs 302, 308–9
careers in sport marketing 353–4
cause-related marketing 280
celebrities *see also* athletes; names of celebrities
endorsements by 208, 274–5
over-exposure 274
cereals, sponsorship by 293–4
chambers of commerce, data from 73
Channel Nine 208, 219, 221
Channel Seven 219
Channel Ten 111
characteristics of sport products 8–12
Chevrolet 273
China 275–6 *see also* Beijing Olympics
choice of licensee 330
Cityscape Program 298
Clarke, Michael 291
'clean stadiums' 24
climate issues 61–2
clothing purchases 84
club membership
Australian Football League 157–8
canvassing views of 159–60
measure of success 349
'C'mon Aussie C'mon' 181
Coca-Cola 96, 223, 287, 288
cognitive effects 288, 289
Collingwood Football Club 353
Commercial Economic Advisory Service of Australia 221
commitment to licensing 330
communications
advertising as 198–9
AIDA (Awareness, Interest, Desire, Action) model 180, 267, 292–3
channel 178–9
direct marketing and 187–8
expectations management 167
gaps in 161–2
information processing model 180
innovation-adoption model 180
licensing programs, in 331
message 178–9, 203–4, 272–3
model 178–80
objectives 202
outcome 180
planning for 311
receiver 178
source 178, 179–80, 272–3
targeted placement 179
community accessibility 121
community expectations 16
community sport *see* local sports
comparison advertising 205
competition
competitive advantage 35–6
competitive forces model 27–8
information from competitors 72
intensity of 28–9
market share 198
pricing strategies 129
complaint-inducement mechanisms 170
complaints, tracking and monitoring 168
concurrent control 347
connectedness 248, 260
Connolly, Chris 307
constraints on pricing behaviour 129–30
constraints on sport consumption 62
consumer-to-consumer sales 258
consumers
access to information 75–6
attitudes and behaviours 71–2
bargaining power of 29
behaviour 46–7
buying behaviour 288, 290, 305
decision-making process 47–51
differentiating service quality and satisfaction of 158–60
expectations 166–70
intention to purchase 279
involvement 10, 15, 51
needs 6–7, 14
perceptions 158–9, 160
relational approach to 157–8
satisfaction of 154–74
understanding 44–66
content in new media 247–8

broadcasting and content extensions 252–3
contractual agreements 331
control 345–55
cooperation 10
coordination of marketing 345–55
copy testing 210
Copyright Promotions Group 332–3
core products 95, 334
corporate citizenship 280
corporate responsibility *see* ethical behaviour; social responsibility
cost
  cost–volume–profit relationship 127–9
  effectiveness 230
  per thousand (CPM) 209, 230
  per thousand involved (CPMI) 230
counteract strategies 296
counterfeiting 322
creative strategy 204–6
credibility 272–4, 315
Cricinfo 256
cricket
  attendance levels 4–5, 45, 69, 98
  Cricket Australia 4, 6, 13, 38, 145, 176–7, 187, 211
  economic impact 98
  market development 5
  market segmentation 84–5
  measuring success of 350–1
  one-day cricket 4–5, 6, 14, 38, 96, 107, 109, 176
  popularity of 38, 45, 291
  promotion of 176–7
  Test cricket 69, 96, 291
  Twenty20 cricket 5–6, 14, 38, 63, 69, 96, 176, 351
  World Cup 4, 291, 332
  World Series Cricket 13–14, 176–7, 350
crisis management 302–3, 308–9
critical trading radius 71
Cultural and Recreational Services 97
cultural groups 63
Currie, Lisa 293
customer relationship management (CRM) theory 158, 181, 188, 258
customers *see* consumers
cycling 158, 305–6

da Silva, Neymar 273
Dally M medal 302
Danaher, Professor Peter 239
data collection and analysis 72–4, 78–80
  direct marketing 188–9
  sources 72–4
day-after-recall (DAR) interviews 210
decision-making process 64–6
decline phase 106
'defensive marketing' 158
definition of marketing 6–7
definition of sport marketing 16–17
Delgado, Carlos 97
delivery gap 161–2
demand 122
Demetriou, Andrew 246, 307
demographics
  data about 72–3, 75
  segmentation by 81–2
  television audience 225–7
  trends 27
demonstration advertising 205
digital advertising 206–7, 210
digital marketing 187
digital television 234–7
digitisation 245–6
direct experience 58
direct marketing 187–9
  database and outcomes 188–9
disadvantages of sport sponsorship 267–8
disconfirmation of expectations model 165
disintermediation 247
Disney Corporation 324
distributed campaigns 203
distribution 145–6
  internet 243–4
  new media 247
  sport products 9, 11–12
diversification 6, 38–9
diversion goals 56
dog racing 45
drug use in sport 302, 305–6, 309–10

e-commerce 257–8
economic issues 27, 60 *see also* pricing
The Economist 22, 23
economy, sport contribution to 98, 131–2
effectiveness
  advertising 210–11
  sponsorship 285–300
Electronic Word of Mouth (EWOM) 251
emails 188
endearing features 59
endorsements by athletes 179–80, 208
England *see* Britain
English Cricket Board 252
Enten, Harry 306
environmental inputs 59–62
environmental marketing factors 26–30
ESPN 220, 254, 256
Essendon Football Club 302
esteem goals 56
ethical behaviour 15–16, 280, 310 *see also* social responsibility; unethical behaviour
ethnicity 57, 58, 88
Europe
  Champions League 270, 287
  soccer clubs in China 39
  soccer in 39, 151, 304, 333
  sponsorship levels 264

evaluation
  advertising
    effectiveness 210–11
  influence on consumers 157
  promotional mix 192–3
  public attitudes 304–8
  service quality and
    consumer
    satisfaction 158–60
Evans, Cadel 291
event sponsorship 275–6, 290–2
exchange process 6–7
excitement goals 56
expansion of sport codes 71
expectations 165, 166–70
  managing in new
    consumers 167–8
experience in decision
  making 55
experience qualities 156–7
experiential benefits of
  sport 56
experimentation, data
  collection by 79
exposure 279, 288–9
external forces in product
  competition 26–7
external inputs in decision-
  making 59
external secondary data 72–4
extreme sports 83, 279–80
eye-tracking 279, 289

face-to-face presentations 187
Facebook 75, 101, 250, 251,
  252, 255, 257, 277–8, 279
facilities 11, 137–53
  advertising at 199–200, 207
  capacity 151–3
  'clean stadiums' 24
  mystique of 11
  physical evidence for
    products 143–4
  planning 140–3
  signage 207
fake merchandising 322
family factors 59–60
fan development
  strategies 194–6
fan engagement 14–15
  social media 250
fan forums 256–7
fantasy sport 254–5
Fearns, Colin 151
Federer, Roger 271–2
feed-forward control 347
feedback 160
  control 347–8
fence signage 207
Fennessy, Mark 221
FIFA World Cup *see* Soccer
  World Cup
final price 132–4
finance industry
  sponsorship 266
financial quality control 325
financial stability 352
Finchem, Tim 273
'Find Your Greatness'
  campaign 212
Fisher, Andrew 235
fitness centres 141–2
fixed costs 128
flyers 207
focus 39–40
focus groups 79
football *see* Australian Football
  League; National Football
  League (US); rugby
  league; rugby union;
  soccer
Football Federation of
  Australia (FFA) 36, 37,
  217
Forbes 272, 275
Ford Motor Company 288
Formula One motor
  racing 275
  advertising sales 229, 231–2
  protests against 118
  ratings 231
Fountain of Youth
  Foundation 320
four Ps of marketing 7–8
Fox Sports 113–14, 217
Foxtel 222
free-to-air networks 220–1,
  233–4
Freeman, Cathy 291
frequency vs. reach 201
Friedman, Edward 333
full-menu marketing 84
function-based
  similarity 287–8
funding, from governments 26

gambling and organised
  crime 302
game mechanics 258
gaming advertising 208
Gatorade 206, 273
Geelong Football Club 288
gender differences
  sport participation 57
General Motors 293
generic demand 177
generic strategies 39–40
geographical location 60, 75,
  298–9
'George Costanza night' 185
Gibson, Adam 94
Gillette Champions 272
Gilmore, Sir Ian 214
giveaways 184
'global' sports celebrities 274–5
goals and objectives
  advertising 202
  development of 191–2
  licensing programs 329–30
  marketing 346–7
  pricing 119–20
  promotional 177
  public relations 304–5
  sponsorship 266–7
  sport organisations 31–3
Godfrey, Paul 96–7
Godsick, Tony 271
Gold Coast Suns 66–7
Gold Coast Titans 155, 157
golf 70–1
  PGA tour 273
GoodSports program 214
Google Hangout 250
Gorman, Lyall 37

governing bodies 6 *see also* names of governing bodies
government intervention
  competition and 26
  funding 118–19
  hallmark events 131–2
  legislative 27
Grand Prix *see* Formula One motor racing
Greater Western Sydney Giants 12, 134–5
Greenberg, Todd 309
GreenEdge 158
Gridley, Heather 214
gross rating points 223–5
growth phase 106, 108
The Guardian 306

hallmark events 107, 131–2, 217
'halo' effect 169
Harmison, Chuck 114
Heineken 269–70, 287
Henry, Thierry 272, 274
Herald Sun 307
heterogeneity of services 99
Hewitt, Lleyton 293
high-involvement purchases 64–5
Holding, Michael 69
Holyfield, Evander 275
homes using television 222
'home-win guarantee' 155
horse racing
  advertising for 206
  attendance levels 45, 73, 74
  Melbourne Cup 291
  popularity 291
Howard, John 61
Hulu 228
HUMMER 114
Hunter Pirates 113
Hurricane Sandy 278
HUT 222

'I want to be like Mike' campaign 206
IBM ThinkPad 276
identification
  clubs, with 53–4, 166, 169
  trademarks 323
image-based similarity 288
image building 315
image transfer 267, 279
imagery-based advertising 205
IMG 320
imitation advertising 206
Independent Review of Swimming 316
India, cricket in 14, 30, 69, 248
Indian Cricket League 14
individual learning theory 57
industry competition 27–30
infomercials 205
information search by consumer 49
information sources 49–50
information systems 33–5
ING New York City Marathon 277–8
innovation 121
inputs to decision making 47, 54–62
Inside Sport 206
intangibility and tangibility 9, 98, 99–100, 156
integrated marketing communications (IMC) 180–2, 258–61
  development of 192
  social media 251
  sponsorship and *see* sponsorship
  sports promotional mix, use in 182–90, 263
intellectual property rights 320, 322
intensity of competition 28–9
interactive marketing 189
interactivity 234–7, 248–9, 257–8
interdisciplinary approach 46
internal capabilities of organisations 30–3
internal inputs in decision making 59
internal processing 47
International Agency Against Doping 217
International Cricket League 30
International Olympic Committee 212, 217, 220, 252, 264, 276, 297, 317–18
International Rugby Board 22, 23
internet
  advertising on 206–7
  distribution via 245, 332
Internet Protocol Television (IPTV) 252
'invisible' aspects of experience 156
involvement, in decision making 51, 64–6
IPSOS UK 290
Ironman series 293
iSelect 155

Jackson, Lauren 94
Jackson, Mike 290
Japan Sports Vision 332
Jefferson, Sean 292
Jones, Marion 309
Jordan, Michael 274, 275
  'I want to be like Mike' campaign 206
junior sports *see also* youth market
  boosting participation in 346
  modifications for 6–7, 38, 349
Juventus 332

Kaka 279
Kellogg's 293, 294
Keneally, Kristina 94
Kind, Paul 208
'kitchen table' administration 12
knowledge gap 162
Kolt, Professor Greg 213

LaRocca, Sal 332

latent publics 306
lead generation 315
learning theory 57–8
Lee, Brett 273
legal protection 331 *see also* contractual agreements
Lenova Group 275–6, 288
Li Ting 276
libraries, data from 73
licensing programs 189–90, 319–42
  branding and 333–7
  building 328–33
  marketing through sport 16
  measuring success of 351
  operational element of 329
  partnership 190
  purpose 320–1
  setting up 338–42
  trademarks 321–8
lifestyle advertising 206
likeability 273
line extensions 96
Liverpool Football Club 207, 273
Livestrong 306
local sports 60, 63, 72–3, 130, 194, 286–8
location dependency 298–9
logos 96–7, 321, 327–8 *see also* branding
London Organising Committee for the Olympic Games 212, 264
low-involvement purchases 65–6
loyalty 95, 158
  programs 188–9
Lycra 177–8

magazines 206, 209 *see also* names of magazines
Magnussen, James 315–16
Major League Baseball (US)
  advertising by 205
  licensing programs 324
  logos in 327–8
  MLB Fan Cave 257
  new media 243
  promotions 185–6
  servicescape 142
Major Professional and Participation Sports 214
males *see* gender differences
management information system *see* marketing information system
management of sport products 12–16
  public relations and 284
Manchester United 221, 251, 273, 332
many-to-many media 246
market development 36
market equilibrium 122–4
market expansion 36
market for sponsors 264–6
market for sport products and services 9
market penetration 36
market research 68–90
  examination of 33–5
  process 77–80
  public attitudes 304
  purpose 69–70
  satisfaction, into 168–70
  service quality 101–3
  strategy and 70
market sensitivity to price 121–7
marketing 6–7
  ambush 211–12
  channels for 148–50
  constraints on 118–20
  contribution 5–6
  control of 346–52
  'defensive' 158
  definition 6–7
  digitalised content 245–6
  direct 187–9
  effect on sport consumption 60
  function of 145
  implementation of strategies 345–55
  mission 76–7
  new media and 249–50
  'of' and 'through' sport 16–17
  'offensive' 158
  opportunities, identification of 21, 25 *see also* SSMPP
  outsourcing 14
  theory 157
marketing information systems 33–5, 70–2, 85, 87
  data sources 72–4
Mashable 255
mass media 60–1, 244
massed strategies 203
maturity phase 108
maximum shareholder value 120–1
Mayweather, Floyd 275
McDonald's 215, 322
McGeoch, Rod 263
McGrath, Glenn 291
McIlroy, Rory 273, 275
McLachlan, Gillon 307
McLean, Brock 307
measurement
  satisfaction 165–6
  sponsorship effectiveness 287–90
  success 348–52
  television audiences 222–7
media
  database of 311
  definition 244
  direct marketing and 187
  public relations and 311–14
  selecting 206–10
  strategy for 203–5
  technologies 61
media buys 219
media conference 312–13
media relations 310–11
media releases 311–12
Melbourne Commonwealth Games 295
Melbourne Cup *see* horse racing
Melbourne Football Club 302, 207

Melbourne Park 95, 113, 144
Mercedes-Benz 198
merchandising 324, 332, 351
message strategy 203–4
Mighty Ducks of Anaheim 324
MISs 33, 70–2
  data sources 72–4
missions *see also* goals and objectives
  marketing 35–40, 76–7
  sport organisations 31–3
Mitchell, Harold 221
Mixed Martial Arts (MMA) 254
mobile applications 236–7
mobile devices 75, 236–7, 245, 252–3
modelling
  communications 178–80
  consumer behaviour 51–62
modifications of sports 6–7, 38, 349
Molik, Alicia 293
money-back guarantee 155
Mornington Peninsula 70–1
Motivation Scale for Sport Consumption (MSSC) 55
motives for sport consumption 55–6
motor sports
  attendance levels 45
  Formula One 98, 118–19, 229–32
multi-purpose facilities 151
multiculturalism 26–7, 58 *see also* ethnicity
multiple segmentation 84–5

names, property rights in 320–1
narrowcasting 233
NASCAR 252, 253, 273
National Basketball Association (NBA) (US) 94, 155, 218, 221, 273, 332
  NBA League Pass 252–3
National Basketball League (NBL) 5, 79, 94, 105, 106, 113
  attendance declines 112
  expansion of 5
  live internet coverage 94
  product development 94, 111–115
  product life cycle 106–9
  television audience 115
National Broadband Network (NBN) 245
National Football League (US)
  cost of television rights to 218
  licensing program 328–9
  social media 251
  Super Bowl 198, 227–9, 336–7
National Rugby League (NRL)
  community presence 346
  expansion 71
  mission 32
  naming rights 86
  new media and 243–4
  popularity of 291
  promotions 155
  public relations 302
  rationalisation strategy 15
  State of Origin 208, 222
  substance use by players 302
  television 219
  virtual advertising 208
nationalism 304
negative disconfirmation 165
networking 250–2
new entrants to market 30, 62–3
new media 242–61, 350–1 *see also* technological change
  definition 244
  dimensions and characteristics 246–9
  interactive marketing and 189
  sponsorship trends 279
'new' sports 279–80
New York Knicks 332
New York Red Bulls 257
New York Times 305
New Zealand Rugby Union (NZRU) 23
newspapers 206, 209
'niche' sports 279–80
Nick Faldo Golf Company 331
Nielson Media Research Australia 73, 226
Nielson Television Audience Measurement 227
Nike 212, 274, 275, 294, 298, 332–3
Nine Network 231
non-price factors 127
non-publics 307
non-verbal cues 178
'Norman factor' 349
Nou Camp Stadium 144
Novak, Lisa 97
Nugent, Leigh 316

objectives *see* goals and objectives
O'Brien, Dr Kerry 214
observation, data collection by 79
Ofcom 235
'offensive marketing' 158
Olajuwon, Hakeem 274
Olympic Games 131–2, 314
  ambush marketing 211–12, 296–8
  Australian swimming team 315–16
  Beijing 264, 276, 280, 322
  brand value 336
  Calgary 296–8
  facilities 138, 140–1
  growth phase 109
  London 94, 121, 131, 138, 179, 205, 211, 212, 214, 264–5, 315–16, 320, 322
  Los Angeles 131
  merchandise 150
  registered trademarks 322
  Salt Lake City 217, 277, 298
  Seoul 265

Olympic Games (*continued*)
- Sydney 61, 217, 263, 295, 322
- TOP sponsors 264–5, 276, 288
- Turin Winter Olympics 276

The Olympic Partner Program 264, 265, 288
on-field success 95, 348–9
one-day cricket *see* cricket
one-to-many media 246
online advertising 206–7, 210, 257–8
online betting/gambling 257–8
online communities 256–7
online sales 257
opportunities and threats 25, 30, 191
organisations
- control of product 160–1, 347–8
- government policy, implementing 26
- licensing programs 321
- management of service quality and satisfaction 166–70
- market research in 75–6
- modification of sports 6–7
- multi-faceted consumption awareness 156–7
- opportunities through new media 243–5
- publics of 306–8
- reputation 314
- social media 251, 259–60

Organised Crime and Drugs in Sport 302
outdoor advertising 207
over-exposure 274
OzTAM data 73, 222, 226, 227, 239–40

Packer, Kerry 13, 79
'part-time marketers' 145
partial cost recovery 120, 121
participants *see* players
participation 163, 349
Participation in Sport and Physical Activities, Australia 72
pay television 11, 219, 222, 227, 233–4
PBL Marketing 14
PCM framework for sport consumer behaviour 51–5
- inputs 54–5
- stages 52–4

peer influence 60
Pele 205
people meters 225–7
perceived service 102–3
perceptual maps 103
performance goals 56
perishability of services 99
personal inputs 57–9
personal selling 186–7
personalisation 157, 248
personality
- choice of sport and 49–50

Pettigrew, Professor Simone 215
philanthropy 280
physical evidence 143–5
physical source, trademarks and 323
Pinterest 255
place dependence 130 *see also* geographical location
planning
- facilities 140–3
- process and stages 21 *see also* SSMPP

players *see also* athletes; celebrities
- bargaining power of 26
- information from 72
- sponsorship of 271–5

political interventions 61
Ponting, Ricky 291
Port Adelaide Football Club 12, 126
positioning 86–7, 103–5
- defining 103–5
- establishing 105

positive disconfirmation 165
post-purchase outcomes 50–1
posters 207
Premier League, Barclaycard sponsorship 286–7, 292
The Premiership 287
presentation of findings 78
press releases 203, 312
pricing 9, 117–36
- competitors' strategies 129
- discrimination via 132
- elasticity of demand 124–5
- membership packages 134–6
- sport products 9
- standardised 29, 39–40

primary data 74
problem recognition 49
procedures 289–92
process *see* distribution
product life cycle (PLC)
- curve 106–7
- stages 108–9
- variations from curve 108–9

product placement 208
production and consumption 99
products *see* sport products
professionalisation of sport 12–13, 181
profit maximisation 120, 130
program ratings 222–3, 231
promotion 7, 175–96
- communications model 178–80
- defining 177–8
- evaluation and measurement 192–3
- factors 193
- fan development strategies 194–6
- objective development 191–2
- physical evidence and 144–5
- planning process 191
- process 190–3
- promotion mix 132, 193, 303, 304–5, 317
- resource allocation and budget 192

situation analysis 191
sport products 9
strategic, integrated promotional mix 180–2
strategy development 170–71
tools for 182–90
use of 181
promotional licensing *see* licensing programs
promotional strategy 177–8
Protheroe, Chris 333
psychographics 75, 82
Psychological Continuum Model (PCM) framework for sport consumer behaviour 51–5
inputs 54–5
stages 52–4
psychological inputs 55–6
public attitudes and opinions 304–8
evaluation 305–6
public interest, policies linked to 308–11
public relations (PR) 183–4, 173, 249, 301–18
advantages and disadvantages 315–16
defining 303–4
management functions 303
objectives 304–5
proactive 308–9
reactive 309–10
sport 304
publicity 11, 183–4, 313–14
publics of sporting organisations 30, 31, 306–8
purchase decisions 50

quality of service 101–3
dimensions 102, 103
quality of sport products 87, 93–95
measuring 351–2
trademarks and 324, 325
QUESC 163

racism 304
radio advertising 207, 209
Rafter, Pat 73, 291
ratings points 223–5
reach vs. frequency 201
reactive public relations 183, 304, 308–10
Real Madrid 39, 144, 279
recall of advertising 210, 335
recognition of advertising 210, 335
Reebok 298
RegionalTAM 227
registered trademarks 335–6
relationship marketing 157–8
relationships in licensing programs 331
religious groups 61
RepuCom 279
reputation management 314
research
cognitive 289
design 79–80
sport sponsorship 278–80, 290
resourcing for licensing programs 330–1
response model 180
responsiveness 102, 147, 162
return on investment (ROI) 278
return on objectives (ROO) 278
A Review of Culture and Leadership in Australian Olympic Swimming 316
revitalisation of product 108
rewards programs 189
Ricciardi, J.P. 97
right to associate 266–7, 286
Robinson, Mark 307
Ross, Stephen 243
Roy Morgan Research Centre 73–4, 291
Royal College of Physicians 214
royalties 321

rugby league 32, 42, 96–97, 236–37 *see also* Australian Rugby League
rugby union *see also* Australian Rugby Union
attendance levels 42, 45, 62
Bledisloe Cup 23, 24
growing profile 24
shift from amateur code 23, 24
Super 15s 24
tensions 23
Tri-Nations Series 24
video games 326–7
World Cup 22–4, 229
rules, modifications of 6 *see also* modifications

S-Comm Australia 266
sales growth maximisation 120
sales objectives 202
sales promotion 149, 184–6
Salt Lake City Olympics 217, 277, 298
Samsung 288
San Jose Sharks 330, 337
satisfaction of consumers 155, 164–6 *see also* consumers
effect 164
expectations and 'disconfirmation' 165
link to primary variables 164
measuring 165–6
modelling 164
'Save Albert Park' group 118
SBS 217
Schumacher, Michael 275
Scott, Adam 273
season tickets 167–8
expectations of holders 167–8
induction programs 168
seat-sharing 84
'second-screen' experience 236–7, 253–4
secondary data 72–4
segmentation 80–5
variables 81

service groups 61
service/s
'churn' 155–6, 167
classification 99–100
definition 98–9
delivery models 147–8
'expected' and 'perceived' gap 102–3
quality *see* service quality
service gap 161
sport as 97–100
sport services definition 156–7
technology and 101
service quality 160–4
concept of 160–1
differentiating consumer satisfaction and 158–60
management 101–3, 166–7
measuring 162–4, 351–2
modelling 161–2
servicescape 142
SERVQUAL 162–4
servuction 145–6, 156
Seven Network 229
Shazam 235, 237
Sheedy, Kevin 134–5
Shine Australia 221
short message services (SMS) 187
'Simply the Best' campaign 181
situation analysis 30–1, 191
Sky Sports 253
slice-of-life advertising 205
SMART objectives 33, 77, 352
smartphones 227, 236
Smith, Tommy 59
snowboarding 86
'So you think you know Lenova?' campaign 276
soccer
A-League Football 37, 88–90, 217, 230, 256, 284
attendance levels 45
Football Federation of Australia 6, 36, 37, 217
globalisation of 5
licensing programs in Europe 333
live broadcasts 217
positioning and challenges 88–90
racism and 304
ticket sale revenue 139
Toronto FC 37–40
UEFA 304, 333
Soccer World Cup
advertising at 205
ambush marketing 211
brand value 337
economic value 131
integrated public relations campaign 305
live streaming 253
McDonald's sponsorship 215
sponsorship 277
television 217
social interaction via sport 56
social learning theory 57–8
social media 14–15, 75, 279
access to information through 75
advertising 206–7, 228
classification 15
definition 250
disadvantages 278
networking and 250–2
poor decisions 252
social networking sites 75
social responsibility 15, 280
see also ethical behaviour
social trends 27
Softball Australia, staff employed by 353
South Sydney Rugby League Club 15
SPEED 56, 65
Spong, Doug 83
SPONSEFFECT model 292–4, 295
sponsorship
activation 277, 291
advantages and disadvantages 267–8
ambush marketing 294–8
attracting and implementing 262–84
benefits to sponsor 263, 269
communication vehicle 59
corporate brand image 276–7
current research trends 278–80
effectiveness of 285–300
expenditure on 264
global growth 264
goals 266–7, 287
individual athletes 271–5
industries as sponsors 265
integrated marketing approach 263, 275–8
international and local effectiveness 276–8
location dependency 298–9
market for sponsors 264–6
marketing 'through' sport 16
measure of success 350
naming rights 270, 288
Olympic Games 264–5, 276, 288
properties 290–2
reciprocal relationship 263–4, 288
research firms 290
right to 'associate' 266–7, 286
sponsee goals 267, 269, 288
sponsor goals 267, 269, 288
sponsorship myopia 281, 350
sport products, of 11
strategic importance 280–1
telecasts, of 217
television 232
types 290–1
vertically integrated portfolio 277
what is 263–4
win–win situations, creating 268–71
Sport Interest Inventory (SII) 55
sport management

'administrator' culture 13
importance of marketing in 12–16
volunteers 12
sport marketing
definition 16–17
sport organisations *see* organisations
sport products 9, 93–116
branding *see* branding
characteristics of 8–12, 94–7
'churn' 155–6, 167
definition 156
development of 38, 105–9
differentiation between 35–36
diversification of 38–9
extensions to 95, 160
life cycle curve 106–9
marketing 3–17
perceptions, mapping 104
positioning 103–5
product mix 130
quality 95
service, as 97–100
stages of life-cycle 108–9
unpredictability 10
sport servuction model 145–6, 156
sport-specific information 76
SportBusiness in Numbers 265, 266
SPORTFIVE 253
sportplaces *see* facilities
sports facilities *see* facilities
Sports Illustrated 206
sports magazines 206, 209 *see also* magazines
sports programming on television 219–20
sports tourism 98
sportscape 140, 141–2
SPORTSERV 163–4
spot packages 232
Spotify 255
SSMPP (strategic marketing planning process) 24–6, 40–1, 354–5
eight steps 25
environment, understanding 26–30
marketing opportunities, identification of 25
strategy determination 25
strategy implementation, evaluation and adjustment 25
Stadium Australia 24
stadium experience 243–4
staff 146–7, 352–3
standards gap 161–2
Starch Readership Test 210
Stephenson, Terence 215
Stoner, Casey 74
straight sell advertising 205
strategic sport-marketing planning process 21–43
subscription markets 157–8
substitute products 27, 29
Summer's Biggest Dress-Up Party campaign 176–7
Sun Tiantian 276
sunscreen advertising 200
Super 15s 24, 26, 32, 42, 71, 88, 107
Super Bowl 198, 227–9, 251, 336–7
Superleague dispute 30, 347
suppliers, bargaining power of 29
supply, price sensitivity and 122
surveys 78
AFL 160
attendance 45–6
SERVQUAL 162–4
sustainability 35
Sweeney Sports & Entertainment Report 73, 291, 293–4
swimming
Australian interest in 302
Olympic Games 302, 315–16
sponsorship 293–4
Swimming Australia 6, 316
Swisse 179, 205
switching cost 29
SWOT analysis 30–1, 191
Sydney Blue Sox 159–60
Sydney Kings 113, 114
Sydney Morning Herald 302, 309
Sydney Olympics 217, 295, 322
Sydney Swans 67, 126, 270
symbolic association advertising 206

tangibility and intangibility 9, 98, 99–100, 156
target audience rating points 223, 231
target markets 85–6, 306
Taylor, Mark 61
team identification 169
TEAMQUAL 163–4
technical evidence advertising 205
technological change
communication formats 181
digital television 234–7
digitalisation 245–6
impact 245
new media 242–61
sports distribution 11
telemarketing 186–7
television 5, 109–10, 216–41
see also pay television
advertising on 207, 209, 219, 227–33
audience measurement 73, 218, 223
broadcast rights 217
colour, introduction of 13
commercial 218
corporate clients 219
digital 234–7
effectiveness of advertising 230–3
exposure measurements 288–9
live coverage 4, 217
marketing and 218–19
measurement technology 218

television (*continued*)
measuring 222–7, 350–1
online challenge 221
program ratings 218–19, 222–3, 231
programming 219–21
protectionism 220–1
sport-television relationship 218–19, 237–8
top 20 programs 224
worldwide rights 241
tennis
attendance levels 45
Australian Open *see* Australian Tennis Open
Davis Cup 293
popularity of 293–4
Wimbledon 121, 122, 124, 217, 235
Test cricket *see* cricket
testimonial advertising 205
Tew, Steven 23
Thorpe, Ian 291, 294, 320
ticket packages 157–8
ticket purchasing platforms 257
'Tiger Woods' factor 349
time-dependence 132
Toronto Blue Jays 96–7
Toyota 270–1, 293
Trade Marks Act 321
Trade Practices Act 294
trademarks 321–8
advertising 324
functions 323–4
identification 323
licensing 321–8
licensing agreement 325–6
licensor and licensee perspective 326
merchandising 324
quality 324
registration 322
sources 323–4
sport products and 321–3
Trickett, Libby 291
Turner, Bob 113
Twenty20 cricket *see* cricket
Twitter 75, 101, 228, 236, 250, 251, 255–6, 277–8, 279
Tyson, Mike 275

UEFA 304, 333
Ultimate Fighting Championship (UFC) 251, 252, 255–6
UN Inter-Agency Task Force on Sport for Development and Peace 280
'Unbelievable' AFL campaign 181
Uncle Toby's 293–4
unethical behaviour 296 *see also* ethical behaviour
unique selling proposition (USP) 204
Unitam devices 227
United Kingdom *see* Britain
United Nations Inter-Agency Task Force on Sport for Development and Peace 280
universities, data from 73
University of Manchester 214
University of New South Wales 214
University of Western Sydney 213, 215
unpredictability of sports outcomes 10
usage segmentation 84
user control 248
user generated content 250

Valenzuela, Michael 214
value
brand 336–7
licensing 327
sponsorship 288–9, 294
variable components of place 139–40
variable costs 127–8
Veeck, Bill 155
venues *see* facilities
Victorian Football League 5, 11–12
Victorian Titans 113
video games 326–7
virtual advertising 207–8, 235
Visa 277, 288
voluntary administration of sport 12–13

Warner Bros. Consumer Products 333
Waterhoue, Gai 59
websites 260–1
Wembley FC 252
'What are you #DrivenBy' campaign 273
'Where's Lenovo?' 276
White, Dana 255–6
Wide World of Sports 231
Wimbledon final 122, 124, 235
win–win situations 268–71
Winfrey, Oprah 306
Woods, Tiger 272–4, 275, 349
World Assembly of Public Relations 303
World Cups *see* cricket; rugby union; Soccer World Cup
World Series Cricket 13–14, 176–7, 350
World Swimming Championships 316
World Wide Web *see* internet
wrestling 317–18

YouTube 75, 228, 252, 255

zapping 230
zero disconfirmation 165
Zidane, Zinedine 277
Zone Marketing 333
Zulueta, Pilar 333